D1130299

THOMAS TENISON
HIS LIFE AND TIMES

Thomas Tenison, Archbishop of Canterbury.
Contemporary engraving from a portrait by Mary Beale.

THOMAS TENISON
ARCHBISHOP OF CANTERBURY
HIS LIFE AND TIMES

By

EDWARD CARPENTER
M.A., Ph.D., B.D.

Published for the Church Historical Society

LONDON
S · P · C · K
1948

To

The Reverend Dr. Claude Jenkins, Regius
Professor of Ecclesiastical History in the
University of Oxford, and Canon of Christ
Church ; and the Reverend Dr. Norman
Sykes, Dixie Professor of Ecclesiastical
History in the University of Cambridge :
In grateful acknowledgment of their help
and encouragement.

MADE IN GREAT BRITAIN

CONTENTS

v

LIST OF ILLUSTRATIONS

PREFACE

THE writing of this book accompanied me in London throughout the war years, and helped me to preserve some measure
of sanity in a world far from sane. The life of Thomas Tenison may
at first seem remote from the tumultuous days of the twentieth
century, but the more discerning reader may discover many
interesting affinities. He will read of refugees flying from French
aggression; of a Church of England in which some wiser and more
liberal spirits were seeking a comprehension in the interests of the
Dissenters; and of an Archbishop who tried to adapt the liturgy to
the needs of his own age, and "thought that the narrow notions of
all the Churches had been their ruin". He will also observe the
Protestant Churches of Europe feeling after some kind of union
with each other, and he will notice how party passion within the
Churches prevented any effective action, until the calm of the
eighteenth century descended.

If it is true that we learn from history that we do not learn from
history, then this work has been written in vain, and the enjoyment
it has given the author is its only justification.

The Rectory,   EDWARD CARPENTER.
Stanmore, 1947.

INTRODUCTION

THOMAS TENISON died in 1715, and in the same year there appeared *Memoirs of the Life and Times of the Most Reverend Father in God, Dr. Thomas Tennison.* This work is principally concerned with defending the Revolution of 1688 and in justifying the Whig attitude to the disputes in Convocation. As to its author, we might have suspected either Edward Tenison, Archdeacon of Maidstone, and a grandson of the Archbishop's uncle Philip, or Thomas Green, Archdeacon of Canterbury, were it not that the work includes many inaccuracies which they most certainly would have avoided. Thus the writer makes an error of two years in the date of Tenison's birth (1634 instead of 1636); he knows nothing of his private ordination by Bishop Duppa in 1659, but says that "upon the Restoration of the Church of England, with the Royal Family, he was Ordain'd Deacon and Priest"; he ascribes the elevation of Dr. Offspring Blackall to the see of Exeter in 1708 as due to the initiative of Archbishop Tenison, whereas in fact he strongly opposed it. We may say of the author, then, that he was a convinced Whig of the latitudinarian school, but that he was not very intimate personally with the Archbishop.

In 1720, John Le Neve devoted a short article to Archbishop Tenison in his *Lives and Characters of the Protestant Bishops of the Church of England*, the material for which, he writes, was "communicated [to him] by the Right Reverend White [Kennett], Lord Bishop of Peterborough, from notes taken from his Grace's own Mouth or Papers". This article does not add much to the *Memoirs*, although it furnishes us with some personal details.

In 1753, Robert Masters, in his *History of the College of Corpus Christi*, included a short memoir on Tenison, but he adds little to the above except that he provides a rather inaccurate list of Tenison's works, and suggests other sources of material.

From these three authorities—plus a few references to the Archbishop in contemporary histories—the articles in A. Chalmers' *Biographical Dictionary* (1816) and G. Cunningham's *Lives of Eminent Englishmen* (1835) have been drawn.

The writer of the article on Tenison in *The Dictionary of National Biography* (W. H. Hutton) has relied mainly on the above, assisted by the British Museum Catalogue of the Archbishop's works, certain publications of the Historical Manuscripts Commission, contemporary diaries, and information about the family supplied by C. M. Tenison, the nearest representative of the Archbishop. The latter gentleman himself drew up in 1914 a short volume, Notes for the Life of Thomas Tenison, but this work, though using the sources mentioned above, quoting liberally from Tenison's works, and drawing on the publications of the Historical Manuscripts Commission, makes little use of the available manuscript sources. It has never been published, being intended as "Notes" for some more comprehensive work.

Except for these short monographs, Tenison has been more or less ignored, and no authoritative life, based on manuscript sources, and using the methods of modern scholarship, has yet appeared, although an author wrote not many years ago that "it is much to be regretted that we know so little of the life of the Archbishop".[1]

The reason for this neglect, perhaps, lies in the fact that most people have tended to dismiss Tenison—following the lead of Jonathan Swift, who never forgot or forgave the Archbishop's refusal to support his elevation to the episcopate—as a "dull man", and as such hardly worthy of attention. True it is that most of Tenison's controversial works make rather heavy reading in our day, and that the Archbishop's later semi-official retirement at Lambeth during Anne's reign lacked the spiritual dignity of Ken at Longleat, or the dramatic interest of Atterbury at St. Germains: yet it is equally true that people have been content to repeat Swift's estimate quite uncritically, without any detailed study of the Archbishop's life.

The following biography has been largely drawn from manuscript sources, and amongst these the Tenison and Gibson MSS. in Lambeth Library and the Act Books of the Archbishop of Canterbury come first in importance. Around these manuscripts this work has been largely constructed, and hardly a chapter but owes something to this collection. Tenison was very systematic in the discharge of his archiepiscopal responsibilities, and he frequently made experimental drafts of his letters before finally dispatching them. Many of these drafts—often written in the most difficult hand, and on odd scraps of paper—are still at Lambeth, together with many letters which he received.

[1] Peter Cunningham, *The Story of Nell Gwyn*, 1927, p. 153.

By an injunction in his will, Tenison instructed his executors to destroy the "several Books and Papers in a deal Press marked B, and a deal Box marked M" within ten days of his decease, and "not to suffer any Person to look into these or any of those Books and Papers". We cannot help wondering as to the nature of the information thus destroyed.

Other manuscript sources have been invaluable for filling in the picture. The State Papers (Domestic) have provided details of the Archbishop's official duties, while Gibson's letters to Bishop Nicolson (in the Bodleian) furnished many personal references of unique interest, including a description of Tenison's last illness. The minute books of the S.P.G. and the MSS. of Archbishop Sharp, which I came to know of through the kindness of the Rev. A. T. Hart, should also be mentioned. I have been fortunate in securing access to the parochial registers of the various livings which Tenison held, and the information which they provide is essential to the understanding of one who did so much as Archbishop to improve the standards of parochial life.

Very valuable have been the various publications of the Historical Manuscript Commission, especially the Hastings MSS. in connection with Chapter 10, "Deprivation and Suspension", where the MSS. at Lambeth proved obstinately silent.

Histories and contemporary diaries have also supplied much useful material (as the bibliography at the end of this work shows), amongst which Evelyn's and Clarendon's diaries, Narcissus Luttrell's *A Brief Historical Relation of State Affairs*, Simon Patrick's *Autobiography*, Burnet's *History of my own Time*, White Kennett's *Complete History of England*, Lathbury's *History of the Convocation*, and Sharp's *Life of John Sharp* deserve special notice.

Contemporary pamphlets, of course, have provided material of first-rate importance, particularly in relation to the Anglican and Catholic controversy, the struggle over comprehension, the cases of Bishops Watson and Jones, and the disagreement about lay baptism.

As to more modern works, Montagu Burrows' *Worthies of All Souls* and Professor N. Sykes' *Queen Anne and the Episcopate* (E.H.R., vol. 50) have given me a general background for Chapter 12 and Chapter 7, Part II, as well as introduced me to material I could not otherwise have obtained.

PART I

CHAPTER 1

"OUR FATHERS THAT BEGAT US"[1]

THE family of Tenison, Tennison, or Tennyson [2]—for sixteenth-
and seventeenth-century scribes wrote the name as they
pleased—was one of considerable antiquity in Holderness in
Yorkshire, which was probably the original home of the family.
The name, which is said to be of Danish origin,[3] and is still found
in Denmark, appears in the Coram Rege Rolls for 1343, when
John Tennison charged certain persons with taking forcibly his
goods and chattels at Paulflete in Holderness to the value of £40.
In 1344 he was plaintiff in a similar action. In 1361 John Tennyson
of Welwick, in Holderness, caused one Maud Bochard to be indicted for stealing his corn and barley to the value of thirteen
shillings and fourpence. In 1503 a John Tennison graduated B.A.
at Cambridge (no college given) and proceeded to M.A. in 1506.
In 1522 Dominus Thomas Tenyson became Rector of Sutton in
Holderness and resigned in 1528.

The earliest proved Tenison ancestor of Archbishop Tenison is
William Tenyson of Ryhill in Holderness—close to Paulflete above
mentioned—who made his will on 15 September 1528, and died
almost immediately after, as it was proved on 30 September
following. By his wife Beatrice, he had an only son John Tennyson
of Ryhill, who was of full age in 1528, when, with his mother, he
proved his father's will. This John Tennyson died in 1546, between
3 August, the day on which he made his will, and 10 November,
when it was proved. He married Margaret, daughter of Christopher Thornton of Ryhill and sister of John Thornton, M.P. for
Hull, and was father of Christopher Tennyson (styled in the
subsidy rolls "Tenison") who was under age in 1546 and died in
1580. His will is dated 1 March of this year and it was proved
on 29 July. By his wife Elizabeth he had, amongst other children, a
son and heir John Tenison.

[1] The material in this chapter (except where otherwise acknowledged) comes
from an unpublished MS. of C. M. Tenison, Notes for the Life of Thomas Tenison.
[2] In C. Parkin, *History of Norfolk*, 1775, iv. 330, we even read "Tomison".
[3] It has been suggested that the name "Tenison" comes from "Thane's son",
but nobody really knows. Garter King at Arms in 1660 described the family as
"ancient".

This John Tenison was born about 1563 and was mentioned in his father's will in 1580 as a student at Cambridge. He was admitted a pensioner at Peterhouse on 7 June 1578, and matriculated the same year. He became B.A. in 1582, M.A. in 1585, B.D. in 1594, Fellow in 1589–98, and Bursar in 1595.[1] He was ordained deacon and priest by the Bishop of Peterborough (Richard Howland) on 25 November 1593.[2] We get an interesting insight into his character from Mullinger's *History of Cambridge University*. In 1584 a letter arrived from the Crown "recommending one John Tenison, a Master of Arts (*sic*), for the next vacant Fellowship", and Richard Belt, himself a royal nominee, "appended his name to a reply in which Dr. Perne and the Fellows jointly deprecated the restraint put upon them . . .; for, as it was pointed out in the protest, it was required by the Statutes that a Candidate for a Fellowship should be poor and of a humble and quiet spirit"; whereas, say the petitioners in particularizing John Tenison's disqualifications, "of late the thirds of his mother have fallen to him,[3] besides a Lease, as we are informed, yielding a yearly rent exceeding the rate of living allowed by our Statutes; he having otherwise of certain Worshipful friends very good and sufficient allowance by the year. And during the time of this his suit, he hath showed some manifest tokens of dispositions neither quiet nor humble".[4] He did not get his Fellowship for some years (till 1589) so the protest of the petitioners was for the time being successful.

In 1597 he was presented by Queen Elizabeth to the Rectory of Downham, Ely (now known as Little Downham to distinguish it from Downham Market), which became vacant through the death of Richard Perne. He ministered there till 1639, when his signature in the register ceases and it is assumed he resigned office, probably because of old age and the growing unsettlement of the times. He died in 1643, aged eighty, and was buried on 25 September of that year in Trinity Church, Ely.[5] He married in 1597 Anne, eldest daughter of Philip Haldenby of Haldenby—a very old family of royal descent. From this union there came three sons, the eldest being John, father of the future Archbishop, and Philip.

[1] J. and J. A. Venn, *Alumni Cantabrigienses*, 1926, Part I, iv. 214.
[2] *Ibid.*
[3] By reason of her remarriage in 1583.
[4] J. Bass Mullinger, *History of Cambridge University*.
[5] *Alumni Cantabrigienses*, iv. 214.

Philip Tenison was baptized at Downham on 26 April 1612.[1] He was admitted a scholar of Trinity College, Cambridge, in 1631, and became B.A., 1632, M.A., 1635, and D.D., 1661. He was presented to the living of Barton in Cambridgeshire in 1637, which he held till he became Vicar of Wethersfield in Essex in 1642. In 1647 he was appointed Rector of Hethersett in Norfolk, from which he was ejected during the Commonwealth when he suffered a term of imprisonment. Owing to this persecution of the episcopal clergy, he set up a school at Bawburgh in Norfolk, where he remained till he was appointed to the Rectory of Foulsham at the Restoration, and was made Archdeacon of Norfolk the same year. It is interesting to notice that Philip married Anne Mileham (eighth daughter of Sir Gregory Mileham), whose sister Dorothy became the wife of Sir Thomas Browne (1605–82), author of *Religio Medici*.[2] Philip Tenison died on 15 January 1661, and was buried at Bawburgh.[3]

John Tenison (his brother) was born in 1599, and was admitted a pensioner at Peterhouse on 2 April 1614. He matriculated that year, became Perne Scholar 1614–21, B.A., 1618, M.A., 1621, B.D. 1630, and Fellow, 1621–31.[4] In 1624 he was appointed curate to the parish of Cottenham in Cambridgeshire by the Rector, Leonard Maw, who became Bishop of Bath and Wells in 1628 and died the next year.[5] John Tenison retained this position under the succeeding rector, and also when John Manby, chaplain and son-in-law to Francis White, Bishop of Ely (1631–38), was appointed to the living in 1635. John Manby was turned out of Cottenham when it was sequestered by the Westminster Assembly, and the sister and brother-in-law of Oliver Cromwell resided in the rectory, being joined for a short time, so it is said, by the Protector himself.[6] Manby was restored with the return of Charles II and John Tenison, despite his other preferments, continued to act as curate, at least for some years.

In 1637 John Tenison was appointed Rector of Mundesley in Norfolk, a small village on the sea coast, and in 1641 he became Rector of Topcroft in the same county. During the Commonwealth, however (we are now quoting his son Thomas), he was "turned out of his Living of Mondesley (*sic*) in Norfolk, as an Adherer to King Charles the Martyr; a Person, one of whose

[1] Parish records.   [2] See p. 14.
[3] *Alumni Cantabrigienses*, iv. 214. [4] *Ibid.*
[5] *D.N.B.*, xxxvii. 110.   [6] Parish register and *Alumni Cantabrigienses*, iii. 964.

names was Gubbard, recommending himself to the Committee at Norwich as a man who had a zeal for the same Cause in which they were engaged, took possession of the Living and received all Profits but restored nothing".[1]

John Tenison's unhappy plight was by no means exceptional. The saintly Dr. Hall, Bishop of Norwich, was himself reduced at this time to a state of complete destitution, and some eighty clergymen in Norfolk were ejected from their livings, while after the ordinance came out that "no sequestered minister should be allowed to teach in a private school, there was nothing left but penury for most of them, and the widows and families of many had to be relieved by charity, some even coming upon the parish".[2] Fortunately, however, John Tenison appears to have remained undisturbed in his rectory at Topcroft, since he continued to sign the registers there from 1641 to 12 November 1670.[3]

On 9 March 1662, he was presented to the Rectory of Bracon Ash near Norwich (to which his son Thomas had been presented in 1661), but he appears to have continued to make his home at Topcroft, where he died on 25 June 1671, aged seventy-two, being buried in the church two days later. A simple grave-stone, placed there by his son, records the death of "Mr. John Tenison, B.D., sometime fellow of St. Peter's College in Cambridge, rector of Topcroft and Braconash".[4]

He had married at Rampton in Cambridgeshire, on 22 May 1631, Mercy, eldest daughter of Thomas Dowsing of Cottenham, gentleman, by Sarah Hills, his wife. From this union came Thomas, the future Archbishop of Canterbury and the subject of the following biography. To him, the only surviving son, John Tenison left under his will dated 17 February 1671, and proved 16 April 1672, "all my books and gowns and coats, and the great tanker and salt, and the two rings I wear on my finger". He bequeathed his copyhold in Thurston, Norfolk, to his wife for life,[5] with remainder to his son, the sole executor, and to "the said Thomas and his wife, my copyholds in Hempnall, Topcroft, Woodton, and Denton".[6]

---

[1] T. Tenison, "A True Account of a Conference", 1688, preface.
[2] *Victoria History of Norfolk*, 1906, ii. 291.
[3] Parish registers.
[4] C. Parkin, *History of Norfolk*, v. 1168.
[5] She died at Topcroft and was buried there on 7 August 1682.
[6] John Tenison's will.

CHAPTER 2

A PARISH PRIEST

Part I

IT was into an England governed on the principles of "Thorough" that Thomas Tenison was born on 29 September 1636, at Cottenham, a village in the fen district of Cambridgeshire which was also the home of the Pepys family. He was baptized three days later in the large parish church where his father was curate.[1]

Laud had been some three years Archbishop of Canterbury when Tenison was born, and in his own forthright yet blustering manner was trying to preserve the Church from what he regarded as the virus of Puritanism and the slovenliness of the apathetic. He turned the money-changers out of St. Paul's Cathedral, ordered the communion table to be placed at the east end of churches, and in 1637 branded Prynne on the cheeks with the letters "S.L.", a deformity which this witty and irrepressible Puritan described as the "Stigmata Laudis".

In matters of civil government, Tenison's early years saw the growing estrangement between the King and Parliament. Enraged at the activities of Laud, and conscious of their increasing power, the Puritans contested the king's right to levy taxes without the consent of Parliament; hence the stand of Hampden on the issue of Ship Money. But for Charles there could be no turning back, and his march into Scotland in 1639, accompanied by Laud,

---

[1] The following is a copy of the baptismal certificate.

1636 on ye second day of Oct.	Thomas	John & Mercy	Tennison	Cottenham	Curate

It will be noticed that "Tenison" is here spelt with two "n's". This variant is frequently found, but we shall follow Tenison's own usage. The register from which the above extract is taken bears at the end of the year the signature of John Manby, Rector, and the two churchwardens. An elder brother John Tennison was also baptized at Cottenham on 2 September 1632, but he seems to have died in infancy. Katharine Pepys endowed a school here and left a sum of money for charity. Tenison also remembered in his will the place of his birth, and left to the poor people of Cottenham £10. See *Memoirs of the Life and Times of Thomas Tennison*, p. 120. The village was nearly destroyed in 1676 by fire, which burnt out more than two-thirds of the buildings. The date of Tenison's birth is given by Le Neve, *Lives of Protestant Bishops*, i. 236.

5

to impose upon its people a prayer book which the Archbishop had helped to draw up, was the beginning of that tragic journey which led to final disaster—after those nightmare years during which he sacrificed both Strafford and Laud, raised his standard at Nottingham and suffered eclipse at Naseby. Thomas Tenison was twelve years of age when on 30 January 1649 Charles stepped out of a window of the Banqueting House at Whitehall, and was removed from a world, in which at least he had borne adversity with dignity, with the enigmatic injunction "Remember" on his lips. The Long Parliament, meanwhile, had made short shrift of the Church, and many clergy were in extreme want; but Thomas was fortunate in being safe at school, since his father had "interest enough to get him admitted as one of Archbishop Parker's scholars in the school at Norwich, a seminary at that time of high repute under the able mastership of Mr. Lovering".[1]

From the free school at Norwich, Thomas went up to Corpus Christi College, Cambridge (then Bene't College), on 22 April 1653—Cromwell having two days previously expelled the Long Parliament—where he was admitted a scholar upon Parker's foundation, and matriculated on 9 July 1653, at the age of seventeen.[2]

This choice of a university, following the family tradition, was a step which influenced Tenison for the rest of his life. For many years England had been, and was to continue to be, a scene of religious strife. Laud, although he had showed surprising tolerance to some intellectuals (Chillingworth, for example), yet stood for a rigidly organized episcopal system, which was to be supreme in matters of decency and order. The Puritans were equally rigid and intolerant in their views on church government, and the principle of dissent, once admitted, led to a multiplication of sects, each claiming divine sanction and infallible guidance. But the very menace of these conflicting and mutually exclusive theologies, each anathematizing the other, led some thoughtful minds to consider the possibility of lifting religion out of the maze of doubtful doctrines and divine decrees, into the serener atmosphere of universal principles. William Chillingworth found in the

---

[1] Cunningham, *Lives of Eminent Englishmen*, iv. 224. In Tenison's will we read: "To the six Norwich Scholars of Archbishop Parker's Foundation of which I once had the Honour and Benefit of being a Scholar and Fellow, Forty Shillings a piece yearly". *Memoirs of Life and Times*, etc., p. 11.

[2] Cunningham, *Lives of Eminent Englishmen*, iv. 224.

Scriptures, interpreted by reason, the final authority for religion, and John Hales of Eton fell back on the individual judgment, insisting that "every man must bear his own burden". This line of thought was given a philosophical basis in the middle years of the century by a remarkable group of men known to history as the Cambridge Platonists. It was to these men that Tenison was now introduced when he went up to Cambridge in 1653. Many a time, as a young student, he must have heard Benjamin Which-cote, Provost of King's, lecture in Trinity Church, and he could hardly fail to be impressed by the force and lucidity of his teaching, expressed in such pregnant phrases as: "Heaven is first a temper and then a place"; "To go against reason is to go against God; reason is the divine governor of man's life; it is the very voice of God".

A more direct influence on Tenison, however, was Ralph Cudworth, Master of Christ's College, whose refutation of Hobbes in *The True Intellectual System of the Universe* enjoyed an enormous contemporary reputation, and hardly deserves the complete oblivion into which it has been allowed to fall. Though Tenison may not have appreciated to the full the philosophical insight of these men, he yet learned from them a respect for reason, and a practical tolerance (not extended to Roman Catholics, however!) which were to remain with him throughout life.

Tenison graduated Bachelor of Arts in the Lent term 1657, but the uncertain state of the times, and the rigours to which the episcopal clergy, including his own father, were then being subjected under the Puritan domination, induced him to study medicine. But despite this temporary expedient, Thomas's heart and soul were with the Church of his fathers in its time of suffering. The unsettlement of the Commonwealth period made an impression upon him never to be forgotten. In his eyes the beheading of the King was "an execrable Murther", "the cutting off the Lord's anointed".[1] Cromwell was "the Spectre of Authority which walk'd at Whitehall", and his rule stood condemned as a time of "laxation of Discipline", "great and black Hypocrisies", and "religious Frenzie".[2] Yet during this time, so he wrote later, the Church of England was "still in being, though in Adversity. She had strong vitals and did not die, notwithstanding there was some Distemper in her Estate. And great numbers of the Church-men, by their constant Adherence to their Principles, under

---

[1] Tenison, *An Argument for Union*, 1683, p. 25.   [2] *Ibid.* p. 12.

publick Contempt and heavy Pressure, gained daily on the People".[1]

So great was his attachment to this Church that it was into its ministry that he was ordained privately at Richmond by Dr. Brian Duppa (1588–1662), Bishop of Salisbury, at a time when the future was never more uncertain, Oliver having died and the army then quarrelling with the Rump Parliament. Bishop Duppa was one of Archbishop Laud's protégés, and had been a great friend of Charles I., spending many weary hours with him before his execution. During the Commonwealth he lived in privacy at Richmond, but he took a great interest in the fate of the dispossessed clergy, and frequently held private ordinations. Tenison's letters of orders were not given out till after the Restoration, though at the time they were entered into a private book of the Bishop's.[2] The fact that Tenison was ordained at such a time shows a firm intention to enter the ministry of the Church of England as well as sympathy with its episcopal traditions.

Of Tenison's academic career there is not much to tell, for he appears to have been a conscientious rather than a brilliant student. He became Master of Arts in 1660 (which degree was incorporated at Oxford on 28 June 1664), Bachelor of Divinity in 1667, and Doctor of Divinity in 1680. He had been pre-elected to a Norwich Fellowship at his College on 29 February 1659, and was admitted Fellow on the death of one William Smith on 24 March 1662, becoming a tutor and university reader in 1665.[3] Amongst those to whom he acted as tutor at Corpus Christi were William Briggs (1642–1704), a famous oculist who wrote a treatise on "The Theory of Vision", and Thomas Montagu, fifth son of Tenison's patron, Edward Earl of Manchester. Tenison took an active part in the affairs of the College, voting regularly on the election of the Fellows, and he maintained throughout life his affection for his "alma mater". This he showed in many small ways. He subscribed £72 in respect of a mortmain licence, and

---

[1] Tenison, *An Argument for Union*, 1683, p. 29.

[2] Le Neve, *The Lives and Characters of the Protestant Bishops of the Church of England*, 1720, i. 237. Le Neve gives as his authority for this story of Tenison's ordination, and for his article as a whole: "MSS. notes concerning him [Tenison] communicated by the Right Reverend White [Kennett] Lord Bishop of Peterborough, which were taken from his Grace's own Mouth or Papers". There is no record of Tenison's ordination either in Duppa's register at Salisbury (which is defective) or in the Act Books. White Kennett himself, in his "register and Chronicle, Ecclesiastical and Civil" in 1728, says (I.626) that he heard this account of Tenison's ordination "from his own Mouth".

[3] R. Masters, *The History of the College of Corpus Christi*, 1753, i. 392; also *Alumni Cantabrigienses*, iv. 214.

contributed £50 towards the rebuilding of the brew house. Later, when Vicar of St. Martin's, he provided funds for the paving of the hall with stone; and "wainscotted very elegantly with oak that Norwich Fellowship Chamber where he himself had dwelt".[1]

Dr. Spencer (1630–93), Master of the College, was a great friend, and when in 1686 he appeared to be in a precarious state of health and "it was feared that the College and their MSS. might fall into the hands of the Papists, Mr. Cory, one of the Fellows, a person well skilled in old writing, was employed at the instance of Dr. Tenison, carefully to copy some of those relating to the establishment of the Protestant Religion—which copy has since been presented to the Dean and Chapter of Ely, and is now in their possession".[2]

Spencer was a learned Hebraist, an admirer of the Cambridge Platonists, and very tolerant in his attitude towards the Nonconformists. He and Tenison had therefore much in common, and the Master was indebted to his friend's kindness for a loan of money when he was pressed by his cousins. Tenison was the sole executor of Spencer's will, and he is therein spoken of as "my ancient friend", and is left the testator's book *De Legibus Hebraeorum* with full right and property therein. When the Master was buried in the college chapel in May 1693, Tenison, then Bishop of Lincoln, attended the funeral, and he later prepared the *De Legibus Hebraeorum* for the press, though its publication was prevented during his lifetime by "divers accidents". When it eventually appeared, it may be said (together with Spencer's *Dissertatio de Urim et Thummim*, 1669) to have "laid the foundations of the science of comparative religion, by tracing the connection between the rites of the Hebrew religion and those practised by kindred Semitic races".[3]

Despite these connections at Cambridge, Tenison was not destined for an academic career, and his first ecclesiastical preferment came when he was presented to the rectory of Bracon Ash, a small village some six miles from Norwich. He resigned this, however, in favour of his father, on being presented, in 1662, to the important living of St. Andrew the Great in Cambridge, by the Dean and Chapter of Ely, the Dean at this time being Dr. Wilford, Master of Tenison's College of Corpus Christi, and the living having once been held by Cudworth's father. It was his first

[1] R. Masters, *The History of the College of Corpus Christi*, 1753, i. 164.
[2] R. Masters, *ibid.* p. 14.
[3] *D.N.B.* liii. 378.

real experience of parochial responsibilities, and it enabled him to exercise an influence both on the town and university. His task was not made easier, although he was given a chance to show his mettle, by a visitation of the plague in 1665, during which year the parochial registers record numerous deaths. Tenison's conduct, at a time when most people, including Isaac Newton, fled from Cambridge, elicited general admiration, and an eighteenth-century historian writes:

"Pestilence broke out with such violence that none ventured to continue here but Mr. Tenison, one of the Fellows (afterwards Archbishop of Canterbury), two scholars and a few servants; for whom a Preservative Powder was brought and administered in Wine, whilst Charcoal, Pitch, and Brimstone were kept continually burning in the Gatehouse. The former not only resided here, but what is very extraordinary, attended upon the care of St. Andrew's, the Parish of which he was then Minister, with perfect safety to himself during the whole time".[1]

During Tenison's incumbency, there occurred the death of a prominent citizen, Christopher Rose, High Sheriff, and twice Mayor of Cambridge, who over a number of years had been a great benefactor to the Church. Rose showed his appreciation of Tenison's ministry by leaving him a bequest, and Tenison placed an extract from the will in the parochial register.

Tenison resigned the living of St. Andrew's in 1667, and the parishioners displayed their gratitude by presenting him with "a large silver Tankard, and upon it St. Andrew's Cross and this Inscription, Gift of St. Andrew's Parishioners 1667 in Cambridge. Tho. Wiseman, Nic. Settle, Churchwardens, 1667".[2]

During the next few years preferment came readily into Tenison's hands, which seems to suggest that he was now making valuable connections. It was customary for rising clergymen to attach themselves to some powerful family, and Tenison, following the prescribed course, had become chaplain, at the time of the Restoration, to Edward, second Earl of Manchester[3] (1602–71). This Earl had been a leader of the Puritans during the Long Parliament, securing Lincolnshire for the Parliament in 1644, but owing to his negligence at the second battle of Newbury,

---

[1] Masters, *History of Corpus Christi*, i. 161.
[2] Le Neve, *The Lives and Characters of the Protestant Bishops of the Church of England*, 1720, p. 237.
[3] Son of Sir Henry Montagu, first Earl of Manchester (1563–1642), who wrote the famous *Contemplatio Mortis et Immortalitatis*, 1631.

he was charged by Cromwell in the House of Commons with incompetence in the prosecution of the war, and as a result resigned his commission in 1645. He opposed the ordinance for the King's trial, and retired into private life when the establishment of the Commonwealth became inevitable, remaining in obscurity until he was restored to honour and position at the Restoration.[1]

In 1667 the Earl of Manchester appointed Tenison to the rectory of Holywell and Needingworth in Huntingdonshire, Tenison marrying in December of that year, Anne, daughter of Dr. Love, Dean of Ely, and Master of his old College (1596–1661). The exact date of his institution is not recorded in the parochial registers, and Tenison himself seems to have acquired a lease of the advowson, since he appointed himself and his successor John Knighton (who later became Sub-dean of Lincoln).

The records of this parish bear witness to Tenison's undoubted zeal in the discharge of his duty. He was the first rector to keep a parochial register, and it was his custom to place his signature at the end of the entries for each year. The records included in this first volume (for the years 1667–1746) show a total of 1,053 baptisms (yearly average 14), 360 marriages (yearly average 5), and 1,242 burials (yearly average 16). It is interesting to notice that the highest figure in two of these is recorded during Tenison's incumbency, 27 baptisms in 1676, and 37 burials two years later.[2]

In 1672, Tenison, with his customary thoroughness, drew up a deed and terrier of all lands belonging to the Church, and signed the document on 2 April. We shall have much to say later of Tenison's charitable bequests. His generous spirit here showed itself in a "Tenison Charity" for the poor, which is still in existence,[3] and a fund for the parish church, the yearly value of which now amounts to £3 1s. 4d. He also presented the parish with a characteristic gift—a collection of statutes in two volumes, dated 1632 and 1667, both bearing the inscription: "The gift of Tho. Tenison to ye parish of Holywell". Nor was Mrs. Tenison behind him in generosity, for she gave to the church a Book of Common Prayer (folio edition 1669), inscribed: "The gift of Mrs. Anne Tenison to the Parish of Holywell for ye use on the more solemn times".[4]

[1] D.N.B. xxxviii. 27.
[2] Holywell Parish Records.
[3] Its terms of reference have recently been revised by the present rector.
[4] Holywell Parish Records.

Tenison was as yet quite unknown to the general public, but he now first claimed its attention in *The Creed of Mr. Hobbes Examin'd*, written in 1670, and dedicated, naturally enough, to the Earl of Manchester.

It was the materialistic determinism of Hobbes which had largely induced the Cambridge Platonists to embark upon a philosophical enquiry into the nature of religion, and opposition to his conclusions runs throughout all their works. The serious nature of his attack on religion had been particularly recognized by Ralph Cudworth, who regarded it almost as his life's work to refute him. But *The True Intellectual System of the Universe* was an erudite treatise lacking system, and as such not likely to commend itself to the rank and file of the clergy. Tenison, therefore, determined to attempt something smaller and more succinct, for though Hobbism was out of favour during the reign of Charles II, that Indian summer of Royalism, yet the force of his cold logic remained. No matter what lip service Hobbes might pay to the forms of the Christian religion, Tenison recognized that the nature of his arguments was to deny its validity.

Tenison cast his work in the form of a dialogue between Hobbes and a student, and his general manner of argument and arrangement of his material show clearly, that though he was not possessed of a highly original or speculative mind, he had yet read widely, was more at home with the Greek philosophers than his opponent, and could concentrate on the subject in hand with vigour. He began by accusing Hobbes of maintaining the "corporeality" of God, in which case, he said, the divine Being must be identified with the world, and "so the universe might be worshipped as God"; and Pharaoh, Herod, and Judas, "not to say Mr. Hobbes himself", must be parts of God. Following his Cambridge teachers, he denies that human reason is incapable of judging the divine actions, but insists that it is "an eternal and universal standard". Turning to the philosopher of Malmesbury's political speculations, Tenison writes:

"He hath form'd a model of Government, pernicious in its Consequences to all Nations; and injurious to the right of his present Majesty: for he taught the people, soon after the martyrdom of his Royal Father, that his title was extinguished when his adherents were subdued; and that the Parliament had the right for that very Reason, because it had possession".[1]

---

[1] Tenison, *The Creed of Mr. Hobbes Examin'd*, 1671. Preface.

The Creed of Mr. Hobbes Examin'd certainly gave the lie to a ridiculous rumour that Tenison himself was a Hobbist, and Hunt, in his *History of Religious Thought*, regards it as "perhaps the most sensible reply" made to this philosopher.[1] It soon went through two editions, and may have contributed to the condemnation of the *Leviathan* by the University of Oxford on 21 July 1683, as one of "certain pernicious books and damnable doctrines".

The success of this first publication encouraged Tenison to follow it up with a *Discourse on Idolatry* in 1677, and *Baconiana*, published in the following year.

That Tenison should have appeared as the enthusiastic admirer of Bacon is interesting, particularly since most of the Cambridge Platonists took up a "neutral" attitude in relation to the works of this great man. Perhaps Tenison was influenced by Dr. William Rawley (1588–1667), Bacon's "learned Chaplain", with whom he was on terms of some friendship; or it may be that he had studied the works of Joseph Glanvill (1636–88), author of *Scepsis Scientifica*, which did so much to familiarize students with the importance of the inductive method.

Certainly Tenison's admiration for Bacon was unbounded, and in assessing his work he placed him above Copernicus, Father Paul the Venetian, Galileo, Harvey, and Gilbert,[2] and paid him the following noble tribute:

"Easie it is to add to things already invented; but to invent and to do it under Discouragement, when the World is prejudiced against the Invention, & with loud Clamour hooteth at the Projector; this is not an undertaking for Dulness or Cowardice. To do this argues an Inquisitive and Sagacious Wit; a mind free from slavish prepossession; a piercing judgment able to see through the mists of Authority; a great Power in the Understanding, giving to a man sufficient courage to bear up the Head against the common Current of Philosophical Doctrines, & Force to beat out its own way in untravelled

[1] Hunt, *History of Religious Thought*, i. 402.

Tenison apparently contemplated dealing with Hobbes again some years later, for in 1680, Wallis (Professor of Geometry at Oxford, who exposed Hobbes' claim to have squared the circle) wrote to him as follows: "I received yours of Nov. 25, and I approve the Designe. The Life you speak of I have not seen. Nor do I know that I ever saw the man. Of his writings I have read very little, save what relates to Mathematics. By that I find him to have been of a bold, daring Fancy (to venture at anything). But he wanted judgment to understand the Consequences of an Argument & to speak consistently with himself". See Wallis to Tenison, Nov. 30, 1680. Lambeth MSS. 930, f. 55. De Quincey in his *Murder as one of the fine Arts* introduces Tenison in a dialogue with Hobbes.

[2] Tenison, *Baconiana or Certain Genuine Remains of Sir Francis Bacon*, 1678. Preface.

Places. With such intellectual ability was the Lord Verulam
endu'd; . . . and he has been happy in being follow'd, by
Men of the ablest Understandings, with singular Success; & the
Society for improving of natural Knowledge do not at this day
depart from his Directions, though they travel further than
Death could suffer him to adventure".[1]

Tenison's *Baconiana* is still not without interest and it has undoubtedly proved useful to many subsequent students of Bacon.

The other work, a *Discourse on Idolatry* (there is an examination
of it in Chap. 3), was "some part meditated and the whole
revised in the castle of Kimbolten", the seat of the Earl of
Manchester. It was the first of Tenison's many published attacks on
the Church of Rome.

Perhaps we may anticipate the years to notice here that in 1685
Tenison appeared as the editor of "Certain Miscellany Tracts
written by Sir Thomas Brown (*sic*) Kt. and Doctour of Physick
late of Norwich".[2] We have already seen that Tenison's uncle
Philip married Anne Mileham, a sister of Lady Browne, and this
appears to have made him intimate with the family. Thus in
January 1664 Edward Browne was present when Tenison preached
in St. Luke's Chapel, Norwich, and some years later Sir Thomas
in a letter to this same son says: "Mr. Tenison, I told you
had written a good Poem 'Contra Huius saeculi Lucretianos'
illustrating God's Wisdome and providence from Anatomie and
the Rubric and Use of Parts, in a manuscript dedicated to me and
Dr. Lawson[3] in Latin, after Lucretius his Style".[4]

Sir Thomas Browne died in 1682 and Edward (his eldest son)
passed on to Tenison his father's unpublished papers with a view
either to the "suppressing or publishing of them". Tenison
decided to place a selection before the public since "many who
had taken of the fruits of his former studies were covetous of more

[1] Tenison, *Baconiana*, p. 15. This book consists of: (a) List of Bacon's works;
(b) "Baconiana Bibliographica"—extant judgments of him, etc.; (c) papers written by
himself referring to his books; (d) papers written by others relating to his books and
life; (e) an extract from Abraham Cowley's poem to the Royal Society. As to Bacon's
undignified fall, Tenison made the charitable comment (p. 16): "Whatsoever his
Errors were, or the Cause of his Misfortune, they are over balanced by his Virtues,
and will die with Time. His Errors were as some Excresencies which grow on those
Trees that are fit to build the Palaces of Kings".
[2] "Certain Miscellany Tracts written by Sir Thomas Brown Kt. and Doctour of
Physick late of Norwich", 1685, ed. T. Tenison.
[3] Dr. Lawson was Tenison's brother-in-law, he also having married a daughter of
Dr. Love, Dean of Ely. Tenison wrote the "Epistle Dedicatory" of his *Discourse on
Idolatry* from Dr. Lawson's house in Mincing Lane in London.
[4] This poem never appears to have been published and no trace of it now exists.
See Edmund Gosse, *Sir Thomas Browne*, p. 163.

of the like kind", and the author himself seemed to have intended publication. These papers consisted of "occasional essays", in letter form, on subjects so various as "The Fishes eaten by our Saviour with the Disciples after the Resurrection from the dead", and "Of Languages and particularly of the Saxon tongue". Tenison was careful to point out in his preface that these essays "were rather the Diversions than the Labours of his Pen", though he was certain they would commend themselves by their "Learning, Curiosity and Brevity" to all except those "with such a Niceness of Imagination as no wise man is concern'd to humour". As to Sir Thomas, the editor "chose to be silent", though he had had "the hapiness to have been for some years known to him".[1]

It was this connection with Sir Thomas Browne which, probably, led to Tenison's being chosen upper minister of St. Peter Mancroft in Norwich in 1673, this church being then, as since, the centre of religious life in the city. In 1595 the parishioners of St. Peter Mancroft had established their right to appoint the minister, a privilege which now resides in the parochial church council. Tenison had already preached in the church a year before his appointment, so that he was no stranger to the congregation. He held this office for some eighteen months, during which time he received £142 in salary, paid to him quarterly by the church-wardens.[2] It is characteristic of him that during his short stay he should have given several valuable books to the church library, which are now unfortunately lost. A portrait of the future archbishop still hangs in the sacristy of the church. It was while he was at St. Peter Mancroft that Tenison made the acquaintance of Thomas Green, father of Thomas Green, D.D., later his domestic chaplain.

Part II

Tenison was now a man of rising importance, and this was recognized in 1672 when he became a chaplain-in-ordinary to the King.[3] His public career, together with his Cambridge loyalties, had shown him to be a conscientious Protestant, wholehearted in his attachment to the Church of England, yet broadminded and

[1] "Certain Miscellany Tracts written by Sir Thomas Browne Kt.", 1685. Preface. Tenison later contemplated writing a life of Sir Thomas Browne, but was forced to give up the idea because of his many other labours.
[2] St. Peter Mancroft, Norwich. Parish records.
[3] *Alumni Cantabrigienses*, iv. 214.

practical in his attitude to the Nonconforming parties. In his many livings, he had discharged his duties with great zeal, and his reward came when on 8 October 1680, he was nominated to the important living of St. Martin-in-the-Fields (its income was from £900 to £1,000 a year), on the promotion of Dr. Lloyd to the bishopric of Coventry and Lichfield. It had been offered first to Simon Patrick, an energetic church reformer, Vicar of the neighbouring church of St. Paul's, Covent Garden, and Dean of Peterborough, who on declining it wrote to Dr. Thorpe, chaplain to the Archbishop of Canterbury, urging him to use his influence on behalf of Dr. Tenison. Thus Dr. Patrick writes in his *Autobiography*:

"When I came to town the Lord Chancellor sent for me, and made me that noble offer: Which I told him I could not thankfully enough acknowledge, but my parish had lately been so extraordinarily kind to me, that I could not with decency remove from them to another. Besides I told him I doubted whether I should be able to perform the duties of so great a parish: but if he would not think me too bold, I would recommend one to him that had strength of mind and body to undergo so great a charge and named Dr. Tenison, whom I perceived he had heard of, and afterwards told me that he would bestow it upon him. Of which I wrote first to the Doctor, and blessed God for placing so good a man in that great Station, who is now deservedly advanced to the highest dignity in the Church".[1]

Tenison was at his best in a position where organizing activity and a conscientious application to detail were required, and as Vicar of St. Martin's he undoubtedly found full scope for his abilities. Burnet summarizes his work at St. Martin's as follows:

"Tenison carried on and advanced all those good methods that he [Lloyd] had begun in the management of that great cure; he endowed schools, set up a public library, and kept many curates to assist him in his indefatigable labours amongst them. He was a very learned man, and took much pains to state the notions and practices of heathenish idolatry to fasten that charge on the Church of Rome.[2] And Whitehall lying within that parish, he stood as in the front of the battle all King James' reign; and maintained as well as managed that dangerous post with great courage and judgment, and was held in very high esteem for his whole deportment, which was ever grave and moderate".[3]

[1] Simon Patrick, *Autobiography*, p. 83.
[2] See Chap. 3.
[3] Burnet, *History of my own Time*, ii. 338.

As Vicar of St. Martin's, and as a religious controversialist, Tenison now became a public figure, and his contemporaries were undoubtedly impressed with the care and diligence which he displayed in the administration of his large parish. John Evelyn, the diarist, who as a frequent worshipper at St. Martin's now first became acquainted with Tenison, thought him "one of the most profitable preachers in the Church of England, being also of a most holy conversation, very learned and ingenious". So conscientious was he that Evelyn adds: "The pains he takes, and care of his parish, will, I fear, wear him out, which would be an inexpressible loss".[1] The parish of St. Martin's was certainly a large one, and some idea of its population may be seen in that during the month of December 1685 (we take this month quite at random from the parochial records) there were 77 baptisms, 144 burials, and 4 marriages.[2] Congregations were large, and when Evelyn received the Communion on Sunday, 7 October 1688 (after Tenison had preached a very militant Protestant sermon), he was one "of near 1,000 devout persons".[3] Services were

---

[1] Evelyn, *Diary and Correspondence*, ii. 174.

[2] St. Martin-in-the-Fields. Parish register.

[3] Evelyn, *Diary and Correspondence*, ii. 280.

We find from a document at Lambeth (Lambeth MSS. 1035) that the collection at this service amounted to £10 1s. 0d. In this document there is an account of all the offertory monies received and disbursed by William Cleer, senior church-warden of the parish for the year 1688. We quote it below, though it should be noted that it is not a complete account of all offertory monies, but only those which passed through the hands of William Cleer.

"The Account of Mr. William Cleer Senior Church Warden of the Parish of St. Martin in the Fields in the County of Middlesex of the Offertory moneys received and disbursed in the year 1688.

April 29		2	2	6
May 6		7	7	0
May 10		25	3	0
May 13			8	6
May 20		1	2	0
Ascension Day May 24			10	0
May 27			11	0
June 3 Whitsunday		8	15	3
June 10 Trinity Sunday		6	10	6
July 1		10	11	6
Aug. 5		6	10	6
Sep. 2	7 o'clock prayers	7	2	0
Sep. 20 At the Sacrament this morning after 8		1	1	6
Oct. 7		10	1	0
Oct. 21 At Sacrament this morning at 8 o'clock		1	0	0
Oct. 28 At Sacrament this morning at 8 o'clock		1	0	0
Nov. 4 ,, ,, ,,		9	4	6
Nov. 18 ,, ,, ,,		1	0	0
Nov. 25 At the Sac. this morning at 8 o'clock			15	0
25 At Sac. immediately after divine service		1	10	0
Dec. 2 At the monthly Sac.		9	8	0
16 At Sac. immediately after 7 o'clock prayers			10	0

numerous, and there were regular celebrations of Communion on the first Sunday in each month, as well as frequent celebrations after "divine service", and what was termed "7 o'clock prayers".

It may help the reader to gain a more vivid impression of Tenison's ministry at St. Martin's if we quote a few typical instances of his pastoral care. As we shall see later, he was deeply concerned with the wider political issues of the day, but it was as a parish priest that he commended himself to a man of such wide humanity as John Evelyn.

The zeal with which Tenison discharged his parochial responsibilities often led to his being called in to visit the death-bed of the penitent. In December 1681 he ministered to the notorious informer Edward Turbeville (1648?–81) when he was dying of smallpox,[1] and a few months later he attended at the death-bed of Thomas Thynne of Longleat (1648–82), "Tom of Ten Thousand"—"that very wild young gentleman", as Godolphin describes him. This eccentric figure, first James' supporter and then Monmouth's, was fatally injured when driving down Pall Mall, on 12 February 1682, by a certain Königsmark, one of his wife's suitors.[2] Tenison was immediately summoned, and first saw the wounded man between eleven and twelve o'clock at night, when he "discoursed with him about the state of his soul", and prayed with him till the last.[3]

Present with Tenison was the Duke of Monmouth: they were to meet again a few years later at an even more dramatic scene.[4]

16 At Sac.	..	..	..	..	..	divine service		15	0
23 At Sac.	..	..	..	..	..	7 o'clock prayers		10	0
25 At the Sacrament	..	..	..	..	..	..	13	19	6
30 At Sac.	..	..	..	..	..	7 o'clock prayers		15	0
Jan. 1 At the Sacrament	..	..	..	..	..	..	1	12	0
6 At the Sacrament	..	..	..	..	..	..	7	3	6
20 At Sac. immediately after 7 o'clock prayers			..	..	1	0	0
Feb. 3 ..	..	..	..	..	..	..	6	15	0
17 At Sac.	..	..	..	..	..	..	1	2	0
24 At Sac.	..	..	..	..	..	..	1	4	0
Mar. 3 At monthly Sac.	..	..	..	..	..	6	13	0
17 At Sac. immediately after 7 o'clock prayers			..	..		19	0
24 Palm Sunday At Sac.	..	..	..	..	..	1	1	0
29 Good Friday	..	..	..	..	..	..	7	8	0
31 At a Sac.	..	..	..	..	..	..	7	8	0
31 At a Sac. the 28 March when Bp. of Exeter ordained 5 priests and deacon ..				..	..	..		8	6
April 7 Low Sunday ..	..	..	..	..	..	..	5	12	0

[1] H.M.C. 10th Report. App. 9, p. 174.
[2] There is a vivid representation of the scene on his memorial in Westminster Abbey.
[3] Simon Patrick, *Autobiography*, p. 92.
[4] J. H. Jesse, *Memoirs of the Court of England from the Revolution in 1688 to the Death of George the Second*, 1843, i. 366.

Perhaps there is no more striking testimony to Tenison's sympathetic nature than that he should have been sent for by Nell Gwyn (1650–87)—the favourite of Charles and the "witty Nelly" of Pepys—during her last hours. Pall Mall, where she resided, was in the parish of St. Martin's, and it was probably through the good offices of Dr. Richard Lower (1631–91), the most noted physician of the day,[1] that she was introduced to Tenison. Dr. Lower was a sturdy Protestant, and as James later observed, "did him more mischief than a troop of horse". He was frequently with Nelly, and would "pick out of her all the intrigues of the Court of King Charles II". In November 1687, Nelly fell ill with apoplexy. She immediately called for Dr. Tenison and he was with her to the end, encouraging her "in all contrite symptoms of a Christian anxiety".[2]

Nelly had drawn up her will on 9 July 1687, but three months later she added a codicil written on a separate sheet of paper and headed: "The last request of Mrs. Ellen Gwynne to his Grace the Duke of St. Albans [her son] made October the 18th, 1687". In this she asked :

"that Dr. Tenison preach her funeral sermon; that there be a decent pulpit cloth and cushion given to St. Martin's; that the Duke would pay into the hands of Dr. Tenison one hundred pounds to be disposed of in his discretion for the use of the Poor of St. Martin's and St. James', for taking any poor debtors of these parishes out of prison, for cloathes for the winter and other necessaries, as he shall find most fit; that, for showing her charity to those who differed from her in Religion, fifty Pounds be put into the Hands of Dr. Tenison and Mr. Warner, for the benefit of the poor Roman Catholics of St. James' Parish".[3]

The Vicar of St. Martin's, to his great credit—the controversy with Pulton was then engaging his attention[4]—carried out Nelly's wishes. Peter Cunningham, her biographer, writes:

"Good Dr. Tenison, too, complied with her request, and preached her funeral sermon; but what the Doctor said—except that he said 'much to her praise'—no one has told us. The Church was doubtless crowded—all apprentices who could obtain leave from their masters for such a lesson were there, and perhaps many a wet eye was seen—for Nelly was a good subject,

---

[1] *D.N.B.* xxiv. 203.
[2] P. Cunningham, *The Story of Nell Gwyn*, 1927, p. 157.
[3] Considering the temper of the time, this shows a rare charity.
[4] See ch. 3, pt. II.

and the then Vicar of St. Martin's was an impressive preacher. It was bold in Tenison to preach such a sermon and on such a person; but he knew the worth of Nelly and was not afraid".[1]

He did not escape censure, however. "Some mercenarie people printed and employed hawkers to cry in the streets a sham or largely transmogrified discourse which the Vicar himself was obliged to denounce as a forgery". This he did by inserting the following notice in a pamphlet he was issuing at the time in connection with the Catholic controversy: "ADVERTISEMENT. Whereas there has been a Paper cry'd by some Hawkers, as a Sermon preached by D.T. at the Funeral of M. E. Gwynn, this may Certify, that that Paper is the Forgery of some Mercenary People".[2]

The sermon was not soon forgotten and it was later brought up against him at the time of his elevation to the see of Lincoln.[3]

Tenison's diligence in visiting the dying led to a somewhat mysterious incident in 1684. On 10 June, the following letter, written in a "made and counterfeit hand", found its way to the Vicar of St. Martin's:

"Sir,

This is from an unknown hand, but it's to let you understand that one Sergeant Ramsay lyes a-dying, & desires some Divine to come to him to unburden his conscience about the murder of Sir Edmund Godfrey;[4] he lives in your Parish in Yorke building. Justice Dew can tell you more, he lives in Suffolk Street; if you have courage to own the Protestant cause, do your duty, visit him".

Tenison's suspicions were aroused. He sent his chancel-keeper to make enquiries, who discovered that Sergeant Ramsay "had long since left that House and was gone into the Country".[5]

As Vicar of St. Martin's, Tenison appears to have been an assiduous visitor, and in later years he used to tell an interesting story of a rather curious experience. One day, he said,

"a young woman came to him to visit her dying father in a Yard or Lane in King's Street, Westminster, and importuning him much to go with her; She said that her Father lay

---

[1] P. Cunningham, *The Story of Nell Gwyn*, p. 158.
[2] Tenison, *A True Account of a Conference*, 1687, p. 100.
[3] See ch. 6, p. 121.
[4] Sir Edmund Berry Godfrey (1621–78), justice of the peace, was a zealous Protestant and received the first depositions of Titus Oates. He was murdered a month later. Two Catholics and a Protestant were later hanged at Tyburn for the crime, but they were almost certainly innocent. *D.N.B.* xxii. 31.
[5] Le Neve, *The Lives and Characters of the Protestant Bishops*, p. 238.

under the Horrour of having cut the King's head [Charles I].
When he came, the Person was dead and no Confession was left
in writing, nor any other Account to be got, but that the Person
had been a sort of Butcher or Cattle Driver at St. Ives in
Huntingdonshire, was sent for by Oliver Cromwell about the
end of 1648, had ever since lived obscurely by a feigned name
and received a Yearly Pension which died with him".[1]

Many years after this incident Tenison asked his friend,
White Kennett, to make some enquiries as to the whereabouts of
the daughter at the Griffin or Green Dragon Tavern in Fleet
Street, but the house had changed hands and he could discover
nothing".[2]

In his pastoral labours Tenison's advice was often sought
on personal problems, and we quote the following as typical,
although it shows, perhaps, an exceptionally nice conscience
in the enquirer. A certain couple were engaged to be married,
but the lady, on her own initiative, broke off the engagement and
married another, who soon died, however, and left her a widow.
The former lover now wrote to Tenison to know whether he was
free from any obligations to the lady, and could himself enter into
matrimony.[3] Even so stern a moralist as the Vicar of St. Martin's,
we feel, could hardly forbear to reply in the affirmative.

Clergymen, apparently, were asked out in those days as much
as now, although not all modern invitations are so interesting
as the following:

"1683 Tues. 29 May,
Sir,
    The King's Birth Day having been annually kept by divers
Noblemen and Gentlemen, Born in the Parish of St. Martin in
the Fields, you are directed to continue that custom, and give
them a Meeting at the Sun Tavern in the Strand, on Tues. the
29th of May, 1683 by Eight of the Clock in the Morning, there
to receive your Colours, and from thence to return to Dinner
to the Tavern aforesaid".[4]

Despite his "many curates", Tenison soon came to feel that
the parish was too large, and that efficiency would be best

---

[1] White Kennett, *A Complete History of England*, 1719, iii. 187.
[2] *Ibid.* Among Tenison's papers at Lambeth, there is a letter (930, f. 21) dated 30
October 1696, which relates that King Charles, when he came out onto the scaffold,
told Bishop Juxon that one of the disguised executioners was Grey of Groby, son of
the Earl of Stamford. He could tell this by his hand.
[3] Lambeth MSS. 933, f. 371.
[4] *Ibid.* 954, f. 12.

promoted by splitting it up. There was undoubtedly a real quickening of church life at this time, due partly to the stimulation of the Roman Catholic attack, and also to the high standard of duty which such men as Sharp, White Kennett, and Tenison set themselves. Consequently, in 1685 in the first parliament of James II, an Act was passed for "making part of St. Martin's Parish, Westminster, a distinct parish of itself by the name of St. James' Parish, and Dr Tenison was by the same Act constituted its Rector, which he held together with that of St. Martin's until his promotion to the see of Lincoln and above six months after by commendam".[1]

Tenison was now vicar of two parishes, and had working under him a numerous staff of clergy; but he still did not regard the provision of churches as adequate to deal with a rapidly increasing population. To remedy this he himself in 1687 built a private chapel of ease in Swallow Street, now St. Thomas's, Regent Street,[2] and in 1689, encouraged by his success in the case of St. James', he attempted to create another parish. Perhaps with a certain relish, he determined to preach the Protestant word in a former Catholic conventicle. As part of his proselytizing activities, James had established a church for "mass priests" on Hounslow Heath, and Tenison thought that if he could secure its removal (which seemed possible now that William was on the throne), this might provide a church for the new parish. He was so far successful as to obtain permission to re-erect this wooden structure in Conduit Street, which he did almost entirely at his own expense. On 18 May 1689 Tenison had the satisfaction of being the first to preach in this church on its new site, and amongst a distinguished congregation on this occasion was John Evelyn, sitting in a gallery intended for his son's family. The Vicar of St. Martin's took as his text Ps. xxvi. 8: "Lord, I have loved the habitation of thy house, and the place where thine honour dwelleth", and in bringing the sermon to a conclusion he announced that the church would be made "a parish Church so soon as the Parliament sate, and was to be dedicated to the Holy Trinity in honour of the three and undivided Persons in the Deity".[3]

[1] Le Neve, *The Lives and Characters of the Protestant Bishops*, p. 241.
[2] This chapel was rebuilt in 1702, but not consecrated till 1869.
[3] Evelyn, *Diary*, ii. 314. Evelyn writes that Tenison concluded his sermon by exhorting his congregation "to attend to that faith of the Church now especially that Arians, Socinians and Atheism began to spread among us".

Tenison had already decided to appoint one Stringfellow as its first vicar, and on 18 May this clergyman preached a sermon in which he "modestly insinuated the obligation that they had to that person who should be the author and promoter of such public works for the benefit of mankind".[1]

Tenison's hopes, however, were disappointed, since despite this favourable beginning, he was unable to secure the creation of a new parish and the church remained a chapel in private hands. What he intended was later secured, though he was then Archbishop of Canterbury, when under an "Act for building fifty new Churches in London", a church was built between Conduit Street and Hanover Square. The first stone was laid to this building on 2 June 1712, and the parish of St. George, Hanover Square, was carved out of St. Martin-in-the-Fields.

Part III

To his contemporaries, Tenison's stay at St. Martin's was marked by two events, both almost of national importance, namely, his founding a free library and a school in the parish. It is not easy for us, now that libraries are numerous, to appreciate the difficulties which confronted the ordinary student in those days. Owing to the elaborate and solid nature of the bindings, books were expensive, and the poorer clergy found it very difficult to obtain them. Evelyn, a student himself, complains in his diary that "it is a great reproach that so great a city as London should not have a public library belonging to it", and he thought that one should be placed in St. Paul's if "ever finished".[2] Tenison was first confronted with the need in his own parish, where there resided many clergymen, mostly "governors to young gentlemen or chaplains to noblemen". He was distressed to find that they spent most of their time "frequenting taverns or coffee houses" (the vogue of the latter was beginning), and with that conscientious diligence so typical of him, he went out of his way to remonstrate with them but received the reply that "they would study and employ their time better if they had books". To meet this demand, Tenison determined, in 1684, to erect a free library in his parish (having in mind, possibly, the library of St. Peter Mancroft, Norwich), and he stated his reasons for so doing (in a printed pamphlet) as follows:

[1] Evelyn, *Diary*, ii. 314.   [2] *Ibid.* p. 227.

3

"Dr. Tho. Tenison having considered that in the precinct of the Cities and Liberties of Westminster there are great number of Ministers and other studious persons and especially in the parish of St. Martin's where besides the Vicar and his assistants, there are several Noblemen's Chap[ns] perpetually residing; as also there is not in the said precincts (as in London) any Shopp or Stationary, fully furnished with Books of various Learning, or any public Library, excepting of St. James which belongs to his Majestie and to which there is no easie access, that of Sr Rob. Cottons (which consisteth chiefly of Books relating to the Antiquities of England) and the Library of the Dean and Chapter of St. Peter's Church, Westminster (wch is as the other are) inconvenient for the use of all the said precinct . . . He the said Dr. Tenison hath been inclined upon the above considerations in case the Gentlemen of the Vestry sh'd approve of it to erect in that place a Fabrick for a public Library for the use of the students of the above mention'd precinct at his proper costs and charges, and to make some settlement for the support of the said Fabrick and towards the maintaining of the keeper of the said intended Library".[1]

In accordance with this scheme, the Vicar of St. Martin's first sought the advice "of his worthy Friends ye gentlemen of the Vestry . . . and desired their concurrence for ye governing of that library by such Methods as he should judge convenient". It did not take the vestry long to approve such an excellent scheme. They agreed that the site in Castle Street was convenient for the purpose, and that the erection of a library on this spot would not prove prejudicial to the users of the churchyard.[2] Empowered to proceed, Tenison next met John Evelyn and Sir Christopher Wren on 23 February 1684, when a plan for the library was submitted by Sir Christopher, and an estimate of the expense made. Building operations began in the spring, and when Evelyn visited the library after its completion, on 15 July, he was very much impressed with its appearance and writes in his diary: "The Books with backs gilt are set on the shelves: there be divers tables set in convenient places for the use of such as read or transcribe".[3] The Archbishop of Canterbury, under the terms of its constitution, was made visitor of the library, and nine trustees were appointed from the parish of St. Martin's, among whom the vicar and churchwardens were always to be included.

[1] B.M. Add. MSS. 24, 692, f. 13.
[2] *Ibid.* 38, 693, f. 148.
[3] Evelyn, *Diary*, ii. 227.

It was further stated that the librarian must be in priest's orders, and that persons privileged to use the library were the vicar and lecturer of St. Martin's parish, the schoolmaster and usher for the time being, the clergy of St. James' and St. Anne's, Westminster, and the king's chaplains. The cost of building and furnishing the library appears to have been borne entirely by Tenison, who left a settlement for the support of the fabric and the salary of the librarian. Unfortunately, however, he left no money for the purchase of new books, so that when in 1777 a visitor saw the library, he described it as being in the same condition as at Tenison's death.[1]

Tenison was himself an enthusiastic collector of books and manuscripts and remained a life-long bibliophile. We have already seen how he collected manuscripts relating to Bacon and edited a volume called *Baconiana*.[2] In 1695 he bought the MSS. belonging to the scholar Henry Wharton, after his premature death, and deposited them in the Lambeth library, to which he left by will all his books "both Printed and in Manuscript", such as should be "judged worthy for that Place by Dr. Gibson, Rector of Lambeth, and Mr. Ibbot my Library keeper and Mr. Clavering my other Chaplain".[3] These manuscripts are now at Lambeth, but are "named after the librarian instead of the collector".

Not all of Tenison's collections, however, are at Lambeth, since one of his reasons for founding the library at St. Martin's was to make a large number of his books and manuscripts accessible to students, particularly those books "which he regarded as most representative in English history". This library, as we have seen, was catalogued by Edmund Gibson in 1692, and we are thus given an indication of Tenison's wide range of interests. Amongst the many MSS. deposited there, we may notice the following: a note-book belonging to Bacon, relating to his private affairs in 1608–09; a copy of *Polychronicon* of Ranulf Higden (d. 1364), translated by John de Trevisa, a large folio fourteenth-century MS. on vellum; a noted Sarum Missal; a tenth-century MS. known as "Prudentii Liber de Pugna Vitiorum et Virtutum cum Glossis", which had eighty illustrations in outline, forming a complete school

[1] In 1692 Gibson catalogued the manuscripts at St. Martin's library in his *Librorum Manuscriptorum in duabus insignibus Bibliothecis; altera Tenisoniana Londini; altera Dugdaliana Oxonii Catalogus*. These manuscripts consisted of those belonging to John Ware, which the Earl of Clarendon had purchased while Lord Lieutenant of Ireland, and deposited in St. Martin's Library; and other MSS. collected by Tenison.
[2] See p. 13.
[3] *Memoirs of the Life and Times*, etc., p. 123.

of costume of the times; a " Psalterium" of the thirteenth century, superbly illustrated by an English artist, containing many figures and numerous capital letters; and a medieval treatise against miracle plays. Among the printed books (over six thousand in number) there were: *Flores Historiarum per Matthaeum Westmonasteriensem*, printed in 1567 from the Merton Priory MS; a large quarto volume *Libri duo Samuelis et Libri Duo Regum*, printed in 1518 and once belonging to the celebrated scholar Ludolf; a *British Chronicle in old English from Brutus to the year 1417*; a volume of English poetry compiled by John Gower (1325–1408); a copy of *Recorda Parliamenti*; a book of Irish poetry; a folio volume of Chaucer; *Piers travels, writ by himself*; certain tracts of John Wycliffe; and many rare pamphlets relating to the Quakers.

Instances of Tenison's enthusiasm in this field could be multiplied. Le Neve relates that in 1708 the Dean and Chapter of St. Paul's purchased, for the use of the cathedral, the library of William Gery, Vicar of Islington, the catalogue of which ran into fifteen written leaves. The price demanded was £450 but the Chapter could only find £200. Fortunately, Tenison came forward and provided the deficit, and the commissioners for rebuilding St. Paul's expressed their "thankful acknowledgments to his Grace for the said Benefaction".

The scheme of setting up a library was but part of the Vicar of St. Martin's complete plan, and its success encouraged him to continue with an experiment which he had already embarked upon, somewhat tentatively, in 1683. Tenison possessed a real enthusiasm for education, and in this year he had founded a small, "perfectly free" school in his parish, "from which", he wrote later, "great Benefit hath arisen both in relation to the Ease of the poor Housekeepers, and the learning and good Manners of their children". Tenison now determined to enlarge this scheme, and "to attempt something greater in this way". Accordingly, in co-operation with his friend and neighbour, Dr. Kennett, Vicar of St. Paul's, Covent Garden, he drew up a printed paper, dated 14 April 1688, setting out their aims at length, and circulated it among their friends and parishioners.[1]

---

[1] Lambeth MSS. 932, f. 80. One of the printed papers was sent to Sir Samuel Morland (mathematician and inventor, 1625–95), who acknowledged it as follows: "About a week after you did me ye favour to visit me, one of ye gentlemen, who came along with you, brought me a printed paper which I suppose was drawn up by your directions, to inform all persons concerned of your pious intentions of erecting two Free Schools and by what methods they shall be managed". (Lambeth MSS. 931, f. 7.)

In this it was stated that

"the Dean of Peterborough and Dr. Tenison (their Parishes
of Covent Garden and St. Martin's having anciently been but
one) have agreed (so far as concerneth these parishes) to settle a
School, with the help of some Judicious and Charitable Persons,
under the Library of the Parish of St. Martin's for boys of the
said Parish and Covent Garden. And the said Dr. Tenison
with the said Dean of Peterborough, and the like charitable
help, does purpose in the Tabernacle nigh Golden Square in
St. James' Parish to settle another school for boys of that parish
alone, there being as yet no Public School there. Both Schools
(by God's assistance) will be opened the week after Easter Week,
and they will be managed by the same Methods".

It is a duty, we feel, to quote these "Methods" in full.

"1. The Children shall be duly instructed in the Principles of
Church Religion, and Care taken that their Manners be formed
accordingly.

2. Such as have learnt already shall be taught true Reading
and Writing, with singing Psalms according to the Grounds of
Music.

3. Youth being generally design'd in this great Place for
Trade and Navigation, they shall be taught Arithmetick and
other parts of Practical Mathematicks.

4. They shall be instructed in the Latin and Greek tongues,
as far as is necessary for the employment for which they shall be
found fit.

5. They that have a special genius that way shall be instructed
in such learning as may fit them for the Universities.

Masters are provided, of Piety, Ability, and Diligence, for the
carrying on of these Ends: and they shall be Maintained without
any charge to the Persons who send their Children, Provided
their Fortune be not so apparently Great, that to spare them
would be an abuse of Charity. And for such who are both
able and willing, what they give shall be put in a common Stock
towards the support of the Respective Schools, and towards
the putting out of such Poor Boys for the Universities, as shall
be judged by the said Doctors, and the Masters of the Schools,
to be of very promising Parts and good Temper".

The school at St. Martin's (in the room underneath the library)
was proceeded with immediately and opened on 23 April 1688.[1]
Two masters were appointed, an upper and a lower, the former
having £30 a year salary, with an additional £10 a year for
teaching the juniors to write. He acted also as librarian to the

[1] Luttrell, *A Brief Historical Relation*, i. 437.

free library, for which he was to receive a further £10 a year. This educational experiment proved a complete success, and "Archbishop Tenison's Grammar School" is still in existence, having been moved to Kennington in 1928.[1]

Tenison always took a great personal interest in the school and among his papers at Lambeth, there is a beautifully bound interleaved volume of some of his sermons (1700), with translations of them into Latin and Greek, made, it says, by scholars "in the school und^r S. Martin's Library".[2] He was constantly on the lookout for boys of promising talents, and while Vicar of St. Martin's he took an interest in one Michael Bull, the son of a trumpet maker, whom he sent to the school and after he had acquired "a sufficient competency of classical learning", provided for him at his own College of Corpus Christi.[3]

Tenison went to considerable pains to secure adequate and conscientious teachers for his new school, and the first upper-master he appointed was John Postlethwayt (1650–1713), who later (1697), through the influence of Tenison, became Head-master of St. Paul's School.[4] We quote from the interesting letter of recommendation which the Archbishop wrote on his behalf:

"I have known Mr. Postlethwayth nigh 20 years. He hath long been Upper Schoolmaster of St. Martin's. I have never known him wilfully absent for two hours on any day in school-time. He is a man of great abilities and learning, and particularly in that which relates to Grammar, in the Knowledge of the Hebrew, Greek and Latin tongues. He is of very even temper and one who studieth the Temper and Genius of Youth.

[1] The funds of the school became so low in the middle of the nineteenth century that the Governors were forced to sell the library to maintain the school, thus unfortunately dispersing Tenison's collection of manuscripts. The school prospectus writes: "Unfortunately, much early history is lost owing to the destruction of the records of the meetings of the Governors, and it is difficult to give details prior to 1847. In 1868 the site of the building in what was then Castle Street, Leicester Square, was compulsorily acquired for the erection of the National Portrait Gallery. The Governors, therefore, bought Hogarth's old house in Leicester Square. A new building was designed by Mr. Marrable, and opened by the Duke of Northumberland in 1881".

[2] Their names were Edward Abbott and John Wallis.

[3] Masters, The History of Corpus Christi, pp. 256, 327. Michael Bull appears to have had an interesting history. He became one of Tenison's chaplains, but he did not go with the Archbishop to Lambeth, since his services were invaluable at the college and also because of "the great Clamour raised against him as a person of Latitudinarian Principles from his pressing the Objections in Disputations more warmly than was thought necessary, and from a sermon preached before the University on Private Judgment in Matters of Religion". Tenison eventually presented him to the Rectory of Sisted in Essex. See Masters, p. 256.

[4] Luttrell, A Brief Historical Relation, iv. 273.

His Scholars are in awe of him by Reason of his grave deportment and good Discipline; but he doth not terrify them with
Severity [1] . . . He is very careful of the Religion and Manners
of those under his care, and taketh pains with divers of them
every Lord's Day before Church time. His Conversation is
serious and discreet and hath nothing of Pedantry in it. I have
said very much of him, and yet cannot do him justice in
saying less".[2]

This enthusiasm of Tenison for education led to his being
consulted by others equally interested. Thus Viscount Lonsdale,
himself it would seem contemplating the foundation of a school,
wrote to Tenison when Archbishop, and received from him a reply
dated 14 July 1696, stating that he "had been inquiring after
such a Schoolmaster as might be fitt for the carrying on of your
great and good design", and hoped he had discovered one
in Mr. Coe of St. Giles, though this gentleman was not "perfectly
to my mind".[3]

In 1700 Tenison enlarged the educational endowment which,
as we have seen, he had already founded in St. James' parish.
On 10 September of this year he deposited £500 with nine
trustees (amongst whom were John Moore, Bishop of Norwich,
Dr. Wake, Rector of the parish, and Sir Isaac Newton) to allow
"a Chapel or Tabernacle [in King Street] to be ever hereafter
used as a Public Chapel or Oratory for divine service according
to the liturgy of the Church of England". This £500 was to be
invested in land and houses, and its revenue was to provide "two
able ministers", licensed by the Bishop of London, a reader to
say divine service in the chapel daily, a clerk, and a sufficient
number of schoolmasters "to teach and instruct poor boys,
Natives and Inhabitants of the Parish of St. James, Westminster".
It was laid down that these pupils must include six poor boys of
the parish of St. James' between the ages of nine and fourteen,
who were to be taught reading, writing, accounts and mathematics. The first meeting of the trustees took place on 7 March
1700, when the reader and schoolmaster already doing duty
were continued. From then on the trustees met regularly,

[1] Perhaps Tenison had in mind Dr. Busby (1606–95), headmaster of Westminster
School.
[2] B.M. Add. MSS. 1039, f. 94.
[3] H.M.C., 13th Report, Part VII, 106. During a conference at Lambeth on
27 December 1697, Tenison confessed: "I have much to do to find Schoolmasters
for my own Schools". Fulham MSS. Virginia Box III. 187.

Tenison presiding as long as his health allowed. Their deliberations were often interesting. On 7 July 1702, for example, they
decided that no boy was to be admitted with "a remarkable
blemish, impediment or deformity". By 1704 numbers had
increased to fifty-three (thirty-six being "free boys"), and as a
new school house had been erected over the "Watch House",
the school was now divided into two, thirty going into the new
premises. In 1715 a query arose as to whether Tenison's "poor
Boys, Natives and Inhabitants of the Parish of St. James" could
be interpreted to include boys not actually born in the parish.
Tenison gave it as his ruling on 5 April (it was the last he ever
gave) "That his Will and Meaning was, To have Poor Boys,
Natives and Inhabitants, have the Preference; and that in Case no
Natives be presented in some reasonable Time to the Trustee
Presenter, such poor Inhabitant's Son might be presented;
but not to be a Precedent".[1]

Tenison's devotion to matters educational was no passing
enthusiasm. Towards the end of his life he founded a school
for the education of twelve poor girls in the parish of Lambeth [2]
and as late as 1713 he was occupied in establishing another
charity school in Croydon. The premises in this latter case
were an adapted stable and in his papers at Lambeth there is a
report on the building operations dated 25 August. The scheme
was successfully carried through, and the school, situated in
the north end of Croydon and designed for the education of ten
poor boys and the same number of girls, was opened on 25 March
1714. For its endowment he purchased a farm at Limpsfield in
Surrey, valued at £42 a year, and he bequeathed to the school

---

[1] "Extract of Deed of Settlement of the School and Chapel in King Street", 1814.
In 1854 this school was moved to a house in Cambridge Street and was closed in
1870, when the funds were merged with those of Archbishop Tenison's Grammar
School.   See M. A. Burgess, *A History of Burlington School*, 1924, p. 18.
    We may note here, perhaps, that Tenison was a visitor of Dulwich College, and
took a great interest in the school. In 1695 he admonished the chaplain for immorality
and heresy, and made exhaustive enquiries into the management of the school a few
years later (Lambeth MSS. 953, f. 39).
[2] Tenison mentioned this school in his will as follows: "And whereas I have
erected a school at the West End of the said Churchyard, for the Education of Twelve
Poor Girls of the said Parish of Lambeth, and appointed Mrs. Mary Davis Mistress of
the said School, I do hereby give and devise the said School House and Ground
whereon it is erected, unto the said Dr. Edward Tenison etc. for the Advantage of the
said School for teaching of Twelve Poor Girls; . . . Also the Number of poor Girls
shall be increas'd as the Revenue of the Estate will conveniently bear". He also left
to the school a portrait of his "dearest Wife", in token of the "great affection . . .
and prudent Care" she had shown for the school. See *Memoirs of the Life and Times*,
etc., p. 118.

£400 to be laid out in land for the enlargement of the charity. The revenues from these sources increased in the nineteenth century, and as the old schoolhouse was no longer adequate, a new building was erected in 1892 on a space adjoining the old house, which was then let by the trustees. New premises were again built in 1928.

There exist at Lambeth the rules which Tenison himself drew up for the regulation of his school, which we quote in full as an appendix. The master and mistress, he laid down, were to be convinced Christians and regular communicants; the children were to be taught the catechism, and each was to have a Bible and Prayer Book; the boys were to be taught reading, writing, and arithmetic, the girls spinning, knitting, and sewing; they were all to be sent to school "cloathed, whole and clean".

As a result of Tenison's generosity and initiative, there are now three schools bearing his name, the Archbishop Tenison's Grammar School at Kennington, the Archbishop Tenison's Central School at Croydon, and the Archbishop Tenison's Girls' School at Lambeth. He may therefore claim an honoured place among educational pioneers. The Charity Schools founded at the end of the seventeenth and the beginning of the eighteenth century, a modern teacher has written,

"form an interesting educational development, midway between the Renaissance foundations of the sixteenth century, and the national, state-aided system of the nineteenth. They stand, midway, not only in point of time, but also in origin and outlook. The Renaissance foundations depended upon the generosity of individuals, and their founders looked upon education as the liberator of man's spirit, but it was a liberation to which only the intellectually able could attain. The State aimed at providing an irreducible minimum of education, from which all children could benefit. In origin, like the Renaissance foundations, the Charity Schools owed their existence to private generosity, in outlook they resembled the State system. Their aim was primarily moral improvement.[1] It was desirable that the children of the poorer classes should be taught to read, since in this way they could the better understand and supplement the teaching of the Church; it was desirable that they should be taught a useful trade, and simple arithmetical calculations, since they could then become

[1] This could hardly be said to be the aim of twentieth-century State-aided education.

self-supporting. Hence, for girls, reading, simple arithmetic, and domestic training, leading up to domestic service, or apprenticeship in one of the needlework trades, formed the curriculum".[1]

This is doubtless substantially true, but there was in Tenison a great deal of the renaissance spirit, and he took particular care to encourage the poor boy of ability to go on to the university.

Throughout his life any scheme for the increase of educational facilities received his favourable consideration, and his papers abound with numerous such suggestions. Education was almost in the air. We take as typical a paper presented to him entitled: "Means for raising a Fund for purchasing general and parochial Libraries".[2] This paper suggested that the Archbishop and bishops should recommend such an appeal for money to their clergy, who in their turn were to enlist the support of the local gentry. The money so collected was to pass through the hands of the archdeacons to the bishops, and an account of the whole proceedings, including a list of benefactors, was to be drawn up by each diocese. Booksellers, it was thought, might be asked to co-operate in this scheme, and authors requested to give free copies of their own works. Lastly, and this is most interesting, a committee of bishops and professors of the universities, and eminent London clergy, was to draw up a list of recommended books. The scheme, admirable as it may seem, does not in this complete form appear to have been put in operation. Perhaps Tenison felt that he was too frequently circularizing the clergy for money, particularly on behalf of the Protestant refugees. That such a scheme was proposed, however, shows that there were people interested in encouraging the reading of good books, and anxious for some national scheme to secure this. Parochial libraries were, in fact, springing up in England at this time, thanks largely to the inspiration of Dr. Bray (1656–1730), and through his labours the Society for the Promotion of Christian Knowledge came into existence in 1699, a society which also did much to inspire the foundation of charity schools throughout England. The problem was to see that these parochial libraries did not fall into neglect through the apathy of the clergy. To secure this a Bill placing them under episcopal control was brought before the House of Commons in 1704, entitled: "An Act . . . to preserve

---

[1] M. A. Burgess, *A History of Burlington School*, p. 3.
[2] Lambeth MSS. 933, f. 51.

Libraries that have or shall be erected by charitable contributions in small parishes in England".[1] The preamble of this proposed Act stated that the provision for the clergy was so mean in many parts of England that they could not afford to buy books, to remedy which charitable persons had settled libraries in several parishes. It was therefore suggested: (1) That such libraries should be preserved according to the founder's bequest; (2) that all clergy using such libraries should enter into bonds to observe such rules as the bishop drew up, and if books were removed, then the incumbent could bring an action to recover them in the name of the bishop; (3) that the bishop be empowered to inspect such libraries at his visitation, or at any other time; (4) that a new incumbent coming to a parish where such a library existed should be required to draw up a complete list of the books, sign it, and send it to the bishop to be entered into a special register; (5) that any rules necessary to regulate these libraries in addition to those contained in the benefactor's bequest should be drawn up by the bishop.[2]

Tenison approved the principle of the Bill, but was a little concerned as to its precise terms, especially in relation to the power it gave to the diocesan bishop. Thus on 18 February 1704, he wrote to Spencer Compton (1673–1743, later Earl of Wilmington), who was introducing the Bill into the Commons: "I am not against the Design of it", he said, "but I think it breaks in upon the Jurisdiction of the Queen, the Archbishops, Divers Deans, and others, in their Peculiars, letting in upon them the Bishop of the Diocese and his officers".[3] He therefore requested that he might see Compton, and that the Bill should be "much amended" before it came up to the Lords "so as to have no opposition in our House".

Whether as a result of this intervention we do not know, but the Bill never appears to have become law, although a similar Act was passed in 1709 "for the better preservation of Parochial Libraries in that part of Great Britain called England". Under this Act, "the Incumbent of every Church to which such a parochial library was attached was made personally responsible for the good keeping of the collection, and for a

---

[1] Lambeth MSS. 929, f. 117.
[2] *Ibid.*
[3] Tenison to Compton, 18 February 1704. Quoted from Notes for the Life of Thomas Tenison, by C. Tenison, p. 86.

safe transfer to his successor. He was likewise compelled to maintain a complete catalogue of the volumes in his care".[1]

After this anticipation of the years, we return in the next chapter to Tenison's career.

[1] An interesting letter was sent to Tenison on 11 February 1699, "concerning the education of youth". (Wheeler to Tenison, Lambeth MSS. 929, f. 49.) In this the writer suggested that "all Cathedral and Collegiate Churches in the Nation having schools annexed to their Foundations be made in every Diocese the only Nurseries for gentle or learned education". These schools were to be inspected by the dean and bishop. The Grammar Schools, on the other hand, were only to teach the children of husbandmen. Tenison, himself a product of Norwich Grammar School, was hardly likely to sympathize with this scheme.

Tenison's concern for propagating knowledge can be seen in his patronage of the Boyle lectures. These famous lectures, which consisted of a course of eight sermons to be preached annually, came into existence as the result of a codicil attached to Robert Boyle's will in 1691, the design being "to prove the truth of the Christian Religion against Infidels, without descending to any controversies amongst Christians; and to answer new difficulties, scruples, etc.". For the remuneration of the lecturer, who was to be elected for a term not exceeding three years by the Archbishop and others, Boyle assigned the rent of his house in Crooked Lane. The fund, however, proved uncertain, and had it not been for Tenison's generosity, the scheme would have lapsed. The Archbishop "provided a yearly stipend of £50 per annum for ever, to be paid quarterly, charged on a farm in the parish of Brill in the county of Bucks". Tenison's choice of lecturers was in many cases particularly happy. He and Evelyn were mainly responsible for choosing Richard Bentley as first lecturer, who took as his subject "A Confutation of Atheism". Tenison also chose Clarke, and spoke enthusiastically of his lectures "On the Being and the Attributes of God". Dr. George Stanhope (1660–1728) dedicated his Boyle lectures on "The Truth and Excellence of the Christian Religion asserted against Jews, Infidels and Heriticks", to the Archbishop who had encouraged him. See Nichols, *Literary Anecdotes of the Eighteenth Century*, iii. 99. John Strype, we may notice, found in Tenison a generous patron, and in return dedicated to him his *Annals of the Reformation*.

CHAPTER 3

Part I   The Catholic Menace

TENISON became Vicar of St. Martin-in-the-Fields in 1680, when the political and religious condition of the nation seemed again to be approaching a crisis. It was the year which saw the defeat of the Exclusion Bill in the House of Lords (through the firmness of Lord Halifax, the "Trimmer") and the definite emergence of the Whig and Tory parties. The barely concealed Catholic policy of Charles II, and the war in Scotland against the Covenanters, brought religious controversy to the forefront and Tenison entered into it with energy, his church becoming a rallying ground for the Protestant national spirit. It is to this aspect of his career that we now turn.

Charles had been now some nineteen years returned from his travels, and these years had given him a rich experience of men and things, which was to stand him in good stead for the rest of his reign. The King found the English people in two minds, and he made the most of their dilemma. They wished to cripple the Dutch as commercial rivals—an ambition which he himself probably shared—and at the same time they feared the absolutism and Catholicism of the French King Louis XIV, who was himself the sworn enemy of the Dutch. To fathom the real desires and intentions of Charles II is a task which many historians have set themselves, but in which none, it may be, have succeeded; the mainsprings of human action are often mysterious and hidden from us. His political creed, it has been said, was almost that of a later statesman, "that there was nothing new, nothing true, and that nothing very much mattered". Probably he was the complete sceptic, but as destiny made him a king, so he appears to have gained a cynical satisfaction in maintaining his royal power and outwitting his parliaments. The pattern of the age was the French court, which Charles himself knew at first hand, and Bossuet, the Gallican Chrysostom, maintained that Protestantism in religion led to republicanism in politics; certainly the condition of Europe in his day seemed to bear him out. To most contemporary observers the future seemed to lie with the absolute monarch, and not with parliamentary institutions. "In France and Spain, in the German states, even in happy Scandinavia, royal power had been for more than a century on the increase; all medieval systems of estates, of which our parliament was only one, had gone to the wall; and in all these countries order had been all the better kept, and prosperity had been greater than in the Middle Ages, when monarchs were limited ".[1] Charles, albeit a little indolently, accepted this thesis in his own cynical way and longed for the splendour of Versailles. Although he was determined not to go on his travels again, this did not prevent him from imitating the grand monarch, and wishing to make England Catholic in religion (after the Gallican pattern, of course) and autocratic in government. His problem—it was the problem of all the Stuarts—was one of money, and here Louis himself was only too anxious to help him. The French monarch, intent on the destruction of the Netherlands, a stronghold of republicanism and Protestantism, both anathema to him, was only too ready to buy English neutrality by supporting Charles against his Parliament—or if need be, Parliament against Charles. The secret Treaty of Dover (1670) between the two monarchs provided material for anxious speculation, and despite British mercantile ambitions the parliamentary and Protestant ideals became bound up with the support of the Netherlands, while a war against France had the added advantage of depriving Charles of French money, thereby compelling him to summon Parliament. In such a situation, power must eventually go either to the King or Parliament; the *via media* of Clarendon or Danby could not be permanent.

Thomas Tenison remembered with horror the oppression of the Commonwealth, and in this respect he was a friend of the monarchy, but Roman Catholicism was, and remained till the end of his days, his major fear. In its system he saw a menace to liberty, religious and political, and to the whole national way of life. It was the identification of monarchy with Romanism which led him to move a long way from the loyalty of the early years of the Restoration. True, the attack on the Church of England was indirect under Charles, and cunningly concealed, for the "merry monarch" had no intention of losing his crown even to save his soul. Still his reign began, and James' rule increased to a fury, a controversy between divines of the Church of England and the Roman communion, which led to the

[1] C. R. L. Fletcher, *Introductory History of England*, ii. 299.

production of pamphlets innumerable. The public devoured them with eagerness, and debated them in the coffee houses. As we turn over their pages to-day, and disturb the dust which has settled on them, we cannot but wonder how these polemics could ever have caused such excitement. In all these pamphlets—and this applies equally to Tenison's—there is not an argument which had not already been expressed with more force and lucidity by Chillingworth and Hales, or on the Catholic side by Bellarmine. Tenison repeats himself, argues frequently "in a circle", quotes with wearisome monotony from the Fathers, as if to admit that the principles in debate between Catholic and Protestant had already been adequately defined, and the real controversy exhausted. Tenison sees clearly enough the points of division—he has studied Hales and Chillingworth much too thoroughly not to be aware of this—but he fails to go directly to the heart of the problem, and consequently falls into the error of dissipating his energies, by cutting off a twig here or a branch there, rather than attempting to fell the tree at its roots. Nor is Tenison unique in this respect; and it is because of this that Fowler, Clagett, Gee, Scott, Linford, and a host of others are but forgotten men to whom no amount of special pleading can give life. Why then, we ask, were their works read with such enthusiasm by their contemporaries? The answer is to be found in the political events of the day. It was the power with which Catholicism was armed at Whitehall, and the policy of Louis XIV towards his Protestant subjects, which made the controversy such a living issue. People wanted to be kept instructed and informed as to its progress, and even apprentices (see p. 51) were not averse to discussing the theology of Luther. When the political situation changed with the final defeat of Jacobite hopes early in the eighteenth century, and the death of Louis XIV, interest in the controversy disappeared, and Catholicism remained only as a bogey to appear at inconvenient moments now and again.

Tenison wrote three works during the reign of Charles II which were in the main concerned with the Catholic controversy; in the reign of James II his energies increased with the pace of political events. The Roman Catholics, on their part, recognized in him an implacable foe, and his friend, Simon Patrick, went so far as to warn him on one occasion that "a Roman priest said in a private house that they would take some course with him . . . if they met with him in the night, or could get him out under pretence of visiting some sick person, or some such means".[1]

Some examination of Tenison's labours in this field will be necessary if we are to give a true picture of the man and his work. Certainly, in his own eyes, his anti-Catholic activities loomed very large, both as Vicar and Archbishop. We shall be more concerned, however, with the circumstances attaching to the publication of his works than with their content, since they are distinguished by no new approach, nor do they offer us old truth in a novel form.

All controversy between Protestant and Catholic in the seventeenth century centred around four simple problems, and the vast literature was in this respect but variations around these themes:

1. The question of "religious certitude", or "the means whereby the truths of revelation are conveyed to our understanding".
2. The distinction between "points fundamental and not fundamental".
3. The question whether the Apostles Creed contains "all points necessary to be believed".
4. Whether separation from the Church of Rome constitutes "schism and heresy", and whether Protestants ought not therefore in charity to become reunited to that body.

These points may be more summarily subdivided under two heads: the source of religious truth, and the sum or character of this truth.

Tenison's first theological work of importance was a *Discourse on Idolatry*. This volume set out to be a full length enquiry into the origin and spread of idolatry throughout the world, a practice which, he wrote, was "so scandalous to the Christian Religion, and (as some use it) so extremely ridiculous, that the very statue, had it any apprehension, would modestly bow itself and prevent the adorer". This work was written in 1677, the year when Shaftesbury was sent to the Tower, and Charles and Danby appeared to have triumphed. It was published the next year, and bore a dedication to Robert, Earl of Manchester, in whose family Tenison "had had long dependence", and in whose castle of Kimbolton ("a place where his Lordship does yearly offer new matter to the admiration of Travellers who speak with such praise

[1] S. Patrick, *Autobiography*, p. 197. See also p. 37.

of the Villas of England") the "Book itself, some part of it, was meditated, the whole revised".[1]

The work is of course now valueless, coming as it did before the days of any scientific study of comparative religion, but we propose to quote it more liberally than some of his later works, since it provides us, thus early in his career, with Tenison's attitude to many matters of religious interest.

He began by pleading for a liberal approach, and in terms instinct with the growing rationalism of the time, he wrote: "God is a Being absolutely perfect; and the better he is understood, he is worshipped with the more rational Religion and with the profounder Reverence".[2]

He then went on to enquire into the nature of superstitition, and defined it rather clumsily as "a corruption of public or private worship, whereby men (actuated by servile motives) perform or omit, in their own persons; or urge upon, or forbid to others, anything as in its nature religious or sinful, which God hath neither required, nor disallowed, either by the Principle of right Reason, or by his revealed Will".[3] Many rites merely serve to distract our attention from other and more important things, while most Catholic ceremonies, such as "the watchings of women on the eve of the Nativity", are quite "unfit for the solemnity of Divine worship", and "look more like the play of Children than the Worship of Christian Men".[4]

Tenison was well aware, however, that the boundary between worship and superstitution had to be drawn somewhere, and he agreed that there were some usages, such as the sign of the cross which, though not commanded by God, were yet "acceptable to him, if our high estimation of them, and our indiscreet zeal in their use or imposition, does not become the dead fly in the Spikenard".[5]

In the leisurely manner of those days, Tenison found time to embark on an historical enquiry into the origin and development of idolatry in Greece, Palestine, and Rome, which culminated, as it was meant to, in a long and specific attack on the idolatries of the Roman Church, in proof of which he quoted extensively from the Roman breviaries.[6]

To the worship of the image of Christ, Tenison devoted a chapter, and after pointing out that he was not against anything

[1] *Discourse on Idolatry*, 1678. Preface. [2] *Ibid*. p. 1.
[3] *Ibid*. p. 4. [4] *Ibid*. p. 6.
[5] *Ibid*. [6] *Ibid*. p. 190.

"which may be serviceable as an help to devotion", he condemned those "who, in our late unhappy Revolutions, defaced such Pictures and brake down such Crosses as Authority had suffered to remaine entire, whilst it forbad the worship of them".

Among such external acts of reverence as Tenison approved, there were included, naturally: (1) bowing to the altar, (2) kneeling at the Sacrament, (3) reverencing the name of Jesus.[1]

Of Tenison's works, we must confess to having read the *Discourse on Idolatry* with most pleasure. Though far too mechanical in its attitude to religion (inevitable in Tenison's day, although his friend Spencer was laying the foundations for the study of comparative religion), it is yet the work of a scholar as well read in the Fathers as in contemporary apologetics both Catholic and Protestant. Throughout he holds a middle position and we are reminded of the *via media* as set forth in Hooker's *Ecclesiastical Polity*. While anxious to expose the Roman Catholic position, he is equally anxious not to fall into the iconoclastic position of the Dissenters. In the heaping together of fact upon fact, and an obvious delight in the minutiæ of information, the *Discourse* bears some resemblance to Warburton's "mass of ill digested learning", the *Divine Legation*, although, of course, it is not so comprehensive in character.[2]

The work betrays an interest in knowledge for its own sake, particularly in its speculations on early religion, and the scholar is not yet subordinated to the controversialist. As more responsible preferment came Tenison's way, his opportunities for study grew less, and his later works bear a more pronounced *ad hoc* appearance, besides being more vehement in character. The fact that Tenison's first two works, however, were a volume on Bacon and a reply to Hobbes, seems to suggest that he might have remained a scholar had the Government not seen fit to prefer him.

Tenison's second attack on the Catholics came in 1681, a few days after the Oxford Parliament had been dissolved, when he preached a sermon at St. Sepulchre's Church, London, before the Lord Mayor, "Concerning Discretion in giving Alms".[3]

[1] These were, as might be imagined, the very points in dispute between the Church of England and the Dissenters.
[2] Thomas Bray, in his *Bibliotheca Parochialis*, 1697 (p. 53), includes Tenison's *Discourse* as a work "setting forth the design of Christianity . . . to dispossess Satan of his usurp'd Dominion and Tyranny over Mankind, which before our Saviour's coming into the world was almost universally enslav'd to him by Idolatry, Superstition and filthy Lusts".
[3] Tenison, "Concerning Discretion in giving Alms", 1681.

This sermon attracted a good deal of attention at the time, for though its main thesis was the foolishness of indiscrimate alms-giving (on which Tenison had a lot of excellent things to say,[1] and on which he had a right to speak), it degenerated into an attack on Catholic charities and a reply to the Romanist conten-tion that the suppression of the monasteries, together with the general unsettlement of the Reformation, had created social problems of great urgency which the Elizabethan systems of workhouses failed to remove. To this latter argument Tenison replied that in fact it was "the indiscretion of the Monasticks (by feeding the slothful, the superstitious, the Enthusiastick, the Fryars Mendicants, the Pilgrims and loytering wanderers of that Church) which provided objects of Burthen and expence for those of the Reformation".[2]

Catholic charities were "fanciful and vap'rous . . . an irra-tional waste",[3] he argued, while Protestant charity was essentially "publick and reasonable", in that it provided for the education of children, the correction of offenders, the employment of the idle, and the procuring "relief, shelter, care and oversight" for the sick and aged. In all these things, he concluded, let us be practical and systematic: "Let us conquer foolish pity and irra-tional compassion. That affection is put into men by nature to keep their reason from languishing, and not to pervert it".[4]

This sermon could hardly fail to arouse a great deal of indigna-tion among the Catholics, and Tenison himself admitted later that he "was not surprised at the offence which some have taken at the sermon; for it touches a very tender part when it touches their gain". It was not till 1687, however (when another controversy recalled this earlier sermon and a second edition was published), that a reply appeared in "Good Advice to the Pulpits", written by John Gother, who described Tenison's remarks on indulgences as a malicious slander,[5] but did nothing to refute the particular instances of this abuse, which Tenison had cited at length in the printed edition of his sermon.

[1] As for example, "Discretion considereth the time of giving Alms. It hath respect to the Seasons of great Sickness, of great Losses, of Scarceness of Work and of Dearness of Provisions. It hath especial regard to diligent men just sinking in their fortune, who may often be kept above water by a very little help, when a hand is opportunely reached towards them".
[2] Tenison, "Concerning Discretion in giving Alms", p. 20.
[3] Ibid. p. 20.
[4] Ibid. p. 44.
[5] Gother, "Good Advice to the Pulpits", 1687, p. 4.

Another and more important critic appeared at this time in the person of Andrew Pulton, the Jesuit (of whom we shall hear a great deal later on in this chapter). In the course of one of his "afternoon exercises" on 27 November 1687, at the "Savoy Mass House" (to quote Tenison's description) Pulton accused the "eminent doctor" of laying a "calumny" on the Church of Rome, namely, that the Pope granted his Bulls of Indulgence for sins unrepented of. "Now I say that this is notoriously false", he said, "for I would fain have the Doctor to discover by whom these Bulls have been granted? what time? in what place etc.? or else 'tis a palpable imposture".[1]

Such a challenge (and opportunity) could not be allowed to pass unnoticed, and John Williams (1636?–1709), later Bishop of Chichester, replied in "An Apology for the Pulpits," Tenison adding as an appendix "A Defence of Dr. Tenison's Sermon on Discretion in giving Alms".[2] Tenison's reply to Pulton was certainly very much to the point. "The Reader has a further Exemplification of Mr. Pulton's Method in disputing or managing a Conference",[3] he wrote. "He has proofs given him, and he takes no notice of them, and goes on asking, Where are they etc. I had cited the Book, the Indulgence, the Pope that granted it; and he cries out, by whom was it granted? at what time? and what place? This 'tis to have been refined by Travel, and to have studied Eighteen years out of the dull Air of England".[4]

It is impossible, as we have seen, for Catholics and Protestants to engage in controversy without the question of authority coming to the fore, and many Anglican and Roman divines during the reigns of Charles II and James II devoted a great deal of their energies to dealing with this difficult, if well worn, subject. In 1683, Tenison gave his views at large concerning it in an anonymous work *A Discourse concerning a Guide in Matters of Faith*, which was republished under his own name in 1687.[5] Briefly he contended, with Chillingworth, that in the last resort men will

[1] Quoted. Williams, "An Apology for the Pulpits", p. 6.
[2] John Gother replied once again with "Pulpit Sayings or the Character of the Pulpit Papist examin'd, in Answer to the Apology for the Pulpits", 1688. Williams, not to be outdone, had the last word in "Pulpit Popery true Popery", 1688. Gother (d. 1704) began life as a Presbyterian, became a fervent Catholic, and his *Spiritual Works* (ed. 1718) have often been reprinted.
[3] See Part II of this Chapter.
[4] Williams, "An Apology for the Pulpits", p. 6.
[5] Tenison, *A Discourse concerning a Guide in Matters of Faith*, 1687, p. 36. This work was republished in 1738 and 1848, the latter being the latest date for any edition of Tenison's works.

and must be judges for themselves. Thus the "guide" was not exclusively to be found in the early Church, nor in Councils, nor in "a present Church declaring to particular Christians the Sense of the Church of the former Age"; nor yet in those "who with disdainful insolence contemn all Authority, even that of the sacred Scripture itself . . . and pretend to an infallible Light of immediate and personal Revelation". The only objective guide was Scripture, although "it needed to be interpreted with caution, since in finding out the Scriptures the Church gives them help, but it does not by its authority obtrude the sense upon them".[1]

When this work of Tenison's appeared, the reign of Charles II was drawing to its close, and constitutional and religious problems were becoming inextricably united. The King's policy of "wait and see" triumphed with the collapse of the constitutional opposition in 1683; and the execution of Russell and the University of Oxford's declaration "that the doctrine of passive obedience even to the worst of rulers was a part of religion" were symbols of his victory.

What would have happened had Charles lived to survive James is a question which we must leave to the more imaginative historian. As it was, his death on 6 February 1685, brought to the throne a monarch who, though not devoid of some ability, was yet lacking in the arts of statesmanship. More significant for future events, James II was genuinely interested in religion, and had neither the wish nor the temperament to play the *politique*. Charles knew how far to go and he was prepared to wait his time, and if necessary, to withdraw. He concealed his intentions behind a mask of cynical frivolity, and to the last (like Queen Elizabeth) he could sense the temper of his people. James, however, was a Catholic by conviction, devoid of political judgment, and a bigoted believer in the divine right of kings. True, many of his subjects paid lip service to this erastian dogma, but James, with incredible folly, determined to use it in support of a fully-fledged and openly-avowed Catholic policy. Had he possessed all the tact which he so singularly lacked, he might have delayed, but he could not have averted, the inevitable disaster.

The political and religious issues thus became clearly defined, and the pace of events, after James' accession, grew more rapid from day to day. Two days before Charles' funeral at Westminster

[1] Tenison, *A Discourse Concerning a Guide in Matters of Faith*, p. 45

Abbey, Tenison preached before the Royal Household, but the King himself was absent, having "gone to Mass publicly in the little Oratory at the Duke's lodgings, the doors being set wide open".[1]

On 8 April, Evelyn writes: "I went to London to hear Dr. Tenison at Whitehall—it being a Wednesday in Lent. I observed that though the King was not in his seat above the Chapel, the Doctor made his three 'congés' which they were not used to do when the late King was absent, making then one bowing only".[2]

The Vicar of St. Martin's now increasingly threw his energies into the struggle with the Catholics, and his church became more than ever a Protestant stronghold. In April 1686 we find him interesting himself on behalf of his friend Dr. John Sharp, whose Protestant zeal had incurred the royal disfavour. John Sharp was born in 1645 of a Puritan father and a Royalist mother, and he retained throughout life the signs of this double origin. He preached with the forthrightness and simplicity of the Puritan, yet with the scholarship and in the traditional form of the Anglican divines.[3] In 1675 he was appointed Rector of St. Giles-in-the-Fields, which he retained when he became Dean of Norwich in 1681. His forceful preaching made him popular in London, but its anti-Catholic character brought him into disfavour with James, although he became Chaplain-in-ordinary to the King on 20 April 1686. Provoked by the tampering of the Roman Catholics with his parishioners, Sharp preached two sermons at St. Giles on 2 and 9 May 1686, which were interpreted by many as reflecting on the King himself. To his friend, Burnet, Sharp denied that he had any such intention, and he even went to Court to submit the notes of his sermon to royal inspection, but was refused an audience. Instead, the King ordered Compton, Bishop of London, to suspend the Rector of St. Giles-in-the-Fields, but the Bishop (according to Burnet), though declining to do so (and consequently being suspended from his episcopal functions by the Ecclesiastical Commission), privately advised the Rector of St. Giles, when they met at Doctors' Commons on 18 May, "to forbear the pulpit for the present".[4]

Tenison was infuriated at what he regarded as a shackling of Protestant liberty, and "used several Endeavours with some of the

[1] Evelyn, *Diary*, ii. 211.   [2] *Ibid.* p. 219.
[3] *D.N.B.* li. 408.   [4] Burnet, *History of my own Time*, iii. 100.

nobility,[1] in vain, to obtain a liberty of preaching for his neighbour". Not to be outdone, Tenison persevered so far as to explain the whole position to Mr. Pepys (the diarist), a "good-natured Man with Wife and Children who went fully to the King and prevailed with his Majesty to restore him to the Exercise of his Office; till which time he [Dr. Sharp] had a Guard or Centinel to attend his Lodgings".[2]

A last and desperate effort was now being made, with royal support, to win England back to the Catholic fold, and thus to achieve the impossible. It is not surprising, therefore, that the reign of James marks the age, *par excellence*, of Protestant and Catholic religious controversy—that is, if we estimate excellence in terms of the number of pamphlets produced. Catholic protagonists could, for the last time till the nineteenth century, come boldly before the public and plead their cause. Tenison was by no means averse to this kind of paper warfare, and we need not take too seriously his own confession that controversy was "as unwelcome to him as the trouble was to those of old time, who when they were employ'd in offering sacrifice, were forced to turn aside, and drive from the Altar the greedy Fowls and the impertinent Flies".[3] A natural lover of argument, Tenison took a very serious view of the contemporary situation, and his protest against what he regarded as the insidious attacks of the Catholics came from a burning conviction.

Such a dangerous and insidious attack Tenison thought he detected in "The Protestant's Plea for a Socinian", a pamphlet published in 1686 and written by Abraham Woodhead, a Catholic controversialist and formerly a priest in the Church of England.[4] The importance of this small work lay, not in the examination of Socinian opinions which it contained, but in the principles upon which it based an indirect attack on the Church of England. Socinian opinions (the denial of the pre-existence of Christ before

[1] Probably with Sunderland and Middleton.
[2] White Kennett, *A Complete History of England*, iii. 483. The incident as we have related it comes from the above authority and White Kennett almost certainly received it from the lips of Tenison. Other versions, however, are to be found in Burnet, *History of my own Time*, iii. 100, and Evelyn, *Diary*, ii. 255, 7. In the latter we read: "On July 1, by the advice of Jeffrys he [Sharp] left London for Norwich; but when he returned to London in December, his petitions, revised by Jeffrys, were received and in January 1687 he was reinstated".
[3] Tenison, "The Difference betwixt the Protestant and Socinian Methods", p. 6.
[4] Abraham Woodhead died in 1678 but the "Protestant's Plea" was a reprint in the form of a separate pamphlet of the "Fourth Discourse" of his *Guide in Controversies*, published in 1673. See "The Difference betwixt the Protestant and Socinian Methods", p. 7.

He was conceived in the womb of the Virgin Mary by the Holy Spirit) had been freely expressed by certain sects outside the Church of England during the Commonwealth (that period so fertile in religious speculation), and the Socinians then ranked with other Independents as a distinct party. The prevalence of this heresy in England gave the writer of this pamphlet an excellent opportunity to contend that there must be some final authority in matters of religion, in order to correct the wayward fancies of individual thinkers. Such an authority the Catholics had ready to hand in the Church, whereas the Protestants, who professed to find it in Scripture, in effect left the whole question to private judgment, which meant "that instead of the Roman Church here setting up some men (the Church Governors) as Infallible in necessaries; here is set up by them every Christian, if he will, both infallible in all necessaries; and certain that he is so".[1] It followed that the Church of England, in practice, was bound to breed Socinians, and other heretics, because it lacked any authority to restrain individual licence.

The Vicar of St. Martin's recognized the dangerous character of such an attack, and he replied in a pamphlet, "The Difference betwixt the Protestant and Socinian Methods", written in 1686 and published the next year. Tenison is anxious to deal with what he knew to be the crucial part of his opponent's attack, the question of authority, but it is not easy here to state precisely what he does maintain. At times he seems to infer that ultimate authority resides in a General Council. "A Protestant submits to the Decrees of a Council", he writes, "no further than he is convinc'd that the same Council is rightly constituted, and that her definitions are founded on the Word of God".[2] He does not state, however, who in fact is to determine whether the definitions of a Council are in agreement with the Word of God, although in practice "a Son of the Church of England reverenceth the first four General Councils of which Nicea is the first".[3] His whole position on this difficult question of authority is necessarily obscure, though he agrees with Chillingworth that if men will but use their reason then they are "following God".

Finally, Tenison replies to the criticism that when once the authority of the Roman Catholic Church is denied, "no man can

---

[1] "The Protestant's Plea for a Socinian", p. 9.
[2] Tenison, "The Difference betwixt the Protestant and Socinian Methods", p. 49.
[3] *Ibid.* p. 50.

be assured that any parcel of the Scripture was written by divine inspiration". Here, it is interesting to note, our author falls back on a purely empirical test. "The experience of innumerable is against it, who are sufficiently assured that the Scripture is divinely inspired, and yet deny the infallible authority of your Church or any other".[1]

The position of Tenison, it will be observed, is *per se* one that cannot easily be reduced to precise form, largely because he is really arguing against any exact or determinable authority in matters religious. In the last resort the Church of England claims a reasonable authority over reasonable minds. Scripture, Councils, Articles combine to express a faith so reasonable that the honest enquirer is not forced to deny his reason to be reasonably convinced. The object presented by faith to the believer (and we quote Tenison here) is "truth" and its end is not, as Spinoza asserts, the "quiet of human society" but the welfare of the soul.[2]

The controversy between the Catholics and the Church of England was certainly absorbing Tenison's energies at this time, and he felt strongly (particularly in view of the general thesis of his *Guide in Matters of Faith*) that all Protestants should be instructed in the importance of the matters in debate and be able to give a reason for the faith that was in them. Such instruction had already been attempted in the case of the Church of England's quarrel with the Dissenters, for here a few of the London clergy (prominent among whom was Tenison) had reduced "the matters in debate with the Dissenting Party to a certain number of Cases . . . in the plainest and most inoffensive manner that they could, to shew them how little cause they had to separate from our Communion upon any of those pretences which were said to be the cause of separation".[3] As a result of this guidance, so Tenison claimed, "several for whose sake these Discourses were principally intended, have declared themselves abundantly satisfied, both with the strength and temper that appeared in them".[4] The success of this publication encouraged Tenison "to run through the principal Points of difference between the Papists and the Church of England after the same manner, that those who had not the leisure or opportunity to consult larger

[1] Tenison, "The Difference betwixt the Protestant and Socinian Methods", p. 58.
[2] *Ibid.*
[3] *The Present State of the Controversie between the Church of England and the Church of Rome*, 1687, p. 4.
[4] *Ibid.*

Books, might here in a short time be led to a true knowledge of the Controversie, and stand the firmer in truth, by being better acquainted with the grounds of it".[1] By this means he was sanguine enough to hope that even some Catholics, "who had hitherto been detained in those Errors from want, not so much of a will to embrace the Truth, as a Light to discern it by, might possibly take this opportunity of seeing with their own eyes, and discover that way of Error, in which their ignorance or their prejudices had so long detained them".[2]

Tenison had, in fact, begun this experiment in the reign of Charles II, but the accession of James created a new situation, and the Vicar of St. Martin's, with his collaborator Dr. Clagett, "thought fit to be on the Defensive side, and for some time published no more Discourses of this kind, but waited to see whether the Gentlemen of the Roman Communion would make any Attacques . . . or be contented that the Controversie should rest as it was".[3] Despite difficulty, however, Tenison and Clagett published in 1687 what might be called a bibliography under the title: *The Present State of the Controversie between the Church of England and the Church of Rome, or an Account of the Books written on both sides.* Its purpose may, perhaps, be best expressed in Tenison's own words: ". . . Because you [i.e. the intelligent Protestant] desire an account of all that has been done of this nature, I will let you know how far they have advanced in this design and give you a catalogue of the tracts, tho' not just in order as they came out, yet in that order which seems to have been design'd and is most natural for you to peruse them".[4] There then followed a list of the books and pamphlets which had appeared in the last few years relating to this religious controversy, and a few critical comments upon them. It would be too much to expect this task to be undertaken in an impartial spirit —and it was not! Tenison's list was certainly an extensive one, and the topics dealt with reflected the contemporary situation. Amongst them were the following: the difference between the Protestants' separation from the Church of Rome and the Dissenters' secession from the Church of England; the authority of the Church in interpreting the Scriptures; the necessity of a visible succession from Christ for

[1] *The Present State of the Controversie between the Church of England and the Church of Rome*, 1687, p. 4.
[2] *Ibid.*
[3] *Ibid.*
[4] *Ibid.* p. 5.

infallibility in such interpretation; the existence of such a visible
succession in the Church of England; "Maryology"; the corruption of the Church of Rome; Communion in one kind. That
Tenison should have collaborated with Clagett in a work of this
kind is indicative of the interest and care with which he followed
the controversy as a whole.

In June of this year Tenison again appeared as the opponent
of Roman claims in connection with a reply to Cardinal Bellarmine. This great Italian theologian (1542–1621) had fixed the
pattern for Catholic apologetics, especially against Protestants,
in his famous three-volume work *Disputationes de Controversiis
Christianae Fidei adversus hujus temporis Haeretics* (1581–83), which
became almost a textbook for Catholic defenders of the faith.
In the course of this work Bellarmine enumerated what he
called fifteen "Notes" of the true Church,[1] and a group of
Anglican Churchmen (which included Linford, Williams, Payne,
Freeman, Fowler, Clagett, Stratford, Patrick, Thorpe, Scott, and
Sherlock) decided to reply to these one by one. Hence there
appeared a collection of pamphlets, and amongst these one from
the pen of Tenison, "The Tenth Note of the Church Examined
viz. Holiness of Life". In this brief work Tenison maintained that
holiness was a prerogative of no one Church, but that it was a
characteristic of all those Christians who were "separated from
the unbelieving and wicked world" and were "incorporated by
Baptism into the Spiritual Society of the Christian Church".[2]

Part II   "Our Rambling Talk"

Anglican apologetics against Catholic attack was now admitted
(and not without reason) to be a field in which Tenison could at
least hold his own. He had directed his studies towards this end,
and as the quarrel between Protestant and Catholic kept pace
with James' more determined Catholic policy, so did his zeal and
activity increase. It was owing to this enthusiasm that the Vicar of
St. Martin's now became embroiled in a very heated controversy

---

[1] These were (1) catholicity; (2) antiquity; (3) duration; (4) multitude and variety
of believers; (5) succession of bishops; (6) agreement in doctrine with the primitive
Church; (7) union of members among themselves with the head; (8) sanctity of
doctrine; (9) efficacy of doctrine; (10) holiness of life; (11) miracles; (12) prophecy;
(13) confession of adversaries; (14) unhappy end of Church's enemies; (15) temporal
felicity.
[2] Tenison, "The Tenth Note of the Church Examined viz. Holiness of Life", 1687,
p. 234.

with the Jesuit, Andrew Pulton. We are tempted to pass over this not too edifying exhibition of ecclesiastical warfare, which, as well as being long drawn out, is extremely difficult to disentangle owing to the conflicting reports which each side circulated; but we encourage ourselves, however, with the thought that this controversy illustrates in bold relief the temper of the two parties at the end of James' reign, and gives a vivid picture of a method of theological disputation, not infrequently resorted to in those days.

Conferences between Protestants and Catholics were, in fact, quite fashionable, and in 1686 Stillingfleet and Burnet had crossed swords with the Romanists in a "Conference about Religion", subsequently addressing a discursive theological letter to a certain "Lady T", in whose interest the conference had been held. Princess Anne, writing to her sister the Princess of Orange on 29 December 1686, reported a similar debate as follows: "The Lord Treasurer told me the other day, the King commanded him to hear a dispute; and that he heard one between two of their priests, and Dr. Jane and Dr. Patrick of our side; and by it, that he was the more confirmed of the truth of our religion".[1]

Andrew Pulton (1654–1710), foremost English Jesuit of the time, was by virtue of his position an opponent worthy of Tenison's mettle. Born in 1654 of Catholic parents, he had studied the "humanities" in the College of the English Jesuits at St. Omer, and entered the Society of Jesus in October 1674, studying theology at Liège. When James embarked upon his definite policy of recovering England to the faith, a Jesuit College was opened at the Savoy in the Strand on Whitsunday 1687, and Andrew Pulton and Edward Hall were appointed the first masters.[2] This college was intended to form a centre for the new proselytization of England, or as a zealous Protestant of the time expressed it from his point of view, it was erected "on purpose to poison the youth of the city and suburbs with Popish principles".[3] It was, in part, to counteract the influence of this school that Tenison set up his own at St. Martin's. Not the erection of this Catholic academy, however, but the following rather curious incident gave rise to the controversy which we are about to relate.

[1] Princess Anne to Princess Mary, 29 December 1686. Quoted, B. C. Brown, *Letters of Queen Anne*, 1935, p. 21.
[2] *D.N.B.* xlvii. 35.
[3] Simon Patrick, *Autobiography*, p. 215.

One morning in September 1687, while Tenison was at his house in St. Martin's Churchyard, he was interrupted by a Mr. Uppington and his apprentice John Smith, who waited on him "about business in the way of his Trade". Being informed the day before that this apprentice "was departing from the Church of England having been at Mass nigh two Months before",[1] Tenison elicited from him "that Mr. Pulton the Jesuit was the person in whose Lodgings he had been and that he had perswaded him by his Arguments".[2] Tenison immediately asked the nervous youth, by now somewhat tongue-tied, what these arguments were, and he managed at length to blurt out, rather incoherently, that Luther had contradicted himself in his own works, and had been persuaded not to go to Mass by the devil. Tenison saw that it was useless to prolong the discussion, and advised Mr. Uppington to send the boy back to his father in the country, since he "was reported to be a man of condition and zealous".

As a result of this and similar conversions, the Catholics, according to Tenison, became openly jubilant and "great boast was made in the Neighbourhood about Mr. Pulton and odds were offered that Dr. T. would not meet him". This led to negotiations between the two, although there were frequent delays and many difficulties, since a few days later (so the Vicar of St. Martin's complained) he and Mr. Uppington waited in vain for the arrival of two priests "at a time and place mutually appointed".[3] Tenison became somewhat perturbed after this disappointment but consented to another meeting, being persuaded by Mr. Uppington that "if Mr. P. were not met, it would be said because none dare meet him; and upon that motive how inconsiderable so ever to men of sound sense, the matter turned".[4] Hence negotiations were resumed and it was finally agreed that Tenison and Pulton should engage each other in public debate. There was to be "little Company and no Noise", the former to bring with him only Mr. Uppington and his wife, the latter a friend and the youth John Smith. Preparations were soon completed and on the day, Thursday 29 September 1687 (Tenison's birthday), "when the hour came he broke away abruptly from two Eminent Divines D[r]. S[herlock?] and W. W[ake?] without so much as

---

[1] This seems to suggest that the meeting may have been pre-arranged.
[2] Tenison, "A True Account of a Conference", 1687, p. 1.
[3] Ibid.
[4] Ibid.

letting them know about what business he was going". Thus he arrived at the appointed place "without either Friend or Servant".[1]

Pulton's account of the preliminaries to this encounter differs in some details from that which we have quoted above, and the two versions are not very easy to reconcile. He says that on Monday 26 September a youth called asking him to debate on Thursday with Dr. H[orneck?]. He agreed to the proposal, and it was not until the Thursday morning that he learnt that his opponent was to be Dr. Tenison.[2]

What exactly happened when the two first confronted each other it is very difficult to determine from the conflicting accounts which the combatants have left behind them.

Tenison claims that Pulton came in "with nine or ten after him", amongst whom "he espied in the room, which was of a sudden crowded with people, Mr. Meredith, whom he look'd upon as next to a priest", and four others whom he took to be priests.[3]

Pulton writes that he came with one witness only who was not a priest; that Tenison entered the room alone, whereupon he offered to have the hall cleared, but the Vicar of St. Martin's desiring that the "man of the house" might be present, it was agreed that Pulton should have one witness and he chose Meredith.[3]

Both accounts then agree that Tenison objected to Meredith on the grounds that he was converted when very young to the Church of Rome, and consequently was "possessed with a spirit of fiercer bigotry than those who were Romanists from the beginning".[5] Edward Meredith (1648–89) was, in fact, a well-known Catholic controversialist, who had changed his religious allegiance when companion to Sir William Godolphin on an embassy to Spain. His presence at this conference arose out of a chance meeting with Pulton on the Thursday morning, when he decided that the Jesuit must take someone with him to observe what passed "and hinder as much as might be the bad effects of such Misrepresentations as experience shows are hardly avoidable on such Occasions". To Tenison's objections against him,

[1] Tenison, "A True Account", p. 4.
[2] Pulton, "A True and Full Account of a Conference", p. 1.
[3] Tenison, "A True Account". Preface.
[4] Pulton, "A True and Full Account", p. 2.
[5] Tenison, "A True Account", p. 5.

Meredith replied that "he knew not what the Doctor called young, but it was not till he had gone through one of the best and most careful schools in England, and spent above three years at the University and as many in Spain".[1]

The preliminary skirmish being more or less disposed of, there followed a debate lasting some two and a half hours, which was as acrimonious as it would have been amusing had any been able to abstract themselves from the passions which the controversy aroused. The room was packed to overflowing, and a number of schoolboys were present. Applause was frequent and prolonged, so much so that Pulton complained that "the Crowd and the Noise gave such an Interruption that the Closeness of Discourse which was intended could never take place". Tempers ran high: interruptions from onlookers were frequent, and while the conference was taking place, a ridiculous rumour went round that "Father A.P. was in danger of being killed", and an earnest Roman Catholic even brought a constable along, who soon seems to have satisfied himself, however, that there was little danger.[2] Later in the debate Tenison entered into a private and heated argument with Meredith "which lasted some time, A.P. not being able to obtain of the Doctor a prosecution of the Question in debate".[3]

It may not be without value to give a *résumé* of the main lines of the discussion.

Pulton began in the orthodox Catholic manner by indulging himself in a polemic against Luther, as one who frequently contradicted himself in the course of his writings, particularly on the subject of the Sacraments. To this attack Tenison replied that the validity of Protestant sacraments did not rest on the consistency of Luther. "Our Church", he said, "depended not upon Luther, but Christ".[4] Moreover, the Roman Church itself was not consistent in its sacramental teaching, since it had not always fixed the number at seven. Pulton here interposed that if the Church of England did not find its authority in the works of Luther, but in the Scriptures, then it must be able to prove: (1) that the Scriptures were a sufficient rule of faith; (2) that the volumes which we now possess "truly are such". The Church of

[1] Meredith, "Some further Remarks on the late Account". Preface.
[2] Tenison, "A True Account", p. 24.
[3] Pulton, "A True and Full Account", p. 7.
[4] Tenison, "A True Account", p. 7.

England, Tenison protested, received the Scriptures from the universal Church; to which Pulton interjected that since in Tenison's view a large part of the universal Church, namely, the Church of Rome, was corrupt, how could he be sure that a pure Bible had been preserved; for "if one should bring a Deed into a Court of Justice, attested only by Lyars and corrupted Witnesses, although never so many, it would never make good any Action in Law or find credit with any not corrupted Judges".[1] The Vicar of St. Martin's saw the difficulty but refused to be cornered. "There were true Christians", he said, "of an uncorrupt Doctrine at such a Time as the Reformation began", and he appealed to the witness of the Greek Church. Appeal to the Greek Church was a doubtful expedient, replied Pulton, particularly seeing that this Church had gone out of its way to anathematize many of the doctrines of the "pretended Reformation".

The speakers then turned to the question of "transubstantiation" and the "real presence", into which intricacies, however, we will not follow them. Tenison here asserted that the Church of England remained firm in the faith of the first four centuries, while Pulton countered with a host of quotations from Justin, Irenaeus, and Ambrose *De Sacramentis*, to all of which authorities Tenison observed sarcastically: "should one come to pay me £20 and the first half crown which he brought me prove nought, I would suspect all the rest". There then ensued a long and minute enquiry into the various texts quoted, and a discussion of the metaphysical theory used to support transubstantiation, in the course of which Tenison asked: "whether it was true Philosophy to say, there was whiteness without a white thing, and breaking without a thing broken and the body of a Man without the dimensions and figure of such a body".

Such difficult subjects, however, proved too much for the tempers of those concerned, and the conference ended, apparently, in general disorder, personal abuse replacing argument, and Tenison adding to the rising temper of the gathering by accusing Pulton of "tampering" with the scholars at the Savoy, and expressing surprise "that anybody would entrust their children with him", since "there was no credit to be given to Papists being by their principles Breakers of their Word". Upon this outburst, the Catholics saw their opportunity and shouted as a body: "This reflects upon the King", whereupon the Protestants

[1] Pulton, "A True and Full Account", p. 5.

retorted that it was a "knavish trick to bring his Majesty into the debate".[1] The hubbub now reached its zenith: debate was no longer possible, and Tenison, Pulton, and Meredith retired into an adjoining room where a private wrangle went on until they finally dispersed.

This conference, as might have been anticipated, was but the prelude to a fierce and prolonged paper warfare. A newsletter of the day reported: "On Thursday last was held a conference between Dr. Tennison of St. Martin's and Mr. Pulton a Jesuit of the Savoy, upon the subject of a brazier's son in Long Acre who had embraced the Roman Faith, it being to render satisfaction to the parents of the lad, but it being managed with great heat, it came to little effect".[2]

Conflicting rumours of what had happened were soon circulating in the city. Mrs. Uppington (wife of the apprentice's master) told Tenison that she received a visitor who wanted to be "satisfied in these Questions; Whether there had not been a Conference there? whether there had not been five Ministers of the Church of England there against one Jesuit, who put them all to silence? whether Mr. U. and Mrs. U. were not stagger'd in their Religion upon this Conference? Whether a Gentlewoman of the Church of England was not after the Conference fallen distracted?"[3] Mrs. Uppington, naturally, was able to assure her visitor that "there was but one Minister there, and no putting of him to silence, and no distraction", whereupon the other confessed that "the aforesaid Stories were us'd by a Roman, as Arguments to turn her". Pulton, on his part, bitterly protested that the next three days following the conference were filled "with reiterated reports of his being run down, and silenced with five, eight, fifteen of his fellow Jesuits, and of the Doctor's putting many Questions to him without being able to obtain any Answer".[4] He therefore felt that he must make some public protest against such mis-statements, and on the following Sunday afternoon (2 October) at the Savoy, he addressed his congregation as follows: "I believe you have heard of a late Conference, in which I was concerned. It is not the way of Catholicks to make a great noise of such Matter; but if the Protestants make a stir

[1] Tenison, "A True Account", p. 23.
[2] Devonshire MSS. H.M.C. 1924, I. 269.
[3] Tenison, "A True Account", p. 25.
[4] Pulton, "A True and Full Account", p. 23.

5

about it, then next Sunday in this place, I will give you an Account of that which pass'd in that Conference".[1]

This pulpit reference led to Pulton's being waited on by Tenison (accompanied by Dr. Clagett, a noted controversialist)[2] at the Jesuit's lodgings in the Savoy, on 3 October at half-past five in the afternoon. A rather heated interview then followed. Tenison complained that Pulton had " opened the scene ", while the Jesuit protested against "the Dirt that was cast upon him by the Papers and Words in Coffee Houses". Finally, as they bade farewell and "took leave civilly one of another", Pulton court-eously "invited them to taste of their Beer", an invitation which we think it a great pity Tenison declined on the grounds of "haste".

During the next few days following the interview, a series of letters passed between the disputants, each one bearing witness to a mutual rise in temper. They could not agree as to what they should discuss, and on 8 October Pulton sent off to Tenison the notes he had drawn up on the conference; since "having there-fore agreed to wright [sic] I thought myself first bound to disabuse the world in reference to matters of Fact of St. Michael's day . . . and the Impudent Lyes of 5, 10, and 15 Jesuits being silenc'd running up and down the Town and Kingdom". [3]

What was inevitable from the beginning had therefore now taken place, and Pulton was distributing his own account among his friends. Interest in the controversy was consequently growing, and when the Jesuit stood up to preach in the Savoy on Sunday, 9 October, there was a large and excited congregation to hear him. Many perhaps were disappointed, for his remarks were most artfully restrained. "I know it is to be expected", he began, "I should now speak of a late Conference I had; but the Dr. having since been with me, to acquaint me he had not taken any measures about speaking thereof in the Pulpit, desir'd therefore that I would not; to which I promis'd him; so, for your information of what passed there, you are to expect it from Methods which may be concluded on".[4]

Tenison, as soon as he heard of this statement, regarded it as singularly double-edged, since it seemed to imply that he had visited Pulton " to beg of him to say nothing of the Conference, as

---

[1] Tenison, "A True Account", p. 35.
[2] He died the following year of smallpox.
[3] Tenison, "A True Account", p. 43.
[4] *Ibid.* p. 39.

being afraid that the Truth should come out"; and as such, he complained, it was being interpreted. Hence, on Monday (10 October), Tenison wrote a third letter in a somewhat wearisome correspondence, and announced the completion of his own version of the conference. "If I have touch'd upon any Infirmity of yours", he wrote, "I presume it will be the more easily pardon'd, seeing I do not spare myself".

Three more letters were sent, and everything was now ready for the paper battle. The seconds were out of the ring. Time had been called, and the rules for theological warfare, which prescribed a seeming reluctance to appear in print, had been meticulously observed. Thus for the next few months there appeared a battle of pamphlets, containing wearisome examination of particular points, and equally wearisome patristic quotations. The conference itself (or what Tenison preferred to call "our rambling Talk") was almost forgotten in an increasingly intricate maze of minor questions.

Pulton was first in the field with "A True and Full Account of a Conference held about Religion Between Dr. Tho. Tenison and A. Pulton, one of the Masters in the Savoy".[1] The Jesuit, it must be admitted, was at some disadvantage when it came to waging a battle with the pen in the English language, a fact of which he was so conscious that he began his first pamphlet: "A.P. having been Eighteen years out of his own Country, pretends not yet to any Perfection of the English Expression or Orthography; wherefore for the future he will crave the favour of treating with the Dr. in Latine or Greek, since the Doctor finds fault with his English".[2] Macaulay was certainly justified in describing his spelling as "deplorable", and a contemporary satirist expressed his disgust in a couplet:

> Send Pulton to be lashed at Busby's school,
> That he in print no longer play the fool.[3]

Pulton's first pamphlet was some eighteen pages in length, and he introduced it with a preface addressed to "The Indifferent Reader", containing an account of the incidents, previous and subsequent to the conference. We have already remarked on the

---

[1] This pamphlet, we are informed on the fly-leaf, was "published by authority"; the printer was Nathaniel Thompson "at the Entrance into Old-Spring Gardens, Near Charing Cross".

[2] Pulton, "A True and Full Account". Preface.

[3] Macaulay, *History of England*, ii. 110. Note.

difficulty of reconciling this account with Tenison's, and particularly in the story of the debate itself, we are struck with the success of the writer, until "bidding the Dr. Goodnight, [Pulton] Desir'd him to be more wary another time, how he objected things that must naturally oblige his Adversary to so severe a Recrimination".[1]

Tenison's version appeared very soon after, dated 17 October, under the title: "A True Account of a Conference Held about Religion at London Septemb. 29, 1687 between A. Pulton Jesuit and Tho. Tenison D.D., As also of that which led to it, and followed after it". This pamphlet (which bore the imprimatur of the Archbishop of Canterbury) is of interminable length, some eighty-three pages. He dedicated it "To the Parishioners of St. Martin in the Fields and St. James' Westminster", whom he asked not to pass judgment on the conference till they had read the following pages. The pamphlet was a veritable encyclopædia of all the facts relating to the controversy. It contained an account of Tenison's visit with Dr. Clagett to the Savoy and reproduced the letters which passed between Pulton and himself, as well as the Jesuit's "True and Full Account" with Tenison's comments in an adjacent column. There then followed a description of the debate agreeing in its general outlines with Pulton's, but reversing, of course, the role of victor and vanquished.

The Vicar of St. Martin's made it particularly evident that tempers ran high, and he himself admitted that he went further than he would have done in a less excited atmosphere. He confessed that when Mr. Pulton talked of being hanged, in the heat of the moment he did reply: "Mr. P. you use a very scurvy word; and you put me in mind of a saying of the late Lord Faulkland, You are apt to hang and to damn; but if they whom you hang were no more hang'd than they whom you damn were damn'd, few men would fear either your hanging or your damning".[2]

Tenison was undoubtedly fortunate in possessing a very retentive memory, which stood him in good stead during the debate, and in the controversy afterwards. Pulton (on his own admission) was not so blessed, although it is a little surprising to find that

[1] Pulton, "A True and Full Account", p. 18.
[2] Tenison, "A True Account", p. 13. As to Pulton beating the table and saying he would be hanged, he confessed in his next pamphlet ("Remarks of A. Pulton", p. 25); "A.P. grants both the Words and the Actions to be true; and though he seem'd then to be justly provok'd: Yet he confesses it to have been a Fault, and desires none may take occasion of Scandal from it, but rather learn, how in the greatest Provocations, Men ought to moderate their Passions".

he could not remember the name of the presiding Pope at the Lateran Council of 1215, a lapse of memory which made Tenison remark to Meredith: "Why do you bring a man who has not common skill in history?"

The ball was now properly set rolling and no one could stop it, particularly as there were others anxious to give it a kick. Pulton, in his account, had dealt very severely with one of Tenison's supporters, "the facetious schoolmaster", whom he accused of making "wry Mouths and antick Postures". It came as no surprise, therefore, when there appeared "The Vindication of A. Cressener, Schoolmaster of Long Acre, From the Aspersions of A. Pulton, Jesuit and Schoolmaster in the Savoy, Together with some Account of his Discourse with Mr. Meredith". This work goes some way to support Pulton's criticism, in that it is written in a facetious vein throughout, the writer admitting that he could not help smiling now and again during the conference, since "he that could be so grave as to deny himself the liberty of a Smile at the singularity of A.P.'s Reasonings hath really a greater share of Mortification than ever A.C. could pretend to".[1]

It was now Pulton's turn to renew the attack, and he did so (on 4 November) in "Remarks of A. Pulton, Master in the Savoy, upon Dr. Tho. Tenison's late Narrative with a Confutation of the Doctor's Rule of Faith, and a Reply to A. Chresner's [sic] pretended Vindication". This pamphlet Pulton himself addressed to the parishioners of St. Martin-in-the-Fields and St. James', Westminster, and in it he accused Tenison of having "notoriously misrepresented matters of fact", thereby "stuffing his whole Narrative with several false Aspersions reflecting not only on any particular Person, but also on the whole Society whereof I am a Member". Tenison, in his "True Account", had made much of his father's sufferings during the Commonwealth period.[2] To this Pulton replied with dignity:

"Now to shew how great Favour the Priests and Jesuits found with the Committees of those Times, I take the Liberty to inform the World that my Father had six Uncles Jesuits; and yet was not only himself committed to Prison by the Rebels for his Religion, and his Loyalty to the King; but his house was also for a long time possess'd by a Committee Minister, and two of his Brethren were for three years Educated in

[1] "The Vindication of A. Cressener", 1687, p. 2.
[2] See Chapter 1, p. 3.

another Committee Minister's house at Kettring in Northamptonshire, where they were oblig'd, being under Age, to go to
Schismatical Service. Nor do I believe any one Family in
England was more frequently Pillag'd, or more severely
sequester'd, than Ours; yet I bless God, I am so far from
having my Indignation thereby rais'd against that Party, or
entertaining any Hatred towards them, that I rather glory in our
having had occasion to suffer for our King, and our Religion".[1]

Pulton then proceeded to go over the same well-trodden
ground yet once again. The triviality of the matters now in
debate can be seen from the fact that Pulton took the trouble to
publish the affirmations of several witnesses on oath testifying that
he went unaccompanied by any Jesuit to the Spring Gardens—
to prove which "a Gentleman zealous for the Truth will allow a
Guinea a Head for every one that shall be proved to have been of
A.P.'s Company".[2]

Turning to the subject at issue in the debate, Pulton once more
indulged in a fierce attack upon Luther as "most filthy in his
Language and Writings, most disrespectful and insolent towards
Princes; one infamous for his intimate Familiarity with the
Devil; and in short, one, whose Principles and Practices are
absolutely destructive of all Piety, Religion, Civil Government
and Morality".[3] He then attacked Tenison's rule of faith (i.e.
the Scriptures and the definitions of the Councils), and maintained
that this position led inevitably to an appeal to the individual
conscience, with the paradoxical result that Tenison "must grant
to each particular Member what he denies to the whole".[4]

Referring to the charge that the Catholics supported a foreign
jurisdiction, Pulton declared himself content to leave this "to the
Judgment of his most sacred Majesty who alone can be injured
by that assertion".[5]

Before releasing his reply to this second pamphlet, Tenison
took the opportunity to publish a translation of *Six Conferences
concerning the Eucharist*, written by Mons. de la Placette. In his
short foreword to this edition, Tenison explained that he placed
it before the public at this time, because Pulton had claimed
"that the Principles of Philosophy which contradict the doctrine

[1] Pulton, "Remarks of A. Pulton, Master in the Savoy". Preface.
[2] *Ibid.* p. 2.
[3] *Ibid.* p. 12.
[4] *Ibid.* p. 17.
[5] *Ibid.* p. 31.

of Transubstantiation were to be renounced ".[1] He referred Pulton to this treatise and promised a more complete reply, which he soon gave in "Mr. Pulton considered in his Sincerity, Reasonings, Authorities, or a Just Answer". The parishioners of St. Martin's and St. James' were once again favoured with a third treatise dedicated to them, but Tenison intimated that this would probably be his last, as he did not envy his adversary "the Honour of throwing the first, and the second, and the third handful of Dirt".[2] The Vicar of St. Martin's was by this time aware that the battle of pamphlets was growing a little tedious and he endeavoured to add interest to this one by a somewhat heavy attempt at humour. This he attempted at the expense of "Katherine", whom Pulton had quoted as a witness to his arrival at the conference accompanied only by Meredith. In the course of a long passage, Tenison suggested that if this good lady were present during the debate, she "must have come by some unsuspected way, such as the Chimney or the Key Hole: And if there she remain'd, she must have put her self into the shape of some such thing as a Table, a Chair or a Candlestick".[3]

Tenison then proceeded in his customary manner on a long and minute examination of Mr. Pulton's "chief reasonings and authorities" in relation to Luther, the rule of faith, the Lateran Council, and the antiquity of Popery in England. We hope we may be pardoned if we do not follow him into this excursion. Suffice that it showed his seriousness and patience, although he himself was a little weary by this time, for he concluded: "Perhaps my Readers have already taken compassion on themselves and left off some Pages before they have come at this. And I think it is time to relieve myself, after having been concern'd in a Controversial matter which in the nature of it I do not much relish; and which by the length of it, has created in me a most ungrateful Satiety".[4]

[1] The publication of this translation drew forth a Catholic reply in "A Full Answer to Dr. Tenison's Conference Concerning the Eucharist" (1687). Tenison, with characteristic energy, answered with "Of Transubstantiation: or a Reply to a late Paper called, etc". (1688).
[2] Tenison, "Mr. Pulton considered in his Sincerity, Reasonings, Authorities, or a Just Answer".
[3] *Ibid.* p. 2. These remarks were not allowed to pass unnoticed, and it is interesting to find that the lady herself replied in a very sarcastic paper: "A Full Discovery of the False Evidence Produc'd by the Papists against the most reverend and learned Doctor Thomas Tenison". This pamphlet is possibly one of the earliest of its kind which purports to come from a woman.
[4] Tenison, "Mr. Pulton considered in his Sincerity, Reasonings, Authorities, or a Just Answer", p. 100.

One person, however, had yet to add his contribution before the controversy died down. Edward Meredith, the ardent Catholic convert, could hardly be expected to remain silent, and early in 1688 he published: "Some Farther Remarks on the Late Account Given by Dr. Tenison of His Conference with Mr. Pulton. Wherein the Doctor's Three Exceptions against Edward Meredith are examin'd, Several of his other Misrepresentations laid open, Motives of the said E.M.'s Conversion shew'd, and some other Points relating to the Controversie occasionally treated." Of all the pamphlets connected with this controversy, we confess to having read this with most pleasure. Its style is clear, its wit effective, and it is more concerned with the principles than with the trivialities of debate. With typical ingenuity, Meredith asked of his Protestant readers one thing only, namely, that they really would be Protestants, "since Nothing . . . is so primarily essential to Protestants, as to conclude both themselves and their Leaders Fallible, and in consequence of this to distrust both". Of Tenison's controversial writings, Meredith remarked rather unkindly that "altho' his part of the Conference hath been lick'd since its Birth into as much shape as it was capable of, yet after all this paternal industry it is but an homely creature still, and neither does us much harm, nor (I am verily persuaded) would it have appeared to the Doctor himself worthy of Publication, had it not been in Virtue of that Instinct whereby the Cow thinks her own Young ones the whitest".[1]

As Tenison had objected to Meredith's presence on the grounds that he was a convert,[2] so the latter used the opportunity to make his pamphlet an informal apologia for his conversion. The weakness of the Protestant position, he maintained, lay in the unrestrained licence which it was bound (if consistent) to grant to individual speculation, and this must lead logically to no Church at all.[3] "Amidst these doubts I confess ingenuously", he wrote, "that what our English Doctors have made so light of, was of great moment with me, viz. That the Church of England affirmed that Salvation might be had amongst the Roman Catholics; but the Roman Catholics absolutely denied that the like was to be had amongst them. . . . In a word I considered that if the Protestants were true, I should be safe with the Roman

[1] Meredith, "Some Farther Remarks on the Late Account", p. 4.
[2] See p. 52.
[3] Meredith, "Some Farther Remarks on the Late Account", pp. 28, 29.

Catholics: but if the Roman Catholics were right, I could not be so with the Protestants".[1]

To call him a "bigot", he continued, because he had changed his religious allegiance was only true if the word were synonymous with "zealous": if it were meant to imply that he would never hear another point of view, then this was disproved in that he had already left one communion for another. Dealing with Tenison's claim that the Scriptures constituted a rule of faith,[2] Meredith replied that this could not be so, since "the Difference of Sense in the several Translations of the Bible which are now in Being, is an undeniable proof that the Scripture does not manifest itself to us by its own Lustre (as pretended) at least in all its parts".[3]

Meredith's pamphlet was certainly expressed in an ingenious manner throughout, and his discernment may be seen in his recognizing Chillingworth as "the subtlest of them all, and the Fountain Head from whence Dr. St[illingfleet] and most others of our Modern Controversie Writers had derived their Notions".[4]

The controversy (at least as far as the main combatants were concerned) had now spent its force, although a minor battle remained to be fought around a pamphlet entitled "Speculum Ecclesiasticum or an Ecclesiastical Prospective Glass", written by Thomas Ward (1652–1708), a character not without interest. A prolific controversialist, although the exigencies of English grammar often proved too much for him, he began life as a Calvinist, became a convert to the Church of Rome, and obtained a commission in the Papal guards. Returning to England in 1685, he took a leading part in the controversies of the time, and was thought by Dr. Tillotson to be a Jesuit in disguise, and to have been "bred a Cambridge scholar and exchanged his black coat for a red one". Ward was not directly concerned in the dispute between Pulton and Tenison nor does he appear to have been present at the conference, but he became involved through Pulton's quoting one of his works, the "Speculum Ecclesiasticum", a treatise which endeavoured to prove the doctrines of the Church of Rome from the Scriptures "and the Testimonies of the Fathers

---

[1] Meredith, "Some Farther Remarks on the Late Account", p. 30.
[2] As a matter of fact Tenison did not make this exclusive claim for the Scriptures, in this respect departing from Chillingworth. See p. 47.
[3] Meredith, "Some Farther Remarks on the Late Account", p. 61.
[4] Ibid. p. 41.

for the first 500 years". Tenison felt that some reply ought to be made to the "Speculum", "not so much with respect to the Author, but to the Jesuit who used the Pamphlet", but as Ward was a soldier, he felt it hardly "decent" in him to reply, and so suggested to Henry Wharton, "a Young Man and not of years enough to be a Priest",[1] that he should take the matter in hand. Hence Wharton replied in: "The Pamphlet entitled Speculum Ecclesiasticum or an Ecclesiastical Prospective Glass Considered in its False Reasonings and Quotations".[2] This short work of Wharton's inevitably evoked a reply from Ward under the title, "Monomachia or a Duel Between Dr. Tho. Tenison, Pastor of St. Martin's and a Roman Catholick Souldier", in which he denied indignantly that he had ever been to Cambridge or had "turned his black coat into a red one". "If he had told you", he wrote, "that I preach'd the last Sunday in St. Martin's Church in his Gown, and his Reverence mounted the Guard in my Red Coat it had been every whit as true as the other". Ward also added a further contribution to the controversy a few months later in "The Roman Catholick Souldier's Letter", which induced "C.D." (Tenison himself) to condescend to men of low estate and reply in "An Answer to the Letter of the Roman Catholic Soldier".

So ended the controversy which arose out of the meeting between Pulton and Tenison at the Long Acre on 29 September 1687. How many people were induced to change their religious allegiance as a result of it, we do not know, though it is natural to ask what happened to the young apprentice, John Smith, who was the indirect cause of the whole proceedings. At first it seemed likely that he would persist in going over to the Roman communion, for Dr. Horneck, who saw him on 13 October, reported to Tenison that he saw "Stubborness, Ill nature and Sulleness in his Face", and that "he seem'd to intimate that he was already gone over to them".[3]

Time, however, inclined him to see things in a different light, and perhaps it is not uncharitable to suggest that the Revolution of 1688 was not without its effect. The following letter which he wrote to Tenison on 15 February 1689, witnesses to his complete restoration into the fellowship of the Church of England.

[1] Henry Wharton (1664–95) later became well-known as a scholar: his death at the age of thirty-one was a great misfortune to English scholarship.
[2] "The Pamphlet entitled Speculum Ecclesiasticum . . . considered". Preface.
[3] Tenison, "A True Account", p. 79.

"I have been ye only cause of ye great trouble you have had in ye late conference held about religion, and for all what was then said, and you and Dr. Horneck had said before, I obstinately continued in ye Romish persuasion, but God be praised, I am now convinced of ye great error committed in forsaking ye Church of England and adhering to ye Church of Rome. I doe therefore resolve stedfastly to ye Church of England for ye future. I doe most humbly beg your pardon for my many and great offences against you, and I return you thanks for all you have done to bring me back".[1]

He also drew up another paper, in which he stated that he had decided to leave the Church of Rome because he was convinced of the evil of such practices as the adoration of the Cross and the Blessed Virgin Mary, the preaching of purgatory and the making allegiance to the Pope necessary for salvation.[2]

This conference between Tenison and Pulton is not altogether without interest and importance. It shows clearly the temper of the times, and the strenuous efforts which the Catholics were making to commend their cause to their fellow countrymen during James' reign. It was, in fact, though they could not be aware of it, the last open attempt which the Catholics were able to make to proselytize in England till the nineteenth century released them from legal disabilities. The principles on which Pulton based his arguments in this conference represented an attack in all departments on the individualism ushered in by the Renaissance and Reformation. Shorn of the embellishments, hair splittings, and subtleties with which both sides obscured their arguments, the Catholics were attacking, the Protestants asserting, the right of private judgment. The ideals for which both parties stood were, in the political circumstances of the time, mutually irreconcilable, and it was James' folly which enabled the instinctive Protestantism of the English people to win the day. Thus the zeal of both parties may be understood, when we recognize the importance of the subjects in debate.

As far as Tenison personally was concerned, the conference was certainly not without its significance, for it marked him out as a defender of the Church of England in days when at court it was not profitable to be so.

Conferences of this kind were by no means uncommon, although this one, because of the public nature of the debate,

[1] Smith to Tenison, 15 February 1789. Lambeth MSS. 1029, f. 8.
[2] Lambeth MSS. 1029, f. 9.

attracted more attention than any other.[1] Tenison's success (or reputed success) [2] led to his being consulted by others in affairs of a similar nature, and in January 1688, for example, he received a letter from Dr. Horneck, a London vicar and German by birth. In this case Dr. Horneck had already met his adversary once, and "after two hours rambling discourse for hee stuck to nothing: Hee desired we might have another meeting, and that we should write down our objections and answers, which I agreed to, not that I am fond of such conferences, for I see no good come of them, but that they might not have anything to object against us that we decline a Conference".[3] Accordingly, a further meeting was arranged for 4 January, and Horneck begged Tenison's support on this occasion "to beare part of the fatigue", the more so as he had a cold upon him. Unfortunately we know nothing of this conference: if it took place, as seems probable, it was a private affair in Horneck's own house, and the public were not admitted.

Tenison's proselytizing zeal secured for him a notable convert at this time in John Taffe, formerly Father Vincentius of the Order of Capuchins of the mission of Ireland. His public conversion and reception into the Church of England took place on 15 June 1688,[4] in the presence of Tenison, the two churchwardens of St. Martin's, Oliver Trebern and John Woodman, and a certain Peter Menel of Clerkenwell Green. The form of recantation to which Taffe subscribed was drawn up by Tenison, and in the course of this long document he confessed "that the twelve last Articles in ye R. Creed (commonly called ye Creed of Pope Pius) are neither true nor necessary doctrines, but on ye contrary, false and perillous to ye souls of men as also that the worship in that Church consonant to them is aequally false and dangerous". He concluded: "Also I do unfeignedly and heartily desire to be received into ye Externall Communion of the said C. of E.

---

[1] See p. 50.

[2] There were some who accused Tenison "of being foiled in his Conference with Pulton the Jesuit, for want of Capacity to defend so good a Cause, and having committed too many blunders in his Writings, to be reckoned either a man of good sense or extraordinary Learning". See Higgons, *Remarks on Burnet's History*, p. 186.

[3] Horneck to Tenison, 3 January 1688. Lambeth MSS. 1029, f. 7.

[4] Taffe, in 1695, stated that he "recanted before Mr. Tenison . . . the day the Bishops were sent to the Tower" (i.e. 8 June). From a private note of Tenison's (Lambeth MSS. 1029, f. 13) in which he writes, "June 15, 88, John Taffe . . . of Ye Order of Capuchins of ye ministry of Ireland renounced . . .", and from the actual recantation to which Taffe subscribed (Lambeth MSS. 1029, f. 11), it is certain that it took place on 15 June. Either his memory played him false, or he referred to a more informal recantation before Tenison which may have preceded his official recantation in the presence of the Vicar and churchwardens of St. Martin's.

professing that I will, (by God's blessing) continue in the same all ye days of my life".[1]

Conferences and conversions, however, began to lose interest. The Revolution of '88 turned men's thoughts in other directions, and the practical question of government and the inclusion of the Dissenters engaged men's minds. The accession of William and Mary drove Catholic propaganda underground, but Tenison's energies in this field were not exhausted (they never were!), and late in 1688 he published two more works dealing with the Catholic controversy, the first of which was a symposium under the title: *Popery not founded on Scripture*. This volume contained nineteen separate articles, all dealing with the scriptural authority for certain Catholic doctrines and practices, including the following: the supremacy of St. Peter (Patrick); the worship of Angels (Gee); transubstantiation (Williams); the sacrifice of the Mass (Kidder); auricular confession (Linford); prayer in an unknown tongue (Scott); the celibacy of the priests (Payne); purgatory (Bramstone); the visibility of the Church (Resbury). Tenison edited the volume, and supplied an introduction on the relationship of the Bible to the present controversy.

The reformists were often contemptuously styled the "biblists", he said, but so far from resenting this, they accepted it as a "mark of honour", for had not St. Athanasius declared "that the Holy and Divine Scriptures are of themselves sufficient for shewing the Truth".[2] Unfortunately, Tenison went on, "as the Authority of the Papacy increas'd, the Use of the Scriptures decreas'd in that Church; which being possessed of an unhappy Privilege of a Chair in the Imperial City, began too early to set itself up as a Kingdom of this World".[3] With the advent of the Reformation in England, the Bible was placed in all churches, with the result that the Catholics themselves now "began to appeal to the Bible for their new Doctrines and to fight against the Protestants with weapons taken out of their own Magazine".[4] Hence it was necessary to acquaint the public with the relation of the Scriptures to the various Catholic practices, which consequently formed the aim of the following volume.

[1] Lambeth MSS. 1029, f. 11. Taffe's career in the Church of England was by no means a happy one. See Lambeth MSS. 1029, f. 15, and Kenyon MSS. H.M.C. 10th Report, IV. 321.
[2] *Popery not founded on Scripture*, 1688, p. 5.
[3] *Ibid*. p. 7.
[4] *Ibid*. p. 9.

The other work published by Tenison at this time was his own somewhat laboured translation of J. de la Placette's *Of the Incurable Scepticism of the Church of Rome*. To translate such a lengthy volume for the benefit of the English reader illustrates yet again Tenison's industry and patience. It is unnecessary for us to enter here upon an analysis of this ponderous work, particularly as it does not come directly from Tenison's pen. Suffice, perhaps, to set out its object in its own words:

"1. That it is most false what is pretended with so much confidence that the Church, at least in the sense by them understood, cannot err. 2. That granting the Church cannot err, this her infallibility is of that Nature, that both itself labours with inextricable difficulties, and confers certainty upon nothing else. 3. That our faith relieth upon far more firm foundations, and that nothing is believed by us, which is not both certain in itself and such as the certainty of it cannot be unknown by us".[1]

Part III   Years of Vigilance

Tenison's fear of the Catholics proved to be a life-long passion. It arose from an exaggerated respect for their power, as the following estimate, which he drew up in 1683, makes abundantly clear:

"The Romanists are a mighty body of Men; and though there are intestine Fewds betwixt the Secular and Regular Clergy, as likewise betwixt the several Orders, yet they are all united into one common Politie, and grafted into the one stock of the Papal Headship. They are favoured in many places by great men; they have Variety of Learning; they pretend to great Antiquity, to Miracles, to Martyrs without number, to extraordinary Charity and Mortification; they have the Nerves of worldly Power, that is, Banks of Money, and a large Revenue: They have a Scheme of Policy always in readiness; there are great numbers of Emissaries posted in all places for the convey-ing of Intelligence, and the gaining of Proselytes; they take upon them all shapes, and are bred to all the worldly Arts of Insinuation".[2]

Tenison never realised that the danger, so real in 1688, had largely disappeared in 1715, and throughout the whole of his

---

[1] Tenison, *Of the Incurable Scepticism of the Church of Rome*. Preface.
[2] Tenison, "An Argument for Union", 1683, p. 19.

archiepiscopate, he regarded it as his special responsibility to keep a close watch over the Catholic population.

For years after the Revolution of '88, the Catholics remained suspect as potential rebels and it was the policy of the Government to keep a check on all their activities. Tenison was foremost in advocating this policy, and through the diligence of one Spence "employed in the secret affairs of the Post Office", letters passing between Catholics both in England and abroad were intercepted and forwarded to him for inspection and report. The Archbishop seems to have been particularly interested in "secret service" work of this rather unsavoury nature, and the Earl of Shrewsbury writing to the Earl of Portland on 21 August 1696 (in connection with two intercepted letters), reported that he found the Archbishop "stored with tools for that business and well skilled in it; but neither he nor I having very fine fingers, he has promised to engage one whose fidelity he can be answerable for, and who is already adroit, but he will assist him with his skill". In addition to this, he added, "The Archbis[hop] knows how to set up the engine for imitating hands, but thinks it so dangerous an art that, unless his Majesty commands him, I perceive he is desirous it should be discovered to nobody, but die with him, being confident that he is now the only person alive that is perfectly master of that secret".[1]

In 1696 and the following year the Government were particularly uneasy since, in Spence's opinion, a Jacobite plot was being hatched, and charges of complicity in such intrigues were even brought against Shrewsbury.[2] Tenison was always unduly nervous and credulous where Jacobites and Catholics were concerned. He regarded it as his especial task to keep the Council alive to the danger, and he laid any information he received before it, no matter how insignificant it might seem.[3] In August 1697 this undue nervousness led to his paying exaggerated attention to the story of one Price, an informer, who told the Council with real gusto of a scheme which he claimed to have discovered for seizing Dover castle with fifty men, and hanging out "a flag next day which would be a sign for the French to land". Price confessed that he himself was selected to carry the plan to King James, and that he had arranged for five hundred men to be in

---

[1] Shrewsbury to Portland, 21 August 1696. Portland MSS. H.M.C. II. part i. 386.
[2] *D.N.B.* lv. 301.
[3] See Somers to Trumbull, November 1696. Devonshire MSS. H.M.C. II. 713.

readiness to reduce Dover if it did not surrender.[1] The Lord
Chamberlain gave it as his opinion that it was "all stuff and
signified nothing", while even Tenison found it difficult to believe
that the Earl of Yarmouth (1652–1732), a supporter of James,
could have been partner to such a hair-brained escapade. The
Archbishop, however, was for proceeding with the investigations
and he undertook the interrogation of Yarmouth when he
appeared before the Council on 21 September. The enquiry
proved farcical and both the Attorney-General and the Solicitor-
General agreed that no prosecution could be possible on the single
evidence of such a dubious character as Price.[2]

Tenison was also interested at this time in the case of one
Metcalf, a Roman Catholic, who (to quote Dryden) was "commanded to appear before the Council for printing a pamphlet of
two sheets in Latin concerning a project of some of our Clergy
to live in common, that thereby they might be helpful to such of
our Communion as are in want". Dryden wrote to his friend Sir
William Trumbull, Secretary of State, requesting his "moderation" in this affair, since Metcalf was a "young man", this was
his "first offence", and particularly as "My Lord Archbishop is
pleased to represent the action as dangerous".[3]

William's views on religious toleration, as we shall see later,
were well in advance of his time, and it was not his wish that even
Roman Catholics should be excepted from the Act of Toleration,
for he would gladly have extended to all his subjects the privileges
which he had obtained for the Dissenters.[4] But this could not be,
and towards the end of his reign feeling against the Catholics
grew worse. After the Peace of Ryswick, in 1697, great numbers of
Popish priests fled to England, and it was rumoured that William
had bound himself by one of the secret Articles to relax the penal
laws against the Catholics.[5] The House of Commons became
alarmed, and the Parliament of 1700 passed a disgraceful act
against them which, so J. R. Lumby comments, "at the present
day can hardly be read without astonishment". Under this Act,
all Roman Catholic priests were banished under pain of perpetual imprisonment, and it offered £100 for information which
should lead to the conviction of any one of them performing the

[1] S.P.D. William III. 23 August 1697. 8B, p. 327.
[2] Ibid. 23 September 1697. 8B, p. 392.
[3] Dryden to Trumbull, 18 August 1697. Devonshire MSS. H.M.C. 1924. II. 761.
[4] Hallam's Constitutional History, 1827, iii. 177.
[5] Ibid. p. 178.

offices of his Church. It required every person brought up in the Roman religion or suspected of it to take the oaths of allegiance and supremacy, and to sign the Declaration of Charles II against transubstantiation; in default of which they were to be incapable of purchasing, inheriting, or holding any estate, and that which they might already possess was to become the property of the next of kin, being Protestant. A Church historian writes:

"The design of the Bill was to force the Catholic landowners to sell their property and thus to destroy that class altogether. But its very severity helped to defeat its object. The spirit of liberty was strong in the nation and the judges hesitated to enforce a law as tyrannical as the edicts of the French government against the Protestants. Fortunately the Act was found to be drawn up in terms so indefinite as to be easily evaded and there is scarcely a single instance on record of any loss of property under it. From the time of the passing of this Act, which relieved the minds of the timid from the fear that the King and the nation were drifting into Popery together, till the end of William's reign not long after, no restrictive measures were taken against Roman Catholics. As a class they were shunned and neglected a good deal, both at this time and for nearly a century after. Hatred of Rome long continued to be as it had become in James II's reign, a ruling passion of ploughmen and artisans. As members of a communion so generally detested, the Catholics and particularly those whose property kept them in the country, were compelled to lead very lonely and secluded lives, especially as their well known leanings towards the exiled royal family caused them to be avoided by their neighbours as persons whose acquaintance, never very desirable, might now and then bring them into serious difficulties".[1]

An effort was made in 1705 to render the Act of 1700 against the Papists effective, but the motion was lost in the House of Commons by a large majority, a fact which indicates that passions did not run so fiercely as five years previously.

The constant distrust of the Catholics as concealed Jacobites, and the fantastic rumours as to their numbers and activities, still made many conscientious Protestants uneasy. Tenison's apprehensions were certainly not diminished by receiving a letter in October, 1705, from a correspondent in Germany, reporting that he had recently visited the Jesuit College in Hildesheim and

---

[1] J. R. Lumby, *Compendium of English Church History*, 1883, p. 60.

6

had been told that "there were more emissaries of that order in England at this time than we believed"; and that "near half the priests of the Abbey of Lambspring, who are all English, are lately gone for England, since these vipers had some designe in hand at present".[1]

In view of this supposed "increase and boldness of the Catholics", Tenison, supported by the House of Commons, secured an order in council, dated 4 April 1706, requiring that "a distinct and particular account should be taken of all Papists and reputed Papists in the Kingdom".[2] The archbishops accordingly circularized all the bishops, requiring them to find out what advowsons, right to presentation, or schools were in Catholic hands, and to proceed against any of the clergy who declined to co-operate.[3] The response to this circular letter seems to have been very unsatisfactory, so much so that on 15 July 1706 Tenison sent a further letter to the bishops complaining of "ye backwardness . . . in ye Execution of ye Former", and urging them "to be very punctuall in answering ye contents of it".[4]

The Archbishop himself never needed exhortation to be on his guard, as two typical instances will show. In 1708 there appeared a pamphlet from the pen of a certain Dr. Bernard under the title "An Exact and critical Account as to every particular, in what manner, and how far ye Book of Common Prayer is taken out of ye offices of ye Church of Rome".[5] The writer appears to have been a beneficed clergyman in the diocese of Lincoln, and Wake, the Bishop, drew up a report of the matter. As to the performance itself, Tenison did not think very highly, and writing to the Bishop of Lincoln on 3 August he commented: "Popish Bernard has now vented his wrath in print against ye Ch. of England in such mann^r that I think he is not capable of doing it mischief . . . I believe his Insolence must have some check by ye Court, but if he be deprived (as he deserves) before his poor creditors be payed; they will be ye sufferers".[6] The pamphlet, however, commanded more attention than the Archbishop seems to have thought likely, and he wrote anxiously again to Wake on 30 August: "Dr. Bernard's printed paper in wch he defies the Ch.

---

[1] Gwynne to Tenison, 6 October 1705. Lambeth MSS. 930, f. 222.
[2] Ibid. f. 83.
[3] Ibid.
[4] Tenison to Wake, 15 July 1706. Christ Church. Lincoln Correspondence. Wake Papers.
[5] Ibid. 7 September 1708.
[6] Ibid. 3 August 1708.

of England is much spread and makes a mighty noyse here, insomuch that if there be no proceeding against Him in ye ecclesiastical Court upō yt Account, ye Clamour . . . wch is now begū, will grow into an ĩsupportable Outcry, both frō Friends and Enemies. I hope therefore yr Lp will begin something of this nature with speed". Wake, accordingly, commenced proceedings against Bernard without delay, and the Archbishop expressed his satisfaction in a letter written on 7 September,[1] and followed this up by another on 17 September.[2] He was "glad", he said, that the Bishop had "order'd a Prosecution" since "Neglect would not have done ye business in a case so public and of such a nature".

In 1709, Tenison heard rumours of a Roman episcopal visitation near Chester, and he immediately made investigations, receiving a report from one Joseph Holme on 3 November. The facts, Holme stated, were as follows:

"The first week in July (wch was the next week after my Lord of Chester held his Visitation here) Bishop Smith came to Mr. Walmsleys, Lower Hall, in Salmesbury within my Parish and confirmed there on Friday, Saturday and Sunday 8, 9, 10 of July. . . . The number of Papists that were there was very great. Mr. Hull, my Curate at Salmesbury tells me that he sees multitudes goe that way past his house, some on foot, some on horse back, most of them with little children in their Arms; But the greatest Concourse was on Sunday because the Bishop was to preach that day. The neighbouring Protestants seemed to take little Notice of that matter, it being no Novelty with them, the Bishop having been there on the same occasion about 5 yeares".[3]

It was, of course, Tenison's earnest wish to "restore" Roman Catholics to the bosom of the Anglican Church, and particularly was this his desire where they were men of some position. He endeavoured, naturally enough, to make Protestant capital out of such conversions, as, for example, when he received Lord Dumbarton (1687–17 ?) into the Church of England on 24 January 1709, in his Chapel at Lambeth. At this ceremony the Archbishop was assisted by his two chaplains Dr. Sydal and Mr. Ibbot, and he used an elaborate form of service which he had

[1] Tenison to Wake, 7 September 1708. Christ Church. Lincoln Correspondence. Wake Papers.
[2] *Ibid.* 17 September.
[3] Holme to Tenison, 3 November 1709. Lambeth MSS. 930, f. 27.

himself drawn up. Standing at the Communion table, Tenison first addressed the congregation on the importance of the occasion, whereupon after prayers, a psalm, and an examination, Lord Dumbarton was made a member of the Church of England in these words: "I, Thomas, by divine permission Archbishop of Canterbury, upon thy solemn Profession, and earnest Request, do by virtue of my Pastoral Office in this Province, receive thee into the Church of England in the name of the Father and of the Son and of the Holy Ghost, Amen".[1] The Archbishop concluded by instructing his convert to present himself at Communion as soon as possible.

The need of a regular form for use on such occasions as these was widely felt, particularly as there appears to have been a number of conversions in the first few years of the eighteenth century when Romanism had ceased to be either profitable or heroic. True, there was laid down by statute a public form of "submission and declaration to be made in Church of conformity to the Queen's Laws and Statutes" but there was no official form of reconciliation to the Church of England. The provision of such an order was thus left to the individual bishops and Bishop Kennett records that he had seen over one hundred such forms. To impose unity on this diversity, the Queen instructed Convocation in 1710 to draw up "a Form for receiving Converts from the Church of Rome", and as nothing was immediately done, she repeated this order in March 1714. As Tenison possessed in manuscript the form which he had been using for some years, he now took the opportunity of placing it before Convocation, but internal dissension prevented this rather unmanageable body from coming to agreement. The death of the Queen a few months after having given the order led to the dismissal of the Tory ministry, and to the closure of the debates caused by a small minority in the lower house of Convocation, who wanted "to make the Form serve as a Test upon Protestant Dissenters including in it not merely a recantation of Popery but of Schism".[2]

Despite its lack of official authority the form drawn up by Tenison became widely used and it was republished as late as 1827, when the editor noted that "whether from the great authority of the Prelate who composed it, or from the attention

---

[1] Lambeth MSS. 933, f. 61.
[2] "Archbishop Tenison's Form for receiving Converts from the Church of Rome ", p. 3.

paid to it by Convocation, it has continued in use to this day".
Dr. Chandler, Bishop of Durham (1730–50), and Beilby Porteus,
Bishop of London (1787–1808), both adopted it as a semi-official
form in their dioceses. In view of its wide use it may not be
without interest to glance at the order of Tenison's form.

The ceremony, he directed, was to take place in the presence
of the minister (or bishop if possible), and was to be recorded in
the parish register. It began with the priest addressing the congregation from the Communion table:

"Dearly beloved, we are here met together for the reconciling
a convert, lately of the Church of Rome, to the Established
Church of England, as to a true and sound part of the Holy
Catholic Church. Now that this weighty affair may have its
due effect, let us in the first place humbly and devoutly pray
Almighty God for his blessing upon us, in that pious and
charitable office we are going about".

There then followed a number of collects and psalms until
the following questions were put to the convert, who was standing
meanwhile outside the Communion rails.[1]

1. Was he persuaded that the Scriptures contained all the
doctrines necessary for eternal salvation? 2. Did he believe all
the articles of the Apostles' Creed? 3. Was he sorry he had not
hitherto followed the way of the Scriptures? 4. Had he now
resolved to live righteously? 5. Did he desire to be received
into the Church of England "as a sound part of the Holy
Catholic Church"? 6. Did he renounce all the errors of the
Church of Rome, and 7, the last twelve articles of the Creed of
Pope Pius IV? 8. Did he acknowledge the supremacy of the
King in all matters ecclesiastical according to the thirty-seventh
article of religion? 9. Would he receive the Sacraments according to the sense of the Church of England? 10. Would he
honestly conform to the liturgy of the said Church?

After these questions the priest said the following prayer on
behalf of the convert: "Almighty God, who hath given you a sense
of your errors and a will to do all these things, grant you also

[1] In the form which Tenison used for Lord Dumbarton there was inserted here:
"I am verily persuaded by that wch you have declar'd to me in private, that your
Conversion to the Truth and Purity of ye Religion established in the C of E is heartie
and sincere. But inasmuch as with ye heart man believeth and with the mouth confession is made unto salvation in order to the satisfaction of others of ye flock & ye
setting forth thereby ye public honour of God: I think it fitt to propose to you the
following questions to ye intent that you may make playn & open Answers to them
before this Assembly". Lambeth MSS. 933, f. 61.

strength and power to perform the same, that he may accomplish his work which he hath begun in you". After pronouncing the absolution from the Communion service, the priest then took the convert by the right hand and said: "I . . . do upon this thy solemn profession and earnest request receive thee into the Holy Communion of the Church of England".

The increasing weakness of the Catholic body in England, apparent during the early years of the eighteenth century, by no means induced a corresponding apathy in the Archbishop, and he doubtless welcomed the proclamation in 1711 for enforcing the penal laws against them. We are fortunate in possessing the draft of an address, stressing the need for vigilance, which the Archbishop drew up for the clergy of his own diocese, probably in the last year of his life. It is one of the most revealing documents which we have from his pen, and he seems to have intended that this *Oratio* should constitute something of an apologia for his life-long policy towards the Catholics. It comes, therefore, fittingly at the close of this chapter, and we quote from it at length.[1]

"My endeavours (I thank God) have bin very heartie, in order to ye suppressing of fals doctrine & imoralitie, & the promoting ye Truth & Holiness, tho' they have not bin allwaies crown'd with success: And [being] particularly concern'd yt Popery is ye mother of a numerous offspring of evills of an high nature, I have not bin wanting in giving discouragement ever to ye Appearances of It. But I observe with grief of heart, that there are, notwithstanding, Leanings & dangerous *approaches* to It, both amongst you & in other parts of my Province. I should be a very negligent watchman, if I should not give you *warning* of ye perill & exhort you not to listen to ye directions of *blind & Crafty Guides* who would lead you into ye pit of destruction. You will say perhaps, that ys would have bin seasonable Admonition whilst we had over us two Popish Kings; but that now we have a Protestant Head over a Protestant Body, it may seem a fals alarm; I believe ye Contrary & the grounds of my belief are the following".

He then went on to expatiate on the large numbers of people who were devoted to the interests of the Pretender, "so many yt they are not to be computed by any Calculation". These men foolishly protested that they would "rather be Papists than Presbyterians", when in fact there was "no necessity for being

[1] Lambeth MSS. 1037, f. 17. We have transcribed it from a very rough draft in Tenison's own hand, and much of it is in note form. It is very difficult to decipher.

either". Moreover, there was an increase in literature which supported some of the Catholic tenets. "There are Books written", he commented,

"by professed Protestants wch shew the warping and leaning of ye Authors towards Popery, by wch ye many are seduced especially wn this comes from ye Pens of clergymen who have gained some reputation for their learning. There are Books written by Professed Papists and Pretended Protestants in wch ye holy Reformation is industriously blackened and derided. Henry ye 8th is ye chief mark against whom they let fly their bolts tho' a severe Papist in all other respects, except the Supremacie in poynt of peculiar Interest. But that which gave edge to their Design, was not so much his vicious Life as his becoming an instrument in God's hands in beginning to demolish ye Idoll of ye papacy and thereby preparing ye way for others to reform ye corrupt state of ye Church".

More insidious, perhaps, was the fact that many "pretended Protestants" held "Popish Tenets under ye notion of ye doctrines and practices of ye primitive Church". Amongst these doctrines were auricular confession, prayers for the dead, and unction during sickness. Particularly in Holy Communion these "pretended Protestants" taught "the presence of ye very natural substance of ye body and blood of Christ", alleging as justification the actual words spoken by Jesus. "But is our Faith", Tenison asked, "to be guided by ye words, rather than by the sense and meaning of them? hath not Christ said, I am ye door, I am ye true vine, my Father is ye husbandman? Did not our Saviour speak to his countrymen in concise Hebraisms, to wch every new occasion made?"

But this tendency towards "Romanisation", Tenison maintained, came only as a later development in the Reformation. "From the beginning", he said,

"it was not so, as is evident from Abp Cranmer's exercise Book of ye sacrament of ye Eucharist. He and our first Reformers knew best their own Principles in wch they founded their Proceedings. Since they slept in ye Ashes of their Martyrdom, others have taken further, tho' not safer steps. One must allow many of them to have bin Great Men yet we cañot but declare without uncharitable censure that those great Men have greatly erred. Amongst ym I reckon Archbp Laud & Bp Cosin (I am persuaded) did lean this way upõ believing it would heighten devotion in Communicants, whilst they apprehended their Saviour to be personally present. But ye true Fayth is sufficient to produce these effects without any Enthusiastic amusements wch rather blind than edifie ye devout. He who believes that wn Xns associate, & in ye Ld's supper make a solemn memorial of ye Sacrifice of Christ, & partake in worthy manner of ye Elements, they receive in especiall manner the benefit of Christ's Passion, & ye assistance of his blessed Spirit, these have abundant helps to devotion, & receive a greater blessing than ye very flesh and blood of Christ could conveigh . . . to the soul, ye nourishment of wch is spirituall food".

This document is a pathetic reminder, if nothing else, of how Tenison was living in a past age. While he was defending his flock from an imaginary foe, the Deists were making inroads into the fold.

CHAPTER 4

THE BLOODLESS REVOLUTION

THE political situation during James II's brief reign rapidly became worse and worse. At his accession James was not really unpopular, for while the Scottish Parliament "annexed the excise to the Crown for ever, and voted James a revenue exceeding by one-third that enjoyed by his brother", the English Parliament at once settled on him an income as large as that granted to Charles II.[1] James suffered the misfortune, however (in addition to his own personal incapacity), of inheriting difficulties both at home and abroad, prominent among which was the embarrassment of the French alliance. As to his own foreign policy, he seems at first to have been undecided, and to have sought a *rapprochement* with William of Orange—a very wise thing to do, since such an alliance would have been popular in England, where fear of France was the dominant political passion.

This flirtation with the Dutch was not entirely without result, for it led to the dismissal of the Duke of Monmouth from William's court, and, as a consequence, to his foolish and tragic attempt to secure the English throne.[2] Monmouth, "whose astonishing beauty of form" was more than offset by his lack of stability and political judgment, set sail from Santfort on his desperate attempt on 24 May 1685, accompanied by some eighty-three men, who included Lord Grey, Fletcher of Saltoun, and Ferguson. The party landed at Lyme Regis on 11 June—but there is no need here to relate this unhappy chapter in English history or to tell of the Duke's assumption of the royal title by claiming "a legitimate and legal right to the Crown"; of the defeat of Argyle in the north, and the Duke's final eclipse and capture at

---

[1] *D.N.B.* xxix. 188.

[2] This was not Monmouth's first attempt at rebellion for he was deeply implicated in the Rye House plot of 1683, which resulted in the flight of Shaftesbury and the execution of Russell and Armstrong. Armstrong, whom Sprat called "a debauched atheistical Bravo", was arrested at Leyden, and on being brought back to England was sentenced to death within a few days by Jeffrys at King's Bench, despite his claim for a fair trial. He was attended by Tenison on the scaffold (Friday 20 January 1684) and gave him a written paper protesting his innocence. *D.N.B.* ii. 100. See also Portland MSS. H.M.C. I. 380.

Sedgmoor on 5 July. No trial was necessary, as an act of attainder had already been passed against him, and his execution was directed to take place the day after he was lodged in the Tower of London. There then followed the famous interview with the King, at which Monmouth appears to have professed the most abject repentance, even to the extent, so James afterwards alleged, of offering to become a Catholic, if his life were spared. Political expediency, however, demanded his death, and James remained firm, even denying a day's respite.

It was in these sad circumstances that Monmouth, the night before his execution, was waited on in the Tower by Bishops Ken and Turner, to whom the Duke "spoke with sorrow at the bloodshed he had occasioned", and also admitted that Charles II had "often in private denied to him the truth of the report as to the marriage of his mother".[1] He declined to express regret at his connection with Lady Wentworth, however, which he declared to be morally blameless, and as a consequence Bishops Ken and Turner refused to grant him the comfort of the Sacrament.[2]

In his extremity, the Duke himself asked the King that he might see Tenison. The two were probably quite well acquainted, for Monmouth was a not infrequent worshipper at St. Martin's when in London, and the Vicar of St. Martin's (as we have seen) had attended the Duke's great friend, Thomas Thynne, on his deathbed in 1681.[3] In response to this appeal, Tenison went to the Tower on the morning of Monmouth's execution. Bishop Ken and Hooper were talking to him but the Duke drew Tenison aside to the window, and (according to Tenison's own account, given to White Kennett in 1713) "held a long conversation with him too much upon his own follies".[4] Tenison was anxious for Monmouth to make a full confession, and in the course of his examination he mentioned a report that the Duke himself had preached while in the army. Monmouth still possessed some spirit: "No", he replied, "I never preached; nobody preached but Ferguson, and he very foolishly many times; that Man is a bloody Villain". The Doctor next reminded him that he should reconcile himself to his Duchess even at this late hour, but the Duke protested that "his Heart

[1] White Kennett, *A Complete History of England*, 1719, iii. 437.
[2] *Ibid.* Another account says that these two bishops found him "fearfully insensible of his sins of rebellion". *Life of Bishop Ken by a layman*, 1854, p. 289.
[3] See Chap. 2, p. 18.
[4] White Kennett, *Complete History*, iii. 437.

had been turned from her because in his Afflictions she had gone to Plays and into Publick Companies", thus showing that she had never loved him. Tenison, warming to his task, charged him with his relationship with Lady Wentworth, which the Duke freely admitted, but protested "that he had no children by her; but he had heard it was lawful to have one wife in the Eye of the Law and another before God". As might be expected, the good Vicar of St. Martin's was much distressed at such an heretical view, and producing a Bible, he "laboured to convince him of the Falsehood and the ill Consequence of such a Principle". To this fervent exhortation, Monmouth replied with pathetic simplicity: "Well, but if a man be bred up in a false Notion, what shall he do when he hath but two hours to live?" Despite this disapproval of his sentiments, the Duke was not deterred from pulling out a gold watch, and urging Tenison to take it to Lady Wentworth in his name, a request which the Doctor "positively refused", declining to be "concerned in any such message or token to her". Although shocked at his somewhat irregular views, Tenison yet admitted later that the Duke did not seem at all "profane or atheistical", but "had rather a cast of Enthusiasm in him; for he had a silly Charm in a bit of Paper under the Stone of his Ring which was pulled out after his Death and was said to have been given him by some German reputed a Conjurer, which Charm was to save him in a Day of Battle, or other imminent Danger". Owing to the Duke's obstinacy, Tenison, like the two bishops, refused him the Sacrament, but the Duke does not seem to have been very zealous for it.

When this interview was concluded, Tenison and the other ecclesiastics attended Monmouth to the scaffold on Tower Hill, where a large crowd was assembled. The four of them (Ken, Turner, Hooper, and Tenison) "press'd him to the very last to make a particular Confession of his Crimes, and to acknowledge himself guilty of Rebellion against his lawful Prince by invading his kingdom". Monmouth made no direct reply, but protested that he died a Protestant in the communion of the Church of England. Again the Churchmen exhorted him: "My Lord if you be of the Church of England you must acknowledge the Doctrine of Non-Resistance to be true, which Publick Satisfaction they declared to be a necessary condition of his Repentance, and that they could not pray for him with that Cheerfulness and Encouragement they should, without this particular Acknowledgment and detestation of his Rebellion".[1] This he steadfastly refused to do, nor would he utter any "public and particular condemnation" of his misdeeds: rather he attempted once more to vindicate his relations with Lady Wentworth, although after some hesitation he added an "amen" to an oft-repeated prayer for the King. There is something rather disgusting in this united attack on a dying man; but the tragedy of his brilliant yet sordid career was now to be brought to its untimely end when, after a disgraceful scene, John Ketch, the executioner, severed his head at the fifth attempt. His body was then removed and buried in St. Peter's Church in the Tower.

The whole episode created great excitement at the time, and owing to the circulation of conflicting reports as to what the Duke had said in the Tower, and on the scaffold, the four churchmen concerned published a small pamphlet containing the Duke's statement, and why he had been refused the Sacrament.[2]

The four divines were accused by many contemporary pamphleteers of "unfeeling conduct",[3] particularly when Monmouth was on the scaffold, but Burnet says of the Vicar of St. Martin's:

"He [Monmouth] was much better pleased with Dr. Tenison who did very plainly speak to him with relation to his public actings and to his course of life. But he did it in a softer and less peremptory manner, and having said all that he thought proper he left those points in which he saw he could not convince him, to his own conscience and turned to other things fit to be laid before a dying man".

Tenison's part in this unhappy affair makes it evident that although in opposition to the Court on its religious policy, he was by no means prepared, so early in James' reign, to countenance open revolt. Catholicism he opposed wherever found; but rash and irresponsible attempts at rebellion he as firmly condemned.

Monmouth's revolt, from the ease with which it was suppressed, seems to have encouraged James, urged on by the Jesuits, to be more ruthless than ever in his Catholic policy, and he proceeded

---

[1] Sacheverell, *The Loyal Catechism*, 1710, p. 24. This exhortation to the Duke of Monmouth later provided useful propaganda material for the Jacobites and High Churchmen; hence Sacheverell's reference to it. Tenison, doubtless, would have claimed that circumstances alter cases.

[2] "An Account of what passed at the Execution of the late Duke of Monmouth". See Somers' tracts, IX. 260. The Bishops of Ely and Bath and Wells, and Tenison and Hooper themselves witnessed to a document in which Monmouth declared that the title of king had been forced on him against his will, and also that the late King had told him he was not married to his mother. See Illustration, facing p. 131.

[3] *Life of Bishop Ken by a layman*, pp. 289, 296.

to embark upon it with an energy which alarmed the old Catholic families of England and even Innocent XI. His policy was now to remove Catholic disabilities by means of the dispensing power, for which he had already obtained judicial sanction by packing the bench of judges, and to admit Catholics to the Council board. He was optimistic enough to hope for Nonconformist support, since they, equally with the Catholics, would benefit under these dispensing acts. James placed Catholics on the commissions of the peace, and freely introduced them as officers into the army. On Christmas Day 1686, the new chapel at Whitehall was opened and placed in the charge of Father Petre. In Scotland a similar policy was pursued and on 18 February 1687 James issued a proclamation granting the right of public worship to all Nonconformists (though with a few irksome restrictions), at the same time suspending all laws against Catholics.

Excitement in London was now running high, and the Church of England clergy were fully alive to the dangers which beset them. There could be no doubt, now, of James' intentions, for he had cast all caution to the winds. So eager was he to proselytize that he attempted a conversion in his own family, a fact which we learn from Tenison. Mary, the daughter of James and the wife of William of Orange, was known to be a strong Protestant, and was thought to have sympathized with Monmouth if not encouraged him in his attempt upon the throne. James' relations with his daughter had never been cordial, and about this time he endeavoured to shake her Protestantism by sending over to her a long letter "by the hand of one Father Gosse, earnestly desiring her to consider of the Unity and Authority of the Catholic Church and to confer with the said Father on these points". Mary, however, was quite equal to the occasion, and on receipt of the letter (so Tenison later told White Kennett) "she retired to her Closet and drew up an excellent Answer without any assistance; giving the reasons of her being a Protestant and of resolving to continue so; and touching at most of the unscriptural and irrational Tenets of Popery".[1]

Events were now rapidly approaching a climax. On 27 April 1688, James published his second Declaration of Indulgence which reaffirmed his religious policy, and he declared his intention of assembling Parliament before November at the latest. Such a Declaration in the known state of the nation was rash in the

[1] White Kennett, *A Complete History of England*, note, iii. 492.

extreme, but his next order, namely, that it should be read in the churches on two successive Sundays, was an act of incredible folly. The London clergy needed little encouragement to become openly rebellious, and Simon Patrick records that the predominant feeling was one of "great perplexity", and that the order to read the Declaration was "greatly abhorred". Informal meetings of the rank and file of the clergy began to assemble to discuss the situation, and two such gatherings took place at Ely House in the presence of the Bishop of London.[1]

Tenison was one of the leaders in this agitation, and on 11 May he was present at a gathering in the Master's House in the Temple at the invitation of William Sherlock. The position of the London clergy was here discussed, and it was agreed "that the Bishops should be desired to address the King", although the clergy would not formally approach the bishops, but would submit to their leadership.[2] The bishops, or most of them, were as enthusiastic as their clergy, and on the following day a few of them met at Lambeth, where there sat down to dinner the Bishops of London, Ely, Peterborough, Chester, St. David's, and the Earl of Clarendon. The meal was an uncomfortable one, and they ate in embarrassed silence, "nobody caring to speak" since the last two bishops (Chester and St. David's)[3] were known to be very much in favour with James. These two, however, began to feel that their presence was unwelcome, and not caring to implicate themselves in an agitation which they disapproved, they took an early opportunity to depart after dinner. It was when they had gone that Tenison joined the company by invitation of the Archbishop, and he was present throughout the discussion which followed, a fact which shows the prominent position which he held among the London clergy.[4] The company then proceeded to discuss the whole position relative to the reading the Declaration of Indulgence, and they unanimously "resolved not to do it". To secure common action and a united front, they decided to get into touch with as many bishops as were then in town, and to write to the others before they petitioned the King.

On Monday, 14 May, another meeting of the London clergy took place at the Temple, and those present decided to stand firmly against the reading of the Declaration, after Tenison

[1] Simon Patrick, *Autobiography*, p. 131.
[2] *Ibid.*
[3] See Chap. 10.
[4] Clarendon, *Diary*, 1688. Saturday 12 May, ii. 171.

had given them an account of the meeting at Lambeth on the Saturday and had assured them that "if they were generally resolv'd not to read it, the Archbishop had promised to ask the King not to exact it".[1] Twenty clergy were then chosen to feel the pulse of their London brethren before the next meeting, amongst whom Tenison was appointed to wait on the incumbents neighbouring St. Martin's. In the meantime, absent bishops were hurrying up to London, and the rumour already began to spread that the clergy had refused to read the Declaration.[2] On Thursday morning, 17 May, the London clergy met once again, this time in a house in St. Paul's churchyard, in order that they might receive the reports of those who had solicited their brethren. From these investigations it was found that seventy had definitely declared they would not read the Declaration, while the rest had either spoken "dubiously" or could not be found. Dr. Patrick then made a list of these seventy names and took it to the Bishop of Peterborough ("who lodged hard by") in order that he might give it to the Archbishop.[3]

After this meeting Tenison and Patrick proceeded to the Earl of Clarendon's house,[4] from whence, after they had dined with the Earl and the Bishops of St. Asaph and Ely, they all went off to Lambeth. The Archbishop there informed them that he intended to meet the leaders on the following day, and asked them to be present, while urging them to keep it as a day of fast and prayer. Hence, on Friday, when Tenison and Patrick, accompanied by Dr. Grove, went to Lambeth, they found themselves in the company of the Archbishop, five bishops,[5] Dr. Stillingfleet (Dean of St. Paul's), and Dr. Tillotson (Dean of Canterbury). After joining together in morning prayer, they entered immediately upon a consideration of the whole subject which was perplexing all their minds. Various expedients were suggested, but it was finally agreed that "they should move by way of a petition to the King from the Archbishop of Canterbury and the Bishops present". The terms of the petition were then drawn up and all affixed their signatures except Compton, Bishop of London.[6] There remained to decide how the petition

---

[1] S. Patrick, *Complete History of England*, iii. 131.
[2] Clarendon, *Diary*, ii. 172.
[3] S. Patrick, *Autobiography*, p. 132.
[4] Henry Hyde, second Earl of Clarendon.
[5] The Bishops of St. Asaph (Lloyd), Bath and Wells (Ken), Ely (Turner), Peterborough (White), and London (Compton).
[6] He was under sentence of suspension by the Court of Ecclesiastical Commission.

was to be presented, and here it was agreed that the bishops should all go in a body to Whitehall.

After evening prayer, and further fortified with a meal, they proceeded to the royal palace a little after six o'clock. Tenison remained with Grove and Patrick at Lambeth till after eight o'clock, so anxious were they to learn "what the success would be", but it was not until the following morning that they were told what had happened at Whitehall.

The King was "abroad" when the bishops arrived at the palace, and it was nine o'clock before he returned, when they were admitted immediately, and received "very kindly at first". The petition was then solemnly presented. "Oh", exclaimed James, "I know the hand, it is my Lord of Canterbury". He began patiently to read the document, but when he came to a paragraph which declared against his dispensing power his "countenance altered" and he fell into a "great fury". "What," he shouted, "the Church of England against my dispensing power! They that always preached it". The bishops, on the defensive, protested that "they never preached any such things, but only obedience and suffering when they could not obey". "It surprises me", replied the King, "I did not expect an address of this nature from you", and turning more directly upon the Bishop of Ely he added: "Here are some I did not expect to see on such an occasion. Have not I supported you? This is a step to rebellion! This is a step to rebellion!" A little taken aback, perhaps, by his vehemence, the bishops declared that "they were ready to lay down their lives at his feet", and the Bishop of Bath and Wells (the saintly Ken), kneeling down, pleaded: "Did not I go down to suppress a rebellion? Hath not my family always been loyal? And can I be guilty of such a crime?" "Well", remarked the King finally, in dismissing them, "I will keep this in memory; I will never forget it. . . . If I alter my mind you shall hear from me; but I expect to be obeyed".[1]

The scene now appeared to be set for an open breach between the King and the Church. The Declaration was due to be read by all the clergy in London on 20 May, and by the country clergy a fortnight later, which meant that the latter would be able to follow the lead of their brethren in the city. Sunday, 20 May, was a day of great excitement in London. Churches were crowded, and Tenison, in conjunction with nearly all the London clergy

[1] S. Patrick, *Autobiography*, p. 135.

of any importance, omitted to read the Declaration: only in the
Abbey, where the versatile Thomas Sprat was Dean, was it solemnly
if hastily read. There then followed those great scenes in English
history which the glowing pen of Macaulay has made live again—
the arrest of the seven bishops, their imprisonment in the Tower,
and their triumphant acquittal amidst great enthusiasm on 30 June.

While these stirring events were happening in England, James'
position abroad was also deteriorating. Relations between the
King and William of Orange were going from bad to worse, while
the pardonable pride of the English monarch prevented an alliance
with Louis. It was the beginning of the end when a letter (taken
over by Admiral Herbert dressed in the clothes of a common
sailor) was sent to William on the day of the bishops' acquittal
inviting him to come over to England. Tenison was an early
confidant in this scheme, as befitted a leader of the London clergy,
and throughout this difficult period he acted as a liaison between
the rank and file of the clergy and the episcopal bench. On
8 August the Vicar of St. Martin's entertained Simon Patrick and
other clergy in the city, and during a discussion afterwards at
Patrick's house he told them the exciting news that the Prince of
Orange "intended to come over with an army to our relief from
the danger in which we were".[1] With characteristic caution he
proceeded to give counsel, already indicative, perhaps, of a nation
of shopkeepers. "He advised me", Patrick wrote afterwards, "to
carry all my money and what I had valuable out of London; for
none could forsee what confusions we might fall into . . . and he
gave me such assurance of it that I followed his advice".[2]

James at the eleventh hour became conscious of his peril, and
made one last desperate effort to retrieve his position with the
country at large—but it was too late. On 22 September he
informed the Bishop of Winchester (Mews) of his intention to
take the Church of England under his protection. He then
appealed for support against the Dutch invasion, and on
29 September issued a general pardon, from which, however,
once again with incredible folly, he omitted the clergy as a
corporate body. London was still in a welter of excitement and
churches were full to overflowing. The Catholics, on their part,
conscious may be that their liberty was precarious, were making a
last rally and on 30 September a preacher at the Savoy, probably

[1] S. Patrick, *Autobiography*, p. 138.
[2] *Ibid.*

Pulton,[1] delivered a very open attack on the Church of England.[2] The temper of London at this time may be judged in that the Jesuit was unceremoniously dragged from the pulpit by certain Protestants present, and handled "very coarsely"—an incident which "created great disturbance in the city". Tenison took the opportunity to appear as the Protestant apologist and in a crowded church at St. Martin's he replied specifically to this jesuitical attack in a sermon which endeavoured to show that the Scriptures were the only rule of faith, and that their perfection was above all tradition. Evelyn, who was present at this service, records that afterwards "near 1000 devout persons partook of the Communion".[3]

Upon hearing that William of Orange had made a declaration on 29 September promising a free parliament, James granted further concessions. Dismissed officials were restored in both Church and State; the Court of Commission was virtually abolished; and corporations received back their charters; but nothing could now save him. The King's folly had played into William's hands, and although James (again declining French help) attempted defence measures with some energy, he discovered he could not rely on his army. William, meanwhile, landed at Brixham, south of Torbay, on 5 November, and the King proceeded to Salisbury, but the treachery of Churchill and Grafton, to mention only two among many, unnerved his resolution, and made him think his plight hopeless. He forthwith returned to London, and entered into negotiations with William, but fearing for his life, he left London in panic in the early hours of 11 December, and ignominiously threw the great seal in the river.[4] It was the end of an epoch.

---

[1] See Chapter 3.
[2] Evelyn, *Diary*, ii. 280.
[3] *Ibid.*
[4] James embarked at Sheerness, but was brought back to Faversham and it was not until 22–25 December that he finally escaped with Berwick to France.

CHAPTER 5

COMPREHENSION

THE unprecedented circumstance of a fleeing James and an invading William created a situation which called for urgent deliberation. It soon became apparent that there were divided counsels on the episcopal bench. The bishops had been united in withstanding the Catholic pressure of James, but the situation was now entirely changed and in a manner which some of them had hardly anticipated. Sancroft, Archbishop of Canterbury, sincere and rigidly orthodox, scarcely disguised his apprehension at the extreme course which events had taken, although he went so far as to sign a declaration on 11 December at a meeting of peers in the Guildhall, which requested William to assist in securing peace and a free parliament. The Prince of Orange, however, had firmly made up his mind that he would accept no "barren sceptre", and it became clear that he would claim the throne *de jure* as well as *de facto*. Sancroft soon began to feel scruples, and was convinced that his oath of allegiance forbade his associating in any such procedure. He was willing to declare James unfit to reign, and he was prepared to co-operate in setting up William as *custos regni*, but further than this he definitely refused to go. Such a step, had it not been ruled out by William's refusal even to contemplate it, might have commended itself to some of the bishops; but Tenison, whatever his private misgivings,[1] was in favour of admitting openly the *de facto* situation, namely, that the throne was vacant.

The Vicar of St. Martin's was naturally enough an interested spectator of these events, and on 17 December we find him with Simon Patrick in his parlour in the little cloisters at Westminster, discussing the contemporary scene. It was a "very rainy night", but suddenly a knock was heard at the door, and Lloyd, Bishop of St. Asaph, was shown in. "Whatever makes your Lordship come abroad in such weather, when the rain pours down as if Heaven and earth would come together?" enquired Patrick. They were not kept long in doubt, for Lloyd brought news with him which might well induce him to defy the unkind

---

[1] See p. 92.

weather. He had been at Lambeth, he said, and had been sent by the bishops to wait upon the Prince of Orange "to know when they might all come and pay their respects to him". "But", enquired Patrick, with a question which must have been in Tenison's mind as well, "had the Archbishop of Canterbury consented to this step?" "Yes", Lloyd replied, "he made some difficulty at first, but assented at last and ordered him to go with the message".[1]

Hence, the bishops waited on the Prince of Orange the following day, but at the last moment the Archbishop failed to appear, for a reason obvious enough although Lloyd remarked "that the Lord only knows why he did not go along with them".[2]

As might be expected in these circumstances, pressure was brought to bear on the Archbishop in the hope of inducing him if not to wait upon the Prince, at least to send him a message. Amongst those who attempted to persuade him to do this were Tenison and Clarendon.

The Earl of Clarendon (1638–1709), the second earl of this name and the eldest son of Edward Hyde, seems at this time to have been waiting upon events, although he was determined for the present to appear as a strong supporter of the Church of England. In this mood, he called on Tenison on 3 January 1689, and they went together to dine with the Archbishop at Lambeth. Clarendon began by reproaching his Grace for not going to see the Prince, to which the Archbishop (so Clarendon reports) replied: "Would you have me kill myself? do you not see what a cold I have?" Clarendon admitted that the Archbishop "indeed had a sore one", but he suggested to his Grace "that it would do well if you would excuse your not waiting on the Prince by letting him know what a cold you have, and that you will wait on him when it is gone". Conversation then turned to the Convention which was summoned to meet on 22 January and which would be called on without delay to make some decision on the existing situation. Particularly there was a growing feeling in some quarters that the Dissenters, who had so sturdily supported the Church in its struggle against the Catholics, should receive some public recognition, and Clarendon therefore asked the Archbishop "whether he should not think of preparing something by that time on behalf of the Dissenters?", Tenison adding that "it would be expected by the public that something would be offered

---

[1] S. Patrick, *Autobiography*, p. 141.   [2] *Ibid*.

in pursuance of the petition which the bishops had presented to the King". The Archbishop replied to these exhortations in a truly episcopal manner. He was well aware, he said, of the content of the petition, and he believed every bishop intended to make it good, when an opportunity should be offered of discussing these matters in Convocation; but till that time should come, and without a commission from the King, it was highly penal to enter into such Church matters.[1] What the Archbishop said was, of course, correct from a strictly legal point of view: although since an extra legal step had already been taken in the calling of William, so an extra legal step would be equally necessary (no matter what appearance of law it might be given) to restore order and a settled constitution. If James II were still king *de jure*, no one could deny that William occupied the position *de facto*, and that upon his shoulders the responsibility of government would fall. Sancroft promised Tenison and Clarendon, however, that he would keep the subject in mind, and regarding the Dissenters, he said he would be willing "to discourse" respecting them with any of the bishops or clergy who might come to him, although he himself believed that the Dissenters would never agree amongst themselves as to the conditions which would satisfy them. Tenison agreed with the Archbishop's last observation so far as to suggest that "the proper way of proceeding was, not that the matter should be discussed beforehand with the Dissenters, but that the bishops should propose such concessions in parliament as would be advantageous to the Church whether accepted by the Dissenters or not". The Archbishop finally returned to his original point and repeated "that when convocation should meet, these matters would be considered. In the meantime he knew not what to say, but would think of what had now been proposed by them".[2]

One thing was now plain: if Sancroft would not co-operate in getting things done, then things would have to be done without him. He might choose not to be a partner in these events, but he could not prevent them.[3] Tenison was known to be whole-hearted in his championship of the claims of William, and a rumour circulated round London that Compton, the Bishop, had "by his

[1] Clarendon, *Diary*, ii. 240.
[2] D'Oyly, *Life of Sancroft*, ii. 413. Sancroft's attitude is discussed at length in E. Cardwell, *A History of Conferences and other Proceedings connected with the Revision of the Book of Common Prayer*, p. 401.
[3] Sancroft's last public appearance was at a large meeting of bishops and lay peers at Lambeth on 15 January 1689.

advice altered severall collects in ye book of Common Prayer concerning ye King, and that his lordp. required all the ministers in London to read them".[1] As a result of this rumour Sir Thomas Clarges, a supporter of James II, wrote to the Vicar of St. Martin's on 17 January 1689, expressing the hope that the report was not true, since he had always regarded Tenison "as a wise, pious, and honest man", and reminding him that the Prayer Book could only be legally altered by Act of Parliament.[2]

On 11 January Tenison was present at a meeting in Ely House which included the Bishops of St. Asaph and Peterborough, the Earl of Clarendon, and Drs. Patrick, Sherlock, Scott, and Burnet. The latter boldly proposed that the best policy was frankly to regard the Crown as forfeited. Three days later Tenison attended a meeting at St. Paul's, when its Dean, the Bishop of St. Asaph, the Dean of Norwich, Patrick, and himself consulted as to what concessions might bring the Dissenters "into our communion".[3] At this informal assembly it was agreed "that a bill should be prepared to be offered by the Bishops, and the matter was drawn up under ten or eleven heads".[4]

On 22 January the Convention met, and the Throne, as Burnet had suggested, was declared vacant. On 15 March Sancroft issued a Commission which virtually empowered his suffragans to perform the rites of coronation. It was now, obviously, but a matter of time till the Archbishop was suspended, and this was done on 1 August 1689. On 1 February 1690, he was deprived in company with five other bishops and four hundred clergy.

Thus the "Glorious Revolution" of 1688 was accomplished without bloodshed, although, perhaps, at the expense of a few uneasy consciences among the clergy. Tenison himself admitted to Clarendon in January 1690, that there "had been irregularities in our settlement; that it was to be wished things had been otherwise; but we were now to make the best of it, and to join in support of this government for fear of worse".[5]

There were urgent problems, however, awaiting settlement, and amongst the most pressing, as we have seen, was that relating to the Dissenters, the more moderate of whom, it was felt, might be won back again to the "Ecclesia Anglicana". Tenison was

---

[1] Clarges to Tenison. 17 January 1689. Lambeth MSS. 930, f. 7.
[2] *Ibid.*
[3] S. Patrick, *Autobiography*, p. 241.
[4] *Ibid.*
[5] Clarendon, *Diary*, ii. 300.

himself a foremost protagonist of all such schemes for comprehension, and the position of the Dissenters was a subject which had already claimed his attention in a pamphlet, published some six years earlier (1683), under the title "An Argument for Union, Taken from the True Interest of those Dissenters in England who Profess and call themselves Protestants". As this work, whose purpose was "the persuading of Dissenters to Joyn in the Exercise of Constant Communion with the Church of England", sets out at large his views on this major ecclesiastical problem of the day, we propose to devote a few pages to an examination of its contents.[1]

"I take it for granted", he began, "that the ready way to overthrow a Church is first to divide it"; but such divisions were equally unfavourable to the Dissenters, for if they wished to establish themselves as a national church, they could only do so by accepting the supremacy of one of their sects: but, alas, "Presbyterians, Arians, Socinians, Anabaptists, Fifth-Monarchy Men, Sensual Millenaries, Behmenists, Familists, Seekers, Antinomians, Ranters, Sabbatarians, Quakers, Muggletonians, Sweet Singers, might associate in a Caravan but could not joyn in the Communion of a Church".[2]

At the moment, however, the divisions among the Dissenters were worse than they had ever been. Some of their opinions were mutually contradictory, and the ministers of Lancaster and London had themselves declared that "a Toleration would be a putting of a sword into a mad Man's hand".[3] There could be nothing permanent or organic in any union they might achieve, and there would always be a tendency for the stronger to swallow up the weaker party, as could be seen in New England. Even George Fox had admitted "that he never lik'd the Word Liberty of Conscience, and would have no liberty given to Presbyterians, Papists, Independents and Baptist".

Nor was a "general sufferance" the way to lead to truth (even if it were practicable), since the "suffering divers Errours" was not the way to reform them.[4] An insistence on immediate

---

[1] Tenison, "An Argument for Union", 1683. Tenison protested at the outset: "This Argument is here offered . . . in the Spirit of Christian Charity, and without any design of exposing or exasperating any person who differs, in his Notions, from the Sense of the Writer. For he would rather lie at the Feet of the meanest Man who is overtaken with an errour, than spurn insolently against him", p. 2.

[2] *Ibid.* p. 4.

[3] *Ibid.* p. 13.

[4] This might almost have come from the pen of Bossuet!

guidance introduced an anarchical principle into government, as could be seen in the following statement of a prominent Dissenter: "In Reformation do not make Reason your Rule nor Line you go by. God's Worship hath no Ground in any reason but God's will".[1]

If, further, the Dissenters had as one of their main objects the removal of Popery out of England, then their methods would not so easily lead to this desirable end as those of the established Church, since "against all this Craft and Strength what (under God) can Protestants oppose which is equal to the power of the Church of England? A Church, Primitive, learned, pure and not embased [sic] with the mixtures of Enthusiasm or Superstition".[2]

From the above generalizations Tenison drew the following practical conclusions, which bring this pamphlet to a close. If the Dissenters by their present separation were not likely to obtain either of their purposes—the rooting out of Popery, or the establishment of themselves—then "they ought both in Prudence and Christianity, to endeavour after union with us".[3] "I bessech you", he pleaded,

"make such Advantage of this Juncture. Sit down and think once more of the Nature of this Church. Confer with the Guides of this National Religion; read without Prejudice the Books commended by them to you.[4] Peruse seriously the Books which Authority hath set forth. . . . Do as the antient Non-conformists did, who would not separate though they feared to Subscribe . . . Do more for the Peace of God's Church than for a Vote, or Office, or fear of Legal Penalty. Come as Christians to the Sacrament, and not as Politicians. If all would do constantly what they can in Conscience do sometimes, they would create a better Opinion of themselves in the Governours, and move them to all due favour, and hinder all the destructive breaches amongst us".

This pamphlet shows admirably Tenison's general attitude to the Dissenters and how vividly he remembered the unsettlement of the Commonwealth. It may be argued that the obvious way out

[1] Tenison, "An Argument for Union", p. 40.
[2] Ibid. p. 20. The following somewhat sarcastic comment of Tenison's is perhaps worth quoting: "It is at least my private Conjecture that if the Revenue of the Religious Houses which were dissolved had been judiciously applyed to the service of Men, either weak in mind, or indisposed by Temper, or singular in their inclination amongst the Reformed, there might have been a Diversity here (I mean such as there is in our present Colleges) without a Schism".
[3] Ibid. p. 40.
[4] See Chap. 3, p. 47.

of the religious maze was to grant a general toleration all round; but such a solution, as the above pamphlet illustrates, was simply not practical politics at the time. Religion was not only a matter of private devotion, but it affected parliamentary and constitutional issues. People of the various schools of religious thought were not prepared to tolerate each other, and the religious anarchy of the Commonwealth made loyal Anglicans determined not to encourage diversities which could be so disastrous. What Tenison and the most broad-minded of his fellow churchmen wanted was a comprehensive national Church, preserving episcopal government and an ordained priesthood, respecting tradition and scholarship, yet tolerant enough in spirit to include the more reasonable of the Dissenters. Thus within the Church Tenison stood for comprehension and toleration, without he stood for its broad principles and invited others to conform.

We return now to the attempt at comprehension which was made in 1689.

Tenison naturally enough was enthusiastic on its behalf, but, as we have seen, he thought that the bishops should decide on certain definite proposals before discussing the matter with the Dissenters themselves. We need to remember that at this time Dissent had not yet come to be regarded as an inevitable accompaniment of a national Church, and that many people still thought of schism as an accident of history which might be removed by wise and prudent statesmanship. Certainly in 1689 the times seemed not unfavourable for such an attempt. A united opposition to James' Catholic-absolutist policy had brought all Protestants together as never before, and the seven bishops had been the heroes, not only of Churchmen, but of the nation as a whole. Never before, or since, has the Church been so popular, nor so identified with the liberties of the people. It remained to use this opportunity to secure some generous gesture from the authorities of the Church of England, a gesture which should encourage the Dissenters to forget their scruples and conform. So Tenison felt, and talking to the Earl of Clarendon one afternoon late in April, he declared himself so strongly in favour of comprehension, that Clarendon (cautious as ever), expressed his surprise "that so good a man should be so fond of it".[1]

Nor were Tenison and the Whig school generally alone in wishing this. Even Archbishop Sancroft, on 1 July 1688, before

[1] Clarendon, *Diary*, ii. 275.

the Revolution, had urged on the bishops in his own province the need for encouraging friendly relations with the Noncon-formists, in order to secure some unity of action against Catholic encroachments. A definite though tentative scheme had in fact then been drawn up, and Sancroft, Lamplugh (Archbishop of York), Tenison, Patrick, and a few more had embarked upon a review of the liturgy.[1] The revolution and accession of William and Mary interrupted this work, but those who favoured it took encouragement from the fact that William, in his declaration from the Hague on 10 October 1688, declared himself in favour of "such laws as might establish a good agreement between the Church of England and all Protestant Dissenters, and cover all those who would live peaceably under the government from all persecution on account of their religion". Encouraged by these assurances, a body of dissenting ministers waited on William as soon as he was lodged at St. James', and were given the same promises "that he would use his utmost endeavours for promoting a firm union among Protestants".[2] The Dissenters themselves preferred a legal toleration, and Dr. Bates,[3] when they presented their address to the new King and Queen, desired their Majesties "to establish a firm union of protestant subjects in the matters of religion by making the rule of Christianity to be the rule of conformity".[4]

William was not primarily interested in nice differences of theology, his main concern being the destruction of the French menace, but he was undoubtedly anxious to heal the schism at home, and "to abolish religious and political distinctions . . . by raising Protestant Dissenters to a capacity of civil employment".[5] His policy, therefore, was to use Parliament to this end, and under his inspiration two Bills were introduced, one "for exempting their Majesty's Protestant subjects dissenting from the Church of England from the penalties of certain laws", and the other "for

[1] R. Masters, *History of Corpus Christi*, p. 393.

[2] Addressing both houses of Parliament on 1 March, William went so far as to say: "I shall put you in mind of one thing which will conduce much to our settlement, as a settlement will to the disappointment of our enemies . . . I know you are sensible there is a necessity of some law to settle the oaths to be taken by all Persons to be admitted to such Places. I recommend it to your care to make a speedy provision for it; as I doubt not you will be sufficiently against the Papists, so I hope you will leave room for admission of all protestants that are willing and able to serve". See Cobbett, *Parliamentary History*, v. 183.

[3] Dr. Bates (1625–99), a leading Dissenter.

[4] Birch, *Life of Tillotson*, p. 167.

[5] *Ibid.*

COMPREHENSION

uniting their Majesties Protestant subjects".[1] William, however, could abstract himself from the theological passions of his day in a way that the majority of Englishmen could not. Anglican sentiment once again rallied round a Church which was said to be in danger, and the wise intentions of William were in part forced to give way to the narrow prejudices of less far-seeing men.

The first Bill, it is true, the famous Toleration Bill, became law, after several amendments, on 24 May, and in view of its importance we quote the following abstract of its clauses.

"First it repealed the penal laws of Elizabeth and James I against Dissenters, provided they took the oaths that Parliament prescribed. The laws against Papists, passed in the reign of Charles II (1673), were expressly excepted from this repeal. The Act provided that persons convicted of recusancy should be discharged on taking the oaths of allegiance to King William and Queen Mary, and that no one so taking them should be liable to any forfeiture or to prosecution in any Ecclesiastical Court, except such persons as had met together for religious worship with locked doors, by which offence they excluded themselves from the benefits of the Statute. For the relief of Anabaptists (Baptists), it was made sufficient for them to take the oaths and subscribe the Articles of Religion, with the exception of the 34th, 35th, 36th, part of the 20th, and part of the 27th Article. Justices of the peace were empowered to tender the oaths to any person attending a religious meeting, and to commit to prison without bail anyone who refused to take them. Quakers, whose scruples forbade them to take an oath, were allowed to make a Solemn Declaration of Allegiance and Profession of Faith instead. Papists and persons who denied the Trinity, were expressly excluded from all the advantages of this Act. For the protection of religious meetings it was made criminal to disturb them in any way, while at the same time, to prevent abuse of this privilege, no such meeting was to be held with locked doors. Lastly, no place was to be used for public worship without a certificate from the Bishop, the Archdeacon, or a Justice of the Peace, which certificates these persons were obliged to grant on application being made to them".[2]

The second, a Comprehension Bill, which had as its purpose the admission of Dissenters into the Church by altering and modifying the ceremonies and the liturgy of the Church of England and by

[1] E. Cardwell, *A History of Conferences and other Proceedings connected with the Revision of the Book of Common Prayer*, 1840, p. 406. See also Cobbett, *Parliamentary History*, v. 212.
[2] J. Rawson Lumby, *Compendium of the English Church from 1688–1830*, 1883, p. 27.

making the necessity of observing them less strict, was unsuccessful in getting through the House of Commons, which instead petitioned the King for the summoning of Convocation.

It was now obvious to William that he could not at the moment use Parliament to secure his will in this matter of comprehension, and he was therefore forced to adopt some other expedient. The only possible alternative seemed to be to induce the Church of England authorities themselves to make the Church more palatable to the Dissenters, so that they might be induced to re-enter the national Church, and thereby recover their full civil liberties. Tillotson, the Dean of Canterbury, felt that it would be unwise to initiate discussion on this subject in such a body as Convocation, where party divisions and private passions would probably hinder effective discharge of business, and make it far too unwieldy a machine to deal with such a delicate situation. Tillotson on his part maintained that "it would be best, as had formerly been done, for his Majesty to authorise by his Letters Patent, several of the most eminent clergy to consider of some method of healing the wounds of the Church, and establish a durable peace; so that what they agree upon being laid before a Convocation, might first have their sanction and then that of parliamentary authority".[1]

After much hesitation this method of procedure was adopted, although the decision to act by way of commissioners called together by the royal prerogative aroused intense opposition from some Churchmen, and a protest against it was entered by the Earl of Stamford in the House of Lords under eight heads.[2] The word "commission", owing to the abuse of royal power under James II, had unfortunate associations, and the opposition was by no means confined to Parliament when it became generally known that the King had instituted a Commission to ten bishops and twenty dignitaries of the Church, allotting to them the task of preparing "matters to be consider'd by the Convocation". As we shall be devoting some pages to an examination of the work of this Commission, and the reactions of certain people to it, we quote the exact terms under which it was summoned:

"Whereas the particular forms of divine worship and the rites and ceremonies appointed to be used therein, being things

[1] Birch, *Life of Tillotson*, p. 180.
[2] Cobbett, *Parliamentary History*, v. 213. One of these heads was the exclusion of the laity from the Commission.

in their own nature indifferent and alterable, and so acknow-
ledg'd; it is but reasonable, that upon weighty and important considerations, according to the various exigency
of time and occasions, such changes and alterations should be
made therein, as to those that are in place and authority,
shou'd from time to time seem either necessary or expedient:
And whereas the book of canons is fit to be review'd, and made
more suitable to the state of the Church; and whereas there
are defects and abuses in the ecclesiastical courts and juris-
dictions, and particularly there is not sufficient provision
made for the removing of scandalous ministers and for the
reformation of manners either in ministers or people; And
whereas it is most fit, that there should be a strict method
prescrib'd for the examination of such persons as desire to be
admitted into holy orders both as to their learning and manners :
we therefore, out of our pious and princely care for the good
order, edification and unity of the Church of England, committed to our charge, and for the reconciling as much as is
possible of all differences among our good subjects, and to
take away all occasions of the like for the future, have thought
fit to authorize empower and require you . . . and any nine
or more of you, whereof three are to be Bishops, to meet from
time to time as often as shall be needful, and to prepare such
alterations and amendments of the liturgy and canons, and
such proposals for the reformation of ecclesiastical courts and
to consider of such other matters, as in your judgments may most
conduce to the ends above mentioned so that the Things by
you so considered, and prepared, may be in a readiness to be
offered to the Convocation at their next meeting, and when
approved by them may be presented to us and our two Houses
of Parliament, that, if it shall be judged fit, they may be
established in due form of law".[1]

The scope of the Commission was certainly comprehensive,
none other in fact than a review of the liturgy, canons, and
ecclesiastical courts of the Church of England, although the
immediate purpose was to assist in an accommodation with the
Dissenters so that they might re-enter the national Church. It was
not in any sense to be a repetition of the Savoy Conference of 1661,
when the facilities for debate offered to the Dissenters encouraged
them to make what some members of the Church of England
regarded as extravagant demands. This time amendments to the

---

[1] Birch, *Life of Tillotson*, pp. 180–181. Also *The Revised Liturgy of 1689*, edited by J.
Taylor, 1855, p. v.

liturgy were to be decided upon by the commissioners themselves (all Anglicans) as a result of their own deliberations, and the
Dissenters were to be presented with the *fait accompli*. The
commissioners (whose names we add as a footnote)[1] included a
list of men whose talents, as a whole, the Church could not easily
rival at many other periods in its history. The inclusion of Tenison
among this body was an obvious choice, both on account of his
particular interest in the question of comprehension, and also
because of his position as a leader of the London clergy. Before
the Commission met, Tillotson (then Dean of Canterbury),
who was expected to play a leading part in the deliberations,
drew up a list of what he called "concessions which will probably
be made by the Church of England for the Union of Protestants",
and sent a copy to the Earl of Portland on 13 September 1689.
As these are of interest in view of what was actually decided, we
quote them as follows:[2]

1. That the ceremonies recommended in the liturgy or
canons be made indifferent.[3]

2. That the liturgy be carefully revised with the purpose of
leaving out the apocryphal lessons, and correcting the translation of the psalms.

3. That instead of all former declarations and subscriptions
made by ministers, that it be enough to promise to submit to the
doctrine, discipline, and worship of the Church of England,
as it shall be established by law, and promise to teach and
practice accordingly.

4. That new ecclesiastical canons be made, particularly to
provide for a reformation of manners in both ministers and
people.

5. That the delays of the ecclesiastical courts be remedied
and excommunication be taken out of the hands of lay officers
and placed in the hands of the bishop, who is to use it only for
very serious offences.

---

[1] Lamplugh (Bbp. of York), Compton (London), Mews (Winchester), Lloyd (St.
Asaph), Sprat (Rochester), Smith (Carlisle), Trelawney (Exeter), Burnet (Salisbury),
Humphrey (Bangor), Stratford (Chester), Stillingfleet (Dean of St. Paul's), Patrick
(Bishop elect of Chichester), Tillotson (Dean of Canterbury), Meggott (Dean of
Winchester), Sharp (Dean of Norwich), Montague (Master of Trinity College),
Kidder (Dean elect of Peterborough), Aldrich (Dean of Christ Church), Jane (Reg.
Prof. of Divinity at Oxford), Hall (Marg. Prof. of Divinity at Oxford), Beaumont (Reg.
Prof. of Divinity at Cambridge), Goodman (Archd. of Middlesex), Beveridge (Archd.
of Colchester), Batteley (Archd. of Cant.), Alston (Archd. of Essex), Tenison (Archd.
of London), Scott (Preb. of St. Paul's), Fowler (Preb. of Gloucester), Grove (Preb. of
St. Paul's), Williams (Preb. of St. Paul's).
[2] Birch, *Life of Tillotson*, p. 12.
[3] i.e. "the controverted ceremonies". See p. 104.

6. That in the future those who have been ordained in foreign reformed churches be not required to seek reordination to render them capable of preferment here.

7. That for the future, none shall be capable of holding a benefice in the Church of England "that shall be ordained in England otherwise than by bishops": but that those now ordained by presbyters shall not be asked to renounce their orders, but shall receive ordination from a bishop in some such terms as: "If thou art not already ordained, I ordain thee".[1]

The Commission opened its sessions on 10 October 1689, at ten o'clock in the morning, in the Jerusalem Chamber, but it was soon apparent that some of the commissioners were unwilling or reluctant to serve. The Archbishop of York, the Bishops of Carlisle and Exeter, Drs. Beaumont, Montague, and Batteley neither appeared at the first meeting nor subsequently.[2] Thus only twenty-four commissioners were present at the first session (when a discussion on the Apocrypha took place), and at the second session on 18 October dissension began. Thomas Sprat, Bishop of Rochester, immediately arose and questioned the authority of the Commission, "whether they did not fall under the statute of præmunire in meeting according to it". For himself, he said, he could not feel secure, particularly in view of his own experience on a Commission in King James' reign, unless he were reassured by the opinion of twelve judges. Moreover, he stated, this Commission was "to prevent Convocation and it could not be taken well by them to be called together to confirm that which they had had no hand in".[3] Dr. Jane (Regius Professor of Divinity at Oxford) took his cue from Dr. Sprat and declared that the Bishop of Rochester had convinced him of the doubtful status of their proceedings.

Such a challenge to the legality of the Commission could hardly be ignored if it were to continue its sessions, and Simon Patrick, now possibly feeling the dignity of his recent appointment to the See of Chichester, replied at length to Sprat's arguments. There was no comparison, he maintained, between the present Commission, which was only to advise, and the former Commission in James' reign. The Commission on which they were

[1] A copy of these suggestions, undated, is to be found amongst the Lambeth MSS. 954, f. 31.
[2] Parliamentary Papers 1854, vol. 50. "Copy of Alterations in the Book of Common Prayer prepared by the Royal Commission for the Review of the Liturgy 1689", p. 95.
[3] Ibid. p. 96.

now serving had no designs whatever against the authority of Convocation, but was intended simply to lighten the work of that Assembly, whose approval of all that the commissioners advised was necessary before anything could be submitted to Parliament. As to the opinion of the judges, the King had consulted them before he determined on this method of procedure.

The stage seemed to be set for a full dress quarrel, and tempers began to rise. The Bishop of St. Asaph took a practical step and moved "that those who were not satisfyed about the Commission might withdraw and not be spies on the rest", whereupon Dr. Jane immediately rose to leave, but was persuaded to remain.[1] One member then proposed that since the legality of the Commission had been called in question, matters should be debated as before a private committee: but to this it was rightly objected that as the terms under which they met entitled them only to meet as a Royal Commission, so they might well fall under the Act of Præmunire if they went outside it. At last, despite some opposition, it was agreed to get down to business, and the work of the previous session was resumed.

After this second meeting, the Bishops of London and Worcester, and Drs. Alston and Williams dined with the Bishop of Chichester, and were joined later by Tenison and Dr. Grove. These constituted themselves into an informal subcommittee, and they went through the prayer book services together, and examined certain suggested alterations in preparation for the next session.

The Commission had begun its labours in rather an undignified manner, but its subsequent sessions were on the whole characterized by a firm and honest resolve to do something to make the English liturgy, if not entirely acceptable, yet not so unacceptable to the more reasonable of the Nonconformists. Such an aim did not represent their sole hope in meeting, for as Stillingfleet was careful to point out to them: "We sat there to make such alterations as were fitt, which would be fitt to make were there no Dissenters and which would be for the improvement of the services".[2]

To Tenison, it must be confessed, the primary object was to heal the religious schism within the body politic by a gesture at comprehension; and a mediating liturgy, he thought, would be the best way to secure this. Hence, throughout the meetings of the Commission he never lost sight of this primary intention. To

---

[1] Parliamentary Papers, vol. 50. Copy of Alterations, p. 97.   [2] Ibid. p. 103.

shorten the work of the full sessions, a division of labour was
agreed upon, and Tenison on his part undertook "to collect the
words and expressions throughout the liturgy which had been
excepted against", and it was his task to propose others in their
place "which were more clear and plain and less liable to
objection".[1] The former part of the task, which required wide
reading and a conscientious application to detail, was peculiarly
suited to Tenison's temperament and he took it very seriously.
The alterations which he suggested, and the reasons for them, are
interesting and worth quoting. "Thine honourable true and only
Son", he suggested, should be changed to "thine only begotten
Son", since "honourable" was essentially a civil term. The
response in mattins and evensong which follows "Give peace in
our time, O Lord", ("Because there is none other that fighteth
for us, etc.") was to be altered because of its "predestinating"
suggestions, to "That we may serve thee without fear all ye daies
of our lives". All high-sounding titles applied to civil princes of
which Tenison found many in the prayer book ("most gracious",
"most religious", etc.) were to be deleted and the simple word
"Sovereign" used instead. The phrase in the prayer for the
king, "Grant that he may vanquish and overcome all his enemies",
Tenison revised, since it was of "too large an extent if the Kings
engage in an unjust War", to "Prosper all his righteous under-
takings against thy enemies". It was, perhaps, not surprising that
he changed the words (in the prayer for the clergy and the
people), "who alone workest great marvels", to "who alone art
the author of good gifts", since the former expression was "subject
to be ill interpreted by persons vainly disposed". The "healthful
spirit of thy grace" he changed to the less expressive form, "the
holy spirit of thy grace", as "healthful" was an obsolete word.
Finally, the collect which begins, "O God, whose nature and
property", he deleted, "as full of strange and impertinent
expressions, and besides not in the original but foisted in since by
another hand".[2]

These alterations of Tenison's may appear pedantically trivial and
unimportant, but they do bear witness to a liberal if rather literal
mind, which did not regard the English liturgy as descending

[1] Parliamentary Papers, vol. 50. "Copy of Alterations", p. 97. See also Birch, *Life
of Tillotson*, p. 190. In 1683 Tenison had written ("Argument for Union", p. 37):
"It is true, each Church is capable of improvement, by the Change of obsolete Words,
Phrases and Customs, by adjusting discreetly some Circumstantials of External Order".
[2] Birch, *Life of Tillotson*, p. 194.

8

fully fledged from Heaven, but rather as requiring revision
to meet specific needs. The Vicar of St. Martin's worked assi-
duously on the Commission, and out of eighteen sessions and six
subcommittees which met between 10 October and 18 November
he was absent only once;[1] nor was the part which he played in the
deliberations an unimportant one. At the third session (Friday
18 October) he opened the proceedings by reading over his list
of difficulties in the prayer book services, with his proposed
amendments, and after this there was a discussion on ceremonies
during which tempers rose, and Dr. Aldrich, Dean of Christ
Church, walked out "to return no more".[2] This acrimonious
debate concerned a problem which loomed large in the eyes of
contemporaries, and had even received the attention of Parliament, namely, the posture in which to receive the Sacrament of
Holy Communion. The question was a difficult one because many
Dissenters abhorred the practice of kneeling, owing to its Romanist
and idolatrous associations.[3] After a long discussion at this session,
and we quote the exact words of the report, it was agreed "that
for those that scrupled kneeling . . . it should be some Posture of
Reverence and in some convenient Pew or Place in the Church so
that none but those that kneel'd should come up to the Rails or
Table. And that the Persons scrupling shou'd some Week Day
before come to the Minister; and declare that they cou'd not kneel
with a good Conscience".[4] A similar tolerating clause, we may
notice, was decided upon as regards the use of the cross in
baptism.

At the eighth session (28 October) the subject of baptismal
regeneration came up for a lengthy discussion, this being a
question which divided many Churchmen from Nonconformists
and hence of particular interest to Tenison. In the interests of
the latter, the Vicar of St. Martin's favoured either the leaving
out from the baptismal service the concluding part of the phrase
"regenerated by the Holy Spirit", or including some explanation
of the words, since they seemed to imply an actual change. To this
suggestion the more rigid of the commissioners replied "that the
Phrase had been antiently applied to Baptism and if there were

[1] Compton, Bishop of London, was the only member to be present at all the
eighteen public sessions.
[2] Birch, *Life of Tillotson*, p. 192. Neither Drs. Aldrich nor Meggott came after the
third session. Henry Aldrich (1647–1710), we may notice, enjoyed a contemporary
reputation as a musical composer.
[3] Parliamentary Papers, vol. 50. "Copy of Alterations", p. 97.
[4] *Ibid.*

not more in Baptism than in the outward washing, it would give
away the cause to the Anabaptists".[1] Tenison then complained
that this argument was unsound since the regeneration mentioned
was a federal regeneration; apart from which the expression
should be deleted for practical reasons, since it was strongly
objected to by all those who maintained the impossibility
of falling from grace, and was thus a great bar to union. This
disputed point proved a veritable thorn in the flesh, and it was
debated again at the next session on 30 October. Tenison,
supported by Stillingfleet and Goodman, pleaded once more that
it should be deleted or revised as a gesture to the Dissenters, and
particularly that this should be done in the thanksgiving prayer
in the Confirmation service. The more orthodox repeated that the
doctrine of regeneration was common to all the Reformed
Churches, and that if it were changed in this case, then the
Catechism would likewise need revision. Between such conflicting
views there could be no agreement, so the question was left to be
decided by Convocation.

On 1, 3, and 6 November the commissioners "met to consider
the business of re-ordination", which Kennett wrote "held us a
long time".[2] It was a difficult subject. Dr. Fowler complained
that the Nonconformists wanted to be heard, but Stillingfleet
protested that they could not say more than they had already
expressed in their writings. A middle course (see p. 108) was
pursued but the "hypothetical clause" to be inserted in the form
of ordination met with opposition both from those who accepted
and from those who rejected Nonconformist ordination.[3]

The zeal with which Tenison entered into the business of the
Commission made it difficult for him at times to set a seal upon his
lips, and it is not surprising that he found it particularly hard to
restrain himself in the presence of Dr. Beveridge, a life-long opponent of comprehension. Thus during one discussion on the consecration prayer in the Communion service, Tenison went so
far in attacking Beveridge that the latter immediately rose to
leave in great indignation, and it was not until the Vicar of
St. Martin's had asked his pardon that he was persuaded to
remain.[4]

Yet despite such occasional displays of temper, the sessions

[1] Parliamentary Papers, vol. 50. "Copy of Alterations", p. 100.
[2] Quoted, Cardwell, *A History of Conferences and other Proceedings*, etc., p. 417.
[3] Parliamentary Papers, vol. 50. "Copy of Alterations", pp. 102–104.
[4] *Ibid.* p. 100.

were comparatively quiet and harmonious and "proceeded very unanimously and without any heats".[1] The last session was held on 18 November when a debate took place on the legal status of the Commission itself, whether it now ceased to exist, and what was its relation to Convocation. Burnet asserted that since Convocation (under the act of submission in Henry VIII's reign) could no longer enter upon any business except that which was proposed to it by the king, so now its scope was limited to accepting or rejecting the findings of the Commission. This view is interesting, and may be contrasted with that put forward by Tenison,[2] who maintained that the Commission in no way limited the work of Convocation. This last session appears to have come to an end in a rather informal way, for when someone proposed that there should be a form of subscription to its findings, it was discovered that there was no longer a quorum present, so nothing more could be done.[3]

It may be of value to give a brief *résumé* of the recommendations of this Commission, since, although they have been printed in a parliamentary paper, they are not widely known. They were as follows:

1. That the chanting of divine services in Cathedral Churches be discontinued in order that the services may be made intelligible to the common people.

2. That some "proper and devout" psalms be chosen for Sundays, in addition to those used during the course of the week.

3. That the apocryphal lessons, and those of the Old Testament which are "too natural", be left out, and others appointed in their stead by a new calendar, "which is already fully settled, and from which is deleted all the legendary saints, and others not directly referred to in the service book". (Nos. 4, 5 concern the use of the cross at baptism, and the posture for receiving the sacrament: see p. 104.)

6. That a rubric be made declaring the intention of the Lent fasts to consist only in extraordinary acts of devotion, and not in distinction of meats.

7. That the rubric which obliges ministers to read or hear Common Prayer publicly or privately every day be changed to an exhortation to the people to frequent these prayers.

[1] Birch, *Life of Tillotson*, p. 199.
[2] See Chap. 5, p. 111.
[3] Parliamentary Papers, vol. 50. "Copy of Alterations", p. 108.

8. That in order that the "Absolution" in Morning and Evening Prayer may be said by a deacon, the title "priest" be altered to "minister", and the words "and remission" omitted.

9. That the "gloria Patri" be not repeated at the end of every psalm. (Nos. 10, 12, 13, 14, 15, 16 contain the alterations already quoted as the work of Tenison.)

11. That the "Benedicite" be changed to the 128th Psalm and other psalms be likewise used for the "Nunc Dimittis".

17. That "the Collects for the most part . . . be changed for those which the Bishop of Chichester has prepared, being a review of the old ones with enlargements, to render them more sensible and affecting".[1]

18. That if any minister refuse the surplice, the bishop, if the parishioners desire it, and the living "will bear it", may substitute one in his place that will officiate in it.

19. That if any desire to dispense with godfathers or god-mothers, then their children may be presented in their own names for baptism.

20. That with respect to the creed of St. Athanasius "lest the wholly rejecting it should by unreasonable persons be imputed to them as Socinianism, a rubric should be made setting forth, or declaring the curses denounced therein, not to be restrained to every particular article, but intended against those who deny the substance of the Christian religion in general".[2]

21. That it be left to Convocation to decide whether the "reading Psalms" of Lloyd and Kidder, or the translation in the Bible be used.[3]

---

[1] It is hardly a matter for regret that the book of Common Prayer escaped the burden of these collects by Simon Patrick. They are invariably exceedingly lengthy, and lacking in the dignity and rhythm which we associate with the older collects. Few will dissent from Macaulay's strictures upon them, and Patrick would have done well to remember Tenison's words: "Nor did the long continued Prayers [of the Puritans] help men so much against Distraction as those short ones, with Breaks and Pauses in the Liturgy". ("Argument for Union", p. 38.)

[2] The rubric reads: ". . . The Condemning Clauses are to be understood as relating to those only who obstinately deny the substance of the Christian Faith".

[3] These propositions (quoted in Birch, *Life of Tillotson*, p. 193, and Cardwell, *A History of Conferences and other Proceedings*, etc. p. 429) come from the Tanner Collection of MSS. (CCLXXXII. 222) in a volume containing many papers in the handwriting of Archbishop Sancroft. Cardwell writes: "Whether the MS. was preserved by the Archbishop or only by Bishop Tanner, it clearly may be considered of high authority. It is remarkable that no notice is taken in it of the important point of re-ordination which the Commissioners certainly debated, and according to the statement of Dr. Nicholls were willing to concede". (Nicholls, *Apparatus ad Defens. Eccles. Angl.*, p. 95.) Actually the document quoted in the text ends: "In the Litany, Communion Service etc. are some alterations made, as also in the Canons, which I cannot yet learn so particular an account of, as to give them with the rest; as perhaps I may hereafter be able to do".

As to the ordination of those Dissenting ministers who wished to officiate in the Church of England, this was the most difficult subject with which the Commission had to deal, and certainly the one which aroused the fiercest passions, both among the commissioners and at the Convocation which followed. Till the time of Charles II, so Cardwell writes,[1] "ordination conveyed by presbyters though resisted by the governors of the Church had never been disowned by the legislature", and it was a matter of principle with most of the Dissenters to vindicate their position by insisting on the validity of their own ordinations. Tenison, according to his own biographer, was "inclined not to insist on the Re-ordination of them, alledging, that they ought not to shew less Regard to the Vocation of Presbyterians Ministers, than to that of Roman-Catholick Priests, whose Ordination was never question'd upon their joining in Communion with the Church of England".[2] There were many on the Commission, however, who, though eager for comprehension, were not prepared to abandon the principle of episcopal ordination, and despite

"all that was alledg'd by Dr. Tenison, and the others, who spoke in Conformity to Reason and Justice on this Head, the Majority in Commission thought it more proper to keep a middle Course, which was, First, with Respect to Romish Priests, to leave it undecided, whether their Ordination was good or no: But because they were not obliged to give Credit to their Certificates, that therefore such of them, as for the Future, should turn Protestants, should live in Lay-Communion only, unless they were re-ordain'd to a legal Title of any Church or Cure: And, Secondly, That tho' they did not determine the Ordination of Presbyterians to be altogether invalid, yet they thought it necessary for their Ministers to receive Orders from a Bishop, who in Conferring the same, might add a Clause to the common Form, as the Church had already ordain'd in the Case of uncertain Baptism to this Effect; If thou art not already Ordain'd, I Ordain Thee etc. and this was the greatest Concession that ever was made by the Commissioners".[3]

Few will regret that these recommendations, as they stand above, did not become law, and Burnet himself, who "was very anxious at the time for changes", admitted later "that the

[1] Cardwell, *A History of Conferences and other Proceedings*, etc., p. 418.
[2] *Memoirs of the Life and Times*, etc., p. 13. That this was Tenison's position rests solely on the author of *Memoirs of the Life and Times*, and seems a little difficult to reconcile with the general ethos of "An Argument for Union" and also Chapter 15, p. 338.
[3] *Memoirs of the Life and Times*, etc., p. 14. This is discussed at length in A. J. Mason, *The Church of England or Episcopacy*, 1914, p. 2844.

providence of God was displayed in the proceedings which led to a refusal to make alterations in the Liturgy".[1] True there were some excellent things in the recommendations, and the general spirit of tolerance which they breathe is more often admired than emulated. Yet they bore the impress of the rationalism of the time, and unfortunately it was rationalism of a not very æsthetic kind. We tremble to think what an irreparable loss the English Church would have sustained if the singing of the daily offices in our cathedrals had been everywhere abandoned; or if Patrick's lengthened collects had been inflicted upon the worshipper. On the other hand, it may well be a matter for regret that the conciliatory clauses, designed to promote a "comprehension", were never put to the test. It seems only fair to the commissioners to admit that they did their work in a large and liberal spirit and tried honestly to deal with the questions which prevented many Dissenters from rejoining the communion of the Church of England. They made a genuine effort to understand their difficulties, and Tenison, as we have seen, collected the "exceptions" which Puritans before the civil war, or Nonconformists after the Restoration, had made to the Anglican services.[2] There seems little reason, on the whole, to doubt the statement of Birch, Tillotson's biographer: "Matters were well consider'd and freely and calmly debated: and all was digested into an entire conviction of anything that seemed liable to any just objections".[3]

---

[1] Lathbury, *History of Convocation*, p. 334.

[2] In addition, Birch records (p. 190) "they had likewise many propositions and advices which had been offered at several times by many of our Bishops and Divines upon those heads of which Bishop Stillingfleet had made a great collection". While the Commission was sitting, one Samuel Snowdon sent to Tenison on 14 November an interesting "Abstract concerning alterations in the Liturgy and matters to be considered in Convocation". Amongst the suggestions are the following: (1) The services are too long and should be cut down. (2) It would be better to have psalms in the new translation. (3) The three "controverted ceremonies" should be left optional. (4) The Lord's prayer is too often used. (5) The prayers for the King and the Royal Family should be revised so that they "may be indifferently us'd (without either regrett or sin) in any reigne whatever". (6) The burial service is unreal when said over profligates. (7) So are the statements concerning regeneration in the baptismal service. (8) It is wrong to make all the clauses of the Athanasian Creed essential. (9) Alternative reading of verses of the psalms is a mistake. (Lambeth MSS. 937, f. 13.)

[3] Birch, *Life of Tillotson*, p. 190. The preceding account of the Commission of 1689 and its work has been drawn from: (1) A diary of the meetings of the commissioners kept by Dr. Williams afterwards Bishop of Chichester. (2) A complete and official list of the alterations suggested by the Commission. (The originals of both of these are in the library at Lambeth; the latter consists of an interleaved prayer book with the 1662 and the revised liturgy facing each other. In 1854 it was published as a parliamentary paper.) (3) Lathbury, *History of Convocation*, pp. 313–333. (4) Cardwell, *A History of Conferences and other Proceedings connected with the Revision of the Book of Common Prayer*, 1840. (5) *Memoirs of the Life and Times*, etc.

The meetings of the above Commission inevitably aroused intense hostility at the time in some quarters, and this found expression in a contemporary pamphlet: "A Letter to a Friend containing some Quaeries about the new Commission". The writer, who styled himself "the Quaerist", maintained that the setting up of a Commission was prejudicial to the authority of Convocation and could never be tolerated by Parliament.[1] As for the commissioners themselves, he said, their very personnel condemned them for they were almost without exception "assuming men" who would regard themselves as "bound in honour to defend what they had done", especially since they had "Tenderness and Moderation enough to part with everything but their Church Preferments", and had been eager to demand "Latitude to conform to a Church de Facto which had Power on its side".[2] Moreover, the Quaerist argued, under the terms of the Commission nine men established a quorum, so that the Church might be "chang'd and alter'd and transform'd by Nine Men". Nonconformists, no matter what was offered them, would never return to the Church of England, but were determined to carry on with their ordinations. The times were certainly difficult, "the persons of Men in a Vehement Fermentation", and it was not an opportune season to persuade even the more moderate Dissenters to conform. If certain "Reverend Prelates", not named in the Commission (i.e. Sancroft and his followers), were to appear at the Convocation which was to follow, the commissioners would not dare to bring up their proposals.

This pamphlet, as will be seen, came from the pen of a High Churchman of non-juring sympathies. The Commission, in his eyes, was of too erastian a character and too likely to jettison the historic faith in the interest of civil unity, for any good thing to come out of it.

As a result of these criticisms, and also because of the disagreement within the Commission itself, evident at its first three sessions, Tenison replied with "A Discourse Concerning the Ecclesiastical Commission". This document is important in that it may be regarded as a semi-official apologia by the commissioners for their own work.

Tenison began by stating plainly that although he had never

[1] "A Letter to a Friend containing some Quaeries", pp. 4, 5. This letter has been ascribed to William Sherlock, Dean of St. Paul's. (Lathbury, *History of Convocation*, 1853, p. 326.)

[2] *Ibid.* p. 4.

entertained a good opinion of the Ecclesiastical Commission in
King James' reign, yet he was prepared to argue of the present
Commission: (1) That it was agreeable to the law of the land.
(2) That it was not prejudicial but useful to Convocation. (3) That
it tended to the well-being of the Church. (4) That the present was
a "fit juncture for putting the design into execution".[1] Tenison
then proceeded to elaborate these four points.

1. The Commission, he said, "was founded upon a legal
bottom; for it is undoubtedly a right of the King to call any
number of his subjects together to advise concerning such
things as he shall think fit to propose to them". Such a method
of procedure could be justified by precedents, for the Book of
Common Prayer itself was compiled by a Commission in the
time of Edward VI.

2. A Commission which met before a Convocation could in
no sense be prejudicial to that body. No comparison could be
drawn between the status and constitution of Convocation and
Parliament,[2] and even if there were an analogy, "no Member of
Parliament who either by Himself or by Advice prepares an
useful Bill is by either House reprehended when he asks leave to
bring it in".[3] A Convocation could not commence its proceedings with a committee appointed by itself because without
the King's warrant it was not allowed to deliberate on any single
matter. Nor were the members of the Commission such as would
desire to restrict the rights or endanger the liberty of Convocation, since they were all churchmen of ability and learning, and
would themselves sit in Convocation. Yet even if all the
commissioners were, in fact, men of "ill design", their power
remained merely that of recommending to Convocation.

3. Tenison then quoted the exact terms under which the
Commission met (see p. 98), and made the following observa-
tions upon them: (a) All Churches, no matter how well
founded, admitted at certain times of alterations and improve-
ments. (b) There had been numerous revisions in the past,
e.g. 1662. (c) The present design was for the advantage and
support of the Church of England with respect both to Conformists and Nonconformists, and changes were as necessary
now as after the Restoration, since even the enemies of the
Commission admitted the need for the reform of the ecclesiastical
courts. "It is true", Tenison remarked, "the present Churchmen have given their Assent and Consent to the last Book of

[1] Tenison, "A Discourse concerning the Ecclesiastical Commission", p. 1.
[2] This is interesting in view of later convocational disputes.
[3] Tenison, "A Discourse", etc., p. 5.

Common Prayer, but even that consent is to the Preface of it, in which it is set forth that there are in Churches, Circumstances which may from time to time admit of Alterations. Neither can any man reasonably think that when they assented and consented to the Use of the Book, as containing nothing that was unlawful, they intended to declare that everything in it should be unalterable".[1]

4. As to the Dissenters, if it were intended to do anything for them, it should be done now, and undoubtedly the leading Dissenters were as anxious for this as members of the Church of England.

Tenison concluded his Pamphlet with a threefold request: (1) That those who knew of the Commission only through hearsay, would do something to acquaint themselves first hand with its real nature. (2) That they would refrain from passing judgment till they had done so. (3) And lastly, addressing himself to the Quaerist, he pleaded: "I entreat him to make some Christian Reflections upon his Letter and primarily to consider whether he hath not been angry without a cause, judged rashly, done to the commissioners what he would not have done to himself, and endeavoured to lead others into like offences".[2]

Tenison's pamphlet expressed admirably the position of all those who were anxious for some kind of comprehension. It could hardly be expected that it would go unanswered, and a reply soon appeared in "Vox Cleri, or the Sense of the Clergy concerning the making Alterations in the Established Liturgy, including Reflections on a Discourse concerning the Ecclesiastical Commission". The writer of this pamphlet maintained that no matter what alterations were agreed upon, they would no more satisfy the Dissenters than in time past. "Now to what purpose", he asked, "should we begin when we cannot see the end. Is it not better to endure some inconveniences (as in all Constitutions some will be) than to expose ourselves to certain mischief. And what can we expect when the Alterations in 1661

[1] Tenison, "A Discourse", etc., p. 20.
[2] There were many who shared Tenison's hopes, and while the Commission was sitting he received the following anonymous letter, typical, doubtless, of others, asking him "whether different forms may not be used for variety; whether some of the collects may not be left indifferent, and the surplice and the sign of the cross be yielded to the scruples of the Nonconformists. Whether some express allowance be not convenient in several things which now in many places are grown customary without one? Such are sermons in the afternoon; the liberty which is taken of ye prayer before ye sermon. Whether some expedients are not to be found out to restore the credit of episcopacy to the vulgar". Quoted, Lathbury, *History of Convocation*, p. 328.

had no competent effect but were rejected with scorn".[1] The proposed changes, on the contrary, so far from contributing to peace would but add to the present perplexities by inflaming men's passions, and it would be better for Convocation to have nothing to do with them, because it "will be to their comfort, that they did not grant their Hands to the pulling down the Church upon their own Heads".[2] Moreover (and the writer here raises a real difficulty), it would be a doubtful blessing if certain alterations which encouraged some Dissenters to conform, provoked a number of Churchmen to secede. As the author of another contemporary pamphlet expressed it: "You seem to have forgot one main thing, and that was to make up your Chancel Door; for it may so happen, that more Conformists may go out at that, than grave Dissenters will go in at the other".[3]

The setting up of the Commission, and the Convocation which followed, produced a spate of pamphlets, a list of which we add as a footnote below.[4] Most of them are deservedly forgotten, but one, we feel, has an interest quite apart from the historical situation which called it forth. We refer to a "Letter to a Friend relating to the present Convocation at Westminster", written by Humphrey Prideaux,[5] in which he makes a bold plea for the revision of the liturgy, not so much on the ground of contemporary expediency, but from the nature of liturgy as such. Prideaux admitted that a too frequent alteration of a liturgy was not to be desired,

[1] "Vox Cleri, or the Sense of the Clergy", 1689, p. 19.
[2] Ibid. p. 23.
[3] "To the Reverend and Merry Answerer of Vox Cleri", 1689, p. 10.
[4] In favour of the Commission:
    Tenison, "A Discourse concerning the Ecclesiastical Commission", 1689.
    Prideaux, "A Letter to a Friend relating to the present Convocation", 1689.
        "An Answer to Vox Cleri", 1690 (attributed to William Payne).
        "A Just Censure of Vox Cleri".
        "Remarks upon the Two Letters".
        "Vox Regis et Regni or a Protest against Vox Cleri".
    Against the Commission:
    "Vox Cleri, or the Sense of the Clergy Concerning the making of Alterations in the established Liturgy; with some Remarks on the Discourse concerning the Ecclesiastical Commission", 1690 (published anonymously but written by Thomas Long, Prebendary of Exeter).
    "Vox Populi", 1690.
    "Remarks from the Country on two Letters relating to Convocation".
    Bassett, "Two Letters and a Vindication".
[5] The authorship of this pamphlet has been disputed. Bishop Barlow, in his own copy which he left to the Bodleian, wrote: "Writ by Dr. Kidder, Dean of Peterborough, who had been a dissenter". Kennett (Complete History, iii. 591) supposed it to have been written by Tillotson; but the evidence of Prideaux's son, who ascribes it to his father, may be taken as conclusive. (Article on Prideaux, Universal Dictionary.)

"because an unsteadiness as to these, although in outward circumstances only, which are always alterable, may to many become an argument against the whole. For there being multitudes among us not being able to distinguish between what is circumstantial, and what is essential in our worship, what is in the power of the Church to alter, and what is not, they are apt to call every alteration, though in things merely indifferent, and which the variation of time has made wholly insignificant to the first end of their establishment, to be a change in religion".[1]

Then followed a plea for revision, as relevant perhaps now as then, and we hardly need apologize for quoting it in full:

"As to the Liturgy of our Church, I freely acknowledge and I think no man can contradict me herein, that it is the best which was ever yet used in any Christian Church, but that it should therefore be so perfect as not to be capable of amendments and alterations for the better doth by no means follow. For nothing of humane composure can be such, especially in a thing of this nature, where progress of time and alteration of circumstance frequently produce a necessity of correction as more certainly in our Liturgy they very often doe. For the language in which it is wrote, being constantly *in fluxu*, as all other living languages are, in every age some words that were in use in the former grow obsolete and some phrases and expressions formerly in grace and fashion, through disuse become uncouth and ridiculous, and always to condemn these in our Liturgy without correction, would be to bring a disparagement upon the whole, and expose to contempt the worship of God among us. Besides there are several things in one age may conduce to devotion, which through variations of times and circumstances may not be born[e] in another; several things which may be the proper matter for prayer at one time, which may not be in another, and all these things call for alteration and amendments whenever they happen. And therefore I am so far from asserting, with some of our Brethren in this particular, that our Liturgy ought not to be altered that I think it absolutely necessary, from the above mentioned particulars, that it be always at least once in thirty years brought to a review for this purpose.[2] . . . For in truth it is not ancient usage, but the necessities and exigencies of the Church that are the reasons of all its constitutions and establishments, which are to be framed in every age as will best sute

---

[1] H. Prideaux, "A Letter to a Friend", etc., p. 34.   [2] *Ibid.* p. 50.

with the promoting of the honour of God and the edification of his people, to which abundance of things might very well serve in primitive times which will not now".[1]

We have seen that the deliberations of the Commission were conducted in an orderly fashion, and without "undue heats", but the same cannot be said of the Convocation which followed on 21 November, when it soon became apparent that a large number of the clergy disagreed violently with the proposed changes. Significant at the outset was the election of Dr. Jane (who had left the Commission in disgust after the third session) as Prolocutor of the Lower House by a majority of over two to one against Dr. Tillotson, who was favoured by the Court. It does not fall within the scope of this work to relate the stormy scenes which accompanied the brief life of this assembly. Suffice that it became obvious to William that the alterations proposed by the Commission would not be accepted (despite the effort of "Dr. Tennison, Fowler, Kidder etc. to make the clergy drop their too violent Animosities to their Christian Brethren")[2] and that to persist in the attempt to force them upon a reluctant Convocation would be to increase and not allay religious discord. The times were unfavourable: the persecution of the episcopal clergy by the Presbyterians in Scotland, and the stern opposition of the Non-jurors to the proposals of the Commission, did not create an atmosphere favourable to calm discussion. William, as a statesman, gave way: Convocation was adjourned from 13 December to 14 January and soon after was dissolved with Parliament. The King did not summon it again so that it never passed any judgment on the recommendations of the Commission.[3]

That Tenison was disappointed with the failure of this attempt at comprehension, there can be no doubt. He was wholehearted in its support, and had spared no pains to promote it: but he never afterwards tried to challenge this verdict.[4] He realized that the time was not yet, and he preferred, in later years, not to discuss the Commission and its failure. Some time afterwards,

[1] H. Prideaux, "A Letter to a Friend", etc., p. 60.
[2] *Memoirs of the Life and Times*, etc., p. 18.
[3] Lathbury, *History of Convocation*, p. 333.
[4] Among Tenison's papers at Lambeth there is one called "Pensée d'un Théologien désintéressé . . . Touchant la réunion des Presbytériens à l'Eglise Anglicane" (Lambeth MSS. 932, f. 76). In this document the writer, a French Protestant, comments upon the satisfaction which this Protestant disunion in England gave to the Jesuits, and suggests that in the Anglican Confession of 1562 there is a mean of effectual unity.

there passed into his hands in the form of an interleaved prayer book, the proposals which the Commission had drawn up, but he was always careful not to let others peruse them, and he refused to allow them to be published. "If they came to be public", he explained, "they would give no satisfaction to either side, but be rather a handle for mutual reproaches, for one side would upbraid their brethren for having given up so much; while the other would justify their nonconformity, because those concessions were too little, or, however little, not yet pass'd into a law".[1]

Thus comprehension ceased to be practical politics, at least for the time being, but a compromise had already been found in the practice of occasional conformity, by which the Nonconformist who communicated once a year avoided the disabilities imposed by the Test Act, and was granted (in the main) the same legal privileges as a member of the Church of England. Tenison gave this *via media* his warm support, but it was anathema to the Tories and High Churchmen, who could do little to oppose it, so long as William, the firm friend of the Dissenters, remained on the throne. Anne's succession, however, somewhat changed the ecclesiastical temper, and the Tories were encouraged to make many attempts to prevent the Dissenters from "short-circuiting" the Test Act.[2] Firm against all such attempts stood Tenison, then Archbishop of Canterbury.

In the first session of Anne's first Parliament, a Bill to prevent this occasional conformity passed through the House of Commons and was sent up to the Lords on 2 December, much to the consternation of the Dissenters.[3] The Lords, however, "were so little fond of this bill, that apprehending it or some other bill they did not wholly like might in time be tacked to a money bill by the Commons, they passed a vote 'that it would be an Infringement of the Privilege of their House'." Tenison, among others, "strenuously opposed it by causing several amendments to be

---

[1] Birch, *Life of Tillotson*, p. 190.

We may, perhaps, note here that at the request of this Commission Tenison prepared a book of family prayers, but although many later tried to persuade him, he would not consent to its publication. "Though he was sensible", he said one day to Prideaux at Lambeth, "of the great occasion there was for it, and the service it might do Religion, he thought it had best be done with the concurrence of Convocation, which would make it be received with greater authority". This book of prayers passed into the hands of the Bp. of Chichester, Dr. Williams, but seems to have been burned at his death. See *Life of Humphrey Prideaux D.D.*, 1748, p. 64.

[2] The Test Act provided that none should be in office in any corporation who had not within the year previous to his nomination communicated in the Church of England.

[3] Cobbett, *Parliamentary History*, vi. 59.

made",[1] but as the Bill in certain of its clauses dealt with the fixing of fines, so the House was accused of "meddling with money". Thus there was a conference between both Houses, and the Upper House searched records, but as the Lords stood to their amendments, and "the Commons likewise adhered to their disagreement with the Lords' amendments, the bill was lost for this time".[2]

In 1703 it was again introduced in an amended form into the Commons. A heated debate then took place in which a great deal of animosity was displayed against the Whig bishops in general and Tenison in particular, Sir John Pakington, the alleged though improbable original of Addison's Sir Roger de Coverley, observing sarcastically:

"I did wonder to hear so many bishops against this Bill but that wonder ceased, when I considered whom they owed their Preferment to; the Archbishop of Canterbury, I think, was promoted to that see by Lord Sunderland's Interest; and being asked what Reasons he had aganst this Bill replied: he had not well consider'd the Bill, but my Lord Sunderland[3] told him it ought not to pass. This was a very weighty reason for the head of our Church to give; and yet, I daresay, none of them could give a better. One would be provoked by the late behaviour of the Bishops, to move for leave to bring in a Bill for the toleration of Episcopacy; for, since they are of the same principles with dissenters, it is but just, I think, that they should stand on the same foot".[4]

The Bill passed through the Commons by a majority of 223 to 140 on 7 December, but Tenison with fourteen other bishops secured its rejection in the Upper House by a majority of twelve, after Burnet had given vent to his feelings in a long speech.[5]

Still the Tories remained obstinate, and in 1704 Mr. Bromley (member for Oxford University) introduced a similar Bill into the Commons. What the Upper House had feared in 1702 seemed

---

[1] *Memoirs of the Life and Times*, etc., p. 102.

[2] Cobbett, *Parliamentary History*, vi. 91. Wallis wrote to Tenison from Oxford on 22 December 1702 (Lambeth MSS. 930, f. 52): "I am not sorry that the Bill concerning Occasional Conformity, hath end with some Rubs in the House of Lords. I think it our common Interest to compose these differences, rather than to make the breach wider".

[3] The *Memoirs of the Life and Times*, etc., p. 103, here reads: "Lord Somers" (d. 1716) who was at this time a strong Whig. The vehement and absurd nature of this attack on Tenison shows the violence of religious and political passions at this period.

[4] Cobbett, *Parliamentary History*, vi. 155.

[5] *Ibid.* p. 168.

now likely to take place. The extreme Tories in the Lower House tried to tack it to a Land Tax Bill, in order, as Sir Thomas Littleton said, "to throw a necessity upon the Lords to pass it". The Commons itself, however, rejected this particular expedient by 251 votes to 134, though it passed the Occasional Conformity Bill, despite strong opposition, by 179 votes to 131.

The Archbishop of Canterbury once again led the opposition to the Bill in the Lords, and we are fortunate in possessing a summary of his speech with which we bring this chapter to a close:

"The Noble Peer that spoke last has consider'd the Reasons that are given for the Occasional Bill itself; but I must confess that I can see none that Satisfie of the Necessity of it. I think the Practice of Occasional Conformity as used by the Dissenters so far from deserving the title a Vile Hypocrisy, that I think it the Duty of all Moderate Dissenters upon their own precepts to do it. I think that however it may be disapprov'd by some rigid Dissenters, it ought to be encourag'd by all good Churchmen, as a likely means to bring them over. The employing of Persons of a different Religion from the Establish'd, has been preach'd in all Countries where Liberty of Conscience has been allow'd. That we have gone further already in excluding Dissenters than any other Country has done, That whatever reasons there were to apprehend our Religion in danger from the Papists, when the Test Act was made, yet here does not seem the least Danger to it from the Dissenters now. But on the other hand I can see very plain Inconveniences from this Bill at present. As it is brought in this last Time indeed, they have added a Preamble, that though it was put in the first Edition of the Bill, was left out in the second. viz. That the Act for Toleration should always be kept inviolable. But the Toleration Act being to take away all the Penalties that a Man might incurr by going to a Separable Congregation and the Occasional Bill being to lay new Penalties upon those that do it, how they can say that this is not in itself a Violation of the other, I cannot very easily comprehend; I doubt it will put People in mind of what pass'd in France when every Edict against the Protestants began with a Protestation; That the Edict of Nantes ought always to be preserv'd inviolable, till that very Edict in which it was in express Words repealed. At a time that all Europe is engag'd in a bloody and expensive War: At a Time that this Nation has not only such considerable Foreign Enemies to deal withal, but has a party in her own

Bowels, ready upon all Occasion to bring in a Popish Pretender, and involve us all in the same, or rather worse Calamities than those from which with so much Blood and Treasure we have been freed. At a time that the Protestant Dissenters (however they may be in the wrong by separating from us) yet are heartily united with us against the common Foes to our Religion and Government. What Advantage those who are in earnest for defending these things, can have by lessening the Number of such as are firmly united in this common Cause I cannot for my Life imagine. Therefore I am for throwing out this Bill, without giving it another Reading".[1]

It remains only to state that the Bill did not pass.

The Tories had yet to realize their full strength under the favour of Anne, however, but when the Bill against Occasional Conformity finally obtained the approval of Parliament in 1711, and the Schism Act,[2] introduced by Lord Bolingbroke into the House of Lords, became law on 25 June 1714, Tenison, owing to failing health, was not present.[3]

When both were repealed in 1719, he had been over three years in the grave.

---

[1] *Memoirs of the Life and Times*, etc., p. 103.

[2] By this measure, no person was allowed to teach publicly or privately without first signing a declaration of conformity, and obtaining a licence from the bishop of his diocese, which licence was not to be granted unless he could produce a certificate that he had received the Sacrament according to the rites of the Church of England for a year previous. Anyone without such a licence was liable to be imprisoned without bail.

[3] Cobbett, *Parliamentary History*, vi. 1356.

CHAPTER 6

A DIOCESAN BISHOP

Part I Bishop of Lincoln (1692–94)

THE successful outcome of William's bid for the English throne inevitably brought into royal favour those who had welcomed and worked for his accession. Prominent amongst these was Thomas Tenison, and his name was one of a list of ten clergymen whom Burnet recommended to William, most of whom secured important preferment.[1] It was not long before he received a sign of favour. On 26 October 1689 he followed Stillingfleet, promoted to the see of Worcester, into the Archdeaconry of London, this preferment being in the gift of the Bishop of London. As Archdeacon of London, Tenison took precedence over his four other brethren[2] and he had under his jurisdiction all the parishes in London (except certain peculiars of the Archbishop of Canterbury, the Bishop of London, and the Dean and Chapter of St. Paul's),[3] and three parishes in Middlesex—"all which Parishes of his Jurisdiction he visits by himself or his Official, Twice every Year; swears the Churchwardens every Easter; receives their Presentments, and proceeds judicially thereupon; and yearly receives Procurations of the Clergy, who are Incumbents of those Churches". Besides these duties "he likewise proves the Wills and grants Letters of Administration of Intestate Goods, of such as die within the said Parishes, not having 'Bona notabilia'", except in parishes subject to the "Commissary of London ".[4]

How efficiently Tenison discharged these responsibilities during the two years and five months of his office, we cannot tell, as it is impossible to get access to records from the Bishop of London's

---

[1] Clarke and Foxcroft, *A Life of Gilbert Burnet*, p. 257. The others were: Tillotson, Sharp, Wake, Stillingfleet, Patrick, Fowler, Sherlock, Ayrshott. Burnet also warned William against Hall and Watson.

[2] The Archdeacons of Essex, Middlesex, Colchester, and St. Albans.

[3] Newcourt, *Repertorium Ecclesiasticum Parochiale Londinense*, writes that there were thirteen peculiars belonging to the Archbishop of Canterbury, one (St. Botolph without Bishopsgate) "which in all ecclesiastical matters belongs to the Bishop of London", and four to the Dean and Chapter of St. Paul's.

[4] Newcourt, *Repertorium Ecclesiasticum*, etc., p. 56.

registrar.[1] He was succeeded by William Stanley on 5 March 1692.[2]

Thomas Barlow, Bishop of Lincoln, died on 8 October 1691— a diocesan who in life was as much distinguished for his scholarship as for his almost total neglect of the diocese. No man had more claim on the goodwill of William and Mary than Thomas Tenison —Vicar of St. Martin-in-the-Fields and St. James', Westminster, and Archdeacon of London—and a contemporary writes that he was "recommended to their Majesties by his Exemplary Piety, and his great Moderation towards Dissenters; when their Majesties still endeavoured by all gentle (which indeed are the most effectual Methods) to bring them over to the National Church".[3] Such a good Whig, however, could hardly expect his nomination to go unchallenged, and we are not surprised to find that the Earl of Jersey, Master of the Horse, did his best "to prejudice the Doctor in her Majesty's Opinions, out of Design to gain her Interest for a friend of his own", namely, Dr. Scott, Rector of St. Giles-in-the-Fields. To do this (we quote the story, though it appears rather naïve) the Earl reminded the Queen when "she was speaking in terms of respect of Dr. Tenison, that he had some weeks [4] before deliver'd a notable Funeral Sermon in praise of Mrs. Eleanor Gwyn, one of King Charles the second's late concubines". Mary was not to be so easily shocked, however. "What", she cried, "I have heard as much. This is a sign that that poor unfortunate Woman died Penitent, for if I can read a Man's Heart through his looks, had she not made a truly Christian and pious End, the Doctor could never have been induc'd to speak well of her".[5]

So Tenison "was prevail'd with to accept the Bishopric of Lincoln" (White Kennett says "after the rejecting of better Offers"),[6] and he took with him a reputation for conscientious diligence and Protestant zeal. All good Whigs rejoiced.

On 27 October 1691, a warrant for a *congé d'élire* was issued to the Dean and Chapter of the Cathedral Church at Lincoln,

---

[1] I made a personal visit, but in vain.
[2] Newcourt, *Repertorium Ecclesiasticum*, etc., p. 64.
[3] White Kennett, *A Complete History of England*, iii. 34.
[4] It was, in fact, three years eleven months previously!
[5] *Memoirs of the Life and Times*, etc., p. 25. Tenison, as we have seen, attended Eleanor Gwyn on her death-bed. The story goes that when some of the parishioners of St. Martin's raised objections against her burial in the crypt, Tenison offered his own grave for the purpose.
[6] White Kennett, *A Complete History of England*, iii. 676.

with a letter missive "recommending Dr. Thomas Tenison D.D. one of the Chaplains in Ordinary, to be by them chosen a bishop of that see".[1] He was duly elected on 11 December and the warrant for the royal assent to the election was granted on 14 December.[2] The new Bishop was reluctant, presumably for financial reasons, to resign immediately his livings of St. Martin's and St. James' (for setting up in a bishopric was always a costly business), particularly since his removal to Lincoln meant his resigning the Archdeaconry of London.[3] Hence he secured a grant in December 1691, which enabled him to hold these livings in commendam till 1 July of the following year.[4]

Tenison was consecrated to the episcopal order in Lambeth Chapel on 19 January 1692, by Archbishop Tillotson assisted by the Bishops of London, Worcester, and Ely, and the sermon was preached by William Stanley, later Dean of St. Asaph. In the course of his address the preacher, having in mind the character of the new Bishop, extolled the virtues of moderation, and urged "that to this purpose they ought not to be forward even to censure one another, much less openly to oppose one another, and break into Parties".[5] "And particularly let us pray God", he concluded, "to send that excellent Person, now to be received into that Order, a double Portion of his Spirit, large as his mind, and suitable to his Charge; that he may be as Eminent and useful in this, as he hath been in his former Station, and may long continue a light to our Israel".[6]

As a parish priest Tenison was noted for the energy with which he discharged his duties. There was certainly much for him to do at Lincoln, for Barlow had resided during his long episcopate at the palace near Buckden, and was so little seen in other parts of his diocese (it is doubtful if he ever visited the city of Lincoln!) that he was contemptuously styled "the Bishop of Buckden". Tenison now brought the same diligence and concentration to detail, which had proved so successful in his parishes, to bear on the whole of his diocese.

The first task was to restore some kind of order into a charge which Barlow's apathy had neglected, and his controversial spirit

---

[1] S.P.D., William and Mary, 27 October 1691.
[2] Ibid. 19 December 1691.
[3] Ibid. 11 October 1689.
[4] Lambeth MSS. 952, f. 78.
[5] W. Stanley, "A Sermon preached at the Consecration", etc., p. 23.
[6] Ibid. p. 28.

embittered. This Tenison attempted in his first visitation which
he began at Hatfield Church on Wednesday 26 April 1693, and
concluded at Dunstable on Thursday 8 June. On Tuesday 16 May
he visited the Dean and Chapter of the Cathedral in the Chapter
House. After this, he spent some five and a half weeks getting to
know the rank and file of the clergy and the parochial conditions
in his diocese, during which time he visited five archdeaconries
(Huntingdon, Buckingham, Leicester, Stow, and Lincoln), over
fifty deaneries, and held his enquiries in nineteen different
places, travelling in all over 420 miles.[1] The procedure of such
visitations is well known, but may perhaps be mentioned briefly.
Tenison first sent out "Articles of Enquiry" to the vicar and
churchwardens of every parish which he intended to visit, and the
replies to these questions were given to him in person when he
came to the archdeaconry.

The new Bishop believed firmly in using his archdeacons and
their courts to inaugurate his policy of reform in the diocese
and to make the ordinary church machinery operate. Hence on
18 November 1693, he wrote to the Archdeacon of Leicester,
asking that he might have an "Account of the Names and the
Crimes of all such persons as were detected and presented in the
last visitation". The Archdeacon, perhaps a little flustered at this
unaccustomed sign of episcopal activity, replied through his clerk
that he would forward a "faythfull account . . . with all
expedition", excusing himself meanwhile as he was busy sending
out the demands for the tenths.[2] Such a request seems to have
stirred the Archdeacon to some activity, for a little later Tenison
received information that investigations had been started into the
irregular conduct of one Mr. Grove, Rector of the parish of
Witherly in Leicestershire. We propose to quote this case at length
as an example, doubtless, of what happened in many others.

[1] Lambeth MSS. 954, f. 1. The following is an account of his progress. The Archdeaconry of Huntingdon visited on 26 April in Hatfield Church; the Archdeaconry
of Buckingham, 28–29 April in Aylesbury Church, 2 May in Buckingham Church;
the Archdeaconry of Leicester, 4 May in Harborough Chapel, 5 May in St. Martin's
Church, Leicester, 8 May in Melton Mowbray Church; the Archdeaconry of Stow,
13 May in the Consistory Court; the Archdeaconry of Lincoln, 10 May in Grantham
Church, 12 May Consistory Court; the Dean and Chapter of Lincoln, 16 May in the
Chapter House; the Archdeaconry of Stow, 18 May in Gainsborough Church; the
Archdeaconry of Lincoln, 20 May in Caistor Church, 22 May in Ludborough Church,
24 May in Horncastle Church, 26 May in Boston Church, 30 May in Bourn Church,
31 May in St. Mary's Church, Stamford; the Archdeaconry of Huntingdon, 2, 3 June
in All Saints' Church, Huntingdon, 7 June in St. Paul's Church, Bedford, 8 June in
Dunstable Church. See Lambeth MSS. 954, f. 61.
[2] J. Stephens to Tenison, 4 December 1693. Lambeth MSS. 942, f. 65.

Tenison immediately directed that an enquiry should be held in Grove's parish, and this was done, the former year's church-wardens, together with those who had been admitted at the visitation, and the promoter, being presented with the articles "and admonished to give in their answers".[1] The four church-wardens were unanimous in their declaration

"that Mr. Grove was a man of very civill and sober life and conversation, much inclined to doe any act of charity and kind-ness to any of his neighbours, exactly constant in the perform-ance of his Ministerial Functions and Offices and given to good hospitality".

But, they added in their report (perhaps to cover themselves),

"since they were summoned about the matter, they have been informed . . . that Mr. Grove's Father, a Shropshire gent. of good Quality coming to see his Son, they were both by Mr. Chittwin of Grindley . . . envited to dine wth him, where by Mr. Chittwin's over kindness he was surprised and overtaken in Drink, but say they never knew or heard that he was ever so before, and by the character he hath both from his own parish-ioners and Neighbour Clergy he should not be any such man".[2]

This report was forwarded to Tenison on 4 December by James Stephens (clerk to the Archdeacon of Leicester), who added on his own account:

"On Thursday last being att Madame Wollaston's (neare unto Wytherley) a person of good Quality, Aunt to the Earl of Pembroke, I met Mr. Grove, who wth a great deale of Trouble and sorrow ingenuously confessed the unhappyness of that fact as the greatest trouble and misfortune that ever befelle him in his Life, and did not goe about in the least to extenuate it but sayth he was not soe well dealt with all as he might have expected to have been in a gentleman's house where he was too much pressed and imprudently complyed to Drink too much strong drink wch should be a caution to him all his life. I doe believe by what I heare (if yr Lordship shall please to require it) he will be able to procure a good certificate of his life and conversation. . . . And if yr. Lordship shall please that Mr. Grove shall be cited and yr Lordship's letter objected to him, you may have his Answer, and he will confesse the Fact upon which he must lie under a Monition wch I am prone to forsee he will be very cautious in observing".[3]

---

[1] Stephens to Tenison, 4 December 1693. Lambeth MSS. 942, f. 5.
[2] Ibid.
[3] Ibid., f. 56

Grove certainly had many supporters in his parish, and on 28 December General Vincent, one of his flock, sent the following letter to the Bishop. We quote liberally from it, as it provides an interesting glimpse into the church life of the period:

"May it please yr Ldship.

I having formerly experienced yr Lordship's Candour emboldens me to be further troublesome to you in behalf of my Neighbour Mr. Grove who as I understand hathe been very much misrepresented to Yr Lordship viz. as a great frequenter of Ale houses and getting drunk, does continue so for ye space of 10 days and in ye mean time neglects ye care of souls which he hath undertaken. This is indeed an heavy charge and did I believe it to be true I would not open my mouth in his vindication: but having had personal knowledge these 8 years past, and living not above two mile distant from him, I can testify this for him yt there is not a person in all yr Lordships Diocese yt hath been more constant in performing all parochial Dutys than he hath been; he is a constant preacher every Lord's day, twice even in ye depth of winter, which scarce any of his neighbouring Clergy are and as to ye other pts. of his accusation viz. his being a common drunkard I would intrete yr Lordship, to allow me to speake in his defence yt it's a scandal he deserves not. I question not but by God's Grace he will make good his promise to yr Lordship of being cautious for the future; therefore let me beg of yr Lordship not to give occasion to ye Enemys of ye Church to triumph over his Warrior's Reputation, by hearkening to an accusation wch is in a great measure false and inflicting punishment accordingly".[1]

The testimony of the churchwardens and the petitions of the parishioners prevailed. Tenison tempered justice with mercy, accepted Grove's promise to be "cautious for ye future", and allowed him to remain at Witherly, which he did till his death at the age of ninety in 1745.[2]

The above case may appear trivial and unimportant, but it is indicative of Tenison's general policy of keeping a close eye over his clergy, and where slackness or irregularity was proved, of applying ecclesiastical censure. Examples could be multiplied.[3]

[1] Vincent to Tenison, 28 December 1693. Lambeth MSS. 942, f. 16.
[2] Henry Grove was Rector of Witherly from 1689 to 1745. He married one Marie Buchnade, the daughter of a former rector. Parish Records. See also J. Nichols, *The History, etc., of Leicestershire.*
[3] Instances of incumbents informed upon seem to be fairly common at this period. We quote the following from Tenison's papers at Lambeth. (a) Certificate of the inhabitants of the Parish of Snave of Mr. Brushnell their Minister: 14 September

Thus George Vaux, one of his clergy, who had fallen into "ill fame", waited on the Bishop on 3 February 1693, and was induced to resign his living into his diocesan's hands, on condition (we quote Vaux's own words) that he was granted "Ys favour, yt I shou'd continue till Candlemas and receive ye profit without any molestation, bec. yre would then be due to me as much as would discharge ye cure and Taxes".[1] Vaux's difficulties, however, were not to disappear so simply. Things had already gone too far, for while he journeyed to wait on Tenison, an ecclesiastical court was already proceeding against him, and a report of their findings awaited him on his return. Considerably "discouraged" and very much "indisposed for several days after by reason of ye sharpnesse of the weather", he went himself to the Court at Rushden, in hopes that it might be induced to reverse his suspension, "considering", so he wrote to Tenison, "yt yr L'shp. promis'd me ovr & ovr yt I shou'd enjoy that living till Candlemas wth out any trouble wtevr"; but despite this, he complained, "wn I came yre [i.e. to the Court] I found myselfe in worse Circumstances than before. Whereupon . . . things have bin carried on so severely agst. me quite contrary to yr Lp's Intentions & promisse". As a result of the Court's decision, Vaux was unable to collect any dues, and on 3 February he wrote indignantly to the Bishop complaining how much he had depended on his lordship's promise, and asking that he might have a letter from him giving him authority to collect the dues from his tenants.[2] What happened in Vaux's case we have been unable to discover. The incident certainly helps to show that efforts were being made to secure a measure of efficiency amongst the parochial clergy in the diocese of Lincoln.

To be fair to the clergy of this diocese we need to remember that the tasks which confronted them were by no means easy. There had been much unsettlement of late, and in 1690 seventeen clergy from the diocese were deprived for refusing to take the oaths of allegiance, while "there was another and much larger body of nonjurors in the county among the popish recusants".[3] As to the condition of many of the churches we learn that

1695. Lambeth MSS. 942. (b) Certificate given by Nic. Toke of Mr. John Lodge, Rector of Bocking, 11 October 1695. Lambeth MSS. 942, f. 105. (c) Certificate given by the neighbouring clergy of Phil. Jones A.M. Vicar of Addington in the County of Surrey, 14 October 1695. Lambeth MSS. 942, f. 10.

[1] Vaux to Tenison, 3 February 1693. Lambeth MSS. 953, f. 16.
[2] *Ibid.*
[3] *The Victoria History of the County of Lincoln*, 1906, p. 69.

"in some . . . the Common Prayer was seldom read, or not
the whole, or not in due order, and the fasts and feasts of the
church unaccountably neglected. The churches were in some
cases wholly disused and in more nastie condition than any
cottager would keep his house, and communicants still expected
to be served in their seats in spite of the great inconvenience of
consecrating in the alley of a church and delivering the bread
and wine over the heads and treading on the feet of those that
kneel. Among the moral defects against which the clergy were
warned intemperance has a prominent place, and alehouse and
taverns evidently still offered temptations. But the covetousness
of men of great preferments which led them to cheapen curates
and contract with them for £20 to £30 a year was still more
severely censured and stigmatised as a scandalous practice
which makes scandalous curates".[1]

To meet such problems Tenison believed in the application of
the law both secular and ecclesiastical, and later as Archbishop
he refused on more than one occasion to use his influence to
prevent clergy being prosecuted in a secular court, when their
offence fell within its jurisdiction.[2] In the diocese of Lincoln,
however, even the most diligent of the clergy were handicapped
by the unsettlement of the Commonwealth, and the consequent
multiplication of sects. As an illustration of these difficulties we
quote the following interesting extract from a letter of Edward
Bowerman, Vicar of Caddington in Bedfordshire,[3] written on
17 December 1692 in response to an enquiry from Tenison as to
conditions in his parish. It gives a glimpse into the life of a country
parish which more official documents do not always provide, and
its interest may perhaps excuse its length.

"Your Lordship commands me to write at large to you and
Acquaint you with the State of ye People committed to my care
and ye folly and madness of such of them as are most remarkable, with my weak endeavours among them. I most willingly
obey, because I shall have an opportunity to let your Lordship
see how much I need your assistance.[4] . . . I found ye people

[1] *The Victoria History of the County of Lincoln*, pp. 70, 71.
[2] See S.P.D. William III, 22 July 1697.
[3] See *Alumni Oxonienses*, i. 409.
[4] The parishioners claimed the right to nominate their own vicar, and were much
offended when the Dean and Chapter of St. Paul's, the patrons, set aside their choice.
After the death of his predecessor, the parishioners in fact appointed themselves as
the real incumbent "and it was a matter of surprise to them", Bowerman wrote, "in
ye midst of their hopes, to see me who was altogether unknown to any of them,
come among them".

over run with ignorance and irreligion and wholly unconcern'd
for their souls, that one would think they had conversed their
lives with ye wild men of America not with Englishmen and
Christians, and many of them not acquainted with ye very
principles of ye Christian Religion; when I discoursed with
some of the more knowing sort, they were so far from relishing
ye severer Precepts of Christianity that I could scarce convince
them anything was their duty that gave any disturbance to
their carelessness and ease, or thwarted their inclinations:
and antient Custom is in such esteem among them that they
often plead it for irreverence. Ye Minister of Kensworth told me,
that a Christmas last, looking out of his Chamber window, he
discovered some potts of ale conveyed into ye Church, as he
supposed to ye Ringers there, & unwilling to allow such
practices he went to them, found them in ye chancell, drinking,
smoking and making merry; he also told me that they used to
play at Cards on ye Communion Table, and to defile ye Chancel
by easing of Nature there, as if they had been in an house or
office; ye Glaziers, he said, frequently made use of ye Communion Table to work on: in Easter last, when ye Parishioners
were met to chuse Churchwardens at Flamstead [another
neighbouring church] ye minister at his coming in was amazed
to behold a great number of people in ye Church and Chancell
with their Hatts on, smoking and drinking, and when he
expressed his indignation at their profane rudeness, ye Clark
very gravely (with his pipe in his mouth) told him that it was
their custom there these three score years. They have every
year on that day a sort of Fair in ye Churchyard, and another
in Whitsun week! In Lent last at Eaton [another parish near
Dunstable] while ye minister was preaching a funeral sermon
. . . two came into ye Church and arrested one of ye Congregation who after great disturbance and many blows, was rescued
from them chiefly by ye valour of a woman who with much
activity flew over the seats and with great bravery set upon and
overcame the disturber. My congregation is increased to above
200 and ye number of communicants at Christmas last was 24:[1]
there were not many at my first coming, ten in ye Parish that
had ever received ye Sacrament; many of them had strange
notions, and mean and contemptible thoughts of it. One
Butterfield, who died about a year since, used to take it by
himself in brown bread and small beer: another said he would
soon as drink the devil's health as receive ye Sacrament . . .

[1] The population of the village in 1801 was 1073. Carlisle, *Topographical Dictionary
of England*, 1808.

another replied that she understood what belonged to ye Sacrament as well as I did. I asked her why was ye Sacrament of the Lord's Supper ordained; She answered that Christ had ordered that women that were brought to bed sh'd receive it and this was all ye account she could give me of it . . . During ye time of ye solemn office of Baptism one Hossey, a farmer, stood up, and taking a man that sate next to him, repeated ye words of Baptism after me, making in derision, a cross upon ye man's forehead".[1]

This letter shows only too well the legacy of the Commonwealth period, which with its emphasis on individualism had led to an independence in religion which spurned the traditional forms of Anglican worship. Edward Bowerman's parishioners at this time had doubtless ejected their own minister, and appointed one more or less of their own choosing: hence they were loath to surrender this privilege into the hands of the proper patrons, the Dean and Chapter of St. Paul's.

Finance was then, as now, a problem which oppressed many of the clergy, and at this time it was aggravated by strong sectarian feeling. The following letter from one Marshal, Vicar of Cockerington St. Mary's with Alvingham, written to Tenison in December 1693, is typical of many which the Bishop doubtless received.

"I blush to acquaint you how the Revenues of my Vicaridge are curtail'd by ye Enemies of our Church, how an Anabaptist has engross'd ye greatest part of ye Lordship, who, I am confident, would almost ruin himself to hinder me of my dues; and how Mr. Scrope had 60 Acres in his own hand last year, wch formerly paid three pounds ye annū Tythe, for which his steward will needs perswade me there is but three shillings sixpence due wch I must take or have nothing. The trouble of these Livings would be an intollerable burden were it not attended with some delight and an honest Ambition to do good; but ye vexations I have in collecting ye Revenues belonging to him yt waits at ye Altar, make me ready to yield, and perhaps were it not for this Consideration that I was ordain'd to a Cure I should not be willing to preach twice every Sunday and give twelve pence a day for a horse, for a small (but troublesome) Income of £20 ye Annum. But I offend your Lordship's patience by these tedious complaints and therefore begging pardon for my rudeness shall cease to be further troublesome"[2]

[1] Bowerman to Tenison, 17 December 1692. Lambeth MSS. 933, f. 9.
[2] Marshall to Tenison, 16 December 1693. Lambeth MSS. 952, f. 13.

This letter was conveyed in person to the Bishop at Buckden, with a request that the young man who took it might be admitted to Holy Orders. "The Bearer thereof, together with the ensuing Lines", Marshal wrote,

> "most humbly present themselves to your Lordship's Candour, not without some confidence that your Goodness (which is never more illustrious than when it extends itself to the most undeserving Objects and delights and triumphs in new Experiments and discoveries of its own greatness) will excuse ye importunities and imperfections and grant ye Requests of both. The young man has not acquired any good habit of speaking, nor I believe will ever become a Chrysostom, but I hope that upon your Lordship's Scrutiny he will be found to be more than either his words or gestures do at first promise; and yt being under ye Eye and direction of a kind Uncle he may be considerably serviceable to ye Church",[1]

and doubtless, we can't help surmising, to his uncle. Whether the request was acceded to we cannot tell, nor is the young man's name quoted. We must leave to another chapter Tenison's attitude to this question of ordination.[2]

Tenison remained active throughout his three years at Lincoln, and we get a glimpse of his energy in the following extract from a letter written on 19 September 1694 to "ye honourable Mrs. Buscawen at her house in Amen-Corner, London".

> "I have bin latelie in the Fenns as fare as Spalding in South-Holland in Lincolnshire", he wrote, "A Country wch people speak dismally of, but it has agreed with me very well, & I found the People better Christiās then I expected, & good numbers were confirm'd. I am now as soon as the Ordination is past, thinking to prepare for London, & then I shall sometimes interrupt my Friends at Amen-Corner".[3]

Tenison did not stay at Lincoln long enough to do more than begin the work of reform, but he certainly prepared the way for the more solid achievement of James Gardiner (1637–1705), who would have found his task more difficult had he immediately followed Barlow. On the whole, there seems to be little reason to doubt the substantial justice of the somewhat

---

[1] Marshall to Tenison, 16 December 1693. Lambeth MSS. 953, f. 13.
[2] See Chap. 7, p. 144.
[3] Tenison to the Hon. Mrs. Buscawen (now spelt Boscawen), 19 September 1694. Private Papers.

Anne, wife of Thomas Tenison, Archbishop of Canterbury, and daughter of the Rev. Richard Love, D.D., Chaplain to King Charles I, and Master of Corpus Christi College, Cambridge,

I declare yt ye Title of King was forct upon
mee & yt it was very much contrary to my opinion
when I was proclaimd.   For ye Satisfaction of
this world I doe declare that ye Late King told me that
Hee was never married to my Mother.
Haveing declard this I hope yt the King who is now
will not let my Children suffer on this Account. And to
this I put my hand this fifteenth day of July
1685.
                                        Monmouth

        Declard by Himselfe & Signd in the presence of Us.

                        Jran: Elie.
                    Tho: Batherbrly
                    Tho: Tenison
                    Geo: Hooper

Declaration by the Duke of Monmouth acknowledging his
illegitimacy, written on the day of execution, showing the signature
of Thomas Tenison.

eulogistic summary of his work given by his contemporary biographer:

"Having been Consecrated and put into possession of the see of Lincoln, this truly primitive Bishop began to make a narrow inspection into the abuses that had been unredress'd by his Predecessor, and to seek out for the same Opportunities of dispensing his Charity there, as he had laid hold in his own Parish, which he before had the care of . . . he began incessantly to do the work of an Evangelist, and other Things requisite to so great and high a calling, as making a strict Inquisition into the Behaviour of his Inferior Clergy, causing his Archdeacon to make a narrow Inspection into any Breaches made upon the Canons by Parish Officers etc. enquiring into the Wants and necessities of the Poor and providing for this after the most ample but legal Harvest".[1]

White Kennett says the same thing, though more briefly, when he states that he "restored a neglected large Diocese to some Discipline and good Order".[2]

Part II Archbishop of Canterbury (1694–1715)

On 22 November 1694, Archbishop Tillotson died, recommending Tenison as his successor, and the Bishop of Lincoln, after having refused an Archbishopric in Ireland,[3] followed him to the primacy, once again, if we can believe White Kennett, with great "Reluctancy".[4] On 6 December he kissed hands on his promotion and on the 8th he "received the compliments of the nobility and gentry". News of the appointment soon got abroad and a newsletter to the Earl of Derwentwater written on 8 December stated:

"On Thursday night last before the Council rose his Majesty was pleased to nominate Dr. Tenison, Bishop of Lincoln, to the Archbishopric of Canterbury, to the general satisfaction of all, he being esteemed a person of great learning, piety, charity and wonderful moderation, and one who in the last reign was a common mark to the Romish priests and Jesuits".[5]

Evelyn paid tribute in his diary on 9 December: "I had news that my dear and worthy friend Dr. Tenison, Bishop of Lincoln,

---

[1] *Memoirs of the Life and Times*, etc., p. 20.
[2] White Kennett, *A Complete History of England*, iii. 676.
[3] See Chap. 16, p. 364.
[4] White Kennett, *A Complete History of England*, iii. 676.
[5] S.P.D. William and Mary, 8 December 1694, vol. 85, p. 290.

is made Archbishop of Canterbury, for which I thank God and rejoice, he being most worthy of it for his learning, piety and prudence".[1]

The appointment was not unexpected, though Queen Mary, supported by Burnet, "pressed the King and Shrewsbury to name Stillingfleet", but without success, since "Tenison was preferred as less high in his notions and temper" and also, perhaps, as more robust in health.[2]

Garth expressed the feelings of all good Whigs when he wrote later:

> Within this isle for ever must I find
> Disasters to distract my restless mind :
> Good Tenison's celestial Piety
> At last has raised him to the sacred See.[3]

Tories, of course, were not so pleased, and some of their comments were far from flattering, as for example:

> Tho' his old solid Grace was preferr'd 'cross the water
> For tacking the Tyde, and well trimming the matter,
> Yet does it not follow that the Church of St. Martin
> Makes her Rectors all Prelates for being uncertain.[4]

Tenison was elected Archbishop of Canterbury on 15 January 1695, and this was confirmed on the following day at St. Mary le Bow, London, when there were present the Bishops of London, Durham, Winchester, Coventry and Lichfield, Rochester, Exeter, Salisbury, Bangor, and Ely.[5] He deferred his installation, "being satisfied there was nothing depended on it", until 16 May when he went down to Canterbury "and was installed in person" in the Cathedral, the first to be so since the Reformation.[6]

For the next twenty years Tenison was to hold this position of pre-eminence in the Church of England, and if he sometimes lacked imagination, he certainly displayed great industry in the

---

[1] Evelyn, *Diary*, etc., ii. 333.

[2] Clarke and Foxcroft, *Life of Gilbert Burnet*, p. 329.

[3] Garth, *The Dispensary*, 1699.

[4] Quoted, Hearne, *Collections*, ii. 358. Other Tory comments were equally unfavourable. Thomas Bruce, Earl of Ailesbury (1655?–1741), writes in his *Memoirs* (1890), i. 299: " . . . when he was promoted it was commonly said that they had advanced a good parish priest (for that was all he was good for) to make the worst of Archbishops; for the see of Canterbury was never filled so unworthily since the first institution, and I do not scruple to say that it was Doctor Thomas Tennison that without sense or judgment, arrived to that high station . . . [p. 300]. In reality they advanced him for what he really was, a very tool. He lived many years despised by all people of one party or the other that had good sense".

[5] "Act Books of the Archbishops of Canterbury", IV, 530, 531, 536.

[6] E. Sydall to Wake, 11 January 1716. Christ Church. Lincoln Correspondence. Wake Papers, I.

first years of his archiepiscopate. We propose to devote the rest of this chapter to a brief account of his internal administration of the diocese of Canterbury.

Immediately after his enthronement in Canterbury Cathedral on 16 May 1695, Tenison embarked on a visitation of his diocese, and confirmed as he went. We are fortunate in possessing an "Account of ye Primary Visitation" which we append below.[1] It shows that he began at Canterbury, on the same day as his installation, with an examination of the Dean and Chapter of the Cathedral, and that he concluded his visitation on 24 May at Sittingbourne. In Tenison's register there is a list of the articles which he submitted to the Cathedral Church of Canterbury. They are eleven in number and deal comprehensively with the life of the cathedral clergy, being particularly explicit concerning the residence of the Dean and the Chapter, their other preferments, their regular preaching at the Cathedral, and their taking of the oaths. The number, superintendence, and instruction of the choir boys, the condition of the grammar school, the repair and upkeep of the fabric of the Cathedral—all these are also diligently enquired into.[2]

[1] Lambeth MSS. 954, f. 61.

An Account of the primary Visitation May 1695

Date	Place of preach.	Deaneries Vis.	Dean. Conf.	Places of Conf.	Numbs.
16	Christ Church Canterbury				
17	Christ Church Canterbury	Dean and Chapter	Sandwich Westbere	Christ Church Canterbury	350
18		Dean and Chapter	Bridge Dover Eltham	Christ Church Canterbury	560
19	Christ Church Canterbury		Canterbury	Christ Church Canterbury	1200
20	St. Margaret's Canterbury	Canterbury Sandwich Westbere	Canterbury	Christ Church Canterbury	44
21	St. Margaret's Canterbury	Bridge Elham Dover	Canterbury	Christ Church Canterbury	206
22	Ashford	Charing Lympne	Charing Lympne	Ashford	590
24	Sittingbourne	Sittingbourne Sutton Ospringe	Sittingbourne Sutton Ospringe	Sittingbourne	724
					3674

[2] Tenison's register, Lambeth MSS. The Archbishop, we may perhaps notice here, presented to the cathedral "a decent and beautiful Throne" in wood, carved by Grinling Gibbons. Le Neve (p. 25) says that "the Joyners Bill of work done by John Smallwill came to £174 8. 2., and the Carver's [Gibbons] work £70". This throne lay unused in the crypt for many years, but was re-erected in the cathedral in 1892, and is now in the south transept to the choir.

During this first visitation Tenison confirmed no less than 3,674 persons and on one occasion he administered the rite to 1,200 people in the Cathedral and himself preached the sermon. All the confirmations during this visitation were held in the Cathedral, except on two occasions, when the Archbishop confirmed 590 people in the parish church at Ashford, and 724 in the parish church of Sittingbourne.

Tenison took particular care in the matter of confirmation, and endeavoured to see that it was all performed "decently and in order"—a difficult thing to ensure in view of the large numbers who received the rite. We are fortunate in possessing an account of his practice in this respect from Thomas Brett, who as an incumbent in the diocese of Canterbury must have observed it at first hand. His testimony to Tenison's thoroughness is of particular value, in that Brett had little sympathy with the Archbishop's Whig principles.[1] He writes:

"Our former Archbishops have thought it sufficient once in seven years or thereabouts to send some other Bishop to Visit and Confirm for them, this was done by Archbishop Sancroft; others as Archbishop Sheldon and Archbishop Tillotson have neither come themselves nor sent any other, but his present Grace of Canterbury has almost kept to the strict Letter of the Canon and visited us very frequently, and performed the office of Confirmation with the greatest Order and Solemnity imaginable; not in a hurry or huddle [sic] as I have seen it done in some other places, where hundreds have been confirmed by the Bishop that neither heard the Exhortation made, nor gave any Answer to the Questions put to them, and probably knew nothing of the Matter. But his Grace, my present Lord Archbishop, caused the Chancell Doors to be shut, and admitted the people Parish by Parish, and none came in but in the Company of their own Minister, who stood by them whilst the Preface to the Confirmation was read, and when the Questions concerning their Ratification of their Baptismal Vow was put to them, he took care that every one of them should answer with an Audible Voice according to the Directions of the Liturgy, and satisfied the [Arch]Bishop that every one he had brought to be Confirmed did so Answer. And all this was done and the whole Office read to every Company particularly after they were admitted into the Chancell. So that nothing could be more solemn, Decent and Regular. However there lies the Misfortune, that his Grace's time would not permit him to

[1] See Chap. 9, p. 203.

Visit and Confirm at more than five principal Towns of his Diocese, so that at least one half of the People could not be brought to receive this Ordinance".

Brett concludes by saying that Tenison "has done more than any other of his Predecessors for these hundred years".[1]

As for ordinations, it was not customary at this time for the Archbishop himself to ordain, and only on five occasions do we find record of his so doing, once, we may notice, during the above-mentioned visitation. A list of those for whom he obtained ordination from other bishops (taken from the " Act Books etc. of Canterbury ") will be found below.[2] From this list it will be seen

[1] Brett, T., *Account of Church Government and Governors*, 2nd ed., 1710, p. 244.

[2] Date	By whom ordained	Number	
1695 Feb. 28	Bp. of London	1 D[eacon]	
May 19	Archbishop of C.	1 P[riest]	
1696 May	London	1 D	
1697 Feb. 20	Rochester (or any other bp.)	1 D	
May 25	Rochester	1 P	
June 11	London	1 P	
Dec. 15	London	1 D	
1698 Mar. 16	Gloucester	2 D	
Mar. 17	London	1 P	
Oct. 5	London	1 P	
1699 Feb. 25	Archbishop of C. (in Chapel at Lambeth)	2 D	
Feb. 28	London	1 P	
Mar. 3	London	1 P	
Sep. 19	London	1 P	
Dec. 18	Ely	1 P	
1700 May 22	London	1 P	
May 25	London	1 P	
1701 Dec. 18	Archbishop of C.	1 P	
1702 Feb. 15	Archbishop of C.	1 P	
Sep. 14	Lincoln	1 D	
[?]	Gloucester	1 P	
1704 May [?]	London	1 P	
Trinity Sun.	London	1 P	
1705 May	Chichester	1 P	
1704 Dec. 22	London	1 P	
1705 May	Chichester	1 P	
1706 Aug. 11	Archbishop of C.	1 D	
Sep. 17	Lincoln	1 P	
1707 May	.	1 D	
1708 Jan. 21	Norwich	1 P	
1712 Mar. 13	Norwich	1 D	
Dec. 18	London	1 P	
Dec. 19	Norwich	1 D	1 P
1713 May 27	Norwich	1 D	
May 29	Ely	1 P	
Oct. 2	Norwich	1 P	
Dec. 16	Norwich	1 P	
Dec. 19	Norwich	1 D	
1714 Feb. 18	Norwich	1 D	
Sep. 16	Norwich	1 P	
Dec. 16	Norwich	1 P	1 D
1715 Mar. 2	Lincoln	2 P	
May 2	Bangor	1 P	

that it was the practice of the Archbishop, as he was "not ordaining this solemn season", to grant letters dimissory to one of his brethren. The responsibility for ordination, in theory at least, then rested upon the ordaining bishop and the injunction was invariably added in the register: "if after examination he shall find fit".[1] Usually, those whose ordination the Archbishop secured through letters dimissory were licensed to work in his own diocese, although there were exceptions, as, for example, when a student was ordained in 1704 to serve as a chaplain on H.M.S. *Weymouth*.

Tenison believed firmly in reserving ecclesiastical preferment in his diocese (as elsewhere) to those who were thorough-going in their Protestantism, and by this he understood a supporter of the Revolution and an upholder of the Act of Uniformity. Thus Thomas Atkin and Edward Derring, when ordained deacons by the Archbishop in the chapel at Lambeth on 25 February 1699, declared their attachment to the Act of Uniformity in the following terms: "I . . . do declare that I will conforme to the Liturgie of the Church of England as it is now by law established", and this declaration was duly entered into the register.[2] The Archbishop was always vigilant in this matter, neglect of which was one of the charges against Thomas Watson.[3] Thus when John Gray, one of his clergy, applied to him in 1699 for collation to the Vicarage of Terring, he "first subscribed and declared as in and by the Act of Uniformity is enjoyned ye sev¹ Oaths of Fidelity and Allegiance to his Matie . . . denying all Foreign Jurisdicon, agst Simony, for Canonical Obedience and of Residence".[4]

In 1706 Tenison issued another series of "Articles of Visitation and Enquiry to be administered to the Churchwardens and Sidesmen of every Parish within the Diocese of Canterbury". These articles were of the usual kind, except, perhaps, that they were a little more comprehensive in character than those issued by some bishops. They consist of the following sections:

1. The church and its properties (font, communion table, etc.). Of interest here is the order to provide (in addition to the

---

[1] Archbishop Wake writes, however, in his "Directions in relation to Orders" (5 June 1716): "That you [the Bishops] admit not any person to holy orders upon letters dimissory, unless they are granted by the bishop himself, or guardian of the spiritualities *sede vacante*; nor unless it be expressed in such letters, that he who grants them, has fully satisfied himself of the title and conversation of the person to whom the letter is granted". Quoted, R. Phillimore, *The Ecclesiastical Law of the Church of England*, 2nd ed., 1895, i. 113.
[2] "Act Books of the Archbishops of Canterbury", IV, 613.
[3] See Chap. 10.
[4] "Act Books of the Archbishops of Canterbury", IV, 603.

register for baptisms, weddings, and burials) a book in which there could be entered "strange" preachers and the name of the bishop who licensed them.

2. The churchyard, houses, and glebe.

3. The ministers. Here the questions are numerous. The churchwardens were asked if the minister was regularly licensed; if he resided on his cure, and how long during the year he was absent; when absent, who then served the cure; whether he wore a surplice "and other habit according to his degree"; whether he used the offices as prescribed in the Book of Common Prayer reverently "and with an audible and distinct voice"; whether he celebrated communion three times a year, baptized regularly, visited the sick and catechized the youth; whether he announced fast days and four times a year read the act against profane swearing; lastly, was he sober, and studious and did he avoid unlawful games?

4. Parishioners. The questions under this head provide an interesting comment on contemporary manners. Were the congregation reverent in church; were there any loiterers, or any who never attended a place of worship? How many failed to communicate three times a year; was there any quarrelling over seats in church? Were there any assemblies of Dissenters or Papists in the parish?

5. Parish clerk and sexton.

6. Schoolmasters and schools. The questions here, when we remember Tenison's enthusiasm for education, are particularly instructive. What schoolmasters were there in the parish, he asked; were they licensed, and did they bring their children to divine service? Was there a hospital, almshouse, or free school? Were there any in the parish who practised physic and midwifery, and were such duly licensed?

7. Ecclesiastical officers. The questions here were mainly concerned to see that these people faithfully discharged their legal duties. Particularly we may note the following: Did the ecclesiastical officers see that any who lectured or ministered in the diocese first subscribed, in the presence of the bishop, to the three articles mentioned in Canon 36? Did peculiar and inferior courts exhibit the original copies of wills into the Registry Office of the diocese?

8. Churchwardens and sidesmen. Once again we are here given an insight into contemporary procedure. Were the churchwardens of the parish yearly chosen by joint consent of the minister and parishioners or one by the minister and the other by the parishioners? Had the preceding churchwardens

delivered up a just account of the monies? Did they, with the curate, provide sufficient bread and wine for communion, and did the churchwardens ever dispose of money at the offertory without the concurrence of the minister?[1]

Right up to the end of his days the Archbishop kept in touch with the needs of his diocese through his archdeacons, particularly Thomas Green, Archdeacon of Canterbury,[2] and his kinsman Edward Tenison, Archdeacon of Maidstone. He always preserved a zealous and watchful eye over the behaviour of his clergy and although the state of his health in the latter years of his life more or less confined him to Lambeth, this did not prevent him working through his subordinates. In November 1715, for example, he received information that a certain Benson, Curate of Deal: (1) refused to use the prayer for the king; (2) was a great party man; (3) employed a curate named Funifer, who had turned Papist in the reign of James II. Tenison immediately instructed John Bowles, a justice of the peace, to conduct investigations, which he appears to have done with some thoroughness. As a result, the "Mayor, Juratts and Common Council men of Deal" testified that Benson was loyal to the existing dynasty, and never meddled with politics,[3] while Bowles himself (supported by Thomas Hone, a fellow justice of the peace) affirmed that he did in fact use the prayer for the king.[4] Benson also wrote to the Archbishop on his own behalf enclosing a certificate from his parishioners, and also from William Stanley (1647-1731), Dean of St. Asaph, who, having employed him as a curate for nine years in Hertfordshire, testified to his general good behaviour.[5] For himself Benson pointed out: (1) that he had come to Deal as the result of an invitation from Archdeacon Green; (2) he had always held and expressed loyal sentiments; (3) when he left out the collect for the king (as on Christmas Day) he did so only for the sake of brevity as he was single handed; (4) as to his curate Mr. Funifer (a) he had found him there when he came, (b) he didn't know he had been a Papist, and (c) the parishioners liked him.[6]

---

[1] "Articles of Visitation and Enquiry", etc., Tenison, 1706, pp. 1-6.
[2] Thomas Green (1658-1738), later Bishop of Ely and Norwich. Brett, writing in 1710, said that Tenison had made three visitations of his diocese. *Account of Church Government and Governors*, p. 235.
[3] Lambeth MSS. 941, f. 54.
[4] *Ibid.*, f. 55.
[5] *Ibid.*, f. 56.
[6] Benson to Tenison, Lambeth MSS. 941, f. 57. Benson does not seem to have been the vicar of Deal, for there is no reference to him in the parish records.

The charge certainly appears to have been without sufficient foundation and the result of personal malice.

Poverty amongst incumbents was as much a feature of the Church in Tenison's day as now, and he did his best to alleviate cases of acute distress. He was able to do this in a small way through a legacy left to him and Simon Patrick "to be laid out in some works of charity", and they decided to use it "for the Benefit of poor Vicars towards supporting their insufficient Maintenance". Thus for several years "they distributed the sum of One hundred Pounds among Twenty poor Vicars, one half in the diocese of Canterbury, the other in Ely, in equal portions of Five pounds to each vicar". In 1697 Tenison and Patrick made over the principal (which then amounted to about £2,400) to Sir Nathan Wright, Lord Keeper, and to other trustees, in order to make the fund "secure and continual".[1] We may also note here that by will Tenison left £1,000 to the governors of Queen Anne's bounty, on condition that they added another £1,000 for the augmentation of five stated livings in the diocese of Canterbury.[2]

With Thomas Green, his Archdeacon of Canterbury (whose father he had known when he was the minister of St. Peter Mancroft), Tenison was on terms of close friendship, a fact which can be seen from his leaving him in his will "one of ye great gilt Tankards wch I bought at Bp. Barlow's executors". Hence Green was only too pleased to co-operate with the Archbishop in his efforts to secure efficiency in the parochial clergy. This is illustrated in such a letter as the following, written after he had undertaken a visitation in the Archdeaconry of Canterbury in September 1715:

"I came home on Saturday night from my Parochial Visitation wch was three days sooner than I intended, being so much wearied with ye fatigue of a whole fortnight's continual motions, yt I thought it better to defer ye rest for three or four days than run ye hazard of a feaver, wch I was in some fears of. On Thursday next I intend to proceed on ye remaining 15 Parishes having visited 55 in this last fortnight. I shall think my trouble and charge doubly recompensed by ye good effects wch I hope from it. Everybody is sensible of ye alterations it has produced in ye Churches and houses, so great, yt I

---

[1] White Kennett, *The Case of Impropriations and of the augmentation of Vicarages*, 1704, p. 310. It was Tenison who persuaded White Kennett to write this volume.
[2] Lambeth MSS. 952, f. 29.

believe I may without vanity say, yt as to ye former especially, there is no Diocese in England will be to compare with that of yr Grace for ye cleanness and decency of them. It has raised an ambition in ye Parishes of striving wch shall make their character finest. I have been received everywhere with all imaginable respect and civility. I have observed several things wch I think it proper to be layd before your Grace, but that I will do all together when I have finished ye whole; And if ye weather holds good, I will endeavour to come up to London for a few days to wait upon yr Grace wn I shall be able more conveniently to represent all things to yr Grace than I can do by letter".[1]

Green continued his visitation the following week and on 25 September informed the Archbishop that he had completed his task, and that he would soon be in London with "many things to lay before yr Grace & Severall to begg your advice in".[2]

It was probably in this last year of his life that Tenison took a tender farewell of the clergy of his own diocese in an *Oratio*, in the course of which he recalled his own work among them, particularly in relation to the "catholic menace". We quote the opening paragraph of his draft:

"It hath pleased Providence, much beyond my Expectatiō & my merit to make me a Shepherd to a Flock. The same h[as] given me constant inclination to watch over It & to bless my endeavours with some success. Till my health & str[ength] declined with my years, I visited you in person, & since ye decay of ym, I have done so by 2 of my worthy Bps my Bn. I am sensible yt ye time of my finall departure is drawing on & yt I shall see yr Faces no more in that public manner. Something, however, I would attempt, in order to ye expressing my tender Love towards you & my Solicitude for yr spiritual Benefit. If you have seen any evill in my Example I solemnly charge you studiously to avoid it, if any Good . . . imitate and give God glory. I have often thought of the insignificance of my talents & ye weight of my Employment & wished in my hart yt I had rather been a literal then a metaphorical Shepherd. But yet, it was my hopes & my comforts yt ye almighty & most merciful God would vouchsafe me his assistance & generously accept of ye sinceritie of my endeavours".[3]

[1] Green to Tenison, 20 September 1715. Lambeth MSS. 953, f. 107.
[2] Green to Tenison, 25 September 1715. Lambeth MSS. 941, f. 49. These letters show that though Tenison was confined to Lambeth at the end of his life, he by no means lost touch with the affairs of his diocese.
[3] Lambeth MSS. 1037, f. 17. See also Chap. 8, p. 76, for his strictures on the Catholics, which form the main part of the above "Oratio".

PART II

CHAPTER 7

THE REFORM OF THE CLERGY

IT is not easy, as sometimes supposed, to generalize on the condition of the Church of England when Tenison became Archbishop of Canterbury. The preceding fifty years had been a time of unrest and excitement. The Church had experienced power under Laud, persecution under the Commonwealth, and privilege under the Clarendon Code. The cynicism and immorality of the age, if it called out the protest of some of the better minds, also led to a low conception of office within the Church. Contemporary pamphlets, even if they must be interpreted with caution, give us a vivid picture of some abuses. In 1689 a pamphlet which had already become notorious was republished under the title of *Lachrymae Ecclesiae*.[1] The author was a zealous churchman, and he particularly inveighed against the mis-government of the bishops, and the selfishness of the clergy. It was their remissness which occasioned the tears—the sins of simony, non-residence, and pluralism, to say nothing of profanity. He reminded absentee incumbents that Christ's command was that they themselves should preach the Gospel, and not that they should send their curates to do so. The keynote of the whole attack was struck by the frontispiece, in which an afflicted woman with a church in her hand uttered the lamentation, "All seek their own".

Another pamphlet, published about the same time, "Mrs. Abigail; or an Account of a Female Skirmish between the Wife of a Country Squire and the Wife of a Doctor of Divinity", expresses the same point of view though in more violent language. The writer complained bitterly that the rank and file of the clergy were recruited from the lower orders, that they married chambermaids, and yet set themselves up as the equal of the squire! The form of this attack is contemptible, but it does show that the Church had lost respect.

As Archbishop of Canterbury, it was Tenison's especial care to safeguard the welfare of the Church as a whole; to endeavour to improve the personnel of the clergy; and to enter into relations

[1] This pamphlet was first published in 1663 under the title of "Ichabod" and was attributed by some contemporaries (and Dean Plumptre) to Bishop Ken; but his authorship is rejected by Round and Anderdon.

with the Government for the mutual advantage of both Church and State. It is to his efforts to do this that we shall devote the following chapter.

Tenison entered upon his archiepiscopate at what may appear both a fortunate and an unfortunate time. The death of Mary in December 1694 deprived the Church of a real friend, who was genuinely interested in its reformation; but it also had the effect of throwing William into a chastened mood,[1] and making him resolve [we quote Burnet] on "becoming an exact Christian". Tenison, just promoted to the primatial see, determined to use this favourable opportunity and he called the king's attention to "the great Necessity of Preserving and Restoring the Discipline of the Church; and prevailed with his Majesty to issue out . . . Injunctions [3 February 1695] drawn up by himself, and given by the King's Majesty to the Archbishops of the Realm, to be communicated by them to the Bishops and the rest of the Clergy".[2] This thoroughly erastian procedure was the translation into practical terms of the king's undoubted constitutional position as "supreme in all causes, ecclesiastical and civil", and it was a method which the Archbishop welcomed to supplement his own authority. These "Injunctions" were eighteen in number and comprehensive in character. They aimed at a general enforcement of the canons, and represented, perhaps, what Tenison hoped his archiepiscopate might achieve. Tenison was a practical man and believed that the reform of the Church could only come through efficient administration. The first six of these "Injunctions" (which we shall quote later)[3] dealt with the enforcing the canons which regulated ordination. Then came the following:

(7) "That the Bishops shall reside in their Dioceses, and shall take care to oblige their Clergy to such Residence, as the Laws of the Land and the Canons do require, particularly the 41st Canon". (8) That those keeping curates employ only such as are licensed by the bishop of the diocese, and none are to serve without a licence. (9) That the "Abuses occasioned by Pluralities," be suppressed by seeing that only those hold them as are legally qualified, and that these fulfill the requirements of the law. (10) That the bishops superintend the lives of the clergy. (11) That the bishops oblige their clergy to hold public prayers ("not only on Holy Days"), and also to celebrate Holy Communion frequently. (12) That the bishops require the clergy to

---

[1] See Chap. 17, p. 402.   [2] *Memoirs of the Life and Times*, etc. p. 42.
[3] See p. 145.

see that "the Lord's Day be Religiously observ'd" and that they themselves set a good example. (13) That the bishops require the clergy to visit the sick, and (14) to catechize the children. (15) That the bishops confirm regularly at the triennial visitations. (16) That the archdeacons undertake their visitations personally and live within the bounds of their jurisdiction. (17) That no commutation of penance be allowed except by express order of the bishop "which shall be declared in open Court", and all such commutations to be devoted to charitable purposes. (18) That no licence for marriages without banns shall be granted by any ecclesiastical judge without first taking oaths of two sufficient witnesses, and also security for performing the conditions of the licence according to Canons 102 and 103.[1]

If these "Injunctions" did nothing else, they certainly showed that the new Archbishop, in so far as he could, intended to enforce the canons, and that he was eager to co-operate with the secular authorities to do this. Their practical result, of course, depended on how far the bishops acted on them in their diocesan administration. Tenison therefore proceeded to follow up these "Injunctions" with a "Letter" written on 16 July 1695, in his capacity as metropolitan, to the suffragan bishops of his own province "recommending such Rules and Orders as if well observed, would tend weightily to the Peace and Honour of the Established Church".[2] These "Rules and Orders" which Tenison had drawn up in co-operation with a few bishops at Lambeth, and concerning which he consulted Sharp, Archbishop of York,[3] were modelled on the "Injunctions", but they were more explicit and dealt with matters of social as well as ecclesiastical importance. We quote a short summary of them.

(1) That the bishops take special care to see that the late acts of parliament against profane cursing and swearing be publicly read, and that they be referred to in the sermon. (2) That all other relevant acts be read in church. (3) That the bishops require the clergy in their prayer before the sermon to keep to Canon 55, since some omitted the king's title and others did not pray for the bishop. (4) That they require the clergy to catechize on Sunday afternoons. (5) That they be careful when licensing to benefices to prevent all simoniacal

---

[1] See Chap. 13, p. 290.   [2] *Memoirs of the Life and Times*, etc., p. 53.
[3] Writing to Sharp, on 4 July, Tenison said: "I am thinking of a Circular Lr for ye Bps of my Province; when I have finished it I will send you a Copy of it; but because that may not be till I can hear from your Grace again I desire you to send me such heads as come into your mind for my better information. If we hitt upon ye same things, it will however be so far useful as to confirme me in my opinion".

covenants in respect of glebe, tithe, or houses, and also to prevent artificial bargains by bonds of resignation. (6) That the bishops try to ensure that the salaries paid to curates be proportional to the value of the benefice. (7 and 8) That the bishops keep an eye on dilapidations, especially where there are pluralists who do not keep constant residence. Particularly did this responsibility rest upon the archdeacons, who should remember that those dispensed from residence were required to look after the parsonage house and the chancel of the church. (9) That the bishops endeavour to see that only those become surrogates who are qualified by the canons, and that illegal marriages or licences be prohibited.[1] (10) That when a minister moves out of one diocese into another, the bishop give an accurate character of him to the other, who is not to license him till he has seen it.

From these "Injunctions" and his "Letter", it will be seen that two problems loomed very large in Tenison's eyes: the securing a competent and loyal clergy and the keeping of pluralities within the bounds of the law. It is to a discussion of these that we now turn.

The ideal of the best churchmen in those days was not what we should now call a "vocational" ministry, but they were content if the clergy were serious and sober men, devoted to the interests of the Church and the Protestant Succession, and diligent in the discharge of their responsibilities. Bishop Gibson, for example, was at first reluctant to abandon a legal for an ecclesiastical career, and seems only to have done so when a little disillusioned with the prospects of the former. Tenison himself studied medicine, and Edward Tenison, a relative, writing to the Archbishop in 1713 as to the future of his son whose own inclinations were towards the law, suggested that he would send him into the Church if the Archbishop felt he would live to provide for him.[2] Such an attitude did not offend, although it was Tenison's desire that the clergy should be recruited from the best students of the day, for to produce candidates for Holy Orders was still considered the main function of the universities. Tenison did not always take an extreme view in this matter, however,[3]

---

[1] See Chap. 13.

[2] Edward Tenison to T. Tenison, 23 November 1713. Lambeth MSS. 953, f. 104. He writes ". . . but if I were so happy as to have a prospect of your Grace's life being continued till he could be qualified, I should above all things delight to dedicate him to the Service of the Church; for then I might hope for leave for resigning one of my livings, and thereby promise myself the comfort of seeing him my successor".

[3] See Chap. 12.

though when three Warner Exhibitioners at Balliol College applied to him for their allowance of £25, he granted their request, but warned them that he was "resolv'd to sign no more till ye Exhibitioners declare that they will study divinity".

The brilliant pen of Macaulay has fashioned in the main most people's conception of the country clergy during the latter part of the seventeenth and the early part of the eighteenth century. In the famous third chapter of his *History of England*—partly based on John Eachard's satirical work, *The Grounds and Occasions of the Contempt of the Clergy and Religion inquired into*, published anonymously in 1670—Macaulay says of the country rector that he was in general not regarded as, and indeed was not a gentleman: "often it was only by toiling on his glebe, by feeding swine, and by loading dungcarts, that he could obtain daily bread"; he was ill-informed, and grossly prejudiced, and he was a passionate supporter of the Tories. Macaulay contrasts with these country clergy the eminent divines to be found "at the Universities, at the great Cathedrals, and in the Capital". A more detailed and documentary study of this period, however, has done much to modify this estimate[1] (though Lecky alleges its "substantial accuracy"[2]) and Abbey and Overton write: "The wholesale censure of the whole body of the parochial clergy in the early part of the eighteenth century has been far too sweeping and severe".[3]

The responsibility for ordination in Tenison's day (as now) rested solely on the ordaining bishop, and if he were conscientious he would first satisfy himself that the college authorities (if the ordinand were so fortunate as to have attended a university) approved the prospective minister of the gospel, before he embarked on his own personal examination. Tenison saw the paramount necessity of enforcing the canons which regulated admissions to Orders, and in the "Injunctions" to which we have already referred, he set aside the first six to dealing with this problem. We quote a short abstract of them:

(1) That the 34th and 35th Canons concerning ordination be observed. (2) That every person to be admitted to Holy

[1] The first assailant of Macaulay's estimate of the country clergy was Churchill Babington in his valuable study: *Mr. Macaulay's Character of the Clergy in the latter part of the Seventeenth Century considered*, published in 1849.
[2] Lecky, *England in the Eighteenth Century*, i. 97, footnote.
[3] Abbey and Overton, *The English Church in the Eighteenth Century*, ii. 66. See also J. Beresford, *The Diary of a Country Parson*, 1926, i. Introduction.

Orders signify his name and place of abode to the bishop fourteen days before ordination so that enquiry may be made, and that he appear at the latest in Ember Week so that those selected may join together in prayer and fasting. (3) That each bishop make certain that all those ordained have a real title with a proper maintenance. (4) That each ordinand bring with him a certificate of his age taken from the parochial register. (5) That the part of the 34th Canon requiring a certificate concerning the manner of life of those seeking ordination be strictly enforced, and that the bishop exhort the clergy to be careful in the granting of such certificates. (6) That every bishop transmit between Michaelmas and Christmas to the Archbishop of the province, a list of persons ordained during the year in order that a public register may be drawn up.[1]

Tenison's "Letter" is even more explicit concerning ordination, as it might well be, since it was addressed (10 July 1695) to the bishops of his own province. In this document he urged them "to ordain no Man Deacon or Priest who hath not taken some Degree in school, in one of the Universities of this Realm unless in some extraordinary case"[2]—advice as relevant to-day perhaps as then, and representing in both cases a counsel of perfection not possible to enforce. As to letters testimonial, the bishop must not accept them unless a clause specifically be inserted by the testifier that the person was fit for Holy Orders.

Tenison also took the opportunity, in this "Letter", to particularize as to the returns which he required to be sent to Lambeth. After ordination, between Michaelmas and Christmas, the bishop must send a return under his own hand "attested by the Archdeacon and such other Clergy as assisted at the Ordination", containing the full name, place of birth, age, college, and degree of those ordained, as well as to what title and upon whose letters dimissory. Such particulars, Tenison wrote: "I undertake and promise to cause to be enter'd into a Ledger Book for that Purpose. By this means Counterfeit Orders may be detected, & Men who come up for preferment may be better understood and distinguished".[3] Such a book would indeed have been very valuable, but it is doubtful whether the proposal was carried

[1] *Memoirs of the Life and Times*, etc. p. 42. Compare these with Archbishop Wake's "Directions in relation to Orders", 5 June 1716, quoted in Phillimore, *The Ecclesiastical Law of the Church of England*, i. 112–114.
[2] *Ibid.* p. 53.
[3] *Ibid.* p. 58.

into effect. Such a discipline would not have been very easy to enforce.[1]

Too often the bishops were content with a formal obedience to the canons but not always so. Thus William Lloyd, when Bishop of Lichfield, complained to Tenison in 1697 that the authorities of St. John's College, Cambridge, gave letters testimonial simply stating that the student had behaved "modeste et studiose". Such a certificate, he maintained, was not sufficient to satisfy the canon, and their testimonials were further defective in that they were not given under the seal of the college. Hence he begged a ruling from the Archbishop. "I do thereby humbly desire yr Grace", he wrote, "to make them give their testimonials in ye words of ye Canon, or as may come up to ye sense—or be pleased to tell me yt you judge their form to be sufficient, and then I will acquiesce".[2] The point was an important one, and Tenison wrote to Dr. George Oxenden, Regius Professor of Civil Law at Cambridge and his Vicar-General, asking advice. His reply was emphatic: "The Certificate his Ldp. mentions I believe was so given because the College w'd not give a better: therefore it was justly refus'd and must allwaies be refused".[3]

The thoroughness of the bishop's personal examination of the candidate varied, of course, according to the diligence of the diocesan. Such an examination, when undertaken, was designed to test, not only the learning and intelligence of the ordinand, but also his views on certain burning religious and political questions of the day. Tenison was assiduous in this particular discharge of his duty, and we are fortunate in possessing some of the examination papers which he set to candidates for orders (or would-be pluralists). We quote as typical the two following extracts (one of which has answers attached):

(a) Unde origionem duxit Oratio dominica?
 Qua Lingua vel scripta vel dictata fuit oratio dominica?
 Repetas istius modi orationem latine.
 Repetas istius modi orationem graece.
 Quo sensu dicitur deus Pater Noster?
 Quare . . . affirmatur Patrem nostrum esse in Coelis?
 Suntne alii, praeter hunc Deum, Invocandi?

[1] No trace of such a book exists at Lambeth, unless *Notitia Episcopatuum* (Lambeth MSS. 1023, see p. 191) was designed for this purpose; but if so, it was not thus employed.
[2] Lloyd to Tenison, 31 May 1697. Lambeth MSS. 930, f. 45.
[3] Oxenden to Tenison, 2 June 1697. Lambeth MSS. 942, f. 138.

Quo sensu intelligenda est: Santificatio nominis dei?
Quid est voluntas dei? [1]

(*b*) Quid est peccatum contra conscientiam?

Peccatum contra conscientiam est cum persuasi sumus illud peccatum esse et contra Dei mandata tamen libenter committimus.

Et quid est Peccatum quod non est contra conscientiam?

Peccatum quod non est contra conscientiam cujus malitiae non sumus conscii vel de cujus natura animus noster saltem haeret in ambiguo.

An Peccata inter se differunt quoad iniquitatem cum peccatum nihil sit aliud quam legis transgressio?

Affirmo Peccata inter se differe quoad iniquitatem. (1) Peccata infirmitatis . . . differunt a peccatis commissis contra notitiam. (2) Peccata habitualia differunt a peccatis subitariis et commissis violenta tentatione.

The candidate was not expected to write long answers since he was given a paper with the questions written down and a space provided under each for a short reply. Such an examination would, of course, eliminate candidates without any theological qualifications, though no one could claim it to be particularly exhaustive.

It was the custom of the Archbishop to examine all those who desired to be instituted or collated to a living, and Gibson later summarized his usual practice (for the benefit of Archbishop Wake, his successor) as follows:

"All Institutions were granted by *Fiats* to ye Vicar General; ye party to be instituted having first been examin'd at Lambeth, and having exhibited his Orders, testimonials etc. at ye same place, with ye usual subscriptions, Oaths etc. in ye presence of his Grace. The whole business of *Collation* was perform'd, as it is in other places, by ye Archbp. only; with this difference, that for several years past[2] it hath been done in his Chamber; but, heretofore, it was given in ye Chapel (his Grace sitting within ye Rail in a Chair, and ye party collated kneeling without) with some *Collects* suitable to ye occasion".[3]

---

[1] Lambeth MSS. 952, f. 31. This paper is drawn up in Tenison's own handwriting. In its entirety it consists of seventeen questions, and is by far the most comprehensive we have found.

[2] This was written in 1716.

[3] Christ Church. Lincoln Correspondence, Wake Papers, I.

The examination which preceded institution would often be of a semi-political nature, and this can be seen from an example taken when Tenison was Bishop of Lincoln. In August 1694, Robert Kilburn applied to Tenison for institution to the Rectory of Sleaford, and was examined by the Bishop himself in the presence of three witnesses, one being a friend of the examinee. Tenison's first question concerned the external symbols of the faith as contained in the Articles of Religion. Kilburn managed to answer it, though not without difficulty. The bishop's second question was more insidious: "Quaenam est doctrina ecclesiae Anglicanae de civili magistratu secundum articulos religionis?" An awkward pause followed, during which a struggle went on between comfort and conscience: the latter triumphed and Kilburn replied: "Non recte respondebo". It is perhaps unnecessary to add that Kilburn did not become Rector of Sleaford.

Sometimes, of course, the examination was designed to test general intelligence, as it certainly was in the following case. In 1700 Tenison was required, under a writ from King's Bench, to institute a "fitt person" to the living of Stanton Fitzwarren in the diocese of Salisbury. The patron wished to present it to one Sims and the Archbishop accordingly recommended him to Burnet. The latter proceeded to examine him and sent the following report to Tenison:

"I wish you had taken Mr. Sims under examination that you might have been satisfied of the incredible grossness of his ignorance for I examined him with all possible softness and candour before four witnesses: he could not answer any one question tho' the plainest that could be put to him. I took all in writing signed by four witnesses and yet he has got the Latine Articles so by heart that he tongued the first half verbatim but in the second half he lost his thread and writ nonsense".[1]

Hence Burnet asked Tenison to nominate someone else for the living.

To what extent these "Injunctions" and "Rules & Orders" produced practical results it is not easy to determine. Certainly mere exhortation was not enough by itself, and Tenison realized

[1] Burnet to Tenison, 29 July 1700. Lambeth MSS. 952, f. 73. In his *Notitia Episco-patuum* (Lambeth MSS. 1023) Tenison transcribed another letter which he received from Burnet on this question: "There came frō you an Mr. Sims on ye 16th Instant who was us'd wth all ye gentleness, & examin'd with all ye fairness imaginable. But I found him very far from being sufficient in learning, as will appear to any competent judge; you shall see his performance undʳ his own hand".

this for he used the courts to insist on discipline and encouraged others to do the same.[1] He was convinced that to restore order to the disturbed life of the Church, the machinery of ecclesiastical government, working from the bishop through the archdeacon, must be put into operation: the fault lay not so much in Church machinery as in the failure of those responsible to work it. As to one of the most serious abuses of the day, that of pluralities, Tenison by virtue of his office as Archbishop was able to assert a certain measure of control. When Bishop of Lincoln he had already taken a stand against this abuse, and refused his consent to a dispensation from residence for one of the king's chaplains, Dr. Temple, justifying his action in a letter to Archbishop Tillotson and waiting on him at Lambeth. It is significant that although this Archbishop, under pressure from Sir Richard Temple, was willing to allow a dispensation, no such grant was in fact made.[2]

The control of pluralities was no new problem, and as early as 1215 the Church had expressed its mind definitely when it laid down "that whosoever shall take any benefice with *cure of souls*, if he shall before have obtained a like benefice, shall 'ipse jure' be deprived thereof, and if he shall contend to retain the same, he shall be deprived of the other; and the patron of the former, immediately after his accepting of the latter, shall bestow the same upon whom he shall think worthy".[3] This represented, of course, a counsel of perfection, and as so often happened in the case of canon law its sternness was modified by a papacy

---

[1] Thus the Archbishop, for example, supported Humphrey Prideaux, when Archdeacon of Suffolk, in his efforts to insist on residence and an effective discharge of parochial responsibilities. On one occasion Prideaux, encouraged by Tenison, forced a certain Keen, who had held a benefice in Suffolk for some fifteen years, to reside on his cure—though the Archdeacon hoped "that the intemperance which [Keen] hath too long indulged, will soon make way for a better man". (Prideaux to Tenison, 16 October 1695. Lambeth MSS. 942, f. 108.) The Archdeacon also appealed to the Archbishop to ensure that one Powel, who had been convicted by himself of various crimes and consequently deprived by the Bishop, should not succeed in getting this sentence reversed by the Court of the Arches, to which he had appealed. Powel appears to have been a somewhat bizarre figure, to say the least. "He was ye person", Prideaux wrote to Tenison, "that about 2 years ago was bound over to ye Old Bailey for a very scandalous act of incontinency with a certain Dutch woman and thereby gave great occasion for many to reflect upon ye whole order for ye sake of his crime, and his conversation at his living hath been all of ye same piece. I have proved upon him above 20 attempts to lewd acts and some of them aggravated by as bad circumstances; . . . he had a bastard layd to his charge". (Prideaux to Tenison, 16 October 1695. Lambeth MSS. 942, f. 108.)
[2] Tenison received a letter from Lambeth stating that "his grace [i.e. Tillotson] is very sensible of the Abuse of Qualifications obtained at Court by Chaplains Extra-ordinary" and had spoken of it to her Majesty who "for the future hope[d] to stop it". (Fairfax to Tenison, 5 July 1694. Lambeth MSS.)
[3] Phillimore, *The Ecclesiastical Law of the Church of England*, ii. 898.

anxious to indulge particular individuals or to meet existing conditions. At the Reformation, when papal jurisdiction in England was abolished, the Dispensation Act of Henry VIII gave authority to the Archbishop of Canterbury "to grant dispensations and licenses in both provinces where the Pope used to grant them, in cases which are not contrary to the Holy Scriptures and the laws of God".[1] This archiepiscopal authority to grant dispensations was further qualified, so far as pluralities were concerned, by the Canons of 1603 (No. 41) which Tenison always regarded as defining the extent of his powers. It laid down that

"No licence or dispensation for the keeping of more benefices with cure than one, shall be granted to any but such only as shall be thought very well worthy for his learning, and very well able and sufficient to discharge his duty; that is, who shall have taken the degree of a master of arts at the least in one of the universities of this realm, and be a public and sufficient preacher licensed. Provided always, that he be by a good and sufficient caution bound to make his perpetual residence in each of his said benefices for some reasonable time in every year; and that the said benefices be not more than thirty miles asunder; and, lastly, that he have under him, in the benefice where he doth not reside, a preacher lawfully allowed, that is able sufficiently to teach and instruct the people".[2]

It may, of course, be objected that Tenison himself, during his pre-episcopal years, was a parochial pluralist, but we need to remember that it was not the holding of pluralities as such (he thought there was "a Necessity of many of them") but the abuse of pluralities which he condemned, namely, the granting of dispensations: (a) to people not qualified by law to hold them; (b) under conditions which failed to fulfil the canons. Tenison's policy was simply to enforce the law (although he thought it too lenient);[3] and to restrict pluralism and non-residence to the limit of the statutes and canons which regulated them. Since a dispensation from the Archbishop was necessary before a person could legally hold two ecclesiastical benefices, Tenison was able

---

[1] 25 Hen. VIII, cap. 21 (1534).

[2] Phillimore, *The Ecclesiastical Law of the Church of England*, ii. 900.

[3] Burnet even wished all pluralities to be abolished and drew up a Bill to this effect. Prideaux, however, persuaded him to attempt something a little less drastic, and a Bill was introduced into Parliament in 1691 to reduce the distances between benefices to "five miles distance, measuring it by the common road from one Church to another"; but "the Lords were so fond of their privilege of qualifying Chaplains for Pluralities that . . . they would not allow the bill so much as to be read once in their house". See *The Life of the Reverend Humphrey Prideaux*, 1748, pp. 81, 82.

to exert a measure of control.[1] Yet despite this enforcing of the legal requirements, Tenison granted no less than six hundred and forty dispensations during his archiepiscopate of twenty years. The fact that only those of a certain university status, chaplains to the king or noblemen, were eligible to hold them, shows that the privilege was more or less confined to those who could bring some interest to bear on their behalf, though it is true that in many cases the combined income of the livings was small. The applicant, moreover, had first to be approved by the bishop(s) in whose diocese(s) the livings were situated. From what follows we shall see that the Archbishop by no means granted dispensations as a matter of form, but that he submitted each case to a close examination, and endeavoured to enforce the law. Among the "Injunctions" which he persuaded the King to issue in 1695,[2] Tenison laid down the main lines of his own policy as follows:

"That you [i.e. the bishops] use the most effectual Endeavours to suppress the great Abuses occasion'd by Pluralities, and restrain them as much as you can, except where the Parishes lie near one another, and the Livings are small, that all qualifications be carefully examin'd: We [i.e. the King] being determin'd to have no Chaplains to be qualify'd by us, but such as do attend upon us: And that due Caution be taken before any Faculty be granted; and that such Persons as are legally qualify'd, shall reside at least two Months in the Year in each of their Livings, and provide a Curate to serve where they are not in Person, with a due Maintenance, to be determin'd by the

[1] To what precise extent the powers of the Archbishop were limited by law was a subject of nice debate at the time, and Tenison consulted the learned Stillingfleet, Bishop of Worcester, on this subject. Could the Archbishop, Tenison enquired, still refuse to grant a dispensation "in the case of a person qualified by Law for a Dispensation for Plurality of Benefice". Tillotson, Tenison's predecessor, had apparently felt that he could not, and complained to the Bishop of Worcester that on one occasion he was "forced into the granting a fiatt against his Will by a great Man". Stillingfleet maintained, however, that the "law left it to his [the Archbishop's] Discretion as it is plain it doth, but so as upon complaint he is bound to assert a just cause". The procedure, said Stillingfleet, was as follows. A person qualified to hold pluralities, but refused by the Archbishop, must seek redress from the Lord Keeper, who would require the Archbishop to certify into Chancery why he had declined. Then, Stillingfleet wrote, "if the Ld Keeper allowed the Reason to be good and sufficient, the Archbp. is discharged but if he allows it not then a write of Injunction comes out . . . so that judging what is a reasonable cause of denying a Dispensation rests in the Ld Keeper upon Complaint". The matter thus turned on whether the Archbishop could bring a "good and sufficient" reason other than one which was definitely so named in the canons. Stillingfleet here thought that the Archbishop might do so. See Stillingfleet to Tenison, 4 December 1694. Lambeth MSS. 929, f. 102.
[2] See pp. 142, 143.

Bishop of the Diocese, unless the two Parishes lie so near, that the Incumbent can constantly serve both Cures".[1]

Tenison's own practice in this matter of dispensations was set down at length by his chaplain, Edmund Gibson, who was in a position to observe it at first hand. He described it as follows:

"When the late archbishop was applied to for a dispensation, he proceeded in the following manner. The person who desired it, first acquainted the secretary with his desire and delivered into his hands the necessary instruments: viz., his Orders, both priest and deacon (his grace having found in one instance a person really ordained priest who had never been deacon); his Testimonials from the neighbouring clergy or college; a qualification from some nobleman registered in the Faculty office and attested to be so registered; or else a certificate from one of the universities of his being Bachelor of Divinity or Law; a certificate of his being Master of Arts complete; the presentation to the second living; and the bishop's certificate concerning the value and distance of the benefices. In the Forms wch our late Archbp expected from his Suffragans, their *Consent* was expressed;[2] . . . The instruments being all in due form; his grace directed the person praying the dispensation to be examined by his chaplain; if an Oxford man by the Oxford chaplain; and if a Cambridge man by the Cambridge chaplain. His method of examination was the writing on a sheet of paper seven or eight questions, or as many as were judged requisite, (sometimes by himself, but generally by the chaplain), and spaces for the answers being left,[3] to put the person examined in a room by himself, with pen, ink, and paper, and a Bible and Concordance; that he might set down his particular answers to every question. His grace was very frequently importuned to grant dispensations to persons without coming up to London themselves; but very seldom yielded in that particular; especially of late, since ye instance at Exeter of a Clergyman sending up a Certificate from his Physician, yt he could not travel without danger to his life, and afterwards declining to answer ye questions enclosed by his Grace to Canon Gilbert, and in the end contenting himself

[1] *Memoirs of the Life and Times of Thomas Tenison,* p. 44.
[2] Commenting on this giving of their consent by the bishops, Gibson wrote: "I humbly conceive [it] an Invasion of ye Right invested in the Archbishop of Canterbury by ye Faculty Act; and is, in many cases, a difficulty upon ye Suffragans who can scarce be willing to take upon himself ye *whole* burden of *denying* that favour, but may be supposed to signify his opinion more freely (if there be need to ask it) by a private Letter".
[3] See p. 147 for examination papers already quoted.

with Institution to ye 2d Benefice which was ye better. The answers being approved, the secretary prepared a petition which was signed by his grace and directed to the Faculty Office".[1]

We now turn to the Act Books of the Archbishop which illustrate the above policy. The consent of the bishops of the dioceses was expressed in a variety of ways from the formal "being recommended by the Bishop of ——", "the Bishop of the Diocese consenting", to a more explicit approval, as in the case of one Richard Simon who, it was carefully recorded, was "particularly recommended by the Bishop of Salisbury and three neighbouring clergy".[2] The personal examination by the Archbishop's chaplain was also noted as, for example, in the case of Richard Kay, who applied for a dispensation to hold the livings of St. Anne's, Sutton Broughton, and Shepeshead in Leicester, and was "first examin'd and approv'd by Mr. Edmund Gibson, his Grace's Domestick Chaplain . . . he bringing the consent of both of his Diocesans together with other sufficient Testimonials".[3] The wishes of the diocesan bishop were sometimes a determining factor when the Archbishop himself might have demurred. Thus when "Farewell Perrie", a chaplain to the Earl of Winchelsea and already Vicar of Little Bedwin (in the diocese of Salisbury) and St. Peter's, Marlborough, was presented to the Vicarage of Willesford (also in the Salisbury diocese), the Archbishop granted a dispensation in this rather exceptional case, but insisted that Perrie first resigned the rectory of St. Peter's, Marlborough, and it was recorded in the Act Book that the dispensation was granted "at the Earnest and repeated requests of Gilbert Ld Bp of the sd. Diocese".[4] As another example of a similar nature we may, perhaps, quote the case of Hugh Todd, Vicar of Arthuret in Cumberland (value £120), who applied in July 1699 for a dispensation to hold in addition the living of Penrith, twenty-two

---

[1] Christ Church, Wake MSS. Epist. 6, Canterbury 1.

[2] "Act Books, etc., of Canterbury", Lambeth MSS. V, 29. A typical letter of recommendation from a bishop is the following from Bp. Patrick written on 4 August 1700 (Lambeth MSS. 942, f. 150): "The bearer hereof Mr. Wharton my countryman and townsman was presented by me lately to a small Rectory in Lincolnshire. He is now presented to another by a Lady, which is but a mile from mine, both wch will make but a competent maintenance. I desire your Grace will be pleased to grant him a fiatt for a Dispens. to hold them both. I have qualifyed him myself, as my Chaplain, out of kindness to him and his relations. I have no place void but one whom I had formerly qualifyed resigned his patent, haveing now no use of it".

[3] "Act Books of the Archbishops of Canterbury", V, 25.

[4] Ibid. IV, 540.

miles distant and worth £70. The Archbishop granted a dispensation but stated in the Act Book that he did so "at the special Instance of the Bp of Carlisle who promised to give £500 for the good of Penrith".[1]

In many cases where he gave a fiat, Tenison insisted on certain conditions being fulfilled, and these were placed on record in the Act Book. We quote the following example. Edward Williams, chaplain to the Earl of Sunderland and Vicar of Terring (valued at £50), which though in the diocese of Chichester was a "peculiar" of the Archbishop of Canterbury, was presented by the patron John Coke to the Vicarage of Goring. The Archbishop granted the dispensation on 4 July 1704, but he insisted on Williams signing the following declaration:

> "Whereas a Proposal was made by Mr. Coke of Petworth my Patron of Goring, That I should reside at Goring. This appearing to yr Grace unreasonable and having obtained Mr. Coke's Approbation of it, and his entire Resignation to yr Grace's pleasure, I do sincerely and solemnly promise by ye Grace of God to make my constant Residence at yr Grace's peculiar".[2]

Another and similar case may be quoted from the year 1706. Thomas Ferrar,[3] Rector of Steeple Gidding, applied for a dispensation to hold in addition the living of Sawtry St. Andrew. As a result of his customary investigations, Tenison discovered that Ferrar was already an illegal pluralist, possessing both the Rectories of Little Gidding and Steeple Gidding without any dispensation. Thus the Archbishop directed that Ferrar should first resign the Rectory of Little Gidding before he could do anything in the matter, and not until this was done did he grant Ferrar a dispensation (on 20 December 1706) to hold the Rectories of Steeple Gidding and Sawtry St. Andrew.[4]

Perhaps we may be pardoned for quoting one further instance of conditions being attached to a grant of dispensations. Daniel Ayshford, chaplain to the Bishop of Hereford, and Vicar of Harley in the diocese of Salisbury, was presented by the Lord Keeper to the Rectory of Swincombe in the diocese of Oxford, the two livings being some eight miles apart. Tenison wished

---

[1] "Act Books of the Archbishops of Canterbury", IV, 605. See note 1, p. 158.
[2] Ibid. V, 135.
[3] One of the famous Ferrar family. What would Nicholas have thought of the dispensation?
[4] "Act Books of the Archbishops of Canterbury", V, 232.

Ayshford to reside in the latter parish and when he allowed a dispensation on 29 May 1706, he caused Ayshford to sign the following document:

"Whereas I Daniel Ayshford M.A. and Vicar of Harley in the County of Berks and Diocese of Sarum am presented by my Ld Keeper to the Rectory of Swincombe in the Co. and Dio. of Oxon upon wch Rectory there is no convenient House for the Rector to dwell in, and having obtained a Disp. from his Grace Ld Arch Bp of Canterbury to hold both the said Livings of Harley and Swincombe till the repairs and buildings shall be finished upon the Rectory of Swincombe aforesaid: [I] Do hereby sincerely promise that on or before the 29 day of September wch shall be in the year of our Ld 1702 I will resign the sd Vic. of Harley if thereunto required by his Grace the Ld Archbishop of Cant. the Bp of Sarum & the Bp of Oxon for the time being, or any two of them, in Witness whereof I have sett my hand the 29th day of May 1696".[1]

According to the Canons of 1603, a dispensation could be granted only where the livings were situated within thirty miles of each other. In many cases the parishes were stated in the Act Books to "lie contiguous to each other", but parishes twenty miles apart were by no means exceptional, and in one case the distance was seventeen miles when the combined incomes amounted to £240. It is interesting to note that at times there was a difference of opinion as to whether parishes came within this geographical limitation. William Dobson, President of Trinity College, Oxford, and Rector of Cliddesdon in the Diocese of Winchester (worth itself £140) was presented by the Fellows of his College to the Rectory of Garsington (worth £160) a village some five miles out of Oxford. This rectory was annexed to the headship of Trinity College, and Sir Thomas Pope (1507?–59), founder of the college, had erected there "a house of retreat for the students in time of pestilence", which, writes S. Lewis the topographer, "was completed at a subsequent period and displays some good specimens in the late English style". In due course, Dobson applied to the Archbishop for a dispensation (February 1705), stating that the above parishes were twenty-seven miles apart. Tenison, perhaps hoping that Dobson might resign the Rectory of Cliddesdon, declined on the grounds that he had received information that the two livings were, in fact, more

---

[1] " Act Books of the Archbishops of Canterbury ", IV, 541.

than thirty miles apart. Dobson, however, was a man of determination, at least in these matters, and he protested that Cliddesdon was "distant from his former Rectory about 27 miles as was abundantly certifyed by the Inhabitants of both places and others"—a statement glaringly inaccurate.[1] The Archbishop at length gave way and the dispensation was granted on 16 February 1705, although it is interesting to note that whereas in the first entry Cliddesdon was valued at £200, the sum was now reduced to £140.[2]

From what has been said it is apparent that Tenison kept a watchful eye over all grants of dispensations, and did not regard the consent of the diocesan bishop as excusing his own personal enquiries. Instances of his care could be multiplied. Thus when Robert Gould, Rector of Shankton (valued at £72) in Leicestershire, was presented to the rich living of St. Peter's Lamport in Northamptonshire (worth £250), both livings being in the gift of Sir Justinian Isham, he was interviewed by the Archbishop himself, who finding him to be "very deaf" refused to grant a dispensation. Gould returned, however, with a certificate from his patron and one Palmer "importing that his deafness was not constant and Habitual" and he managed to secure his licence.[3]

The Act Books simply record the fact of the dispensation to hold two livings, not the reason why the grant was made, although this was usually given in dispensations from residence. For example, Humphrey Drake, Vicar of Gillingham, was excused residence in 1695 "during his Grace's pleasure . . . [since] the sd. Vicarage is notoriously known to be situated in an unwholesome air".[4] There seems little reason to doubt that in most cases dispensations to hold two livings were a concession to human weakness, although even reformers such as Prideaux saw a necessity for them in certain cases.[5] As a whole, however, they

---

[1] The distance is in fact thirty-four miles as the crow flies, and much more by road.

[2] "Act Books of the Archbishops of Canterbury", V, 206, 209.

[3] *Ibid.* p. 312. Apropos Gould's coming up to London to see Tenison and the reference to such journeys on p. 153, we may notice a short letter from Lloyd, Bishop of Lichfield, to the Archbishop, in which he requested that a Mr. Skrimshaw might be spared the ordeal of an interview since "he has never been to London in his life". Lloyd to Tenison, 7 August 1697. Lambeth MSS. 930, f. 43.

[4] "Act Books of the Archbishops of Canterbury", IV, 438. In one case we do find, in reference to a dispensation to hold two benefices, that Richard Forster was licensed to Beckley and Crondal both in Kent because "the Air of the former was inconsistent with his health". (*Ibid.* p. 577.) See also *Alumni Oxonienses*, ii. 517.

[5] *The Life of the Reverend Humphrey Prideaux*, p. 80.

were more marks of favour than helps to necessitous clergymen (who often lacked interest to obtain them), and it was by no means uncommon for the combined incomes to total more than £300.[1] Often, as we have seen, the scruples of the Archbishop were reflected in the Act Book. Thus one incumbent, dispensed to hold two livings worth over £250, promised "to give the profits of the sd. Rectory to the Church thereof",[2] while another undertook to "keep a Curate resident . . . and allow him such a salary as his diocesan shall approve of".[3] Many, of whom we have no record, were possibly refused by the Archbishop, as, for example, William Whitfield, who was unable to secure from the Archbishop a dispensation to hold the living of Ewhurst in Surrey with St. Giles', Cripplegate, although his claims were urged by the Lord Chief Justice of the Common Pleas.[4]

[1] We quote the following from Tenison's archiepiscopate. IV, p. 599—combined value £240; p. 603—£210; p. 571—£300; p. 604—£190; p. 592—£260; V, p. 312—£250.

[2] " Act Books of the Archbishops of Canterbury", IV, 548.

[3] *Ibid.* p. 593. Among Tenison's papers at Lambeth (951, f. 15) there is a cartoon contrasting a "Careful Resident" with a "Careless Non-Resident" with a poem underneath. Of the former it says:
"He yt the Charge and Cure of Souls doth mind
    Will heavy 'nough the weight of one Church find".

[4] Lambeth MSS. 952, f. 118. It must not be thought that because the dispensations granted conformed to the statute, therefore the legal requirements were always carried out, or that only those legally dispensed held more than one benefice. We have already noticed a case of illegal pluralism (p. 155), which probably had gone on for years, and might never have been discovered had not the pluralist been presented with a third living. The following letter from William Lloyd to Tenison (1705) provides an interesting commentary on what existed in some dioceses, although we ought to add that the letter was written under the stress of personal injuries from some of his clergy: "There are but 2 others in my Diocese [Worcester] yt have dispensations. One of them is my son. But of him there is nor justly can be any complaint; for he spends and gives in his parish to ye full of wt he receives from it. I speak of his parish in my Diocese. For ye other, yt was formerly his Unkle's, he lets him take ye Profits, discharging ye Cure. I do not hear yt ye Jacobites complain of it. Another yt has a dispensatiō lives at one of his Churches, and yt within a mile of ye other Church, and serves both of ye Churches himself both morning and evening to ye great content of both of his parishes. There is another yt holds 2 Rectories wth out Dispensation. One is 6 7s 3 ob. in ye King's books, ye other just 7; I believe yt both do not yield him 10 a year, and ye Churches are very well serv'd. I cannot say this of them before mentioned, nor especially of ye 4 witnesses. One of them, who is Sr. Jon. P's Chaplain, Mr. Stevens, holds by Dispensation a Rectory at which he lives . . . and a Vicarage about 20 miles dist. . . . At this Vicarage he never comes so much as once in a twelve month but keeps a Curate there, who is no doubt ye cheapest he could get for he allows him only £10 a year, wch together with £20 for serving a Cure belonging to Merton College is all that he has to subsist, himself and a Wife and 7 Children. The Curate has taken a cours to wash down sorrow with drunkeness and his Family either beg or are very near starving. Of ye rest of ye Knot, there is not one yt observes ye 3 Provisoes in his Dispensation, or any one of ym as far as I can learn. The 3 Provisoes yr Grace may see at large if you please in yor [*sic*] Secretaries hands. They are to this purpose. 1. He shall reside so as to keep Hospitality and to relieve ye poor for 2 months. 2. He shall preach in the parish Church at least 13 times a year. 3. He shall

It was this diligence in executing the law which led to Tenison's making a protest to the Queen herself in 1712. The Crown, we must notice, was able in virtue of its prerogative to grant dispensations by royal warrant, although this power was very sparingly used.[1] The last case which Tenison could discover occurred in 1676 when a John Whitehall was granted a dispensation by royal warrant "notwithstanding any Statute, Canon, Custom or Constitution to the Contrary". For over thirty years, therefore, no dispensation had been granted on a royal warrant, till in January 1712 Anne decided to use her prerogative to

keep a Curate and give him such salary as the Bp of the Diocese decides. . . . There is one Mr. Hodges, yt has a great living in the Lichfield Diocese and would now have a greater in this to hold with it. I believe my Ld Bradford and some others will desire to be heard before he has a dispensation. And I think ye young man's Qualifications ought to be well considered". (Lloyd to Tenison, 2 June 1705. Lambeth MSS. 931, f. 1.) We may note that Hodges did not secure this dispensation: although another Hodges obtained one to hold the Rectory of Harvington (Worc.) with St. Mary's, Warwick.

[1] The use and history of this royal prerogative was very carefully investigated by Tenison himself. When the statute for Dispensations and Pluralities was enacted in the reign of Henry VIII, he wrote "there was a great want of Secular Pastors and no encouragement was judg'd too great for them, and so widespread was the abuse from dispensations in the Middle Ages that this Act was judg'd a considerable step at first toward a Reformation". At the beginning of Elizabeth's reign so many of Mary's clergy "stood against the Reformation that the labourers in it were few tho' the Harvest was great and upon this Emergency the distances [between livings] were widely extended". But with the progress of learning, the number of clergy increased and in 1576 the Council of Queen Elizabeth deliberated whether "not only to suppress undue and illegal Faculties, but also whether the distance should not be reduced to Twenty miles, It having been before restrain'd to 26 soe far as the Canons of 1571 had any validity". In 1580 the Lower House of Convocation proposed that none should have dispensations for plurality of benefices except a Master of Arts of four years' standing, who was known to be a good preacher, and that such men should reside on each benefice "for some reasonable proportion of time". In 1584 a canon was made by royal authority which limited the distance between benefices to thirty miles, and in 1586 (circa) there was a project before Convocation to petition Parliament to limit the distance further to twenty miles, but "private and party Interest" (so Tenison commented) "occasion'd a slowness in the Growth and ripening of such matters in the publick reformation". In the Parliament of 1587, Lord Burleigh said "that he was not so Scrupulous as absolutely to like the Bill agst Pluralities wthout any Exemption, for he did favour both learning and wish'd a competent reward to it, and therefore would like to allow a learned man to have two Benefices soe that They were both in one . . . Diocese, not one in the Diocese of Winchester and another in the North where the severall Diocesans would have no regard for them". Again in 3 Jac. 1 and 16 Car. 1 there were Bills "for regulating of Abuses in Pluralities" before Parliament and in the first year of James I a canon passed by Convocation (No. 41) fixed the distance at thirty miles, though statute law was left as it was. True, this canon was sometimes dispensed with in the reigns of James and Charles, but "sparingly . . . and upon extraordinary occasions and in favour of extraordinary persons". After the return of Charles II, it was not surprising, perhaps, that many loyal clergy were rewarded with pluralities, although Tenison thought that the number of priests and deacons was more than enough to supply all the vacancies then existing. In Archbishop Sancroft's time there was probably one case of a dispensation upon a royal warrant (1678) but the last definite case which Tension could find was that granted to John Whitehall in 1676.

enable a certain Borradall to hold the livings of Market Deeping
in Lincolnshire and Foulsham in Norfolk, which were well over
thirty miles apart.

On 24 January the Archbishop was waited on at Lambeth by
Sir Jacob Astley (patron of Foulsham) and Borradall himself.
An account of this interview, apparently drawn up by the latter,
was published from his papers in the *Gentleman's Magazine* of
1783, and we propose (despite some inaccuracies which it possibly
contains) to quote this curious document as it stands:

"Sir J. A. My Lord, I am come to wait on your Grace in
behalf of Mr. A. B——le, to whom I have given the presentation
of Fowlsham in Norfolk, to desire your dispensation, that he
may hold that living together with Market Deeping, of which
he is now rector.

Abp. C. Sir, you come at a very bad time, for my wife is
ill, and I am very much out of order myself.

Sir J. A. My Lord, I am sorry to find your Grace indisposed,
but hope you'll excuse my coming at this time, since it is upon
a very urgent occasion, in obedience to the Queen's warrant.

Abp. C. The Queen's warrant! pray what do you mean,
sir?

Sir J. A. Being informed that your Grace's dispensing power
was limited to 30 miles, we therefore made our application to
her Majesty for a royal dispensation.

Abp. C. This is a very wicked thing, and I wonder you
would undertake it. Aye! 'tis a very wicked thing indeed.

Sir J. A. The power of dispensing without distance was given
to the Crown by the same Parliament that gave the Abp.
of Canterbury to dispense for 30 miles.

Abp. C. 'Tis a very wicked thing.

Sir J. A. I am informed your Grace executes your dispensing
power; and why not the Queen hers?

Abp. C. Hers! I'm sure 'tis a very wicked thing, and ought not
to be done.

Sir J. A. My Lord, shall I call the gentleman up? You may
hear him speak for himself.

Abp. C. No, no. I will not see him; I am sure he is a very
wicked person, and I had as lief see anything else.

Sir J. A. My Lord, he has the Queen's warrant to your Grace.

Abp. C. Warrant! I had rather he would come up and cudgel
me, than bring me that; for I am resolved not to do it, let the
Queen do what she pleases. I'll sooner go to prison first—I had
never such a wicked thing put upon me in all my life before.

Sir J. A. If your Grace please to let the gentleman come up, you may hear what he will say for himself.

Abp. C. Well, let him be called up then.

Enter Mr. B. This is the substance of the discourse that passed before I came in, as I received it from Sir J. A.

Mr. B. My Lord, I beg your Grace's blessing.

Abp. C. I can't bid God bless you, Sir, for you are a very wicked man. How durst you do such a thing as this? I must tell you, you are a very wicked man, and I can't pray God to bless you.

Mr. B. I have brought the Queen's warrant to your Grace; will you please to see it.

Abp. C. Read the warrant. Oh! you are a very wicked man! I'll never suffer it. How dare you do so? Well we've come to a fine pass! I am sure good King William would not have done it. No! he promised me he would not; for 'tis an unreasonable thing, and not lawful.

Sir J. A. What is confirmed by Act of Parliament cannot be unlawful; this is the Queen's undoubted prerogative, and certainly she may exercise it when she pleases.

Abp. C. The Queen may do her pleasure. I'll write to my Lord Bolingbroke about it, but will never consent to do it, let them do what they will. For, if I suffer them once to break in upon me, I know not where they will stop—But hark you, Sir, How can you supply these two livings, hah?

Mr. B. The one I will serve myself, and will take care to provide a sufficient curate who shall serve the other.

Abp. C. I tell you, 'tis an unlawful thing, and cannot be done, if they be above 30 miles distant—Pray how far are these two places distant from one another?

Mr. B. Between 40 and 50 miles, my Lord.

Abp. C. Ah! abominable! 'Tis a very wicked thing. King William abhorred such things. Aye good K[ing] William! I tell you sir, I'll never do it, do what they will.

Mr. B. If it be not unreasonable for your Grace to grant dispensations for 30 miles, why may not the Queen do it, if they be above, since it is equally impossible to supply two livings in both cases.

Abp. C. I tell you I never did it all my life and never will.

Mr. B. I am informed that King William granted his warrant in the like case, my Lord, and it was obeyed.

Abp. C. Who told you that? I am sure K[ing] William was a better man than to do such things. 'Tis a very wicked thing!

Sir J. A. I can assure your Grace there was a royal dispensation granted in King William's reign.[1]

Abp. C. Pray, Sir, urge me no more; for I tell you I won't
do it.

Sir J. A. I can't but take your Grace's refusal unkindly,
since I never heard of such a thing being denied before;
and I am the more concerned, in regard I am the patron of the
living, and the gentleman a near relation.

Abp. C. I can't tell how to help that; but I won't suffer the
great ones to swallow up the little ones, no, not I. Besides,
pluralities are only for men of distinguished merit. Here was
t'other day, Dr. B——g's son, a very good man, and he came
to me to get one living; and you, who are so much his junior,
have gotten two. This is very fine!

Mr. B. This will equally hold against all pluralities, be
they ever so near together; and the farther they are off, they
are generally the better served; because when two livings
lie near together, they are generally served by one minister,
and by this means both are frequently neglected; whereas at
such a distance, there must of necessity be kept a sufficient
curate to officiate at that upon which the incumbent does not
reside. And as for the Gentleman your Grace mentions, I am
his senior in the university, was his schoolfellow, and know
him very well.

Abp. C. Well, well, 'tis all one, I'll not do it. Pray let me
have your name, and an account of your College and degree.

Mr. B. My name is A. B. about seven years ago of Jesus College
in Cambridge. My degree LL.B.

Abp. C. I wonder people don't understand themselves
better than to trouble me when my wife is so ill. I wonder
people should be guilty of so much indecency. But we are come
to a fine pass!

Sir J. A. This is the same living I gave your uncle, Archdeacon
Tenison.

Abp. C. I remember it; He had that living before Dean
Astley, but I can't allow this gentleman to have it. I don't keep
public days.

Sir J. A. Your Grace's humble servant. I am sorry we have so
much disturbed you.

Abp. C. Well pray God bless you, Sir Jacob, but let me hear
no more of this wicked thing. I hope you'll concern yourself no
more in it.

A true Copy A. B——le".[2]

[1] See later p. 163.
[2] *Gentleman's Magazine*, 1783.   Vol. LIII, pt. 2, 670, 671.

The Archbishop's feelings may be inferred from the report of this interview. It was plain to him that Borradall was not "above the common Levell of the ordinary Curate of the Diocese", and could not "modestly pretend to an Extraordinary Favour". Tenison felt he must make a protest and on 31 January 1712 he wrote at length to the Queen from Lambeth.

He began by excusing his not waiting on her in person, but as for some time she had been "graciously pleas'd to permit [him] to address her by Writing", so he felt he must communicate with her on the recent royal grant of a dispensation. "I cannot but perswade myself", he said with great candour,

"that your Maj^{tie} has bin surprised in this Grant and haveing heard your Maj^{tie} at the beginning of your Reign declare to me your aversion to such distant pluralities; I am upon this account under great Concern. I am not against all Canonical Pluralities; I think there is a Necessity of many of them till by the progress of your Maj$^{tie's}$ great Bounty to the poor Clergy and other means their maintenance becomes sufficient and that those who preach the Gospel may live of the Gospel. I dispute not your Majtie's Prerogative in this matter of a Royall Dispensation yet firmly hope that in Instances which may appear at any time either inconvenient or mischievous to this Good Church, the milder professions of your wisdom and Goodness will moderate your Power".

Tenison then embarked upon a historical account of the statutes and canons which regulated pluralities, and referring to William and Mary, he commented:

"I know it to have been their opinion that the distance of six miles was much more expedient than that of Thirty and indeed if the distance was some way shortened, and the time of residence lengthened, It is my poor opinion that it would tend much to the true Interest of the Established Church. . . . The affecions of the Sheep would not be so much alienated from the Pastor as principally loveing the sheep. The common Scoffers of Pluralities under the odious phrase of Ecclesiasticall Monopolies would be in some degree silenc'd, separate Meetings would not be so commonly set up in such places, and by the Parishioners frequented even in despite to the Pastor whilst the cheapest Curates are notwithstanding the care of the Bishops too often chosen especially by Lay Improprietors, some of wch have sometimes allowed but five or six pounds a year for the service of the Church, and such haveing no well fix'd place of abode and a poor and precarious maintenance, are powerfully tempted to a kind of vagrant and dishonourable life, wandering for better subsistence from Parish to Parish even from North to South". Hence the Archbishop expressed the hope that "after the Crowd of present and most important Affairs wch may be some impediment to Recollection becomes less pressing; Your Matie will call to mind when I waited upon You upon this subject at the beginning of your Reign, You were pleas'd most freely and graciously to assure me I should have no trouble from you on this Account and that Thirty miles distant was great enough".

In the present case, Tenison went on, there was "noe Emergency" or "special features" and he therefore hoped the Queen would forbear to use her prerogative. Market Deeping was a market town, and Foulsham was worth £100.[1] Borradall himself was only a young man, merely a bachelor of laws (whereas the canons required a master of arts), nor was he possessed of any conspicuous ability.

Regarding his own practice and position in these matters, Tenison pointed out that the statute of 25 Hen. VIII granted to him a power of dispensation after examination of the "causes and the qualities of the persons procuring dispensations"; and the Canons of 1584, confirmed in 1603, required that dispensations should be granted "to such only as shall be thought very well worthy of his learning and very well able and sufficient to discharge his Duty". The Archbishop confessed that he could not testify this of Borradall, and he concluded his long letter to the Queen with these words:

"If a door for Royall Dispensations (which your Matie's great wisdom and goodness hath hitherto shutt) should be once again open'd, there being already such an overflow of supernumerary Clergy, Your Matie will be perpetually troubled with unwelcome Importunities, and much prejudice will accrue to that Good Church of wch your Matie is the Nursing Mother & in which I am plac'd (how unworthy soever in other respects) as a Watchman or Shepherd in order to the promoting the Benefit of that Flock and to the Securing it (as far as in me lyes) from any detriment. Whilst I doe my duty sincerely in this way and no longer, I shall depend upon Your Matie's protection

---

[1] Tenison's uncle, Philip Tenison, Archdeacon of Norfolk, was at one time Rector of the Parish of Foulsham, being presented to it as a compensation for "his great sufferings in the late evil times". B.M. Add. MSS. 35, 508, f. 113. See Chap. 1, p. 3.

and encouragement; without that, my Gray hairs would soon be brought with sorrow to the Grave, towards wch I am hastening, But from wch may God long preserve Your Matie for the manifold advantage of Church and State. Soe prayeth with undissembled fervency Madm. Your most dutifull, most humble Subject and Servant".[1]

This letter was certainly explicit and candid: it shows clearly Tenison's genuine distaste for pluralities, and his sincere desire to prevent the abuse of them. We may also detect, perhaps, signs of an estrangement between the Court and Lambeth, not entirely due to the inability of the Archbishop to wait on the Queen in person. Ten days later the Archbishop wrote to Wake, Bishop of Lincoln, expressing his dismay. "I am much out of order", he wrote, "and my poor wife still worse. I need not to have my affliction added to by seeking for pluralities and who are scandals to their p's orders. There is one Borradall of Market Deeping who has procured [?] a Royal dispensation to hold yt Living in yr dio. with Foulsham nigh Norwich. I hope a stopp is put to ye matter: I would desire to know whether he hath bin with yr Lp. He is a very good Hors-Coursier: That's ye Character I have heard of".[2]

The Archbishop, however, had the satisfaction of seeing his intervention successful. Anne had the interests of the Church at heart, and she proceeded no further in the matter, so that Borradall remained simply Rector of Market Deeping: it was not until George I was on the throne and Tenison had been some four years in his grave that Borradall secured a dispensation to hold the Vicarage of Boston in Lincolnshire with his former cure.[3]

[1] Tenison to Queen Anne, 31 January 1712. B.M. Add. MSS. 35, 508, f. 113.
[2] Tenison to Wake, 10 February 1712. Christ Church. Lincoln Correspondence. Wake Papers, I.
[3] "Act Books of the Archbishops of Canterbury". Tenison's earnest desire to encourage conscientious clergymen may be seen in the requirements which he laid down for livings in his own gift. In 1704, for example, he purchased the Rectory of St. Peter, Duxford, in the county of Cambridge from the widow of the late incumbent, and two years later gave the presentation of it to Corpus Christi College. He enjoined that whenever it became vacant "they should present such an one as he should nominate during his life, and afterwards either the Master, one of the Fellows (without regard to seniority) or some other pious Clergyman who they should think most fit and most likely to promote the glory of God". Masters, *History of Corpus Christi College*, p. 179. Perhaps more explicit was the condition upon which he made over the presentation of the Rectory of Stalbridge in Dorset to the same College in 1697. Here he stated "that as often as it became void after his decease, they should elect one of the twelve Fellows to the same, such an one as they in their Consciences shall think most fit . . . and by reason of its being a very good subsistence alone for a clergyman, he further

order'd no Dignitary of any Church, or who has any other Rectory, Vicarage etc. shall be presented to it; and that whosoever takes it shall give a solemn promise in writing, that he will not accept any other with Cure of Souls without resigning it". Masters, *History of Corpus Christi College*, p. 197. It may not be out of place to notice here that Tenison because of "the Difficulties put upon the Country Clergy, by want of an easy Recourse to the Articles, Canons and Statutes by which they were to regulate their Offices and Lives", went to the trouble and expense of publishing a "Manual" entitled *A Collection of Articles, Canons, Injunctions etc. together with several Acts of Parliament concerning Ecclesiastical Matters ; some whereof are to be read in Churches*. The book was published in 1699, and the Archbishop himself contributed a short preface "showing the considerable use of it especially to those in Holy Orders". Such a volume certainly met a real need, and John Wallis, professor of Geometry at Oxford, expressed his pleasure "with the collection of Articles which yr Grace hath caused to be printed for the ease of the Clergy". (Wallis to Tenison, 31 August, 1699. Lambeth MSS. 942, f. 151.) It was a useful little work, and Tenison told Sharp that he was moved to compile it in part because Sharp had informed him of a clergyman of his province indicted for not reading certain acts which in fact he did not possess.

CHAPTER 8

THE CROWN, THE ARCHBISHOP, AND THE EPISCOPATE

Part I   William III

THE relationship of the episcopate to the Crown in the matter of ecclesiastical appointments was one which at times occasioned difficulty (for preferment was a valuable royal weapon for winning over opposition) and we propose to devote the following chapter to a discussion of this subject.

When William secured the throne in 1689, it became an obvious and necessary axiom of government that high ecclesiastical preferment should be given only to those clergy who were whole-hearted in their support of the Revolution. William at first was guided in his selection by Burnet and the bishops (who owing to the nonjuring schism were in part of his own choosing), and in the remorse which he undoubtedly felt after the death of Mary in 1694, he particularly resolved to encourage "a pious and laborious clergy".[1] This good resolution, coupled with his so often being solicited by place-seekers "which he was not at all times able to resist" (and his frequent absences abroad), induced him to set up a small Commission consisting of the two Arch-bishops, the Bishops of Salisbury, Worcester, Lichfield, and Ely, who were sworn in the Court of Chancery on 29 April 1695.[2] These were to "recommend fit persons to all ecclesiastical prefer-ment", and the King exhorted them "to seek out the best and worthiest men they could find that such only might be promoted". The intention was undoubtedly excellent, though Burnet was sceptical. "This has a very good appearance", he wrote at the time, "and if it is continued by the King and is well managed by us it may have happy effects, though I confess my hopes are so sunk with the Queen's death that I do not flatter myself with further expectations".[3]

We do not know very much concerning the history of this first Commission, except that Burnet's prophecy seems to have come

---

[1] Foxcroft, *A Supplement to Burnet's History of my own Time*, p. 406.
[2] Luttrell, *A Brief Historical Relation*, etc., iii. 466.
[3] Foxcroft, *A Supplement to Burnet's History of my own Time*, p. 40.

to pass. The Commission certainly met and deliberated as is evident from the correspondence of the day, but there were difficulties, both within and without, from the beginning.

It was especially important that unanimity should be preserved on the Commission itself, and this meant, in particular, that Tenison, Sharp, and Burnet should work harmoniously together. Burnet was a militant Whig, anxious to use the Commission to exclude the possibility of Tory preferment. Sharp and Tenison had been fellow clergy together in London during the troublous days of James II, and we have already seen how that they stood together against Catholic pressure; but somehow Tenison never appears to have been easy with his brother Archbishop, even during the early years of his archiepiscopate, when he consulted him quite freely. From the first, Tenison was suspicious of him as a High Churchman, and also because of his connection with the Finch family; besides which a difference of temperament probably led to a mutual antipathy. Sharp was free and easy in his manner: Tenison found self-expression difficult, and was inclined to keep his own counsel. Yet when Tenison was first promoted to Canterbury, he appears to have been genuinely anxious to co-operate with Sharp, although the attempt gives the appearance of being somewhat self-conscious and studied. Thus in February 1695, we find Tenison writing that he hoped to see Sharp before the next session of parliament began, and adding: "It seems to have been our great failure, that we have not, by consultations, digested our matters relating to the good of the Church and state before we are to use them".[1] At another time he says that he very much needs Sharp's "consultation and advice". Many letters thus passed between Lambeth and Bishopsthorpe, but the Archbishop of York appears to have felt somewhat of an outsider on the Ecclesiastical Commission, and he was never intimate with William. It frequently happened that the Commission met in London and agreed on a nomination while Sharp was away at York, so that Tenison communicated with Bishopsthorpe merely for confirmation. In 1696, for example, when the Bishopric of Worcester became vacant, Tenison wrote: "We shall have more discours of this when we have more time. But I think neither of us have had an hour to spare for some weeks. I shall send you our sense about the filling the Bishopric of Worcester as soon as we have met. . . . We think the next is the Bishop of Lichfield

[1] Tenison to Sharp, 2 February 1695, The Lloyd-Baker-Sharp MSS., L 52.

but he demurs".[1] Instances could be multiplied, the more so as the years went by. In 1701 Dr. Gee was recommended for a prebendal stall at Westminster by the Commission "presuming upon yr Grace's [Sharp's] consent", and in the same letter Tenison said that they were thinking of Wake for the Deanery of Exeter and Willis for Lincoln. "We hope", he commented, "we have hitt upon yr Grace's mind".

In 1697, feeling between Sharp and Tenison grew particularly strained. In this year the Deanery of York became vacant, and Sharp was very anxious to place Henry Finch, brother of Sir Heneage Finch, first Earl of Nottingham, to whom he had been tutor, in this position so close to himself. Hence as soon as he heard a report of the Dean of York's death, Sharp wrote to Tenison, only to receive a reply on 29 April that the Archbishop was "loth" to do anything till the report of the Dean's death was confirmed, and that he "forsaw difficulties". William III, it appeared, was by no means prepared to acquiesce in this appointment, largely because he suspected Henry Finch and his brother of being involved in the "Lancashire plots"; nor was Tenison himself very zealous for it. The situation proved a difficult one, and as Sharp came to realize that this special wish of his was not to be gratified, so did Tenison feel it incumbent on him (not for the first time in similar circumstances) to make an explanation. Hence on 14 May, the Archbishop of Canterbury wrote a long and rather uneasy epistle to Sharp, in which his anxiety is apparent. He had passed on to the King, he said, the Archbishop of York's "earnest recommendation" of Mr. Finch, despite the difficulties which "were never of my making", but arose from the king's distrust of him; but had received from his Majesty the categorical reply that he did in no way approve this promotion of Lord Nottingham's brother. This reply, Tenison said, "made it impracticable for me to do more than I have done". "Yr Grace", he commented, "will think it hard not to be gratify'd with a dean you have long desired, and could take most content in: but I need not explain to yr Grace the Obstructions; I would to God they had never bin, I would none of them"—and that was "ye naked truth". "I believe I shall be blamed on all sides", he concluded somewhat petulantly, "as I usually am upon Promotions", but "going as I allwaies do, by God's help, to my Conscience, I shall not be disturbed".

[1] Tenison to Sharp, 22 November 1701, Lloyd-Baker-Sharp MSS. L 70.

The Archbishop of York (naturally) received the other side of
the story from Henry Finch in an embittered letter written on
May 22, which contained an account of an angry interview he
had had with Tenison two days previously.[1]

But Finch was passed over, and it was not till Anne was on the
throne, and Tenison's influence counted for little, that Sharp's
wish was gratified.

This was not the only difficulty, however, which the Commission had to face in this same year. In September 1697, a
prebend of Windsor fell vacant and Princess Anne immediately
wrote two letters to Tenison. In the first she reminded him of his
promise "yt when anything fell he would remember Dr. Pratt
who is indeed a very worthy man",[2] and in the second she
announced the death of the Dean of Guernsey, and hence the
vacancy of a prebendal stall at Windsor, adding: "I cannot help
mentioning Dr. Pratt again to you, hopeing you will let ye King
know my desires concerning him: who I do not doubt but will
easily grant so reasonable a thing when ye case is truly represented
to him, wch I shall wholly depend upon your kindness for".[3]

Tenison got into touch with Sharp on the following day,
informing him of the vacancy, the Princess's request, and also
Sir William Trumbull's desire to secure the prebend for his
brother. "The Lady Anne", the Archbishop wrote, "is a very good
friend to ye Church, and would not be pleased with a disappointment".[4] Sharp and the other commissioners replied supporting
Dr. Pratt (he was tutor to Anne's son, the young Duke of
Gloucester) and the Archbishop then passed on to the secretary
of the Council the commissioners' "unanimous decision in laying
Dr. Pratt before the King as a Person whose Preferment would be
so agreeable to ye Princess". Tenison was particularly anxious
to promote friendly relations between William and Anne, so that
we can imagine his dismay when he received a letter from the
secretary, naming various candidates for the vacant prebend,
but excluding any mention of Dr. Pratt—an omission which
forced him to conclude that William was "unwilling to contrive
ye matter with ye Princess".[5] Tenison immediately got into
communication with Bathurst on 28 September, drawing his

---

[1] Finch to Sharp, 22 May 1697, Lloyd-Baker-Sharp MSS., B 4.
[2] Anne to Tenison, 1 September 1697. Lambeth MSS. 930, f. 210.
[3] Ibid. 930, f. 211.
[4] Tenison to Sharp, 2 September 1697, Lloyd-Baker-Sharp MSS., L 55.
[5] Lambeth MSS. 930, f. 193.

attention to this passing over of one "of whō much was said" in his last letter.

"I think it proper", he stated, "to acquaint you that I have latelie receiv'd Letters frō all ye Cōmissioners (ye AB of York, ye Bps of Lichfield, Worcester, Sarum and Ely) in wch they all agree in laying Dr. Pratt before the King. . . . So that (you see) I cannot, in Form and as a Cōmissioner, lay any other Man before the King but him, tho' 'tis certain his Majestie's finall determination must govern the Affair. I desire that this may be represented to his Majestie to whom, without necessitie, I would not by any means have given a second trouble".[1]

This united stand by the Commission proved successful and Samuel Pratt became a Canon of Windsor and held this position till his death in 1723.[2]

This instance does not mean, of course, that the Commission experienced difficulty of this kind all the time, for much of its business was of a more routine nature. Thus when the King was requested by Lord Wharton in 1698 to appoint a Mr. Hibbons to the crown living of Marsh Gibbon in the county of Berkshire, he referred the matter automatically to the ecclesiastical commissioners.[3]

In the following year (1699) the original Commission lapsed, probably owing to the death of Stillingfleet, but it was renewed 28 October 1699, when his place was taken by John Moore, Bishop of Norwich. It may not be without interest, in the light of subsequent events, to glance at the terms under which the Commission met, particularly as they were largely the same as "those contained in the last ecclesiastical commission", and were in part drawn up by Tenison himself.[4] The general purpose of the Commission was said to be "for recommending to his Majesty

[1] Tenison to Bathurst, 28 September 1697. Lambeth MSS. 930, f. 202.
[2] *Alumni Oxonienses*, ii. 573. Samuel Pratt also became Master of the Savoy in 1697 and was presented to the Deanery of Rochester in 1706. He published in 1696 a treatise on the problem of restoring the currency. *D.N.B.* xlvi, 295.
[3] S.P.D. Will. III, 29 May 1698, 8C, p. 275. Other examples could be quoted. When Sir G. Markham presented a petition from the corporation of Newark "on behalf of one they desire may succeed in that vicarage when it is vacant", the request was referred to Tenison in order that he might "consider whether the person proposed be fit to be recommended by the Ecclesiastical Commissioners" (S.P.D. Will. III, 2 May 1698, 8C, p. 225). When the Bishop of Lichfield was translated to the see of Worcester in 1699, it was the Ecclesiastical Commission which successfully petitioned the King to remit the payment of first fruits. S.P.D. Will. III, 27 April 1699, 8D, p. 148.
[4] There is a corrected copy of the terms of this Commission at Lambeth in Tenison's own handwriting.

persons to succeed to any bishopric in England or any other ecclesiastical preferment in England above the value of £20 in his Majesty's Books, in his gift".

In the absence of the King overseas, minor preferment in the royal gift was to be disposed of by the commissioners themselves, and their "hands and seals" were to be deemed sufficient "under the great seal" to appoint. As to more important preferment, however, this was not to be the case. The Commission was to recommend to the King, but he was under no obligation to accept its nominees and was still left free to choose whom he wished. What appears to have been restricted was the soliciting the King directly through the Secretaries of State, since it stated categorically that "if at any time we [the King] be moved in like manner by any Person whatsoever our Pleasure is that neither of our principal secretaries of state shall present any Warrant to us for our Royal signature in such a Case until our Commissioners have been acquainted therewith and have given [their] Opinion and Recommendation as aforesaid".[1]

One thing was fairly obvious. Unless the King were to ignore the recommendations of the Commission, the advancement of Tory High Churchmen to important ecclesiastical preferments would be rendered almost impossible. The powers of the Archbishop of Canterbury on the Commission should also be noticed. His presence was necessary to constitute a quorum, and to him belonged the right of a casting vote.

We have seen that the terms of the Commission were too vague to limit the king's power, and this meant that the successful working of the experiment depended on how far the King, in practice, accepted the recommendations of the Commissioners. No men of any independence or self-respect could be expected to meet regularly for the purpose of giving advice, if such counsel was as often ignored as accepted. It was not long, however, before the reconstituted Commission had occasion to complain, and things came to a head in May 1700. Early in this month a clergyman "was recommended to the ecclesiastical commissioners, with the approval of the King, whose character would not bear inspection". The Commission received the message with dismay. The indignant Burnet was for standing firm, but Tenison seems to have been reluctant to go to extremes. The former, in militant

---

[1] S.P.D. Will. III, 28 October 1699, 8D, p. 27.

mood, tried to rally the Archbishop and wrote: ". . . it is part of my daily prayers to God for you that yr Grace may be directed and animated upon this occasion to act suitably to your post".[1]

The preferment was the living of Greens-Norton, in the king's gift, and the person nominated was the brother of a certain Colonel Wood. Writing to the Archbishop of York, Tenison confessed that William had given "especial directions wch the Commissioners here will follow tho' somewhat heavily"—a statement which suggests that Tenison's own approach to the King had been somewhat lacking in vigour. This is also born out by his admission that he informed the King that "he might over rule our Representation if he did not approve of it", and received from him the ambiguous reply: "I do not care to break in upon ye Commission, but I would have this done by ye Commissioners upon my direction".[2]

The Commission, notwithstanding the Bishop of Salisbury's prayers, gave way: it might have been different had he been Archbishop. Burnet complied some days later in the following curt epistle: "I return you the form with my hand to it. I hope your Grace will let the King know how hard it was for us to comply with his pleasure in this matter, and that he will be pleased not to put such things too often upon us".[3]

But worse was to follow. On 22 May the Archbishop received the following terse note from Lord Jersey, Secretary of State and a noted Tory (brother to Elizabeth Villiers), who it will be remembered had endeavoured to prevent Tenison's elevation to the see of Lincoln.[4]

Hampton Court 22 May

"My Ld
His Maj. has been pleased to cõferr ye Prebend of Worcester now vacant upon Mr. Stappylton, and has accordingly ordered me to acquaint Yr Grace of it, yt you may impart it to ye rest of ye Comĩissioners, and give ye necessary directions thereto".[5]

Mr. Stappylton, chaplain to Lord Jersey, would appear to have been a perfectly deserving person, but there could be

[1] Burnet to Tenison, 2 May 1790. Lambeth MSS. 953, f. 72.
[2] Tenison to Sharp, 14 May 1700, Lloyd-Baker-Sharp MSS., L 2.
[3] Burnet to Tenison, 13 May 1700. Lambeth MSS. 953, f. 69.
[4] See Chap. 6, p. 121.
[5] Lord Jersey to Tenison, 22 May 1700. Lambeth MSS. 941, f. 157.

no denying that the king's action "expressly contravened the terms of the Commission which specifically forbad the secretaries to approach the King without previous sanction of the Commission".[1] The normal procedure had in this case been reversed, and the Commission was being instructed whom to recommend. On the next day the Archbishop sent a copy of the above letter to all the members of the Commission, enclosing the following brief note from himself: "I send yr Lp a Copy of a Lr wch I receiv'd yesterday desiring next post to hear frō you yt I may ye better know wt answer to give ye King". As a postscript Tenison rather weakly added: "Mr. Stapylton (My Ld's Chaplain) is a good man. I can't say so of Mr. Smalwood who was recommended by another Ld. ye person dead is worthy Dr. Hopkins".[2]

What had happened was obvious. Lord Jersey, eager to secure a prebend for his own chaplain, and, perhaps, equally desirous of short-circuiting the Whig junto, had gone directly to the King before even the commissioners knew of the vacancy, and had induced him to decide on the appointment independently. The tone of the Archbishop's note, and his endeavouring to gild the pill with a somewhat timid addition, show that he foresaw difficulty from at least one member. He was not left long in doubt of the opinions of the commissioners. Simon Patrick, Bishop of Ely, replied on 25 May with a letter complacently cynical. "If his Mtie hath been pleased to conferr the prebend of W. as my Ld Jersey wishes upon Mr. Stapleton", he wrote, "I do not see what we have to do in the matter. But if there must be the formality of our mentioning him to his Mtie, I am ready to oblige him".[3]

Gilbert Burnet, Bishop of Salisbury, had too much of the Scot in him to be so obliging and he wrote on the same day the following very outspoken letter:

"I hope your Gr. looks on this letter as the superseding our Commission and that accordingly you will carry it to the King and deliver it up, for I am sure this destroies the effect of it. I wish your Grace had maintained your ground upon the first attack, but now it is too late to strugle [sic] if this person is not quite laid aside and an effectuall stopp put to all things of this kind for the future. We are under much obloquy already,

[1] Clarke and Foxcroft, *A Life of Gilbert Burnet*, p. 374.
[2] Lambeth MSS. 941, f. 157.
[3] Patrick to Tenison, 25 May 1700. Lambeth MSS. 941, f. 158.

and I am sure we will become justly so if we are only to skreen
the recommendations of a lewd Court. However for my part,
I beg leave to be left out if yr Grace thinks fit to continue the
Commission on such terms. I thought to have writ to Your Gr.
upon other Subjects but I will mixe nothing with this that I
may leave Your Gr. full freedome to shew it or make what use of
it you please".[1]

Two days later John Moore, Bishop of Norwich, the newly-
appointed member, replied to the Archbishop, expressing the
same sentiments as Burnet, albeit in a little less abrupt
manner.

"I am sorry", he began, "his Majesty should be moved
to anything which may tend to weaken if not break his
Commission—he granted it with prudent advice, and it has
proved both advantageous to his service, and beneficial to
the Church. So far as I have been able to observe, the Comis-
sioners have only recommended persons to his Majesty for
places in the Church, who have been best qualify'd in respect
of their piety, wisdom and learning to fill them, and who have
been longest employed in his service, and when on these
considerations men receive preferment there will be good
ground to hope the Church may prosper and the King be well
served. Such things I humbly conceive Your Grace will be
pleased to lay before his Majesty, and represent the different
presentations yt Dr. G. and Mr. St. have to his favour; that he
may perceive what great preference in point of merit and service
the one ought to have of the other, but Mr. St. being known to
your Grace to be a good man, if his Majesty insists, I presume
his pleasure should be comply'd with. On the other hand, I
apprehend the Commissioners can show no complyance in the
promotion of Mr. S. or any other person, who hath a bad
character, for such complyance will be utterly inconsistent
with that trust the King has reposed in them. So long as his
Majesty shall be pleased to continue me in his Commission,
I shall according to my ability wth all faithfulness endeavour to
serve him and the Church".[2]

Moore, it is true, agreed to continue to serve, but he clearly
showed his dismay at the king's action. One letter only was
completely complacent (unless we include the first) and this came
from John Sharp, Archbishop of York. In view of what happened

[1] Burnet to Tenison, 25 May 1700. Lambeth MSS. 930, f. 159.
[2] Moore to Tenison, 27 May 1700. Lambeth MSS. 930, f. 110.

in 1697 in connection with Henry Finch, its irony is understandable:

> "I have the Honr. of Yr Grace's Letter", he wrote. "I
> think there needs no deliberation about an answer to it. I
> suppose there are none of the Comers but will readily acquiesce
> in the King's pleasure, when He thinks fit to nominate to his
> own Preferments. But I believe Yr Grace thinks it for his
> Majesty's service to put him some times in mind of the
> Expectancys of his own Chaplains".[1]

How Tenison represented the feelings of the Commission to the
King we do not know, although it seems probable that he did
it in person. This appointment, however, seems to have been the
end of the Commission. Preferment was too valuable a royal
asset for it to be controlled even by those who were, in fact, the
king's best friends. The Commission wished to promote only
Whigs:[2] the Crown at times was anxious to bribe Tories. We
read of no more recommendations by the Commission after the
above date, which meant that the Archbishop could now only
petition the King informally. Patrick expressed his opinion
on the state of affairs rather gloomily in a letter to Tenison
in August 1701: "We cannot serve his Mtie", he complained,
"unless he will countenance those whom we recommend to him,
purely because they have deserved well of him, and have no
friends to make their worth known".[3] As it was, the death of
William on 9 March 1702, changed the whole ethos of affairs in
Church and State.

Part II   Anne

The accession of Anne introduced a novel factor into ecclesiastical politics.[4] The new Queen was devoted to the Church of
England, and soon after her accession she complimented those
"who had the happiness to be of our Church", since she herself
"had had her education in it and had been willing to run great
hazards for its preservation". Concerning her public policy,
she affirmed that "her own principles must always keep her
entirely firm to the interests and religion of the Church of

---

[1] Sharp to Tenison, 29 May 1700. Lambeth MSS. 941, f. 161.
[2] Except perhaps Sharp.
[3] Patrick to Tenison, 4 August 1701. Lambeth MSS. 942, f. 170.
[4] The rest of this chapter has been largely drawn from N. Sykes, "Queen Anne and
the Episcopate". *English Historical Review*, L, 433-464.

England, and would incline her to countenance those who had the truest zeal to support it".

As part of this loyalty to the Church, Anne had been taught to distrust the Whigs, and she responded readily to this tuition. Burnet writes that the Queen "had from infancy imbibed the most unconquerable prejudices against the Whigs, having been taught to look upon them all not only as republicans who hated the very shadow of royal authority but as implacable enemies of the Church of England". All this the Queen herself expressed succinctly to Sarah, Duchess of Marlborough, in these words: "I know the principles of the Church of England, I know those of the Whigs, and it is that and no other which makes me think as I do of the last".

Believing such things, Anne could hardly submit to such a measure of control as William had, in theory at least, agreed to. The new temper soon made itself felt. "'Tis said", recorded Narcissus Luttrell on 26 March 1702, "her majesty will herself dispose of all ecclesiastical preferment belonging to the Crown as they become vacant, and not leave it to the Archbishop of Canterbury and 5 other bishops as the late king did".[1] The author of the *Memoirs*[2] writes: "Upon the Accession of a New Sovereign to the Throne, it was but natural to see new Faces at Court, and several of the old Ones dismiss'd from it, so that it was not to be suppos'd, that the Archbishop who was so great a Favourite of King William, should be equally possess'd of the good Graces of his Successor, that had restor'd several of the Ministers that were outed in the late Reign, to their former places in Council".[3]

It was necessary, however, for Anne to have advice upon ecclesiastical matters, and as she knew she could not get the kind she wanted at Lambeth, so she turned to York, with the result that Sharp succeeded "alone to the royal confidence and counsel in all affairs relating to the church". Community of sentiment bound them together, as well as the attractive personality of the Archbishop of York: both were devoted to the interests of the Church, and it was this primary allegiance which gave rise to and controlled their Toryism. So securely did Sharp establish himself in Anne's confidence "that she would rarely give her

---

[1] Luttrell, *A Brief Historical Relation*, etc., v. 157.
[2] *Memoirs of the Life and Times*, etc., p. 101.
[3] *Ibid.*

promise without his advice, and generally speaking, consent first obtained".[1]

Tenison was soon made aware of his changed status when he waited on the Queen in connection with the coronation. She insisted that Sharp be invited to preach the sermon, and showed great concern for his personal comfort in making the journey from York to London.[2]

The disposal of preferment, however, could not in practice resolve itself into a mere matter of royal nomination, and the alliance between Anne and Sharp—no matter how much they might wish to assert its non-party character—was forced to take account of the existing political situation. The Queen and the Archbishop of York, both of whose interests were religious, did not always see eye to eye with Robert Harley, a moderate Tory, and St. John, an extreme one, whose Church policy was dictated by their political ambitions. Opposed to them were Marlborough, and his confidential ally Sydney Godolphin, whose main preoccupation, in domestic politics, was to secure parliamentary support for their foreign policy. To do this it was necessary to conciliate the Whig clergy, and particularly to obtain episcopal support in the House of Lords. Hence in practice the royal pleasure had to take some account of ministerial claims by making concessions to those actually in charge of the conduct of the Government.

The first few appointments of the reign showed that Tenison's advice was neither solicited nor required. On 22 June 1703, William Nicolson (at this stage in his career a zealous Tory) was made Bishop of Carlisle; on 31 October 1703, George Hooper (prolocutor of the Lower House of Convocation) was created Bishop of St. Asaph and translated to Bath and Wells in March 1704; on 16 July 1704, William Beveridge was consecrated to the see of St. Asaph; and on 5 March 1705, George Bull became Bishop of St. David's.

All these clergymen were consistent High Churchmen and sponsored by Sharp.

On 1 March 1705 James Gardiner, Bishop of Lincoln, died, and Tenison decided to exert himself to the utmost to stem this tide of Tory promotions, by securing this see—where he had himself laboured—for his old friend William Wake. He accordingly

---

[1] Sykes, "Queen Anne and the Episcopate", *E.H.R.*, l, 435.
[2] Tenison to Sharp, 28 March 1702, Lloyd-Baker-Sharp MSS., K3.

wrote to Wake, then Dean of Exeter, who had before refused similar invitations,[1] to know "with plainness and without loss of time, whether he would accept" the bishopric if offered to him. Sharp, on the other hand, was energetically soliciting the Queen on behalf of his friend Sir William Dawes, for whom he hoped to obtain some episcopal experience so that he might follow him at York. The political circumstances of the time also added to the excitement of this trial of strength. Parliament was dissolved on 5 April: the extreme Tories set out with enthusiasm to crush the Whigs and raised the cry that the "Church was in danger". Godolphin, back again in the Whig fold, was "exceedingly firm" in pressing Wake's claims on the Queen, and on 16 July 1705, she finally gave way, signed the congé d'élire to Lincoln, and also the letter missive nominating Wake. It was, doubtless, with a peculiar satisfaction, that Tenison, assisted by the Bishops of London, Salisbury, Norwich, and Chichester, consecrated Wake to his old bishopric on 21 October 1705, in the Chapel at Lambeth.[2]

This contretemps did not bring Sharp and Tenison any closer together, and in the course of a letter which the Archbishop of Canterbury sent to his brother of York on 24 July 1705, he observed rather despairingly: "I hope we shall one day agree . . . If not, I'm sure on my part Charitie shall prevail; and I think it will in Yr Grace also".[3]

Tenison and the Whigs, a little reassured, hoped that this victory might be the prelude to better things, and a contemporary Whig writes that "a reaction set in" and the Archbishop of Canterbury had "a much better Reception at Court than during the first years of the Queen. He was thereby again empower'd to recommend such Persons for spiritual Dignities to the Throne as were of his healing Principles".[4] On 10 February 1706, Beaw, Bishop of Llandaff, died, and on 4 June John Tyler, Dean of Hereford, a solid Whig, was nominated to succeed him.

The Whigs did not have to wait long, however, before they

[1] In 1699, for example, Somers wrote to Tenison that "My Ld of Kent came to me and in the most passionate and earnest manner desired me to give St. James' (wch was void by ye advancement of Dr. Wake to ye Bishoprick of Oxford) to Dr. Hickman". (Somers to Tenison, undated 1699. Lambeth MSS. 930, f. 13.) Wake wrote to the Archbishop on 9 April 1699, and though saying, "I shall give myself up to yr Grace's disposall", he yet added at the end of the letter: "I am sure I neither desire the Honour of a Bishop, and am afrayd of the Office and Duty of one". Lambeth MSS. 942, f. 146.
[2] J. Le Neve, The Lives and Characters of the Protestant Bishops, etc., i. 256.
[3] Tenison to Sharp, 24 July 1705, Lloyd-Baker-Sharp MSS., B 9.
[4] Memoirs of the Life and Times, etc., p. 101.

were made aware how ill-founded was this optimism. Within seven months three vacancies were created through the deaths of Mews of Winchester on 9 November 1706, Stratford of Chester on 12 February 1707, and Patrick of Ely on 31 May. In addition, the Regius Professorship of Divinity at Oxford became vacant through the death of Dr. Jane. Anne saw her opportunity and determined to fill the vacancies according to her own inclinations. Trelawney, Bishop of Exeter, was translated to Winchester, and the Queen privately offered Exeter to Offspring Blackall and Chester to Sharp's protégé, Sir William Dawes.

Tenison felt keenly his own ignorance and impotence at Lambeth while these things were depending, but Somers, the former friend of William III and a strong Whig, championed a more energetic policy and advised the Archbishop to wait on the Queen. Hence on 19 January, Tenison wrote to him:

"I'll speak my mind freely as I have always done. Tomorrow I would be glad, at our Charterhouse meeting, to understand how far, if at all, I should speak to my Lord Treasurer upon this subject, before I wait on the Queen. For I would serve him 'in omnibus honestis'. And I think the letting him know (what I have heard even in my retirement) from all quarters, how ill the Ex[ete]r project sounds, may not be disservice. But I'll suspend my Judgment till tomorrow".[1]

Tenison's visit to Anne left no doubt in his mind as to the queen's attitude to the Whigs, and to her disinclination to accept any advice from Lambeth. "My discourse", he wrote to Somers, "was short, it being said to me on my entrance on it, that the thing was already determined, though the person was not declared".[2]

Somers, however, felt strongly that the Archbishop must make a stand and on 3 June he tried to rally him in a very outspoken letter, urging him to take a bolder and firmer line:

"I hope your Grace", he began, "will allow me also to put you in mind that Norwich becomes void,[3] and that if time be lost, or if modesty prevails, it will (as in other cases) be wrong disposed of and the Church and State will be undone. The Archbishop of Canterbury cannot be ill used always, unless he will be a party in it in some measure himself. If the way of

[1] Tenison to Somers, 19 January 1706–07. Somers papers in possession of Corporation of Reigate.
[2] Tenison to Somers, 23 January 1706–07.
[3] Through the proposed translation of Moore to Ely.

talking to the Queen be made difficult or be uneasy to your great candour, the way of writing may in some degree supply, in case it be done with that plainness and vigour which becomes your great station and which other people's insincerity and ill disposition makes absolutely necessary. Pardon, my good lord, this great plainness. The juggling, and trifling and falseness I have of late observed, have made so great an impression upon my mind, and have so deeply afflicted me that I may speak imprudently, but since it is very honestly I hope I shall be forgiven. I have been not a little vexed, when I have remonstrated pretty strongly upon occasion of the talk of supplying late vacancies, to have been told that the Archbishop is principally at fault, who does not speak plainly and fully to the Queen, when the Archbishop of York never suffers her to rest. I know too good a reason for the different behaviour of the two persons, but since that is objected, I should hope there should not for the future be any cause given to repeat that objection".[1]

Tenison, however, did not choose to invite a repetition of his former interview, though he followed Somers' advice so far as to write a tactful letter to the Queen, which by no means, however, satisfied the demand for "plainness and vigour". In this letter, written on 12 June, he began by asking the Queen (perhaps with some irony!) to excuse his "long absence" from the Court since he was suffering severely from the gout. "My confinement", he said, "is the more grievous to me because at this time so many ecclesiastical matters are depend^t and I can so little attend them . . . I can do so little myself, but my office and character call upon me to do what I can". He then turned to the immediate question, the filling of the vacancy at Norwich, and spoke as became a good Whig, albeit a little nervously: "I am in especiall manner concern'd for ye see of Norwich in wh I was a Minister, & where I know ye decided people are as apt to rū into Extremes as in most other places. God hath, hitherto, exceedingly prosper'd y^r Majesty in that [illegible] course of moderation in wh you have proceeded: And I cannot suffer myself to think that you will not be allwaies the same". Concerning the episcopal bench as a whole, he reminded the Queen that it was "ye good Temper of ye prest. Bishops and their appearing for ye true interest of their Coūtry" which had "chiefly gained them respect". "But if it should come to pass at any time by any means", he warned her, "that such

[1] Somers to Tenison, 3 June 1707. Arch. Wake. Epist. 7. Canterbury II.

should come upō that Bench as should make it warp (wch may God avert), Episcopacy itself would be in danger of falling".[1]

The Archbishop now realized that his own influence at Court was almost nil, and he accordingly resorted to other expedients in an effort to secure his will. In connection with the vacancy at Ely he had heard rumours that Moore, Bishop of Norwich (for whom the Queen declared she "had a kindness"), was to succeed to that see, and he now suggested that this Bishop might use his good offices in the interests of the Whigs. "I have pressed him to drop in a word", he wrote to Somers, "about a successor, if it were but to this effect, that the having an improper successor would much abate the comfort he would otherwise have in Ely. As yet he has said nothing; but promises to do something this afternoon. For my part, I am very lame, and if I could go abroad, I do not know whether I should not do more hurt than good".[2]

Still the appointments to the vacant sees were not made public, and the uncertainty and delay added to the excitement, which was not confined to the clergy. Marlborough himself was forced, in the midst of his other cares, to take notice of the crisis, since it was calculated to affect his position in Parliament, and Godolphin observed to him on 27 June:

"The Queen has indulged her own inclinations in the choice of some persons to succeed the bishops which gives the greatest offence to the Whigs that can be; and though the Whigs were, from other things, in a disposition to lay more weight upon it than in truth the thing itself ought to bear, yet it must be allowed, taking all circumstances together, to be a very great contretems".[3]

Most of the Whigs had resigned themselves to the fact that two sees were already lost to them, but they now began to fear for a third. Marlborough, on his part, expressed his anxiety to the Queen, only to receive the following curt reply:

"I cannot think my having nominated Sir William Dawes and Dr. Blackall to be bishops is any breach, they being worthy men, and all the clamour that is being raised against them proceeds only from the malice of the whigs. . . I believe you have been told, as I have, that these two persons were recommended to me by Mr. Harley, which is so far from being

---

[1] Tenison to Queen Anne, 12 June 1707. Lambeth MSS. 930, f. 195.
[2] Tenison to Somers, 17 June 1707. Somers Papers.
[3] Godolphin to Marlborough, 27 June–8 July 1707. Coxe, *Memoirs of the Duke of Marlborough*, ii. 158.

true, that he knew nothing of it till it was the talk of the town. I do assure you these men *were my own choice*. They were certainly very fit for the station I design them; and indeed I think myself obliged to fill the bishops' bench with those that will be a credit to it and to the Church".[1]

The fact that Blackall and Dawes were "in themselves men of value and worth", and that Anne had chosen them, mattered little to Marlborough. What weighed with him was that they were Tories, and with all the emphasis that he could command he wrote to the Queen on 15 September, "to protest in the presence of God Almighty that he was persuaded, that if she continued in the mind that he thought her now, and would not suffer those that had the honour to serve her, to manage her affairs agreeably to the circumstances of the times, her business must inevitably run to confusion".[2]

Such a solemn warning from such a man could not be completely ignored, and even before it had been written Tenison was "in no pain" about Norwich, though he regarded Exeter and Chester as virtually disposed of. Further delay in the announcement of the appointments made some Whigs more optimistic than the Primate, but they were destined to be disappointed for it was at last made public that Dawes had been nominated to Chester and Blackall to Exeter. Maybe it was not only gout which induced Tenison to act by commission and absent himself when these two were consecrated bishops in Lambeth Chapel on 8 February 1708.[3]

The Queen had certainly demonstrated her power to make appointments independent of her ministers: yet it had been a struggle, and her next few appointments showed also the limitations of this power. She had been made acutely aware of the strength of Whig feeling, since the administration "realised the necessity of insisting on the right to nominate ecclesiastical as well as civil appointments, for the dissatisfaction of the clerical supporters threatened to break up the incipient Church-Whig party". The result of this Whig pressure soon bore fruit. The Queen assured the Cabinet Council that in future promotions she would consult the wishes of her ministers, and as a result Charles

---

[1] Anne to Marlborough. Coxe, *Memoirs of the Duke of Marlborough*, ii. 158.
[2] Marlborough to Queen Anne, 15 September 1707. Coxe, *Ibid.*, ii. 158.
[3] Le Neve, *The Lives and Characters of the Protestant Bishops*, etc., i. 257. Le Neve says, "his Grace being at that time indispos'd".

13

Trimnell went to Norwich, and Potter—Tenison's nominee— to the Regius Professorship of Divinity at Oxford.

The fortunes of the Whigs were now rising, owing to the exigencies of the foreign war, and this enabled Marlborough and Godolphin to persuade the Queen to reconstitute the ministry on a party basis. Harley and St. John were dismissed; Somers became Lord President of the Council in November 1708, and Wharton Viceroy of Ireland. Thus when Beveridge, Bishop of St. Asaph, died on 5 March 1708, it occasioned no surprise that William Fleetwood, a solid Whig, was consecrated to the vacant see on 6 June 1708.

Even now, however, there was no clear (or secure) field for the Whigs, for when Williams of Chichester died on 24 April 1709, the Whig ministers were unable to secure the appointment for Richard Willis, whom Tenison recommended. The only satisfaction the Archbishop could wring from the Queen was the promise that the new bishop "should be a person acceptable to his friends".[1]

On 13 November Thomas Manningham was consecrated Bishop of Chichester, but a few days previously, on 5 November, the fate of the Whigs both clerical and lay was being determined for the rest of the queen's reign by a sermon preached in St. Paul's Cathedral by the notorious Dr. Sacheverell. The Whig ministers, when in office, had tried to insist (though in vain) on their right to promote both in Church and State. Anne accepted this principle willingly now that the Tories came into their own. As a consequence the Whigs promoted no more bishops until Anne was "as dead as Julius Cæsar". A devoted Whig wrote concerning Tenison at this time:

"The Remainder of this Great and Holy Man's Life from 1709, when he saw an approaching Change in Matters of State coming on, till the Day of the Queen's Death, was one continued Scene of Sorrow and Sollitariness: And he beheld in his Retirement at Lambeth, as an Addition to the Afflicting Pains of the Gout, with which he was grievously tormented, the Glories of a Reign which had been blessed with a continued Series of Prosperous and Successful Events, sinking into its last Declension by means of Corrupt and Evil Practices".[2]

The failure of the Church-Whig alliance left many bitter feelings behind amongst the Whig clergy. Their support, and particularly

---

[1] Sykes, "Queen Anne and the Episcopate". *E.H.R.*, L, 446.
[2] *Memoirs of the Life and Times*, etc., p. 110.

that of the bishops in the House of Lords, had been necessary
for the Whig ministers to continue in office, since they were
"essentially the party of a minority"; yet during this very period
when they were kept in power by such support, Tory clergy had
been promoted to episcopal office. Tenison, on his part, had always
acted with the utmost loyalty to his lay allies, never entertaining
terms from any other quarters, though Gibson wrote to Wake:
"If a change should happen at Lambeth (and by these frequent
returns of the gout both they and we have reason to feel it too
near) the Whig Clergy may probably be admitted, if not invited,
to terms there, wholly independent from those gentlemen by whom
they are now so scurvily used".[1] But the Archbishop's loyalty
to the Whigs was a matter of conscience, and the principle
(again we are quoting Gibson), "upon which he acted in the whole
course of his administration and from which he never could be
driven by the continual clamours of the Tories about the danger
of the Church", was the conviction "that there was no way to
preserve the Church but by preserving the present establishment
in the State, and that there was far greater probability that the
Tories would be able to destroy our present establishment in the
State, than that the dissenters would be able to destroy our
establishment in the Church".[2] Sharp's intimacy with the Queen,
however, meant that Tenison was dependent upon the Whigs
in the ministry to secure his own nominations to high office in the
Church—and this was where they had failed him. "As to our
Court friends", Gibson complained angrily, "I wish them
well for the sake of the cause they are in, as I think it right in
the main; but as to their persons, we have no reason to be
concerned at their fall whenever it comes, if the same cause
can be tolerably carried on without them, since they so visibly
drop and disown us. And yet I cannot see that they are so
far established as to be in a condition to despise the interest
of their Church friends, how meanly soever they may think of
it".[3]

Perhaps Tenison and the Whig clergy as a whole did not
fully appreciate how determined Anne could be, particularly in
those things which she thought concerned the welfare of the
Ecclesia Anglicana.

[1] Gibson to Wake, 12 August 1709. Arch. Wake Epist. 17 Christ Church, ii. f. 242.
[2] Gibson to Nicolson, 3 December 1717. MSS. Add. A 269, f. 72 (Bodley).
[3] Gibson to Wake, 12 August 1709. Arch. Wake Epist. 17 Christ Church, ii. f. 242.

From 1710 till the Queen's death, the Whigs, both clerical and lay, found themselves in the wilderness, and Tenison neither possessed influence himself nor had any ministers to put his case. All episcopal appointments went to the Tories, although the moderation of Harley—who preferred a mixed ministry—did much to prevent the promotion of too extreme men. Thus the first few appointments, John Robinson to Bristol and Philip Bisse to St. David's in 1710 (the latter being translated to Hereford in 1713), and Adam Otley to St. David's (1713) were all his work. It was Harcourt, however (who had defended Sacheverell in 1710), who forced upon a very reluctant Queen the nomination of Atterbury (leader of the Tory clergy) to the see of Rochester, vacant on the death of Sprat, 20 May 1713. "I never knew the Queen do anything with so much reluctancy", writes the Earl of Dartmouth, "as the signing his congé d'élire. She told me she knew he would be as meddling and troublesome as the Bishop of Salisbury, had more ambition, and was less tractable. I told her, I thought she had a right notion of the man, therefore wondered she would do it. She answered, Lord Harcourt had answered for his behaviour, and she had lately disobliged him by refusing the like request for Dr. Sacheverell; and feared if she did not grant this, she must break with him quite; which she believed I would not think advisable. I told her I really thought anything was more so than letting such a 'boutefeu' into the Church and the house of Lords".[1] Atterbury would co-operate with none but Tories, and his naturally militant spirit raised embittered controversies wherever he went. Harley was anxious to steer a more middle course.

As a whole, however, it was Harley who had the last word, except when the Queen's purely personal wishes prevailed. Thus Harley secured, in 1714, the bishopric of London for John Robinson, Bristol for George Smalridge, and Chester for Francis Gastrell: but it was the Queen's own appointment when, out of respect to Sharp's wish, Sir William Dawes followed him in the Archbishopric of York.

Treasurer Harley's path, however, was a difficult one, for his moderation aroused the fierce opposition of Bolingbroke, Harcourt, and Atterbury, who had the effrontery to accuse him "of not being a sincere Christian". The passing of the Occasional Conformity Act in 1711 (as the result of an unholy alliance between

---

[1] Burnet, *History of my own Time*, Dart. ed. 1833, vi. 176.

the Tories led by the Earl of Nottingham and some refractory Whig lords) and the "infamous" Schism Act in 1714 [1]—which was, in fact, a definite attack on the revolution settlement—showed the intentions of Bolingbroke and the strength of the extreme Church-Tory party.

It was these extreme measures, however, with their implied threat to the Hanoverian succession, which evoked a reaction amongst those Tories who were not prepared to welcome the "King over the water". William Nicolson (Bishop of Carlisle) and Sir Jonathan Trelawney came round to a Whig position, and even Sir William Dawes, Archbishop of York, joined the Whigs, taking with him all the Tory bishops save three "courtiers", in a declaration in the House of Lords on 5 April 1714, that the Protestant Succession was not in danger.

But the end of an age was at hand. In July of this year the Queen was taken ill: she accepted Harley's resignation, and was aroused from stupor to place the staff of office in the hands of the Duke of Shrewsbury.

It may be that Tenison failed to make an adequate distinction between the Toryism of such as Sharp, which was devoted to the interests of the Church, and the militant Toryism of Atterbury which found its centre of loyalty at St. Germains: but to the Archbishop of Canterbury, the one was the first stage on a road which led to the other, and living at a time when at any moment the Pretender might appear at our shores, he was not inclined to make nice distinctions. The practical way, he thought, of showing loyalty to the Protestant Succession was to be a Whig; and to preserve the Protestant Succession was the one thing needful to prevent either the religious anarchy of the Commonwealth, or the attempted Romanization of James II. Sharp, who professed to be above parties, in practice recommended only Tories to Anne: [2] Tenison was more candid and openly identified the security of both Church and State with devotion to Whig principles.

This cleavage on the bench, and amongst the rank and file of the clergy, did much to impoverish the life and witness of the Church: it led to the suppression of Convocation, and to the dissipation of energies which might have been more profitably employed in adapting the medieval constitution of the Church to the needs

[1] See p. 119 for its terms.
[2] It was to Sharp that Tenison said on one occasion: "Brother, you know that I was always a greater Church-man than you; but e'en take the name of the Church, whilst I keep to the Constitution of it". Masters, *The History of the College of Corpus Christi*, p. 396.

of the day, and in doing something to stem the break-away from the Christian faith.

The death of Anne and the accession of George I did not remove Tenison's isolation, for Lord Townsend favoured a mixed ministry, and was anxious to win over the Tories. An indication of this was soon seen in the struggle that went on at the Court before John Wynne was appointed to the bishopric of St. Asaph and Richard Willis (so often rejected) to Gloucester, both in 1714. These appointments were such as the Archbishop did not disapprove, for both were zealous Whigs—in fact he had tried in the late queen's reign to secure the promotion of the latter—but the Archbishop felt keenly his impotence to influence the Court during the negotiations. "While the business of St. Asaph was going on for Dr. Wynne", Gibson wrote at the time,

"our good old Patriarch plainly told them they might do what they w'd, but for his part, he knew not what to make of a *motley* Bench and a *motley* Synod. He seems to be a good deal uneasy at these doings and I can't but say but in my opinion he sinks in strength and spirits, which I hope is only the effect of his great fatigue on Coronation day. His not being able to be often with the King is unspeakable mischief to the Comōn cause. I doe not hear there was much opposition in the case of Gloucester [Dr. Rich. Willis] but St. Asaph was opposed to the last, first for Mr. Hill; then for the satisfaction of the Clergy, that it might be a Tory, and not a Whig, and after that when neither of these would drive, that at least it might not be St. Asaph who had made himself particularly obnoxious to the other side".[1]

[1] Gibson to Nicolson, 27 November 1714. MSS. Add. A 269, f. 36 (Bodley).
This reference to Mr. Hill [a writer on the side of the Lower House in the convocational disputes (?), see p. 251] is interesting, because Tenison had been somewhat disturbed a short time previously, on hearing a rumour from Doctors' Commons that this man was to succeed John Moore (died 31 July 1714) in the bishopric of Ely. Hill was certainly *persona non grata* to the Archbishop since as Registrar to the Admiralty he had lived as a layman for many years. On 5 October 1714, Tenison wrote in strong terms to Townsend pointing out that Canon 76 forbade any priest or deacon voluntarily to relinquish his office or live afterwards as a layman. "I am much Mr. Hill's friend", he protested, "But much more a Servant of ye King and to the Constitution in Church and State. That such an Advancement will also disoblige thousands of ye K's good subjects is the opinion, my Lord, of yr affect. and faithfull Servt". Moreover, the Archbishop stated, he had heard that on the Sunday before, many London pulpits had been ringing with the cry that the Church was in danger and that a new Sacheverell had come to London. "I believe", he warned Townsend, "that nothing will ripen their design of making this government uneasy as they did King William's than ye filling of ye Bpric of Ely on ye abovesaid manner". (Tenison to Townsend, 5 October 1714. Lambeth MSS. 930, f. 196.) It was doubtless with genuine relief that Tenison was able to secure the translation of William Fleetwood, a conscientious Whig, from St. Asaph to Ely. Tenison's settled concern to favour the

Thus even under George I there was at first by no means a
clear field for the Whigs, and many of the party began to feel it
prudent to accommodate themselves to the new state of affairs.
The old Archbishop, so Gibson tells us, did not like "the posture of
Affairs at Court", nor the divided counsels which existed within
the Whigs themselves. Church matters, he thought, were at
"6ˢ and 7ˢ", and when Thomas Sherlock was "taken reeking
hot out of the midst of the Tories . . . to be cast immediately
into a nest of Whigs" (i.e. was made Dean of Chichester, 1715),
Tenison feared for the future. For better or worse he did not live
to see it.

In his relations with his brethren the bishops, it was Tenison's
constant preoccupation to encourage them to be good Whigs,
and to be zealous in the discharge of their duties; but the bitterness of the disputes in Convocation, and the Tory nominations of
Anne, acting on the advice of Sharp, made his position difficult,
and his relations with the bishops were often of a formal character
and conducted through his chaplains. He was conscientious almost
to a fault, serious and sincere, yet political and religious differences
cut far too deeply in him and in others to enable (or predispose)
him to win the confidence of those bishops who did not share
his Whig principles.[1]

It is true that we find him writing to Sharp in October 1700,
at the beginning of the Convocational disputes, that "'twill
be very necessary for ye Bps to meet oftenʳ than they do wn in
Town for ye good of ye Monarchy and ye Ch. & ye com[mon]
Xy"[2]—but such a desire was shipwrecked by the cleavage between
Tenison and Sharp which became acute when Anne ascended the
throne. Human nature being as it is, it is perhaps not surprising
that the Archbishop should have resented his virtual exclusion
from a Court where Sharp was always so welcome a visitor.

At times, moreover, Tenison himself could act in a somewhat
arbitrary manner towards his colleagues, as the following incident
shows.

Whig clergy may be seen in the following small incident. Nicolson requested Tenison
(1712) through John Sharp, Archbishop of York, to grant a Lambeth degree to his
nephew, one Pearson. Tenison replied with a peremptory refusal, but the uncle let
the Archbishop know that Pearson was a strong opponent of Atterbury, and that
"his principles [were] . . . far from Tory lengths", with the result that a little later
Nicolson was informed that the degree had been granted. Gibson to Nicolson,
30 May 1712. MSS. Add. A, 269, f. 16 (Bodley).
[1] Nearly all Tenison's letters have a rather stiff formality about them, even when he
is doing his best to avoid this.
[2] Tenison to Sharp, October 1700, Lloyd-Baker-Sharp MSS., Q 41.

In August 1711, the Bishop of Bangor (John Evans—a strong Whig) was in Chichester, and Tenison requested him to hold a confirmation for the several parishes near the city, and to notify the neighbouring clergy of the event. The Bishop of Chichester (Thomas Manningham, a Tory) could hardly interpret this as other than a public rebuke, although Gibson assured him, on behalf of the Archbishop, that "ye Bp of Bangor was not sent down on purpose, but having resolved on a visit to ye Dean, his Grace thought he might confirm at one or two of your Churches while he staid here, without much trouble to himself". Tenison had done this, Gibson explained, "only on Supposition yt ye Bp of Chichester did not Confirm about this time; Soe that it was plain his Grace meant noe disrespect, and there was not the least ground for such an Interpretation".[1] At first Thomas Manningham, though not "very easy in ye matter", merely remarked that he "himself would not confirm till after harvest". Later, however, so Gibson reported to Tenison, he became "much out of humour that his Grace should employ another Bishop, which he said noe Archbishop had ever done; adding that he was very ready to doe it and had ordered another Confirmation of his own at another Church in Chichester ye same day".[2]

If Tenison intended his action as a rebuke, it was certainly very effective!

Francis Atterbury, when Dean of Carlisle, was almost as much a thorn in the flesh of the Archbishop as he was to the bishop of the diocese, and it was this fact, among others, which helped to draw Nicolson, Bishop of Carlisle, into the fold of the Whigs. In 1707 Nicolson, in the midst of violent disputes with the Dean, decided to visit the Chapter of Carlisle, only to meet with a protest from Dr. Todd, one of the Chapter (urged on by Atterbury), who insisted "upon the invalidity of King Henry VIII's Statutes, maintaining that the Queen and not the bishop was the local visitor".[3] Nicolson replied by suspending and excommunicating Todd, who thereupon moved the court of Common Pleas for a prohibition, and obtained it "unless cause shewn". Tenison regarded these proceedings as a serious attack upon the authority

---

[1] Gibson to Tenison, 31 July 1711. Lambeth MSS. 941, f. 28.
[2] *Ibid.* I have been unable to discover any more information concerning this rather curious incident.
[3] *Letters on Various Subjects to and from William Nicolson,* ed. J. Nichols, 1809, p. 365.

of the bishops of the "new foundations" and on 2 February 1708 he sent the following circular letter to the bishops:

"I doubt not but all my suffragans are apprised of what is doing in the case of the Bishop of Carlisle. Though he is not of our Province, I take it to be a common cause, and of great concern to this Church; which will never be quiet so long as that evil generation of men who make it their business to search into little flaws in antient Charters and Statutes, and to unfix what laudable custom hath well fixed, meet with any success. I write not this as if I suspected your zeal in such a case; but to assure you of my ready concurrence with you, in any proper means whether by Bill or otherwise, to make this excellent Church safe in this point, both now and to late posterity. Such provisions are to be endeavoured in a good Reign, lest in an evil one we feel the want of them".[1]

What Tenison hinted at was achieved, when some time later "An Act to empower her Majesty to amend, alter and approve, the local Statutes and Ordinances of Cathedral and Collegiate Churches" was passed, which established the validity of the local Statutes given by Henry VIII to his new foundations.[2]

At one period in his archiepiscopate Tenison seems to have attempted to keep in touch with the special problems in both provinces by drawing up a central register which he called "Notitia Episcopatuum". This consisted of a vellum book of some two hundred and fifty pages, neatly divided up into sections for each diocese. The Archbishop clearly intended this book to be the means of securing a measure of co-ordination, and he may have provided it as a result of his promise to the bishops in 1695.[3] It is difficult, however, to detect any classification in the things entered, nor does he appear to have used the book very long. Among the subjects included there are the detection of false letters of orders, the question of the presentation to a living, the citation of the Bishop of St. David's on 23 August 1695,[4] and the discovery of a Popish schoolmaster in Winchester.[5]

It was one of Tenison's many responsibilities to see that the bishops as an order were well represented in the House of Lords, particularly when the government especially needed their support.

---

[1] *Letters on Various Subjects to and from William Nicolson*, p. 365.
[2] *Ibid.* p. 379.
[3] See Chap. 7, p. 146.
[4] See Chap. 10.
[5] Lambeth MSS. 1023.

If they desired to be absent, Tenison expected them to get the consent of the Crown or arrange for a proxy. Thus we find William Nicolson (1655–1727), Bishop of Carlisle, asking for leave of absence from Parliament, and receiving the reply that his request was "in many respects very Reasonable and he will doe wt he can to make it pass easily at Court and amongst the Bishops". "Her Majesty", so Gibson commented, who conveyed the message,

> "is of course to be applied to for leave, but if there be any difficulty it will be among the Juniors of the Bench, and you may, I find, leave it to his Grace to keep them in humour for the time you desire, on condition you don't exceed that and contrive matters so as to be able to come up to Town sooner if his Grace and the Bps shall find that there is a necessity or great occasion at, or soon after, the opening of Parliament, tho' he hopes and believes no such occasion will happen".[1]

As a matter of fact Nicolson did come up to London in October.

Again in 1712 Tenison was "pressing all the Bps to be at the opening of Parliament", and told Nicolson that there was "a good deal of difference between his person and Proxy".[2] The Archbishop would, perhaps, have preferred it later the other way round in the case of Atterbury!

Tenison lived long enough to see many changes resulting in much unsettlement, and it became more and more his policy to preserve the essential framework of the Church, while making it more efficient here and there. Schemes of doubtful expediency found little encouragement from him, as, for example, a plan to divide up the Bishopric of Lincoln and erect a new Bishopric of St. Albans—which has since been done. The proposal was briefly as follows. The new bishopric was to include Hertfordshire, Bedfordshire, and Buckingham. At the next episcopal vacancy in the Diocese of Rochester, the see was to be removed to St. Albans, while that part of Rochester which was in Kent (some ninety-eight parishes) was to be annexed to the diocese of Canterbury. In return the Archbishop of Canterbury was to surrender all the "peculiars" which belonged to him in other dioceses to the bishops concerned. Tenison was certainly by no means sympathetic to such an invasion of prescriptive rights. His

---

[1] Gibson to Nicolson, 15 September 1702. MSS. Add. A. 269, f. 3 (Bodley).
[2] Gibson to Nicolson, 30 December 1712. MSS. Add. A. 269, f. 19 (Bodley).

comment, scribbled across the document itself, was brief and to the point:

"I can by no means approve of this Scheme—T. Cantuar: A Chimere".[1]

---

[1] Lambeth MSS. 933, f. 60. For another point of view, see T. Brett, *Account of Church Government and Governors*, 1710. He pleaded for the creation of suffragan bishops, especially in the diocese of Canterbury, since "his Grace . . . (being a Privy-Counsellor, and one of the Principal Ministers of State) is so continually involved in Matters of National Concern, that he can have but little time to think of his peculiar Diocese" (p. 235).

CHAPTER 9

THE NONJURORS

NO man of his time, we imagine, found it more difficult to understand the point of view of the Nonjurors than did Thomas Tenison. In the light of his definite Whig principles—and these remained his firm convictions throughout life—the nonjuring approach to the problems of the day must have appeared almost incomprehensible. To profess allegiance to a Roman Catholic monarch seemed to Tenison to defeat the very purpose for which James II had been expelled, since the Church could never be secure except under a Protestant sovereign. As it was the monarch's duty to protect the Church, so Tenison felt no scruples in taking the oaths of allegiance to a King (and Queen) whose accession he regarded as a timely intervention of Providence, and soon after the Revolution he took part in the negotiations with Sancroft.

From the moment it became certain that William would be content with nothing but the throne, Sancroft decided to stand aside and his last public act was to join, with the rest of the bishops, in a request to William to call a free parliament. Henceforth, he refused to do anything but remained at Lambeth, absenting himself from the Convention Parliament at which he would have had an opportunity of putting forward his own scheme for a regency—though this would certainly have been in vain. No appointment was immediately made to the six sees held by nonjuring bishops in order to give them an opportunity of changing their mind.

Early in 1691, however, it became obvious that new appointments must be made, and it was in these circumstances, after Sancroft had been deprived, that on 23 April, Tenison, in company with William Lloyd, Bishop of St. Asaph, dined with Lord Clarendon and then went on to see Sancroft at Lambeth. Conversation was at first quite general although, to quote Sancroft's words to a friend, he "soon saw in ye Bp's solemn gravity what news he was big wth but stav'd him off for half an hour wth comon discourse as brisk as I could contrive it".[1]

---

[1] Sancroft to Lloyd, 24 April 1691. Quoted, *Life of Bishop Ken by a layman*, 1854, p. 582. Tillotson delayed his election and consecration till May 1691, because right up till the last moment he was reluctant to be made "a wedge to drive out Sancroft".

Eventually, of course, the talk turned to the matter of the new appointments and Tenison and his companions had the unpleasant task of confirming Sancroft's worst fears.

The interview showed plainly that the Archbishop had irrevocably made up his mind not to conform, and it was not long before Tillotson was raised to the primatial see and the other bishoprics were filled.

The position of the deprived bishops in relation to the Church was certainly an extraordinary one. Nobody, not even the most extreme Anglican erastian, could logically deny that Sancroft and his five brethren were still in some sense fathers of the Church.[1] They were under no ecclesiastical censure as such, but had been deprived of their territorial jurisdiction by an Act of Parliament. The schism thus created, although to contemporaries it appeared a political necessity, was both regrettable and dangerous: regrettable in that it deprived the Church of England of many of its most serious and disinterested clergy: dangerous in that it provided a rallying point for those whose political allegiance was with the King over the water.

Early in his archiepiscopate Tenison had occasion to censure the activities of some among the nonjuring communion. In 1695 the Whigs were horrified to discover a plot to assassinate the King and as a result some five people were condemned to death. At the execution of two of their number, Sir John Friend and Sir William Perkin, three nonjuring clergymen gave them absolution by laying on of hands, despite the fact that they were "glorifying in their crimes". This action seemed to approach dangerously near a condoning of rebellion, and the Court and the Whigs were filled with some alarm. Tenison felt he must take some official cognisance of this irregularity, and he called together the bishops then in town to his palace at Lambeth. They proceeded to draw up a declaration

"wherein they censured the Performance of this Office of the Church without a previous Confession made, and Abhorrence expressed by the Prisoners of the heinous Crime for which they died; as extremely insolent, and without Precedent in the Manner and altogether Irregular in the Thing itself; it being a manifest Transgression of the Church's Order, and a profane Abuse of the Authority of Christ; since Mr.

[1] Nine English bishops refused to take the oath of allegiance to William and Mary, but three of them died before their deprivation.

Collier,[1] Mr. Snat(t) and Mr. Cook (the three clergymen) must look on the Persons absolv'd as Impenitents or as Martyrs".[2]

Collier did his best to justify their action in a series of pamphlets, but his two brethren suffered an indictment from King's Bench and on 7 April 1696 were committed to Newgate. The Archbishop of Canterbury was unwilling, however, that they should further suffer, particularly as the official position of the Church had already been vindicated, and he used his influence with the Government to secure their release.[3]

Such a strong supporter of the Revolution as the Archbishop inevitably viewed with the strongest condemnation all those who plotted against the security of the throne, and when dealing with these, his influence was usually on the side of justice rather than mercy. Such an occasion occurred in 1697 in connection with the trial of Sir John Fenwick, when the Archbishop himself came in for a great deal of hostile comment in some quarters.

Sir John Fenwick would undoubtedly have consulted his own and the nation's security if he had remained permanently out of England after the establishment of William and Mary in 1689. A natural love for intrigue, however, and perhaps the excitement of living dangerously, made this psychologically impossible. The friend and supporter of James II, and the introducer of the Bill of Attainder against Monmouth into the House of Commons, he never acquiesced in the Revolution, but was a constant source of embarrassment to the Dutch King. A contemporary writes: "Sir John Fenwick was all along an open declared enemy of the Government. He had not only taken several opportunities of affronting Queen Mary in places of public resort, but had persisted in repeated insolences and riots".[4]

It is not surprising, therefore, that in 1696 he became implicated in the plot against William in which Sir George Barclay and Robert Charnock suffered. Fenwick himself was arrested later when escaping to the coast, and on being brought before the King, he artfully made a confession which implicated the Whigs. For this and other reasons, it was decided to proceed against Fenwick by a Bill of Attainder, a method of procedure which Tenison in the

---

[1] Jeremy Collier (1650–1726) later became a nonjuring bishop. He wrote an *Ecclesiastical History of Great Britain.*
[2] *Memoirs of the Life and Times*, etc., p. 60.
[3] *Ibid.* p. 59.
[4] Calamy, *An Historical Account of my own Life*, i. 338.

circumstances approved, although Smalridge (later Bishop of Bristol) regarded it as "a method of punishing . . . not of the common road, and such . . . as has been condemned by those who have judged cooly".

Robert Nelson, the nonjuror and "a particular friend of the Archbishop", tried to use his influence with Tenison to save Fenwick's life but received the following stern reply:

"My very good friend, give me leave to tell you that you know not what spirit that man nor I am made of. I wish for his nor no man's blood; but how can I do my duty to God and my King, should I declare a man innocent (for my not being of the side of the Bill will convince the World that I think him so) when I am satisfied in my own conscience, not only from Goodman's evidence, but all the convicting testimonies in the world, that he is guilty".[1]

Thus Tenison led the bishops in supporting the Bill of Attainder, and "not only voted but spoke for it with the eloquence and courage of St. Paul".[2] The Tories, on their part, maintained that it was "unknown to that time" for prelates to vote "in cases of blood"[3]—a prohibition, however, which the Whigs claimed applied only to "trial by one's peers", and not to such statutory proceedings.

Despite his strong views on the nonjuring schism, however, and his constant vigilance in preventing suspected Jacobites securing ecclesiastical office,[4] Tenison did not decline to enter into a correspondence with Dodwell, which the latter initiated in the hopes of some kind of reconciliation. It is to this correspondence that we now turn.

[4] See p. 77.

[1] Calamy, *An Historical Account*, etc., i. 338.
[2] H.M.C. Marquis of Bath MSS. 1904, i. 100. Tenison was the only one of the Lord Justices to vote for the Bill. The Archbishop, however, did not welcome ill-considered support for it by the bishops as the following story shows (quoted, C. Tenison, Notes for the Life of Thomas Tenison, p. 56): "When the division was about to be taken in the Lords, the Bishop of Chichester [Dr. John Williams], newly-appointed thereto on Tenison's recommendation, and consecrated the day before the third reading, made all haste to be present in order to vote, and please the Court. While robing himself hurriedly in the Bishops' Chamber, Tenison said to him, 'Brother, Brother, you'll overheat yourself. What's the reason of all this pother?' 'Nothing, may it please your Grace', replied Williams, 'but I am fearful lest the Bill against Sir John Fenwick should be read before I could take my place in the House'. 'Fye, my Lord', replied Tenison, 'you might have spared yourself that labour, since you had not an opportunity of hearing the merits of the Cause at the first and second Readings; but since, as I perceive, you are come to give your vote, pray Brother, come in along with me that you may hear it read once before you do it'".
[3] Thomas Bruce, Earl of Ailesbury, *Memoirs*, i. 300.

Henry Dodwell (1641–1711) was a leading nonjuring layman, and had been deprived of his Camden professorship of ancient history at Oxford on his refusal to take the oaths. Henceforth his home at Shottesbrook near Maidenhead in Berkshire became a centre of the nonjurors, where his kind hospitality and great learning were ever at their disposal. Dodwell was a great letter-writer and an indefatigable controversialist, and on 29 August 1700 he entered into correspondence with the Archbishop. The occasion of his writing was ostensibly to urge Tenison to use his influence to secure resident bishops for the American plantations, but his real purpose was more probably contained in his concluding paragraph:

> "I had formerly flattered myself I had some interest in you, before this present unhappy Schism. And your favours were such as to make me believe I was not mistaken in it . . . I know not how even yourself can judge it as a reason of displeasure, that I defend the Rights of your Function against your Person".[1]

Tenison replied in such a way as to encourage Dodwell to carry on the correspondence and to indulge a hope that he might act as a mediator between the Archbishop and Bishop Lloyd of the nonjuring communion. Hence on 25 November Dodwell dispatched his second letter to Tenison.[2]

"In confidence of the place I have enjoyed in your favour in your private station", he began, "and the encouragement you have given me (as I understand by others) by an information left where you thought it would reach me, I presume to beg a favour which you are more concerned to grant than I am to request it". He then went on, rather in the manner of a school-master, to point out that the Archbishop's championship of the secular power might one day recoil on his own head. He reminded him of Bishop Fisher's advising Henry VIII not to be too enthusiastic in advancing the authority of the Pope, and continued: "The impartiall consideration of this will not only let you see how our Fathers' case is intermingled with your spiritual Interests, but how much more it is so, rather to make an honourable composition with them, than to let the Dispute fall". The actual particulars of any agreement must, of course, be negotiated by Tenison directly with the deprived fathers.

---

[1] Dodwell to Tenison, 29 August 1700. Lambeth MSS. 930, f. 38.
[2] Dodwell to Tenison, 29 November 1700. *Ibid.* f. 39.

The intention of Dodwell's letter was certainly admirable although its method of expression might have been more diplomatic. We quote Tenison's reply, sent on 5 December, in full, particularly as it shows the courtesy with which he could treat a rather tactless letter.

"I had acknowledged ye receipt of yrs of Nov. 25 before ys time if ye trouble ye Gout has givē me had not in some measure hindered me. This (I thank God) is an easie day. There was no need of an Apology for ye writing wth relatiō to my character; my old Acquaintances are encourag'd to use ye same freedō they us'd to do . . . For ye matter of yr Lr it is plaȳ it is of moment; but still there is some obscuritie in it because you descend not to particulars; and perhaps you yet cañot do so. As soon as you cā I hope you will. You speak of *Composition* & *Terms.* I cañot yet master enough of the purpose of these wds as they stād in yr Lr. If any Propositiōs tending to ye good of God's Ch[urch] be sent by yr hand I shall . . . let you know wt my sense is of ym and how I can go in thē".[1]

It was now necessary, if the matter was to go any further, for Dodwell to be more explicit, and this he attempted in a long letter written on 29 December. The first part of this epistle dealt with his own personal position in respect of the negotiations, and the second with the concrete proposals.

"When I proposed a Composition upon Terms with our invalidly deprived Fathers", he began, "I studiously declined mentioning the terms, and I gave my reason why I did so. I thought your Brethren and them the proper Judges what terms were fit to be proposed or graunted on either side for themselves and their Brethren. . . . Yet I cannot imagine how such a Motion can begī except from Private Persons who may adjust[?] the power to the Body, or those who have the power of them. For my own part I pretend to nothing that may qualify me for it, but my hearty good will to both partyes and to our late mother the Church of England. . . . I beg therefore your favourable interpretation of what you have encouraged me to propose and that you take it only as materials to be considered between you and our Fathers".

Then followed the concrete proposals in which he first discussed what kind of settlement should be attempted if William "favoured the reconciliation". Dodwell here suggested that the "Fathers"

[1] Tenison to Dodwell, 5 December 1700. Lambeth MSS. 930, f. 40.

14

should be allowed grace under the Act by which they had been deprived. This Act permitted twelve persons to hold their positions (and a third part of the income) without taking the oaths. There were now only three "Fathers" left who would be affected by this, and they, as a matter of fact, were those for whom the favour had been designed in the Act of Parliament. Even if these Bishops were thus allowed to take advantage of the aforesaid Act, they would still suffer in being deprived of part of their income and their seat in Parliament. It might be, of course, that they would not accept these terms, but this was unlikely since "the great thing necessary to be insisted on will be their administering the Discipline of their Dioceses for which they must be responsible to God".

He next proceeded to discuss what settlement should be attempted if William did not favour the above scheme. Once again he insisted that whatever was decided must come as a result of direct negotiations between the Archbishop and the deprived fathers, though Dodwell himself here showed a con-ciliatory spirit, not, alas! shared by the extreme wing of the non-juring party. "The only Practicle way I can think", he wrote, "for putting an end to this unhappy Schism will be to Article with them for a Voluntary Resignation", by which they would "quit their claim to their undoubted Rights for Peace's sake and oblige themselves to make no successors as to their Episcopal Power, that the controversy may end with their lives". To make such an arrangement possible, the consciences of the deprived bishops must be satisfied on the questions of passive obedience, "our doctrine of the Church's Independency of the State", and the prayers "by ours taken for immoral". Concerning these difficulties, Dodwell boldly suggested that there might well be an agreement to differ.

He brought his long letter to a conclusion with the following words: "These things I humbly propose to be considered and corrected by yr better judgment . . . If you can come so far as to agreement in Essentials, you may then deal immediately with our Fathers in adjusting matters of less importance".[1]

This letter certainly contained concrete proposals and as such had much to commend it; but it showed a failure to under-stand the realities of the contemporary political situation. Regarded as articles of peace the proposals were vitiated by

---

[1] Dodwell to Tenison, 29 December 1700. Lambeth MSS. 930, f. 41.

demanding an admission of error on the part of those responsible for the deprivations, and this confession was basic to the terms throughout.

Tenison was some time in deciding on a reply, and he may have consulted some of the bishops, though there is no extant reference to this in his correspondence. Dodwell, meanwhile, grew impatient, and sent off the following letter to the Archbishop on 15 February 1701.

"Upon the encouragement of yours I presumed to propose some things for making up the unhappy schism. But as I said without any authority from our Fathers, onely as materials to be cultivated by you and them in order to a solid Peace. Though I earnestly desire a happy event, yet I do not write this with any design of precipitating your counsells. I onely desire to know whether you have received that Letter and what you desire to do concerning it. When you have resolved on something practicable for the preserving those liberties of the Church which are essential to its subsistence in a State of Persecution for which you must be responsible, I shall then, if you please, hand your Proposalls to our Fathers".[1]

It is unfortunate that we do not possess the precise terms of the reply which the Archbishop sent to Dodwell some time between 15 February and 20 May. We only know that it was of such a nature as to make Dodwell regard the affair at an end. Tenison, it would appear, was too convinced a Whig, too sincere an erastian, to undertake the difficult task of accommodating nice consciences in this matter of political loyalty. Dodwell and his school were in the paradoxical position of being politically monarchist and yet ecclesiastically anti-erastian. To Tenison such a phrase as "a persecuting state" (true of the Commonwealth or the reign of James II) had no meaning when applied to the England of 1700, and a Church "independent of the state" was to him a wide and straight path leading to anarchy. Certainly in such days of party passion, when Jacobitism was still the major political fear, it would not have been easy to include within the State Church a body of clergy who, though loyal to its religion, were yet hostile to the "supreme governor".

Tenison's reply evoked a final and rather bitter letter from Dodwell on 20 May.[2] He began by saying that he was not surprised

[1] Dodwell to Tenison, 15 February 1701. Lambeth MSS. 930, f. 42.
[2] Dodwell to Tenison, 20 May 1701. *Ibid.* f. 43.

at the rejection of his first proposal (i.e. a legal inclusion of the fathers) since it depended "on the favourable disposition of one who was not bred in her" (William). As to the second proposal, however, he remarked: "I rather doubted of the consent of our Bishops (whom I had not consulted about it) than yours. They were thereby to yield what you neither had nor could take from them, as well as what they had been deprived of by the lay Power. Yet the consideration on which they were to do this was as much for your Spiritual Interest as theirs, the securing the common Rights of Episcopacy in general".

The position, he reminded Tenison, was similar to that in which the early Church found itself and he rebuked the Archbishop for trying "to disable this body to subsist without Princes".

He brought his letter to an end with a personal exhortation to Tenison which certainly lacked nothing in frankness:

"I am loath to warn you", he wrote, "how your neglecting so fair proffers may provoke God to remove opportunitys when he finds you so neglect and despise them . . . It is not proposed that you should concern yourself in the opinion of our Fathers in secular affairs, but in their Communion which is a duty I do not know how you can avoyd. If you will not do even this, we must have Schism in the Church as frequent as there are Revolutions in the State. If you will do nothing on your part to qualify you for Union with us, our Fathers will have performed their part, & you alone must be answerable for the Consequences of it. I am sorry thus to be excluded from all hopes of reconciliation. It may force ours to a means of firmer peace".[1]

It is easy to blame Tenison (if it was he who turned down the proposals—Burnet also may have had something to say), but calmer reflection bids us refrain from a hasty judgment. In the jurors and nonjurors we have before us two opposed ideals of Church government, the one erastian and the other "independent", both hitherto kept within the Church (paradoxically enough) through its state connection and historical traditions. Yet in 1700 it was this very state connection which formed the subject of controversy. One party found it at Whitehall, the other at St. Germains. Passions ran too high for a simple agreement to differ, particularly so long as many Jacobites were actively engaged on behalf of James: nor could they unite on a more fundamental union. Tenison with his usual caution may well have regarded the

---

[1] Dodwell to Tenison, 20 May 1701. Lambeth MSS. 930.

preservation of "revolution principles" as too important to admit of any compromise, and the nonjurors too small a minority to justify such a dangerous experiment.

It might have been thought that the death of James II in 1701 would make things easier for the nonjurors, but the abjuration oath (designed against the claims of the "pretended Prince of Wales"), passed in one of the last parliaments of William's reign, prevented any possible happy results from the death of the "King over the water".

Despite his rigid opinions, Tenison by no means acted towards individual nonjurors in an unfriendly spirit, as may be seen in his relations with Thomas Brett, a prominent member of this body, which may be taken as typical. Thomas Brett (1667–1743) began life as a Whig and experienced no difficulties in taking the oaths to the Government in 1689. He succeeded his uncle in the family living of Bettshanger and it was while there that Tenison offered him the Vicarage of Chislett, worth £70 a year, and "since he acquainted him at the same time that he designed something better for him, he indulged him in holding it by sequestration". Brett on his part very much appreciated the kindness of the Archbishop in this matter and wrote to him on 24 October 1704:

"I return you my thanks", he said, "for your last obliging letter. I shall take care faithfully to perform all ye conditions required, except that of furnishing a room unless yr Grace insist upon it, after I have acquainted you that there is a Tenant in ye Vicarage House put in by Mr. Trent, who has a spare room ready furnished in which I may lay as often as I have occasion".[1]

On 12 April 1707, the Archbishop, still supposing Brett to be a conscientious Whig, collated him to the Rectory of Ruckinge. Brett, however, had been steadily moving in the direction of High Church principles, and the Sacheverell trial seems to have determined him never again to take the oaths. In 1711 his principles found public expression in a sermon on the "Remission of Sins", (preached in "Mr. Higgs Chapell"), "in which the High Church doctrine of priestly authority was advocated in the strongest terms".[2] Tenison, as soon as he heard of it, was somewhat disturbed, and talking to William Quarles, expressed his fears as

[1] Brett to Tenison, 24 October 1704. Lambeth MSS. 953, f. 133.
[2] Quarles to Tenison, 5 December 1711. Lambeth MSS. 941, f. 30.

to the consequences. Quarles made enquiries and writing to the Archbishop on 5 December he reported that a person present (Onslow) could not "say he remember'd the words your Grace was pleased to repeat to me, only that in generall he urged the necessity of the Absolution of the Priest much further than is consistent with the doctrine of the Church of England".[1] Tenison now wrote to Brett himself, who replied by enclosing a copy of the offending sermon, which, he said, he had found it necessary to publish in his own defence. Should the Archbishop wish to see him, he said, he would be willing "as at all times" to obey his Grace's order. It lies outside the scope of this present work to relate how this sermon was only saved from a public condemnation by Convocation through the intervention of Atterbury, the prolocutor.

To Brett, the accession of George I, followed by an Act of Parliament requiring the oaths to be taken again by all those holding office in the Church, created a fresh problem, and he wrote to Tenison desiring leave to resign his livings. The Archbishop "answered very kindly that he would advise him to consider further of it, and not to do rashly what he might afterwards repent of".[2] Thomas Brett, however, had not come to this decision suddenly; he insisted on his resignation being accepted, and was soon received into the nonjuring communion.

He comes before us once again in connection with Tenison when, upon his visiting a sick nonjuror in Faversham, the Archbishop received a complaint from the parish priest. Reluctantly Tenison felt compelled to admonish Brett that "if he heard any more complaints he should be obliged to lay them before the King and Council", a typical warning from an erastian Primate.[3]

---

[1] Quarles to Tenison, 5 December 1711. Lambeth MSS. 941, f. 30.
[2] Nichols, *Literary Anecdotes*, etc., i. 408, 409.
[3] *Ibid.*

CHAPTER 10

DEPRIVATION AND SUSPENSION

Part I   The Bishop of St. David's

TENISON may well have thought himself unfortunate in inheriting, as Archbishop of Canterbury, the prosecution against Thomas Watson, Bishop of St. David's. The story of this Bishop makes extraordinary reading and illustrates only too well how party feeling in those days could give rise to personal animosities, in which hatreds nearly all else was forgotten. Tenison's connection with this unfortunate business was largely of an official character, and in the narrative which follows it is but rarely that we can catch a glimpse of his personal reactions. Still, the prosecution proceeded in the particular manner it did because the Archbishop willed it, and never once did he waver in his determination to carry it through to a successful conclusion.

Thomas Watson was born at Ferriby near Hull in 1637, his father being a seaman, and it was from this side of the family, perhaps, that he inherited a violent temper and a frankness which were to bring him so much trouble in later years. From the grammar school at Hull he went to St. John's College, Cambridge, and became a Fellow in 1660. At college he gained some notoriety as a "pupil monger", and a rumour later gained currency, probably groundless, that he kept a grocer's shop under another name.[1] He was soon presented to the living of Burrough Green in Cambridgeshire and made himself a prominent figure in the county by his vehement and zealous support of the Government and the Court party. In 1678, particularly, his activities occasioned hostile comment in some quarters, when he "was very useful to promote the Interest of Sir Levinus Benet and Sir John Cotton, riding up and down the Country about it and using all sorts of Arguments to the householders".[2] In 1679 he was created a justice of the peace, a position which he undoubtedly used in the interests of the Court party. When in this year the saintly

---

[1] B.M. Add. MSS. 5841, f. 15. Most of the following biographical details come from the Cole MSS. in the B.M.

[2] B.M. Add. MSS. 5841, f. 15. See also "The Case of many Protestant Freeholders and Inhabitants in the County and Town of Cambridge", p. 5.

Sir Thomas Gascoign (a Roman Catholic) was arrested on a charge of conniving to murder Charles II, Watson did not hesitate to declare his satisfaction at his acquittal, speaking "with great Contempt of the Witness against him".[1] He never troubled to conceal his hatred of the Presbyterians, and when at the time of the Titus Oates conspiracy some people spoke to him of their "Apprehensions of the hellish Principles of the Papists, he desired the Presbyterians might be ranked with them, for that he accounted all alike . . . 'for the Devil will have both'".[2]

With these pronounced views, it was no wonder that many Protestants accused him of putting the laws into operation against the Dissenters, but of refraining to do so where Roman Catholics were concerned. Such behaviour, however, if it made him unpopular in the country, gained him the favour of James II, who was then engaged in a struggle to secure control over the Church and the Universities. The result of this favour was seen in Watson's consecration in Lambeth Chapel on 26 June 1687, to the bishopric of St. David's. In extreme Protestant circles many rumours as to the reasons for his appointment soon began to circulate. Some maintained that it was due to the influence of Henry Jermyn (1636–1708), Baron Dover, a dissolute Roman Catholic and the idol of the fashionable world. Others said that he had obtained it by purchase, while the fantastic rumour circulated in certain quarters that Eleanor Gwyn was responsible, since Watson was reported to have entertained her at his chambers in Cambridge.[3] Already Whig animus against him was extreme and his enemies reported him to have said on taking up his new station: "That it was a poor Bishoprick, but that he was resolv'd to get Money one way or other".[4] In Cambridge, particularly, feeling against Watson grew very bitter, and as the tide of resentment against James II ran higher, so did he find his position more and more difficult. Despite this, however, he never compromised in his loyalty to James, and did all in his power to promote the reading of the Declaration of Indulgence in his own diocese. A contemporary account of his attitude during this reign may, perhaps, be quoted at length, though it should be noticed that the very violence of the language suggests a somewhat partial critic:

[1] B.M. Add. MSS. Cole 5831, f. 1480.
[2] Ibid.
[3] "A Summary View of the Articles", etc., p. 1.
[4] Cole MSS., B.M., 5836, f. 16, and "A Summary View of the Articles", etc., p. 1.

"Upon the unhappy death of the reverend and learned Dr. John Lloyd, our late bishop of St. David's, in the last reign, Dr. Thomas Watson of Cambridge, a man of a scandalous character in the University and preferred by Papists to succeed him was pitched upon to carry on the intended ruin of the Church; which we presently perceived by his infamous behaviour in that reign [James II], which he has continued until this happy Revolution. He began his government with so much fury and violence against some of the clergy, with so much craft and insinuation towards others, that we stood upon our guard against him. The first thing he did when he came down to his diocese was to press the so well known address upon his clergy. . . . His next errand was to urge the reading of the declaration for liberty of conscience; the refusers he threatened with dragoons and deprivation".

To add to his crimes, so this philippic continues, Watson

"publicly justified the pretended Prince of Wales his legitimacy within these two months, and that by several expressions at the time of his pretended birth; if his lordship were strictly examined, it is to be concluded he could give some account of the imposture, and that he is acquainted with, and a partner in the cheat; for when the news of his birth came to Brecon, (where his lordship then was), he prohibited the bells and bon-fires, saying he was sure it could not be true, for to his knowledge the queen was not to be delivered till a month after, and then he would persuade the nurse, whom he owned to be his acquaintance, to teach his royal highness to say St. David's the first thing he should speak upon; for which he did not doubt King James would give him £5000 to repair his cathedral".

Few people to-day, except the incurable romantic, support the contemporary fiction of the warming pan, nor can we place too much confidence in an accuser who ends his charges:

"In one word there is scarce an action of his life that is not infamous and which savours not of baseness, Popery, or Atheism; he brings about all his Villanies by lying and slander, and employs only the notorious branded rogues in the country as his instruments to trepan and abuse the clergy".[1]

During the anxious days which preceded the landing of William, Watson was in communication with Henry Jermyn,

[1] Bod. Tanner MSS. 146. Quoted, Howell, *State Trials*, xiv. 447.

writing to him on 18 October and receiving the reply that preparations were well in hand to resist the invader.

"I give your Lordship", Jermyn wrote, "many Thanks for your Letter and enclosed Papers, and am sorry to hear the Dutch invasion continues yet. I was in hope that Damage they have received with fowl Weather and the Winter Season now, would have altered those Resolutions: however I make no question that his Majesty's Forces are now in such Order as will soon make them repent their undertaking".

The downfall of James was the beginning of Watson's own reverse of fortunes. He had backed the wrong horse, and with such conviction that there could be no turning back. As it was, unlike such men as Nathaniel Crewe, Bishop of Durham, he was too high spirited to wish to do so. He could expect no support now in high places, and he soon experienced the result of his isolation.

The Revolution was immediately greeted in Cambridge by a demonstration against him. The "rabble" in the neighbourhood of the parish of Burough Green appear to have taken matters into their own hands, and to have given vent to their "liberation" by a personal attack on the Bishop from which he was with difficulty rescued by some Fellows of the University.[1] Watson, however, was no weakling, and he had the courage not to court what he had previously despised. It might have been thought that he would associate himself with the nonjuring clergy and refuse the oaths: but although some contemporary accounts suggest that he had scruples, he complied with the law in this respect, although perhaps the Whigs would have preferred him to go into the nonjuring wilderness. It is not surprising that he was excepted from the Act of Pardon and Indemnity (a fact to which he is said to have referred as "a great honour done unto him"), and that Burnet particularly warned William against him.[2]

Holding such extreme views, Watson's position in his own diocese was bound to be difficult: it was made more so by his haughty temper and unrestrained avarice. Reports of his conduct

[1] B.M. Add. MSS. 5821, f. 40. Anthony Wood says (*Ath. Oxon.* ii. 1170): "Upon Dislike of his Person and for that he had been recommended by my Lord Dover to King James II he did suffer and induce many affronts and intolerable abuses from the Rabble in Dec. 1688 just after ye sd King had left England for France. By his Picture, both in the Masters Lodge in St. John's College and at Mr. Ward's house, he is represented as a fair handsome Man in his own Hair".

[2] See Chap. 6, p. 120, note 1.

began to get abroad, and lost nothing in the telling. It was said, for example, that the Roman Catholics in the diocese regarded him as their bishop, and that he held his confirmations with the full Roman Catholic ritual. He was reported to fast on Saturday, and at the Communion Service to stand "in the posture of adoration at the time of the distribution of the elements with his hands elevated, his back set against the altar, to the great scandal of the congregation in the Cathedral".[1] He was said to pray simply for "William and Mary, King and Queen", never to pray for them in his own private chapel, and to have instructed the sub-chanter in the cathedral to omit the versicles after the anthem.

That such stories were in part inaccurate is almost certain: but they do suggest that his conduct was tactless in the extreme. Reproached, so the story went, with covetousness, he replied "that he could not help it, and that it was not in his nature to be otherwise", since "he was hardened against what any man should say against him".[2]

But certain more definite charges soon began to be made, some personal and frivolous, others legal and decidedly serious. Among the former we may perhaps class the anecdote that when his nephew John Medley, while taking divine service in the cathedral, stumbled over some of his words, the bishop interjected with great heat: "God damme's, God damme's".[3] Among the serious charges were simony and extortion. The sub-chanter of the cathedral, for example, confessed publicly that the Bishop had offered him the Vicarage of Llanryan, on condition that he gave his lordship ten guineas for continuing as tenant of the palace lands, which he had already rented for some years. Two schoolmasters, Griffiths and Barnet, alleged that the Bishop had seized £5 a year belonging to the college at Brecon; and many declared that he was in the habit of extorting money at his collations, ordinations, and institutions. To his own tenants he was said to have behaved in a most arbitrary manner, particularly in the case of one Vaughan who, when asked to produce his lease, saw it destroyed before his face, and was forced to pay £20 for a new one.[4]

Certainly his behaviour seems to have been of a kind calculated

[1] Howell, *State Trials*, xiv. 447.
[2] *Ibid.*
[3] *Ibid.*
[4] *Ibid.* p. 450.

to give offence,[1] and his visitation of the diocese in 1691, aimed particularly against the Whig clergy, added to his unpopularity.[2] He might have weathered the storm within his own diocese, had it not been that his attitude in Parliament placed him in permanent hostility to the Government. During the year 1692 he consistently opposed the Court party in the House of Lords, and never missed an opportunity of embarrassing the Ministry. The difficulty in which he was known to stand with the Court, thus encouraged his opponents to make a united attack against him in connection with the fees which he had taken from Jeremiah Griffiths on his presentation to the benefice of Dyssarth. Griffiths brought his charge before the grand jury of the county of Brecon, and as a result Watson was found "to be guilty of extortion for taking of excessive fees", and a *billa vera* was laid against him.[3]

Writing from Abergwilly to his friend and patron, Theophilus Hastings, seventh Earl of Huntingdon—a strong Jacobite[4]— Watson said that he had come the previous Thursday to his own house "where I think to confine myself to prevent what I may suffer by the Jealousies etc. of men".[5]

It might have been expected that Watson would now definitely see the red light and give no further cause for complaint—but nothing appears to have been further from the case. In 1694 he announced his intention of insisting on the residence of his chancellor, residentiary canons, and beneficed clergy, many of whom, he declared, had been lax in discharging the duties of their offices. Whatever may have been Watson's motives, few could deny the need for such a purge, since the diocese was still suffering from the regime of William Lucy, a former bishop (1660–77), who had "lived in a woeful and culpable omission of many of the direct and important as well sacred as other duties of his office". He had neglected confirmations, exacted exorbitant fees, and

---

[1] This may be seen from a pamphlet of the time in which "Ten Modest Quaeries, etc." were put to the Bishop. These questions concerned mainly Watson's activities during the reign of James II. From this examination the writer began to wonder whether "the same charge that Paul gave to his son Timothy do's not stand good still: That a bishop must be sober, of good Behaviour, given to Hospitality, apt to teach, not given to Wine . . . nor covetous". See "Ten Modest Quaeries, etc.", p. 3.

[2] T. Watson, "Articles to be enquired of . . . in the triennial visitation of . . . Thomas, Lord Bishop of St. David's", 1691.

[3] Howell, *State Trials*, xiv. 447.

[4] The Earl of Huntingdon (1650–1701) was a volunteer in the French Army, 1672; Privy Councillor, 1683; and imprisoned for an attempt to seize Plymouth for James II. in 1688. He was again imprisoned on suspicion of treason, 1692. *D.N.B.*, XXV, 135.

[5] Watson to Huntingdon, 18 August 1692. H.M.C. Hastings MSS. 1930, II, 225.

"filled his Cathedral with non-residents and preferred royalists exclusively to benefices in the diocese".[1]

Nothing at this juncture, however, could have been more calculated to arouse the indignation of the clergy of St. David's, particularly as Watson's action was known to be directed against the Whigs, amongst whom the chancellor, Robert Lucy (son of the bishop), was the particular enemy of the new regime in the diocese. Robert Lucy, on his part, eagerly seized this opportunity to rally the clergy around him, and to petition Archbishop Tillotson to enquire into the practices of the Bishop. The result was that on 24 July 1694, the Archbishop "appointed Commissioners to visit the bishopric of St. David's", and this was followed by Tillotson formally suspending the Bishop on 21 August.[2] Despite this suspension (the law always sat very lightly on him), Watson continued to collate, until "he was cited before the Archbishop, begged pardon and submitted". Tillotson, meanwhile, continued his investigations of the articles against him, and regarding them as substantial in character and supported by a great deal of evidence, he determined to proceed further against him if necessary.[3]

It was at this rather critical stage in the proceedings that Tillotson died, leaving to Tenison the invidious task of carrying on the investigations. Watson, on his part, immediately appealed to the new Archbishop to remove the suspension under which he suffered, and Tenison, although determined to proceed with the case against him, "readily consent[ed], being desirous to treat him with all possible tenderness".[4] Thus Watson wrote to Huntingdon on 14 February 1695: "My suspension was taken off last Saturday upon my submission which I thought far more advisable than to contend with my superiors, and I am, I think, in Statu quo. I do, as I did, and have such respect as I expect".[5] Thus Tenison placed Watson in full charge of his diocese once again, but the period of suspension does not appear to have moderated his zeal, nor did the fact that investigations were proceeding restrain his animus against several of his clergy. With incredible folly, he continued his efforts to remove Lucy, until he

[1] *D.N.B.*, xxxiv. 251. He was Bishop of St. David's from 1660 to 1677.
[2] Howell, *State Trials*, xiv. 959.
[3] *Ibid.*
[4] *Ibid.*
[5] Watson to Huntingdon, 14 February 1695. H.M.C. Hastings MSS. 1930, II, 243.

drove the chancellor in self-defence to bring a charge of mal-administration and simony against him.

Henceforth the procedure in this case becomes very complicated, and it will be necessary for us to distinguish (1) the question of judicature; i.e. where Watson should be tried; from (2) the substance of the charges brought against him.[1]

We begin, then, with a brief relation of the legal machinery which was set in motion against the Bishop.

The question of judicature, as can be readily understood, bristled with difficulties, so much so that had it not been for political feeling against Watson, it seems probable that the prosecution would not have been successfully carried through. The first problem, a complicated one in view of Watson's status as a member of the House of Lords, concerned the court in which he should be tried. Tenison, in this respect, determined to assert his own jurisdiction as Metropolitan of the Province of Canterbury, and by a citation dated 23 August he summoned the Bishop to appear before him—i.e. to the Court of Audience [2]—at Lambeth, on Saturday, 24 October 1695.[3] When this day came, six bishops and the judge of the Court of the Arches as his assessor sat with the Archbishop, and this, together with the form of the sentence,[4] has led Sir Robert Phillimore to conclude that though legally the court was one of Audience, yet the Archbishop adopted the forms and procedure of the Court of the Arches.[5]

---

[1] It is not always possible to make this clear-cut distinction, because the nature of a particular charge was sometimes the reason for its coming before a particular court.

[2] Luttrell, *A Brief Historical Relation*, etc. 1857, iii. 541.

[3] Concerning this Court of Audience, Phillimore (*The Ecclesiastical Law*, etc., ed. 1895, ii. 923) quotes from Johnson's *Canons* (ed. 1851) as follows: "The Archbishop of Canterbury had formerly his Court of Audience, in which at first were dispatched all such matters, whether voluntary or contentious, as the Archbishop thought fit to reserve for his own hearing. They who prepared evidence and other materials to lay before the Archbishop, in order to his decision, were called auditors. Afterwards this court was removed from the archbishop's palace, and the jurisdiction of it was exercised by the master or official of the audience, who held his court in the consistory place at St. Paul's. But these three great offices (of official principal of the archbishop, dean or judge of the peculiars and official of the audience) are and have been for a long time past united in one person, who keeps his court in Doctors' Commons Hall". Phillimore adds: "The Court of Audience, therefore, has fallen into desuetude. It was, however, distinct from the Court of the Arches".

The origin of this jurisdiction has been carefully investigated in Dr. Irene Churchill's *Canterbury Administration*, 1933, I, Pt. ii. xi. It is interesting to notice that Tenison held the court in person at Lambeth.

[4] See p. 219, note 5.

[5] As to the Court of the Arches, Crosse writes (*Dictionary of English Church History*, p. 154): "The chief of the Provincial Courts were the Court of the Arches and the Chancery Court, the Consistory Courts of Canterbury and York respectively under the Official Principal of each archbishop. The southern court received its name, Court of the Arches, from the Church of St. Mary-le-Bow (de arcubus), in which it was usually

The charges against Watson were then read,[1] but the Bishop immediately objected that he had not been legally served with the process, and even if he had been, he intended to insist on his right as a member of the House of Lords.[2] Watson sensed a hostile atmosphere from the beginning and complained that the Archbishop "seemed concerned that anything seemed to relief [sic] an innocent man".[3] It was therefore clear that the ecclesiastical charges could not be proceeded with until the preliminary question of jurisdiction was settled, and Lucy replied to this move of Watson's by sending to the House of Lords a petition signed by himself and five others on 7 March 1696. In this document they stated that since (a) the Bishop had been excepted from pardon in the late Act of Indemnity: (b) a true bill had been drawn up against him by the grand jury of Brecon: (c) he had committed divers crimes and misdemeanors against the good and wholesome laws of the kingdom: "they humbly pray[ed] their lordships leave to prosecute the said lord Bishop of St. David's for his crimes . . . in such form and course as the laws of this realm do admit of without incurring the displeasure of this honourable house, by reason of the said lordship being privileged therein".[4]

To this petition Watson drew up an answer which was moderate and deferential in tone. He had always regarded it as an unlimited misfortune, he said, to have been excepted from the late act of indemnity, and although the charges now brought against him were so general as hardly to admit of an answer, "he utterly denied that he was guilty of any extortion whatsoever, and doubted not that he should justify himself against the malicious accusation in proper and legal course of law". Regarding his position as a member of the Upper House, he "solemnly promised he would never insist upon his privilege but with submission to their lordships' great wisdom and justice and with all possible regard to the honour of this house".[5]

---

held. The Dean of the Arches was originally the judge of the archbishop's Court of Peculiars which sat in that Church. But after a time this position was always held in conjunction with that of Official Principal, and the holder of both offices came to be known by the title of the less important". Phillimore states (ii. 924) that "the Arches Court exercises the appellate jurisdiction from each of the diocesan courts within the province. It may also take original cognizance of causes, by letters of request from each of those courts".

[1] See pp. 230–4.
[2] Luttrell, *A Brief Historical Relation*, etc., iii. 542.
[3] Watson to Huntingdon, 18 August 1696. H.M.C. Hastings MSS., II, 274.
[4] Howell, *State Trials*, xiv. 447.
[5] *Ibid.*

Thus in due course the question of privilege came up before the House of Lords, and it decided (it was a typical English compromise) not to pass any general judgment, but simply to order Watson to waive his claim, which he agreed to do.[1]

It was now again possible for Tenison to carry on with his own investigations, which he consequently resumed. We are fortunate in possessing a series of letters written by Watson to the Earl of Huntingdon, expressing in frank manner his opinions of these proceedings and his increasing sense of injustice. It is a pity that we have no such insight into Tenison's feelings. The most serious ecclesiastical charge against Watson was that of simoniacal practices with his nephew, John Medley,[2] and the Bishop was therefore anxious that this young man should be allowed to give evidence. Thus on 29 August 1696, Watson reported to Huntingdon:

"This day the counsel argued on both sides whether one who seems *socius* or *particeps criminis* can be a witness for one that is accused of that crime. I did think the argument was on that side because the party is of an unblamable life. . . . But the Archbishop and the Dean of his Arches did more than counsel against the argument, and I see plainly that it will be over ruled not only as to the negative that I made no contract, but as to the affirmative that there were accounts betwixt us and *bona fide* contracted".[3]

This question of Medley's evidence continued to be a bone of contention, and on 8 September Watson reported that the Archbishop had refused to receive "the accounts between him and his nephew . . . thereby cutting off the strongest part of the Bishop's defence",—and this after he had "sat in Lambeth Hall five hours bare headed and took a cold".[4]

Watson recognized in this treatment at Lambeth the penalty of his Jacobite sympathies, and a friend reported that "the Bishop of St. David's is very shy of his old friends, fearing, it may be, that to be seen in their company may be prejudicial to him".[5]

---

[1] Luttrell, *A Brief Historical Relation*, etc., iv. 383.
[2] See p. 232.
[3] Watson to Huntingdon, 29 August 1697. H.M.C. Hastings MSS. II, 279.
[4] Watson to Huntingdon, 8 September, 1697. *Ibid.* p. 281.
[5] Dr. Nathaniel Johnston to Huntingdon, 12 August 1696. H.M.C. Hastings MSS. II, 292. The writer concludes: "However we wish him well believing his prosecution to be unjust and malicious". Johnston (1627–1705), who wrote in 1686, *The Excellency of Monarchial Government*, lived after the Revolution under the protection of Peterborough. Watson encouraged him in his researches into Yorkshire antiquities. H.M.C. Hastings MSS. II, 220.

Watson began to feel that he had acted unwisely in consenting to waive his claim to privilege and this is reflected in the following letter written to the Earl of Huntingdon on 21 September 1696:

"Epimetheus and others were wise too late, and whatever is past I think it better forgot than otherwise. If your Lordship, when I was so pressed, had pleased to encourage the defence, I had never yielded up privilege, and I think very few could have held out longer. Since my last, viz. Wednesday sennight, I was at L[ambeth] and there I think I had the hardest usage. The Commission was granted and one Mr. Ch. Piers was recommended for my n[ota]ry but upon my accuser calling him a Jacobite he was rejected. I told the Archbishop . . . I hoped there was none of that matter in my cause. He said 'Yes' and when I said I was sorry for it . . . he told me there was one article for not giving the oaths".[1]

The political animosity of the prosecution came out more and more as the case went on. "Your servant hath been and is under a strange prosecution", the accused reported on 17 October 1696. "The Articles though many would not contain the malice of his enemies, who in the execution of the Commission stretch their interrogatories to his witness to every part of his life and conversation, as if he was the worst miscreant in nature".[2]

Watson suspected that Lambeth and Whitehall were working hand in hand. "Every fiction and dream of scandal is trumped up and examined", he complained, "and all the care imaginable used to expose and defame him, but the two crimes of sim[ony] and extortion his cor[responden]ts think are, or will be wiped off. Their design now seems to expose him to the displeasure of the Government".[3]

A few months later Watson reported that the case was "flagging", because, as he supposed, "they do not find what they expected",[4] and he wrote to Dr. Johnston "that his nephew the Archdeacon hath the advantage of his adversary".[5] August 1697 saw the Bishop back again in his own diocese and he wrote to Huntingdon: "I bless God I have been very well ever since I saw you and have traversed my diocese more than ever I did to do the

[1] Watson to Huntingdon, 21 September 1696. H.M.C. Hastings MSS. II, 283.
[2] Watson to Huntingdon, 17 October 1696. *Ibid*. p. 283.
[3] Watson to Huntingdon, 24 October 1696. *Ibid*. p. 286.
[4] Watson to Huntingdon, 13 April 1697. *Ibid*. p. 290.
[5] Watson to Johnston, 12 August 1697. *Ibid*. p. 292.

15

office of Confirmation. My affairs stand as they did. I cannot be apprehensive of danger and yet am not secure".[1]

Different friends gave different advice and Watson, as the following letter shows, was doubtful what to do for the best. "I am very sensible of your Lordship's good wishes and concern for me", he wrote to Huntingdon on 16 October 1697. "Some friends think the present Juncture no ways favourable and advise to put in new pleas and delay the matter, others think it more advisable to proceed now, lest after the peace and what shall be done the next sessions, I may be thought unnecessary and power greater".[2]

Perplexed and anxious the Bishop of St. David's decided to let matters go on and announcing his intention to Huntingdon, he reported as follows on 21 October:

"The present alteration and position of affairs have puzzled and altered my thoughts as to my business. . . . I have resolved, notwithstanding the difficulties the present Juncture represents, to adventure and let the hearing go on. I must when the Cause is heard have two common lawyers at least. I have pitched upon Sir William W[illiams?][3] and think to have Serjeant Wright,[4] assuring myself that besides the fees I shall have your interest to engage his friendship and I beg that favour of your Lordship. I think there never was more apparent malice in any prosecution in any age. I hope you will hasten to town. I never desired your assistance more".[5]

It is significant that Sir William Williams and Sir Nathan Wright had both been briefed by the Crown for the prosecution against the seven bishops. The Earl of Huntingdon duly obliged by writing to Sir Nathan Wright on 24 October, his letter admirably expressing the Tory point of view.

"To recommend a cause to a judge", he began, "I know is not allowable. But the occasion of my writing is at the desire of my Lord Bishop of St. David's, who I understand has retained you in his great cause—a prosecution which in my opinion appears full of revenge and malice; indeed he seems to have been marked out for such a purpose. For, though his

---

[1] Watson to Huntingdon, 16 August 1697. H.M.C. Hastings MSS., II, 300.
[2] Watson to Huntingdon, 16 October 1697. *Ibid.*
[3] Sir William Williams (1634–1700) was appointed Solicitor-General during the reign of James II, and appeared for this monarch against the seven bishops. *D.N.B.* lxi. 457.
[4] Sir Nathan Wright (1654–1721) was junior counsel for the Crown against the seven bishops. He became King's Serjeant in 1697. *D.N.B.* lxiii. 120.
[5] Watson to Huntingdon, 21 October 1697. H.M.C. Hasting MSS. II, 302.

learning, piety and prudence preserved him from any imputation of the last reign, yet he was one of the excepted persons in the first general pardon, though never charged with any misdemeanour; which is not to be ascribed to any levity in his metropolitans, because now he is proceeded against with violence upon the articles exhibited against him. All I have to add is that your usual care, industry and elocution in this cause may answer the rest of your pleadings and, if my desires and well wishes may weigh anything with you, I shall esteem it as a particular favour".[1]

Things, however, were not going too well with the Bishop: he began to fear the worst, but refused to let the Earl of Huntingdon persuade him to attempt some kind of compromise. "Your advice in the Gospel",[2] he commented, "had been good in the beginning but so near the end it would betray the cause to offer a reconciliation. And he is so far from making a submission to L[ambeth] that he hath not yet made a visit there or bowed his knee".[3]

This letter did not convince Huntingdon that the boldest course was necessarily the wisest, and he ventured again to suggest the wisdom of some attempt at an accommodation, but succeeded only in eliciting from Watson the following spirited reply:

"I humbly own your Lordship's concern for me, as an instance of your favour and friendship, but if there be no way to stand but by such motions, I must submit to what providence shall think fit for me. I bless God I have consulted my own peace more than interest, and I would not part with the one for the other. I think fear of suffering ought not to make a man forsake his principles".[4]

Though scouting any idea of a compromise, Watson more and more regretted that he had been persuaded to waive his privilege, and began to contemplate asserting it again. He accused Dr. Oxenden before the court of "partiality, enmity, and acting more like an advocate on the other side than assistant of the judge", and told the Archbishop he "would acquaint the House with his complaint". "But as I never yielded to anything more against my judgment", he commented to his patron, "I have

---

[1] Huntingdon to Wright, 24 October 1697. H.M.C. Hastings MSS. II, 303.
[2] Probably Matt. v. 25: "Agree with thine adversary quickly, whiles thou art in the way with him", etc.
[3] Watson to Huntingdon, 6 January 1698. H.M.C. Hastings MSS. II, 305.
[4] Watson to Huntingdon, 3 February 1698. Ibid.

reason to think their unkindness very fortunate, for I gain thereby the satisfaction of proceeding and reserving that, in case I should per nefasque be cast, as my last remedy".[1]

In June things were very much the same, as Huntingdon learnt from the following letter. "My own business is still in suspense. I hope next winter will finish it. I thank God I find nothing in the depositions, and fear nothing but partiality that can do me harm. I have had too much reason to apprehend that, but blessed be God malice hath not been more powerful".[2]

The last letter of this series comes from the Earl of Huntingdon and was written to Watson on 18 November 1698; it shows his fears for the future.

"I am solicitous after your health and grand affair", he wrote, "which I hope will have a happy conclusion. The Bishop [sic] of Lambeth calls for a despatch, which we understand to have no good meaning. If you are distrustful of the event, it were the best course to compound the matter, for it is plain that the public affairs run counter to what good men have so long wished for".[3]

Watson now saw that his condemnation was inevitable if the Archbishop proceeded so far as to pronounce sentence, so, spurning submission, he interposed a protest on 20 February 1699, on the grounds that the charges brought against him were mainly of a temporal nature, and as such did not fall within the jurisdiction of the Archbishop's court. The Archbishop overruled this protest, and Watson then moved for a prohibition for the above reason: (1) that the case was of a temporal character, adding as an independent plea (2) that the case should have been tried in the Court of the Arches.

This question of a prohibition was one which the Court of King's Bench alone could determine, and it came up here in due course, when it decided against the appellant. The Court of King's Bench was at this time presided over by Lord Chief Justice Holt (1642–1710) and his remarks on the Archbishop's jurisdiction are interesting, particularly in view of later developments.

"The Archbishop of Canterbury", he said, "has without doubt provincial jurisdiction over all his suffragan bishops, which he may exercise in what place of the province it shall

---

[1] Watson to Huntingdon, 12 February 1698. H.M.C. Hastings MSS. II, 306.
[2] Watson to Huntingdon, 30 June 1698. *Ibid.* p. 308.
[3] Huntingdon to Watson, 19 November 1698. *Ibid.* p. 309.

please him, and it is not material to be in the Arches, no more than in any other place; for the Arches is only a peculiar consisting of divers parishes in London, where the Archbishop of Canterbury exerciseth his metropolitical jurisdiction, but he is not confined to exercise it there".[1]

That Holt was a learned judge, and one whose conduct was invariably upright and impartial, there can be no doubt.

This further effort to impugn the Archbishop's jurisdiction thus being without avail, Tenison proceeded with the concurrence of the majority of his assessors to give judgment on 3 August 1699, taking no notice when Watson now "resumed his privelege of peerage and pleaded it"; for as he had agreed to waive this in the House of Lords, and had subsequently submitted to the court, so "no regard was had to this since a plea to the jurisdiction of the Court was to be offered in the first instance, but could not be kept up to the last and then made use of".[2] The bishops who were the Archbishop's assessors, then concurred in the sentence which Tenison decreed, namely, deprivation. Burnet, who was perhaps the most vehement of Watson's opponents as he was at all times the most violent of Whigs, would have preferred the court to go further and pronounce sentence of excommunication, since, as he wrote later: "Watson was one of the worst men in all respects, that ever I knew in Holy Orders; passionate, covetous, and false in the blackest instance without any one virtue or good quality to balance his many bad ones".[3] Sprat, Bishop of Rochester, on the other hand (who had leanings towards the Tories), withdrew from the court on the day of sentence since, although he agreed with the Archbishop's right to suspend, he did not think his power extended so far as to deprive.[4] Tenison, however, seems to have been perfectly convinced of his own powers in this respect, and he drew up a long document in which, after rehearsing the Bishop of St. David's various misdemeanours, he passed sentence of deprivation.[5]

[1] Phillimore, *The Ecclesiastical Law of the Church of England*, i. 67.
[2] Burnet, *History of my own Time*, iv. 406.
[3] *Ibid.*
[4] *Ibid.* The author (probably R. Ferguson, see p. 169) of *A Large Review of the Summary Review*, however, goes further and writes that the Bishop of Rochester maintained "that he [i.e. Watson] could not be Legally and Judicially convicted either of Simony or any of the punishable Offences, whereof he had been accused", p. 12.
[5] Howell, *State Trials*, xiv. 467. The terms of the deprivation were as follows: " . . . pronunciamus et per p'ntes declaramus Idcirco Nos Thomas Archiep'us et Judex antedictus p'fatum Thomam Watson Sacrae Theologiae Professorem ab omni honore, dignitate et loco suo Episcopi Eccl'iae Cath'is Meneven cum suis juribus et

It might have been thought that the case was now over; that Watson would retire (albeit a little ungracefully) and that a new bishop would be appointed. Certainly this was the opinion of Dr. William Beaw, Bishop of Llandaff, who wrote to Tenison on 21 August 1699, suggesting that he might succeed to the bishopric of St. David's despite his eighty-three years.[1] Watson's trial had already been going on for some five years, but three factors prevented its coming to an end at this stage. First, Watson's cause was taken up "with great zeal" by many of his own Tory principals who welcomed this opportunity to display their resentment, although Burnet maintains that they were really "ashamed" of him.[2] Secondly, the legal position of the Archbishop in this matter of deprivation was not, perhaps, so obviously clear as Tenison seems to have imagined, and some of the bishops were thought to be a little uneasy at this display of archiepiscopal power. Thirdly, and by no means least important, Watson was a born fighter, and he had no intention of surrendering his see, so long as it was possible by any legal chicanery to hold it.

We now turn to the second part of these proceedings, namely, the efforts which Watson made to secure the reversal of this sentence of deprivation by the Archbishop. The Crown itself could not remain uninterested, for if this deprivation were good in law, another bishop had to be appointed to St. David's, and Watson must forfeit his seat in the Upper House of Parliament. Watson's next move was to appeal against the sentence of deprivation to the Court of Delegates, as a result of which a commission was set up:[3] but the temper of this court made him feel a

pertinentiis universis et ab omni officio et administratione Episcopali et ab omni beneficio ecclesiastico deprivandum amovendum et deponendum fore de jure debere pronunciamus decernimus adjudicamus et per p'sentes declaramus et p'fatum Thomam Watson ab iisdem Honore Dignitate et loco suo Episcopi Ecclesiae Meneven p'dicti et ab omni officio et administratione Episcopali et ab omni beneficio Ecclesiastico (justicia id poscente) deprivamus, amovemus et deponimus per p'sentes p'fatumque. Thomam Watson per p'sentes movendum fore decernimus sicq. per presentes monemus eiq. interdicimus ne in posterum habitum Ordini Episcopali competentem et proprium et ab Episcopis hujus Regni Angliae geri solitum gerere aut induere aut quibuscunq. Insigniis Episcopalibus uti p'sumat sub pena majoris Excommunicationis . . ."

[1] Beaw to Tenison, 21 August 1699. Lambeth MSS. 930, f. 49.
[2] Burnet, *History of my own Time*, iv. 407.
[3] G. Crosse writes (Ollard and Crosse), *Dictionary of English Church History*, p. 156: "The Court of Delegates was created by the Act 25 Hen. VIII. c. 19, which provides 'for lack of justice at or in any of the courts of the arbhbishops of this realm . . . it shall be lawful to the parties grieved to appeal to the King's majesty in the King's Court of Chancery, and that upon every such appeal a commission shall be directed under the great seal to such persons as shall be named by the King's highness. . . like as in cases of appeal from the Admiral's Court to hear and definitely determine such appeals and the causes concerning the same'."

confirmation of the sentence inevitable, and he decided to fall back again on his privilege as a member of the House of Lords. This reassertion of his privilege raised fresh difficulties at this stage, for if Tenison's deprivation were good in law, then Watson had ceased to be a member of the House of Lords and had no privilege to fall back on. The deprived Bishop—it was typical of his character—decided to force the issue, and he appeared in person in the House on 18 November 1699, and took his seat as of old.[1] It was imperative for the House to do something, and it decided on 29 November "that the Bishop of St. David's shall be heard by his Counsel at the Bar of this House on Monday next, at 11 o'clock in the forenoon, what he has to offer in relation to his resuming his privilege in the said cause; where unto the Lord Archbishop of Canterbury may also, if he thinks fit, be heard of his Counsel".[2]

Hence on the appointed days (4 and 6 December) Dr. Walter and Dr. Cook, counsel for the Archbishop, and Sir Thomas Powys, Dr. Oldish, and Sir Bartholomew Shower,[3] counsel for Watson, argued the case in the Lords under the watchful eye of the Attorney-General, who frequently intervened in the debate in the interest of the royal prerogative. For Watson, it was maintained "that the sentence of deprivation (upon which the appeal to the delegates was granted) having been passed by the Archbishop of Canterbury, who had no authority to do it, the Bishop had just reason to protect himself by his privilege as a peer, from the effects of a sentence so illegal".[4] To support this contention it was maintained: (1) The deprivation by the Archbishop was contrary to all former precedents. Stigand, for example, was deprived by a synod, as was Wulfstan, Bishop of Worcester. Since the Reformation, Bishops Bonner and Middleton had been proceeded against in Convocation, while Elizabeth had set up a Court of High Commission with these powers. (2) The Archbishop could not claim such jurisdiction as part of the old legatine authority, as these powers were now lodged in the Crown by 25 Hen. VIII. (3) Nor could the Archbishop assume such a power as part of his undoubted right of visitation, since

[1] Luttrell, *A Brief Historical Relation*, etc., 1857, iv. 584.
[2] *Journals of the House of Lords*, 11 Will. III. 29 November 1699.
[3] Sir Bartholomew Shower (1658–1701) became prominent as a pamphleteer for the Court party in 1683. He was one of the Counsel for the Crown against the seven bishops and defended Sir John Fenwick (see p. 196). *D.N.B.* lii. 61.
[4] Howell, *State Trials*, xiv. 454.

he visited only to discover illegalities, which were then to be proceeded against "in a manner legal and canonical". (4) According to the "reason of the thing", it seemed almost incredible that "the House of Lords should submit their rights of peerage to a single man, since a result of deprivation was loss of peerage, without possibility of appeal to this House".

Sir Bartholomew Shower confined himself to explaining why Watson had decided to resume his privilege of peerage after having first agreed to waive it. The reason for this apparent change of front, he said, was to be found in the manifest injustice to which the Bishop had been subjected by the Court of Delegates, which court included many who had assisted the Archbishop in his sentence of deprivation. In effect, the Bishop had been denied the right of appeal to another court, and this had induced him to "seek protection in his peerage". Moreover, when Watson had first agreed to waive his privilege, he had never suspected that the Archbishop would assert an illegal power of deprivation: but when "instead of admonition he was surprised with an appearance of deprivation, he thought for his own safety he ought to return to his privilege, and out of duty to the House to desire their concurrence".[1] To do so was his only redress, for "a certificate of his deprivation to the Exchequer would have immediately taken away his revenues, and there being in this case no such thing as a writ of error, his privilege, and their lordship's protecting of him in it, was his only sanctuary against the oppression of an exorbitant power".[2]

Such, in outline, was Watson's case, and in its accumulative aspect, it would appear to be a strong one: certainly the Archbishop's counsel did not attempt a very adequate reply, a fact which was apparently obvious to contemporaries, for even one of Tenison's supporters writes that "to every particular . . . it could not be well expected that his grace's counsel should reply; the notice being but short, the case wholly new, and many of the instances and authorities unforseen".[3]

Such as it was, the Archbishop's reply consisted of the following points: (1) It was surprising that the Bishop of St. David's, "after so long a submission without the least scruple, should now begin to dispute the Archbishop's authority".[4] In a civil case,

---

[1] Howell, *State Trials*, xiv. 458.
[2] *Ibid.*
[3] *Ibid.*
[4] This is not true as the letters we have quoted abundantly show.

the jurisdiction of a court must be disputed at the outset, and submission implied legality. Also the fact that Watson appealed from the Archbishop to the Court of Delegates was a tacit recognition of the Archbishop's authority (2) As to the instance quoted against the Archbishop's right to deprive, they were all inconclusive, Stigand, for example, being himself Archbishop and thus no precedent in the present case. But on the whole "a number of precedents cannot be expected in such a case; it is the glory of the English Church not to afford them, and it will then be time enough to produce more instances when his lordship's counsel have named the bishops whose behaviour requires such an exercise of the Archbishop's authority". (3) The statute of citations which limited the right of the Archbishop to summon any person in his province before himself, contained an express exception in the case of a bishop, thus confirming the Archbishop in his ancient authority.[1]

It is perhaps not surprising in the political circumstances that on 6 December, by a "party vote", the Lords decided that the Bishop of St. David's should not be allowed to resume his privilege.[2]

There was, however, still plenty of spirit left in Thomas Watson. The resources of the law were not yet exhausted, nor had he given up the temporalities of his see. Hence he now moved for another prohibition against the Commissioners Delegate to stay their proceedings, and he did so on the following grounds: (1) That by canon law the Archbishop alone could not deprive a bishop. (2) That the Delegates had refused to admit some of his evidence.

There was now another delay until the question of a further prohibition came before the Court of King's Bench. When it did so Chief Justice Holt presided, and under his direction the Court denied a prohibition on the first ground maintaining "that an Archbishop hath power over his suffragan bishops and may

---

[1] An ingenious argument in support of the Archbishop's jurisdiction was put forward by the Attorney-General in the course of the debate, in order, as he said, to safeguard the king's supremacy. By 25 Hen. VIII. the final appeal in ecclesiastical causes, he pointed out, was by way of the Archbishop to the king in Chancery. Hence the king had a right to take cognizance of ecclesiastical causes only in so far as they came to him by appeal, and such appeal was fixed by statute to come from the Archbishop. Thus to deny the Archbishop's right of jurisdiction was to deny the king's right of final judgment which belonged to him as supreme in the Church. The Attorney-General thus concluded: "The King's supremacy and the privilege of the subject are both nearly concerned in the right of the Metropolitan, and to plead against it, is an endeavour (as the law now stands) to take away all possibility of doing justice, and thereby to give an impunity and encouragement to the greater offences". See Howell, State Trials, xiv. 459.

[2] Ibid.

deprive them: that though there may be a co-ordination among the bishops *jure divino*, yet there is a subordination *jure ecclesiastico qua humano*. Regarding the Bishop's second plea for a prohibition (that the Delegates refused his allegations), the question here was whether the Court of King's Bench should issue a mandamus compelling the Court of Delegates to admit Watson's evidence. Here Holt's ruling was quite clear, namely, that the Court could not issue a mandamus to compel another court to proceed according to its own law, and hence a prohibition must be denied on this point also.

It was now no longer possible for Watson to prevent his appeal coming before the Court of Delegates, which it did on 16 February 1700. The proceedings may, perhaps, be best summarized in a minute of the day: "The counsel for the Bishop of St. David's insisting that the archbishop had not jurisdiction in the cause, the Court having considered the arguments on both sides and debated the matter, is unanimously of opinion that the Archbishop had and this Court hath jurisdiction in this cause and doth order the counsel to proceed in the same". It was now merely a matter of time till the Court of Delegates confirmed the sentence of the Archbishop on 22 February.[1]

The Bishop of St. David's, meanwhile, had petitioned Lord Chancellor Somers for a writ of error upon the Court of King's Bench denial of a prohibition, who referred it to the Attorney-General and received the reply that in "his opinion . . . a writ of error would lie in this case".[2] Accordingly, the question came before the Lords and the House, "a little uneasy concerning the whole matter", decided to search their journals and hear counsel whether a writ of error could properly be brought in this case. On 2 March the question was decided in the negative, Lord Chief Justice Holt remarking afterwards that "if the Lords had been of opinion that the prohibition ought to have been granted, yet he would never have granted it".[3]

There now remained to expel Watson from the House of Lords, to seize the temporalities of his see, and to appoint a new bishop, all of which were to occasion difficulty, since although the final result was now inevitable, the business of expulsion provided Watson with fresh opportunities to prolong his case. The deprived

---

[1] Phillimore, *The Ecclesiastical Law*, etc., i. 66.
[2] *Ibid*. p. 69.
[3] *Ibid*.

Bishop displayed once again his customary spirit, and the House of Lords found it necessary to discuss at some length how to eject "Dr. Watson late bishop of St. David's out of the temporalities of that bishopric so that his successor may peaceably enjoy them".[1]

Watson decided on a policy of passive resistance, and he determined to dispute every inch of the way. He refused to accept the confirmation of the Archbishop's sentence by the Court of Delegates, and he refused to pay the cost of the suit—some £1000. For the second of these offences he was excommunicated by the same court, and was arrested by the sheriff of Middlesex on a writ *excommunicato capiendo*. This gave the bishop another opportunity of indulging his litigious spirit, and to secure his discharge he brought a writ of habeas corpus in the Court of Queen's Bench against the sheriff, when his counsel once again repeated the theme song. Watson, they reiterated "was, and now is Bishop of St. David's . . . he was summoned to parliament in the seventh year of King William, and sat there as bishop, as appeared by the record". Since this was so, they argued, a "capias" could not lie against him as a peer, and they declared that they were ready to try the case with the Attorney-General.[2] By amending their plea, and by sheer importunity, they managed to gain their point and a day was appointed for the Attorney-General either to reply or demur. The Attorney-General, when he was acquainted with the position, first protested that he was not ready but later declared that he would not "inter meddle" in the matter (how wise!) and the court, sceptical of the extent of the writ *excommunicato capiendo*, ordered Watson to be discharged.[3]

This release gave the Bishop new hope, and on 9 October 1702, encouraged perhaps by the revival of Tory sentiments under Anne, he sent a petition direct to the Queen. As this document gives a picture of events definitely from the Bishop's point of view we quote largely from its contents.

"Some of the clergy and officers of his diocese", he wrote, "being angry at his attempts to reform non-residence and other disorders complained of in his diocese, raised & spread many false & scandalous reports to make the petitioner odious.

---

[1] This was on 9 March. On the previous day the House seems to have been a little uneasy for it then petitioned the Crown "that the bishopric of St. David's be not filled up for some convenient time". Luttrell, *A Brief Historical Relation*, etc., iv. 621.

[2] Phillimore, *The Ecclesiastical Law*, etc., i. 70.

[3] *Ibid.*

They made use of that ill fame to present articles of simony & other pretended crimes against him. These were so presented to the Archbishop that he was prevailed with to cite the petitioner to appear at Lambeth, and afterward to pronounce sentence of deprivation, with excessive costs against him, which his judges delegates confirmed. The prosecution was wholly malicious, the witnesses untrustworthy, and the evidence insufficient to justify the sentence. The petitioner's witnesses were not allowed to give evidence, and several allegations material to his case were excluded by his Grace's agents and delegates . . . Hence he prayed for a commission of review with a clause of new matter directed to such noble peers, bishops, judges of the Common Law and Doctors of the Civil Law as the Queen thinks fit to hear and determine the case".[1]

This petition, as might have been expected, was simply ignored, and the Crown gave its reply by claiming the custody of the bishop's palace and lands, of which it had been the legal owner since his suspension. Unwelcome as the action of the Crown might have been to Watson, it yet provided another opportunity for him to argue his case, and with magnificent effrontery he refused to surrender his "appurtenances", claiming that he was still Bishop of St. David's. The Attorney-General (on behalf of the Crown) had no option, therefore, but to exhibit an information of intrusion against Watson in the Court of Exchequer, before which court the Bishop appeared on 15 June 1703.[2] Watson protested once again, through his counsel Dr. Phipps (as the rules of pleading then allowed one plea only), that since he was a peer of the realm he could not be deprived by the Archbishop. The Court of the Exchequer gave judgment against this plea, and the Bishop then appealed to the Exchequer Chamber which also decided against him on 24 November 1704.[3]

The end of this interminable legal struggle was at last in sight. Only one thing remained for him to do: he appealed once again to the House of Lords against the last decision and after a preliminary difficulty (due to his attorney being one day late in assigning his error), his case came up on 25 January 1705.[4] The importance of the occasion was realized by all those present, and the Queen herself was an interested spectator. Sir Thomas

---

[1] S.P.D. I Anne, 9 October 1702. 87 A., p. 268.
[2] Luttrell, *A Brief Historical Relation*, etc., v. 308.
[3] Phillimore, *The Ecclesiastical Law*, etc., i. 71.
[4] *Ibid.* p. 60.

Powys and Dr. Phipps once again went through the same ritual to prove that it was not within the power of an Archbishop to deprive a bishop without a synod—but all to no avail. The question whether the whole case should be reheard was negatived by 49 votes to 20.[1]

Even Watson's seemingly inexhaustible resources were now at an end: and well they might be for the case had been going on for some ten years, and it was certainly high time that another bishop was appointed to the see of St. David's. The condition of this diocese may well be imagined, for its remoteness had always made supervision difficult even with a bishop. Now it was becoming more and more disorganized, and this was seen (the Crown could not fail to be interested) in the failure of the Lord High Treasurer to secure the arrears of tenths from its parishes. True, most of the clergy were miserably poor, but some who were not so took advantage of the times to escape payment. Tenison did what he could to preserve some semblance of order, by sending a letter to the archdeacons and clergy on 6 August 1703.[2] He began by pointing out that he had received a complaint from the Lord High Treasurer calling his attention to the failure of the clergy of St. David's to fulfil their financial obligations to the Crown. The Archbishop admitted that they were labouring under a disadvantage in being without a bishop, but he urged them to try and overcome this "by a careful Discharge of . . . Duties in their respective Stations". Those with cure of souls would need no other exhortation, he hoped, than being reminded of the example of Christ: but,

"it may help to quicken our zeal, to consider further, in how much Danger the Souls committed to us are from the great Licentiousness and Wickedness of the Age in which we live: and how much reason we have to fear that this may bring down the judgments of God both upon our Church and Nation. . . . We are now engaged in a dangerous War upon the Success of which, for aught appears to us, depends the enjoyment of our Religion, and of everything that is dear to us; and therefore it very much concerns us to have God our friend and to procure his Favour and Assistance in especial manner at such a time as this".[3]

He concluded by urging them to encourage the magistrates to

---

[1] Phillimore, *The Ecclesiastical Law*, etc., i. 60.
[2] "His Grace the Lord Archbishop of Canterbury's Letter to the Reverend the Archdeacons, etc., of the Diocese of St. David's", 1703.
[3] *Ibid.*, p. 9.

enforce the law; to instruct the youth, and where possible to "procure the Erecting of Charity Schools in which they may be taught to read and to repeat the Catechism".

Such a letter as this was not likely to do very much, unless it were accompanied by some practical measures for its enforcement. Fortunately, the diocese was not to remain much longer without a bishop, for on 5 March 1705, Dr. George Bull was consecrated to the vacant see.

The legality of Watson's deprivation is a question on which legalists themselves, perhaps, will never agree. Dr. Godolphin (1617–78), in his *Repertorium Canonicum*, infers that a bishop may be deprived or removed from his see, but that his character or title cannot absolutely be taken from him, since this is "indelebilis". In other words, he may be legally deprived of that which has been conferred upon him by the State (his civil status and administrative responsibility in the State Church): but his actual ecclesiastical character lies outside such secular jurisdiction.[1] As to the power of the Archbishop, however, Godolphin does not really help us. Dr. Ayliffe (1676–1732), in his *Canon Law* (1726), and Edmund Gibson in his *Codex Juris Ecclesiae Anglicanae* (1713), both declare that bishops may be deprived by the Archbishop, but their arguments have less weight in that they quote the case of Watson as a precedent.

There can be no doubt that a number of contemporaries felt uneasy at this extreme assertion of the Archbishop's authority, and this was illustrated in a pamphlet written at the time: "A Letter to a Person of Quality concerning the Archbishop of Canterbury's Deprivation of the Bishop of St. David's" (1699).

That a bishop could be deprived for simony the writer did not for a moment dispute, but the question was, he said, "whether

---

[1] Phillimore, *The Ecclesiastical Law*, etc., i. 66, writes: "Dr. Godolphin says that the consecration of a bishop is character indelebilis: insomuch that although it should so happen that for some just cause he should be deprived or removed from the see, or suspended 'ab officio et beneficio' both from his spiritual jurisdiction as to the exercise and execution thereof and also from the temporalities and profits of the bishopric: yet he still retains the title of a bishop, for that it is supposed the order itself cannot absolutely be taken from him. [God. p. 49.] (This was the case in the non-juring bishops.) But as to deprivation Dr. Ayliffe says that in England an archbishop may deprive a bishop, if his crime deserves so severe a punishment; and that it is said in the canon law, that a bishop who is unprofitable to his diocese, ought to be deprived and no coadjutor assigned him, nor shall he be restored again thereunto. (Aycliffe, p. 124.) And Dr. Gibson delivers it absolutely that the archbishop has a right to deprive a suffragan bishop; and for the same refers to the case of Lucy and Dr. Watson, Bishop of St. David's which was A.D. 1695 in the reign of William".

a Bishop of this Kingdom is, by the sole authority of his Metropolitan, deprivable for symony".[1] The answer, the writer
maintained, would seem to be that the law "had appointed a
proper Court for enquiring into, and punishing all such Enormi-
ties: nor is there any necessity for recourse to the Legislature".
The writer then entered into an historical survey, from which he
drew the following conclusions:

(1) All deprivations of bishops, etc. used by the law of the land
to be in Councils. (2) Such Councils were called ecclesiastical
when summoned chiefly for spiritual matters. The laity were
by the constitution of the kingdom to be a party to all the
canons which were then passed. (3) Whatever judicial power
was exercised in ecclesiastical or civil Councils, now devolved
upon the House of Lords. Deprivations were judicial acts of
the Council and as such could now be decreed by a judgment of
this assembly. (4) No statute has taken away this jurisdiction.
(5) Whatever jurisdiction the Archbishop might possess did not
extend to deprivation.

A similar point of view was expressed in "A Letter to a Member
of the House of Commons" (1701?), but this epistle displays a
distinct and unrestrained animus against the Archbishop which is
not present in the more legal temper of the former. In fact, the
whole tenor of the pamphlet suggests High Church propaganda
of a particularly violent kind, and especially directed against
Tenison "who hath challenged and exercised a jurisdiction over a
suffragan Bishop which neither our own Laws or Customs,
nor the Canons of General or Provincial Councils do allow to
him". The Bishop of St. David's, it argued, had been (a) excluded
totally and finally "ab officio" and (b) deprived of his benefice,
by a single person not "Vested with a jurisdiction, in Reference
to that Case". All spiritual authority since the Reformation was
vested in the Crown, and flowed from thence, though this did not
preclude the following of older methods so long as these were not
superseded by statute law. The historic method of depriving
a bishop was by means of Convocation—or a Royal Commission.
As to the seizing the temporalities of Watson's see, this was
definitely illegal, since "no Laick can be disseized and dispossessed
of his Freehold or Inheritance unless upon a Trial at Common
Law and by the Verdict of a Jury".[2]

---

[1] "A Letter to a Person of Quality", etc., 1699, p. 3.
[2] "A Letter to a Member of the House of Commons", p. 11.

Here we must leave this vexed question of judicature. Tenison undoubtedly acted on his own authority as Archbishop because of the contemporary situation. Party heats among the clergy were of too violent a nature to allow such a case to come before Convocation, and Tenison had no intention of calling one in 1695 specially for this purpose. Royal Commissions likewise had their difficulties. Certainly the precedents for such archiepiscopal authority were extremely precarious, and perhaps the strongest argument in its support was the ingenious one put forward by the Attorney-General in the House of Lords in the interest of the royal supremacy.[1] To Tenison it may well have appeared, however, that "salus ecclesiae, suprema lex".[2]

It is now necessary to examine the charges made against the Bishop, the respective merits of which were commented upon at length from different points of view in three publications: "A Summary View of the Articles exhibited against the late Bishop of St. David's" (1701),[3] "A Large Review of the Summary Review" (1702), and "the Extraordinary Case of the Bp. of St. David's further cleared" (1703).[4] First, we must notice that the charges brought against Watson included simony; the taking of excessive fees at ordinations, institutions, visitations, etc.; the conferring of orders without administering the oaths, yet certifying under his episcopal seal that the oaths had been taken; the ordaining of men under the canonical age; the abusing of charitable trusts and the detaining a deed of exemplification. For purposes of convenience these may be grouped under three heads: (1) extortion, (2) simony, (3) *crimen falsi*: and it is to the first of these that we now turn.

(1) Extortion. Here some of the charges brought against the Bishop were trivial and such as personal animosity could easily fabricate. Typical among such were allegations that at ordinations he would take all the offertories into his own hands, saying that he would "lay the same out in plate for his chapel", and also that he would keep any gratuities which were meant for his servants,

---

[1] See p. 223, note 1.

[2] Among Tenison's papers at Lambeth (933, f. 31) there is one endorsed and partly corrected by himself, which deals with this question of the Archbishop's right to deprive. Its general thesis is that this power was placed in the Crown by 25 Hen. VIII. and 1 Eliz. and is to be exercised by the king's ecclesiastical judges, which in the case of a bishop can be none other than the Metropolitan who is "Judex ordinarius omnium Episcoporum suae provinciae".

[3] Probably written by Sir John Cooke (1666–1710), who later became Dean of the Arches and Vicar-General of the see of Canterbury.

[4] The following pages have been drawn from these sources.

as, for example, in the case of Robert Douglas, who, given four shillings, found that the Bishop subsequently deducted this from his wages.

More serious, however, was the definite charge that he claimed from the clergy illegal and excessive fees at ordinations, collations, and procurations, in violation of Canon 135 which forbids the bishop taking anything for himself. The evidence against the Bishop on this charge came chiefly from Thomas Powell, his late secretary, who deposed on oath that at two ordinations he received on behalf of the Bishop 5s. for examination, 5s. for subscription, 10s. for orders, 13s. 4d. for the licence to serve the cure "and that the deponents did account with the Bishop for the Fees of the Letters of Orders and Licence aforesaid . . . from all of which proof it evidently appears that the Bishop either took the Fees for Ordinations himself, as Douglas swears, or others received the Fees and accounted to the Bishop for them".[1]

The fees which Watson demanded for collation, it was asserted, were of an arbitrary nature, and in his Registry Office collation was listed at 20s., though this did not prevent his writing to Powell and instructing him to demand £5. Even this figure did not represent the extent of his avarice, for Peter Lewis deposed that he paid £8 14s. 4d. for collation to a vicarage. Many other similar instances were quoted and Walter Williams complained that "the Bishop usually removed several Persons to different Livings upon the vacancy of the first".[2] As an instance of the manner in which Watson conducted episcopal business we may, perhaps, quote the following. Watson had promised to collate David Lewis to the Vicarage of Trelech-ar-Bettwys for which he was to pay £6 as a fee. When he later saw the Bishop he was told that his Lordship had subsequently received a petition from another curate for the living, but he would respect Lewis' claim on payment of 40s. for a licence of non-residence.

To these and similar charges Watson replied that he was allowed by canon law to take fees, even for ordination, and that not law, but custom determined the scale of charges, which consequently varied in different dioceses. As a matter of fact, he said, the fees at St. David's were less than those demanded in the dioceses of Canterbury, Salisbury, and Norwich. At St. David's the fee for institution was £4 10s. and collation £6 10s., as compared with

[1] "A Summary View", etc., p. 16, 9.
[2] *Ibid.* p. 21.

£7 and £10 at Lambeth. Moreover, as to the fees imposed by the Bishop, Watson's secretary Slingsby (who presumably followed Powell) stated that they were taken from a list of such charges, given to him by Robert Lucy (the promoter) as the customary fees for the diocese. Watson himself, in a letter to his secretary, dated 22 December 1688, had instructed him to reduce the fees to £3 16s. for institution and £5 16s. for collation, while as soon as the present process against him began he offered to restore any charges which were found to be excessive.

(2) Simony. This was, of course, the most serious of the charges, and the case against him here concerned the Bishop's relationship with his nephew John Medley. The accusation was, briefly, as follows: Medley in 1687 possessed only a small curacy in Yorkshire worth £30 a year, but through his uncle he was soon presented to two rectories, two prebends, the Archdeaconry of St. David's and the Treasurership of the College of Brecon. Despite this good fortune, Medley remained a most unhappy man,[1] and was "always complaining of want of money". The explanation of this, so Thomas Powell, Watson's former secretary, deposed, was to be found in the following facts. In May 1688 the Bishop collated Medley to the Prebend of Clydey, but the secretary was ordered to receive the rent of £15 and pay it to the Bishop, who also received the fine of £15 paid by one Meyrick to renew his lease on the corps of the Prebend. Medley was twice collated by the Bishop to the Archdeaconry of St. David's in 1690 and 1691, which preferment the Bishop had intended to hold himself *in commendam*, but since "Mr. Medley will take this and let the Bishop receive the profits, 'tis a much better device". Powell, himself a tenant of the corps of the Archdeaconry, alleged that he had paid the first £52 of his rent to the Bishop, as also in 1692 and 1693, making in all a total of £156. Medley on his part never asked Powell for his rent except once, when the former replied: "You know I have paid my rent and to whom". "Ay, my lord, by Faith", said the nephew, "I owe him a hundred Pound, but . . . I hope it will be off at Michaelmas next, and then I shall have it by myself". Medley's hopes, so the prosecution said, were not realized, for all procurations and fees belonging to the Archdeaconry continued to be paid to the Bishop, and in

[1] In his defence Watson maintained that his lack of spirits was due to "the death of a Gentlewoman whom he had entirely Lov'd and intended to have married, and that it was through grief and sorrow for her Decease that he became so, and not because of any simoniacal Transaction". "The Extraordinary Case", etc., p. 31.

August 1693 Watson wrote to Powell: "The Induction fees I am to have till Michaelmas upon a bargain". Later he instructed Powell to delete from the accounts all record of the rental of the corps of the Archdeaconry, though the Bishop was still to receive it. Medley's last simoniacal preferment, it was maintained, was to the Treasurership of Christ Church, Brecon. Medley (so one Griffiths Davis deposed) granted the lease of the corps of this dignity to the Principal, Scholars and Fellows of Jesus College, Oxford, but the rent of the Treasurership, some £60, was paid to the Bishop.

As a result of the above three simoniacal transactions, Watson was said to have received £531 and Medley only £10.

It is necessary, since these charges of simony were the most serious made against Watson (and the cause of his deprivation), to examine his defence with some care.

In general, Watson did not deny that he had received money from his nephew, but asserted that this "was not by reason of any simoniacal contract between them, but in consideration of several sums of Money which had been really lent to him and paid out by the Bishop for him, and having long before executed a Bond for part of the same, after he was possessed of his Benefices, he [Medley] granted to the Bishop full power and authority to receive the Rents of some of them for his own Reimbursement".[1] These expenses the Bishop set down as £300 for the marriage portion of Medley's two sisters; and £40 for his education at Cambridge, besides other large sums. As to these particulars, and this is not without importance, Medley categorically stated that they were true, "and reckons it an injustice done both to the Bishop and himself in refusing to hear him". Thus the Bishop's nephew had publicly authorized the Bishop to receive his rents: it was all legally done, and it "has been unexceptionally as commonly practis'd for any Ecclesiastical person who is legally possess'd of any Benefice to convey a right of receiving the Rents to whom he pleaseth". Yet despite this, so Watson maintained, Medley never paid all his debt of £748 2s. but only £531 of it.

Such was Watson's defence. There are questions we should like to ask both sides. Why was Medley not allowed to give evidence, thereby drawing from Watson's counsel the remark that "it was in vain to endeavour any vindication if the proof

[1] "The Extraordinary Case", etc., p. 34.   See also this chapter, p. 214.

would not be admitted".[1] Where was the document which "publicly authorised" Watson to reimburse himself, and what was its form? It is clear that according to the nature (precise wording) and the legal validity of this document, the proof of a technical charge of simony depended. If Medley was known to be a supporter of his uncle and thus suspect (though if what the prosecution said was true he had no particular reason for being so), then equally so were Lucy and Powell his avowed enemies. That Watson behaved in a manner liable to create suspicion and unworthy of his office is certain: that he may have technically fallen under the offence of simony is possible: but further than this we should hesitate to go.

(3) *Crimen Falsi.* In this last charge it was maintained that the Bishop had certified in various letters of orders that the necessary oaths had been taken, whereas in fact they had been omitted. Numerous instances were alleged but it will be sufficient perhaps if we quote one. Edward Williams and James Harris deposed that they were ordained deacons by the Bishop on 24 September 1693, and that they took the oaths written on a paper in which William and Mary's names were not mentioned, although their letters of orders stated that the legal oaths had been taken— "praestitis juramentis in hac parte necessariis et requisitis". Fifteen others had been ordained with them and in no case had the legal oaths been taken. To this charge Watson replied that the articles of subscription had been gone through on the day previous to ordination (the oath of allegiance being taken in the Hall at Abergwilly), and that consequently on the latter day only the oath of supremacy had been tended. Also, Watson asked, if the above were true, why did only two come forward and object, and why did the Archbishop not allow the rest to be examined? As a matter of fact, the Bishop stated, one candidate was refused because he would not take the oaths, while there were several present who were prepared to swear that the necessary oaths had been taken. It was this accusation of *crimen falsi*, we should notice, which gave the attack against Watson such political momentum, and in this respect made his deprivation possible.

Such, in brief, were the charges brought against Watson, and the replies which he made to them. It is by no means easy to sit in judgment, particularly if we adopt contemporary

[1] Watson to Huntingdon, 18 August 1696. H.M.C, Hastings MSS. II, 274.

standards as our criteria. We wonder, on both sides, exactly
how much depended on the mere attestation of witnesses, and
how far Watson, as he complained, was hampered in his defence.
That the Bishop would not have been deprived, be his faults
never so black, if he had been a good Whig, seems tolerably
certain from the case to which we shall devote the second part of
this chapter. The opposition against him in his own diocese,
which was in part occasioned by the Bishop's own forthright
but avaricious character, was able to proceed to the lengths
it did because of the strength of the Whig backing which it could
command. We can at least understand the following contemporary
view:

> "Admitting all that was Depos'd against the Bishop of St.
> David's was true . . . yet that would not have justified the
> Archbishop's sentence of Deprivation: And therefore the
> depriving of him on such trivial Accusations would make an
> unbiassed man suspect that these Offences were assigned
> as the cause of it: yet the true reason was, his so often dissenting
> from, and opposing his Grace and some others called spiritual
> Lords in the House of Peers".[1]

Watson, as we have seen, was already regarded with intense
suspicion by the "low church party" when he went to his
diocese, and the expulsion of James II was bound to make his
position more difficult unless he were willing to accommodate
himself wholeheartedly to the new régime. His accommodation, however, was little more than a legal fiction, and even as
late as 1696 when the process against him was well under way,
he refused to join the "Association" (formed to defend the throne
after the discovery of the assassination plot), because membership
involved a declaration that William was "rightful and lawful
king". Besides being politically *persona non grata*, Watson undoubtedly had his eyes on "this world's goods", or, as one of his
supporters somewhat euphemistically described it, he was "of a
Frugal disposition". His letters to his overseer show with what
care he kept in touch with the management of his estates, and
that their financial return was an ever-present preoccupation.
We cannot forbear a smile, perhaps, as we read an epistle from his
overseer, who, in telling the Bishop that he had let one of his
mills to a substantial Dissenter, slyly observed that this could

---

[1] "The extraordinary Case", etc., p. 20.

be "no great objection in the Way of Trade".[1] Watson's own
pluralities were by no means more flagrant than the usually
accepted standards of his day, though it might, of course, be argued
that his "simoniacal contracts" made such an expedient unnecessary. This chapter abundantly illustrates that Watson was in
all things vigorous, robust, obstinate, and completely without
tact. There was as little of the statesman in him as in his master
James: and it was a combination of all these things which made
the opposition against him in his own diocese begin with a personal
revolt, headed by Lucy, the son of a former bishop. Whether this
man, as Watson's supporters maintained, was of a low moral
character living in adultery and guilty of many criminal acts,[2]
we cannot now determine: certain it is, however, that he stood
for the interests of the old cathedral order—indolent, apathetic,
non-resident, living handsomely off fees and charges, and allowed
to thrive under previous bishops. Watson came as an avowed and
violent Tory into this nest of Whigs, and, in his own blustering and
interested way, he championed efficiency no matter from what
motive. Personal and political considerations thus made him
determine to purge the cathedral and to restore order, and
we have already seen how he attempted to do this. In 1694 he
declared that he intended to insist on residence among the
cathedral clergy, and at the same time he set about removing
Lucy, the *fons et origo malorum*. Had his ambition been simply
one of securing efficiency, he might have weathered the inevitable
storm: but as it was, his violent temper, his extreme avarice, his
sympathy with the nonjurors and the King over the water, his
preference for Tory clergy—all these things enabled his incensed
Whig clergy to induce the ecclesiastical authorities to act. Upon
his own admission, particularly in relation to his nephew Medley,
his conduct was liable to grave suspicion, and the number of
separate charges brought forward against him made so ominous a
list as to suggest a large measure of guilt. Hence his trial and
deprivation. Essentially this was a political judgment, and we
cannot help feeling that the charge of simony was not proved
beyond doubt, any more than was the Archbishop's right to
deprive him on his own authority.

So far as Tenison himself was concerned, he seems to have
been at first anxious for Watson to have opportunity for replying

---

[1] Baker to Watson, B.M. Add. MSS. 5831, f. 271.
[2] "The Extraordinary Case", etc., p. 3.

to the charges against him, though determined to assert his own right of jurisdiction. Thus quite early in the proceedings a friend wrote to Watson saying:

"A person who came lately from Lambeth and converseth pretty freely with the Archbp. told me, That tho' the Archbp had been slow in his proceedings against yr Ld for which he is generally blamed by his own Friends, and allegeth in his Excuse, that he is resolv'd to leave your Ld no ground of Complaint, by hearing all that can possibly be alleged for you: yet the sentence at last will be heavy. He did not speak this as the Archbishop's Opinion, but he was very positive in what he say'd and pretended good authority for it".[1]

Yet Tenison from the very passion of his own Whig sentiments could not be an impartial judge, and may well have convinced himself early in the proceedings that Watson must be deprived and hence that the charges must be true. It is significant that Tenison was never communicative about the case: he behaved as a good Whig in an official capacity and preferred neither to talk nor write about it.[2]

The reader, from the material which this chapter provides, may feel inclined to accept Clarke's verdict (the biographer of Burnet): "Neither Tenison nor Burnet possessed the judicial capacity. They could not at will divorce intellect from passion: or regard the legal aspects of a case in abstraction from all prepossessions, whether moral and emotional, political or religious".[3]

Certainly Burnet wanted no compromise; though Tenison fired the gun (in virtue of his office), it was perhaps Burnet who loaded it.

---

[1] B.M. Add. MSS. 5831, f. 213.

[2] There are no references to the case in his letters.

[3] Clarke, *A Life of Gilbert Burnet*, p. 358. As regards the rest of Watson's life we may, perhaps, quote the following from a sympathetic contemporary: "The Bp lived hospitably, and beloved by his neighbours at Wilbraham after his Deprivation; . . . Yet notwithstanding his living constantly in the country and among his own Tenants, such was the spirit of Faction and Party that being excommunicated by the Archbp of Canterbury whose officers' fees he would not pay, on his Death, as I was informed . . . the Family was obliged to carry him out by stealth and privately at Midnight, and to bury him, tho' in a Church of his own Patronage, without service, attended by his own Servants and Tenants for fear of an Opposition from disorderly and riotous People. He died June 3, 1717, at Great Wilbraham and was put in the Ground the Night following in the Chancel under the South Wall, close to it and within the rails of the Altar. When I was there in 1748, there was nothing over his grave but the common Bricks: but his great Nephew told me he designed to lay a handsome marble over him. On his coffin was put: T. W. B. St. D. aged 80 died the 3 of June 1717". See B.M. Add. MSS. 338, f. 16.

Part II   The Bishop of St. Asaph

The case which we are now to relate forms an interesting comparison with that which has gone before, since the offending Bishop, Edward Jones (1641–1703), was a Whig, and confessed his guilt.

Edward Jones was born in July 1641 at Llwyn Ririd near Montgomery and from Westminster School he proceeded to Trinity College, Cambridge. He went over to Ireland as domestic Chaplain to the Duke of Ormonde and was appointed Master of Kilkenny Free School, where he numbered amongst his pupils the future creator of Gulliver. He became Dean of Lismore, and in 1683 was appointed Bishop of Cloyne. He escaped somewhat hastily to England during Tyrconnel's administration under James II, but his consistent "Whiggery" gained him the bishopric of St. Asaph in 1692, although some would have preferred Dr. Wake.[1] As to the condition of this diocese when Jones succeeded to it, we learn that William Lloyd, his predecessor, left it in good order, and during his stay of twelve years had done everything he could to improve the personnel of the clergy. So helpful, in fact, was he to Jones that when the latter first came to the see "he inform'd him of the whole State of the Diocese, and gave him the exact Character of every Clergyman in it, and how every Person was qualify'd for his Lordship's future Favours".[2]

Dr. Jones was translated to St. Asaph in November 1692 and made his first visit in April the next year. For a time he seems to have acted upon the suggestions of his predecessor, but discontent soon began to display itself. Men without "Learning or Degrees" were given the best preferment: there were complaints of corruption, of oppressive treatment, and a total neglect of the welfare of the diocese. A court case which arose out of the presentation to a living caused grave public scandal, and gave fuel to the rising flames of resentment. John Price, the Bishop's brother-in-law, was made Dean of St. Asaph (in trust for the Bishop's son, for whose upkeep at the university the money was to be used), and was collated to the Rectory of Llansantffraid on 20 August 1696,

---

[1] The writer of "A Short Narrative of the Proceedings", etc. in the Preface suggests that there was a third candidate, "A Person . . . of great Learning, Integrity and experience. But this worthy and Rev. Person had incurr'd the unpardonable sin of appearing in the Convocation of 1689 against ABp T . . .'s measures" (i.e. the Comprehension).
[2] "A Short Narrative of the Proceedings", etc., 1702, p. 2.

the rector, one Edwards, being ejected. This incumbent, however, determined not to submit to such treatment without a protest, and he sued for an ejectment before the grand Session in Montgomery to recover the possession of his rectory. Edwards succeeded in proving simony and obtaining the verdict. Price could hardly accept this ruling without implicating the Bishop, and he retaliated by bringing an ejectment against Edwards and his tenants in the Court of the Exchequer, but without success.[1] In effect, Jones had now been twice condemned by the ruling of a court, and in the first instance before Sir Joseph Jekyll.

Edwards' success encouraged others to air their grievances, and so serious were these, that thirty-eight of the most prominent beneficed clergymen of the diocese laid a full complaint before the Archbishop of Canterbury under thirty-four heads in March 1697, with the following preamble:

"We . . . most earnestly desire Humbly to Represent to Your Grace the deplorable State and Condition of this Diocess [sic], occasion'd by the numerous and enormous Miscarriages which have often been reported to us all, and some of us have observed, in the Conduct and Government of our present Diocesan. The particulars in the Schedule annex'd (which we humbly offer to your Grace's Consideration) are such of our Bp's Practices as have fallen under the general Remarks and Censure of the whole diocess, and we cannot but with extream Grief be apprehensive, That by such public Scandal, our holy Religion must be expos'd, and our Labours made Ineffectual, unless some seasonable Stop be put by Authority to these growing Evils, which otherwise, by reason of our Bp's Right of Collating to almost all our Livings, may be a means to leave worthy men unprovided for; and in time to fill the Diocese with corrupt and ignorant Clergy-men. Whenever therefore, your Grace for the sake of Religion and of this poor Diocese, shall think fit to make Enquiry into the Truth of those scandalous Reports of our Diocesan that have obtain'd so much Credit, and have so much lessen'd his Esteem among the Gentry and others of this Diocese, we shall be all ready and willing to give your Grace our utmost assistance, and to procure such Proofs as we do not doubt will satisfy your Grace".[2]

Tenison saw immediately that something must be done, and he first suspended the Bishop, while ordering a metropolitan visitation for July 1697, and appointing as commissioners John

---

[1] "A Short Narrative of the Proceedings", etc., 1702, p. 28.   [2] Ibid., pp. 5, 6.

Hough (Bishop of Lichfield), Humphrey Humphreys (Bishop of Bangor), and Dr. Oxenden, his Dean of the Arches. Plans for the visitation were drawn up, and Hough, writing to the Archbishop on 31 May, reported that he and his colleagues would begin with the Dean and Chapter of St. Asaph, among whom, he said, "we shall meet with all or most of ye rurall deans and others of ye Chief men of ye Clergy out of ye severall parts of ye diocese, by whom we may be informed what matters are to be enquired into at all ye severall places where we are to visit". He suggested, moreover, that since the commissioners could not for some time go into the diocese and when they did, would not remain there all the time of the suspension, jurisdiction should be placed in the chancellor of the diocese, Dr. Wynne, in order that he might "attend ye carrying on of ye ordinary business of ye Eccl.cal Court".[1]

The commissioners at length began their visitation in July 1697, and reported that the charges against Jones had been exhibited on 20 July 1698. Tenison determined to proceed, as in the case of Watson, by asserting his own jurisdiction, but Jones' connections with the Court party led to many delays in bringing him to trial.[2] After a delay of a full year, the Bishop of St. Asaph appeared before the Archbishop at Lambeth on 23 June 1699, but it was not until 5 June 1700 that the formal hearing commenced.[3]

It is at this stage, perhaps, that we may conveniently look at the charges brought against the Bishop, to some of which he later confessed his guilt. They may be treated summarily under four heads.

(1) Corruption of the clergy by ensnaring them to commit simony. Amongst many such accusations we quote the following as typical. (a) John Griffith, Vicar of Llangerniew (worth £60), applied to the Bishop for the living of Llansannan (£80). The Bishop pointed out the difference in income and stated "that the Deponent must be grateful if he would be preferred by him". (b) Dr. Robert Wynne when he applied for the Deanery of St. Asaph was asked if he would make over to the Bishop the first year's profit from the Deanery. In these transactions the

---

[1] Hough to Tenison, 31 May 1697. Lambeth MSS. 930, f. 45. See also Oxenden to Tenison, 2 June 1697. Lambeth MSS. 942, f. 138.
[2] Burnet, *History of my own Time*, iv. 407.
[3] Luttrell, *A Brief Historical Relation*, etc., iv. 391. "A Short Narrative of the Proceedings", etc., p. 6.

Bishop's favourite expression was "that his Lp had resolv'd to prefer those only that would approve themselves grateful".[1]

(2) Simony actually committed.[2] (a) Griffith Evans, the Bishop's curate at Dyssarth, was collated to the Vicarage of Llandrillo in September 1693 on condition that he remitted one year's salary which was owed to him. In 1695 he was made Vicar of Dimerchion on payment of thirteen guineas. This case was attested by five witnesses, and Evans himself swore to it in writing. (b) Oliver Owen was forced to pay £40 to the Bishop to obtain possession of the Vicarage of Halkyn and Llandrillo. (c) One, Stodart, was presented to a benefice because a relation had given the Bishop a silver tankard.

(3) Oppression of the clergy.[3] (a) The Bishop forced Robert Lloyd to resign the living of Eglwys-fach (£50) in exchange for a vicar choral's place worth about £30 per annum. (b) The Bishop took the profits of all vacant livings. (c) He preferred the unfit to benefices. For example, "Dyos turn'd out of one Cure for suspicion of Adultery, was afterwards thought fit to be employed as his Ldp's own Curate". (d) He tolerated laymen in office: Robert Jones, curate in the parish church of Llandrillo, was not in orders, nor was Griffith Owen, two years at Abergele, or Oakley, Rector of Aberhavesp.

(4) Misgovernment. (a) He neglected the offices of Confirmation and Communion in the cathedral at St. Asaph. (b) He left the cathedral without an organist for two years and kept his salary. (c) He appropriated over a period of years money left by Bishop Barrow for a free school at St. Asaph.[4]

Jones' defence was not very convincing nor need it detain us long, particularly in view of his own confession. He pleaded before the Archbishop his good character in Ireland and the speech which he made against simony in Newtown at his visitation. Moreover, while at St. Asaph he had printed at his own expense a form of prayer in the Welsh tongue from the catechism, which he had distributed among the poor. As to this keeping the

---

[1] "A Short Narrative of the Proceedings", etc., pp. 15–42.
[2] Ibid. pp. 53–59.
[3] Ibid.
[4] The diocese of St. Asaph was certainly not a very lucrative one so far as the bishop was concerned. This may be seen from the fact that Hooper (Jones' successor) petitioned through the Archbishop on 13 August 1703, that he might be granted a dispensation to hold in commendam (1) The Deanery of Canterbury, (2) a Canonry of Exeter, (3) the Rectory of Landrinio, (4) the Archdeaconry of St. Asaph, (4) Any three other benefices not together worth more than £50 per annum. He later petitioned that he might retain the Canonry until such time as the Archdeaconry and the Rectory of Landrinio were annexed to the bishopric by Act of Parliament. See S.P.D., 13 August 1703. 2 Anne, 87b p. 264.

profits of various livings, he pointed out that he possessed a dispensation to hold three livings *in commendam* if he so wished.

It was thought by some that Jones, like Watson, would be deprived,[1] and Watson's friends rejoiced that though Tenison and his coadjutors would "gladly save" him, yet they "could not".[2] Finally, on 18 June 1701, Tenison passed sentence, and suspended Jones for six months "ab officio et beneficio et ultra donec satisfecerit, etc".[3] Few could help but draw comparisons, and Jones did not make matters easier by declaring that he had only acted in his diocese "pursuant to the example, or under the directions of his predecessor". Tenison himself was reported to have confessed that "if he had been to pronounce sentence some Weeks sooner, he must have Depriv'd him". This uneasiness was reflected in the Archbishop's refusal to restore Jones to his office at the end of six months, when the Bishop appeared at Lambeth with six compurgators, of whom a contemporary writes:

"not one was of his Lps' own Order, and but two Clergymen preferr'd in his Diocess; Whereof one had never been in the Diocess but once to take Possession of a Sinecure his Lp gave him; and the other had a Living with Cure in the Diocese which he has scarce seen these ten years; the third Clergyman was wholly a Stranger; and the other three were Laymen, and not of the Diocess".[4]

Jones could now see that it was necessary to eat very humble pie if he were once more to regain his full episcopal status, and in these circumstances he drew up a confession. We quote this curious document in full:

"I Edward Bp of St. A. do here in the presence of Almighty God in this Court, and before the Most Reverend his Grace, my Lord A—p of C—y, my Metropolitan and Judge hereby confess, that I did not correct Oliver Owen, Clerk, beneficed within my Diocess with Ecclesiastical Censure, upon his being found drunk in my Pallace [*sic*] at St. A. and that I did neglect to punish John Parry, Clerk, accused to me of Crimes

[1] Luttrell, *A Brief Historical Relation*, etc., iv. 560. He writes: "Processe is made against Dr. Jones, bishop of St. Asaph, and it's believed he will be deprived for Simony".
[2] Baker to Watson. B.M. Add. MSS. 5831, f. 2131. He writes: "they [Tenison, etc.] had two Bps now before them; the one of whom they would gladly save, and could not: the other they would gladly deprive and could not".
[3] Luttrell, *A Brief Historical Relation*, etc., v. 63.
[4] "A Short Narrative of the Proceedings", etc., p. 72.

and Excesses Committed by him; and afterwards conferred upon him a Canonry; and I do also humbly confess that by an Instrument under my Hand and Episcopal Seal, I did tolerate one Griffith Owen, a Lay-man, to perform the Office of a Curate, in the Parish Church of Abergeley [sic], within my Diocess of St. A. the Vicaridge being worth 60 1 per Ann. or thereabouts; and that I did likewise tolerate one Robert Jones a Lay-man, to perform the Office of a Curate in the Parish Church of Llandrillo, the vicaridge being worth 40 1 per Ann. or thereabouts; although John Stodart Vicar of the said Vicaridge had not any other Benefice (the Cure whereof he served) and did dwell about 15 miles distant from the said Vicaridge of Llandrillo. And I the said Bp of St. A. do further humbly confess, that I did omit to give the Oaths of Simony to John Price, Clerk, upon his Collation to a Canonry in my Cathedral Church of St. A. altho' he was ready to take the same; and I the said Bp of St. A. do declare, that I am sorry for having offended in the Premises, and do humbly beg pardon of Almighty God and of his Grace the Lord A—p of C—y for the same, and do sincerely promise, That, for the future, I will not offend in the like again; and am also heartily sorry for having given occasion for any suspicion of Simoniacal Pravity, in bestowing any Benefices within my Diocess; and do sincerely promise, that I will not do any thing to give the least occasion for any the like suspicion in the future. And whereas my Absolution from the Sentence of Suspension has been retarded, by reason that I the said Bp of St. A. had declared, that I have acted in my Diocess pursuant to the example, or by the directions of my Predecessor, or to that effect; I do acknowledge to have uttered the said words rashly and inconsiderately; and I do declare, that I am sorry for the same; and I will sincerely perform my Pastoral Office with a good Conscience in all things thereto appertaining; God being my helper. Wherefore I the said Edward Bp of St. A. do humbly pray that I may be absolved from the Sentence of Suspension, and that I may in all things be restored to my Episcopal Office.

Lect. & Subscript. per me
E.A." [1]

His request was at length acceded to and Tenison restored him to his diocese on 5 May 1702. It is somewhat ironic, after what we have related, to read that Jones conducted a visitation

---

[1] "A Short Narrative of the Proceedings", etc., p. 74.

on his return to the diocese and brought his address to the clergy
to an end with these words:

"Lastly I think myself bound in Conscience to mind you
of several solemn Vows and Oaths you have taken, and which
some of you best know how you have kept. First when you were
ordained Deacons and afterwards when you were made Priests,
and particularly when you were instituted to any Living you
solemnly vowed reverently to obey your Ordinary and Diocesan.
I shall not determine the extent of these Oaths and Vows, and
the obligations they have upon the Conscience; but leave you to
reflect on your late behaviour: and tho' I heartily forgive all
that has been done particularly against me, yet I must not
pretend to discharge such sacred Oaths and Vows as they relate
to God Almighty, to whom alone application must be made for
entire Absolution; and I shall heartily pray that he may
forgive you all, for I am for charity that it may have its perfect
work as the Apostle saith 'Charity suffereth long and is
kind'".[1]

As for Jones himself, we need say no more except that he
died on 10 May 1703, at his house in Westminster, and was buried
in the parish church of St. Margaret's, without inscription or
monument.

This case, it is obvious, provides a very interesting comparison
with that which we have before related. In both it was the
Church of Wales which suffered, and in both the bishops concerned
aroused the opposition of those clergy, particularly in the cathedral,
who had been preferred by the previous diocesans. Both were
brought to trial before the Archbishop in person as the result of
petition leading to a metropolitan visitation: both were accused
of financial oppression and simony, though the Bishop of St.
Asaph was also charged with a general neglect of his diocese:
both were condemned to punishment.

It is the differences, however, which are more instructive,
and we notice at the outset, that although Jones preferred laymen
to office, no charge of not tending the oaths to the Government
was made against him. Watson was an advanced Tory, a supporter
of James II, and a sympathizer with the nonjurors. Jones was an
equally staunch Whig, and in favour at the Whig Court. Watson
came as a Tory into a diocese neglected and corrupt, where Whig
sentiment predominated in the clergy and where the opposition

---

[1] "A Short Narrative of the Proceedings", etc., p. 77.

was designed both against his Toryism and reforming efforts. Jones, on the other hand, came as a Whig into a Whig diocese which his predecessor William Lloyd had left in an improved condition. The opposition which he aroused was in no sense political nor did it gather momentum from such a source: It came solely from his administrative corruption. Thus charges of neglect were not preferred against Watson as they were against Jones. When summoned before the Archbishop, Jones acquiesced in the Archbishop's jurisdiction, while Watson certainly did not. In the former case delay was caused by the favour of the court, in the latter by Watson's legal protests. When sentence came to be pronounced, Watson was deprived (and later excommunicated): Jones suspended and after eleven months restored to his see. Watson always strenuously denied his guilt, Jones admitted his in a written confession.

Such contrasts could not escape the criticisms of contemporaries and the general Tory attitude was expressed in "A Short Narrative of the Proceedings against the Bp of St. A." (1702). This book (we quote from the preface) was written to provide a public review of the facts, since for

"want of due Information the Bp of St. A. is very spotless in the Eyes of Some, and the Clergy who promoted the Complaint, in order to a Reformation of his Irregularities, are commended by others; a third sort take their estimate of the merits of the whole Cause from the Sentence pronounced in it; and without further enquiry censure the accusations as, frivolous, which 'stricto jure', could produce no severer Censure than a Suspension for six months; which in comparison to Bp W— is but the Penance of a flea bite".

The author then went on to give a history of the proceedings, by no means favourable to Jones, and he concluded by maintaining that the power to try a bishop did not belong to the Archbishop but to a provincial synod.[1]

The writer of "A Letter to a Member of the House of Commons" (1701) likewise contrasted the treatment meted out to the two bishops.

"Whosoever compareth", he began, "the Cases of the Bishop of St. David's and of the Bishop of St. Asaph together, and considereth how much the latter, under scandalous and flagrant offences, is the object of unpresidented [sic] forbearance

[1] See p. 304.

and lenity; while the Other upon accusations less heinous, and in the esteem of many far from being evidently proved, hath been dealt with in an unexemplified manner of severity and vigour, will be tempted to believe that Love and Hatred have a greater influence upon some People in the Execution of Judicial Power than is fairly reconcileable to their Station and Character".[1]

Burnet managed to draw a distinction between the two cases which, in view of Jones' admission of guilt, few people will find very convincing: "Another prosecution followed for simony", he wrote, "against Jones, Bishop of St. Asaph, in which though the presumptions were very great, yet the evidence was not so clear as in the former case",[2] a judgment upon which the Earl of Dartmouth observes:

"The chief difference between their cases was, that Watson took the money himself (being a bachelor), and Jones' wife received it for him. I asked Bishop Burnet myself how they distinguished the crime: he told me, they looked upon one as direct simony, and the other as a simoniacal practice. Knowing the exceeding partiality of the man I told him I always understood before, that simony had been composed of simoniacal practices; which he seemed to take a little unkindly, but gave me no answer".[3]

We must now leave the reader to make his own judgment from the evidence which has been placed before him. Perhaps he will think there is something to be said for Shippen's criticism of Tenison:

"Tho' I were Mute, you must confess I've stood
    Fixt as a rock amidst the beating Flood.
Witness St. Asaph and St. David's Cause,
    Where obstinately I transgressed the Laws,
And did in either case Injustice show,
    Here sav'd a Friend, there triumph'd o'er a Foe".[4]

---

[1] "A Letter to a Member of the House of Commons", p. 11.
[2] Burnet, *History of my own Time*, iv. 407.
[3] *Ibid.*
[4] Shippen, *Faction Display'd*, 1704, p. 3. Among Tenison's papers at Lambeth there is a pamphlet (in manuscript) sent to him by one of Jones' supporters and entitled: "The Bishop of St. Asaph's Case fairly stated". Tenison wrote on the cover of this book: "I know not who wrote this neither have I read it over: but by ye little I did read, I think it favours ye Bp's ill Cause too much". Lambeth MSS. 933, f. 35.
From this chapter we can see that the condition of the Welsh Church at this time was none too happy. Burnet says of it (*History of my own Time*, iv. 407): "The bishops in Wales give almost all the benefices in their dioceses; so this primitive constitution, that is still preserved amongst them, was scandalously abused by some

wicked men, who set holy things to sale, and thereby increased the prejudices, that
are but too easily received, both against religion and the church". Moreover, most
Welsh bishoprics were allotted to Englishmen, who were alien to the Welsh temperament, and had little regard for the spiritual welfare of their flocks. The foregoing
chapter shows the abuses of this system, and a fitting commentary upon such bishops
is to be found in the following letter sent to the Archbishop on 23 October 1703.
(Anon. to Tenison, Lambeth MSS. 930, f. 33.)

"May it please your Grace To grant a Country Parson who thinks himself ye
meanest of his own function to petition yr Grace on behalf of others and himself,
that you would recommend a Welshman always to a Welsh Diocese for it is allmost
morally impossible for an Englishman to answer the expectation we ye clergy have
upon ye next vacancies here in Wales [Llandaff]; We have (more is ye Pity) great
divisions amongst us, and generally our divisions are ye wider, when there is less of the
English tongue understood; some of ye largest parishes belong to ye Bishops as part
of their revenue and when we had Bishops yt could preach in Welsh, and did take
pains to instruct ye people, ye generality of ye people did keep ye unity of ye Church,
it may be, as well as any part of ye nation. But now of late there has bin another
course taken to make choice of perfect strangers to our country and language who
generally have large comendams in England, and seldom see us, and besides by
there living from us, upon all Vacancies of any Dignity, strangers and Englishmen
are ye only Persons yt come in".

Tenison, as a matter of fact, was himself anxious to preserve the national character
of the Welsh Church. Thus, writing to Sharp in connection with the proposed election
of Dr. Evans to the episcopate, he said: "We had scarce any other choice for yt
diocese required a perfect Welchmā, or a Rich man". (Tenison to Sharp, 4 December
1701). Referring to Dr. Bull, who was passed over (see p. 302), Tenison wrote:
"If Dr. Bull had bin a Welchman, I would have bin for him, tho' indeed, he seemed
to me last sessiō extremelie broken". (Tenison to Sharp, 9 September 1701.)

17

CHAPTER 11

THE STRUGGLE IN CONVOCATION

MUCH has been written on the convocational disputes which disfigured the English Church at the beginning of the eighteenth century. It is not the purpose of the following chapter to add unduly to this literature, nor to go over the well-trodden ground again with any degree of thoroughness. Still, no life of Tenison can claim any completeness which ignores this preoccupation of his later years, and this chapter will endeavour to narrate events from his point of view, though it is but seldom that we can catch a glimpse of his personal reactions to them through the mists of official procedure.

Tenison's first experience of Convocation was in 1689, when William gave this assembly a new, though brief, period of life. In the stormy debates of that year, the Vicar of St. Martin's, just created Archdeacon of London, watched his favourite scheme for a comprehension, and the labour which he had devoted to the work of the Ecclesiastical Commission, rendered abortive through the prejudices and passions of an excited clergy. In the pamphlet warfare which accompanied this summoning of Convocation, the Tory clergy emphasized the status and dignity of this historic assembly, and made it clear that they would use it to frustrate William's mediating policy. Tenison in his "A Discourse, concerning the Ecclesiastical Commission" (1689), anticipated the years when he refused to entertain any comparison between constitutional practice in Convocation and Parliament.[1]

The failure of this attempt at comprehension through the opposition of Convocation influenced very largely Tenison's attitude to this ecclesiastical synod for the rest of his life. The reasons for the situation which Tenison inherited when he became Archbishop of Canterbury may be briefly summarized. Constitutionally the status of Convocation had been irrevocably changed when by a private agreement between Archbishop Sheldon and Lord Chancellor Clarendon, in 1664, the clergy gave up their right to separate taxation in their own assembly. Henceforth, the Crown had no financial interest in summoning

[1] Tenison, "A Discourse concerning the Ecclesiastical Commission", p. 5.

Convocation, so that if for any reason the monarch found it undesirable for Convocation to meet, he could dispense with its services without hardship—and this is precisely what happened. William preferred a Convocation which did not deliberate because of the fierce nature of the dissensions within the body itself, struggles which were the inevitable reflection of the conflicting principles of the day. The flight of James and the accession of William had led not only to the nonjuring secession, but also to a less thoroughgoing but sympathetic party within the Church. They rejoiced that the established Church had been rescued from the jaws of Rome, but they feared equally lest it should now be thrown into the arms of the Dissenters; and William's position as a continental statesman preoccupied with the French menace, his desire for comprehension in 1689, and his mediating Bills in Parliament, seemed to give substance to their fears. Hence these "High Churchmen" stressed the rights of the Church and championed the privileges of its constitutional assembly, Convocation, which William, however, at first refused to summon after its brief life in 1689. Their position was a difficult one. The bishops, since they were appointed by the Crown, were, for the most part, Whig to the core (especially after the nonjuring purge), and being generally latitudinarian in theology, they were anxious for some kind of accommodation with the Dissenters. Thus the rank and file of the Tory clergy, in protesting against the erastian settlement of the Revolution, were led into a paradoxical position so soon as they endeavoured to use Convocation to protect the rights of the Church. The Upper House, in which they were hardly represented, was solidly Whig, and supported William's policy of comprehension. Hence they were forced to split Convocation into two, to champion the rights of an independent Lower House, and by so doing to defy their spiritual superiors—whose episcopal status according to their own theories was of the *esse* of the Church—and to play fast and loose with undoubted precedent and constitutional practice. They were forced to become law-breakers to safeguard what they regarded as tradition, to defy the powers of the bishops in order to protect episcopacy. As a consequence, they could not hope to be consistent, with the result that though they first asserted that the Crown was constitutionally obliged to summon Convocation with Parliament under the *præmunientes* clause, they later asserted (when Convocation had been summoned), that it met more under the authority of the Crown than under that of the Archbishop. Logical consistency, however, could not be expected in an age which had fashioned a Revolution based on a practical compromise, and the Lower House of Convocation was not so much concerned with precedent as with power.

Tenison saw only too clearly the practical difficulties in the way of allowing Convocation to meet, and when he became Archbishop of Canterbury in 1694 he followed "the steps of Dr. Tillotson and several others of his predecessors and (no licence being granted by the Court for the transacting of business) he did continue the convocations by moderate prorogations without sitting".[1] There was increasing discontent, however, at this suppression of Convocation particularly among those "who held the views of the majority of the lower house in 1689", and in 1697 there appeared the celebrated "Letter to a Convocation Man", which in the main was the work of Francis Atterbury, whose colourful and dominating personality inspired throughout the Lower House's attack on the bishops. From the publication of this book, in which Tenison came in for a personal attack as being ready to jettison the rights of the Church, dates the immediate controversy which led to the summoning of Convocation. Atterbury based his demand for the restoration of a sitting Convocation "upon the ground not of grace but of right", asserting that the King had no more authority to prevent its meeting than he had to refuse to summon the Parliament, since Convocation met in obedience to the *præmunientes* clause.[2] Hence it was entitled "not only to meet any session of parliament but to sit and transact business without the royal licence".

It could hardly be expected that Tenison, with the practical government of the Church on his shoulders, should embark upon a historical investigation to challenge this position. He was fortunate throughout the whole of the controversy, however, in securing the services first of Wake, then of Gibson, who both undertook this responsibility. Tenison took these men into his full confidence and they became his personal friends at Lambeth. Both of them devoted many hours of patient and (to their credit) honest scholarship to an examination of the history and development of Convocation, and they thus managed to make the controversy

---

[1] W. Nicholls, *Defensio Ecclesiae Anglicanae*, 1708. Quoted, Lathbury, *A History of the Convocation*, p. 343. Burnet (*History of my own Time*, p. 33) writes that it was "kept from doing mischief by prorogations for a course of ten years".
[2] Sykes, *Edmund Gibson*, p. 28.

not entirely a story of wasted effort. Hence, though it was Tenison who publicly in Convocation bore the brunt of the Tory attack, it was yet Wake and Gibson who loaded the gun which he fired, and established his arguments so firmly "that no one since has been able to shake them".[1]

Atterbury's "Letter", therefore, elicited a reply from William Wake, in "The Authority of Christian Princes over their Ecclesiastical Synods", in which he took a strongly erastian line, "asserting that though the King was bound by custom to summon Convocation with every Parliament, yet his 'absolute and free will' alone could determine whether they should be allowed to meet for business".[2] Atterbury, who never seems to have worried unduly when his case was scientifically destroyed, now came out under his own name with "The Rights, Powers and Privileges of an English Convocation", in which he sketched in much greater detail the parallel between Convocation and Parliament.[3]

No matter how weak Atterbury's constitutional thesis might be, the demand for a meeting of Convocation increased in volume, and John Moore, Bishop of Norwich, writing to Tenison in 1700, expressed the hope that no licence would be granted to Convocation for business since "if there should be, it will be thought the effect of Mr. Atterbury's book", although "if a good answer to that book should precede the sitting of Convocation, people will probably meet with more settled and easy minds".[4] William's ministry, however, forced the issue by accepting office in 1700 only on condition that "Convocation should be allowed to meet concurrently with the newly-elected Parliament".

Hence, on 10 February 1701,[5] the Convocation of Canterbury met in the Church of St. Paul's, London, "by the Archbishop's mandate in Pursuance of the King's Writ". The usual formalities were gone through. The litany was read in Latin by one of the

[1] Lathbury, *A History of the Convocation*, p. 324.

[2] Sykes, *Edmund Gibson*, p. 28. Wake was supported by one Wright in a "Letter to a Member of Parliament occasioned by a letter to a Convocation Man"; and Atterbury by Hill in "An Appeal to all True Members of the Church of England".

[3] Wake replied to this work in devastating manner in 1703 in his authoritative treatise, "The State of the Church and Clergy of England in Convocations". Atterbury in his *Correspondence* (iii. 4) maintains that Tenison persuaded L. C. J. Holt to propose to the judges that his work should be censured for intrenching on the royal prerogative. The story, however, appears to be very doubtful.

[4] Gibson MSS. VI. 41, quoted Lathbury, *A History of the Convocation*, p. 346.

[5] Lathbury in his History of Convocation gives the date (p. 346) as 10 February 1700, and many have followed him in this mistake.

bishops; an "eloquent" sermon in the same language was preached by Dr. Haley, Dean of Chichester; and after this they appropriately sang 'O pray for the peace of Jerusalem". The Archbishop, followed by his suffragans, then proceeded to the Chapter House, where "after reading the Royal Writ and the Certificatory of the Bishop of London for Executing the Archiepiscopal Mandate, his Grace in a Latin Speech admonish'd the Lower Clergy to retire and chuse a Prolocutor and present him on Friday the 21st Instant; whereupon they elected Dr. Hooper, Dean of Canterbury, who on the said appointed Day, was presented to the Archbishop and Bishops by Dr. Jane, Dean of Gloucester, and approved and confirmed in the usual Manner".[1]

So far all had gone regularly and in order, but the battle of pamphlets had already inflam'd men's passions and Gibson could foresee "nothing but confusion and defiance",[2] while the personnel of many of the clergy—such as Jane and Aldrich—recalled ominously the Convocation of 1689.

In the next session (25 February) trouble began, for when the Archbishop's schedule of prorogation was brought down to the Lower House, it continued sitting "in contempt of it", and after discussing further business, the Prolocutor "intimated an Adjournment, by Consent of the House, to meet again in Henry VII's Chapel, instead of the Prorogation to meet in the Jerusalem Chamber, as by the Schedule which expressly included the whole Body of Convocation and left no Pretence to separate Adjournments in either House".[3]

It was a deliberate and planned act of open revolt, and Tenison could not fail to regard it "as a Declaration of setting up for a separate Interest and Power, that would break the Union of a Provincial Synod and prevent the good Correspondence of both Houses and so frustrate the common Methods of doing any Business".[4] The attack on the Upper House thus began, and remained throughout, an attack on the position of the Archbishop (the President), and a setting up of the authority of the Prolocutor in his stead. From this moment Tenison's policy in Convocation was dictated by a firm resolve to maintain his constitutional position as head of both Houses, and by so doing to preserve the historic character of Convocation as one body. He recognized the radical nature of the challenge to his power, and was unwilling

[1] *Memoirs of the Life and Times*, etc., p. 78.   [2] Sykes, *Edmund Gibson*, p. 32.
[3] *Memoirs of the Life and Times*, etc., p. 78.   [4] *Ibid.* p. 79.

for the Lower House to conduct business of any kind until it acknowledged its error in this respect. Gibson, meanwhile, was working patiently at Lambeth (he did not become a member of Convocation till 1705) producing the pamphlets which by their careful scholarship, if necessarily in a rather dull way, destroyed the case for separate adjournments which Atterbury had elaborated in "The Power of the Lower House to adjourn itself vindicated" (1701), and his other pamphlets.

We return to the events of the first Convocation. In the fourth session, on 28 February, the Prolocutor and clergy refused to attend Tenison and the bishops in the "Synodical place", the Jerusalem Chamber, which act of revolt "was justly interpreted to be a second Contempt of the President's Authority".[1] Tenison immediately sent for the Prolocutor and with typical bluntness asked him two direct questions: (1) Whether the Lower House did in fact sit after they were prorogued on 25 February? (2) Whether they had met that very morning, without attending in the Jerusalem Chamber to which they had been prorogued? The Prolocutor refused to give an immediate answer, but said "that the Lower House was preparing somewhat to lay before his Grace and the Upper House, concerning the Methods of Prorogation, and some other Things of Form".[2] Tenison received this reply in a not unfriendly way, remarking "that he and his Brethren were ready to receive what should be offer'd by them, and would consider of it, and do upon it what should appear to them to be Just and Right: But in the mean Time, he and his Brethren thought fit to continue the usual Practice".[3]

To prevent any possible misunderstanding in the prorogation, Tenison now changed the schedule (28 February) from the usual "in hunc locum", to "in hunc locum, vulgo vocatum, Jerusalem Chamber". The Lower House submitted but with a *salvo jure* and at the next session on 6 March the Prolocutor, with several of the clergy, paid attendance in the Jerusalem Chamber according to the form of the schedule. On that day the report of the committee of the Lower House, appointed to search the records concerning the prorogations, was presented to the President. In this it was maintained: (1) That it was the custom of the Lower

[1] *Memoirs of the Life and Times*, etc., p. 79.
[2] *Ibid.*
[3] *Ibid.* pp. 80, 81.

House to continue sitting till the Prolocutor adjourned it. (2) That when the Upper House was prorogued or adjourned by the words "in hunc locum", the Lower House "did meet apart from the same, at the same particular Place where it sate last". Further, they found "no Footsteps of Evidence to conclude, that it was ever the Practice of their House to attend their Lordships before the House did meet and sit pursuant to the former Adjournment. But when the House had first met and sate, it had been the constant Practice to attend their Lordships with Business of their own Motion or when they were called to their Lordships by a special Messenger".[1]

Tenison and the bishops had expected some direct answers to the matters of fact proposed in the Archbishop's questions, but the Lower House was determined to assert an "independency", and it proceeded to examine Toland's "Christianity not Mysterious", a work which the author designed as an attack on the orthodox Christian faith.

On 31 March the Lower House again justified its position and voted that it had a right to adjourn itself, which made Tenison remark to the Prolocutor, when this resolution was brought to the Upper House, that "he expected an answer in writing".[2]

It was by this time obvious that the Lower House was determined to be difficult and obstructive as a matter of policy. Towards the end of April, therefore, Tenison decided to prorogue Convocation till 8 May, endeavouring in his closing speech to both Houses to pour oil on the troubled water in the following words:

"We have many enemies, and they wait for nothing more than to see the union and order of this Church, which is both its beauty and strength, broken by those who ought to preserve it. For the maintaining the episcopal authority is so necessary to the preservation of the Church, that the rest of the clergy are no less concerned in it than the bishops themselves. I have thought fit, with the rest of my brethren, to prorogue the convocation for some time. It is a season of devotion, and I pray God it may have a good effect on all our minds. We on our part, are willing to forget all that is past, and to go on with

---

[1] To this paper (says Burnet), a reply was returned by the bishops "in which all their precedents were examined and answered and the matter was so clearly stated and so fully proved, that we hoped we had put an end to this dispute". (Burnet, *History of my own Time*, ii. 282.) It was to do work of this kind that Gibson was busily engaged at Lambeth.

[2] White Kennett, *A Complete History of England*, iii. 842.

you at our next meeting, as well as at all times, with all tenderness and parental affection, in all such things as shall conduce to the good of this Church".[1]

Such words of sweetness, however, did little to deal with the constitutional problems at issue, and "this long prorogation", a contemporary writes, "so irritated the Lower House, that to the admiration of all men by their own authority they adjourned their session to a different day".[2] Thus they continued, in unrepentant mood, to sit with the Prolocutor in Henry VII's chapel, till on the reassembling of Convocation Tenison warned them "that their proceedings in holding sessions after the prorogation were irregular, and that they could not receive anything that had been done in the interval".[3] In reply to a paper handed to the bishops by the Prolocutor, Tenison described the separate adjournments of the Lower House as "the greatest blow to this church that hath been given it since the Presbyterian Assembly that sat at Westminster in the late times of confusion".[4]

Tenison was not without hope of some kind of a settlement, however, and he "condescended" to propose "that a Select Number of the Upper House should consult with the like Number of the Lower in order to settle Matters amicably. But the Lower House declined coming to any such agreement", and the Archbishop then declared "that they would receive nothing from them till those Irregularities were settled".[5]

Prominent amongst the bishops who were for protecting the rights of the Upper House was (naturally enough) that great protagonist of the Revolution, Gilbert Burnet, and this, doubtless, encouraged the Lower House to vaunt its independence by drawing up "Representations of their Sense upon the Bishop of Sarum's Exposition of the XXXIX Articles of the Church of England", which paper they presented to the bishops on 30 May. Tenison's reception of this document was clear and to the point. "If you have any Thing to offer", he told the Prolocutor, "we cannot receive it till the late Irregularity of refusing to meet the Committee of Bishops to inspect the Books of this Convocation be

[1] White Kennett, *A Complete History of England*, iii. 844.
[2] Nicholls, *Defensio*, etc., p. 132.
[3] Lathbury, *A History of the Convocation*, p. 352.
[4] White Kennett, *A Complete History of England*, iii. 845.
[5] Tenison was not entirely without supporters in the Lower House and some of them began to feel that the Prolocutor had gone too far in his separate adjournments, and they petitioned the Archbishop against this practice on 16 May. Lathbury, *A History of the Convocation*, p. 353.

set right".[1] A written copy of this statement was taken back to the Lower House by the Prolocutor who, having consulted his fellow clergy, returned and "waited in the Chamber adjoining the Jerusalem Chamber".

On Tenison's instructions, the Bishop of Bangor (Humphreys) went out and asked the Prolocutor "Whether the Message he was charged with, was to set the Irregularity complained of Right?" The Prolocutor's answer was somewhat ambiguous. "It was something in order to set the Irregularity right", he said, but immediately corrected this to "It was concerning that Irregularity".[2] The Prolocutor and his attendants were then called into the Upper House and Tenison thus addressed them: "If you have any Thing to offer to the setting right the Irregularity we have complained of, we are ready to receive it". The Prolocutor repeated that "It was something concerning it", and then to the amazement of all (except his own followers!) he proceeded to read a paper entitled, "The Humble Representations of the Lower House concerning the Bishop of Salisbury's exposition of the XXXIX Articles". The Bishop of Bangor, in particular, felt that Dr. Hooper, the Prolocutor, had "prevaricated in this Matter", and after a short debate, Tenison reaffirmed "that he and his Brethren could not depart from their Resolution, Not to receive any Thing from the Lower House till the late Irregularity complain'd of was set right".

At the opening of the next session (6 June) Tenison once again received the Prolocutor with apparent firmness stating that "till the Irregularity complained of be set right, I cannot according to the order of this House, receive anything from you"; but he was sufficiently unwise to add that at the "earnest and repeated request of the Bishop of Salisbury", he was willing to peruse what they had to offer concerning this prelate's exposition of the Thirty-nine Articles. Hence these "Representations" were brought into the Upper House in order to gratify the controversial spirit of Gilbert Burnet, but Tenison, on reading them, remarked that they contained "only generals", and that the Lower House should not have embarked on this examination at all.[3]

The next session began on 20 June, and stormy scenes broke out immediately, for after the Archbishop had finished the prayers, the Prolocutor ("with the greatest part of the Lower House attending him") appeared waving two papers in his

[1] *Memoirs of the Life and Times*, etc., p. 83.   [2] *Ibid.*   [3] *Ibid.* p. 51.

hand and offering them both to Tenison. The Archbishop of
Canterbury, however, had already been once deceived by the
Prolocutor, and he now declared firmly "that he could receive
no Paper from him, but that containing the Particularities of
the general Charge against the Bishop of Sarum".[1] The Prolocutor replied artfully that he could not surrender one paper only
without first consulting the Lower House, and he withdrew to
obtain their advice "but never came back with that Opinion,
till Parliament being finally dissolved, the Convocation of each
Province by Writs directed to the respective Archbishops was
accordingly dissolved".[2]

Behind the Tory clergy in the Lower House there were, of
course, Tory statesmen, prominent amongst whom was Robert
Harley, who took the opportunity on 11 August of this year to
write an anonymous and somewhat abusive letter to the Archbishop. Describing himself as a "lay gentleman" whose "mind
and fortune" rendered him independent, he deplored "the
scandalous heats which have been of late among churchmen",
and protested that he had taken the Archbishop's part "in discourse relating to the affairs of Convocation, in hopes that some
happy hours would fall out to make up this breach". Now,
however, he confessed that his "hopes of healing were vanished",
and he foresaw "a dismal prospect of ruin to Christianity and
even morality". Yet despite this unhappy condition of the
Church, the Archbishop could not better occupy himself than in
"disputing whether a Lower House of Convocation can adjourn
themselves", and was busy "trumping up a legatine power".[3]

The first year of the Convocation's life had certainly been a
difficult one for Tenison, and no successful discharge of business
had been possible. It was obvious that the majority of the Lower
House, under the forceful leadership of Atterbury, were determined on an attempt to use Convocation to destroy the supremacy
of the Whig bishops,[4] and in these circumstances Tenison decided

[1] Memoirs of the Life and Times, etc., p. 91.
[2] Ibid.
[3] Harley to Tenison, 11 August 1701. H.M.C. MSS. of the Marquis of Bath,
Longleat, 1904, I, 52. There is some doubt whether the original of this letter was ever
sent to Tenison: it is not to be found at Lambeth. See also Chap. 10 for reference to
legatine power.
[4] Gibson wrote to Wake in 1716: "Your Grace knows very well that the Convocation Controversy was raised on purpose to render the Archbishop, and that part of
the bench which had distinguished itself in favour of the Protestant succession, odious
to the nation; as if they were destroying the constitution of the Church and the
liberties of the inferior clergy". (Gibson to Wake, 4 February 1715–6. Arch. W. Epist.
6, Canterbury I.)

not to bring any business of importance before it. If the Lower House insisted on its right to adjourn, the Archbishop was equally insistent on his right to prorogue. Thus his general rule "was to tell the members of their [the bishops'] side that they might stay at their cures because no business was intended", even though "the other side were summoning up the most considerable of their members to carry on such measures for perplexing the administration in Church and State as they had in their view". The results of this policy, in Gibson's opinion, were disastrous, since it often led to an ineffective defence of the bishops' interests by "the small gleanings in and about London".[1] He felt that Tenison should either give notice "to their friends in the country to come up to the end that they might make a considerable appearance", or else do nothing in Convocation but "only to send a commissary with power to prorogue".[2]

As so often with Tenison, however, he was reluctant to go to extremes, and anxious to tread the middle way. A new Parliament meant a fresh Convocation and it reassembled on 30 December 1701, in St. Paul's, when after a sermon by William Sherlock, Dr. Woodward, Dean of Salisbury, a violent opponent of Burnet, was elected Prolocutor. On 13 January they all met in Henry VII's Chapel, and after a militant address from the Prolocutor, Tenison

"read an excellent speech, exhorting to unity and peace, and reproving the unhappy divisions in the last Convocation, and mentioning this only good effect of them, that it had occasioned the industry of some learned and valuable men who had now enquired into these matters too much before unknown, and had set them in such a due light, that all persons might be satisfied on the rights and customs of holding our Convocations".[3]

On 20 January the clergy met in the nave of the Abbey, and then proceeded to the Jerusalem Chamber for prayers with the bishops, when Tenison informed the Prolocutor that "Henry VII's Chapel was ready for them". Two days later both Houses managed to agree in an "Address to the King expressing their deep Resentment at the French King's declaring the Pretended Prince of Wales to be King of His Majesty's Realms and Dominions", but six days after this was presented to William

---

[1] Sykes, *Edmund Gibson*, p. 49.
[2] *Ibid.*
[3] Lathbury, *A History of the Convocation*, p. 364. Tenison was referring to pamphlets by Gibson and Wake.

at Kensington, an "unhappy occasion widened the Differences between the two Houses".[1]

This new disturbance arose as follows. During the recess the indefatigable Atterbury discovered in the Convocation Books for 1586 the form: "Dominus Prolocutor continuavit et prorogavit quoad hanc convocationem esse continuatam" instead of the customary "Prolocutor intimavit hanc convocationem esse continuatam". It was now decided that this form should be adopted in the minutes of the Lower House. True, some of Tenison's supporters protested against this (3 February), but the majority agreed "that the Words in the Entry should stand as they are, and that this Matter shall not now be further debated".[2] Henceforth it became the usual practice of the Lower House to ignore the Archbishop's schedule when it came down, although one Whig member moved that it was "the Right of this House to have it communicated to them before they entered upon new Business".[3] The opposition to Atterbury in the Lower House, however, now began to rally its forces. A spirited debate took place as the result of one member declaring "that the House hath no Pretence of Right to adjourn itself", and Dr. Freeman, Dean of Peterborough, tried (but in vain) to get this inserted in the journals of the House "as a standing Evidence of their asserting the just Rights and Authority of their Metropolitan and President". The situation was a difficult one, but the parties in the Lower House managed to agree to a temporary accommodation under three heads: (1) That no form of prorogation should be used by the Prolocutor hereafter which was not used before the last Convocation. (2) That the forms of prorogation used by the Prolocutor in the Convocations of 1586 and 1588 should hereafter be used by the Prolocutor "in the Order they lie in the Books, beginning with the first till they are all gone through".[4] (3) That these forms should be pronounced by the Prolocutor when "the House agrees that their Business is over".[5]

A dramatic event now intervened to provide the Lower House with a fresh opportunity of advancing its claims to independence. On 12 February the Prolocutor, Dr. Woodward, fell ill, and assigned Dr. Aldrich, Dean of Christ Church, as his deputy. The Whigs in the Lower House were willing to accept this

---

[1] *Memoirs of the Life and Times,* etc., p. 93.   [2] *Ibid.*
[3] *Ibid.* p. 94.   [4] *Ibid.* p. 95.
[5] *Ibid.*

nomination provided that "Application was duly made to the President to approve and confirm him". Atterbury at first agreed to this procedure, assuring them "that there was no Design of making a common Referendary without consulting his Grace"; but no such application was in fact made.[1] Tenison felt he must take cognisance of this irregularity and calling the clergy together to the Jerusalem Chamber, he spoke to them as follows: "My Brethren of the Clergy; There has happened an Incident of great Moment, which I and my Brethren must take Time to consider of, between this and Saturday next to which I have thought fit to Prorogue the Convocation".

On 13 February, however, the Prolocutor died,[2] and Tenison saw his opportunity and took it. Leaving his company at Lambeth "in haste", he hurried off to Convocation "in order to prorogue 'em without chooseing a new prolocutor",[3] telling them that he "would consider what was to be done".

Tenison determined to use this occasion, "there being no Business depending and nothing in Debate but the Clergy's Pretensions of Exemption from the Synodical Authority and Rights of the Archbishop and Bishops", to dismiss this troublesome assembly for some time, and this he did on 19 February, when he gave a lengthy address to the assembled clergy.

After remarking on the complaints the Upper House had received against the Bishop of Salisbury, the Archbishop turned, naturally, to consider the situation created by Dr. Woodward's unexpected death. "The Choice of a Prolocutor or Referendary", he said, "is equally the Right and Concern of the whole Lower House", but since many members had left London "that they might attend their respective Cures in this Solemn Time of Lent", he did not propose to call them back to Town when there was "no necessary Business to engage them". He proposed therefore "further to deliberate about the Choice of a Pro-locutor and at present to proceed to a Prorogation". As to those who foolishly maintained that the bishops intended "to bring Convocations into disuse", they were "greatly mistaken".

[1] *Memoirs of the Life and Times*, etc., p. 95.
[2] The biographer of Prideaux says of Woodward that "he conducted himself with candour & abilities much beyond what was expected from him". *The Life of Henry Prideaux*, p. 102. Prideaux, we may notice, supported the Archbishop's right to adjourn both Houses, but thought that the Lower House was right in appointing committees "to sit & act on the intermediate days".
[3] Bp. Nicholson's, *Diary* I, 92. Transactions, Cumberland and Westmorland Antiq. Society N.S. 1901.

He concluded his long address with the customary exhortation to peace in these words:

"I beseech you Brethren, to look forward to the Things that make for Peace, and whereby we may Edifie one another, and the Established Church of which by the singular goodness of God we are members. That so those Differences which have continued too long already, may be speedily and happily composed. To which end I heartily commend myself and you to the God of Peace and Unity through Jesus Christ our Lord".[1]

In this speech, Tenison made his policy for the immediate future tolerably plain, namely, to prevent Convocation from deliberating by frequent prorogations. Yet though one supporter of the Archbishop wrote later that "a great Part of the Clergy was entirely satisfied with the Reasons; and thought it a seasonable Juncture to have the liberty of returning to their Churches and Families; and there to expect a Call upon such Emergent Occasions, as should require the Choice of a Prolocutor and the sitting of the Convocation", most of the Lower House, however, defied the Archbishop's prorogation. Two days later they met in Henry VII's Chapel, and made themselves "a sort of Assembly" by choosing a "Moderator or Chairman". Thus when the day came for the reassembling of Convocation under the terms of the prorogation, the Lower House came as a body without a prolocutor into the room adjoining the Jerusalem Chamber, "and there meeting the Bishop of Lincoln, who as his Grace's Commissary, had now Prorogued the Convocation to a further day, they desired his Lordship to carry a Message to his Grace, of their Desire to proceed to the Choice of a Prolocutor". The Bishop of Lincoln, however, diplomatically asked them to express their meaning in writing. A rather unruly episode followed for when one began " 'It was the unanimous Desire of the Lower House of Convocation', a supporter of the bishops expressed the hope that no such Message would be worded in the Name of the whole Lower House. For as they were not a House, and did not Act in that Capacity without a Prolocutor, so it would be more true and proper to let the Message run in the Name of several members of the Lower House", which was accordingly done.[2]

---

[1] *Memoirs of the Life and Times*, etc., pp. 97–99. This speech was published in the form of a pamphlet: "A true Copy of the Archbishop of Canterbury's Speech in the Jerusalem Chamber, Feb. 19 1701/2". 1702.

[2] *Memoirs of the Life and Times*, etc., p. 100.

Another unexpected event now intervened to interrupt their proceedings. On 8 March William III died, and if as Tenison and the Bishops rightly alleged the Convocation was summoned by the Archbishop's mandate in pursuance of the king's writ, then it was automatically dissolved. If, however, as Atterbury maintained, Convocation attended upon Parliament in virtue of the *præmunientes* clause, then it might be argued that it was still in existence. The latter expedient was certainly worth trying and some of the Lower House endeavoured to enlist the support of the House of Lords "to revive the dead Convocation and to declare it still in being", but without success.[1]

Tenison was thus relieved of Convocation again for some time, and he endeavoured to use the interval to make interest with the Earl of Godolphin (1645–1712), the Lord High Treasurer, in order to counterbalance Atterbury's pull with the Tories. During the year Atterbury had been busy with his pen in "A Faithfull Account of some Transactions in the three last Sessions of the Present Convocation", "A Continuation of the Faithful Account", "The Case of the Schedule stated", and "The Parliamentary Original and Rights of the Lower House of Convocation cleared", in all four of which he indulged in a great deal of personal invective, in order (as he explained to a friend) "to inspirit a dull subject".[2] On 19 October, Tenison called on Godolphin armed with a copy of Atterbury's latest publication and endeavoured to convince him "how little inclination the Convocation were like to have towards an accommodation": whereas he, the Archbishop, had "actually taken out of the press some books that had been written and hindered others designed to have been written upon the subject of contention, on purpose to avoid all occasions of increasing the flame and the divisions that had been so violently and unfortunately kindled and fomented in the Church". Godolphin, however, was far too shrewd and experienced to be drawn into a controversy of this kind, or to pass any definite judgment. He replied that he could not "at all pretend to be a judge" of these things but that as "all matters of difference at this time must needs have very ill consequences both in Church and State", he would "not

---

[1] *Memoirs of the Life and Times*, etc., p. 101.
[2] Bp. Nicolson's *Diary*. 29 February 1707–09. Transactions, Cumberland and Westmorland Antiq. Society N.S. IV, 1904.

neglect anything in his power to compass and heal them". Despite this guarded answer, Tenison pressed Godolphin to take a copy of Atterbury's book "and judge if it were possible to be tame and quiet under such provocations". The Peer accepted it but passed it on to Harley for his opinion![1]

The first Parliament and consequently the first Convocation of Anne's reign met on 20 November 1702, and it was immediately apparent that there was to be no release from ecclesiastical warfare. Tenison was anxious to secure the election of a moderate prolocutor who would co-operate in a policy of appeasement, but in opposition to his wishes the Lower House proceeded to elect Dr. Aldrich, "who had always been a constant Voter for Encroachments upon the Power of the President and the Upper House".[2] They then embarked on a quarrel over the address to the Queen,[3] and "the old Sores broke out again with greater Rancour than ever".

Tenison still seems to have been genuinely concerned for some kind of accommodation, and in response to a request from the Lower House he proposed at a committee of bishops and clergy:

"(1) That the Lower House might meet in Committees to prepare business between the synodical prorogations. (2) That when Business should be before the Convocation, the Archbishop with the consent of his Suffragans, should so order the Prorogations that there should be sufficient and convenient Time allowed for considering and finishing it".[4]

This was a generous gesture considering the party heats at the time, but Atterbury, counting on a rising tide of Toryism under the new Queen, did not want an accommodation, and the House consequently "fell into new Disputes about his Grace's Prerogative".[5] The serious nature of the deadlock may be seen in that on the initiative of Viscount Hatton a group of peers met the Archbishops of York and Canterbury, in order to see whether some amicable agreement could be reached. Hatton suggested an informal meeting between the members of both Houses, to which Tenison finally agreed "out of mere compliance to his Lordship's Request", though the bishops as a whole doubted the

---

[1] Portland MSS. H.M.C. II, 48.
[2] *Memoirs of the Life and Times*, etc., p. 102.
[3] Lathbury, *A History of the Convocation*, p. 378.
[4] *Memoirs of the Life and Times*, etc., p. 102. See also Tenison to Viscount Hatton.
[5] Lathbury, *A History of the Convocation*, p. 379.

18

value "of a verbal Conference upon points soe much out of the common Way".

But the Lower House would have nothing to do with a joint committee; instead they proposed that both Houses should concur in an application to the Queen to appoint persons to adjudicate upon the controversy. To this proposal, however, Tenison and the bishops replied firmly "that they could not make any further concessions without injury to their constitution as an episcopal Church".

In these circumstances, Tenison wrote to Hatton on 21 January, and after giving him a narrative of recent events concluded his letter: "Such of my Brethren as I have met with since your Lordships proposed the revival of the Conference, think it in the recent Circumstances more unfit than ever; and I cannot but say, that upon the best judgment I am capable of forming, I am of the same Opinion".[1]

The Lower House had thus decided on its own initiative to bring its constitutional case directly before the Crown (being encouraged in this resolution by the Tory sentiments which prevailed in the ministry) and by this means to short-circuit the bishops altogether. It therefore petitioned the Queen to take the whole matter into her consideration since, after the interruption of Convocation for ten years, many questions had arisen regarding the rights of the Lower House, and the bishops had declined to allow investigation.[2] The Queen acknowledged the petition but never gave any definite reply, possibly because the legal experts did not concur in the judgment which some of the Tory ministry wished to pronounce.[3]

Tory counsels and High Church "notions" (as we have seen) came increasingly into favour in Anne's reign, and the policy of the Lower House of Convocation, taking its cue from Tory practice in Parliament, was to embarrass the Upper House by forcing it to pass judgment on the many controversial questions of the day. Thus the clergy now petitioned the bishops to make a declaration on the divine nature of episcopacy, only for Tenison to refuse an immediate answer on 15 December, explaining that the question was so important that the bishops must take time to consider it.[4] His reply, when it came on 20 January, was very enigmatic in form, though, with an irony which we can

1 Tenison to Hatton, 21 January 1703. B.M. Add. MSS. 29584, f. 101.
2 Lathbury, *A History of the Convocation*, p. 382.
3 Burnet, *A History of my own Time*, ii. 347.
4 Lathbury, *A History of the Convocation*, p. 382.

understand, he commended the zeal of the Lower House on behalf of the upper order. A short time later, Convocation was prorogued with Parliament. It next met in the autumn of 1703, and in the spring of 1704, after protesting against the inadequacy of the law respecting the collection of Church rates (and receiving an assurance from Tenison that a Bill to remedy this "was ordered", with an invitation to come and inspect it at Lambeth), the Lower House presented to the Archbishop a comprehensive gravamen, which it had drawn up during the recess. This document contained detailed criticisms of the contemporary Church in its relation to baptism, marriage, and the general question of discipline. There was certainly need for such complaint and reform, although Burnet felt it would have been better directed against many practices in which the petitioners themselves engaged, such as pluralism and non-residence.[1]

The Archbishop received the petition with the disarming assurance that copies of the representations would be given to the bishops in order that they might make use of them on their visitations, which, he said in his speech proroguing Convocation on 3 April, had never been so frequent or effective since "the last open attempt to introduce Popery".[2]

It was by this time obvious that disputes would last just so long as Convocation continued in being. In the autumn of 1704 Convocation met again for the third time during the first Parliament of Anne's reign and the Lower House proceeded to lament the fact that owing to dissensions "no benefit had accorded from the frequent meetings of Convocation", though for their part they had "neither raised them, nor after their rise omitted any means . . . for bringing them to a regular termination".[3]

The bishops felt that such a complacent narrative of events could hardly be allowed to pass unchallenged, and in reply they went over the proceedings of the last year, and recalled how that as far back as 1689, although the Convocation had a royal licence to undertake a particular task, the Lower House "could not better serve the Church than by declining the business proposed by the King".[4] They concluded by specifying all the irregular acts of the Lower House during several years.[5]

---

[1] Tindal, *Continuation of Rapin's History of England*, iii. 645.
[2] Lathbury, *A History of the Convocation*, p. 387.
[3] "The Complainer further Reproved", p. 2.
[4] *Ibid.* p. 12.
[5] *Ibid.* pp. 14, 15.

Burnet, of all the members of the episcopal bench, was regarded, perhaps, with most hatred, and his position was not made easier by an impetuous temper and a controversial spirit. With incredible folly he now took the opportunity, in a charge to his clergy, to give vent to his wrath by condemning the members of the Lower House as "enemies to the Bishops, the Church and the Country". Once again the Lower House petitioned the President to interpose his authority.

It was Tenison's custom at every prorogation to comment with regular monotony on the irregularities of the session, and on 15 March (having received a message from the Queen on 25 February in which she declared it her intention "to maintain Our Supremacy and the due subordination of Presbyters to Bishops as fundamental parts of the Constitution of the Church of England")[1] he once again embarked on an elaborate review of the many irregularities committed by the Lower House. His patience seems to have been getting somewhat exhausted, and he declared that most of the alleged complaints of the clergy required no answer, while as to the petition against the Bishop of Salisbury, it could not even be considered, since the charge of which they complained was in fact simply a vindication of the lawful authority of the bishops. He promised, however, that although he was determined to maintain the rights of his office, he would not suppress Convocation. In all their actions, he concluded, the bishops would not depart from the articles, rubrics and statutes, and he asked them to remember that the honour of Convocation "could alone be retrieved by departing from unwarrantable claims".[2]

Things were now rapidly approaching a climax. Convocation met again on 25 October 1705, and Dr. Binckes, Dean of Lichfield, "a fiery and hot Zealot for the pretended Rights of the inferior Clergy", was elected Prolocutor.[3] The Tories at the time were engaged throughout the country in raising their customary cry that the Church was in danger, a fact which induced the Upper House of Convocation to declare its satisfaction at the present state of affairs under her Majesty's Government, especially seeing that "several of the foreign Churches were endeavouring to accommodate themselves to our liturgy and constitution".[4] It is

---

[1] B. C. Brown, *The Letters of Queen Anne*, p. 219.
[2] *Memoirs of the Life and Times*, etc., p. 105.
[3] "The Complainer further reproved", pp. 34, 40.
[4] Lathbury, *A History of the Convocation*, p. 105. See Chap. 15, p. 341.

not surprising that the Lower House refused to concur in this declaration but set up a committee of its own to draw up a statement which was carried up by the Prolocutor to the President on 12 November, and contained the ambiguous statement that the Church could be in no danger from her Majesty.[1]

Tenison determined from now on to make no concessions, and he replied firmly that he could not accept this address, but that the Lower House must either consider the address sent down to them, or bring their exceptions in writing. The Lower House declined to do this and there was now a complete breach between the two Houses, and Tenison (appointing the Bishop of Norwich to take his place as Metropolitan) could do nothing but prorogue the assembly till 1 February, although this did not prevent the Lower House from holding its intermediate sessions.[2]

Upon its reassembling, Tenison received on 12 February a royal writ proroguing Convocation "to such time as seemed meet and convenient",[3] a closure which seems to have taken the Lower House by surprise, and so enraged them that it was with difficulty that they were induced to remain until the prorogation had been read.

And so these wearisome disputes went on. Political expediency dictated that the Lower House of Convocation should not deliberate while the Act of Union was before Parliament, and it was accordingly prorogued by royal writ for three months. On meeting again it immediately complained of this procedure in an address to the Queen, maintaining that no such resort to royal writs had been practised by the Crown since the Act of Submission. Tenison himself replied to this assertion on 2 April 1707, quoting precedents to show that similar prorogations had taken place during the meeting of Parliament, and again proroguing Convocation till 10 April, although the Lower House continued its by now customary intermediate sessions. This unconstitutional behaviour led the Queen, on 8 April, to reinforce the authority of the Archbishop by sending him a letter, in which she said that in spite of her former admonition, some of the clergy had declared that the late prorogation, ordered at her command, was "unprecedented and contrary to ancient and constant usage". Such a statement, she protested, was not only untrue, but an

---

[1] Atterbury, *Correspondence*, iii. 273, 274.
[2] Lathbury, *A History of the Convocation*, p. 398.
[3] *Ibid*. p. 399.

"invasion of her Royal Supremacy",[1] and if persisted in would force her to proceed against them by the laws of the land.

This admonition was communicated to the Lower House, although it appeared without its Prolocutor who was said to have gone into the country.[2] Tenison felt that he must take cognizance of such casual behaviour and he passed sentence of contumacy against him, deferring the penalty for a week, by which time, however, Dr. Binckes, resisting the strong pressure of his own supporters, saw fit to make a formal submission and was discharged.[3]

On 18 April Tenison dispatched a circular letter to the bishops, enclosing with it the letter which the Queen had sent to him a short time before. In his own epistle the Archbishop said that he thought it advisable for the bishops to assume the responsibility of acquainting their clergy with the nature of the proceedings in Convocation. They would find it necessary to point out that in the last session the Lower House had made the most extravagant assertion, namely that it had never been prorogued by a royal writ during a session of Parliament from 1532 to 1705. This was simply untrue and did not come very well from those very people who were themselves making an attack on the historic constitution of Convocation. Hence, in justice to "the cause of the royal supremacy" and "in regard to the welfare of the Established Church", Tenison exhorted his brethren to lay the foregoing account before their clergy.[4]

But passions were now too violent for the clergy to submit to discipline through an episcopal admonition, and "the lower house was so refractory that it was not possible to proceed with business".[5]

The situation was rapidly becoming an impossible one, and Tenison seems to have resigned himself to the fact that prorogation through royal writ was the only expedient, if not of keeping the peace, yet of preventing too violent war. Weariness, with the growing bickerings of faction, made the Archbishop himself now a little less respectful of precedents and constitutional procedure than he had been at the beginning of the disputes. He determined to assert his own powers to the fullest possible

[1] B. C. Brown, *The Letters of Queen Anne*, p. 219.
[2] Lathbury, *A History of the Convocation*, p. 403.
[3] *Memoirs of the Life and Times*, etc., p. 107.
[4] Cardwell, *Documentary Annals*, ii. 359–64.
[5] Lathbury, *A History of the Convocation*, p. 404.

extent, and this determination was seen in the new Convocation summoned to meet with the Parliament in 1708 when he was ready for action. In order to make some *modus vivendi* possible, Tenison was anxious for Dr. Willis to be appointed Prolocutor, but the Archbishop was privately advised that "the Fiery Zealots of the Lower House" were using "great Industry" to push forward the claims of Atterbury. Tenison determined at all costs to prevent this "new Insult" upon himself, and brushing aside the usual custom, he prorogued Convocation the moment it assembled, not waiting even for the religious service to take place.

Such a dramatic intervention secured a respite for some time, and Convocation continued to be prorogued during this session of Parliament. But in 1710 Sacheverell was a national hero, a Tory majority had been returned to Parliament, Atterbury was at the zenith of his power, and the Queen wrote again to the Archbishop on 12 December in rather a different strain, appealing for unity in these words:

"We have therefore by Our Royal Writ summoned the present Convocation together with the Parliament, as in all times has been accustomed, that the Clergy might be in business suitable to their sacred function, such as might tend to the advancement of Religion and Virtue, and redound to God's blessing and the public benefit.

"For Our Part, We are ready to give them [both Houses] all fitting encouragement to proceed in the Dispatch of such business as properly belongs to them, and to grant them such powers as shall be thought requisite for carrying on so good and desirable a work, in confidence that Our Royal Intentions in that behalf will not be frustrated nor the ends of such Assemblies defeated by any unseasonable Disputes between the two Houses of Convocation, about unnecessary forms and methods of proceeding. We earnestly recommend that such disputes may cease and We are determined to do all that in Us lies to compose and extinguish them".[1]

In 1711 Atterbury finally signalized his triumph by securing his election as Prolocutor in opposition to White Kennett, the leader of the bishops' party in the Lower House. Tenison was now more or less isolated at Lambeth and this encouraged Atterbury to secure a change in the licence, by which "the Archbishop was not, as was usual on former occasions, nominated president, neither was he consulted previous to its being issued".[2] Thus

[1] B. C. Brown, *The Letters of Queen Anne*, p. 311, quoting S. P. Dom. 44/150, f. 315.
[2] Lathbury, *A History of the Convocation*, p. 409.

Tenison could only interpret it as an intended slight when John Sharp, Archbishop of York, was consulted by the ministry concerning the business to be laid before the Convocation of Canterbury, and he himself was excluded although it related to his own province. Tenison's position as a convinced erastian was certainly a difficult one when the Queen was dominated by such counsels; particularly since it remained his firm conviction that "for doing of any considerable business, her Majesty's licence was necessary, the Act of Submission so requiring"; and that "her Majesty's supremacy over the Synod ought to be asserted more strenuously than has of late been done by some, since unusual forms and methods in Convocation are not so conducive to the end of it as the old one".[1]

It is perhaps fitting for us to leave the Convocation controversy at this stage, not simply because Tenison's subsequent relations with it are related in another chapter,[2] but because the significant period of conflict was over. It was, in fact, but a matter of time till Convocation received its *quietus* from the Whigs in the early years of George I.

The Lower House had always shown a weakness for proceeding against the authors of latitudinarian books, and in 1717 it attempted to vent its wrath on Benjamin Hoadley, a bold and outspoken supporter of the Whig philosophy. Times had changed, however, and High Church Anglicanism seemed more a sentimental attachment to the past than a living (and profitable) faith for the future. The Government decided to remove this anachronism once and for all and "to scatter a little dust over the angry insects". It did this so effectively that the insects were submerged till 1852.

Tenison's part in these convocational disputes is typical. Doggedly and persistently he stuck to his undoubted legal right as president of the historic assembly of the Church. When political pressure revived the sitting Convocation in 1701, he at first did his best to work with it, and though insisting on the law, he encouraged the Lower House to do business. But it was useless to cry peace where there was no peace. The leadership of Atterbury was of too forceful and militant a character to incline the Lower House to come to terms. Through its insistence on the prolocutor's right to prorogue and its determination to conduct itself as an independent assembly, agreement with the Upper

---

[1] Portland MSS. III, 21 February 1714.
[2] See Chap. 14.

House was made impossible. Tenison tried many expedients. He endeavoured to secure the election of a Whig Prolocutor; to set up a committee of both Houses; to pour oil on the troubled waters in speeches of peace: but all proved to be of no avail, and he was driven finally to secure the prorogations of Convocation through royal writ.

It may be thought that if only Tenison had been endowed with more imagination and a greater gift for leadership, he might have been more successful in making the Lower House amenable. This is possibly true, probably untrue. Between both Houses there was a great gulf fixed, the chasm which separated Tory from Whig, orthodox from latitudinarian, Atterbury from Burnet, Aldrich from Kennett. The disputes in Convocation marched in step with the pace of political events, and Tory sentiments in Whitehall led to independent action by the Lower House. Later, when George I was successfully placed on the throne, the Lower House survived as a Tory stronghold (such is the natural conservatism of the clergy), after many parliamentary Tories had begun to steer a more middle course. The situation, therefore, could not remain permanent. The Revolution of 1688 had introduced a division into English religious life with dissent at both ends, from the Nonjuror to the Nonconformist. Inside Convocation all these different theologies and ideologies found representation in a modified form, the latitudinarians being mainly in the Upper House, the orthodox in the Lower. No one—party heats being what they were—could hope to control such an assembly, and certainly such a convinced Whig as Tenison was not the man to try.

The tragedy of it all lies in the fact that the Church found itself in the great age of reason deprived of its own assembly, and it could speak with no corporate voice on such momentous questions as the rise of Methodism, or the need for bishops in the American plantations; and so it fared worse than the ox which "treadeth out the corn". Tenison repeatedly affirmed that he had no intention of permanently suppressing Convocation, and Gibson later regretted its complete suspension, although his own unsuccessful revival of it in 1741[1] showed that the clergy had not yet learnt their lesson.

[1] See N. Sykes, *Church and State in England in the XVIII Century*, p. 2. He writes: ". . . [nor] that Walpole himself in 1741, at the instance of Gibson and other bishops, allowed the Convocation again to sit for debate until a revival of the contumacy of the lower house toward the upper compelled its prorogation".

CHAPTER 12

VISITOR OF ALL SOULS' COLLEGE

THOMAS TENISON, by reason of his office as Archbishop of Canterbury, was brought into intimate contact with the life of All Souls' College, Oxford, and for good or ill, left his mark upon it. This College was founded by Archbishop Chichele in 1437, and in accordance with his directions, "the Archbishop of the time being was to stand in place of the Founder, the sole interpreter of his Statutes, from whom there was no appeal".[1] All Souls' went through what Professor Burrows calls its "golden age" in the reign of Elizabeth, but in the seventeenth century the unsettlement of the times caused a lamentable decline. During the archiepiscopate of Sancroft, the Warden of All Souls' was the sturdy and independent Jeames, and together they fought a successful war against "the horrible impiety of selling Resignations", by which the Fellows, for a consideration, secured the election of their own nominees. Secure in support from Lambeth, Jeames used his veto on the elections of such Fellows, and the Archbishop supported the Warden, when the elections came to him upon a devolution. Amongst those who suffered under the Warden's veto in 1681 was Leopold Finch (son of the Earl of Winchelsea), then a young man, who seems to have retained to the end of his days a liking for intemperate living—but All Souls' was to hear a great deal more of him a few years later.

Warden Jeames died in 1686 at a most critical time in the history of the country and the College, for James II was then using his dispensing power to support his despotism, and "Oxford itself was of all places, exactly that which it seemed most desirable to imbue as speedily as possible with the idea that the Crown was the absolute disposer of all appointments great or small".[2] The Fellows of All Souls' feared lest a Roman Catholic Warden should be thrust upon them, and amongst the numerous persons who solicited for the post were John Dryden, Mathew Tindal, and Thomas Watson, later Bishop of St. David's. The successful candidate proved to be none other than the forementioned

[1] Montagu Burrows, *Worthies of All Souls'*, 1874, p. 28.
[2] *Ibid.* p. 288.

Dr. Leopold Finch, a boisterous Anglican Tory. Rejected for a Fellowship in 1681, he was elected the next year on his promising to live "studiously and regularly", and he distinguished himself in 1685 by raising a troop of horse from the university to do battle (if need be) against the Duke of Monmouth. Immediately on the death of Jeames, Finch presented himself before the King and was promptly given a mandate dated 15 January 1687, appointing him Warden, "any statute, custom or constitution of the College notwithstanding". Thus Finch returned to Oxford as Warden of All Souls', but he never succeeded in securing election by the Fellows, nor would Archbishop Sancroft confirm the appointment.

Finch's devotion to James, however, was not of the kind that was prepared to share the sufferings of his exile. The new Warden was soon *persona grata* with William III, and he became a favourite at Court, being given a prebendal stall at Canterbury. But his impetuous spirit soon embroiled him in a serious quarrel with the College. He had not long been Warden when his customary impecunious condition (not due altogether "to his buying of books") made him determine to stand against Dodwell for the Camden Professorship in Ancient History. To the Warden's extreme annoyance, the latter obtained the appointment by a majority "so narrow" that he could "put his hand on the very man who had robbed him of the prize". The offender was James Proast, Chaplain of All Souls', who had even persuaded two other Fellows to vote against him. The indignant Finch took his revenge the very evening of the election by dismissing Proast from his chaplaincy.

Proast, however, was a man of "high character and resolute spirit", and he put his case before Archbishop Sancroft, who commissioned two bishops to investigate (Lloyd of St. Asaph and Levinz of Sodor and Man), both of whom reported against Finch. "If he is our Chaplaine, I cannot be his Warden", was Finch's curt comment on their findings, a remark, however, which he interpreted only one way. But Sancroft was soon out of office and Proast next petitioned (although in vain) the Dean and Chapter of Canterbury, this cathedral body acting as Visitor during a vacancy in the archiepiscopal see. Upon Tillotson's appointment Proast once more took his case to Lambeth, but there was much delay due to the chaplain's supposed nonjuring sympathies, although at length in 1694 the Archbishop gave judgment. Proast was to be reinstated in his chaplaincy, but the ruling was not clear as to the settlement of the arrears of Proast's income. The chaplain determined to keep up the fight, but he "could obtain no redress either from the Privy Council or at Westminster".

The elevation of Tenison to Canterbury gave Proast fresh hope, and it was not long before he acquainted the new Primate with his grievance. Proast's letters—probably because of his political sympathies—were not entirely welcome at Lambeth, and the Archbishop complained "that they have bin so full of an evil spirit yt they ought to have mett at least with neglect".[1] Tenison, obviously mistaking the character of Proast, proposed to end the dispute by offering "to procure him a Living double ye value to his Chaplaynship", but the Archbishop was forced to confess that the chaplain "seem'd not to regard it".[2]

Thus Tenison was not at first very sympathetic towards Proast, and this can be seen from a memorandum which he drew up at the time. Mr. Proast, amongst other things, he wrote, seemed to aim at:

(1) "ye Removall of Mr. Finch frō his Wardēship"; (2) "ye receiving the mean Profits of his Chaplaynship whilst he was expelled by Dr. Finch"; and (3) "an Additional Salarie to the Stipend of ye Chaplayn of All Souls'."

As to the first of these, Tenison commented:

"I presume He remembers yt Mr. Finch came in King James' time, when (if some of yt noble family had not prevailed for Mr. Finch)", the King "had sent Mr. Dryden thither. And seeing how Archbp. Sancroft and Archbp. Tillotson did not think fitt to stir yt matter, he cañot imagine it so proper for me to do it after so many years".

As to the second, he wrote:

"Ye Case stands thus. The cause was try'd before Abp. Tillotson. Mr. Proast had sentence givē on his side. In yt sentence Mr. Finch was order'd to pay ye Charge of ye Suite wch he did; but for ye mean profits, it is said that these shall be payd, but 'tis not expressed by whome. Wn Mr. Proast applyed to me for Them, I ask'd him 2 Questions. 1. Of whom he demanded them? 2. What sū they did amount to? He answered that he demanded them of ye College . . . The Fellows have answered that they were never made Parties or called in ye Cause, & therefore could not be concerned in ye sentence. The warden

---

[1] Lambeth MSS. 931, f. 48.   [2] *Ibid.*

has bin shewn ye particulars of ye account, and has sd that some of ym are not just. So yt he asks me to fix so nice a thing as propertie (in a Case tryed & determined before I came to ye see) without having it stated what it is, or of whome it is to be demanded ".

Regarding 3. Tenison observed:

"I mentioned his Proposal to ye College but could not at yt time recommend it there because I knew not whether any thing of ye College Revenue could be properly & without prejudice to other services be spared ".[1]

It seems certain that some member of the College, probably Finch, had done his best to prejudice Proast in the eyes of the Archbishop, for Tenison concluded:

"I could not but take notice how unlikelie this was to succeed as proposed by such a Chaplayn as had of late made prayers so scandalously in their Chapel in a kind of race against another, reading them at ye same time (as I think) by their appointment, leaping over ye Absolutiō to overtake ye other who had gott ye start of Him ".[2]

This memorandum probably represents the Archbishop's first thoughts, but a closer investigation seems to have inclined him to take a different view. Certain it is that when he came to give judgment in 1698, he decreed that Proast should receive £100; that his rights should remain unquestioned; and that the stigma of the royal mandate (which had given rise to Proast's oft-repeated gibe that Finch "was no Warden") should be removed.[3] The latter was achieved by the following expedient. The office of warden was declared vacant, and the Fellows met to elect, but by arrangement did not do so, whereupon the appointment devolved upon Tenison as Visitor who accordingly nominated Finch.[4]

In 1702, Finch's excesses brought him to a premature grave, and he was succeeded by Bernard Gardiner (1668–1726), a sincere and devoted Tory, who as sub-warden during his predecessor's régime, had done his best to preserve some kind of order in the college. Yet in character (so Professor Burrows writes) Gardiner "was certainly deficient in 'suaviter in modo'. He appears to

[1] Lambeth MSS. 931, f. 48.
[2] Ibid.
[3] Burrows, Worthies of All Souls', p. 310.
[4] Ibid. Proast, we may note, became Archdeacon of Berkshire and lived to co-operate with Tenison in the founding of the Society for Propagating the Gospel.

have been as conscientious as he was able, persevering and indomitable; but stern and uncompromising to a degree which kept his public life in a continued state of effervescence".[1]

Gardiner decided on a policy of bold reform and immediately declared it "his duty to retrieve what he judged amiss by the most probable and gentle methods". There was much to be done. Sancroft and Jeames between them had successfully restrained the abuse of corrupt elections, but "no sooner had this reform been effected than Bernard Gardiner found another abuse, that of Non-Residence, gradually carrying off these superior men one after another, and depriving Oxford and All Souls' of their services". There could be no doubt that the Founder had contemplated "forty resident Fellows, all pursuing their studies in the College with an occasional exception perhaps for the services of the Crown, under the idea of the Fellowships being resigned if that service became perpetual". Of the forty Fellows, twenty-four were "artists" and the rest "jurists", of whom the latter (mostly London Common Lawyers) had established their right to be freed from the obligation to take Orders—though Gardiner disputed this. Dispensations, however, became the rule. "Physicians, Members of Parliament, Public Servants such as Commissioners of various kinds, were numerous both among the Artists and Jurists. All wanted to retain their Fellowships while they performed their respective functions as non-residents; each Dispensation diminished the number of clergymen, and strengthened the growing dislike to take Holy Orders".[2]

Gardiner felt that he could not conscientiously be a partner to this abuse, particularly as he had sworn to observe the statutes, which definitely laid down that "the twenty-four Artists were to take Holy Orders in two years; and as many of the sixteen Jurists as did not publicly give proof of their embracing the study of Civil law and take degrees in that Faculty were under the same obligation". Nor was he prepared to accept the gloss which interpreted "clericales" as "synonimous with the whole learned part of the nation".[3]

Thus, without consulting the Visitor, he decided to do battle with the Fellows, using as his great weapon of offence the veto which Archbishop Whitgift had secured for Warden Hoveden.

One of the commonest methods employed to evade the obligation to take Orders was for a Fellow to obtain a "physic place".

---

[1] Burrows, *Worthies of All Souls'*, p. 351.   [2] *Ibid.* p. 353.   [3] *Ibid.*

Successive Visitors had encouraged the study of medicine, but a "physic place" had now come to mean, in many cases, a Member of Parliament or a commissioner. Gardiner went so far as to admit that there could be four "physic places" but no more.

Tenison was now forced to turn his attention to this question, as he was solicited by Lord Brook for a "physic place" on behalf of his relative, a Grevile. The Archbishop very wisely referred the matter to the Warden, and Gardiner in reply, on 5 July 1709, agreed that the Founder had mentioned graduates of physics in his statutes, but added : "I looked upon the taking of Holy Orders to be ye chief Design of ye Founder for his artists, and therefore I exhorted them to bend the statutes that way".[1] Tenison was not unwilling to co-operate with the Warden in securing this measure of reform, and he replied on 23 July with the following letter :

> "Upon the whole it is my opinion that it was never intended by the Founder that you should have so many physicians as you have already. The provision he made was for the encouragement of students of Divinity and Law. Therefore although I have a great respect for Lord Brook and his family, I cannot, because I think I cannot justly, advise the shewing favour to Mr. Grevile by approving his having a Physic Fellowship".[2]

But this measure of support accorded to Gardiner in respect of "physic places" did not prevent the Archbishop from entirely disapproving the Warden's rigid practice of putting his veto upon all dispensations. Tenison, following the settled policy of Tillotson, was particularly anxious to leave a loophole for service to the Crown, and he therefore wished the College to use a wide discretion in this general matter of residence.

It was in virtue of such laxity that Christopher Codrington (1668–1710) was able to retain his Fellowship of All Souls' while campaigning on the Continent or later on his return to the Barbados, and that others became chaplains in the Navy; but a line had to be drawn somewhere and Gardiner determined to clarify the position by simply enforcing the statutes, which (he later reminded the Archbishop) he had sworn to observe. Tenison, on the other hand, was content with only a moderate reform, and wished to steer a middle course.

---

[1] Gardiner to Tenison, 15 July. Lambeth MSS. 931, f. 50.
[2] Tenison to Gardiner, 23 July 1709. Archives of All Souls' College, quoted Burrows, *Worthies of All Souls'*, p. 355.

This question of domestic politics in the College was further complicated by the political animosities of the time, for Gardiner was an extreme Tory, and it was this fact which induced Tenison on one occasion to appear in what Professor Burrows has called "an unfavourable light". The circumstances were as follows.

William Blencowe—a son of Judge Blencowe, and grandson of John Wallis, the mathematician—obtained a Fellowship of All Souls' in 1702 through the intervention of the Archbishop.[1] This young man came of a devoted Whig family and was employed by the Crown in deciphering documents at an annual salary of £200. Gardiner regarded this obtaining a Fellowship for one permanently and independently provided for as a grave abuse, and he determined to oppose it. Blencowe was an "artist", and as such under obligation either to take Orders within two years or resign his Fellowship (unless, of course, he could obtain a dispensation), but when he refused to do either, the Warden interposed his veto upon the dispensation which the Fellows were willing to grant him. No one could deny that Gardiner was right according to the strict letter of the statutes, but Blencowe, with the approval of the Archbishop, proceeded to use his political influence to interest the Crown in the matter. As a result, he obtained a letter from the Queen, dated 19 November 1709, and addressed not to the College but to the Visitor. It said:

"Her Majesty's pleasure is that his Grace should restrain the Warden of All Souls', by such means as he should find effectual and proper, from any further vexation of Mr. Blencowe; so that during his attendance in her Service he might quietly enjoy his Fellowship as fully as if he were in Orders and resident in the College".[2]

The historian of All Souls' College writes:

"The Visitor was certainly bound to deal with this communication in an official manner. It was his duty to communicate with the Warden, to require a statement of his reasons in the case, to examine the power of the Veto which he claimed, and to decide as Visitor in the end upon the whole matter. From what we have seen of their transactions with the College we may certainly infer that Abbot, Sheldon or Sancroft would have done so. But Tenison takes no further step than simply to write off to the Warden with all dispatch, declaring

[1] Wallis to Tenison, 22 December 1702. Lambeth MSS. 930, f. 52.
[2] Sunderland to Tenison, 19 November 1709. Quoted Burrows, *Worthies of All Souls'*, p. 357.

Sir Thomas Browne with his wife Dorothy, daughter of Sir Gregory Mileham (and sister of Anne, wife of Archdeacon Philip Tenison, uncle of the Archbishop).

From a panel attributed to Anna Carlisle.

Facing page 278

Richard Love, D.D., Master of Corpus Christi College, Cambridge.

From the original painted for Thomas Tenison and bequeathed by him to the College.

Reproduced by permission of the Master and Fellows of Corpus Christi College, Cambridge.

Facing page 279

and pronouncing Blencowe's service under the Crown a good and lawful an impediment to his taking Holy Orders, and commanding the College to permit him to enjoy his Fellowship fully and freely. His own letter and Lord Sunderland's are to be entered on the College Books".[1]

It certainly appears to have been a hasty act dictated by party allegiance, for Sunderland, Tenison, and Blencowe were all Whigs, and the latter told Gardiner "to his face" that the Fellows "had made a common purse against him".[2]

The Tories, on their part, maintained that Tenison not only acted "without any authority from the statutes, but contrary to those ends for which the power was lodged".[3]

Nor was the above the only case of this kind which came before the Archbishop during this year. As with Blencowe, so with another Fellow, Richard Stephens ("for many years a student of medecine"), Gardiner requested that he should "take deacon's orders within six months from July 13, when the two years were computed to be terminated". Stephens determined to seek redress at Lambeth, and Mark Sayer, a Proctor in the Court of Arches, sent in a certificate on his behalf (11 July 1709), testifying that though by the

> "statutes of the college and especialy that 'de tempore assumendi sacros ordines' all members of the college are to proceed to take orders within two years of their regentship . . . [yet] by other statutes and especially those 'de habitu sociorum' and 'de modo et tempore devoti dicendi horas canonicas', it is permitted that there may be bachelors and doctors of medecine".[4]

As a result of this intervention, Gardiner was summoned to appear at Lambeth on 19 November 1709, and on 10 January 1710 the Archbishop pronounced judgment in favour of Stephens, and ordered that his decision should "be entered in the College Books". In the letter to the Warden communicating his ruling, the Archbishop took the opportunity of observing that there were various other "important matters relating to the College which needed inspection", but these he would "reserve" for his visitation.[5]

[1] Burrows, *Worthies of All Souls'*, p. 357.
[2] Gardiner to Wake. Quoted Burrows, *Worthies of All Souls'*, p. 357.
[3] H.M.C. Portland MSS. II, 529.
[4] H.M.C. MSS. of F. W. Leyburne Popham, 1899, p. 252.
[5] *Ibid.*

The case of Blencowe, however, was not yet finally disposed of, for Gardiner was able to reopen the matter by reason of a change in the political state of the nation. On 5 November 1709, Sacheverell's famous sermon at St. Paul's changed the balance of parties in dramatic manner, and Sunderland's power, seemingly so securely based on the victories of Marlborough, did not long survive the unpopularity of the trial. Hence, in June of the following year, the seals of office were transferred to the Earl of Dartmouth. Gardiner saw his opportunity, particularly since he suspected that the Queen had hitherto acted under pressure from her Whig ministers. The whole temper of ecclesiastical politics was changed, and even moderates, such as Shrewsbury, Archbishop Sharp, and Compton, Bishop of London, rallied to Sacheverell's cause. The Warden of All Souls', with characteristic boldness, sent a petition direct to the Crown, in which, after stating the terms of the statutes in respect of ordination, he prayed that he "may execute them without incurring Her Majesty's displeasure", and further "trusts that she will not allow the pretensions of Mr. Blencowe to be the occasion of suspending the authority of Statutes to the observance of which both he and Mr. Blencowe are equally bound by oath".[1]

The Queen, surrounded by her Tory advisers, "graciously" received the petition and passed it on to the law officers of the Crown for their opinion; but they, perhaps unwilling to embroil themselves in such a controversial matter, advised her to leave the whole affair with the Visitor. There were times, however, when Anne delighted to assert her independence, and in the following March she decided on her own initiative to take a more definite step. True, she followed the advice of the law officers to the letter, but in recommending Gardiner's petition to the Visitor she requested that the "error" into which she had been led by Sunderland should not prejudice the case, and she instructed Dartmouth, Secretary of State, to tell Tenison "that she did not approve Mr. Blencowe's insisting on his being in her service to excuse him from conforming to the Statutes of his College, nor that the letter of Lord Sunderland should be used for that purpose".[2] What subsequently happened is somewhat obscure, but we learn from Gardiner in a letter written some years later to Wake (1719) that "as to any favour procured by Mr. Blencowe from the Queen relating to a Dispensation from Holy Orders it was

---

[1] Burrows, *Worthies of All Souls'*, p. 359.   [2] *Ibid.*

not granted by advice of Her Majesty's Privy Council, but it was formally revoked by Her in open Council, after a public hearing before her Attorney and Solicitor General".[1]

Dartmouth's letter, however, was not given the same prominence as was Sunderland's former epistle. Tenison had ordered that the latter should be transcribed in the college books: he contented himself in the case of the former by sending it formally to Gardiner without comment. The Warden, with understandable satisfaction, did his best to make up for this deficiency by copying it into the "chained Statute Book" with his own hand—an act which drew a protest from Willis and Littleton, two of the Fellows, who wrote underneath that the Warden "had entered the letter without any Orders from the Visitor, and against the opinion of the Fellows and Officers".[2]

Tenison had for some time intended a visitation of the College, and it is to this that we now turn. There had hitherto been only two visitations in the history of the College, one by Cranmer and the other by Whitgift, and now at the beginning of the eighteenth century there were many matters of domestic politics in the College which demanded the Archbishop's attention. Elections to Fellowships regularly resulted in internal feuds (due to political animosities), and these were followed by the Warden interposing his veto, which led to appointment from Lambeth. In 1708, for example, Gardiner unsuccessfully tried to secure a Fellowship for one Nourse (a kinsman of the Founder, and hence, according to the statutes, entitled to special preference). When the matter came to Lambeth upon a devolution, Tenison informed him (if we can believe Hearne) that "he was an impudent young Man for pretending to such a claim".[3]

In 1710 there were more disputes, so that the College was in its usual state of internal dissension when on 3 September a citation was "fixt up wth inside of the College Gate of All Souls' by the Archbp of Canterbury's order for a visitation of the College on the 12th of October next". The contemporary political situation—the Tories were in power—added to the excitement and Hearne (a very prejudiced authority, however) relates that the citation

"was immediately torn down by someone or more of the Warden's agents, and not so much as a Letter left remaining:

[1] Burrows, *Worthies of All Souls'*, p. 360.
[2] *Ibid* p. 361.
[3] *Remarks and Collections of Thomas Hearne*, iii. 67.

so that in the afternoon a little after six o'Clock when the Observer of these Matters went to look upon it he could find no other traces of it than small bits of Paper sticking with some of the Paste with wch 'twas fix'd".[1]

This outburst of resentment, however, could not prevent the visitation from taking place, and it came at a time when the College was divided into two factions under the Warden and the Dean of Arts (Chicheley). On Wednesday, 12 October, "at 4.15 p.m.", Dr. Bettesworth, Dean of the Arches and Vicar-General to the Archbishop of Canterbury, arrived at the College. The Warden did his best to play the host by entertaining him at a "noble supper" in his own lodgings, and on the following morning Dr. Bettesworth proceeded to hold the visitation: but

"nothing else was done that day than calling over the names, and treating the Dean in the Hall at a most magnificent and splendid Dinner. . . . Next day, being Friday at 3 o'clock in the Afternoon, the Dean receiv'd the several complaints each Man had to make in writing and . . . carried them to Lambeth, where this grand affair is to be determin'd when the Archbishop shall think fit to do it".

Meanwhile the dispute between the Tory Warden and the Whig Dean of Arts, Chicheley, was being maintained with increasing fury, and things came to a head in the election to Fellowships. According to the complaint of the Warden, the Fellows, under the instigation of Chicheley, elected to a Fellowship which he had not declared vacant, thus contravening Archbishop Whitgift's Injunctions. Not content with this, the Dean of Arts had declared certain candidates elected to Fellowships without the concurrence of the Warden, whereas such a case of disagreement should have been referred to the Archbishop on a devolution. The Warden felt he must place the whole position before Tenison, and he complained bitterly in a letter sent to Lambeth on 8 November.

"Mr. Chicheley thought fitt", he wrote, "to Pronounce Persons elected who had not my Vote; which indeed is nothing less than betraying his Trust in declaring ye Votes in Scrutiny which he ought not to doe, and this he persisted in after my public monition in the Hall against it. This matter, too, concerning my necessary Vote I am told is layd before your Grace and is now waiting your judgment. If occasion be offered

[1] *Remarks and Collections of Thomas Hearne*, iii. 67.

I shall desire to defend so inherent a Part of ye Warden's Office which may doe good, but can doe no harm to the Societye but I perswade myself that this Insolence against your Grace's right to a Devolution upon a disagreement of ye majoritye of ye Fellows from ye Warden's Vote (which now is, as anciently it has been ye Case) will meet with no Countenance from your Grace: but you will please to assert the statutable Right both of yourself and me by filling the vacancies by Devolution, as they are now before your Grace".

Tenison had been isolated too long from the Court to be intimidated by the fact that the Tories were in power, and his judgment, when it came, was "heavy" indeed, none other than the abolition of the Warden's veto on dispensations.[1] It is certain that this undoubted right of the Warden's had never seriously been questioned till now, and the Fellows as late as 1699, though disputing Warden Finch's power to exercise the office of scrutator at elections, had yet taken care to add that "no prejudice was hereby designed to the Warden, whose negative is still left entire".[2] In the past the veto on election to Fellowships had been held to cover the veto upon dispensations, but now all was abolished.

It is true that Tenison deprecated the non-residence of the lawyers, and confirmed the limitation of the master of physic places to four, all of whom were to be "bona fide" students, and to forfeit their Fellowships if after having obtained a dispensation from taking Holy Orders, they practised at the Bar; but the judgment of the Archbishop established the principle of non-residence, and all that Gardiner could now do was to register a dissent, which the College was able to override. "Nor", writes Professor Burrows,

"when the Public Service was thus so widely thrown open to non-resident Fellows, could the non-residence of the Common Lawyers, which was forbidden by implication in the Injunctions of the Visitor, be long retained. The Veto on Dispensations was gone. From that day forward the Non-residence of the Fellows of All Souls' has been the leading characteristic of the College".

As to the elections, Hearne writes that "Old Tenison of Canterbury has made Mr. Adderly of All Souls' Sub Warden of that College . . . and Mr. Willis[3] and Mr. Littleton Deans,

---

[1] Burrows, *Worthies of All Souls'*, p. 362.
[2] *Ibid.*
[3] Richard Willis, later Bishop of Gloucester, Salisbury, and Winchester (1664–1734).

purely by way of opposition to ye Warden, who has been complimented (to his no small Grief) upon the occasion ".[1]

The story of these events shows clearly how Tenison applied
his Whig principles to all departments of his archiepiscopal
responsibilities. Thus he left his mark on the future development
of the College, but how far it was entirely a matter of party
allegiance which prevented his co-operating with Gardiner may
well be a matter of doubt. It is possible that he regarded some
enlargement of the Founder's intentions as inevitable and
necessary if the College was to play its full part in a changing world;
and if this is so, he has been proved right.

[1] *Remarks and Collections of Thomas Hearne*, iii. 67.

PART III

CHAPTER 13

A REFORMATION IN MANNERS

THERE can be no doubt that the restoration of Charles II was followed by a serious decline in the moral condition of the nation. If Cromwell may be regarded as the presiding genius of the Puritan purge, so royal Charles may take his place as the practical exponent of a moral *laissez-faire*. As to the extent of the reaction, most authorities, contemporary and otherwise, agree. Daniel Defoe, in the *Poor Man's Plea* (1698), protested that "till the nobility, gentry, justices of the peace and clergy will be pleased either to reform their own manners or find out some method and power impartially to punish themselves when guilty, we humbly crave leave to object against setting any poor man in the stocks, or sending him to the house of correction for immoralities, as the most unjust and unequal way of proceeding in the world".[1] A contemporary wrote to Tenison the following letter expressing similar sentiments:

> "The great and amazing Progress that Vice and Irreligion have of late years made in the Nation has filled the Minds of sober and considerable Men with a just Apprehension of the Displeasure of Almighty God: so it has been the Occasion of making many Excellent Laws to prevent (if possible) the spreading of so growing a contagion. But notwithstanding all endeavours, it must be confessed that Vice and Irreligion have still their strongholds. They have been beaten from their Outworks, but no force has been sufficient yet to make a Conquest".[2]

Charles had been openly indifferent, and James was more interested in changing the country's religious allegiance than in improving its morals. The better elements in the nation, however, looked to William and Mary to do something to deal with the situation, and the King, "having brought the war to a glorious conclusion", proclaimed a "new war" against "profaneness" in his speech to Parliament in 1699: "I esteem it", he said, "one of the greatest advantages of the peace, that I shall now have leisure to rectify such corruption or abuses as may have crept

[1] J. Wilson, *Daniel Defoe*, i. 288.   [2] Lambeth MSS. 953, f. 131.

into any part of the administration during the war, and effectually to discourage profaneness and immorality". He imputed the growing misery of the poor "to the Depravation of Manners occasion'd by their loose and idle life", and desired Parliament "to consider whether the growth of this evil was from Defects in the Laws already made or the Execution of them, promising himself to countenance virtue and discourage vice". On 28 November the House resolved that an humble address be made to his Majesty "that he would be pleased to issue out his Proclamation for the suppressing of all Vice and Immorality, and for putting the Laws in Execution relating thereto".

The royal proclamation was duly issued and Tenison, who was "a steady Promoter of Peace and Piety", was especially concerned that the clergy should play their part in stemming this tide of moral laxity, and on 4 April 1699 sent a letter on this subject to his brethren the bishops. In this epistle he began by calling attention to the increase of "vice and profaneness", and to the endeavours which were being made to subvert the principles of "our holy Religion". Hence he exhorted the bishops to persuade their clergy to assist in a general reformation along the following lines:

(1) Let the clergy and their families be above reproach. (2) Let them be prudent in addition to well meaning. (3) Let them acquaint themselves with the rational grounds for the defence of the Christian religion and become familiar with the answers to "the points in debate". (4) Let them meet together and seek the co-operation of the churchwardens and pious laity in the reformation of manners.[1] (5) Let the clergy make contact with the prominent people in their parishes. (6) Let the clergy inform the ordinary of any person who was obstinate in his vices and with whom example and exhortation were found to be ineffectual, in order that ecclesiastical censure might be passed on him: if this also were found to be of no avail, then let the clergy be foremost in placing such a case before the civil magistrate. (7) Let every pious layman be encouraged to report all swearers, blasphemers, drunkards and abusers of the Lord's day, to the magistrates. (8) Let the clergy report an evil liver

---

[1] Sharp, Archbishop of York, complained in a letter to William Nicolson (1655–1727, later Bishop of Carlisle) that many of the clergy had taken encouragement from this fourth injunction to form "Societies for the Reformation of Manners", "though it is certain in that passage", he wrote, "he did not intend the setting up of such formal assemblies under rules and articles as are now formed in many places". Quoted J. Nichols, *Letters on Various Subjects*, etc., 1809, p. 155.

amongst their own number to the bishop. (9) Let the clergy be diligent in catechizing the young and keeping in touch with them as they grow older.[1]

The results of such a letter no one, of course, can determine. John Wallis, Savilian Professor of Geometry at Oxford, welcomed its appearance, and wrote to the Archbishop that "a grave, prudent and exemplary deportment of the clergy, and a serious endeavour jointly and severally to promote religion, is certainly the most effectual course to conciliate a just reverence and esteem to their persons and functions".[2]

The Bishop of Bath and Wells (Kidder) took up the matter with great enthusiasm, but thought that the growth of profaneness could not be checked "till care be taken for the utter suppressing of all Alehouses, alias Hell Houses, in the nation, for whilst these stinking puddles remain, toads and frogs will still be croaking, swearing and cursing, drinking and whoring; robbery and stealing will never be at an end". He would like to see every minister take out affidavits against such as were profane, and return them at the Quarter Sessions.[3]

The Archbishop was fortunate in securing the co-operation of the Government in this "purity purge", and the judges on circuit were instructed by the "Lords Justices in Council" (13 July 1699) to be "careful to punish vice and prophaneness and to encourage in their charges all other magistrates to be zealous in doing the same". Their attention was also called to the above letter which the Archbishop had written to the bishops, and they were instructed "to take notice of it in their charge".[4]

Tenison supported wholeheartedly the Societies for the Reformation of Manners which sprang up in England after 1697 with the object of encouraging people to inform on those who broke the law. It is interesting to notice that Sharp, Archbishop of York, found himself unable to encourage the establishment of these societies because of the dangers which he thought attached to such a method of procedure, although he admitted that there was only too much need for such a reformation in manners.[5]

[1] It is little references like this (9) which recall Tenison's experiences as a parochial clergyman. *Memoirs of the Life and Times*, etc., pp. 66–70.
[2] Wallis to Tenison, 20 May 1699. Lambeth MSS. 930, f. 51.
[3] Lambeth MSS. 942, f. 152.
[4] S.P.D. Will. III, 13 July 1699.
[5] Sharp, *Life of John Sharp*, p. 170. See note, p. 286.

Archbishop Tenison always recognized the power of the printed word and he was therefore anxious to exert a greater control over the press, particularly in view of the increase of literature which took a definitely anti-Christian point of view. We need to remember that at this time freedom of expression was condemned by all parties, despite Milton's noble plea, and even as late as 1696 one Thomas Aikenhead was hanged in Scotland for "railing against God, and cursing Christ".[1] Tenison wished, particularly, to make the law more effective in suppressing "blasphemous pamphlets", and in 1698 he introduced a bill into the House of Lords against atheism, blasphemy, and the printers of scandalous books and pamphlets.[2] In 1702 he revised a similar Bill and submitted it to Robert Harley (then Speaker of the House of Commons) for his criticism. Harley, who, beginning life as a Whig and Dissenter, had by this time suffered a sea-change into a Tory High Churchman, replied in an interesting letter on 8 January 1702.

"I received your Grace's commands", he wrote, "with great respect and duty, and will always be ready to contribute the utmost I can to ye Public Service and particularly to allaying those heats and animositys wch are greatly increased by the many scandalous lying pamphlets wch are dayly propagated by desygning knaves to ye scandal not only of the nation but of common Christianity; Tho' I have no doubt but there are sufficient authoritys given by the Laws in being for suppressing such enormitys, whenever it shall be thought fit to put those laws in execution, yet a new law may perhaps meet some defects. The draught of a Bill wch I herewith return to yr Grace contains very good methods to have a Printer or Author answerable for everything wch is published, but there must be some severer course taken afterwards with the libellous, wch present laws are sufficient for".

Harley concluded by suggesting that Tenison should have it begun in the House of Lords, and he promised that he himself "would support it as best he could".[3]

Apparently, however, the Bill got no further than this tentative stage, for there is no record of its coming before the House of Lords, nor did such a Bill become law at this time.

Tenison, in company with most of the clergy of his day,

---

[1] Howell, *State Trials*, xiv. 918.
[2] Luttrell, *A Brief Historical Relation*, etc., iv. 347.
[3] Lambeth MSS. 933, f. 36.

deplored the general tone of the stage, though he could do little of a practical nature about it. Amongst his papers there are many suggestions from would-be reformers. One, which we may be thankful went no further, empowered the Government to supervise all plays, to force living authors to revise their works, and to constitute a committee to do this where necessary in the case of deceased authors. One injunction to be strictly enforced forbad any gentleman "to go behind the scenes".[1] In 1710 Tenison received "A Letter from several Members of the Society for Reformation of Manners" in which they complained of the plays of John Vanbrugh, who, they said, had already been indicted at Queen's Bench "for several obscene and prophane expressions in the Relapse, the Provok'd Wife, and the False Friend". In particular, they protested against the following rather cynical rejoinder:

"You can't take the Oaths' you're a Jacobite".
"Thou mightest as well say, I can't take Orders
    because I'm an Atheist".[2]

As a result of this general distrust of the stage, we find Tenison, assisted by William Sherlock, Dean of St. Paul's, persuading one Billinghurst to close a play house, which, he said, was "prest on him against his inclinations".[3]

Queen Anne's interest in matters religious is generally allowed to have been as sincere as it was sustained, and on 20 August 1711, she sent a letter to the Archbishop (for communication to the other bishops), in which she deplored the "looseness and corruption of manners", "the neglect of all wholesome discipline", and the "uncommon Industry that hath been used by men averse to all Religion and Goodness". To counteract this, she urged the bishops to assist in putting a stop to the further growth of infidelity and profaneness by enforcing "all such Ecclesiastical Laws and Canons as have been hitherto provided for the well governing the Church and the furtherence of godly living". Especially did she exhort the bishops

"to watch diligently over their Flocks, to be exemplary in their lives, to frame their public discourses to the People upon such subjects as tend most to edification, and particularly to be careful and constant in catechizing those of the younger

---

[1] Lambeth MSS. 933, f. 57.
[2] "A Letter from Several Members of the Society for Reformation of Manners", London, 1710. John Vanbrugh, we may note, was knighted in 1714.
[3] Sherlock to Tenison, undated; Lambeth MSS. 953, f. 114.

sort, and in preparing them as soon as they come to a fit age for confirmation and the worthy receiving of the Holy Communion . . . And if", she went on, "any of the Clergy under your Care shall be found negligent and remiss in discharging these or any other duties of their sacred calling, or shall by disorderly conversation or by any behaviour unbecoming their holy function, lessen the good effects of their ministry, We command that by admonition, censure or otherwise, as the case shall deserve, you endeavour to reform all such neglects and abuses and by that means repress the Scandal and mischief which the Church of God might suffer thereby".

Finally she urged the bishops to encourage the founding of charity schools, and to visit their dioceses in person.[1]

The position of the "Ecclesia Anglicana" as the established Church meant that the clergy were not only ecclesiastical persons but also important civil officials. It was Tenison's policy to insist on the clergy discharging all their responsibilities, and by so doing to raise the general level of national "morale". Particularly was this the case in the question of clandestine marriages to which we now turn.

This problem, which constituted a serious social menace at this time, grew out of the existing historical situation. It was not until the Council of Trent (1545), it needs to be remembered, "that the intervention of a priest or other ecclesiastical functionary was deemed in Europe indispensable to a marriage", and since the authority of the Council was not recognized in England, the Common Law alone continued to regulate the law of marriage until the Marriage Act of 1753 (26 Geo. ii. c. 33). Thus "whilst, in virtue of domestic institutions, a form was enjoined for the more solemn celebration of matrimony, and persons departing from these regulations were liable to ecclesiastical censure, still other and more private modes of contracting marriage were tolerated and acknowledged by law".[2] Before the time of Innocent III, there was no solemnization of matrimony in church, but the husband simply led the bride to his house.[3] Banns, however, were first required in the time of Hubert Walter (1200), but clandestine marriages continued for centuries to defy all ecclesiastical censure. Certain privileges, admittedly, were granted to those who sought

---

[1] Quoted B. C. Brown, *The Letters of Queen Anne*, 1935, p. 338.
[2] Burn, *History of Fleet Marriages*, p. 1.
[3] Hence "uxorem ducere et capere in virum". *Ibid.*, p. 2.

the sanction of the Church, but any marriage according to Common Law remained perfectly legal, and was regarded as indissoluble. Oliver Cromwell, with his accustomed efficiency, instituted in 1653 an obligatory civil ceremony before the justices of the peace, after due publication of banns, and required that a proper entry should be made in the parish register; but this Act, always the butt of royalist wit, was automatically abrogated at the Restoration. In fact, so far did the zeal of some royalists go that they even wished to declare null and void all marriages contracted under the Act of 1653; but an intention "so monstrous could not prevail; and a statute legalising these civil marriages was passed in the first year of Charles II."[1]

After the Restoration, with the return of the "merry Monarch", the number of "informal" marriages increased enormously in London, and it is estimated that "within a few years previously to 1696, many thousands of clandestine marriages were performed; many of them in certain churches and chapels exempted from the visitation of the Ordinary, the ministers of which Churches did generally marry without licence or banns . . . by which practices those laws which had been made to prevent clandestine marriages were rendered ineffectual".[2]

People married in such a way obtained the best of both worlds. Important for them, they escaped the expense and publicity of banns, and yet obtained a quasi legal sanction from Common Law which allowed secular marriage. So long as two different systems of marriage were both "valid", there was bound to be difficulty. It was the obvious policy of Churchmen to insist upon ecclesiastical marriage, and to prohibit any ceremony in an ecclesiastical building or by an ecclesiastical person which did not fulfil the requirements of the canons. Thus, on 17 February 1686, Adam Elliott, Rector of St. James', Dukes Place, was suspended for three years "ab officio et beneficio", for having married or suffered persons to be married in his church without banns or licence, but his suspension was relaxed in May 1687, when he resumed his profitable practice and married at the rate of sixteen couples a day.[3]

---

[1] Howard, *A History of Matrimonial Institutions*, 1904, i. 408, 431.
[2] Burn, *History of Fleet Marriages*, 1834, p. 3.
[3] 5 & 6 Will. In this church between the years 1664 and 1692, some 4,000 marriages were entered in the books; and the number continued to be large, though decreasing, till the Marriage Act of 1753 made such marriages illegal. See Burn, *History of Fleet Marriages*, p. 4.

It seems that the temporary prohibition of weddings at Dukes
Place led to the practice being "taken up by certain real and
pretended clergymen in and about the prisons (principally the
Fleet) not, however, on account of any real privilege or exemption
attaching to these prisons . . . but because these Fleet parsons
were generally prisoners enjoying the Rules of the Fleet, and had
neither liberty, money nor credit to lose by any proceedings the
Bishop might institute against them".[1]

The conditions under which the Fleet marriages were performed have become notorious, as have the characters of those
disreputable ministers of religion who performed them. Such
conditions flourished because before the reign of William III
there existed only ecclesiastical censures to restrain secret
marriages, but the realization of the inadequacy of such penalties,
and a need for revenue, now led to the passing of three Acts, the
first of which in 1694 "imposed on all marriages a direct tax,
graduated according to the ranks of the parties", and empowered
the clergy to keep registers to which the collectors of the taxes
were to have access.[2] This Act, however, proved to be of little
value, because there were places (such as St. James', Dukes
Place) which claimed to be exempt from episcopal control, and
their business was now made even more lucrative by the removal of
competition. Amongst Tenison's papers at Lambeth there is
one which deals particularly with this situation, and demands
that "since ye Clergy of ye Priveleged Places . . . marry dayly
without licence or banns, to ye diminution of Revenue to his
Majesty under ye Paper and Licence Act", the King should
grant a commission "to some loyal subjects during his pleasure,
in order yt these disorders may be regulated", these commissioners
to have "power to require assistance of any bishop in whose
Diocese cognizance of any misdeameanor shall be taken".[3]

Many complained, moreover, that the great price of licences
charged at Doctors' Commons encouraged numerous clergy to
defy the canons.

Hence a further Act was passed (6 & 7 Will. III, c. 6, s. 53)
which included all places within its terms of reference, and required
that all marriages should be solemnized only after publication of

[1] Burn, *History of Fleet Marriages*, p. 4.
[2] 5 & 6 Will. III, c. 21. Under this Act the tax on a duke's wedding (or Archbishop
of Canterbury's!) was £50 2s. 6d.: on a baronet £15 2s. 6d.: a gentleman, £1 2s. 6d.
See Jeaffreson, *Brides and Bridals*, 1872, p. 84.
[3] Lambeth MSS. 929, f. 116.

banns or episcopal licence, the penalty for any clergyman offending against the Act being fixed at £100 for the first offence with three years' suspension from office. Even here, however, there was still a loophole, for many of the people who performed these illegal marriages were not included under "parsons, vicars and curates", and they thus continued to thrive after the passing of this Act, many clergymen allowing them to use their churches "on a consideration".

It was therefore felt that a further Act was necessary and by 7 & 8 Will. c. 35, the fine of £100 was extended to apply to these "unattached" or "doubtful" clergy, and a fine of £10 was imposed on all those who resorted to marriage without banns or licence.

Tenison was in part responsible for the drafting of two of these Acts, and they were submitted to him for final criticism. Thus the original of the last Act which dealt with offending clergymen "who had no benefice, Dignity, living or other ecclesiastical Promotion", contained a clause that they should "suffer other corporal punishment as to the justices before whom they are convicted shall seem meet". The Archbishop felt that to submit even the more worthless of his brethren to such a means of correction would be to lower the dignity of the order as a whole, and he substituted an injunction that they should be "imprisoned by ye space of 1 year without let or privilege".[1]

The general tenor of these acts was to insist on regular marriage by either banns or licence, and to impose penalties both civil and ecclesiastical upon offending clergy and contracting parties. It was apparent, however, that the success of these Acts, either in regularizing marriage or in increasing the king's revenue, depended on how far the clergy in practice would be willing to co-operate in enforcing them. Already three Acts had been found necessary, and the chancellors of the dioceses by issuing blank licences could short-circuit the law altogether and at the same time make detection impossible. The Government realized the necessity of ecclesiastical support, and Tenison was given a "friendly caution" that unless the Church put its own house in order in this respect, it would be done (so the Archbishop wrote at the time) "in another manner than we shall like". This warning encouraged Tenison to send a long letter to the bishops

---

[1] Lambeth MSS. 929, f. 120. He also reduced the cost of a bishop's licence from £8 to £6.

of his province, though from his own enquiries he had satisfied himself that the issuing of blank licences was not practised in the diocese of Canterbury.

He began by reminding them what care the legislature had taken in this matter to prevent clandestine marriages.[1] "The Parliament", he said, "has well done their part and having gone thus far, It is very justly expected that we likewise in whom the great Care and Trust is imposed do performe our Parts towards the preventing of such mischiefs as arise by clandestine marriages and the better securing his Majesty's Revenue on marriage Licences". Particularly he wished to warn them against "a Practice too long tolerated, which . . . is generally used by the Chancellor of the Bishops and other ecclesiastical Judges pretending to have the power to grant marriage licences, which as it is Contrary to the Canons & antient practice so It includes many other ill consequences"—namely, the granting blank licences to surrogates who then administered the oaths to the parties paying for such licences, despite the fact that the presence of the registrar or his deputy to attest such acts was required by Canon 123. This itself, Tenison wrote, "tends to promote clandestine marriages & Stolen Matches & to hinder the detection of them and takes away the benefit of having recourse to the Registers to finde out whether any Licenses of marriages for Stolen Matches were granted and of Ent'ring Caveats to prevent such Matches where Stolen Matches are suspected". He then went on to acquaint them that he had "received many grievous complaints against this Practice both from the Clergy and the Laity", and that "some of the Persons employed in his Majesty's Revenues have likewise complain'd of it . . . as illegal and tending to defraud his Majesty of the dues ariseing from marriage Licenses". He was pleased to be able to say that such a deception was not practised in his own diocese, but, he commented:

"I the more wonder how it comes to pass that it has bin used so long in other dioceses of my Province. I am very sensible of the ill effects of this practice and am very desirous to use such methods whereby it may be quite abolished out of my Province . . . I do therefore earnestly desire yr Lps judicially to command and admonish under pain of Eccl · cal Censures ye Chancellor & Commissarys & such Archdeacons and their officials as pretend to Exercise the power of granting marriage

[1] Tenison to the bishops of his province. Lambeth MSS. 929, f. 74.

Licenses together with the Registrars and Deputys forthwith to revoke and recall all Blank Licenses for the dispensation of the publication of Banns of matrimony which are putt into the hands or Custody of any Surrogates & to revoke & make void all Acts of Surrogacion by which any Ministers of any Churches or any Surrogates are entrusted with blank licenses".

In order that the above might be effectively carried out, he suggested that the bishops should require their ecclesiastical officers to do this within a certain time, and to admonish them never to grant blank licenses for the future "that this abuse of the law may be entirely remedyd & reform'd".

"That I may be satisfi'd of the Effectual Execution of this", he concluded, "I desire yr Lps to Certifye me of what you have done herein . . . & how ye commands & moniĉons have been obeyed, to the Intent that if it be necessary, such further Course may be taken herein as the case may require. I don't doubt but yr Lps will think it highly reasonable that my-Selfe & my Brethren the Bps of my Province should exonerate ourselves in this matter & do what lies in our power to reform this Abuse. So not doubting of yr Lp's due care herein I bid yr Lp heartily farewell".

The abuse, however, was too deep-seated and too profitable to be removed so easily, and it defied episcopal admonition. This may be seen in that we find Tenison writing yet again to the bishops of his province in the reign of Anne, admitting frankly that neither the King's Injunctions of 1695,[1] nor his own circular letter of the same year, had "proved sufficient wholly to prevent the same". Hence he again instructed the bishops to issue the strictest injunctions to all legal officials "that they be very careful to preserve the Rules and Directions prescribed by ye aforesaid Canons under ye several Penalties to be inflicted on them by Law . . . and that they do not suffer any Licence to pass without ye Oath of one of ye Parties to be married, nor any such license to go out of their office without being first filled up".[2]

Tenison realized, of course, that mere exhortation would not of itself restrain such lucrative if nefarious practices, and he declared that in future any notary who allowed a defective licence to pass, would be suspended from his office for six months, and that the

---

[1] See Chap. 7, p. 142.
[2] Lambeth MSS. 929, f. 73.

bishops must send a copy of this letter to all their officials in order that it might be publicly displayed in their registries, as had been done in his own diocese.[1] The Archbishop also enclosed a list of "Injunctions for preventing Clandestine Marriages and all abuses in granting matrimonial licenses", which was likewise to be displayed.[2]

That Tenison did something to prevent the abuse of clandestine marriages seems reasonably certain: but its abolition had to await the Marriage Act of 1753 which did away with the anomalous system which enabled it to thrive.

[1] See "Act Books of the Archbishops of Canterbury", V, 161. Here Tenison records his having acquainted Sir Charles Hedges "Master of our Faculties", of complaints he had received against irregular and uncanonical practices in the granting of marriage licences. The Archbishop therefore ordered: (1) The canons of 1603 were to be enforced. (2) No licence was to be filled up except in the presence of the registrar or his deputy. (3) No licence was to be granted except where one party had taken the oaths. (4) Where either party was under 21, the parent or legal guardian must be present to give consent.

[2] The list was as follows: (1) No persons are to be married within the prohibited degrees, or (2) without banns or licence, or (3) without the consent of parents or guardians (if under 21). (4) No chancellor is to be made a surrogate unless he is qualified by Canon 128. (5) No act for a marriage licence is to be issued by a judge except in the presence of the ordinary, the registrar or his deputy. (6) No chancellor is to seal any blank licence. (7) No licence is to be filled up upon any affidavit unless the registrar is present at the taking of the oaths. (8) A public list of all the fees for licences, etc. is to be displayed on the table in the registry office. (8) Enquiries are to be made at visitations of all persons married without banns or licence, and the ecclesiastical law of excommunication is to be applied to persons present at such clandestine marriages, and the minister responsible is to be punished according to Canon 63.

CHAPTER 14

THEOLOGICAL CONFLICT

IT hardly needs to be said that one of Tenison's most earnest wishes as Archbishop of Canterbury was to keep the theological peace within the Church, a task which was by no means easy, since political and religious passions raged too fiercely to be easily restrained. The Church of England, he thought, had known enough upheaval and controversy; what was required was a period of peace which might best be used to improve the general standard of pastoral efficiency in the body of the clergy. He did not feel, however, that the best way to promote peace was always to be lenient towards heresy, and in his later years he often advocated the intervention of authority to restrain individual and wayward speculations. It is the aim of this chapter to quote a few typical instances of this policy.

Tenison had not long become Archbishop before he was called upon to intervene in a first-class theological squabble. The period of the Commonwealth had provided an environment favourable to theological speculations of various kinds, and among the many heresies then revived was that of Socinianism, which gained many adherents. Interest in these opinions, however, seems to have died with John Biddle in 1662,[1] until they were revived by the publication of a *Brief History of the Unitarians*, by Stephen Nye, in 1687, and *Brief Notes on the Athanasian Creed*, by Thomas Firmin, in 1689.[2] William Sherlock, an indefatigable controversialist and then Master of the Temple, saw in these two works an opportunity of appearing as the grand apologist of orthodoxy, and in 1690 his busy pen produced *A Vindication of the Doctrine of the Trinity*. Unfortunately, a contemporary writes, since "Mysteries of Faith being above Reason are not to be explained by Reason, else they would cease to be Mysteries; it far'd with the Doctor, that whilst he endeavour'd to prove Three Distinct Persons, he

---

[1] The life of John Biddle (1615–62) is a fine example of patient dedication to the truth as he saw it despite continual persecution.

[2] In 1696 Humphrey Prideaux, Archdeacon of Suffolk, wrote to Tenison in connection with the activities of Firmin, who, he said, "in ye beginning of August . . . took all occasions wherever he came to preach up his notions to all manner of people that came his way". Prideaux to Tenison, 2 October 1696. Lambeth MSS. 930, f. 56.

297

was charg'd with proving three distinct Gods; having asserted that there were in the Godhead Three Minds, Three Beings and Three Intelligencies".[1] Thus this book, intended to be a bulwark of orthodoxy, made Thomas Emlyn (1663–1741) an Arian.

William Sherlock had given his many opponents too good an opportunity to be missed. Dr. South, a Prebendary of Westminster, and "a Divine of great Parts but very petulant", attacked his Trinitarian formula with masterful irony in his *Animadversions*, accusing him of Tritheism, a charge which induced Sherlock to reply by denouncing South as a Sabellian. "The Quarrel grew hot", we read, "the two Doctors were learned and witty in their several Answers and Replies, and some of their Seconds began to come in on each side".

While the controversy was at its height, Joseph Bingham (1668–1723), a Fellow of University College, Oxford, "preached a perfectly orthodox sermon on the subject at St. Mary's in which he gave a most accurate sketch of the opinion of the early fathers on the terms 'person' and 'substance'."[2] The friends of Dr. South, however, took hold of the words that "there were Three infinite, distinct Minds and Substances in the Trinity", and complained that they were heretical. On 25 November 1695, the Vice-Chancellor of Oxford, "with some of the Heads of Colleges and Half of ye University", followed up this complaint by declaring that "the sermon contained words which were False, Impious, and Heretical; disagreeing with, and contrary to, the Doctrines of the Catholic Church, and especially to the Doctrines of the Church of England publickly receiv'd".[3]

Tenison was by now somewhat alarmed, and the King also, at what they both regarded as an unnecessary aggravation of religious passions. The judges were consulted, and, to quote the Archbishop's words, they reported that the Vice-Chancellor's act was "a High Usurpation upon his Majesty's Prerogative and a manifest Violation of the Laws of this Realm".[4] Tenison accordingly wrote two strongly worded letters to Adams, the Vice-Chancellor of the university, in the second of which he said that the King regarded their intervention as "unwarrantable and illegal", and had been reinforced in this opinion by the judges.

---

[1] *Memoirs of the Life and Times*, etc., p. 49.
[2] *D.N.B.* v. 48.
[3] Tenison to Adams, 24 December 1695. B.M. Add. MSS. 799, f. 149.
[4] *Ibid.*

"Wherefore", he went on, "his Majesty has commanded me to signify to you in his name that he is not well pleased with what you have done. Nevertheless out of his Tender Love of Learning, and being unwilling to put the least Discouragement upon you or any of the Heads of yr University, he is graciously pleased to pass by this yr Proceedings without further censure; expecting that for the future you will be as regardful of his Authority and the Laws as he will always be ready to preserve yr Rights and Privileges".[1]

Three days later the Vice-Chancellor of Oxford replied, excusing himself in the only way possible.

"It is no small trouble to me", he confessed, "as well as the rest of my Brethren, that we should fall under his Majesty's displeasure. I do assure your Grace that there was nothing more intended by me, then to put a stop to some novel opinions about the greatest Article of our Christian faith. And I dare say, there was not one of us all had the least thought of invading his Majesty's Prerogative in what we did. And therefore I hope Your Grace will do us that justice, as to represent our proceedings in such a favourable manner to his Majesty as we may no longer lie under his misfavour".[2]

The Archbishop felt that the increasing bitterness of the controversy needed an act of authority to restrain it, and he drew up certain "Directions to the Archbishops and Bishops, for the preserving Unity in the Church, and the Purity of the Christian faith concerning the Holy Trinity", which he persuaded the King to issue under the royal signature. The directions were as follows:

"I. That no Preacher whatsoever in his Sermon or Lecture, do presume to deliver any other Doctrine concerning the Blessed Trinity, than what is contained in the Holy Scriptures, and is agreeable to the three Creeds, and the Thirty-nine Articles of Religion.

II. That in the Explication of this Doctrine, they carefully avoid all new Terms, and confine themselves to such ways of Explication, as have been commonly used in the Church.

III. That Care be taken in this Matter, especially to observe the 53d. Canon of this Church, which forbids publick Opposition between Preachers; and that above all Things they abstain from bitter Invectives, and scurrilous Language against all Persons whatsoever.

[1] Tenison to Adams, 24 December 1695. B.M. Add. MSS. 799, f. 149.
[2] Adams to Tenison, 28 December 1695. Ibid. f. 151.

IV. That the foregoing Directions be also observ'd by those who write any Thing concerning the said Doctrine.

And whereas we also understand, that divers who are not of the Clergy, have of late, presumed, not only to talk and dispute against the Christian Faith concerning the Doctrine of the Blessed Trinity; but also to write and publish Book Pamphlets against the same, and industriously spread them through the Kingdom, contrary to our known Laws Establish'd in this Realm: We do therefore strictly charge and command you, together with all other Means suitable to your Holy Profession, to make use of your Authority, according to Law, for the Repressing and Restraining all such Exorbitant Practices: And for your Assistance, we will give Charge to our Judges, and all other Civil Officers, to do their Duty herein, in executing the Laws against all such Persons as shall by these Means give Occasion to Scandal, Discord, and Disturbance in our Church and Kingdom".[1]

The effect of such a document we cannot, of course, determine, but it was probably small. So far as Tenison was concerned with this controversy, it was his general policy to restrain the passions on both sides, though the old controversialist in him was, perhaps, at times not easy to reconcile with the authoritarian Archbishop. When William Payne, for example, a supporter of Sherlock, wrote a sermon on the Trinity and submitted it to the Archbishop, he was not forbidden to preach it, but urged to make it more popular and less technical. It was only when Payne gave people to understand that Tenison had approved the sermon, that the Archbishop intervened and called on him to repudiate this statement.[2] Tenison's concern was for the orthodox position, and he did not necessarily wish to associate himself with either of the sides in debate.

His orthodoxy, however (certainly in his early years), was tinged with a vein of liberalism, particularly when it was related, as in the case of the Dissenters, to the practical needs of the contemporary situation. Such orthodoxy can best be understood, perhaps, in terms of a defence of the Anglican Reformation in the religious, and the Revolution of '88 in the political spheres. Tenison never ceased to remember with disgust the religious anarchy of the Commonwealth, and it was this fear which led him to have little sympathy with speculation for its own sake,

<hr/>

[1] *Memoirs of the Life and Times*, etc., p. 51.
[2] Payne to Tenison, 27 January 1696. Lambeth MSS. 930, f. 19.

and made him anxious to keep controversy within respectable bounds. In reply to an attack on Burnet in the Lower House in May 1701, Tenison and the bishops declared that "private persons may expound the Articles of the Church"—that is, they were free to work within the framework which subscription to the Articles laid upon them. But some thinkers demanded a wider liberty, and there were some bolder spirits within the Church who dared to follow whither the argument led. Here Tenison was at one with the High Churchmen, though he probably did not share their enthusiasm and acted to keep the peace, in condemning them. He himself laid a book entitled *Essays on the Balance of Power* before Convocation,[1] and though the rights of Convocation in this matter of judicial censure were uncertain, neither Toland, author of *Christianity not Mysterious*, nor William Whiston, found much sympathy from this assembly. It is to this latter brilliant but eccentric figure that we now turn.

Whiston is one of the most amusing and interesting men of the time, and his peculiar genius is almost without parallel in any age. The translator of Josephus and the successor of Newton at Cambridge, he yet entered into the most ludicrous absurdities. He discovered that the Tartars were the lost tribe: that the Millennium would come in 1766: that Mary Toft, "the rabbit woman", was foretold in the book of Esdras: and that Prince Eugene by a visit to London had fulfilled some of the prophecies in the Apocrypha. No one, however, ever doubted his disinterestedness, his piety, and his intellectual honesty. Well might he have said: "Quocunque veritas duxit sequi ausus".

On 17 July 1708, Whiston wrote to Tenison and the Archbishop of York from Cambridge explaining that he had lately been "examining with all Care, and impartiality he could the Original Doctrines of Christianity, concerning the ever Blessed Trinity, and the Incarnation of our Lord and Saviour". As a result of these studies he had become convinced "that the opinions of the two and almost first three centuries were very different from those of the fourth and following ones"; that the "Apostolical Constitutions" were the most sacred books of the New Testament; and that the usually accepted doctrines of the Trinity were erroneous. "As to the most proper Method of proposing these Matters to the Publick", he wrote, "I shall have the greatest Deference for your

---

[1] Lathbury, *A History of the Convocation*, p. 349.

Grace's Judgment and Directions", and he hoped that the matter might be "calmly and fairly debated and settled by the Learned, before it came into the Hands of the Ignorant".[1]

The Archbishop of York replied to this letter on 6 August 1708, in a very friendly but candid epistle.

"I must own", he said, "I do by no means approve of the Design which you tell me in your letter you are upon (as thinking that if you do pursue it, you will do a great deal more hurt to the Christian religion among us than you will do good); and being of this opinion, to be sure I can give you no Advice as to the Method in which you should make the World acquainted with it".[2]

Tenison, however, replied on 24 July with a cautious, though by no means prohibitory, letter, the terms of which, it may well be, he later regretted. We quote it in full:

"I received your Letter; but I cannot judge of your Work therein mention'd without perusing it; And I had rather at first see it in Writing than in Print. Perhaps your second Thoughts may be different from your first, after you have drawn them out, and laid them before others, and they have given you their Opinions upon them. Amongst them it seems very proper to me to consult the learned Bp. Bull,[3] who hath shown himself a great Master in this Argument. For Myself, when I see your Scheme, I shall freely and without byas give you my poor Thoughts of it. May the God of Wisdom guide us all in all our Researches and make us wise to Sobriety".[4]

Caution was not one of Whiston's virtues, and neither of the above admonitions prevented his publishing (in Latin it is true) an essay,[5] "De Trinitate", in 1709, as an appendix to his *Sermons and Essays*. As a result of this publication, rumours soon began to circulate that Whiston was an Arian or a Eusebian; but though his friends remonstrated, they failed to check his bold fancies. Once again, as in the case of Joseph Bingham, honest thought

[1] Quoted, *Articles Objected to Mr. Whiston*, p. 30.
[2] *Ibid*. p. 33. The Archbishop of York remarked in the course of his letter: "... if you have any weakness, it is this, that you are too fond of new Notions, and often times lay too great Stress upon them".
[3] George Bull (1643–1710), Bishop of St. David's, had published *Defensio Fidei Nicaenae* in 1685. Cardinal Newman writes in his *Apologia pro vita sua* (Everyman ed. p. 40) that Bishop Bull was one of the formative influences in his life.
[4] *Articles Objected to Mr. Whiston*, p. 31.
[5] Whiston, *Sermons and Essays*, 1709, p. 327. In an edition of this work in the British Museum, Whiston has written against this essay in his own hand: "Omit this Treatise in Future Editions".

was visited with temporal punishment, and Whiston was summoned before the Heads of Houses, banished from the University and deprived of his professorship on 30 October 1710. He removed to London, and undismayed published his *Historical Preface*, which he dedicated to Convocation, and added as a prefix to his *Primitive Christianity Revived*. The ecclesiastical temper of England at this time was orthodox and High Church, and such men as Atterbury and Sacheverell were the presiding genii. Convocation immediately seized hold of this latest work of Whiston's with persecuting zeal, and on 19 March 1711, condemned it in a series of resolutions.[1]

It was in these circumstances that Whiston addressed himself to Archbishop Tenison on 5 April 1711. He did so, he said, because the publication of his *Historical Preface* had called down upon his head the charge of Arianism and had unfortunately disturbed the peace of the Church. He confessed frankly that he tended to express himself with too great confidence and assurance. "As to the manner of my writing", he said, "it is, I confess, too agreeable to the Warmth and Vehemence of my natural Temper, increas'd by an Hearty, and, I am sure, an Honest Zeal for what things so ever at any time appear to me to be True, and of importance in Christianity".

Referring to the charge of Arianism, Whiston admitted that he had not been "sufficiently careful to avoid it", but he denied that it was ever his intention to assert it. He requested, finally, that the Archbishop would recommend the serious investigation of all his works to Convocation or to a committee of learned men. "If once the Matter be brought to that Method of proceeding", he wrote, "I shall exceedingly rejoice; and be ready, whenever I shall be required, to lay all my Papers before their Consideration; and to Correct any Mistakes in them, or retract any Opinions I have advanc'd, that upon Examination shall appear not to be well grounded".[2]

The offending book, with the resolutions of Convocation, were now laid before the Archbishop, and he proceeded to give his opinion upon them in a letter dated 12 April and addressed to the "Right Reverend . . . the Bishops of the Province of Canterbury in Convocation assembled".[3]

---

[1] Lathbury, *A History of the Convocation*, p. 411.
[2] *Articles Objected to Mr. Whiston*, p. 38.
[3] Lambeth MSS. 1029, f. 112a.

He "entirely agreed", he wrote, "that Notice should be taken of the said Book", and in order the better to advise in the matter, he had consulted former precedents. To proceed regularly in their condemnation two points needed to be considered: (1) the censure of the book, and (2) the censure of the person.

As to the first, "two things seem necessary to be done", he commented; (a) to have the book well examined, and "to fix upon the particular Passages, wherein he has asserted his heretical and pernicious Tenets most plainly and expressly", and (b) to "fix the particular places of Scripture and in the Council of Nicea, and the Articles of our own Church, upon which the Charge of Heresie may be most clearly grounded".

As to the second question, the censure of the person, there were three methods of procedure which they must weigh and consider well "in order to judge how far each of them will be safe, and expedient, and how far effectual".

The first method was by way of Convocation, in which court such judicature had been exercised both before and after the Reformation, and which he thought "the most desireable method in the present case", if certain legal difficulties did not make it impossible.

"The second Method of proceeding", he continued "(as I humbly conceive), is for the Archbishop to hold a Court of Audience, and calling to him his Provincial Bishops as Assessors, there to Examine, Proceed and give Sentence, as in his Court of Audience, into which Court he is fully empowered to cite any Person out of the Diocese wherein he dwells, in case that the Bishop or other immediate Judge or Ordinary dare not".

The third method was for the bishop, in whose diocese the accused resided, to cite him into his court; in which case the prosecution could be delegated to the bishop as the "Proper Ordinary", by the Archbishop and Bishops in Convocation, "as hath often been done in Cases of ye like nature".

Concerning these three ways of procedure, Tenison observed that the last two were "most plain and clear as regards legality"; but as the first was the most "solemn and on that account the most proper and desirable", so it should be followed if the queen's judges supported such a method.

The Archbishop handed this letter in person to Charles Trimnell, Bishop of Norwich, to whom he wrote again on 15 April stating that he had found a precedent for the exercise of such jurisdiction by Convocation "as had great Strength in it".[1]

The question of judicature was certainly a difficult one, and Tenison was anxious to tread warily. It was therefore decided that Convocation should first address itself to the Queen condemning Whiston's "several damnable and blasphemous assertions against the doctrine and worship of the ever blessed Trinity", at the same time asking her advice in the vexed matter of jurisdiction. Tenison's meticulous care may be seen in his revision of the form of the petition. In the draft submitted to him for inspection, the Queen was requested "to lay this case before your reverend judges or others whom your majesty in your wisdom shall think fit".[2] Tenison suggested a significant alteration, namely, the changing of "or others whom your Majesty, etc." to "and others", since, he wrote to the Bishop of Norwich: "I believe no Councill will be ready to give their Opinion if the Judges be excluded, or if they should, I am very confident that neither I nor any of my substitutes will be ever induc'd to act judicially upon such opinion if the Judges be left unconsulted".[3]

As a result of this petition to the Queen, Tenison received the following message from St. James's on 8 May 1711:

"We are pleased to find that according to the opinion of Eight of our Twelve Judges,[4] and of our Attorney and Solicitor General, as the Law now stands, a Jurisdiction in matters of heresy and condemnation of Heretics is proper to be exercised in Convocation, and We cannot doubt that the Convocation will now be satisfied they may employ the power which belongs to them in repressing the impious attempts lately made to subvert the foundation of the Christian Faith, which was one of the Chief Ends We proposed to Ourselves in assembling them, which appears from the whole tenor of Our letter of December the 12th . . . We trust that these Our Royal Intentions so often signified will not be without effect".

If the case were to be proceeded with in Convocation, however, certain difficulties still remained which this judgment did not clear up. First of all there was the question whether Convocation, in its judicial capacity, consisted of the bishops only, or the

[1] Tenison to Trimnell, 15 April 1711. Lambeth MSS. 1029, f. 92b.
[2] Howell, State Trials, xv. 703.
[3] Tenison to Trimnell, 15 April 1711. Lambeth MSS. 1029, f. 112b.
[4] The other four thought that while heretical tenets might be condemned by Convocation, yet the authors of them could not be sentenced. See Cobbett, State Trials, xv. 700.

bishops acting together with the Lower House. Secondly, in the case of appeal, by what delegates could the case be tried.[1] In these circumstances, as the Queen had written that she expected Convocation to proceed with the matter, it was thought best to begin simply with an explicit condemnation of Whiston's teaching, and so to follow the Archbishop's advice. Thus the offending book was minutely analysed and the heretical paragraphs quoted, together with the scriptural passages and councils against which Whiston had offended. This document was sent down to the Lower House, which endorsed it except for one proposition, and the whole was then "laid before the Archbishop [on 12 January 1712] to know how best it might be laid before Her Majesty".[2]

Whiston, meanwhile, was becoming more and more angry with the Archbishop for acquiescing in the proceedings against him, and particularly for not allowing him to appear in person before Convocation. Misfortunes were certainly not coming singly to this bold thinker. He had already been hounded out of Cambridge, deprived of his professorship, and condemned by Convocation: but more was to follow. He was now living in London in the parish of St. Andrew, Holborn, and the Rector, the Bishop of Chichester (Manningham), now desired him "to forbear coming to the weekly Communion, on Account of the Debates in Convocation".[3] This prohibition was continued for over a year despite Whiston's protesting in repeated letters to the Bishop and his curate that it was against the law of the land. On 19 April 1711, therefore, he wrote a long letter to the Bishop of London, only to receive a formal reply from his chaplain on 6 August that as he did not live within his jurisdiction so he could not concern himself in the matter. There was now nothing left for Whiston but to petition the Archbishop of Canterbury. He did so, but received a very curt reply, namely, that Tenison "had hoped he would in common Prudence, especially at this time, have restrained from Writing Printing and Discoursing of his dangerous and offensive Matters".[4]

It is not surprising that Whiston gave vent to his feelings in a long and embittered letter to the Archbishop on 9 January 1712. He must beg for a "hearing in his own Defence", he began, "since

[1] Tenison, it will be remembered, regarded the Court of Convocation as final.
[2] Lambeth MSS. 952, f. 89.
[3] Whiston, *Articles Objected to Mr. Whiston*, p. 15.
[4] *Ibid.* p. 17.

the Archbishop had received so many stories against him without giving him ye opportunity of a Vindication". It was useless to complain of his misfortunes, he went on, though he was surprised that the Archbishop had not communicated his former letters publicly to Convocation. Yet some things he must complain of which affected his reputation, and which were so far owing to the Archbishop "that he could apply nowhere else for relief from them". He therefore asked that he might put his case "openly" before his Grace, and that he be allowed "to bring a few friends as Witnesses" on his side.[1]

"This is what I cannot but expect from your Grace's Equity and Justice in ye present Matter", he wrote. "I am, I confess, not a little surpris'd that a person of your Grace's sincerity, prudence and experience should so easily change your opinion of my integrity, as you seem of late to have done, and yt without any other foundation than hearing partial and gross mistakes and misrepresentations of matters of fact, without your once desiring to know the real truth, and what I had to say in my own vindication: especially when Your Grace cannot but be sensible yt in such a case ye like scandals and false reports will of course abound".[2]

Tenison was determined not to become embroiled in a private correspondence with Whiston, and he replied through his chaplain, Benjamin Ibbot, on 15 January.[3]
The Archbishop had refrained from replying to Whiston's former letter, he said, for two reasons. First because Whiston had a habit of publishing other people's letters without their permission, and secondly, because of "the unfitness of it frō the Nature of the Case wch forbids me to intermeddle otherwise than in a Public Capacitie". As to the charge that the Archbishop had not communicated his letter to Convocation, he replied caustically: "I am sorry he has written in ys Lr wt is false concerning his last sent to me at Lambeth and wt upon the least enquiry he might have found to be so". In fact the Archbishop had sent it immediately to his deputy in Convocation where, owing to Whiston's own delay, it arrived after the bishops had risen, and "was not judg'd of Moment enough to be laid before the synod on the following Day".

---

1 Whiston to Tenison, 9 January 1712. Lambeth MSS. 1029, f. 116.
2 *Ibid.* f. 11.
3 Lambeth MSS. 1029, f. 115. See also Whiston, *Life and Writings*, 1749, p. 200.

Concerning Whiston's main request, a hearing before the Archbishop, Tenison made no reply, feeling doubtless that the affair was now the business of Convocation, to whose deliberations we return.

On 8 February 1712, the Bishop of Ely (Moore) reported to Convocation that in response to the Archbishop's order he had laid their judgment before the Queen who had promised an answer. The zeal of the court, however, seems to have somewhat abated: no reply came from the Queen and Tenison once more instructed two of the bishops to wait upon her as soon as possible.[1] The Queen again promised a reply in a few days, but a little later the Lord Treasurer reported to the Bishop of Ely that the Queen "had mislayd the paper containing the judgment of Convocation", with the result that on 20 February the Upper House ordered another copy to be made.[2] The Queen again promised that she would soon give an answer, and, thus encouraged, the patient Bishop of Ely called to collect it on 20 June, "so that it might be subscribed by Convocation".[3] He left the Queen with another promise, which was still unredeemed at the end of the year.

It seemed as if matters would remain thus permanently suspended, but on 18 June 1713, Tenison received a letter from the Earl of Dartmouth, Secretary of State, requesting that the Queen might know the exact position regarding Whiston's condemnation. The Archbishop caused a search to be made of the convocational records, and replied on 20 June,[4] that the paper condemning Whiston's heresies had "not yet been sent back to ye Convocation with her Majesty's Approbation", so that the signing of it had not hitherto been practicable. The Archbishop took the opportunity to ask that the document might be returned to Convocation before its next meeting on 1 July. Although most of the bishops were out of town, and the infirmities of the Bishops of Worcester and Gloucester "had occasion'd their long Absence from the synod", he yet hoped "enough may meet of both Houses for the Signing of it in due and Effectual Form".[5]

Still the Queen did not confirm the censure and many,

---

[1] Moore to Tenison, 10 February 1712. Lambeth MSS. 1029, f. 114.
[2] Lambeth MSS. 952, f. 89, and Moore to Tenison, 21 February 1712. Lambeth MSS. 1029, f. 113.
[3] Lambeth MSS. 952, f. 89.
[4] Tenison to Dartmouth, 20 June 1713. S.P.D. Anne.
[5] *Ibid.*

including Burnet, who had left for his diocese as soon as the condemnation was passed, having never been happy about it, thought "that the true interest of the Christian religion was best consulted, when nice disputing about the mysteries was laid aside and forgotten".[1] The Court, it was obvious, had lost interest, but there were still some others who wished to carry on with the prosecution. Interest in the case was revived when in the winter of 1713 a Dr. Pilling offered himself before Dr. Harward, Commissary of the Dean and Chapter of St. Paul's, as a voluntary promoter against Whiston on a charge of heresy. The Commissary sent the matter to the Dean of the Arches who, as the case did not come to him on appeal, dismissed it. Pilling then managed to persuade the Lord Chancellor to appoint a Court of Delegates which met in full session on 1 July 1714. How long this tedious affair would have gone on before some judgment was reached, we cannot tell. As it was, the death of the Queen enabled the whole matter to be decently interred.

Tenison's part in this rather unhappy episode was typical. Burnet would have preferred no action to be taken, but Tenison, apart from the fact that he wished to co-operate with the Lower House of Convocation when for once this seemed possible, was himself a believer in publicly condemning a heresiarch, if only to dissuade others from following the same perilous path. It is true that when the Tory Earl of Dartmouth first went to Lambeth with the message that the Queen "thought it necessary that some censure should pass upon Whiston and his book", the Archbishop replied that "there were some difficulties and disputes about prosecuting men for their opinions", yet he was genuinely interested in questions of theology and opposed to innovation. Whiston was undoubtedly a difficult man to control, and by temperament he was bound to be a thorn in the flesh of authority: but it is unfortunate that Tenison does not appear to have made any efforts to win his confidence, or by personal sympathy and understanding to influence him. The Archbishop behaved in a public and formal way to a kindly and well-intentioned man who might have responded to more generous treatment.

Tenison's interest in purely doctrinal matters may be seen in another typical action of his in 1711, in connection with a "Book of Common Prayer set forth in English and Dutch Anno 1711, for the use especially of the Dutch inhabiting the West

[1] Howell, State Trials, xv. 716.

Indies, by order of the Society for the Propagation of the Christian Faith in America".[1]

The history of this book is interesting. It had been Archbishop Laud's policy to insist that the Dutch congregations in this country should use the Church of England liturgy, and to make this possible he had secured the translation of the book of Common Prayer into Dutch (by Duez and Hoefnagel), a work, however, which was not published till 1645 in Rotterdam.[2] In 1710 an edition appeared in London, probably through the influence of Archbishop Sharp; "but better known than the purely Dutch translations are the editions of the liturgy in English and Dutch, the 'editio princeps' of which appeared in 1711, entitled 'The Book of Common Prayer . . . English and Low Dutch. Amsterdam. John Crellius. MDCCXI'". The reverse of the title page stated that it had received the "approbation" of the Bishop of London (Compton) and the edition contained a beautiful frontispiece by Adrian van Spiers (d. 1718). The English and Dutch were printed in parallel columns and the Dutch text was that of Duez and Hoefnagel, revised by S. Vandereyken, reader of the Royal Dutch Chapel at St. James. This edition was one of the early publications of the S.P.C.K., and the Society made provision in 1709–10 for an edition of 750 copies, mainly for the use of the Dutch in New York city and the Provinces, which in 1665 had been ceded by the Netherlands to the English.

It was this translation which was left at Lambeth for the Archbishop's perusal in 1711, at a time, however, when he was unfortunately confined to his bed. He got up on 13 May, Ascension Day, and "after he had been up a while, and found that his Eyes would serve him, he called for the above sd Book and turned to the service for the above sd Day".[3] His critical eye soon noticed that there was something wrong with the Dutch version of the collect, and that the ascription to the Trinity was curtailed. His suspicions were further aroused when he noticed that although the book bore the imprimatur of the Bishop of London, yet the printer was John Crellius of Amsterdam, a reputed Socinian. On closer inspection, Tenison found that the whole work "abounded with Faults of divers kinds, amongst which many smelt offensively of the heresy of Socinus", and he therefore acquainted the

---

[1] B.M. Add. MSS. Stowe, 117, f. 51.
[2] W. Muss-Arnolt, *The Book of Common Prayer*, etc., 1914, p. 115.
[3] B.M. Add. MSS. Stowe, 117, f. 51.

Society with his opinion in order that it might secure the "suppress-ing of this Edition of the Comon Prayer Book, so dangerous to the Souls of Men, so scandalous to the Societie and so prejudicial to their glorious design of propagating the true Gospell of our Blessed Saviour".

Tenison gave this private intimation on some day between 15 and 18 May, so that he was somewhat disconcerted when, at a meeting on the latter date, the Society ordered "that 500 Copies of the Dutch and English Comon Prayer Books should immediately be bound and sent to New York". This time the Archbishop intervened with greater emphasis and so effectively that the Society immediately stopped the issue of the books on 15 June, the Secretary "laying before the Board a Letter from his Grace the President, dated from Lambeth 14 inst. . . . imparting his Ldp's desire that all that has been ord.ᵈ in the Minutes of the Society on the 18th May last relating to the said English and Dutch liturgy may be expunged, till it may be determined at the next meeting what shall be done with the said Book".[1] At this meeting the publisher Mr. Vandereyken was called in, but all he could do was to "produce two other Translations of the Liturgy and avow that his Edition agreed with the two former". On 22 June, therefore, the offending minute of the order made on 18 May "was declared null and void for good and weighty Reasons wch he [Tenison] promised to explain to the Society as soon as his health would permit". As his physical condition did not amend very rapidly, Tenison decided to send the Society his opinions in writing, and he did so on 19 July, explaining fully in his letter the nature of his objections to this "pretended translation" of the Book of Common Prayer.[2]

His criticisms, he wrote, were of a threefold character, and were directed against "the Omissions, Alterations, and Additions in ye Low Dutch Columns in wch none are necessary and very many pernicious". He began with the omissions, which in most cases, he thought, were due simply to lack of thought. Of the many examples quoted, we select the following as typical.

(a) Where the English had "one God", "one" was frequently omitted in the Dutch, and sometimes "God". (b) "Jesus" was often deleted from the phrase "Jesus Christ". (c) Little phrases were frequently omitted such as "through the merits and

[1] S.P.G. Minutes.
[2] Tenison to S.P.G., 19 July 1711. B.M. Add. MSS. Stowe 117, f. 51.

21

mediation", from the Collect for the 12th Sunday after Trinity. (d) In most cases where ascriptions were made to the Trinity, especially at the end of the collects, "etc." was used. (e) In the proper preface for Trinity Sunday, the words "without any difference or inequality" did not appear, and here Tenison observed: "Of this omission I was advertiz'd by a Friend and should wonder more at my own Stupidness in overseeing It (as possibly I have done many others) if the multitude of errors wch occurred to me had not brought a bluntness and weariness upon my curiosity".

Some omissions, however, he regarded as of a more serious nature, and particularly he deplored the leaving out the Act of Uniformity in the preface, which if included "our Constitution might be better known and recommended to strangers to our Church which the better it is understood the sooner it will be approved of". Alike unfortunate was the omission of the forms for ordaining priests and deacons and for consecrating bishops, since these were "wise, pious and grave", and might give "those who as yet absent themselves from our Communion a better idea of Episcopacy". "It is true", he wrote, "(& I say it not without grief of mind) we have not yet any Bp of Our Own in the West Indies,[1] but we have some ground to hope that we may have some who may there Reside, Confirm, Govern and Minister in all Holy Things to the greater Good of both Ministers and People".

As to the omissions generally, the Archbishop remarked somewhat caustically that it was the simple duty of a translator "to translate accurately what is in ye Original and not to leave anything out at pleasure".

Tenison next turned to the alterations, and quoted a large number of them. Many, perhaps, were not very important, such as the changing "Papist Conspiracy" to "Gunpowder Treason", and "that we cannot do any good thing without thee" to "that we cannot hold fast": but more insidious was the alteration of "ever one God" to "ever true God", which latter ascription, he wrote, "divers Arians and Socinians may be ready to give to a Deus Factus or made God".

Finally he turned to the additions and here he noticed many instances, some of which "in their own nature" were "laudable", such as the adding "van Hanover" after the Princess Sophia's name in the prayer for the Royal Family, but which "in a pre-

[1] See Chap. 15, p. 350 for this reference to a bishop in the West Indies.

tended translation were an Offence against Truth, Modesty and Publick Authority".

And so, he asked, "after all the Instances of Omissions, Alterations and Additions here produced and possibly others pass'd by unobserved, how can we easily repose a Confidence in Those (when once they shall be discovered) who have shew'd so little regard to Truth and honesty as to have said with assurance to a Person of great and venerable Character who trusted them in this affair, as men of skill and integrity, that this Edition is perform'd with great care and exactness". Nor could one be unduly impressed, he went on, by the fact that it was "formerly translated out of English during ye reign of Queen Elizabeth[1] and now printed a second time, carefully compared with ye English, many mistakes and faults corrected, and by the order of the same Her Majesty publish'd for the use of her Majesty's Low Dutch Court Chappell at St. James . . . The more the pity Kings and Queens have not leysure enough to compare ye Editions of all Our Church Books, though they should happen to have ye skill in all the modern Languages in wch they are set forth". Thus, though a few of the corrections were advantageous, the whole edition was tinged with Socinianism, and the Archbishop concluded his letter as follows:

"And now to wind up this matter wch has been drawn out to so great a length: My first Request is that you would shew some tenderness towards the person of the Editor and at ye same time, set marks of your just indignation upon the Edition. You would not, I believe, burn the Person of an Haeretic if the Law allowed you to use such Severity, much less would you punish in so terrible a manner a poor Creature who seems to have offended rather out of Ignorance, Negligence and Supineness, than Malice aforethought. And yet when I consider the many Instances now produc'd I cannot but be of opiniŏ, that this Edition is fitt to be destroy'd, some way or other, perhaps by a private Flame. My second Request is that, in due time, just consideration may be had of setting forth a true and complete Edition, to wch (if God continues my life) I will readily contribute. For my third and last Request; It is, My earnest desire of your Prayers to God for me that whilst I remain amongst you, he would be pleased to grant me such a measure of Grace, Wisdom and Understanding and Health, as may, in some degree, render usefull my poor but

---

[1] There seems to be no extant copy or reference to such an Elizabethan translation.

hearty endeavours to promote the great Ends of your Excellent Institution wch I have much at heart".

This letter was read to the Board at its next meeting on 20 July at the Archbishop's special request. The members were undoubtedly impressed, and they "order'd that the thanks of the Society be return'd to his Grace for the great care and pains his Grace had taken in perusing the said Liturgy, and for the Zeal his Ldp has testified for the Honour of the Church and of this Society". All the copies of the condemned liturgy were to be sent to the Archbishop "to be destroyed in such a manner as he shall think fit", and as there were "pressing demands" for such a liturgy from New York, Tenison was to be applied to "for directions after what manner and by whom the said Edition shall be prepared".[1]

As a result of this application, the Archbishop went into the whole question with his accustomed thoroughness, and he drew up a report which received the approval of the Society on 21 September 1711. In this document he suggested:

(1) That a "new and more orthodox Impression" be commissioned and "special care" be taken because of the "late miscarriage". (2) That it be referred to a special committee which should consult Mr. Nucella, minister of the Royal Dutch Chapel, and Dr. Coughlan. (3) That the edition be in ordinary type, and that the Queen's Printer be asked to undertake it, if he will do it cheaply enough. (4) That the Society contract to take 750 copies. (7) That the order for the consecration of bishops, the Act of Uniformity, and the Thirty-nine Articles, be included in this edition.[2]

Nucella and Coughlan embarked upon their task forthwith and the Society approved their translation as "perfect" on 18 September 1713. There seems to have been some delay, however, as to its publication, for it did not appear till 1718 and then in an edition prepared at the Hague.

Nor was the rejected edition destroyed in Tenison's lifetime. Through some misunderstanding, the books remained at Lambeth, and it was not until 7 February 1716, that fifteen parcels of "Socianized Common Prayer Books" were "burnt and reduced to Ashes in the Kitchen belonging to the Palace" by the orders of Archdeacon Tenison, the Archbishop's heir.[3]

---

[1] S.P.G. Minutes.   [2] *Ibid.*   [3] *Ibid.*

Tenison's interest in the maintenance of doctrinal orthodoxy
by no means made him take an extreme view on all questions.
This may be illustrated from his attitude to lay baptism, a question
which came to the fore towards the end of his archiepiscopate.
This subject was one which caused much internal dissension
within the Church of England, for most High Churchmen condemned lay baptism as opposed to the practice of the primitive
Church and to the traditions of the Church of England itself;
while Low and Liberal Churchmen took the view that though it was
irregular, yet it ought not to be declared invalid, particularly as
they were eager to welcome Nonconformists into the Anglican
fold. This latter view was expressed forcibly by Burnet in two
sermons preached in November 1710, and as it was these sermons
which in part gave rise to the following controversy, we quote at
length from one of them.

"There is a conceit lately got in among us", he said, "that
denies all who are not Baptized [1] among us to be Christians,
shuts them out of Christ's Covenant, and thinks them no better
than Heathens. A Notion, that tho' it once got into some
Churches, who thought that the Baptism of hereticks was of
no value, and was to be repeated upon their coming into the
Church, yet was solemnly condemned and rejected by the
Churches of God now for above fourteen hundred years. In
Popery the Midwives generally Baptize: Yet tho' this is
against the express rule of the Apostles, that a Woman ought
not to speak in the Church, none of the Reformed ever thought
of Rebaptizing the Persons so Baptized; nor did our Church
at the Restoration ever entertain the least notion of that sort:
But now this is received by many. The common Topick for
supporting this wild unheard of Paradox is, That the Commission to preach and Baptize was given to the Apostles, so
that none but their Successors can pretend to it. But has not
every Christian in Cases of Necessity a Right to Teach and
Instruct another and to persuade him to become a Christian?
And therefore, tho' it is a very just part of the order of the
Church, that none but Persons initiated into Holy Functions
should Baptize and Preach, yet Necessity is above all Rules.
In such a case they may Baptize as well as preach. The faith
of the Trinity gives every Man a Right to Baptize; and this
has been the Sense of the Church for above Fourteen hundred
Years, which in a Ritual Matter is certainly of great Authority.
They reckon'd that Baptism is the Gift of Christ to his Church,

[1] i.e., by episcopally ordained ministers.

when given in the Name of the Father, Son and Holy Ghost. It is Christ's Baptism, be they who give it Hereticks or Orthodox, Clergy or Laity, and in the latter Ages, Men or Women".[1]

Burnet proceeded to publish these sermons and thus rendered controversy inevitable. In 1712 there appeared a pamphlet, "Lay Baptism Invalid", which included as an appendix a letter from the nonjuring Bishop George Hickes. This induced the Bishop of Oxford (Talbot), in a charge to the clergy of his diocese, to refer to "the Notion, which began to prevail too much", namely, "the Invalidity and Nullity of Baptism, administered by Persons not episcopally ordained; a Doctrine that do's at once unchristian all the Reform'd Churches abroad, even those Blessed Martyrs among them who have been Baptiz'd in their own Blood, laid down their Lives for the Gospel, and glorified God by their Death".[2]

The author of "Lay Baptism Invalid" replied to this attack in "The Bishop of Oxford's Charge Consider'd", and the controversy now began to have its repercussion in Convocation, where the question was introduced into the Lower House and many members of High Church persuasion supported the thesis maintained by George Hickes.[3]

It now seemed advisable for the bishops to agree upon some common line of action before the question came to the Upper House of Convocation. Thus, when according to ancient custom the Archbishop of Canterbury invited the bishops of both Provinces to dine with him on Easter Tuesday (22 April), the conversation turned inevitably to this question. Good food seems to have added harmony to the discussion, for all the bishops agreed that lay baptism could not categorically be declared invalid. Archbishop Sharp writes of this meeting in his diary:

"At eleven o'clock I went to Lambeth. We were in all about thirteen bishops. We had a long discussion about lay baptism, which of late hath made such a noise about town. We all agreed that baptism by any other person except lawful ministers, ought as much as may be, to be discouraged; nevertheless, whoever was baptised by any other person, and in that baptism the essentials of baptism were preserved, that is, being dipped or sprinkled in the name of the Father etc. such baptism was valid and ought not to be repeated".[4]

---

[1] Quoted *Sacerdotal Powers*, etc., pp. 2, 3. Contemporary scholarship would confirm the substantial accuracy of Burnet's historical thesis.
[2] "The Bishop of Oxford's Charge Consider'd", 1712, p. 4.
[3] Lathbury, *A History of the Convocation*, p. 419.
[4] Sharp, *Life of John Sharp*, p. 370.

Tenison (and particularly Burnet), "feeling so many bishops unanimous in their opinion, thought it would be of public service if they all joined in publishing a declaration of their sentiments, which would appear as a kind of decision, and might help to make the minds of some men more easy, at least to shorten the disputes then raised upon this question". Accordingly, on 26 April, Tenison summoned a number of his brethren to Lambeth again, when they accepted a declaration which he and the Bishop of Salisbury had drawn up. We quote this document as it exists at Lambeth in Tenison's handwriting, dated 26 April, and headed "A declaration etc. ye Title not yet agreed on".

"Forasmuch as sundry Persons have, of late, by Preaching, writing, and discourses, possess'd ye minds of many People w^t doubts and Scruples about ye Validity of their Baptism to their great trouble and disquiet: We the Archbishops and Bishops, whose names are und^{r}written, have thought it incumbent on us to declare our several opinions in conformity with ye judgm^t and Practice of ye Catholic Church of Christ and of ye C of E in particular that such Persons as have already been baptized in, or with water, in ye name of ye Father, Son and Holy Ghost [1] ought not to be baptized again. And to prevent any such Practice in our respective Dioceses, we do require our Several Clergy, That they presume not to baptize any adult person whatsoever w^{t}out giving us timely Notice of ye Same, as the Rubrick requires".[2]

Tenison was anxious for the bishops to send out this agreed report to their clergy, thus short-circuiting the deliberations of Convocation, and hence on 27 April he forwarded the declaration to the Archbishop of York "in pursuance of the Agree^{mt} made at Lambeth". "I met yesterday", he explained,

"wth some of them; and we drew up a Paper suitable (as we judg'd) to the proposal then made. It is short and plain and

[1] There is inserted here in another hand, "Though their Baptism was irregular for want of a proper administration".
[2] Lambeth MSS. 954, f. 8. There is another draft of the above (954, f. 9) with some interesting emendations in Burnet's hand-writing. He deletes "the Archbishops and Bishops . . . opinions" and replaces it with: "We think it incumbent on us in conformity etc. to declare". He crosses out "And to prevent, etc." to the end of the document, and replaces it with: "Thus we do use Archbishop Whitgift's words . . . not to bring confusion into the Church, for let men take heed that they usurp not the office whereunto they be not called, for God will call them to an account for so doing". Tenison did not adopt these corrections. See draft found among Archbishop Sharp's papers (*Life of John Sharp*, p. 373).

(I hope) inoffensive and (for a begiñing) (as I humbly conceive) full enough. I here enclose a copy of It for yr Grace and of as many others as yr Grace shall think fitt to shew it to. I send ys Declaration unsign'd, because we who were present desir'd first to have ye Opinion of Yr Grace and others who were absent; and should be glad to know whether you would have anything added to It, or alter'd in it; for we affect not ye vanity of dogmatizing . . . I hope for yr Grace's speedy Answer (tomorrow if it may be) because the evill grows, and we have heard of more odd Books and sermōs since we met and of an increase of ye Temptations [?]: and Yr Grace well knows that the more timely ye Check is given, the likelier it is to have (through God's blessing) a good Effect. I comēnd this Affair to Yr Grace's most serious consideration and yr self to ye protectiō of ye great sustainer of souls".[1]

This letter, with its many parentheses, seems to suggest a certain nervousness as to how Sharp would receive it. The letter reached the Archbishop on the evening of the 28th, and he immediately felt that the enclosed declaration went beyond what had been agreed upon at Lambeth on Easter Tuesday. It was one thing, he thought, to decide against rebaptism: another to issue an official declaration to the clergy upon it. Sharp immediately summoned the Bishops of Chester, Exeter, and St. David's,[2] all High Church Tories promoted by Anne, and showed them both the letter and declaration. We relate what happened from the Archbishop's diary:

"About six o'clock this evening, came in the Bishops of Chester and of Exeter and of St. David's, who staid here till nine o'clock. We had a great deal of talk about the Archbishop of Canterbury's proposal, in a letter he had wrote to me, that we should sign a declaration of our judgments, that all persons who were baptized with water in the name of etc. . . . their baptism ought not to be repeated by whomsoever they were baptized. They were all of opinion and so was I, that it was not proper for us to make such a declaration under our hands, for that it would too much encourage the irregular baptisms of the dissenters. And accordingly, after they were gone, I wrote a letter to my Lord Archbishop to the same purpose".[3]

[1] Tenison to Sharp, 27 April 1712. Lambeth MSS. 941, f. 33.
[2] Chester (Sir William Dawes), Exeter (Offspring Blackall), and St. David's (George Bull).
[3] Sharp, *Life of John Sharp*, p. 37.

This letter ran as follows:

"I am entirely of the same sentiments that we all declared we were of, when we had the hon^r to dine with yr Grace the last week: But yet for all that, I can by no means come into the Proposal Yr Grace has now made in yr Letter in that we should all declare under our Hands the Validity of Lay Baptism. For I am afraid this would be too great an Encouragement to the Dissenters to go in their way of irregular uncanonical Baptisms".[1]

This cleavage on the Bench, representing the tension between the Whig and Tory elements, probably came as no surprise to Tenison, and he replied to the Archbishop of York on the following day.

"The paper", he began, "wch was drawn up at the desire of yr Grace and the rest of the Bps by myself and some of them, seems (by the words of yr L^r) not to be thoroughly understood, It being by no means design'd to encourage any Irregularities in Baptism but levelled, in special manner, against Rebaptization. And when It was sent to yr Grace, I sent it with the express Declaration, that we had therefore not sign'd it, because we thought it was not fit to preclude yr judgment with relation to any Addition or Alteration wch might be thought proper to be made. I believe Yr Grace in so weighty a matter as this is, will not think it is sufficient to reject this Proposal without offering one of your own".[2]

It is obvious that there was some misunderstanding here, for the declaration which Tenison maintained had been drawn up at the desire of the Archbishop of York among others appears to have taken him by surprise. Burnet, with characteristic prejudice, accuses Sharp of being "prevailed on to change his mind", after he had first consented to the drawing up of a declaration.

---

[1] Tenison to Sharp, 29 April 1712. Lambeth MSS. 953, f. 32. Also Burnet, *History of my own Time*, ii. 605. He writes: "The bishops thought it necessary to put a stop to this new and extravagent doctrine [viz. the invalidity of lay baptism] so a declaration was agreed to, first against the irregularity of all persons who were not in holy orders [this doesn't appear in Tenison's final draft, only in Burnet's], but that yet, according to the practice of the primitive Church, and the constant usage of the Church of England, no baptism in or with water etc. ought to be reiterated. The Archbishop of York first agreed to this. So it was resolved to publish it in the names of all the bishops of England, but he was prevailed on to change his mind, and refused to sign it, pretending that this would encourage irregular baptism". Lathbury (*A History of the Convocation*, p. 419) has in the main followed Burnet's interpretation, which is clearly not entirely accurate. It may be, however, that Burnet was unaware of the precise form of Tenison's final draft.

[2] Tenison to Sharp, 29 April 1712. Lambeth MSS. 953, f. 96.

It is significant, however, that the Archbishop of York was supported by three other bishops in his attitude.

Hence Tenison was forced to abandon his scheme of circularizing the clergy with an episcopal declaration maintaining the validity of lay baptism, but it was still possible for him to place the document before the southern Convocation. He decided to do so, and he obtained the support of the Upper House as a whole, but the "lower house refused even to take it into consideration". Thus as the declaration had been refused by the bishops independently as an order, and rejected by Convocation, Tenison was unsuccessful in securing any formal pronouncement.

The controversy, meanwhile, was being maintained in a host of pamphlets. The author of "Lay Baptism Invalid" proved a prolific writer, and in addition to "The Bishop of Oxford's Charge Consider'd", which we have already noticed, he published "Dissenters' and other Unauthoriz'd Baptisms Null and Void", and a second part to "Lay Baptism Invalid". From the point of view of learning, the honours of the debate went to the scholar Bingham, who, arguing in support of the Archbishop of Canterbury, devoted a great deal of patient labour to "The Scholastical History of Lay Baptism", published in two parts in 1712 and 1714.[1]

Fundamentally this controversy was a part of the Tory and High Church Anglican protest against the growing rationalism of the eighteenth century. But theological disputation of a highly doctrinal nature was beginning to lose interest. Tenison's preoccupation with the Catholic controversy in his early and formative years prevented his seeing the dangers incipient in the new spirit, and he never seems to have suspected that reason would

---

[1] The following is a list of the more important pamphlets which the controversy produced.

"Lay Baptism Invalid", 1712. Part I.

"Lay Baptism Invalid", 1713. Part II.

"A Supplement to the first and second Parts of Lay Baptism Invalid", 1714.

"Sacerdotal Powers, or the Necessity of Confession, Penance and Absolution, together with the Nullity of Unauthoriz'd Lay Baptism".

"Dissenters and other Unauthoriz'd Baptisms Null and Void", 1713.

"The Judgment of the Church of England in the Case of Lay Baptism and Dissenters' Baptism".

"The Bishop of Oxford's Charge Consider'd", 1712.

"The Judgment of the Reformed in France", 1712.

"The State and Importance of the Present Controversy about Validity of Lay Baptism", 1713.

"The Scholastical History of Lay Baptism", Part I, 1712. Part II, 1714, by J. Bingham.

"Dissertation upon the 8th Canon of the Council of Nicea", 1716, by J. Bingham.

be placed over against faith. Most people longed for religious calm, not out of respect for the "Faith", but because theological squabbles of too technical a nature seemed almost indecent and certainly irrelevant. Hence behind the following injunctions which George I sent to the Archbishops and Bishops on 11 June 1715, and their apparent defence of the Church, the discerning student may perhaps detect the growing secularism of the age. We quote these injunctions as we bring this chapter to a close.

1. No preacher when dealing with the Trinity is to teach other than as the Creeds and the thirty-nine Articles direct.
2. New terms are to be avoided.
3. The 53rd Canon of the Church, which forbids preachers opposing each other publicly, is to be observed.
4. The clergy in their sermons (and (5) in their written expositions) are to avoid references to affairs of state, except on special and authorized occasions.
6. The prayer before the sermon is to be in accordance with Canon 53.
7. All legal means are to be employed to stop laymen writing against the Christian faith, and particularly 9 Will. III, suppressing blasphemy and profaneness, is to be enforced.[1]

These injunctions remind us how often governments set themselves an impossible task.

[1] Lambeth MSS. 933, f. 16. See Chap. 13, p. 288.

CHAPTER 15

Part I The Protestant Refugees

NO man of his time, as this chapter will endeavour to show, felt more keenly the sufferings of his Protestant brethren overseas, than did Thomas Tenison, though this did not prevent him tempering his charity with statesmanlike caution. He lived in the aftermath of the Counter-Reformation, when both the reform of the Papacy and the rise of the Jesuits had done much to stem the tide of Protestant advance. Protestantism stood on the defensive, and Tenison believed firmly that all the reformed Churches of Europe should stand together against the common foe. He first displayed this sympathy in an active manner, not long after he became Vicar of St. Martin's, in connection with the French refugees.

Louis XIV, as we have already seen, regarded a Gallican form of Catholicism as the only branch of the Christian religion compatible with absolutism, and he consequently viewed his Protestant subjects with peculiar aversion. Early in his reign, he had decided "to reduce them gradually, observing the liberties granted by his predecessors, but granting them nothing but these liberties". This negative policy, however, was given a vicious and positive twist in 1685, when Louis committed the cardinal error of his reign and revoked the Edict of Nantes. As a result of this disgraceful change of policy, "all privileges granted to the Protestants by Henry IV and Louis XIV were suppressed; public worship was forbidden to them except in Alsace; their ministers were to leave the realm within fifteen days; and lay Protestants were forbidden to follow them, under pain of the galleys and forfeiture".[1] It is not surprising that many fled in disgust, and amongst these a large number came to our own shores, where they were hospitably received.

It will be readily understood that James II did not regard this assertion of Protestant solidarity by his subjects with too friendly an eye. Tenison determined that his own countrymen should know the full facts of the case, and by such knowledge rise above vulgar prejudice. A book had recently been written by Mons. Claude, a

---

[1] Duruy, *History of France*, ii. 18.

refugee himself, giving in some detail the hardships to which his brethren had been subjected in their native land. Tenison now translated this work into English and published it anonymously in 1686 (without either printer's name or introduction), under the title *An Account of the Persecutions and Oppressions of the Protestants in France*. At such a time, in view of James' Catholic policy, it was a bold thing to do, and the French ambassador in London "was particularly chagrined and at his instigation James ordered the translation to be burned by the common hangman"— a unique penalty, it may be, for the work of a future Archbishop of Canterbury ! [1]

Henceforth Louis XIV became, in Tenison's eyes, the Protestants' bitterest enemy, and the war against him assumed the dimensions of a religious war, a crusade on behalf of Protestantism and the liberties of a free Europe. When, on Tillotson being ill, Tenison was asked to preach before the House of Commons on 5 June 1689 (a "fast day" which was kept "very strictly"), he gave free expression to his indignation against Louis.

> "It is to be confess'd", he said, "that he has caused the Art of War to be considerably improv'd, but in order to the making room for his own Triumphs in the Solitudes of his Neighbourhood. . . . He has terrified Multitudes into a sudden Flight into strange Lands, yet to them more charitable than their Native Country. And for many who could neither escape themselves, nor obtain of him the Privilege of Banishment, he has driven them by a Terror (by mere human strength not to be resisted) into the very worst of all Refuges; I mean, Hypocrisy".[2]

It is now clear that the Romanism of the French King had little in common with the Papalism of Gregory VII, but most contemporary Protestants were on the whole unable to make this distinction.

Tenison, as Archbishop of Canterbury, was faced with a twofold problem: first, to provide relief and protection for Protestants forced to leave their own country as a result of Catholic persecution; and secondly, to deal with the demand from many

---

[1] *Life of Bishop Ken by a Layman*, 1854, p. 328.
[2] Tenison, "A Sermon against self love preached before the House of Commons on 5 June, 1689", p. 26. The preacher concluded with a strong plea for a united effort against Louis in the following words: "May our Councils be wise and steady, in order to the frustration of his devices. May both our Sea and Land forces, prepared against such pernicious self love, go forth in the name of that God, who is truly the Lord of Hosts. May they go forth with Courage and return with Victory".

quarters for some measure of unity, doctrinal and perhaps organizational, amongst the Protestant Churches of Europe. The following chapter,[1] therefore, will fall naturally into this twofold division.

That it was a duty incumbent upon the Church of England to succour Protestants suffering for conscience' sake was a conviction firmly held by Tenison in company with the best minds of his day. As he expressed himself in a letter to the clergy of his province: "The Church of England hath been a Shelter to other Neighbouring Churches when a Storm hath driven upon them. It was such in former times, it hath been so of late, and I question not it will be so in this Instance".[2]

The practical question was how best to raise the necessary money and organize its distribution amongst the various Protestants requiring it. The problem may be seen clearly if we take an example from a small community of French refugees.

French Protestants had been coming over to England ever since the religious wars of the sixteenth century, and they settled down in small communities, thereby greatly benefiting the economic life of this country. With the accession of Henry of Navarre (despite his own acceptance of Catholicism) they secured a legal toleration, and the influx of God-fearing Huguenots into England more or less ceased. The Revocation of the Edict of Nantes in 1685, however, resulted, as we have seen, in renewed emigration, so much so that with these, and the claims of other continental refugees on English charity, the position of the older French exiles became somewhat difficult. The sad condition of the Walloon congregation in Canterbury in 1695, when its desperate plight was brought before the Archbishop, may be taken as typical. This community of some 1,500 persons had been settled in Canterbury since 1595, and it had managed to make itself completely self-supporting, even looking after its own poor. In 1695, however, when it was driven to petition the Archbishop, the silk trade by which it had supported itself in the past was ruined. The community, heavily burdened with parish taxes, had been forced to borrow money in an effort to keep going, and it now found itself heavily in debt. To add to its general distress at this time, the community contained one hundred aged persons, including many widows. It is obvious that this Walloon

---

[1] i.e. Part I.
[2] Tenison, "Letter to the Clergy of the Province of Canterbury", 1709.

congregation created a serious problem for the civic authorities in Canterbury, and similar conditions existed in many other towns. The Walloons inevitably became dependent upon alms, and the grant of £20 or £30 which they received in 1692 alone prevented them from literally starving. It was in these circumstances that they applied (in vain) for help from the money distributed by the Crown to the French Protestants in London, and their plight would have been really desperate had it not been for the generosity of Archbishop Tillotson. Out of the next general collection, fortunately, they were allocated £125, although they felt they ought to have been given at least as much as the sum collected in the diocese of Canterbury.

Tillotson, meanwhile, died, and it fell to Tenison to receive a petition from the Walloon congregation at Canterbury, asking him to do his best to secure for them "a proportionable grant from his Majesty's disbursements".[1]

This request makes the problem clear. Although the collections were made, they were inadequate to meet the need, and the support of these foreign Protestants was, in practice, largely left to the towns where they resided. So long as the old communities of refugees had been self-supporting, their presence was an asset and not a liability: their failure to be so any longer, coupled with fresh incursions in larger numbers, created a new and difficult problem.

In January, 1695, Lord Galway (1648–1720), himself a French Huguenot,[2] wrote to Tenison on this problem, drawing his attention to the serious difficulties in which the French refugees found themselves. He urged the Archbishop to do something for them, particularly as there now seemed "some prospects by the means of a good Peace of their re-establishment in France".[3]

As to the French Committee which had been formed to deal with this problem, Galway felt it could do no good so long as the collection of money was left to be settled by the vagaries of private charity. He suggested, therefore, that the Archbishop should endeavour "to secure a settled fund either from the King or Parliament".

"God hath rewarded your Grace's charity that you have always shew'd towards our poor French refugees", he wrote, "who want now more than ever your Grace's Assistance and

---

[1] Lambeth MSS. 942 f. 91.
[2] His French name was Massue de Ruvigny.
[3] Galway to Tenison, 22 January 1695. Lambeth MSS. 941, f. 115.

relief, and except more speedy care be taken of their maintenance, do see themselves in the most miserable conditions in the world, after having made shift to live for nine years past by the help of charitable persons, and especially of your Grace, who I am sure, will not abandon them at this juncture".[1]

This same general problem claimed the attention of many people at this time, and William Lloyd, Bishop of Worcester, commented upon it a few years later in a letter to the Archbishop, though from a slightly different point of view. He had been assured, he wrote, "out of severall parts of France, yt learned men there are generally extreme sick of Popery; and yt many of them would leave their country if they knew how to live anywhere else; and to chuse they would come into England, but that there is a generall report and belief among them, yt there is neither subsistence to be had, nor so much Protectiō, there being divers Instances of Converts yt came hither for Protection, and were spirited away and carried back into perpetual captivity".[2] To prevent this, he suggested that the French refugees should be boarded out in parts of Carnarvon and Pembrokeshire, where they could live "very comfortably . . . 7 or 8 for £100 a year". To make certain that these hospitable shores should not receive undesirables, no refugees were to be allowed to remain here without the consent "of ye best of ye French . . . in London, and once in England they should be under the inspection of the Bishop".[3]

It hardly seems likely, we feel, that men who were willing to flee from their native land would submit to such restraints in another.

The pressure of events, however, necessitated a nationally organized attempt to deal with the problem. In November 1695, William in his speech to Parliament stressed the need of making provision for the French refugees, and £15,000 was voted out of the civil list for their relief.[4] In the following year, the Archbishop, writing to the Bishop of Lichfield, lamented the ill condition of the Vaudois "in ye hands of their bloody enemies". Protestants in England felt keenly the sufferings of these brethren on the Continent, and a special appeal was made for the support of their

[1] Galway to Tenison 22 January 1695. Lambeth MSS. 941, f. 115.
[2] Lloyd to Tenison, 27 December 1700. Lambeth MSS. 1029, f. 109.
[3] Ibid.
[4] Lambeth MSS. 1122, f. 1.

"ministers and schoolmasters", which enabled £10 a quarter to be paid to them by the Bishop of Lichfield under the direction of the Archbishop.[1]

In January 1699, there was a renewed outburst of persecution, which resulted once more in the flight of many Vaudois and French Protestants from Switzerland. William received a letter from the States General on their behalf, and he replied that he "would gladly do what he thought fit for their relief". Tenison and the Bishop of London (Compton) were accordingly consulted, and it was left to them "to propose the methods they judged the most proper".[2] They met forthwith and decided upon a national collection "for the Vaudois and French protestants coming out of Switzerland", which Tenison supported by a letter of appeal to the clergy. The money thus obtained was paid in to the Lord Chamberlain, and to secure a just allocation of the funds, a Commission for the relief of the Vaudois was called into being on 12 March 1699, under royal licence.

This body met for the first time at Doctors' Commons on 12 May, Tenison presiding and some other fifteen persons being present.[3] The king's patent defining the terms of the Commission was read at this first meeting, and an inventory then drawn up of the monies collected and paid in to the Lord Chamberlain up to 12 May, which amounted to no less a sum than £5,381 13s. 7d. The Commission next considered certain information sent to it from Brandenburg, where many of the refugees from Switzerland hoped to settle. As a result, it was decided that a warrant for £1,500 should be issued "for ye use of ye Refugees in ye Territories of Brandenburg upō ye receipt of ye order of Mr. Stepney who is to be written to",[4] after which Tenison adjourned the meeting till Friday 26 May at 3 p.m.

The actual transference of the above sum of money did not prove quite so simple a matter as might have been hoped. There was much delay, and on 19 May, Tenison anxiously instructed the clerk to write to Mr. Stepney (who seems to have been in charge of these proceedings in Brandenburg) "to know whether any number of them have arrived there that the money may be ordered

[1] Lloyd to Tenison, 19 October 1696. Lambeth MSS. 930, f. 42.
[2] S.P.Dom. Will. III, 20 January 1699.
[3] Lambeth MSS. 1028, f. 1. Those present besides the Archbishop of Canterbury were: the Archbishop of York, the Bishops of London, Rochester, Salisbury, Ely, the Dean of St. Paul's, the Lord Almoner, the Earl of Stamford, Drs. Stanley, Younge, Willis, Hoby, Oxenden, Mr. Bradford, and Mr. Pilcome.
[4] Lambeth MSS. 1028.

22

accordingly".[1] When the commissioners held their second meeting on 26 May, as no report had been received from Mr. Stepney of the arrival of the refugees in Brandenburg, nothing could be done to distribute the £1,500. The money paid in to the Lord Chamberlain up to this date amounted to £8,285 4s. 2d.

The records of the Commission show only too clearly the difficulties with which it had to contend.[2] During the first twelve months the commissioners met ten times, Tenison presiding on each occasion, while the monies paid in to the Lord Chamberlain during this period reached the total of £24,193 19s. 3d. The transference of the money to the refugees in Brandenburg was never easy and the commissioners were often left in doubt whether it had been handed over to the proper authorities. Writing to Sharp on 29 May 1700, Tenison expressed the difficulties only too clearly as follows:

"After all enquiry I cañot find a way by wch ye money for ye Vaudois may be remitted. I hope yr Grace's Agents will find a way by Bill of Exchange from York. That's farr ye safest way. There was once lost upon ye French Brief about 700 l. from Yorkshire wch Mossun ye Secretarie of ye Comīssion rec'd there upon a Counterfeit Order & then ran away & has never bin heard of since. So yt one would use even greater caution there now".[3]

On 23 June 1699, a warrant was issued to one Robert Hackshaw to pay £1,500 directly to the Elector of Brandenburg for the refugees in his territory.[4] This step, however, seems to have caused some dissension among the refugees themselves, and on 14 July it was decided to alter the procedure, and to instruct Stepney to

---

[1] Vernon to Williamson, S.P.Dom. Will. III, 19 May 1699.
[2] The Commission met at the following dates and places.

Date	Place	Present	Sum collected
May 12 ('99)	Doctors' Commons	15	£5,381 13s. 7d.
26	,, ,,	6	£8,285 4s. 2d.
April 24	Chapter House, St. Paul's	6	
June 23	,, ,, ,,	6	£13,419 2s. 0¼d.
July 27.	Whitehall	7	£18,051 8s. 11d.
August 8	,,	6	£18,975 3s. 8¾d.
August 29	,,	—	
August 31	,,	6	£20,419 0s. 1¾d.
December 20	Lambeth	10	
March 6 (1700)	Princes Chambers	—	£24,193 19s. 3d.

(Taken from Lambeth MSS. 1028, f. 1–47.)
[3] Tenison to Sharp, 29 May 1700, Lloyd-Baker-Sharp MSS., L. 70.
[4] Lambeth MSS. 1028.

pay directly to each refugee £20 per head, an amount which was increased to £30 on 8 August.[1]

The commissioners, however, were by no means solely concerned with the relief of Protestant refugees in Brandenburg, since many German Princes appealed for aid, amongst whom the Prince of Hesse Cassel was successful in obtaining a grant. The distribution of the largess was often made difficult in that the claimants fell out among themselves and became jealous of each other. Particularly was this the case with the Protestants of the Vaudois. Divided in their political allegiance, these people were now widely scattered and those on the French side of the river Chisone had settled in Würtemberg. The latter frequently maintained that they were not receiving their fair share of the moneys collected in England, and they were particularly distressed in 1700, when they complained of the exorbitant claims which M. Herwart was putting forward on behalf of those still in Piedmont. So indignant were they that they sent their minister over to England, and he secured interviews with both Lloyd (Bishop of Worcester) and Tenison. The former championed their cause with his customary energy, maintaining "yt these men now in Wirtēberg land are as true Vaudois as those in Piemont [sic]". "Wt is the difference", he asked Tenison in a letter dated 27 December 1700,

"Onely this, yt while those Vaudois on ye other side of Chison still are suffered to continue in their Valleys, and are now only fewer in number than they were 15 yeares since, but otherwise in as good condition now as they were then . . . these poor men on ye French side of Chison now in Wirtemberg land have now more need of charity than they had when it was first given them by her Mt. of blessed Charity. Indeed I am of opinion that those Mins. now in Piemont ought to pay ye Charge of these poor men for the unkinde and unreasonable treatment they have given them".[2]

He suggested as a remedy "a speedy day for ye meeting [i.e. of the Commission] to order this money, yt ye poor men may receive it, and return to their families and friends that want them".

M. Herwart certainly seems to have been somewhat forceful in putting the claims of his own flock, for even the Vaudois

[1] Lambeth MSS. 1028.
[2] Lloyd to Tenison, 27 December 1700. Lambeth MSS. 1029, f. 29.

settled in Frankfort complained of his avarice and alleged that he had managed to deprive them and the Würtemberg Vaudois of the £1,500 which was their due.[1]

That the Commission did good work despite all setbacks may be seen from the following list of moneys which it allocated up to April 1700.[2]

1699	June 23 to	Brandenburg	..	£1,500
	July 27	Würtemberg	..	£1,500
	Aug. 10	Brandenburg	..	£1,500
	Aug. 31	Würtemberg	..	£1,500
	Nov. 23	Hesse Cassel	..	£1,000
	Dec. 20	Würtemberg	..	£1,500
1700	Mar. 11	Würtemberg	..	£1,500
	Apr. 16	For Vaudois and French Refugees to Plantations ..	..	£1,430
	Apr. 20	Würtemberg	..	£1,500
	Aprl 24	Würtemberg	..	£300
	May 8	Hesse Cassel	..	£250
	May 18	To assist voyage	..	£100
	Aug. 29	Würtemberg	..	£1,500
	Sep. 7	Hesse Cassel	..	£1,000
	Nov. 11	For Vaudois settling in Virginia	..	£2,000
	Dec. 19	Würtemberg	..	£1,500
1701	Apr. 22	Würtemberg	..	£500

This list makes no claim whatever to completeness, but it does give some indication of the amount of money collected in England, and the way in which it was distributed. By 6 March 1700, for example, £24,193 had been subscribed, and £8,500 distributed in relief, leaving some £15,693, which further grants by 31 August had reduced to a balance of £5,339. The help given proved a godsend to many refugees and was greatly appreciated, as a letter sent to Tenison from M. Jourdan at Frankfort on 28 November 1699 makes apparent. The grant was particularly opportune in this case, because the Vaudois who had emigrated to this town were quite penniless when they arrived there. "They brought nothing with them", Jourdan wrote, "and having arrived too late to sow anything, they have not been able to reap anything this year. It has been only by the means of charitable collections that they have existed and then only in a miserable way". They

---

[1] Lambeth MSS. 28 November 1699, 939, f. 2.
[2] Lambeth MSS. 1028, f. 1–47.

had been supported on their first arrival, Jourdan said, by bread and money given to them by the Elector of Brandenburg proportionately to their age and sex, and at the beginning of September they had received from M. Herwart the £1,500 which Tenison had sent from England, and this lasted them till the end of October. After this they were given a further £500 out of Tenison's next £1,500, and had anticipated similar treatment under the third allocation, but to their dismay, "M. Herwart thought otherwise". The letter concluded with an appeal for more assistance, and the information that the brethren would be meeting in conference on December 22–24 for the purpose of restoring faith and order, and that he would send a copy of their deliberations to the Archbishop.[1]

Settlement in Germany certainly had its difficulties, and as a consequence some of the refugees were approached with a view to settling them in the Plantations of America. Many were immediately attracted with the proposal, and at a meeting of the Commission on 3 March 1700, it was decided that "whereas several French and Swiss have left Switzerland and are willing to settle in the Plantations, it be ordered that £6 a head be allowed to every 500 of them willing to settle".[2] This resolution was confirmed by an Order in Council dated 5 March, and on 15 April instructions were given that Sir William Ashurst should be paid £1,200, "to be distributed among 200 of them at £6 per head, or to any lesser Number in proportion, when on shipboard, or in order to their settling in some of his Maj. Plantations". It was also agreed that £200 should be allocated for the purpose of building them a church with a resident minister, and in addition £30 "for a Bible and Comon Prayer Books and other books of devotion to be exported thither".[3] Sir William Ashurst's task was no sinecure, and he soon found it expedient to make a rule never to pay out money till the refugees were actually on board ship.

The records of the work of the Commission (those at Lambeth) cease in 1701, although it appears to have met for some time after this date. In the early part of this year the Commission was certainly still busy, and on 25 February it presented the King with a suggested allocation of its funds, which again included

[1] Jourdan to Tenison, 28 November 1699. Lambeth MSS. 932, f. 2.
[2] Lambeth MSS. 1028, f. 8.
[3] *Ibid.* f. 26.

grants to French settlers in New England.[1] A meeting was held as late as Thursday, 1 April 1703,[2] while in June 1706 Tenison was still negotiating for £6,000 to be sent out to Lord Raby, our ambassador in Berlin.[3]

The distribution of relief in the above manner did not, of course (as we have seen), do away completely with dissatisfaction, or prevent private solicitation. Typical of many others was a request sent to the Archbishop on 3 January 1701, from "the ancient French Protestants and Ministers banished from France". The burden of this petition, signed by twenty-six ministers, was that the allowance of £20 per person should be extended to include those over sixty years of age, since the old had been equally persecuted with the young.[4]

The country as a whole was made aware of the needs of the refugees through the general collections which were ordered from time to time. One such collection, for example, took place in 1702, and the Archbishop wrote to the clergy of his Province on behalf of those "who have willingly abandoned their Native Country and all their Careers in this World rather than sin against God and make shipwreck of the Faith and of a good Conscience". The Archbishop admitted that the present occasion was not the most appropriate time for a collection, owing to the havoc wrought by the late storm,[5] but "crying Necessities and extream Want", he urged, "cannot admit of delaies".

Tenison was always careful and systematic in the distribution of the monies collected, and when in 1706 £3,000 was allocated out of her Majesty's bounty "for relief and support of such poor distressed French ministers as are now residing within this Kingdom of England", he insisted on receiving a complete list of all those who were given assistance, in which the name, number of children, and the Church of each family were stated. Those relieved on this occasion were largely widows, and the inventory

[1] Lambeth MSS. 1028, f. 43. The suggestions were as follows: (1) "That £1,200 w'd be well applyed to the 12 Colonies of Vaudois, 6 settled in Würtemberg and 6 in Frankfort under 12 ministers". (2) That £5,400 be employed to build a temple and school for a colony of French Protestants and Vaudois settled in Usingen. (3) That £300 be allocated to the colony of French Protestants at Roshen in New England (£50 for present relief: £50 for next year: and £200 towards establishing an annual pension for the minister). (4) That £500 be set aside for a colony of French and Vaudois refugees who had emigrated to America.

[2] Lambeth MSS. 1028, f. 47.

[3] H.M.C. Portland MSS. II, 94.

[4] Lambeth MSS. 942, f. 167.

[5] Addison recalled this great storm in his poem "The Campaign", which dealt with Marlborough's victory at Blenheim.

distinguished carefully between widows of (a) "ancient ministers", (b) ministers ordained since the Revocation of the Edict of Nantes, (c) "widows newly come of ancient ministers", and (d) "young widows newly come".[1]

At times these French refugees proved an embarrassment to the Archbishop of Canterbury, particularly when there appeared amongst them some who claimed to be prophets and to speak with tongues. It was a phenomenon which Tenison viewed with dismay and suspicion, for it doubtless recalled some of the excesses of the Commonwealth period. He immediately represented to the French authorities what a "great scandall" these "pretended prophets" were to the cause of religion. The refugees themselves determined to put their own house in order: they held a meeting in London "and unanimously resolved to prosecute the said prophets to the utmost rigour of the law".[2]

Refugees continued to come to England spasmodically throughout the reign of Louis XIV, and in 1709 many German Protestants were forced to leave their homes in the Palatinate because of French aggression. To meet this new need, it was again decided to hold a general collection, and Tenison was made chief trustee.[3] He was very anxious that there should be a good response, and he supported the Queen's brief to the clergy of his own province with a letter of exhortation.

"You will herewith receive", he said, "her Majestie's Brief for the better Support and Settlement of many Thousands of distressed German Protestants, who through the repeated irruptions of the French, attended with unmerciful Exactions and Inhumanities, have been forced to quit their native country, the fruitful Palatinate near the Rhine. They have chosen to take Refuge here, being induced thereto by the Excellency of our Constitution and the Justice and Clemency of our Government".

The Church of England, Tenison continued, had always recognized the duty of hospitality, and the Queen herself "with a very tender Care and Regard hath Entertained these Poor

---

[1] Lambeth MSS. 941, f. 4.
[2] Luttrell, *A Brief Historical Relation*, etc., vi. 223.
[3] *Memoirs of the Life and Times*, etc., p. 109. The author here writes: "The following year, 1709, was remarkable not only for great Sums of money given by his Grace, to great Numbers of Poor People of his own Nation during the extremity of a very cold winter, but also his extensive Charity to the Poor Palatinates for whom he was the Chief Trustee, by Letters Patent to her Majesty, and whom he recommended to the Clergy of his Diocese".

Strangers and at no small Expense, sustain'd them by a present Supply, while the Good People in whose neighbourhood they have hitherto been, have comforted them very much by the Effects of their Humanity". Upon the clergy, however, rested this responsibility in particular.

"As to yourself", he wrote, "(together with the rest of my Brethren the Clergy of my Province), I do earnestly and in especial manner, recommend to you the Promoting of this good and necessary Work. I press you with fewer Words, because I expect from the Nature of your very Function, that you will use all your good Offices, in setting this deplorable Case in a clear Light in giving according to your ability; and in doing your utmost to stir others to a cheerful and liberal Contribution. . . . I am sensible that, in these and the like cases, divers Prejudices do and will arise from the Weakness of some, and the cunning Craftiness of Others. You will therefore do well, after mature Consideration, to open the matter judiciously and to show, as you have occasion, that the Increase of People is a means, not of Impoverishing or Weakening a Nation, but of advancing the Wealth and Strength of it".[1]

From this somewhat fragmentary account of what the Church of England, under the careful supervision of Tenison, attempted for the refugees, we may fairly claim that, on the whole, it was an example of good work well done. The money collected was distributed only after much thought and careful planning, and there was a genuine desire, on the part of those administering the funds, to help those really distressed.

The close communication between the various Protestant bodies, which this provision of relief made necessary, brought to the fore the question of union, which, in idea at least, remained dear to the heart of all members of the reformed Churches. In the early years of the eighteenth century this ideal became almost practical politics, the reasons for which may be briefly summarized. First, the successes of the Counter-Reformation placed the Protestant bodies definitely on the defensive. The avowed aim of the Jesuits was none other than the reincorporation of all the lands lost to the Roman See, and already much territory had been restored to the bosom of the Catholic Church. There is nothing so effective as a common fear to produce unity.

[1] *Memoirs of the Life and Times*, etc., p. 113.

Secondly (although this may appear at first to contradict the above), the reformed Churches were in some measure more consolidated internally in Tenison's day, and could thus begin to look outwards. They had never forgotten the universality of the Medieval Church, but so long as they were fighting for their very existence, they had of necessity to insist on the right to dissent. They were now free to work out some of the implications of their faith, although they possessed this freedom only within the framework of the national state which protected them. The fact that some of the Protestant Churches were forced to deal with the problem of dissent within their own communions, made them anxious to seek some wider union and thus to add to their own prestige. Thirdly, the very existence of a refugee problem inevitably tended to bring the Protestant Churches nearer together, particularly the English and German branches. When Tenison was sending out money to Brandenburg for the settlement of refugees in that country, he could hardly help being brought into contact with the heads of the Lutheran Church. Certainly many reformers on the Continent desired some kind of union among Protestants, and Leibnitz wrote to Burnet in 1698, suggesting that a small committee (Burnet, Tenison, and Patrick) should be formed in England to discuss their common faith.

A year later, Dr. Erastus Jablonski, Chaplain to the King of Prussia and superintendent of the Protestant Church in Poland, sent a letter to Tenison as Archbishop of Canterbury suggesting that they might consider together this question of a closer union. Jablonski was not unknown in England, having visited this country twice and residing some time at Oxford, where he had come to entertain a high regard for the English liturgy. Persistently throughout life he pursued two ideals: (1) A union of all Protestant Churches in Germany under the leadership of Prussia. (2) The introduction of the episcopate into the evangelical Church.

These and kindred schemes gained support in Prussia, and there is evidence that in 1700 a plan for some kind of union between the Protestant Churches was tentatively placed before the Archbishop of Canterbury. Among Tenison's papers at Lambeth there are two documents (with various transcripts) in part drawn up, in part corrected by the Archbishop, which outline the terms of fellowship. These two documents are substantially the same, and are both headed "A Declaration offer'd as an Expedient for

Peace between those of ye Augustine Confession,[1] & ye other of ye Reformed Churches". They consist of a series of articles, which the Archbishop has corrected, and to which he has added two different endings. We quote first an abstract of the articles in what we will call document A.

(1) We declare that the Scriptures contain all things necessary for salvation.

(2) "We declare against [this is Tenison's correction of 'we condemn'] all those that hold any other writings, or any unwritten tradition to be of equall authority with the Holy Scriptures".

(3) "We Profess to have a very high esteem [this is Tenison's correction of 'we own'] of the first Four general Councils and judge all things Heretick wch were declar'd so by any of them".

(4) "We declare against the Council of Trent as . . . managed by very bad arts".

(5) "For ye Books of ye new Testament we receive all those wch are comonly own'd as canonical by all Christian Churches".[2]

To the above Tenison has added in his own hand:

"We agree and declare that all those who subscribe the aforesaid Articles shall be received into ye lay comunion of all ye Churches of ye forementioned Confessions reserving to every Church the ordaining of its own ministers, and ye Exercise of these Rites and ye use of those Formes of Prayer yt they judge best for themselves, without reflexion on any other Churches. We agree and declare yt whatsoever Churchman or Laic shall either preach or write against Doctrine contain'd either in ye 39 Articles of ye Church of England or any other of the Confessions publisht in ye Book entitled Harmonica Confessio, He ought to be proceeded against as a disturber of the Publick Peace of ye Church of ye above mention'd Confessions, and as such to be delivered up to ye Agents of ye Prince or state to whose Church he has given such provocation in order to his receiving condyn punishment".[3]

The terms of this addendum are interesting. Each Church is to preserve its own individuality and orders, while the five articles are to be regarded as adequate only for lay communion. Mutual recrimination between the various bodies is to be avoided by a strong erastian policy.

[1] i.e. Augsburg.
[2] The apocrypha is said to be "for example of life and instruction of manners."
[3] Lambeth MSS. 932, f. 82.

Interested in these articles, and it would seem largely responsible for them, was William Lloyd, Bishop of Worcester, and we are fortunate in possessing his own thoughts on their terms of reference, and the safeguards which, he wrote to Tenison, "ought to be provided for in such a draught; yt it may passe, and yt it may do ye good yt is designed".[1] Lloyd was well aware of the difficulties confronting any such attempt at communion, although, as we shall see from the additions which Tenison added to the final draft, the Bishop of Worcester was prepared to make the common denominator of union lower than the Archbishop—that is, he would have asked less of those to be admitted into lay communion with the Church of England. Commenting on the scheme as a whole, Lloyd observed to Tenison:

"1. Yt it may passe, there ought to be no other Terms yn wt will be agreed to by all ye Churches concerned. 2. Care should be taken that they may be such Terms as will suffice for ye receiving of any Person into lay Comūnion in any of these Churches. I say only lay Coīō for more yn yt we are not to hope for and yt alone will suffice for ye Ends of this Union at pres^t. 3. Ye things we ought to provide against are chiefly these two. 1. ye dividing of us among o^rselves by affording such Terms to forein [sic] Protestants as will give occasion to ym yt seek it, for ye breaking of Comūnio. 2. ye laying of a stumbling block in ye way of those yt are well inclined to come over to us out of ye Roman Comūnion".

It was the fifth article, in Lloyd's opinion, which would occasion most opposition.

"There is only one thing in yt Paper", he commented, "wch I am afraid will be objected agst: that is ye last . . . concerning him yt shall write or preach against any doctrine rec^d in any of ye Reformed Churches. I am of opinion yt ye person so offending ought to be put under a Temporall punishm^t and not a Spirituall; but I doubt ye hot men, yt know how hard it is for ye men of their temper to keep within bounds, will open agst such an agreement yt they shall be delivered up to ye Agent of yt King or State whose Church is agrieved".[2]

We now turn to document B, which consists of ten articles, the last four of which are added by Tenison himself. The first five articles are substantially the same as those in document A, except

[1] Lloyd to Tenison, 27 December 1700. Lambeth MSS. 1029, f. 109.
[2] *Ibid.*

that for (5) we find: "We hold the Ancient Creed a true summary", and a sixth is added: "We declare against the Forma Professionis Fidei". Tenison's additions to this document are interesting because they represent a desire to prevent the Church of England seeking union with Protestant sects of a too extreme kind: that is, they seek to safeguard what we may call the more "catholic" elements of the teaching of the "Ecclesia Anglicana". We quote a summary of them as follows:

(7) "We profess our Firme adhaerence to the promises made by us in our name w^n we entered into ye Covenant of ye Gospell by Baptism, continuing to believe ye above sd antient Creed".

(8) We declare against all those who decline the practice of Baptism or regard it as unnecessary.

(9) "We profess that ye Sacrament of ye Ld's Supper is a standing ordinance in ye Church of Christ and a publick Memorial by wch Christians shew their Lord's death till he comes, as also that the bread wch they break and eat in ye ordinance is ye Comunion of ye body of Christ and that the Cup of Blessing we there bless and drink is the Comunion of ye blood of Christ and we promise (by God's grace) to endeavour to be meet and frequent partakers of ys holy Sacrament as God giveth us abilitie and Opportunitie so to do".

(10) We declare against those who maintain that the sacrament of Communion is "indifferent or unnecessary".

The significance of these additional articles is obvious, and seems to suggest that Tenison was not without his misgivings as to the wisdom of the proposed accommodation. The Church of England, he felt, must not be made free for those Protestants who (like so many sects during the Commonwealth) held a non-sacramental creed, but belief in the necessity of both baptism and communion must be the common faith of all those seeking union and not the idiosyncrasy of one body. There is reason to believe that it was document B which the Archbishop accepted as a basis for negotiation, since there is a fair copy of the whole in Latin amongst Tenison's papers.[1]

That Tenison should have felt it necessary to add these "catholic" articles, indicates the nature of the difficulties in the way of union. It might be thought that there could have been an agreement to differ, by which each body preserved its own distinctive features: but Protestantism was just as dogmatic as

[1] Lambeth MSS. 935, f. 22.

Catholicism on the necessity for credal affirmations. The problem for Tenison, as a practical man, was how to accommodate the Protestants abroad without losing the "high Anglicans" at home, for any agreement with "the brethren" on the Continent would be an empty triumph if it were achieved at the expense of dividing the Church in England. It was, in fact, the historical ethos of the Church of England which constituted an opportunity and yet a difficulty in the way of union, a fact which Burnet realized when, commenting to Tenison in 1702 on a scheme of M. Turretin's, he wrote: "God knows we are not at present united enough among ourselves to have much credit abroad".[1]

Hence all these ambitious plans came to nothing, and the failure of the efforts initiated in 1700 seems to have made Tenison more cautious than ever. Thus he probably remained quite unmoved when he received a letter from a French Protestant, M. Jurieu, suggesting that the English Crown should act as the general guardian of Protestant liberties.[1] Yet as Archbishop of Canterbury he corresponded with the leaders of most of the Protestant communions on the Continent, and expressed the most agreeable sentiments. As typical of the many letters which he received, we quote the following from M. Lortie, written on 26 August 1707.

"The Christian spirit of Moderation which has always been conspicuous in Your Grace as in the generality of English Divines, and the Station which by the Divine Grace and Providence You are placed in, make me most humbly to present you the following Address, which either I might not have the occasion to make, or could not so fully or so fitly express, any other way but this. The asswaging the greatest Differences and Controversies amongst Protestants, and evidencing that upon their common Principles they may and ought to unite, cannot but be esteemed an excellent Design and a most useful Work . . . Papists are indeed in the wrong, but the divisions of Protestants are not the more but the less excusable. The being guilty of Schism is reckoned in Scripture among the most damnable Sins, and was judged by the primitive Christians to be so heinous as not to be atoned by Martyrdom. Why do I mention these things, known to all, in all Parties among us? My Lord, it is to apologise for my having made it my chiefest business, since many years, to get into the greatest light the Protestant way of Union".[2]

[1] Burnet to Tenison, 15 August 1702. Lambeth MSS. 930, f. 31.
[2] Lortie to Tenison, 26 August 1707. Lambeth MSS. 932, f. 67.

It is unlikely that Tenison did more than acknowledge this letter with politeness, and express equally admirable sentiments as to the Christian nature of union.

With M. Turretin of Amsterdam, the Archbishop was on terms of some friendship, and in 1706 Tenison favoured him with a collection of his sermons. Turretin replied on 8 October with "a thousand thanks", asking that he might have anything else which came from the Archbishop's pen. He expressed himself, perhaps, a little fulsomely. "Je ne trouve rien", he wrote, "qui m'instruit tant, qui me donne si grandes idées de la Religion, ni qui fasse tant d'impression sur mon coeur, que ces excellents pièces". Turning to a more practical question, he said that as to a union of Protestants, the King of Prussia had a great interest in promoting it, and it would be a real inspiration if the Queen of England would take the leadership in a Protestant alliance consisting of the King of Prussia, the Elector of Hanover, and others of the north.[1]

These letters illustrate the responsibility which many continental "reformers" thought belonged to the Church of England as a "bridge-Church" in this matter of union, and mention of the King of Prussia serves to introduce us to the negotiations concerning a proposed introduction of the English liturgy into that country, towards which Tenison appears to have acted with even more than his customary caution.

Prussia, it must be remembered, numbered among its population both Lutherans and Calvinists, and this found expression at the coronation of Frederick in 1701, when he gave the title of bishop to the two assisting ministers, one a Calvinist (Dr. Ursinus) and the other a Lutheran. Frederick, a sincere Protestant as well as a statesman of ability, conceived the idea of uniting Lutherans and Calvinists in one public form of worship, and he thought that the English liturgy (itself compiled in order to include all Protestants loyal to the throne) might be the best means of doing this. To put his plan into execution, Frederick secured the translation of the English liturgy into high Dutch at the University of Frankfort, and then instructed Dr. Ursinus to write a letter to the Archbishop of Canterbury "to acquaint him with what had been done; and what was intended to be done, and to ask his Grace's

---

[1] Turretin to Tenison, 6 October 1706. Lambeth MSS. 932, f. 80.
On this question of union see also "Pensées d'un Théologien désintéressé . . . touchant la Réunion des Presbytériens à l'Église Anglicane", Lambeth MSS. 932, f. 76.

advice about it".[1] The king's intention, if the scheme met with
due encouragement in England, was to introduce the English
liturgy into his own private chapel and the cathedral church,
and to leave the other churches free, though at the same time
encouraging them to follow the royal example. By such a tactful
method of introduction, the King hoped to win over those German
Protestants who were for drawing up their own liturgy "lest
they should seem to acknowledge a dependence on the Church of
England by wholly using her services".[2]

Ursinus, meanwhile, wrote to Tenison in accordance with the
king's instructions in August 1704, enclosing two copies of the high
Dutch version of the English liturgy (one of which was for the
Queen) and suggesting that the leading ecclesiastics of both
Churches should correspond with each other. Tenison, usually so
systematic and conscientious, did not reply to this letter, and the
reason for this neglect has never been satisfactorily explained. It
has been suggested (though this hardly seems adequate) that it was
due to a "feeling of jealousy on his part of the Archbishop of
York, who had interested himself particularly in this matter, and
engaged the Queen's confidence more than any other prelate".[3]
Others have maintained that he "entertained so mean an opinion
of Ursinus that he refused to answer him".[4] Archbishop Potter
later declared that the letter of Ursinus never reached its destina-
tion, despite the fact that the King of Prussia was emphatically
assured that it had done so. Yet if this last explanation be true, it
seems almost impossible to believe that Tenison would not have
heard of it from some other source, particularly as the Queen
is said to have instructed Lord Raby, her minister at the Prussian
Court, to return her thanks for this sign of favour.[5]

The Archbishop's failure to reply, whatever the reason may
have been, was certainly a calamity. The position of those who
favoured the scheme in Berlin was made very difficult, and the
King frequently asked Dr. Ursinus "what answer the Archbishop
had given to his letter", remarking that he "greatly wondered"
at receiving no reply.[6] In these circumstances it is not surprising

---

[1] T. Sharp, *Life of John Sharp*, 1825, p. 406.
[2] *Ibid.*
[3] *Ibid.*
[4] *Ibid.* p. 407.
[5] Sharp, *Life of John Sharp*, p. 406. If the Queen's translation were enclosed
in the letter to the Archbishop, and the letter was lost, it is difficult to see how she
could have returned thanks.
[6] *Ibid.* p. 407.

that a number of German ministers began to feel that Tenison was not very enthusiastic about it; and Dr. Richardson, the eighteenth-century editor of Godwin's *De Praesulibus*,[1] states that this promising attempt at "inter-communion" broke down through the neglect and timidity of the Archbishop.[2] As an illustration of this apathy, he further relates that Dr. Grabe, a German minister, was sent to England by Frederick in order to obtain ordination, but that he was received so "frigidly" by Tenison, and had so many objections brought against him, that the project was abandoned. This story, as it stands, needs some correction, for Grabe came to England in 1697 and received priest's orders soon after, attaching himself to the nonjuring communion.[3] In 1705 he was in communication with Atterbury (then Dean of Carlisle) urging him to use his influence to bring the King of Prussia's scheme, and his own for consecrating bishops, before the Council; a fact which may well account for the Whig Archbishop's lack of interest in Dr. Grabe and suspicion of his episcopal experiment, particularly as Atterbury was making party capital out of the affair in the Lower House of Convocation by asking for "information on this subject".[4]

Archdeacon Sharp, in his life of his father, John Sharp, Archbishop of York (first published in 1825 and compiled largely from contemporary letters), refuses to place much belief in this and similar stories against Tenison, though he regards it as certain that the Archbishop of Canterbury was not favourably disposed to this scheme, which many in Germany were so anxious to promote. Sharp relates that Dr. Ursinus, when the delay caused by the

---

[1] It was Richardson who received from Archbishop Potter the story of the lost letter.

[2] Godwin, *De Praesulibus*, 1743, ed. Richardson, p. 167. See also Nichols, *Literary Anecdotes*, etc., viii. 250. Here a letter is reproduced from Godwin, a descendant of the antiquary, to one Hutchins, in which he maintains that Richardson in his edition of *De Praesulibus* "charged it upon him [Tenison] very hard", but "for the sake of a legacy of £100, and some evidence produced in favour of Tenison, he retracted what he had said, and the half sheet of his book was reprinted, giving a very different account of Tenison's conduct". The truth behind this story appears to be that Archbishop Potter, under whose patronage the second edition of *De Praesulibus* was published, informed Richardson of the lost letter, "and prevailed upon him to cancel the sheet containing the obnoxious reflections", so that "Tenison is only charged with negligence in the business". See Lathbury, *A History of the Convocation*, pp. 449, 450. Godwin also added in his letter to Hutchins that "Dr. Ayerst, who was at that time chaplain to our ambassador in Prussia, and personally applied to Tenison, usually related the affair to the discredit of Tenison".

[3] *Encl. Brit.* (9th ed.), XI, 25.

[4] Portland MSS. II, 157. Also Lathbury, *A History of the Convocation*, p. 401. In the former authority, there is a very interesting letter written by Grabe to Atterbury on 22 January 1705.

Archbishop's failure to reply became embarrassing, sent over to England "a man of strict veracity and honour in order that he might ask Tenison whether he had received the letter, and to desire him to write something which might be shewed to the King". The emissary could hardly have arrived at a more unfortunate time, for the Archbishop was then considerably agitated at a public pronouncement of a politico-religious nature issued by the University of Helmstadt. Tenison accordingly informed him that "the said letter had never come into his hands", but that he was unwilling "to write anything to Dr. Ursinus", because of the "scandalous report that was at that time spread of the University of Helmstadt having declared, in the case of the marriage of the Queen of Spain, that it was lawful for a Protestant to change communion, which, he said, was a reflection on all the Protestant Churches in Germany, and sufficient . . . to hinder his commencing a correspondence with any of them".[1]

Sharp sees in this incident a possible reason for the breakdown of negotiations, and this, he claims, is born out by papers sent to the Archbishop of York by Dr. Hobart; but for himself he is forced to admit that it seems "too trifling to be true".[2]

In estimating the importance of this story, we must remember that it was some four years previously that the King of Prussia had sent over the translation of the liturgy to England. Perhaps nearer the truth was the verdict of Godwin (a descendant of the antiquary), who, writing in 1767, says that he had been enquiring into "the conduct of Archbishop Tenison relating to this affair", and had satisfied himself on "good authority" that the Archbishop did not proceed with negotiations because of his "timidity and great complaisance of the Dissenters".[3]

It is significant that when the affair was reopened by Sharp (Archbishop of York), Robinson (Bishop of Bristol), and Jablonski, through the mediation of Dr. Ayerst, Chaplain to the English

[1] This declaration by the University of Helmstadt certainly occasioned much hostile comment in England at the time, and the *Post Boy* for 12 and 21 August 1708, was particularly violent. These two copies of this journal are missing from the collection of printed papers at the British Museum, possibly because they were seized by orders of the Government. So unfortunate was the impression created in England by this declaration that Dr. Fabricius wrote on 15 October to Dr. Andrew Snape "clearing the Academy of Helmstadt from some aspersions thrown upon them in an English Newspaper called the *Post Boy*, August 12 & 21, 1708, about a declaration of theirs"; and Jablonski wrote to Tenison on 27 October. Lambeth MSS. 941, f. 20.

[2] Sharp, *Life of John Sharp*, p. 409.

[3] Nichols, *Literary Anecdotes*, etc., viii. 250. The Dissenters would not have welcomed the introduction of episcopacy into a Protestant communion which had separated themselves from it.

23

ambassador at Berlin, Tenison appears to have taken no part in it. The time for union, he thought, was not yet, and the Church of England had too many internal problems to lead the Protestant Churches into the way of peace. As it was, the menace of Catholicism disappeared with the advance of the eighteenth century, while the passions engendered by the Thirty Years' War cooled down, and religious enthusiasm waned. Reason and the growing consciousness of the national state shifted the emphasis away from religion, and Protestant union no longer presented itself as a condition of survival.

Part II   The Society for Propagating the Gospel

Tenison's archiepiscopate has a permanent claim to grateful remembrance, in that it coincides with the definite emergence of what we may call a missionary spirit within the Church of England and its embodiment in institutional form.

The Archbishop himself was undoubtedly genuinely interested in the progress of the Christian Gospel in other lands, and it says much for him, when we remember his cautious temperament, that he encouraged Thomas Bray, right from the beginning, in his efforts to found the Society for Propagating the Gospel in Foreign Parts, declaring that it would be "of the greatest consequences imaginable". We cannot relate here the epic labours of Thomas Bray; suffice that the scheme was approved by the Lower House of Convocation on 13 March 1701, and that he appealed to the King in April, with the result that on 8 June a Royal Charter was issued under which the Society was incorporated.

The first meeting, over which the Archbishop presided, was held at Lambeth Palace on 27 June 1701, and the subsequent meetings for many years (till 1833) were held in Tenison's library at St. Martin-in-the-Fields.[1]

---

[1] There later arose some doubt as to the Archbishop's willingness to continue this arrangement, and on 30 April 1713, a motion was discussed for "providing a Proper Place for the several meetings of the Society". Efforts were made to acquire offices in Lincoln's Inn Fields, but Tenison on being consulted replied: "Brethren you are very welcome to me yourselves. For the Message you come about, seeing the prevailing Party has made so great a Progress in ye Affairs of the Library without asking my Opinion hitherto, I cannot well understand why they do it now, nor do I desire being very ill to give any opinion now farther than this: that as the Society was always welcome to my Library, so they may be still, if they think fitt". (S.P.G. Minutes.)

The Archbishop became the first President of the Society, and he was re-elected to this office annually.[1] He was thus enabled to keep in close and intimate touch with its proceedings, and he presided in person over fifty-three out of the two hundred and sixty-one meetings of the Society held during his lifetime. There can be no doubt that he was whole-hearted in its support, and it was to him in April 1702, that the Queen declared that she would be "always ready to do her Part towards promoting and Encouraging so Good a Work".[2] His interest can be seen in many small matters connected with the life of the Society. We quote a few typical examples.

Many missionaries complained that they were subjected to much ill usage while on board ship, and in May 1704 Tenison took up their cause and insisted that a full report be drawn up.

He seems always to have been foremost in nominating to the Society continental Protestants of reputation, and it was on his proposal that MM. Ostervald, Tronchin, and Turretin (21 May 1703) and M. Bonet (17 September 1708) were made members.[3] It was this connection which encouraged Turretin of Geneva to petition the Society on 28 December 1708, to use its influence to secure liberty for the Protestants in the valley of Pragelas, who had been subjugated by the Duke of Savoy. The Society was eager to do something, and on its recommendation Tenison, the Archbishop of York, and the Bishop of London laid the matter before the Queen.

There were times, however, when the Archbishop felt it necessary to restrain the zeal of the Society, lest it should compromise itself with the Government. Thus when in June 1709 it proposed settling the "poor palatines" in America and providing a minister for them, Tenison gave it as his opinion that "it was not proper to meddle therein till the Government had resolved how to dispose of it".[4] The settlement of these refugees in the plantations led to a great deal of friction between them and the Society's missionaries already at work there. The Archbishop was a man of peace, and he suggested to the secretary that "it might be proper for him when he writ occasionally to any of the Missionaries to exhort them to Temper and Moderation".

[1] It was not till 1882 that under a new charter the Archbishop of Canterbury was made *ex officio* President of the Society.
[2] S.P.G. Minutes.
[3] *Ibid.*
[4] *Ibid.*

The problems confronting the progress of the Gospel in America were certainly many and varied. The Society was eager to do something for the Indian nations "bordering New York", and in April 1710 four Iroquois Indian Princes (or Sachems) presented themselves in England. Tenison was particularly interested and he presided over a select committee at Lambeth which proceeded "to consider that part of the address from the 4 Indian Princes to the Queen which concerned propagating the Gospel among them".[1] This small committee, under the Archbishop's guidance, seems to have gone into matters with some thoroughness, and the resolutions which it drew up are worth quoting:

(1) The design of propagating the Gospel in foreign parts chiefly concerns the conversion of the heathen, and this must be placed first. (2) Itinerant ministers to preach the Gospel should therefore be sent amongst the six Indian nations. (3) "That a stop be put to the sending any more Missionaries among Christians except to such places whose Ministers are or shall be dead or removed, unless it may consist with the funds of the Society to prosecute both Designs".

The committee discussed the whole position relating to the Indians, and received much assistance from Colonel Nicholson, Governor of Virginia. Hence they decided to petition the Queen that the Society be allowed to send two missionaries and one interpreter to the Indians, and that a chapel be built at Tyndwrooghe, and a fort for defence. They added as a postscript "their just Apprehensions that the good desyns of this Society cannot be well carryed on for want of a Bishop to Govern the Clergy in the plantations; and that they are of opinion that the French Kings early sending a Bishop to Canada or Quebec has been one great successful cause of propagating the Popish errors among the Indians in those parts".[2]

The Indian Princes, meanwhile, were the talk of London, and their strange appearance gained them many entertainments which they enjoyed enormously. The Queen presented them with four Bibles, and their last act, before they left for America, in company with Colonels Nicholson and Schuyler on H.M.S. *Dragon*, was to send a letter to the Archbishop, dated 22 May, urging the Society to carry out its promise. The most urgent

---

[1] S.P.G. Minutes.
[2] *Ibid.*
[3] Tenison made the presentation on her behalf. See Luttrell, *A Brief Historical Relation*, etc., v. 576.

practical problem was to secure a suitable minister willing and able to work among the strange conditions of Indian life. There was much delay, however, due in part to the Government's reluctance to subsidize the scheme as it had promised, a difficulty which was eventually overcome by the Archbishop contributing £264 from his own purse. Nothing had been done by the time Colonel Nicholson returned to England in the following year, and the Sachems sent over another petition, dated 22 July. Finally, on 22 February 1712, Tenison announced to the Society that he had chosen Mr. Andrews for work among the Indians, he being of a good character, unmarried, and already familiar with the Indian language. Thus when Nicholson returned to America in 1712, he took back with him a present of twenty guineas and the following letter from the Archbishop, both for the Sachems:

"I have acquainted o^r most excellent Queen wth the contents of y^r L^r; and she is graciously disposed to promote ye good designe to your satisfaction. Yr excellencies will, shortly, not only hear of, but see with yr Eyes, ye good fruits of yr wise Application to her Royal Bounty. Our Societie, also, has had an account of what you have written and will not be wanting in anything towards ye success of that great Affair, the Propagation of ye true Christian Religion in ye regions of America and especially in yours. They now send you, in ye Quality of a minister in ye Church of England, Mr. Andrews, who is looked upon as very fitt for ye office of such a Missionarie. We are persuaded both that He will do his duty as becomes Him, and that you will give your Protection and Encouragement in the doing of it. I most heartily commend you to ye Protection of God".[1]

Andrews, however, by no means found his task an easy one, as a letter written to the Society from Queen's Fort on 25 May 1714, makes abundantly clear. The school which he had started was not going very well. The children soon tired of instruction, and the parents being "over fond" did not insist on their attending. He urgently needed another teacher, and to make matters more difficult, he was constantly being worried by the Dutch, because they resented his exposure of their selling rum to the Indians.

Andrews' subsequent labours are told at length in his reports to the Society, and a year before the mission was suspended in 1719, Governor Hunter assured the Society that his lack of success was by no means due to his "want of care or attendance" but

[1] Tenison to Sachems, 29 May 1712. B.M. Stowe MSS. 119, f. 73.

that from the first the "method would not answer the ends and pious intentions of the Society".[1]

A curious incident which concerns a bequest, and in relation to which Tenison appears to have acted in a rather arbitrary manner, may perhaps be included here.

Amongst the most munificent benefactors to the Society was Christopher Codrington (1668–1710), Fellow of All Souls', whose will contained the following clause:

> "Item, I give and bequeath my two plantations in the Island of Barbadoes to the Society for the Propagation of the Christian Religion in Forraigne Parts, erected and established by my late good master, William the Third; and my desire is to leave the plantations contained therein entire, and three hundred negroes at least always kept thereon: and a convenient number of Professors and Scholars maintained there, all of them to be under the vowes of poverty, chastity, and obedience, who shall be obliged to study and practise physick and chirurgery, as well as divinity, that by the apparent usefulness of the former to all mankind they may both endear themselves to the people, and have the better opportunity of doing good to men's souls whilst they are taking care of their bodies; but the particulars of the Constitution I leave to the Society composed of good and wise men".[2]

The above is taken from the original will in Doctors' Commons, but the words "all of them to be under the vows of poverty, chastity and obedience" do not occur in any printed copy whatever belonging to the Society, nor in fact do they appear in the copy of the will reproduced in the Report for the year the bequest was received—although they are of course to be found in the original conveyance of the property in the archives of the Society. All subsequent books and papers copy the terms of this first Report, so that by the time the actual conveyance was completed (1743),[3] it was quite forgotten that Codrington had intended his

---

[1] *Two Hundred Years of S.P.G.*, pp. 70–72.

[2] Burrows, *Worthies of All Souls'*, p. 340. We may notice that in March 1703 Tenison was elected president of the corporation for promoting the interest of religion in the West Indies, and gave a large sum of money towards the work. Luttrell, *A Brief Historical Relation*, etc., v. 166.

[3] There were many difficulties to be overcome before the S.P.G. finally entered into its inheritance in the West Indies in 1743. Colonel Codrington, a brother of the General, proved very obstructive, and on 18 October 1711, the Archbishop wrote a letter to the Society calling its attention to his "great Concern" for the "bad Condition of the Society's Affairs in the Barbadoes". He suggested that a special sub-committee be set up, and he himself presided over its deliberations at Lambeth.

professors and scholars to be a monastic body, observing the three-fold vows. The precise terms of the bequest, however, were apparently known to some people at the time of Codrington's death, for Bishop Tanner, writing to Dr. Charlett on 21 July 1710, makes the following observation: "I have since seen the clause in his Will relating to the propagation of the Gospel, where his ordering all his Professors and Scholars [at Barbados] to be under vows of poverty, chastity and obedience is very monastic".

It is natural to ask how this "monastic clause" came to be erased "so promptly and conclusively" from all the copies of the original will. "No debate, no motion, no legal opinion, no statement, appears either in the Reports, the Journal of the Board Meetings or the Journal of the Committee Meetings".[1] In the absence of any positive evidence, we are left to conjecture, and Professor Burrows, the historian of All Souls' College, makes the following suggestion: "The Archbishops of those days were auto-cratic in the affairs of the Society. Tenison, advised no doubt by the Lord Chancellor, or some great legal authority, simply scratched his pen through the clause, and took his chance as to the future. He chose to consider this as one of the 'particulars of the Constitution' left to the 'wise and good men of which the Society is composed'".[2]

Taking what he calls a "larger view of the case", Professor Burrows feels that the action was justified, since if the clause were retained, it "would have vitiated the whole bequest". "Whatever might have been possible", he observes, "in other times and places, any attempt to put the condition into execution at that time, and in the West Indies, would have been fatal; or at any rate, the Society may well have thought so. The difficulties they met with from all quarters were enormous as it was; but there was not the slightest element of sympathy with the 'monastic design', either at home or abroad, which could have saved the infant institution from shipwreck".[3]

Whether we regard this excision from Codrington's will as due to Tenison's personal initiative or not, it is certain that it could not have been effected without his approval. From what we have seen of the Archbishop's attitude to anything Roman, it seems quite in keeping that he should have acted in this matter on his

[1] Burrows, *Worthies of All Souls'*, p. 341.
[2] *Ibid.*
[3] *Ibid.*

own responsibility; nor need we be surprised that there is no reference to this somewhat irregular act either in his correspondence at Lambeth or in the archives of the Society.

The Archbishop left the Society under his will £1,000 "to be applied in equal Portions to the Settlement" of two Protestant bishops, "One for the Continent, Another for the Isles in North America".[1] As an explanation of this bequest, he declared that

"until such lawful Appointment and Consecrations are compleated, I am very sensible (as many of my Brethren of that Society also are) that as there has not hitherto been, notwithstanding much Importunity and many Promises to the contrary; So there never will or can be any Regular Church-Discipline in those Parts, or any Confirmations, or due Ordinations, or any setting apart in Ecclesiastical Manner of any publick Places for the more decent Worship of God; or any timely preventing or abating of Factions and Divisions, which have been, and are at present, very rife; no Ecclesiastically legal Discipline or Corrections of Scandalous Manners either in the Clergy, or Laity; or Synodical Assemblies [2] as may be a proper Means to regulate Ecclesiastical Proceedings".[3]

He laid down, meanwhile, that until bishops were appointed in America, the interest on the £1,000 should be devoted to helping infirm missionaries who had been forced to return to England. By the accumulation of interest, the capital sum increased to £18,730, which, invested in government stock, brought an annual income of £560. Under the authority of the Court of Chancery, this was later made available for disabled missionaries, and is now known as the "Tenison Pension Fund".

This bequest is not without interest since it shows Tenison's preoccupation with the anomalous position in which the Church of England found itself in America, due to the historical *milieu* in which its work there had arisen. "As early as 1634 a Commission was formed partly for the regulation of the spiritual and ecclesiastical affairs of the North American Colonies, under the control of the Archbishops of Canterbury and York, the Bishop of London, and others. In the same year an order of the King in Council was obtained by Archbishop Laud for extending the jurisdiction of

---

[1] *Memoirs of the Life and Times*, etc., p. 128.

[2] One might have thought that Tenison would not have been unduly disturbed at such a deprivation!

[3] *Memoirs of the Life and Times*, etc., pp. 128, 129. See also E. Calamy, *An historical Account of my own Life*, ii. 333.

the Bishop of London for the time being to English congregations of clergy abroad". Laud was anxious, however, to make a more satisfactory arrangement, and in 1638 he endeavoured to send a bishop to New England, but troubles in Scotland prevented the furtherance of the scheme. At the time of the Restoration, Dr. Alexander Murray (Charles II's companion in exile) was nominated Bishop of Virginia, and "a Patent was made out constituting him such", but the proposal again broke down through the failure to provide an endowment out of the customs. The creation of the Society for Propagating the Gospel provided the stimulus for fresh agitations to get something done, since the Society was generally regarded as "the most fitting instrument for dealing with this question". It is to the credit of Tenison, that though he proceeded with his customary caution, and insisted that the Society acted only on the advice of all the bishops,[1] he yet consistently supported its efforts, and took the lead in the negotiations with the Government.

The matter was taken up in earnest in 1703, and in its first report (1704) the Society "stated a case for the consideration of the law officers of the Crown", and asked:

(1) whether under the Act 2 Hen. VIII cap. xiii, the Bishops suffragan of Colchester, Dover, Nottingham and Hull might be disposed of for the service of the Church in foreign parts; (2) "whether the Archbishops and Bishops of the Realm would be liable to any inconveniences or penalties from the Statutes or Ecclesiastical laws should they consecrate Bishops for foreign parts endowed with no other jurisdiction but that of Commissary or the like"; (3) whether by the Act of Edward VI for the election of bishops, the Queen might not appoint new suffragans for foreign parts within her dominions.

The Society's efforts were now reinforced by a petition from fourteen missionaries working in New Jersey, dated 2 November 1705, begging that bishops might be sent over to them. The affair was entrusted to the President, Archbishop Tenison, who at the renewed request of the Society laid the matter before the Queen, who asked him to submit a plan. There seemed to be now every prospect of success, and the name of Dean Swift was whispered as the first bishop of Virginia. The Society even went so far in 1711 as to negotiate for the purchase of a bishop's house in Burlington, New Jersey, "in the sweetest situation in the world". In 1712,

[1] See Meeting 15 July 1709, S.P.G. Minutes, when Tenison would not discuss subject because so few bishops present.

on the motion of Lord Clarendon, the Society prepared the draft of a Bill to be offered to Parliament "for the establishment of bishops and bishoprics in America". But it was not to be. The death of Queen Anne came as a real tragedy, for though the Society went on with the scheme and petitioned George I on 3 June 1715, the Rebellion in Scotland, and the fear that many episcopal clergy were concealed Jacobites, led to its being shelved—and so successfully that it was not till 1787 that Charles Inglis was consecrated Bishop of Nova Scotia.[1]

The establishment of the Society for Propagating the Gospel, despite this failure, yet marked a great step forward in the regularizing and fostering of missionary enterprise. Its existence led bishops to encourage men to volunteer for service overseas, and to send their names to the secretary of the Society. On 15 September, 1710, the Society ordered that "when any person offers himself to the Society as a Missionary, particular and immediate notice be given thereof to the President", with his university and degree, as well as the time and place where the proposed missionary was appointed to read prayers and to preach.[2] Nor was this a mere formality, for the Archbishop's insistence on receiving these particulars arose out of his disapproval of the Society's choice in a case that had occurred a few months previously. In May of this year, the Society had accepted one Griffiths as "qualified" to be a missionary, the Archbishop being absent from the meeting when he was approved. As soon as he was informed, Tenison wrote to the Society asking it to do no more in the matter till he was present. It appears that Griffiths had published a pamphlet entitled "A serious and friendly Call to the Dissenters", a work in which the ever watchful eye of the Archbishop had detected "several unwarrantable Expressions in favour of Popery",—than which no offence could be more grievous in his eyes. When confronted with this charge before the Society, his Grace the President being in the chair, Griffiths stuck his ground and refused to admit any shortcomings in the pamphlet, with the result that it was unanimously decided that he "ought not to be admitted as a missionary".[2]

---

[1] Another bequest of Tenison's, perhaps worth mentioning, was his gift of a number of books to the proposed college at Barbados. These included six volumes of the polygot Bible; five volumes of Purchas's *Pilgrimages*; three volumes of the last edition of Foxe's *Book of Martyrs*; one volume of Thomas Aquinas; and three volumes of John Ray's *Catalogus Plantarum Angliae*.

[2] S.P.G. Minutes.

All departing missionaries engaged by the Society were required to wait on the Archbishop of Canterbury to receive his blessing, while the Bishop of London licensed them to the particular part of the Church which they were to serve.[1] Henceforth missionary activity became an officially recognized part of the task which the Church of England set itself, existing in its own right, and more or less independent of the progress of trade. Tenison did his best to keep in touch with this increasing responsibility, and he was often consulted by the Bishop of London on questions relating to the Church in America and elsewhere.

In 1697 he was called upon to arbitrate in the following case. James Blair (1656–1743), a Scotch episcopalian minister, obtained a charter in 1692 to found a college in Virginia, and he became its first President. Internal friction, however, and the hostility of Sir Edmund Andros, the Governor,[2] threatened to undermine its foundation, and complaints were made that Blair had (1) "filled ye Church and the Colledge with Scotchmen, and endeavoured to make a national faction by the name of the Scotch party", and (2) "misapplyed and squandered away money that should have gone to ye building of ye Colledge".[3]

On 27 December 1697, the whole case was argued out before the Archbishop at Lambeth, when Blair, his accusers, and the Bishop of London were present. For two hours Blair defended himself against his adversaries, until the Archbishop turned to the Bishop of London, and said: "Well, I think all the matters have been sufficiently discoursed. My Lord we must take time to consider what is fit to be done upon all this". The Archbishop and Compton showed clearly throughout the hearing that their sympathies were with Blair, and referring to the attempt of Sir Edmund Andros to get him out of his living, Tenison remarked:

"This seems to me a very strange way they have here, that their ministers are not inducted; but may be removed like domestick Servants by a Vote of the Vestry. Who would be a Minister in that Countrey? It must be a very pernicious thing, a minister will not know how to preach against Vice, but some

[1] A. L. Cross, *The Anglican Episcopate and the American Colonies*, p. 35.
[2] Sir Edmund Andros (1637–1714) was Governor of the province of New York (1674–81), New England (1685–89), and Virginia (1692–98), and was recalled in each case owing to disputes arising from the severity of his government. *D.N.B.* i. 411.
[3] Fulham MSS. Virginia Box III, 187.

of ye great men of his Parish may fancy the Sermon against him; and so make a faction to turn out ye Minister, tho' perhaps the sermon was made seven years before".[1]

It was only to be expected that when Tenison came to pass judgment, it was in favour of Blair. In gratitude the Archbishop was elected Vice-Chancellor of the College of William and Mary in 1700,[2] and Blair, writing from Virginia, thanked him for his "undeserved favours", to which, he said, "I owe my present tranquillity".[3]

Throughout the Archbishop's life Blair was a regular correspondent. On 29 May 1700, for example, he sent the following letter concerning the College library.

"I must upon this occasion beg leave to put your Grace in mind of your good intentions to help our Library to some good books. We are of opinion that if Application were made to severall good authors in England, they would enrich it at least with a present of their own books. And the Governors of the College have desired me to signify this much to your Grace that if you will employ any young Schollar there you think fit to ask books for us, we will allow him 20 pound a year for his pains. I have enclosed a Catalogue of what books we have on purpose that your Grace may the better judge what we want".[4]

Blair never seems to have found it easy to establish harmonious relations with the secular authorities, and it is not easy to recognize Sir Francis Nicholson (1660–1728), an able and conscientious colonial administrator, in the following description:

"He governs us, as if we were a Company of galley-slaves by continual roaring and thundering, cursing and swearing, base abusive Billingsgate Language to the degree that it is utterly incredible to those who have not been the Spectators of it . . . I do really believe since Oliver Cromwell there never was a man that deceived so many with a Shew of Religion, which is now turned into a mixture of the grossest hypocrisy . . . I doubt not when your Grace is well informed of the truth of the whole matter, you will have compassion upon us, a most unfortunate Church and People, and contribute your best endeavours for our speedy relief".[5]

---

[1] Fulham MSS. Virginia Box III, 187.
[2] Ibid. p. 143.
[3] Blair to Tenison, 29 May 1700. Ibid.
[4] Ibid.
[5] Blair to Tenison, 13 July 1702. Ibid. II, 78.

Sir Francis Nicholson, on his part, writing to Tenison on 28 July 1702, protested: "I humbly begg yr Grace to believe yt I hope in God yt nothing shall make me desert from endeavouring to doe my duty to my holy Mother ye Church of England, what lies in my power in all respects; particularly as to what relates to ye sd Clergy".[1]

Tenison himself, apparently, found Governor Nicholson by no means unfriendly to the work of the Church in America, and in 1710 Sir Francis thanked the Archbishop for "his Extraordinary Zeale both for Propagating the Christian Religion in America and for ye Civille Interest thereof", and particularly for his endeavours to procure resident bishops, without which "ye Church of England will rather diminish than Increase in North America".[2]

The provision that those working abroad should see the Archbishop before they set out gave Tenison an opportunity to make a personal connection, and thus to encourage the missionaries to send him an account of their work, and to seek his advice. Many responded and we quote the following examples.

On the remote island of St. Helena, there dwelt an English minister in the person of the Rev. Charles Marsham, sent out there by the East India Company, and in response to a letter of enquiry as to the state of religion there, the Archbishop received an interesting reply.

"No body professes any other here than the Church of England", Marsham wrote, "observing the same rites and ceremonies as are observed in England, excepting some few things wch ye nature of ye place will hardly permit. These are therefore to humbly request your Grace how these things that follow may be dispensed with; as first, they seldom will bring their children to be baptyzed in the Church alleging 'tis dangerous to carry them up and down the hills soe young, which are very sharpe and allways attended with troublesome winds and they generally Christen their children less than a week after they are born, and if I refuse to goe to their houses (tho' not upon ye account of sickness) to give them full baptism, they then neglect to baptyze them at all. I have therefore hitherto complyed with their desires, upon ye above mention'd considerations, but humbly beg yr Grace's orders and instructions for the future".

[1] Nicholson to Tenison, 28 July 1702. Fulham MSS. Virginia Box II, 103.
[2] Nicholson to Tenison, 22 May 1710. Lambeth MSS. 941, f. 24.

The writer then went on to say that a similar state of affairs existed as regards burial, and that in the past he had often been requested to bury people on their own plantations and had for the most part complied.

He then proceeded to ask the Archbishop's advice on the difficult question of marriage. The Governor of St. Helena, Marsham wrote, claimed that he was supreme in ecclesiastical affairs, and had instructed him to marry "without banns simply on his licence". If despite this he chose to publish banns, he had first to obtain the consent of the Governor. In the former circumstances, the betrothed pair were required to visit the Governor to obtain the licence, and he in effect married them before the church service took place.

"The Governor is a very good Man", Marsham admitted, "(a French refugee) and One for whom I have a great respect, and fearing lest I might disoblige him, either in refusing to obey his orders, or arguing the case with him, I have (And I hope with no offence to your Grace) hitherto complyed for peace sake, because I look upon the external Rites and Ceremonies of the Church not to be so absolutelie necessary in themselves".[1]

The general wisdom and charity of this letter would seem to suggest that the Reverend Charles Marsham had in him the stuff of which real missionaries are made.

The returning missionary was sure of a warm welcome at Lambeth, and Michael Glyd, minister in Barbados, was quite moved with the reception he received when he called on the Archbishop on 12 May 1700. When he returned overseas, Tenison sent out to him a parcel of books, and writing to the Archbishop from the island on 3 December, he thanked him as follows:

"I hope in the Lord Jesus that the Parting Blessing which you were pleased to administer to me, and your Prayers that you promised me in my Voyage, were to my great avail . . . I most humbly and most thankfully remember the great favour and honour of your kind Reception, that I had from yr Grace when I was in England, and at times waited on you".[2]

Mention of Barbados may serve to remind us that it was the fear of the slave owner lest the Gospel should prove prejudicial to his rights which constituted one of the hindrances to the

[1] Marsham to Tenison, 29 November 1705. Lambeth MSS. 929, f. 52.
[2] Glyd to Tenison, 3 December 1700. Lambeth MSS. 942, f. 165.

spread of the Faith in the plantations.[1] The biographer would like to record that Tenison questioned the owner's whole right to property, but the Archbishop so far as we know felt no such scruples. Rather he himself corrected and revised the terms of an Act of Parliament which declared "that no Negro or other Servant who shall hereafter be baptiz'd shall be thereby enfranchised, nor shall such baptism be construed to be any Manumission of such Negro or Servant".[2] And this Bill claimed to be for "converting the Negroes in the Plantations"!

We are reminded of the relativity of our moral judgments.

Requests of all kinds poured into Lambeth, and we may be sure that the following letter from "Theneriffe" found in the Archbishop a most sympathetic reader.

"The High Station Yo[r] Grace is in and the fervent zeale you have for the purest of Churches makes me as Consul of the Canarie Islands take ye Liberty in the name of his Majesties Subjects here to throw my Self at Yo[r] Grace's feet and implore yo. ffatherly care and Protection of some Persecuted Sones of the Church of England.

Yo[r] Grace will see the state of affairs wth us by what I have writ to ye Hon[le] S[r] James Vernon and considering how plaine ye 28th Article of Peace betweene the Crowne of England and Spaine and ye Cedula annexed to those Articles are to ye Contrary and ye Unreasonableness of Protestants being subject to such a Tribunal as even the Moderate Roman Catholiques themselves will not endure, we cannot doubt of Yo[r] Grace's readey assistance in so just and Holy a Cause.

We are confidant yt Prince who has so often Ventured his sacred Person in asserting our Liberties at home, will not suffer Us to lose them abroad. He that defended the Protestant Religion in General from being utterly Extirpated by a mighty King will not see a part of it ruined by so Illiterate a Clergie as the Inquisition here.

I once more beg Yo[r] Grace's ffatherly Care and Protection in this affair, and that our redress may be speedy and effectual some of us being already Prisoners for not submitting to ye

[1] The Fulham Papers abound in complaints from the missionaries about this.
[2] Lambeth MSS. 941, f. 72. In 1705 we find Tenison negotiating for the redemption of English captives from the Moors, the terms of which were as follows : For thirty-two English captives the exchange to be twenty-six barrels of powder and sixteen slaves; and for thirty-four French Protestants thirty-two barrels of powder, seventeen slaves and three thousand four hundred gunlocks. Portland MSS. H.M.C. II, 225. Also S.P.Dom. Will. III, 11 June 1700.

Inquisition and the rest daily Expecting it, and fearfull yt it may end in wors yn imprisonment: and what Effects this fear of so Unmercifull a Tribunall has had and may have upon the soules of some weak spirited Persons amongst Us, I humbly leave to Yo[r] Grace's Consideration".[1]

There are many indications that there was a quickened interest abroad at this time in the unique character of the Church of England. Luttrell reports on 3 March 1698, that "Sunday last the czar and his priests were at Lambeth house to see the Archbishop ordain a minister of the Church of England".[2] In 1700 it was proposed that some twenty Greek youths should come to England in order to be educated in the faith and practice of the Church. The following request sent to the King on 20 May 1700, on their behalf, is interesting:

"The true primitive religion so early and so long flourishing in the Greek Church, and so successfully propagated in other parts, hath for ages been exposed to the pressure of the Mohametans and the Romish imposture so that many of that distressed Church desire that some of their most hopeful youths should be brought over to England and instructed in the fundamentals of religion and learning, whereby at their return they might be capable to defend the faith: that it has been proposed that twenty such youths might be constantly receiving an education here (four and five yearly being sent back and so many others coming over) and some of these have already been received into Gloucester, who by their extraordinary progress have given the greatest hopes that the design will answer: and praying the King to receive the youths into his protection and to set apart a fund for this great work".[3]

On 23 August 1701, Luttrell reports again:

"A Greek patriarch is arrived here from Turkey with a considerable retinue, having letters of recommendation from the lord Paget [4] and Monsieur Collier the Dutch ambassador; he has been splendidly treated by the Archbishop of Canterbury, and designs to visit the two universities".[5]

---

[1] E. Smith to Tenison, 19 June 1699. Fulham MSS. Virginia Box. III.
[2] Luttrell, *A Brief Historical Relation*, etc., iv. 351. There seems to be no reference to such an ordination in the Act Books. See Chap. 6, p. 135, note 2.
[3] S.P.D. Will. III, 20 May 1700.
[4] William Paget, sixth Baron Paget (1637–1713), was ambassador to Turkey, 1693–1702.
[5] Luttrell, *A Brief Historical Relation*, etc., v. 83.

We conclude with White Kennett's tribute to Tenison's connection with the Society for Propagating the Gospel:

"He was the wisest Director and President of it; He put a Stop to many indirect Motions and Steps made to put us out of the Way, and prevented a great deal of Interruption and Embarrassment".[1]

[1] W. Newton, *Life of White Kennett*, p. 123.

CHAPTER 16

IRELAND AND SCOTLAND

Part I Ireland

THE story of the established Church in Ireland in the seventeenth century is by no means a happy one, for it is marked by changes both in its fortunes and personnel which reflect only too accurately the disturbed political life of England. The Anglican Church, it must be remembered, was in effect the State Church of Ireland, and remained until the nineteenth century the outward and visible sign of English political supremacy. True it is that Cromwell, during the Commonwealth, encouraged the Anabaptists and Independents, who under his rule numbered some seven-eighths of the ministers paid by the State, but this attempt to destroy the supremacy of the Episcopal Church was swept away at the Restoration, which led in a surprisingly short time to the collapse of these bodies. Their privileged position went at once, and the Acts of Settlement and Explanation restored property to all Episcopalians and Catholics who had remained loyal to the Royalist cause. In the general collapse of Nonconformity, the Presbyterians suffered as much as any, although they had consistently been faithful to Charles and greeted his return with enthusiasm. Thus the Episcopal Church, representing a very small percentage of the population and served by 500 ministers (whereas the Catholic priesthood numbered over 3,000), was restored as the only legal church in the island. The Catholics, it must be admitted, were granted (at times) a tacit tolerance, but that was all. It is not surprising that the Episcopal Church, placed in this legal position of privilege and ministering to so few—and these very largely among the more wealthy classes who found it profitable to conform—should soon fall into a state of degradation. Irish bishoprics were bestowed by the English Government, not as rewards for spiritual zeal, nor even to men of superior if selfish abilities, but as polite acknowledgments for services rendered. Clarendon wrote in 1660 of the Church of Ireland:

"The state of the Church is miserable; most of the fabrics are in ruins; very few of the clergy reside on their cures, but employ pitiful curates . . . I find it an ordinary thing for a minister to have five or six cures of souls, and to get them supplied by those who will do it cheapest. Some hold five or six ecclesiastical preferments worth £900 a year, get them all served for £150 a year and preach themselves perhaps once a year. When I discourse with my lord bishops on these things I confess I have no satisfactory answers!" [1]

His concluding statement is significant, for the bishops undoubtedly were the *fons et origo malorum*. Until some effort was made to secure resident bishops genuinely interested in the Irish people and of some ability and energy, nothing in the way of reformation could be expected. Bishops such as Thomas Hacket and Simon Digby (advanced to the episcopate because "he was a great master of painting in little water colours", and pleased the ladies) were hardly likely to leave a name behind them except for indolence and neglect.

The death of Charles II had its repercussions in Ireland, since James did everything he could to promote the Catholic cause and to weaken the Protestants. Richard Talbot, Earl of Tyrconnel (an extreme Romanist and a worthless profligate), was placed in charge of the army and he succeeded in ousting Henry Hyde, the second Earl of Clarendon, as Lord Lieutenant. Thereupon a thoroughgoing Romanizing policy was adopted as regards both the army and the corporations. The Protestant clergy, apart from being officially out of favour, found it difficult to maintain themselves, for tithes were frequently not paid and it was useless to sue for them. Many Protestants left the kingdom,[2] and Catholicism virtually became (as in justice it should) the established religion. How events would ultimately have shaped themselves, we cannot tell. James' flight to France, and his return to Ireland, where he made his last desperate bid for the throne and lost it at the battle of the Boyne, culminated in William's victory after the surrender of Limerick in 1691.

The accession of William led to the restoration of the Episcopal Church in Ireland to its former position. The Roman Catholics were the first to suffer, and it is to the shame of William (contrary to his own real interest) that he allowed the articles of Limerick to be in effect abrogated by the Act of 1697 passed in the Irish Parliament. The Episcopal Church, however, was in no fit

---

[1] Killen, *The Ecclesiastical History of Ireland*, ii. 161.
[2] Among these was Jones, later Bishop of St. Asaph's. See Chap. 10.

condition to reassume a position of privilege, as many honest observers could see only too well. Queen Mary, writing to her husband a few days after the battle of the Boyne, summed up its position somewhat cryptically: "Take care", she pleaded, "of the Church in Ireland. Everybody agrees that it is the worst in Christendom". "During the two preceding reigns", Killen writes, "patronage had been administered with little scrupulosity; and the veriest worldlings had, to a large extent, gained possession of the establishment. Pluralities abounded; so that many parishes had no resident incumbents"[1]—and all this in a country where two-thirds of the population were Catholics, and among the Protestants the Episcopalians numbered barely a half! To make the possibility of reform more difficult, the bishops of the Episcopal Church sat in the Irish House of Lords, so that no Bill could easily pass through this assembly without their support.

William, it must be admitted, was honestly desirous of doing something to improve the character and effectiveness of the English Church in Ireland, and he turned his attention in all earnest to this problem. His first act was to establish a Commission to deal with ecclesiastical affairs in this country, and it was on this body that Tenison, in company with the Bishops of London, St. Asaph, Salisbury, Chichester, Worcester, Oxford, the Dean of Canterbury (Sharp) and the Dean of St. Paul's (Tillotson), gained his first intimate acquaintance with Irish affairs. We quote as follows from the terms of the Commission:

"Almighty God having of his great goodness blest our arms with so much success in Ireland, that it is now almost entirely reduced to our obedience, we esteem it our duty in the first place, to provide for the settlement and the government of the Church there by such rules and orders as may most effectually encourage piety and promote the worship of God. For this purpose we have made choice of you as persons whose judgement, prudence & experience we are well satisfied, and do hereby require you to meet and consult of such means as may be most proper for attaining this great end. We recommend it particularly to you to consider of the ecclesiastical preferments in our said Kingdom, now void, and of all the persons best qualified to fill them in respect of duty, learning, and exemplary life, and fidelity to the discharge of their duty by a due residence upon the place".[2]

---

[1] Killen, *The Ecclesiastical History of Ireland*, ii. 183.
[2] S.P.Dom. William and Mary, 6 November 1690.

The terms of this Commission certainly indicated an understanding of the problem in Ireland. First and foremost, as a *sine qua non* of reform, there must be conscientious, resident bishops, eager to co-operate in any effort to cleanse the Augean stables. No Church could afford to have many men like Thomas Hacket, Bishop of Down and Connor from 1672–94, who, we read, "carried on a system of traffic in benefices with unblushing effrontery. The livings in his gift were sold to the highest bidder. For twenty years he was never seen within the bounds of his diocese; and as during all that time he resided at a place in the neighbourhood of London, he was commonly known as the Bishop of Hammersmith".[1] Such bishops must be eliminated. How long and effectively this Commission worked we unfortunately cannot determine: probably it went the way of most Commissions of this period, yet the mere fact that it existed and included such a personnel, doubtless proved of some benefit to the Church in Ireland. References to the Commission are few and not very illuminating, and the following letter sent to it is typical: "The King having requested you among other things to consider ecclesiastical preferments in Ireland, I [The Earl of Nottingham] am to acquaint you to take care particularly of the Dean of Waterford, and the Dean of Cloyne, Mr. Frank and Mr. King, as persons of whose merits, being very well satisfied, he [the King] is willing to prefer them".[2] The Commission, we may notice, dutifully complied and King, an ardent Whig, became Bishop of Derry in 1691, and Archbishop of Dublin in 1703.[3]

More important is the reference to the Commission in Simon Patrick's *Autobiography*. In this work the author states that the Commission met for the first time in the Bishop of London's lodgings in Whitehall when its terms of reference were read. They resolved upon one thing immediately (a very salutary step),

[1] Killen, *The Ecclesiastical History of Ireland*, ii. 283. Thomas Hacket, we may notice, was deprived in 1694 as the result of the findings of a Commission which visited the diocese of Down and Connor. Tenison, who had just become Archbishop of Canterbury, was appealed to by the commissioners lest "what we have begun with some success be made ineffectual by any powerful solicitation at Court or in Parliament, and that your Grace will extend your fatherly care to the Church of Ireland as well as England". See Lambeth MSS. 929, f. 40.

[2] S.P.Dom. I. William and Mary, 8 November 1690.

[3] King was certainly resident and interested in ecclesiastical matters, albeit a most violent opponent of the Catholics. His *magnum opus* was *De Origine Mali*, published in 1703. Among other appointments at this time, favourable to the interests of the Church in Ireland, we may note the translation of Narcissus Marsh to the Archbishopric of Cashel in 1691 and the promotion of Richard Tenison, a relative of Thomas, to the bishopric of Clogher in the same year.

namely, "to send home the Clergy in Ireland, who were here, to their respective curacies, if they lay in such places as were under his Majestie's protection". Three days later they met again, and "agreed upon such persons as were thought fit to recommend to his Majesty for Bps in Ireland". As to the subsequent meetings of the Commission, Patrick adds (and it suggests that the Commission soon took a secondary place): "several other times we met but I do not remember what was further done".[1]

The Queen herself, as we have seen, took a particular interest in Irish ecclesiastical affairs, and consistently used her influence to secure a higher standard in the personnel of the episcopate. For example, when Henry Sydney (1641–1704), who became Lord Lieutenant of Ireland in 1692, recommended a member of a prominent Irish family for a bishopric, the Queen "when she understood that he lay under a very bad character, wrote a letter in her own hand to Lord Sydney, letting him know what she had heard, and ordered him to call for six Irish bishops, whom she named to him, and require them to certify to her their opinion of that person: they all agreed that he laboured under an ill fame: and till that was examined into, they did not think it proper to promote him: so the matter was let fall".[2]

As part of this move to improve the Irish episcopate, a determined effort was made in 1693 to induce Thomas Tenison to go to Ireland as Archbishop of Dublin. He was then Bishop of Lincoln and had already shown himself able and energetic in this position: moreover, he had connections in Ireland, a branch of his family having settled there, Richard Tenison, Bishop of Clogher, being a relative.[3] On 16 November 1693 Francis Marsh, Archbishop of Dublin, died, and Tenison was approached by the Queen herself in connection with the vacant see. There can be no doubt whatever that the more conscientious of the Irish bishops were anxious that he should join them, and news of the offer soon got abroad. Tenison was placed in a difficult position, torn doubtless between inclination and what may have appeared as duty, and in this dilemma he wrote to his friend William Lloyd, Bishop of Lichfield, receiving the following reply on 19 December.

"For wt you say of ye Archbpric of Dublin, I confess it divides me between 2 when I think of it. On ye one hand to

[1] S. Patrick, *Autobiography*, p. 159.
[2] Burnet, *History of my own Time*, iv. 209.
[3] He was educated at Trinity College, Dublin. *D.N.B.* lvi. 56.

think of how much good you would certainly do, if God send you life and health in yt Kingdome, wch so extremely needs a good Primate and where ye Church does even languish for want of it: On ye other hand ye great good you do in this Kingdome, and ye much more that you may and will do if you live and continue in it. But I see an end of this dispute; if I know Mrs. Tenison, you must continue in this kingdome, for you cannot go out of it. I believe she would hardly cross ye water to Lambeth to see you Archbishop of Canterbury; I had written this before I thought of London Bridge. That way indeed she might foot it about, taking time. But there is no bridge between this and Ireland. Therefore I conclude you must continue in this Kingdome. But then for Ireland, ye well doing whereof in this matter is so great a concern to so many poor soules in yt Kingdome is also of so great moment to ye preservation of this. I doubt not you and others of o^r good Brethren have it deeply in your thoughts. I trust also for Sion's sake you will not hold your peace but speak freely, as God be praised you may, to their Maties. You neither need my advice, nor am I able to advise you, wt to doe or say. But to shew you I would if I were able I send you ye enclosed, wch seems to me to have things in it worth ye considering upon this present occasion. I beseech God to suggest to you, and to direct their Maties, as he in his infinite Wisdome sees best for these Churches and Kingdomes".[1]

Tenison found it difficult to come to a decision, and the matter hung fire for some time. Meanwhile rumours that he had accepted the Archbishopric began to circulate in Ireland. Richard Tenison, Bishop of Clogher, was naturally anxious that his kinsman [2] should come over, and wrote urging him to do so, but receiving no reply, sent another letter on 21 March 1694.

"Tho'", he began, "I have had many joyful letters from Dublin that your Lp is pleased at the Queen's desire to accept of the Arch Brick, yet till I hear that happy News from yrselfe, I can't be satisfyed for I know yr good Lady and other Relacōns wil dissuade yu from it, and both the Clergy and Laity of England will be grieved to part with so great a Blessing, and therefore I dare not urge it any further then I did in my last tho' I still have some hopes that yr great inclinacōns to doe good to our poor Church, will prevayl wth y^u to take it. And I doe

---

[1] Lloyd to Tenison, 19 December 1693. Lambeth MSS. 942, f. 57.
[2] The exact relationship of this branch of the Tenison family with the Archbishop is not known.

assure y^r L^p both Bps and laymen have wrote to me, that your coming would be one of the greatest Blessings that could happen to our Church and Naĉon, and never was any man so earnestly desired as y^u are for in you we think to have our famous Ussher and Bramhall againe, and that under yr Patronage and Government our Church will flourish more than ever".[1]

The Archbishop of Tuam (John Vesey) was even more pressing, and wrote three times to Tenison urging him to accept the Archbishopric.[2]

The Bishop of Lincoln, however, was not to be so persuaded. His "good lady", who appears to have been a woman of some character, and not one given simply "to obey", was obviously reluctant to cross over the water, and it is not uncharitable to suppose that Tenison himself did not want to go "into the wilderness". Considerations of this kind could hardly be stated publicly, nor were they, in fact, the only reasons for his refusal. To the Queen and others he found an excuse in the failure of the Government to do anything about the forfeited estates, a neglect of duty which led to the further impoverishment of an already impoverished Church.

This problem arose out of the following historical situation. During the reign of James II, Catholicism, as we have observed, was openly encouraged, and as a result many livings fell into the hands of Papists, who thus became legally seized of the glebe land and received the tithe payments. After the battle of the Boyne and the final defeat of James II these "Estates" were declared forfeited (although some Catholics were settled in them by the treaty of Limerick), but they were not returned to the Church, thus leaving many clergy permanently unprovided for. There had been many promises that something would be done, but without avail. At last in 1694 an Act came before the Irish Parliament which endeavoured to deal with this question, and Tenison let it be known that he regarded its passing (or some action by the English Government) as the condition of his accepting the Archbishopric of Dublin. "It is certain", White Kennett writes, "that when the vacant Archbishoprick of Dublin was offered to the Reverend Dr. Thomas Tenison, he requested this favour to the poor Clergy as a just motive to his Acceptance of it; that the Impropriations belonging to the Estates of Papists there forfeited to the Crown

---

[1] R. Tenison to T. Tenison, 21 March 1694. Lambeth MSS. 942, f. 64.
[2] See later in this chapter, p. 370.

might be all restored to the respective Parish Churches. And upon the Motion made to his Majesty, he was pleased to say that it was a reasonable Proposition. But some unforseen Difficulties arising it was not executed".[1] These difficulties might well have been foreseen, since they came both from the hostility of the Irish landlords, who set to work to secure the rejection of this remedial Act in the Irish Parliament, and from William's desire to allocate them to his Dutch favourites. On 24 February 1694, Tenison wrote to Tillotson, Archbishop of Canterbury, expressing his fears that "the Act was not likelie to pass", and adding: "If ye Act goes on, I go on with it".[2] It was necessary, however, that Tenison should give some semi-official explanation of his attitude, and he drew up the following "Memorial" in March, while the Act was pending:

"Some while since, he began to imagine that the Act touching the Forfeited Estates in Ireland, would not pass this Session. Yesterday he understood that there was little probabilitie of it passing in ye House of Comͦns, and less in ye House of Lords, many of them having claims to putt in. Ever since Hee considered this matter, he look'd upon ye Clause in ye Bill for restoring ye forfeited Impropriations to ye Church as ye main Spring of his Removal to Ireland, nothing of less fine being strong enough to resist ye Prejudices wch would otherwise obstruct all his Endeavours there, and render them less usefull then they might be here. He is convinc'd (as He finds others are) that this Act, if it does not now pass, will not pass in some Years, seeing, though a Vote of ye Nature was (if He well remembers) made two years agoe, the Matter then went no further; and now when ye Comͦns seem to be at a greater loss for Funds, the Bill moves not. It is true their Majesties have most graciously declar'd that They will do, in this Affair of ye Church what they can; and God forbid that ye high Indignitie of a Mistrust should ever be offered them. But the World do's not expect frō ye best and greatest of Princes what, in ye nature of ye Thing, cannot be done; and He is inform'd, by such as he esteems judicious and impartiall men, that nothing but a Clause in an Act of Parliament hath strength to bring about that wch He has his Eye upō as his onely Motive. He hath bin further assured (though not till within a few daies ago) that ye Glebe belonging to most of ye said Impropriate Rectories has bin long since swallow'd up, and is not to be discover'd; by wch means

---

[1] White Kennett, *The Case of Impropriations*, etc., 170 and 317.
[2] Tenison to Tillotson, 24 February 1674. Lambeth MSS. 929, f. 64.

ye value of what is desir'd for Churches and Scholes [1] is much abated. And, as to ye Remainder, wch consists in Tythes, the Claims wch will be put in, and wch will arise thereupō, will be exceeding many. So that, without ye Power of an Act to adjust such Matters, and sett them at Peace, He fears that Ministers will scarce be encourag'd to hazard their Charges and pains in going to Law. Wherefore upon these Considerations (as well as that of his ill State of Health, ye like to wch in one of his Predecessors, Bp Fuller, was increas'd in Ireland, and upō his coming in to ye air of England amended), He do's humbly hope and pray that their most gracious Majesties will not be offended, if He desires to stay in England, where he resolves by God's blessing to do ye best Service he can to God and their Majesties in his Station ".[2]

This "Memorial" was sent by Tenison to Tillotson, and, we may assume, found its way to the King and Queen. As will already have been anticipated, the Act did not pass, and since the King could not, and the Irish Parliament would not, deal with this problem, Tenison felt himself free (and doubtless welcomed the opportunity) to remain in England.

This question of the forfeited estates long remained a thorn in the flesh of the Irish bishops, and even occupied the attention of Jonathan Swift for a number of years. Bishop King, for example, wrote to Burnet in October 1696, complaining of this grievance:

"We immediately after the Victory of the Boyne", he said, "applied to his Majesty for them, that he would be pleased to restore them to the Church, for the maintenance of the Protestant Clergy, which is very much wanting where those impropriations are. We have been promised fair all along, but instead of giving them to the Church there are several . . . already granted to laymen, and we do understand the rest will be disposed the same way. We have made several attempts to prevent this, and the late Lord Capel undertook our petition, but his death prevented our knowing the success. . . . 'Tis hoped, if these things were laid before His Majesty, he would not refuse so small a request which is not one farthing out of his pocket or any courtier. If therefore yr Lordship could put

---

[1] Tenison had in mind "ye settling a University School upō ye forfeited estates". See Tenison to Tillotson, 24 February 1694. Lambeth MSS. 942, f. 64.

[2] Tenison's health was not good at this time, and we find him complaining to the Archbishop of "violent headaches" (ibid. 929, f. 64). William Lloyd recommended Tenison to consult a physician named Hobbes who is "so honest yt he does not leave himself any occasion to be sent for again". (Lloyd to Tenison, 17 December 1693. Ibid. 942, f. 57.)

your helping hand to further our petition, it would be a very great obligation on the Clergy here, and a real service to his Majesty".

Tenison, to his credit, did not lose interest in this problem when he became Archbishop of Canterbury, and he endeavoured (although unsuccessfully) to get something done. The circumstances of this attempt arose out of the many changes on the episcopal bench in Ireland in 1695, and the consequent "stocktaking" which this entailed.

The Bishops of Down and Connor, Cloyne and Ossory, and the Archbishop of Dublin decided to use the opportunity to secure the return at least of those impropriations "which were not yet passed away by any grant of his Matie's", and a petition was sent over to Tenison on 5 March 1695, asking him to intercede personally with the King.[1] Before anything could be done either by Act of Parliament or other means, it was necessary that the extent of such impropriations should be determined and the Bishop of Cloyne and Ossory wrote to Tenison "that the present value of ye forfeited Impropriations of Ireland which are not yet passed away . . . do not exceed six hundred pounds p.ā.", and that consequently he "could safely assure his Matie that they are much less than one thousand pounds p.ā.".[2] Despite Tenison's representations little was done, although in this year a Bill passed through the Irish Parliament dealing with impropriations arising out of the will of Sir Maurice Eustace. This Bill was brought over to England for the approval of the King, but so great was the apathy concerning Irish affairs (and the avarice) that it remained in the office where it had been deposited till Tenison made enquiries in 1697.[3]

And so the abuse of impropriations went on, and still the Irish bishops went on complaining. Again in 1698 Tenison received a document from Dublin concerning "his Maitie's late promise of grants of forfeited Impropriations to the Church".[4] This paper complained bitterly that when the Bishops petitioned Lord Capel, the impropriations were worth about £800 per annum, but that since this time many more estates had come into the hands of lay people and particularly to the king's commissioners of revenue. It was anticipated, the document went on, that more estates would

[1] Lambeth MSS. 929, f. 65.
[2] Ibid. 941, f. 94.
[3] S.P.Dom. 9 Will. III, 17 August 1697. 86 B, p. 315.
[4] Lambeth MSS. 927, f. 65.

come to the Crown through forfeitures and Tenison was therefore requested to use his influence to secure the return of all
impropriations to the Church; but nothing came of this fresh
attempt.[1]

We return, after this digression, to Tenison's refusal of the
Archbishopric of Dublin. It was some time before this became
definitely known in Ireland, and as late as 6 April 1694, John
Vesey, Archbishop of Tuam, a staunch if somewhat venal
Protestant, still hoped he would come and sent him the following
rather interesting letter:

"There is a report here, wch has much mortify'd the Bp of
Clogher, with whom I frequently correspond, as well as myself,
and many others, and that is yt yr Lordship still demurrs to
wt their Majesties and all good men desire, about yr succeeding
into this vacant see, where you will have opportunities and
abilities of doing ye greatest Good to this Church, at a time yt
it much wants somebody, yt has creditt at Court, as well as good
qualities; we still hope that Industrious and Publick Spirit wch
is yr character and Hon^r will prompt you to consider this, as a
call of Providence, and not suffer you to consult Flesh and
Blood. I hope you will pardon my forwardness in writing this
third time, without hearing from you, on this subject, since it
can proceed from no private interest, having declin'd all applica-
tions for myself, as soon as I heard yr Lordship nam'd in this
matter. We are told you find difficultys in ye forfeited Impropriations, wch we are sorry for on their Majestys' account, whose
enemies magnify on this occasion ye Piety of former Reigns; . . .
but those now forfeited are by the Articles of Lymerick so
few, yt they are scarce worth asking; I hope you will surmount
this obstruction in yr way or pass it by, and come without it,
for you will do much greater service in some more favourable
crises . . . My Ld. we are not only a part of Christ's Church,
but an Image of Yours, reform'd on ye same Faith and Worship
and Governm^t and every addition to our Establishm^t will
enlarge your own Bottom, and strengthen yr security. Scotland
is lost, and if Ireland be so too, how long will you dwell secure
. . . we hope yr Lordship and others will take some care of us,
for your own sakes, but you will never do it so well, as when you
are of us; we shall then hope to have our counsels more
comon and united, wch are now much divided by ye aspiring
of some to high places".[2]

[1] Lambeth MSS. 927, f. 65.
[2] Vesey to Tenison, 6 April 1694. *Ibid.* 953, f. 27.

This letter is particularly interesting in that it expresses the general feeling of neglect, which many Irish bishops felt very acutely. Tenison, maybe, found this letter rather uncomfortable reading, but he was not to be persuaded: "flesh and blood" did prevail, and Narcissus Marsh (1638–1713) was raised in his stead to the Archiepiscopate of Dublin.

Richard Tenison could not conceal his disappointment, although he was sanguine enough to hope that his kinsman might yet come out as Archbishop of Armagh.

"Yr Lp not accepting of Dublin", he wrote on 23 November, "was a very great grief and trouble to this Kingdom. We all looked upon it (as indeed it was) a very great misfortune to us, but we have still hopes to see y^u in Armagh, and that y^u will yet be a great Blessing to this Church and Na͞con for wch we know y^u have a great inclina͞con to doe all the good y^u can".[1]

Tenison's declining to go to Dublin certainly did not lose him the royal favour, for in January 1695 he was elected to Canterbury. There was general satisfaction in Ireland at this appointment, for it was believed that the new Archbishop would now be in a position to promote the welfare of the Church in that country. Sir Henry Ingoldsby (1622–1701) [2] expressed what most of them felt as follows:

"Nothinge could have bin better contrived to mitigate ye sorrowes off ye good people here, then their Majesty conferinge ye Succession off his See on yr Grace. . . . I congratulate yr honor therein and in earnest rejoyce at itt. And wish you (with all my heart) mutch happiness and longe Enjoyment off itt. I once earnestly desired to have had you setled [sic] in Dublin amongst us, but now am better pleased that providence has ordered it otherwise, since yt place wherein yr Lordp can doe much ye most good in, is most agreeable to your nature and most advantadgiouse to ye publike; mutch good might have been done heere, but mutch more wherein you are now fixed; However I hope you'll not forget us here, wherein yr good Word may helpe us and doe us service".[3]

John Vesey, Archbishop of Tuam, also conveniently discovered a providential ordering of things in Tenison's declining to go over to Ireland.

---

[1] R. Tenison to T. Tenison, 23 November 1694. Lambeth MSS. 929, f. 9.
[2] Brother to Richard Ingoldsby, commander of the king's forces in Ireland 1707–12.
[3] H. Ingoldsby to Tenison, 4 January 1695. Lambeth MSS. 941, f. 75.

372 LIFE AND TIMES OF THOMAS TENISON

"Yr Grace's Refusall to come into this Kingdome", he wrote, "was not a greater mortification to me, than it is now a satisfaction. The hand of that Good and Wise Providence is visible in it, wch often denys us in kindness what we desir'd with passion. This High Station in God's Church to wch yor Grace has been call'd with out yor own seeking, affords opportunities of doing good even beyond the sphere of yor imediate Presidency so yt we hope for greater Comfort from your Graces' Influence, than actuall Presence with us. I do therefore most heartily Rejoyce in his Majesty's Choice, for comon and disinterested reasons as well as for ye particular Affection & Duty wch I owe yr Grace, for many favours done to me".[1]

More significant was a letter from Narcissus Marsh (promoted instead of Tenison to the see of Dublin), a prelate who was sincerely interested in the welfare of the Irish Church, and one whom Tenison later described to the King as "a steddie Mā, and faithful to ye Interests of ye Government".[2]

"Your Grace's so generously undertaking to espouse ye concerns of this poor Church of Ireland", he said, "as there may be occasion, hath put new courage and hopes into me; who before was almost ready to sink into despair of ever seeing any great good done amongst us; since we were not much reformed by our calamities, but by ye late succeeding Manners certainly improv'd in Wickedness".[3]

Tenison's elevation to Canterbury certainly made it possible for him to exert an influence on the appointments to Irish bishoprics—that is so long as he himself remained *persona grata* at Court—though how far this influence extended it is not always easy to determine.[4]

The position which he was thought to hold (and the need for his guidance) may be seen in the following extract from an anonymous letter written to him in 1695:

"Since his Matie has been pleased to prevent this mischief for the future by making all promotions in the Church pass

[1] Vesey to Tenison, 25 January 1695. Lambeth MSS. 941, f. 77. The Archbishop of Armagh also wrote to Tenison on 9 February 1695: " 'Tis a great comfort and blessing to this poor Church of Ireland", he said, "to have so good a friend as your Grace placed so near the Healm, where it will be in your Grace's power to assist us from time to time". *Ibid.*, f. 80.

[2] Tenison to William III, 1 January 1698. *Ibid.* 930, f. 200.

[3] Marsh to Tenison, 9 February 1695. *Ibid.* 941, f. 97.

[4] As Bishop of Lincoln, we may note he had been able, on the recommendation of his kinsman, to secure the bishopric of Cloyne for Tobias Pullen (1648–1713). *Ibid.* 929, f. 9.

through your Grace's hands,[1] we have reason to bless God for
such an excellent constitution and to rest o^rselves secure against
all such further impositions, there being no danger now but in
their insincerity whom yr Grace is pleased to confide in and
lest they should prefere their own before the Church's interest
. . . It is certaine my Lord that the Church of Ireland is
under very unhappy circumstances at this criticall juncture.
The Lord Primate is with drawn from business and the others
that should are little mindfull of the Church's interest, so that
except yr Grace be kind as well as vigilant in relation to her
welfare she will probably suffer more in a little time then many
ages will be able to retrieve. The Essays of the late Parliament
(tho' they sat but a few moments) did plainly shew her what she
has to expect . . . But her happiness is this, that no act can
be proposed to her disadvantage here before it passes the
approbation of the Counsell of England, where yr Grace's
Patronage is her surest refuge wherein she may rely with
undoubted safety".[2]

The feeling that Tenison was genuinely interested in Irish
ecclesiastical affairs encouraged the bishops there to consult
him about the problems in their dioceses, and to recommend to
him persons for promotion, though not always with success. Thus
Narcissus Marsh failed to secure through Tenison the appointment
of Dr. Brown to the see of Dromore in 1695, Tobias Pullen,
Bishop of Cloyne, being appointed in his stead.[3]

A typical case of Tenison's care in recommending to appoint-
ments may be seen in 1695, when the bishopric of Down and
Connor became vacant through the death of Samuel Foley (1655–
95). A candidate much favoured in some quarters was Edward
Walkington, Archdeacon of Ossory (though Sharp supported a
Dean Davies), and his name was placed before Tenison. The
Archbishop, with characteristic caution, proceeded to make his
customary investigations, and consequently wrote to Narcissus
Marsh, whose judgment he valued, for particulars of Walkington's
character. The reply, dated 13 January, was somewhat disturbing,
and gives an interesting picture of conditions in the Irish Church:

"In obedience to your Grace's comāands", he began, "I make
bold to acquaint yr Grace that Dr. Walkington was well known
to me about 12 years ago, when I was provost and he ffelowe of

---

[1] The reference may be to the Commission (see Chap. 8, p. 167).
[2] To Tenison, Lambeth MSS. 929. f. 90.
[3] Marsh to Tenison, 9 February 1695. *Ibid.* 941, f. 79.

ye College in Dublin; then I am sure he was a man of very good natural parts, but very little improved by industry; He was a great company keeper, and consequently very seldom in ye college either at prayers or at other duties; and I thought him always to be of a negligent, lazy temper as appeared by ye careless discharge of any office he undertook in ye College. But whether in his company keeping he was given to drinking (if some of his companions would) or were any other way Lew'd I cannot say; more then to this one particular, That I was then inform'd yt he was Chairman of a Company of Wits (as they pretended) who made it their business to censure and ridicule every sober, learned and pious man who would not be like one of them".[1]

No appointment was made to the vacant see for a considerable time, but different pictures of Walkington were given to the Archbishop by the Bishop of Kildare, and Capel, Lord Deputy of Ireland, both of whom Tenison consulted.

The former sent over to England the following testimonial:

"This is to Certifie whom it may concerne that Dr. Walkington, Chaplain to the late House of Commons and now Archdeacon of Ossory is a person that both for his Piety, his Principles and his learning and behaviour well deserves the utmost Encouragement that can be given him; This I am able to Testify upon the knowledge that I have had of him for severall years past, and shall be glad of any other Opportunity to manifest this of him".[2]

Capel supported this judgment and wrote as follows:

"I have consulted severall of the Bishops as well as other persons and by the best Inquiry I can make I find that Dr. E. W. is most proper to succeed in that Bishoprick. He is a very excellent and constant preacher, of a good and sober life, and a man of great moderation and temper, which will render him the more agreeable to the Dissenters in the North where his residence has bin for some years past. He is likewise well related and beloved which will the better enable him to support his Majesty's Title to that Bishopric it being still contested by the deprived Bishop.[3] He was also Chaplain to the late House of Commons, and had as appears by their Journalls both their good will and that of his Exc. the late lord Lieut. And being as I conceive every way qualified to discharge the trust I think

---

[1] Marsh to Tenison, 13 January 1695. Lambeth MSS. 941, f. 65.
[2] Bp. of Kildare to Tenison. 942, f. 98.
[3] i.e. Thomas Hacket, see note 1, p. 363.

myself in duty obliged to recommend him to your Ex^{lies} and
hope he will be acceptable to his Maj. and therefore I desire
your Exc. will please that letters will be sent over in form for his
promotion".[1]

The tone of this last letter suggests that Walkington was very
much *persona grata* to the Government in Ireland, no matter how
much some Churchmen disapproved (he was certainly favoured
by the King),[2] and it is therefore not surprising that whatever may
have been Tenison's own private feelings in the matter, Walkington
was eventually promoted to the vacant see.

The real facts of this case and the way in which ecclesiastical
preferment could seldom be separated from political exigencies,
may best be seen in the following letter which Tenison wrote to
Sharp on 4 July 1695:

"I have had ye fav^r of yr Grace's & in It I found a L^r from
dean davies. That wch he desires cannot be done for my Ld
Capel insists so much upon ye preferring of Dr Walkington to
ye Bpric of Down and Connor that there will (I fear) be no
removing of dr. Ash at ys time. My Ld Capel being made a
deputy & Great things being expected from him in relation
to ye Parliament there, the King will be unwilling to deny his
Request".[3]

In some promotions the Archbishop's personal wishes may
perhaps be discerned, particularly when his relation, Richard
Tenison, was translated to the bishopric of Meath in 1697.
William was at this time on the Continent, and had left State
affairs in the hands of the Lord Justices, of which body the
Archbishop was himself a member. Upon the see of Meath becoming vacant, the Lord Justices of Ireland sent directly to the King
in Holland, asking him to appoint, an irregularity to which
Tenison called the attention of the Lord Justices in England
on 6 May 1697,[4] pointing out that it was "contrary to their instructions".[5] Having thus vindicated the powers of the Lords Justices
under the terms of their Commission, the Archbishop presented a
paper to them on 18 May in which he suggested that the Bishop

---

[1] Capel to Tenison, 28 May 1695. Lambeth MSS. 953, f. 32.
[2] Devonshire MSS. H.M.C. II, 718.
[3] Tenison to Sharp, 4 July 1695. Lloyd-Baker-Sharp MSS.
[4] S.P.Dom. Will. III, May 1697. Tenison was made a Lord Justice on several
occasions when William was out of the kingdom see: White Kennett, *A Complete
History of England*; in 1695 (p. 687), 1696 (714), 1697 (734), 1698 (755), 1700 (784),
1701 (825).
[5] See also Chap. 16, p. 365.

25

of Clogher (Richard Tenison) should be removed to Meath, and the Bishop of Cloyne to Clogher. If, the paper went on, the Bishop of Clogher

> "chose rather to continue in his own Bpr. as some imagined he would, then the Bishop of Cloyne should be removed directly to Meath and Dean Pooley be made Bishop of Cloyne, holding his Deanery in Commendam, because the Bishopric of Cloyne is but of small value. He would quit the Rectory of St. Michael's, Dublin, valued at £600 per annum, and that parish might then be divided into three according to the desire of all the inhabitants: there is but one Church on that side of the water, and there is no doubt that parliament will consent to it".[1]

Such circumstances, however, did not arise, for Richard Tenison, contrary to expectations, accepted the Bishopric of Meath, where he remained till his death in 1705.

Tenison, it is interesting to note, appears to have been in part responsible for disappointing Swift's hopes of preferment in Ireland, in return for which the Dean dubbed him "the dullest good for nothing man I ever knew". Swift was at one time chaplain to the Earl of Pembroke, Lord Lieutenant of Ireland, but when the latter was succeeded in 1708 by the Earl of Wharton, his position became doubtful since it was rumoured that this peer would bring his own chaplain over with him. The Archbishop of Dublin advised Swift to accept the appointment if it were offered him, but to prevent such a possibility "the low Church Archbishop Tenison" persuaded Wharton to take Dr. Lambert over in this capacity.[2] Likewise when the bishopric of Waterford became vacant some time later, and Swift's pretensions were "placed strongly before the Queen and Archbishop Tenison" by Sunderland and Somers, it was the Archbishop of Canterbury again who was in the main responsible for dashing Swift's hopes by securing the bishopric for a devoted Whig, Dr. Thomas Miller.[3]

One of the problems which particularly confronted the established Church in Ireland was the difficulty arising out of its relations with the other Protestant bodies, and especially with the Presbyterians, who represented about a half of the Protestant population. During the repressive régime inaugurated by James II all the Protestants in Ireland had more or less stood together

---

[1] S.P.Dom. Will. III, 18 May 1697. 6 B, p. 157.
[2] Forster, *The Life of Jonathan Swift*, 1875, p. 180.
[3] *Ibid.*

in face of the common attack, until the accession of William led to the dominance once again of the established Church, and the repression of the Dissenters—a policy which was the more disgraceful since the defeat of James II at the battle of the Boyne had been largely due to their efforts. William, moreover, publicly acknowledged his obligation to the Dissenters, and even before the battle of the Boyne doubled the *Regium Donum* which James had previously withdrawn. The Dissenters felt the position the more acutely, since as a result of the revocation of the Edict of Nantes many French Protestants began to settle in Ireland, and in 1692 these (together with other foreign Protestants) were authorized by Act of Parliament to conduct their worship "according to the several rites used in their own country".[1] In addition, numerous Scotch Presbyterians (attracted by cheap farm land) emigrated to Ireland, and began to meet openly in their presbyteries and synods.

On the whole, the bishops of the Episcopal Church in Ireland regarded this rise of Presbyterianism with dismay, especially since William on his part was anxious "to place them under a protection of a legal nature". A Bill to achieve this was in fact introduced into the Irish Parliament by the Earl of Drogheda,[2] and would have passed into law had it not been for their solid opposition to it in the Upper House.

Tenison supported the views of William rather than the prejudices of the Irish bishops, and he wished the established Church in Ireland to do nothing to offend the susceptibilities of the Presbyterians, but rather to establish friendly relations with them by a large-minded tolerance. He elaborated his views in a letter written to his kinsman, the Bishop of Clogher, in 1696, a bishop who seems to have been a strong opponent of the Presbyterians and much renowned for his "constant exercise of preaching, by which he reduced many Dissenters to the Church".

To this exhortation from the Archbishop, Richard Tenison replied in an interesting letter, dated 14 September 1696, from which we quote the following extract:

"I had ye honr of yr Grace's very obliging Lr in July last, and would not yet trouble yr Grace wt an Answer (it being a

---

[1] 4 Will. and Mary, c. 11. Irish Statutes.

[2] The Earl of Drogeda caused some anxiety to Narcissus March in 1697 by receiving the sacrament at Easter, not publicly, but privately in his Castle Chapel, thereby encouraging rumours that he was not friendly to the Church of England. The Archbishop of Dublin wrote to Tenison on 10 April 1697, urging him to exhort Lord Galway, when he came over, to receive the sacrament publicly. Lambeth MSS. 942, f. 133.

kind of Sacrilege to rob ye Publick of any of yr minutes) were it not to assure yr Grace, that I have been long of yr opinion and do think it our interest in this Kingdom, as well as our duty to avoyd all heats and divisions, as far as it is possible wth ye safety of our Church and Religion. That being secured, I am and ever have been as much for moderaçon as any man, And no man in my station has given greater demonstraçon of an easy and indulgent Temper than I have done, no Dissenters being troubled in my county, but for theyr imoralityes (from all over Ulster): in all other respects no man can be more easy to ym and I use ym wth all tenderness and respect in hopes to gain some of ym, wh I bless God I have done. But my Lord I am humbly of opinion (and after so many years experience I may pretend to understand something of this Kingdome) that eye should allways be kept over ym by ye Governmt., and that ye real numbers wch come dayly out of Scotland should be thought of in time, for they are not (as K. C. the first observed) to be hyred at the ordinary rates of Mercenaryes. But my hope is, if God send Peace abroad, a good Army (wch must allways be thought necessary for this Kingdome) will keep all in good Order, as it did in K. C. the seconds time. I might have been admitted into ye Secrets of State if I would, but I thank God I never had the ambiçon to desire it, but did what service I could privately, and gave wt intimaçons I thought necessary to those who were at the Helm and will continue to do so to yr Grace if you require it".[1]

This letter betrays a feeling, common to many in the Irish Church and perhaps justified, that those in England did not really understand the problems with which they had to deal. It must not be thought, however, that anxious as Tenison was to keep the peace in Ireland, and thus to prevent it becoming a happy hunting ground for Jacobite intrigues, he necessarily thought the blame was all on one side. He himself viewed with some alarm the growing strength of the Presbyterians in Ireland and particularly their openly meeting in synods. He therefore thought that a limit must be set to tolerance and that where the Presbyterians stepped outside the law, they should be legally (albeit cautiously) restrained.

---

[1] R. Tenison to T. Tenison, 14 September 1696. Lambeth MSS. 1029.

Some of Richard Tenison's letters to his kinsman strike a more personal note. We quote the following: "Pray give my good wishes and my humble service to yr good lady, whose kindness we must never forget, and to my cousin Faye, and favour me sometime with a line, that I may know how yu doe. I bless God I have had health this sumer to visit the Dioceses of Raphoe and Derry for my Ld Primat, and have had a Parochial Visitaçon through out my own Diocese, and to my great Comfort have confirmed about two thousand of the Scotch". Lambeth MSS. 1029.

Such a case occurred in 1698, when on 1 June John Macbridge, a minister from Belfast, preached a provocative sermon (later published in Dublin) before the Provincial Synod at Antrim. Macbridge, we should note, was not a resident minister at Belfast, but simply a Scots preacher who sometimes ministered to a private meeting. In his offending sermon (we quote Tenison's account) "he asserted a Power in ye Church of calling National and Provincial Synods, and the Obligation of their Acts, without the authoritie or ye sanction of ye civil Magistrate, tho' a Christian".[1] Marsh, Archbishop of Dublin, himself regarded such an open attack on the position of the established Church in Ireland as an affront which could not be tolerated and (again we quote the words of Tenison) he "feared very much that this will occasion heat at a time when he and others are using all possible means to dispose as many persons as they can to Peace and quiet this next sessiō of Parliament".[2]

Tenison determined that both the author and publisher of the tract, which attacked the very principle of an established Church, should be prosecuted at law, and he consulted the Lord Chancellor who upheld him in this opinion. Armed with this legal support, the Archbishop then wrote direct to the King in July 1698, acquainting him with the main facts of the case, and expressing his own and the Archbishop of Dublin's fears "lest ye Scots Presbytery in Ireland take a libertie of holding Synods [Conventicles] wch yr Maj. has not thought fit hitherto to grant to ye Episcopal Clergy . . . because yr Majestie having not during yr Reign called a Convocation in yt Kingdom and ye clergy having severally acquiesced in it, It will seem strange yt those who are not by law establish'd should instruct [?] upon a manner assuming to themselves a Libertie denied to those that are, especially seeing ye former challenge a Right Independent of ye Xtian magistrate as ye Non Jurors also do". Hence he concluded by requesting "that some notice should be taken by Yr Majestie of this illegal proceeding, so far at least, as to comānd yr Lds Justices of England to write to the Js of Ireland to examine into the Tract, and as they find a cause, to discountenance these practices by such methods of procedure as shall occur to them".[3]

Whether this step was taken we cannot tell: perhaps, as often

---

[1] Lambeth MSS. 930, f. 200.
[2] Tenison to William III. Undated 1698. *Ibid.*
[3] *Ibid.*

happened in cases of a similar nature, the whole affair came to nothing.

Tenison's archiepiscopate was not entirely an uneventful one in the history of the Church of Ireland, for early in the eighteenth century one of its most deeply felt grievances was removed when Convocation met in that country for the first time since 1666. Parliament, of course, had frequently been in session, and the clergy maintained that they should legally have been summoned to meet at the same time, a fact which led to a protest from the Irish Bishops in the House of Lords against what they regarded as the virtual suppression of their assembly. Complaints against this suppression were numerous although Tenison speaks in a letter just quoted of the "clergy having severally acquiesced in it". Thus on 5 October 1697, William King, Bishop of Derry,[1] wrote to the Bishop of Waterford:

> "I own a Convocation necessary and I had hot disputes about it in England; but all assemblies that have been long chained up, prove unruly when first let loose; and I am afraid this would prove in our present juncture a reason of abrogating them altogether; which I am afraid will happen, however, and if you have seen Dr. Wake's book against them, for so I reckon it that 'tis intended, you will be of the opinion that little less is designed".[2]

It was obvious for many reasons that Governments in the past had preferred a Convocation which never met, but in 1703 an agitation for its revival (supported by the Tory elements in England) began anew, and a petition was sent to the Queen.

The clergy in Ireland, or most of them, were enthusiastically behind the scheme, and they grew impatient when nothing was done, so much so that Narcissus Marsh (now Archbishop of Armagh) reported to Tenison:

> "The inferiour Clergy viz. ye Deans, Archdeacons and Proctors, who are come up from some parts of ye Kingdom (but four from my Province) to ye Number of between 30 & 40 in hopes of a Convocation, do begin to be somewhat impatient and troublesome, as yr Grace will find by ye enclosed Paper, yt they presented to me yesterday; after ye Arch Bps had at their request waited on my Ld [Lieutenant] to know if he had yet rec[d] any Answers from ye Queen to our Petition, who reply'd

---

[1] William King (1650–1729) became Archbishop of Dublin in 1703 and founded a lectureship in divinity at Trinity College, Dublin. See note 3, p. 363.

[2] Mant, *History of the Church of Ireland*, 1840, II, 96.

That he had rec^d none; but had written to her Majestie ye
night before to desire her Answer. There seems to be a great
ferment amongst ym on this occasion, for wch I am most
heartily sorry. We do all know this comes not from ymselves,
& I dare say yr Grace will easily divine from whence it comes,
without my hinting it to you. I pray God to endue men with
better tempers, and more calm dispositions, which were never
more wanting in this Kingdom yn now, wn we stand in most
need of them".[1]

The Queen, however, who was genuinely interested in the welfare of the Church and under the influence of the High Church
Archbishop Sharp, proved by no means unfriendly, and finally
declared herself in favour of once more summoning this Assembly.

Preliminary difficulties relating to procedure, meanwhile, began
to manifest themselves, and the Archbishops and Bishops of
Ireland were asked to submit precedents, while Tenison searched
the records at Lambeth to lay before the Queen what he could
collect there.[2] He reported on 25 June that he had gone through
his book relating to former Convocations, and that he was
surprised to find that there had been neither synod nor convocation since 1666. "There is nothing more to be found in Ireland",
he wrote, "wch is not contained in it, it being . . . by a person
who transmitted it to me some time since". The project was now
assuming concrete form and on 3 August the Queen wrote to the
Lord Lieutenant asking him for all the forms he could find relevant
to the summoning Convocation. Since this would take some time,
and Parliament was soon to meet, she regretted that she could
not at the moment do as the clergy desired, "however inclined
she was to favour them".

These events had their repercussions upon the Church in
Ireland. Narcissus Marsh, recently translated to the Archbishopric
of Armagh, feared lest William King,[3] his successor in the Archbishopric of Dublin, should place himself at the head of this
agitation for summoning Convocation, and thus try to challenge
his own authority as "Primate of all Ireland". Hence many
letters passed from Armagh to Lambeth in one of which Marsh
said he had met two Irish bishops who "have discoursed ye matter
with the ABp of Dublin, & fully represented to him that there is

[1] Marsh to Tenison. Undated. Lambeth MSS. 929, f. 39. See also R. Mant, *History of the Church of Ireland*, 1840, II, 96.
[2] S.P.Dom. Anne, 3 August 1703.
[3] For William King, see note 3, Chap. 16, p. 363.

no ground for his pretence of precedence and yt ye rest of ye Bps will as one man oppose it".[1] In another letter written over a year later he complained bitterly that the Archbishop of Dublin had left for England, and had declared publicly to the clergy of Dublin, without consulting any of the Archbishops or bishops, "that he would procure ye Queen's Licence for ye Convocation to act and do business". "I fear", Marsh observed gloomily, "yt we are not at this time in a temper to ask and obtain such a favour from the Queen unless all heats and animosities be laid aside, which certainly will prevent business as it had done hitherto". If the Queen should grant a licence, he continued, then he hoped "there would be no innovations in or by it", but that it would be directed as of old to the Archbishop of Armagh, "Primate of all Ireland", and "not be directed to ye four Archbishops by name, because an ill use may be made of it against ye Primate". "Ye presiding in Convocation doth of right belong to him", he said, and in particular he hoped that the licence would not be directed to the Archbishop of Dublin, on the pretext that Convocation met in that city.[2]

Despite all these difficulties, however, Convocation was eventually summoned. Its history lies outside the scope of this book, although we may notice, in passing, that Marsh wrote to the Archbishop of Tuam on 4 July 1705: "'Tis an uncomfortable thing that all assemblies of men can come to some conclusion and agreement, save clergymen; that all that have controversies can write with temper and humanity, only they treat one another with passion and bitterness".[3]

It will be seen that Tenison's archiepiscopate marks no new or striking departure in the life of the Irish Church, and that he left no outstanding impression upon it. It is true that Convocation was restored to life, but though he co-operated in this, he was not sufficiently enthusiastic to initiate it: his own experience of these assemblies may perhaps provide the explanation! What he did, however, was to keep in close contact with the life of the Church in Ireland, and to endeavour through his influence to secure that only diligent and conscientious men were promoted to positions of responsibility. He kept up a correspondence with most of the Irish bishops, who reported their activities to him and consulted

---

[1] Marsh to Tenison, 5 October 1703. Lambeth MSS. 929, f. 28.
[2] Marsh to Tenison, 16 January 1705. *Ibid.* f. 56.
[3] Quoted Relton, *History of the Church of England*, p. 205.

him about their problems. By his own concern, Tenison encouraged them to work together and to carry on with a task which was by no means easy, and he endeavoured, as with Lord Galway,[1] to make the English officials in Ireland sympathetic to the cause of the Church.

Perhaps the most regular of the Archbishop of Canterbury's correspondents was Narcissus Marsh, and his letters give a vivid picture of ecclesiastical life in Ireland at this time. In 1697, for example, he wrote to Tenison as follows, expressing his fears at the arrival of Toland, the celebrated Deist, into that kingdom:

"I wish we may speedily see him [i.e. Lord Galway] again (tho' in another capacity yn formerly) for ye good of this poor unhappy Kingdome, unhappy I have reason to call it on severall accounts but more especially I speak it now, because we have lately had come from England, one whose design seems to be involved [?] agst our religion, by endeavouring to draw men off from it. The persons I mean are one Toland (sufficiently known by his Book agst ye Mysteries of our Religion) who seems very busy in Dublin to make proselytes; and four Muggletonians come not long since from London to this city to set up for gaining converts; who I hope will find none of so little sense as to follow their senseless Doctrines; whom I will watch very narrowly to find if ye law can lay hold of it".

We conclude by quoting at length a letter sent to Tenison on 12 September 1706, when Marsh was Archbishop of Armagh. It may be thought that it paints a somewhat too rosy picture.

"Having finisht my Visitation of ye Province of Armagh I make bold to acquaint yr Grace in brief & in general wt condition I have found ye Church there. I informed yr Grace by letter from Raphoe in wt condition I found yt Diocese, and yt ye Bp thereof (after, by his frequent and publick talk he had rais'd an opposition in the Clergy of this Kingdome yt he would oppose me and had argued ye point (agst my power of visiting) with several of ye Bps, and mine own vicar general, who went to him to dissuade him from his purpose and y[t] more than once) yet appeared at my visitation and submitted without shewing ye least sign of opposition; for which I again return my hearty thanks to God Almighty and to yr Grace.

By all ye rest of ye Bps and their Clergy I was rec[d] with a great deal of respect and civility. As to ye state of ye Church

1 Lambeth MSS. 942, f. 39.
2 The book referred to is *Christianity not Mysterious*, published anonymously in London, 1696. It created a great sensation.

throughout ye whole Province, 'tis much better yn I did believe
or could expect. The number of Non Conformist indeed is
very great but withall ye Congregations of Protestants who
do conform (whereof I made particular enquiries in all places)
are more numerous yn I have found ym than in other parts of
this Kingdome where ye Papists are more numerous yn here;
haply because this part of it is best peopled.

Divine Service is duly and very regularly performed in every
Church twice every Sunday (and on holy daies) except in
some places, where ye Ministers serve two Cures, and in those
they generally serve one in ye forenoon, and ye other in ye
afternoon, and where ye Livings will bear it, I have enjoyned
those men to keep curates, yt each parish may be serv'd twice a
Sunday. And because in some parishes all ye Inhabitants (yt
are Conformists) and in others far ye greatest part of ym, live
at too great a distance from ye Church to come to morning
prayers, if they go home to dinner (they living 2, 3, and 4
miles distance from ye Church) in such places I have permitted
some (who practised it before) and enjoyned others (who did
not) to make a pause of half an hour or an hour, after morning
service and ye sermon is over (which never ends untill betwixt
12 and one of ye Clock) and yn assemble their Congregation
again, and read ye Evening Service and Catechise their
Children before they depart, by which means catechising will be
practised in every Church; as is done in most Churches already
throughout ye whole year.

In all considerable Towns, I have either found or enjoyned
Prayers to be read in ye Churches every day in ye week (indeed
in most of ym I found it done . . .) and in all other places
where any Conformists live near enough to ye Church, I have
enjoyned prayers to be read on Wednesdays and Fridays, where
I found it not done before.

Monthly Comunions in all Towns and quarterly in all
villages, I found mostly practis'd and where not, have enjoyned
ym, if practicable. But for ye use of ye Surplice I confesse 'tis
not generally practis'd thro' this Province, nor does it seem yet
seasonable to require it in all places at once, but may be
introduced by degrees, as I endeavour to do it in mine own
Diocese. For ye parishes will be apt to mutiny, if ye charge of
paying for a surplice should be laid on them in these calamatous
times.

Most of ye Churches (yt are necessary for Divine Service)
are standing and in tolerable good repair; others are rebuilding
and repairing apace, as fast as money can be raised, either upon
ye Parishioners or out of ye forfeited Impropriations.

Ministers houses are most wanting, which is great hindrance to Residence in this Kingdome, where convenient Houses for Ministers to dwell in are not to be rented or purchased. But (thanks be to God) this evill begins to be pretty well removed in this Province by ye Clergy a building on their Glebes: but how 'twill be effected in other Provinces, where ye Clergy have but very few Glebes to build on, God Almighty only knows.

As for ye Bishops, I myself have a large house in Drogheda, where I now am (but am forced to rent one in Dublin). The Bp of Meath hath an old hous within his Diocese, wherein his Predecessors lived, but he hath let it and lives in Dublin, attending ye Council, untill he can build one in a more convenient place. The Bps of Kilmore, Dromore and Clogher have built fair houses for ym & their successors; the Bp of Derry lives in a hous yt wil come out [of] ye see, wn ye lease is expir'd. The Bp of Raphoe carries on ye repairing his hous, wch was far advanced by his Predecessor, it having been burnt by ye Irish at ye time of ye late revolution. Only ye Bp of Down hath no house, but wt he Rents; but intends to build one.

Pluralities are not so comon in this Province as in others, by reason of ye number of Livings, yt may singly suffice to maintain a family, wch in other parts of the Kingdome are more rarely to be found.

And now upon ye whole, I must say, That in this Province (generally speaking) we have an able, orthodox, regular and diligent Clergy; the Bps having taken care to furnish their Dioceses with such men; and to sett all things in order therein by their Parochial Visitations, wch are yearly practised more and more. So yt I can safely say, yt this part of ye Church of Ireland is now in a much more flourishing Condition (I mean as to ye Religious part) yn it hath been for many years; and I pray God it may continually grow better and better, to wch care shall not be wanting.

I will trouble yr Grace with no more at present, but if there be anything wherein yr Grace desires further satisfaction, it shall be done to ye utmost of ye power of etc."[1]

If we compare this letter with Clarendon's condemnation of the Church in Ireland in 1660 and Queen Mary's in 1690, it certainly seems as if some progress had been made; and if this is so, then Tenison may fairly claim a share of the praise.

[1] Marsh to Tenison, 12 September 1700. Lambeth MSS. 929, f. 41.

Part II   Scotland

Tenison's relations with matters ecclesiastical in Scotland were inevitably different from those into which he entered with the Church in Ireland, since the Church of England was not established in the northern kingdom.

The accession of William and Mary was followed by the restoration of the Presbyterian form of government of 1592, and consequently by the abandonment of the Stuart policy of forcing upon an unwilling Scotland (though, perhaps, not quite so unwilling as frequently supposed) an established Episcopal Church. William's interests were not primarily religious, and his main preoccupation in Scotland was to prevent this country becoming a centre of Jacobite disaffection, although so far as was consistent with this policy he was not unwilling to do something for the Episcopalians. In the coronation oath he refused to swear "to root out heretics and enemies of the true worship of God", but "required an assurance that persecution for religious opinion was not intended, and himself made a declaration in favour of toleration". What the King really desired was to unite under his government all Protestant subjects loyal to the Revolution, and to leave to their individual consciences the question of religious faith. The practical problem, however, was a difficult one. After the expulsion of James II, the rabble of southern and western Scotland evicted as many episcopally ordained clergy as it could, and a proclamation by William could do little to prevent this. The King, in domestic matters at least, was a man of peace, and he was anxious to settle upon a formula of subscription which could be taken by all loyal Episcopalians. Thus he wrote personally both to the General Assembly urging it to accept all who signed such a declaration, and to the Episcopal clergy instructing them to make their addresses to this body, after which he would take them under his own protection. The Assembly, however, was more eager to revenge the past than to secure a tolerance of this kind, and it decided that only those Episcopalians should retain their livings who subscribed to the Confession and the Presbyterian form of government.[1]

No matter how intolerant they might be, however, no one could deny that the Presbyterians were intensely loyal, and that

[1] These events are described in detail (from the Episcopal point of view) in "The Case of the Episcopalian Clergy of Scotland". Lambeth MSS. 929, f. 20.

their legal establishment worked for the security of the throne. A few episcopally ordained ministers, who were willing to subscribe to the Confession of Faith and acknowledge the Presbyterian government of the Church, managed to retain their benefices, especially in outlying districts which remained Episcopalian in sentiment: and others officiated in private meeting houses; but the Episcopal Church, as such, was both unofficial and illegal. The position was the more complicated since it contained two distinct parties. One consisted of those clergymen who had taken the oath of allegiance to William and Mary, and were thus loyal supporters of the Revolution of '88. Their quarrel was not with the English Government, but with the Presbyterian Church: they believed in Episcopacy, and since they could not conform to the Kirk they fell under the civil and religious ban of the Presbyterian authorities. The other party, which included most of the Scottish bishops, and a majority of the Episcopal clergy, consisted of those who opposed both the Revolution in England and the Presbyterian form of Church government. These men could not in conscience take the oath of allegiance and they quite definitely associated themselves with the "King over the water", thereby falling under a legal disability in both countries.

Such, in brief, was the state of ecclesiastical affairs in Scotland when Tenison became Archbishop of Canterbury, and it will readily be seen that he was presented with no easy problem. As a believer in episcopacy, and yet a strong supporter of the Revolution, he doubtless experienced a conflict of loyalties. Certainly he could not view with any enthusiasm the eclipse of the English Episcopal Church in the northern kingdom: yet regarding the defence of Protestantism in England (and therefore the Episcopal Church of England) as bound up with the maintenance of the new dynasty on the throne, he could not fail to be cautious in helping a communion in which passive loyalty shaded off into open revolt. It was not a question of the Christian in Tenison being in conflict with the statesman, for religious and secular loyalties were in this matter linked up with each other.

Despite these complications, however, Tenison did feel that the Episcopalian clergy had not received a fair deal, particularly under the Act of 1693 "for settling the peace and quiet of the Church", which William and his representatives had wrung from a reluctant Assembly. He therefore determined to make their grievances known, and he drew up an extensive "Memorial concerning the episcopal clergy of Scotland", which he sent to the King and his ministers.[1]

In his paper he began by maintaining:

(1) That such Episcopal clergy as had taken the Oath of Allegiance, were still in livings (about 400), and prayed publicly for the King, should have further time given them to make provision for themselves and in the meantime should "be protected and preserv'd". (2) That the duration of this interim should be left to the king's discretion. (3) That since many Episcopalians complained that in the proceedings to which they had been subjected by the commissioners on the charge of "scandall", they had not been heard in their own defence, arrangements should be made for them to have a full hearing before they were ejected. (4) That "the Finance arising frō ye Revenue of ye Bishoprics and vacant stipends be methodized" as follows: (a) The revenue of the bishoprics (some £5,000) be put to the use of "such of ye Bishops who now lived in that Kingdom as are not disaffected and are in straits, if they address to ye King in Council or Treasurie or by either of his Secretaries to that purpose, tho' they cañot qualify Themselves according to ye Act June 13 1693 wᵗʰout degrading themselves". (b) "That his Majesty's Bounty may extend to ye Universities of Aberdeen and St. Andrew's, as It has done latelie to ye rest, for ye Encouragement of Professors". (5) "That ye vacant livings (wch are said to be about 200) be filled up with Good men as soon as it may be well done". (6) "That such as have been Rabbled out of their Livings (the nūber of which is said to have bin about 200) qualifying Themselves, be put into such vacant Livings as are any wise judg'd proper for them". (7) "That till They be provided for, they be supported out of ye above said fund, They and their Families being said to be generally in a starving condition".

Tenison then went on to enumerate the four complaints which the Episcopal clergy of Scotland entertained against the Act of 1693.[2] We quote them in full:

" 1. They profess that They scruple the Assurance by reason of some clauses in it (as they speak in a late Address) to them obscure and dark; But are ready to give all Assurances of their loyalty in playn words, and all such as are given by their Brethren in England and Ireland.

---

[1] Lambeth MSS. 929, f. 10.
[2] Under this Act "the admission of Episcopalians was provided for on their taking the Oaths of Allegiance and Assurance, and subscribing to the Confession of Faith and acknowledging the Presbyterian form of Government".

2. They scruple ye Subscribing to ye Presbyterian Government (settled by ye Act June 7 1690) as the *Only* Government of Christ's Church in that Kingdom; It not being said, the only legall Government in that Kingdom.

3. They scruple ye subscribing ye Confession as the Confession of their Fayth; It not being said that It contains the substance of their Faythe; but the phrase seeming to them to imply that it is a Creed, & that all its branches are of Fayth.

4. They scruple subscribing a strict observation of the uniformitie now practiz'd (as ye late Act requires) It restraining (they say) from using at any time in public the Lord's prayer, & the doxologie, & from repeating the Creed, or causing it to be repeated, in baptizing. And from Reading ye playnest chapter of ye Bible to ye People; the present Practice being Otherwise".[1]

This memorandum makes it evident that Tenison was anxious to do his best for the loyal Episcopalians, and that he regarded it as little short of persecution that they should be forced to forswear their belief in Episcopacy in order to secure a legal tolerance. His proposals, it will be seen, were of a purely *ad hoc* character, and made no effort to outline a really permanent settlement, capable of constituting a final *modus vivendi* for the Episcopalians in Scotland. The document was essentially an interim report: it was an endeavour to remove hardship, to prevent hasty eviction, and to provide for the necessities of those already "without visible means of support". As so often happens when memoranda are drawn up, nothing appears to have been done.

If to the Government Tenison was anxious to represent the cause of the Episcopalians in as favourable light as possible, to the Episcopalians he constantly represented the necessity of their taking the Oath of Allegiance. Only those not disaffected could hope for governmental protection, and it was the Archbishop's deliberate policy to prevent the Episcopal Church in Scotland becoming merely a Jacobite fifth column.

An illustration of this concern may be seen in the events of 1695. William III was at this time on the Continent, fighting a war which most contemporaries (and particularly Tenison) regarded as a Protestant crusade on behalf of the liberties of a free Europe. All eyes were fixed on his siege of Namur, and the attempts of the brilliant French commander Villeroy to entice William away

[1] Lambeth MSS. 929, f. 10.

by the victories of Dixmude and Deynze, and an attack on Brussels. Excitement and anxiety in England were intense, since a triumph for Villeroy might well have meant a Jacobite rising. Tenison anxiously scanned at Lambeth the letters which he received from Namur, and was reassured, perhaps, when on 15 August he received "great hopes of good success". London, however, was filled with rumours, and "early one morning it was confidently averred that there had been a battle, that the Allies had been beaten, that the King had been killed, and that the siege had been raised".[1] Events in Flanders, meanwhile, had their repercussions in Scotland, and Tenison was informed (though he hesitated to believe it) "that some of ye Episcopal Clergy . . . who had declared for allegience before dixmunde & deynse [sic] were destroy'd, did upō ye news of yt Treacherie, make a quick turn to a contrary way".[2] The Archbishop was deeply disturbed and immediately dispatched a letter to "Mr Secretary Johnstone", on this question of the allegiance of the Episcopal clergy in Scotland. James Johnstone (1655–1737), Secretary of State in Scotland, was a great friend of William as well as being an extreme and strict Presbyterian. As such he could hardly be expected to regard the Episcopalians with too friendly an eye, although Tenison had extracted a promise from him before he had taken up his office that he would use them "with wisdom and candour".[3] In his letter the Archbishop frankly related what he had heard concerning the conduct of some Episcopal clergy, though many he knew were "very consciencious". "Conscience", he observed, "do's not fall or rise according to ye weather of ye state,[4] and therefore . . . I hop'd that they do and will approve themselves very dutifull to ye establish'd Civil Government and give them demonstrations of their Allegience. I am sure ye King is not desirous to put hardships upon Them, and I hope they will not draw any upon Themselves, but be free both from ye Crimes and ye very suspicions of disloyalty". He concluded by expounding his own Whig philosophy, by reminding Johnstone of his promise, and urging him not to make Presbyterian capital out of the current rumours. "Certainly no Good to ye Church", he said, "can be expected frō a Popish Authoritie and no Peace frō having here two Kings at a time. For myself I depend upon yr

---

[1] Macaulay, *History of England*, iv. 594.
[2] Tenison to Johnstone, 20 August 1695. Lambeth MSS. 930, f. 205.
[3] *Ibid.*
[4] It did for numerous clergy in 1688!

promise that you will use them with w^d & candour; and doubt
not but yt They will be gratefully sensible of it".[1]

The suspense in which England anxiously awaited news was
now soon to be removed. On 26 August Namur surrendered and
all devout Protestants could breathe freely once again. Jacobitism
no longer appeared an immediate menace, and it is not surprising
that many of the Episcopal clergy in Scotland took the opportunity
to take the oaths, and others to reaffirm their loyalty in a
"Declaration of Allegiance" and a "loyal address to his Majesty".

Tenison thought it prudent to forget the past and he acknowledged this gesture in a letter of appreciation written on
28 November. It was a "great satisfaction", he said, to hear of
their expression of loyalty, and the King had received it "very
graciously". It would not pass unrewarded, he promised, since
"ye King will certainly give you his Protection whilst you continue exemplary Christians and good subjects", which, Tenison
added, "I doubt not but by God's Grace you will alwaies be".
He concluded his letter with words of fatherly advice: "Perhaps
there may be some ill men [2] who, being in other Interests, may
reproach you for doing yr duty, But if you suffer for well doing,
happy will you be, and ye shame, will, at least, rest upō yr
Enemies. For my part, I shall be ready at all Times, to do all ye
good offices I can in my station".[3]

It is certainly true that many of the Scottish bishops were
called upon to suffer, and Tenison was made painfully aware
of this in a pitiable letter which he received in the following year
from the Bishop of Glasgow. This unhappy man had been driven
by sheer penury to seek a haven in England, and he was thankful
to accept hospitality in the house of the Vicar of St. Stephen's
Church, Norwich. In these unfortunate circumstances, he wrote
to the Archbishop in June 1696, asking him to use all his influence
with the King to secure his return to Scotland so that he might
at least educate his children: in which country, he promised,
"my peaceable behavious shall be so exemplarie as to influence
such as I have influence upon to demean accordinglie under his
Majesty's Government".[4]

The Bishop of Glasgow's case was, unhappily, only one of many.
The accession of Anne, however, gave new hope to loyalist

[1] Tenison to Johnstone, 20 August 1695. Lambeth MSS. 930, f. 205.
[2] i.e. Jacobite Episcopalians who were in a majority.
[3] Tenison to Seton, 28 November 1695. Lambeth MSS. 930, f. 190.
[4] The Bishop of Glasgow to Tenison, 22 June 1696. Lambeth MSS. 942, f. 126.
26

members of the Episcopal Church in Scotland, for she herself was known to be eager to do something for them. The clergy accordingly petitioned her to move in the matter, and a Bill was introduced into the Scottish Parliament to grant a legal toleration to all loyal Protestants in Scotland, but once again the Presbyterian opposition was so strong and fierce that it had to be withdrawn.

The whole position of ecclesiastical politics was now changed by an event which represented the triumph of reason over the passions of centuries. Scotland, Presbyterian in religion, particularist in sentiment, and (in the north) Jacobite in allegiance, was united with England, Episcopal in religion, and Hanoverian in politics. Tenison was wholeheartedly and energetically in favour of this act of wisdom, and he, with Archbishop Sharp as the other Churchman, was one of the Lord Commissioners appointed on 25 August 1702, "to treat for the union between England and Scotland".[1] This Commission met from 10 November 1702 to 3 February 1705, but its proposals miscarried through the refusal to grant free trade between the kingdoms. In 1705, however, the English Parliament sanctioned the appointing of other commissioners (Tenison was again included),[2] and new officers of state were nominated from Scotland, with the result that fresh terms were agreed upon for submission to the Parliaments in both countries. Tenison attended the meetings of the Commission regularly, and signed the report "gladly". His High Church brother of York did neither. The debates in the English House of Lords on these terms of union began on 10 January 1707, when it soon became obvious that the Act was to have no easy passage, though the opposition was careful to divide only on subordinate issues. The position of the English bishops was beset with difficulties and was maliciously commented upon by the Earl of Nottingham (head of the High Church Tories) in his speech opposing the bill:

"I will venture my life", he said, "in defence of the Church of England . . . But if my Lords the Bishops will weaken their own cause so far as to give up the two great points of episcopal ordination and confirmation, if they will approve and ratify the act for securing the presbyterian church government in Scotland as the true protestant religion and purity of worship, they give up that which has been contended for between them and the presbyterians these thirty years".[3]

---

[1] S.P.Dom. Anne, 23 August 1702 : also *Memoirs of the Life and Times*, etc., p. 107.
[2] *Ibid.*
[3] Cobbett, *Parliamentary History*, vi. 564.

Such an attack had a certain sting in it, for it was not easy to see how the bishops in England could profess an attachment to Episcopacy as a necessary and divine institution, while at the same time seeking union with a country possessing a Presbyterian form which abominated it. Certainly their attitude seemed to make the relevance of Episcopacy depend on facts of geography. The Bishop of Bath and Wells (George Hooper) realized the difficulty and declared that the union came one hundred years too late and should have been carried through at James I's accession.[1] Tenison (it was typical of his statesmanlike approach) regarded the act as a political necessity and was himself largely "instrumental in obtaining the ratification of the Articles in the House", although four bishops in all spoke against the Bill.[2] As to his own attitude, the Archbishop stated clearly in the course of the debate that "he had no scruple against ratifying, approving and confirming it within the bounds of Scotland", since "he thought that the narrow notions of all the Churches had been their ruin, and he believed the Church of Scotland to be as true a Protestant church as the Church of England, though he could not say it was so perfect".[3] This forthright admission by the Archbishop was too frank even for some of the bishops who supported the Bill. The Bishop of Oxford (Talbot), for example, maintained that the Act no more sanctioned Presbyterianism than did a treaty with Louis XIV support Romanism. In fact, he argued, the union would be found to promote Episcopacy in Scotland, rather than Presbyterianism in England.

Tenison realized, however, that his position as Primate placed upon him a special responsibility so far as the "Ecclesia Anglicana" was concerned, and he brought in a Bill (to be appended to the Treaty of Union like the corresponding Act for the Church of Scotland) "for the security of the Church of England". This Bill "gave to existing Acts which protected the Church of England in her rights and monopolies, the character of essential parts of the constitution of Great Britain", but during its passage through the House of Lords it was subjected to criticism from two different quarters. Lord Wharton, taking upon himself to express the feelings of the extreme Whigs, declared with some irony that the Bill was completely unnecessary, since the Scriptures declared

---

[1] Cobbett, *Parliamentary History*, vi. 568.
[2] *Memoirs of the Life and Times*, etc., p. 107.
[3] Carstares, *State Papers and Letters*, 1774, p. 760.

that the Church was built upon a rock and was consequently unassailable. The Tories, on the other hand, complained that the Bill was entirely inadequate to achieve its purpose, and Archbishop Sharp, in company with the Bishops of Durham, Chester, and Rochester, entered a protest because they could not secure the insertion of the Test Act in its terms.[1]

The opposition to the Act of Union in both Houses of Parliament proved to be more vociferous than numerically strong, and it managed to secure the approval of both Houses.

More difficulty, it is interesting to notice, had been experienced in the Scottish Parliament, where Lord Belhaven and Fletcher of Saltoun rallied the nationalist forces with commanding rhetoric—but without success. On 6 March 1707 the Scottish and English Acts of Parliament, ratifying the Union, received the royal assent, and the first Parliament of the United Kingdom met on 6 November, preceded by a service of thanksgiving conducted by Tenison, in St. Paul's Cathedral, the preacher being the Bishop of Oxford.

One result of the Union, not generally much commented upon, was an increase in the use of the English liturgy in the Scottish Episcopal Church. Hitherto prayers had been either extemporary or fixed according to the Prayer Book of Charles I. Now there seems to have been a general tendency to adopt the English liturgy, and as early as 1703, before the Union, we find the book of English Common Prayer being used at Glasgow by a clergyman who had taken the oaths, though as a consequence his meeting place was attacked by a riotous mob. In 1707 the Anglican liturgy was introduced on a large scale into Montrose, Aberdeen, Elgin, and Inverness. The Presbyterians, as might be expected—it was a natural reaction against the Union—grew somewhat alarmed, and the General Assembly of 1707 passed an Act enjoining its members to instruct their people against such a form of service, and urging them "to use all proper means, by applying to the Government or otherwise, for suppressing and removing all such innovations, and preventing the evils and dangers that may ensue thereupon to this Church". Nothing, perhaps, better illustrates the anomalous position of the Union so far as ecclesiastical affairs were concerned, than this illegality of a liturgy in one part of the kingdom which was the legally established form in another.

A further result of the Union was a revival of nationalism in the

---

[1] E. Timberland, *The History and Proceedings of the House of Lords*, 1742, ii. 167. See also G. M. Trevelyan, *Ramillies and the Union with Scotland*, 1932, p. 283.

northern country which tended to make the position of the Episcopalians particularly difficult. This may be seen in the case of a minister in whom Tenison was interested. James Greenshields (an Episcopal clergyman, ordained by Bishop Ramsay of Ross after his deprivation) opened in Edinburgh a place of worship on his own account where the Church of England liturgy was used. As a result, he was summoned before the Presbytery in Glasgow but refused to accept its jurisdiction. His objection was summarily overruled, and he was prohibited from preaching on the grounds that he was exercising his ministry without the authority of the Presbytery and was introducing innovations in worship. Greenshields, who was a man of some spirit, ignored this prohibition and was promptly thrown into gaol. He determined, however, not to accept this treatment without protest, and he appealed to the Lords of Session pointing out that the Scottish Presbyterians in Ireland were granted a toleration; but this appeal was dismissed for the irrelevant reason that he had received his orders from a deprived bishop.[1] Greenshields now decided to take the case as far as he could (he was not without supporters) and he then appealed to the British House of Lords, where his appeal could not have come forward at a more opportune moment. A Tory ministry, High Church to the last degree, was in office, and it was anathema to them that Episcopalians north of the border should be subject to "persecution" from the Presbyterian authorities. It is not surprising, therefore, that on 1 March 1711 the sentence of the Court of Session was reversed and heavy damages were imposed on the magistrates who had closed his chapel. This legal verdict inevitably served to give an impetus to the demand for some alteration in the legal status of the Episcopalians in Scotland. There was talk of a Toleration Act, and others went so far as to suggest Acts condemning irregular baptism, and restoring to lay patrons their right of presentation to livings. It seemed to many Presbyterians as if the Caroline Anglicans were on the eve of using the United Parliament to undermine their establishment, and in their alarm they sent a deputation to London consisting of Carstares, principal of Edinburgh University, and two ministers, Thomas Blackwell and Robert Baillie.

[1] Narcissus Marsh (Archbishop of Armagh) wrote to Tenison on 30 December 1710, stating that Greenshields had asked him to write on his behalf to Lambeth. Marsh reported that Greenshields had been a curate in his diocese, where he had behaved himself very well, and that he had subsequently left for Scotland—since when he knew nothing of him. Lambeth MSS. 1028, f. 110.

Tenison could hardly remain a mere observer of these events, and it was in these circumstances that he drew up another long memorandum for the English Government under the title : "Some proper methods to propagate the English Liturgy in Scotland together with Loyalty to her Majesty and Security to the Protestant Succession".[1] In this paper he maintained that the Episcopal Church in Scotland must be granted a quasi legal establishment, if only to prevent it throwing itself into the arms of the Jacobites. Hence in the first part of the paper he considered "wt number of meeting Houses would be proper to be set up in Scotland, wch may be occasionally augmented, and how they may be supported". The Episcopal Church, according to this scheme, was no longer to exist precariously and irregularly, but was to be legally established in proportion to the numbers of the Episcopal population. Thus Tenison suggested, tentatively, that there should be six meeting houses in Edinburgh and one in each town in every shire, making some forty in all. As regards finance, £40 a year "for those who should sett up in Edinburgh and 20 everywhere else would be a good allowance together wth wt their Congregation would allow them"—all which would amount to about £920 a year. As to the raising of this money, Tenison proposed that the Queen be petitioned to allow those revenues, which formerly belonged to the Scottish bishops and had not been disposed of, to be used for this purpose. These moneys, he estimated would come to £700, but much more if an "Act of Resumption" in respect of these Episcopal revenues were passed through Parliament. The Archbishop felt confident that the Queen "could not refuse" such a request, particularly seeing "she allows £1,200 p. ann. to the Dissenters in Ireland who have no Toleration". The remaining £220 could be made up out of "the money wch is raised here in England for the support of the Scots Episcopal Clergy".

The Archbishop then proceeded to his second question, namely, "what qualifications should be required of those that are to officiate in them". Here he replied pointedly that "as to their Ecclesiastical Qualification" it should be "the same here as in England", and this would have the effect of promoting loyalty. As to their "Civil Qualifications" every clergyman in charge of a meeting house should be required to take the Oath of Abjuration, and although this would send the Jacobite Episcopalians further

[1] Lambeth MSS. 954, f. 32.

into the wilderness, it would remove the reproach of Jacobitism from the Episcopal Church as such. This taking of the Oath of Abjuration must be made obligatory on all, since "it would be very hard and unequal to demand it of them and not of the presbyterian Ministers that enjoy the Benefices". Such legislation he realized would not be sufficient of itself "to protect the clergy in the use of the English liturgy", for a recent case (namely, that of Greenshields) had made it plain that even "the Decree of the Lords of the Parliament" was not able to do this. Nor could loyal Episcopalians expect any protection from their own bishops, since these "now encouraged . . . [none] but professed Jacobites". To make their position finally secure, therefore, the Archbishop proposed that the Episcopal clergy should be protected by "an express Toleration", categorically stated, and that the "barbarous Law be rescinded wch enacts banishment to all . . . Episcopal ministers who baptize children".

Tenison then went on to discuss a problem which he said "most of all concerns the Safety of the C. of E.", namely, what attitude the Government should take to the Solemn League and Covenant. This document, drawn up in August 1643, represented the minimum terms on which the Scotch Presbyterians were willing to make common cause with the Parliament against the King, at a time when Parliament was in desperate need of such an alliance. To loyal Episcopalians it was the price of betrayal, the thirty pieces of silver. The Solemn League and Covenant declared that they (the Covenanters) were "to labour to bring the Churches of God in the three kingdoms to the nearest conjuncture and uniformity in religion, confession of faith, form of church government and directory for worship and catechizing. They were in like manner, without respect of persons, to endeavour the extirpation of Popery, Prelacy, superstition, heresy, schism, profaneness, and everything else contrary to sound doctrine, and the power of godliness". From this date the Solemn League and Covenant represented the ideal of the extreme Presbyterians, although when William granted their establishment as the state religion of Scotland, he refused to sanction this document as the expression of their faith, thus causing the Camerons (and others) to "lament the utter disregard of what they viewed as the chief triumph of their party". Had William wished to do so, he could not risk the alienation of his supporters in England, by giving his approval to a document which condemned Episcopacy in such explicit terms. Tenison, however, was not content merely to remove the offending document, but thought it might be "proper to insert a Clause in yt oath to be taken by the Clergy of Scotland [i.e. Presbyterian as well as Episcopalian] obliging them to renounce the Solemn League and Covenant in so far as by it they think themselves as much obliged as their Fathers yt took it (and actually put it into Execution) to reform the C. of E. in Discipline and Government to conform to their modell".

It is very doubtful how far this suggestion of Tenison's was wise, and some may see in it more of the old controversialist than the accommodating Archbishop. An oath of this kind would have revived animosities rather than brought peace, and might well have served to increase Presbyterian hostility against the Episcopal clergy. It was one thing to omit mention of the Solemn League and Covenant in the settlement; it was another to wring from the Presbyterian ministers an explicit denial of its terms, particularly as it had no legal status in the establishment. The former was prudent: the latter, though perhaps more logical, savoured too much of the ecclesiastical temper, which Tenison so often deplored in others. The situation arose, of course, from the nature of the Act of Union, by which formal consistency had been forced to give way to political expediency: that this Act became law at all was itself an indication that religious passions were cooling down and that the great age of reason was on the way. To Tenison, however (whose formative years had been spent in the latter half of the seventeenth century), the Solemn League and Covenant was no dead letter, but rather a potent factor moulding the attitude of the Presbyterians to the Episcopalians. "The reason" (for requiring a renunciation of the Covenant), he wrote,

"is plain. That the Presbyterian Ministers industriously keep up this principle amongst the people that the Covenant is binding upon them to this day and do oblige the parents att the baptizing of their Children to bring them up in that Faith, and Ministers at their Ordination to express their consent to that belief, yt the Covenant is binding upon them, and it is known that there are six ministers in Galloway and Nithsdale who actually have renewed the Covenant and receave none to the Sacra^{mt} but those yt doe. And att the Queen's accession to the Throne several presbyters entered into a new Covenant much like the former".

Tenison wished to extend this renunciation and the taking of the oath of abjuration (the latter was aimed at the Jacobite clergy more than the Presbyterians) to "all chaplains and schoolmasters whether of publick Schools or privately in Gentlemen's Houses called Governors or Tutors to their children . . . [since] it comes to pass yt the youth who had no being at the Revolution are as bigott as those who took the oaths to the late King James".

The Archbishop turned finally in his memorandum to immediate and contemporary events, and commenting on Carstares' [1] visit to London he remarked that he had come "as the Agent of the Kirk" to co-operate with General Wyhtman to prevent the sending of English chaplains to Scotland. The General, so Tenison alleged, had agreed to support Carstares on condition "that the Kirk should not prosecute the soldiers for imorality wch Mr. Carstares undertook they should not". It was Greenshields' anxiety to secure chaplains, he said, which had contributed to the hostility of the Kirk, and Carstares himself had vowed he would "provide an antidote for his poyson", to do which he had "convinced the Whigg Lords how unreasonable it was to send Chaplains seeing that they had not the liberty to send Presbyterians to the Regiments"—a statement which Tenison observed was quite false since "all the Scots Regiments in Flanders have Presbyterian Chaplains". The results of this policy on the part of the Kirk were lamentable, and as a consequence one Episcopalian general had already instructed his officers "not to submit themselves or soldiers to the Kirk discipline". The Archbishop concluded his paper (it sounds almost ironic) with the information that "Mr. Blackwell was come up to represent to the Queen the grievances of the Kirk, particularly the prodigious growth of the English Liturgy in Scotland".

This paper, as we have already observed, displayed more of the Churchman than we usually find in Tenison's memoranda, and it may in part reflect his growing isolation from the Court and consequent independence.

All the efforts of the General Assembly to preserve the *status quo*, however, were destined to prove in vain, and in the following year the principle of Tenison's paper was established by Act of Parliament. In 1712 a Toleration Bill was introduced into the House of Commons, and passed through this Assembly with a large

[1] William Carstares (1649–1715) was William's chief adviser in Scottish affairs, and was a promoter of the Union.

majority despite the remonstrances of the Scottish Commissioners. In the Lords it was subjected to a severe handling from the extreme Whigs (especially from Burnet) but became law on 3 March. This Toleration Act secured in effect what Tenison had argued for, in that it placed the Episcopal Church of Scotland on a definite legal footing, although it displayed a Caroline animus against the Presbyterians which the Archbishop probably did not share. It was entitled "An Act to prevent the disturbing of those of the Episcopal Communion in that part of Great Britain called Scotland in the exercise of their religious worship, and in the use of the liturgy of the Church of England; and for repealing the Act passed in the parliament of Scotland, entituled An Act against irregular Baptism and Marriages". According to its terms it became "free and lawful for those of the Episcopal Communion in that part of Great Britain called Scotland to meet and assemble for the exercise of divine worship, to be performed after their own manner by pastors ordained by protestant bishops, and who are now established ministers of any church or parish; and to use in their congregations the liturgy of the Church of England, if they think fit, without any let, hindrance or disturbance from any person whatsoever". All clergy both Presbyterian and Episcopal were expressly enjoined, as the Archbishop had proposed, to take the oaths of allegiance and abjuration, and to pray explicitly during divine service for the Queen, the Princess Sophia, and her heirs, as established in the Act of Succession. Tenison does not appear to have been present in the House when the Bill was discussed. Ill health confined him to Lambeth, and thus prevented his attendance at a debate, which in some respects might have been a little embarrassing for him: to Burnet, it may well be, his absence was not unwelcome.

CHAPTER 17

THE HANOVERIAN SUCCESSION

THE accession of William and Mary, after the flight of James II, placed Tenison definitely within the circle of royal favour, and we have seen in an earlier chapter how he became Archdeacon of London in 1689, Bishop of Lincoln in 1692, and Archbishop of Canterbury in 1694/5.

His relations with the two monarchs were inevitably of a close if not intimate nature. All three were sincere Protestants, and Tenison had from the first championed their cause, and laboured on their behalf. Interest as well as common sentiment thus united the throne with a devoted servant who, though maybe lacking in some of the graces,[1] was yet eminent for his loyalty. Tenison, despite occasional weakness,[2] acted on his part towards the King and Queen with a frankness which, although it never seems to have won their affection, yet had as its end the welfare of their persons and the security of their throne. Tenison frequently preached before the Royal Household both at Whitehall and Kensington, as, for example, on Easter Day 1694, when (being then Bishop of Lincoln) he delivered a sermon on the celestial body, and warned his congregation that "the impenitent sinner hopes against all grounds of Hope, if he has expectations of seeing God face to face with Eyes which have been full of adultery".[3]

Mary endeavoured to compensate in her own life for the lack of religious ardour in William, and in the end her constant virtue and affection won the heart of a husband whose response was as cold as his infidelities were frequent. She was not long, however, to endure them. On 20 December 1694, Mary complained of feeling unwell and took to her bed. On the 22nd she seemed better, but on Christmas Day the physicians agreed that she was suffering from a virulent attack of smallpox. The King's grief, so Burnet tells us, was "excessive", and sympathetic crowds blocked all the approaches to Kensington Palace. Tenison was in constant

---

[1] Thomas Bruce, Earl of Ailesbury (*Memoirs*, 1890), complains of his country manner of speech.
[2] See Chap. 8, pp. 172–6.
[3] Tenison, "A Sermon concerning the Celestial Body", 1694, p. 24.

attendance on the royal invalid, and it was from his hand that she received the Sacrament on the day before she died.[1]

William certainly appears to have been genuinely distressed at the death of his wife (she was only thirty-two), perhaps the more so because he had treated her with scant attention, often

[1] Perhaps we may be pardoned for quoting at length Tenison's description of the closing scenes (taken from his funeral sermon), particularly as this extract shows his prose at its best. "Some few Days before the Feast of our Lord's Nativity, she found herself indispos'd. This Indisposition speedily grew into a dangerous Distemper. As soon as that was understood, the earliest care of this charitable Mistress was for the removing of such immediate Servants as might, by distance, be preserved in Health. Soon after this, she fix'd the Times of Prayer in that Chamber to which her Sickness had confin'd her. On that very Day, she shew'd how sensible she was of Death, and how little she feared it. She required him who officiated there [Tenison] to add that Collect in the Communion of the Sick, in which are these Words . . . 'That whensoever the Soul shall depart from the body it may be without Spot presented unto Thee'. I will (said she) have this Collect read twice every Day. All have need to be put in mind of Death and Princes as much as any Body else. On Monday, the Flattering Disease occasioned some Hope though they were but faint ones. On the next Day, the Festival of Christ's Birth, those Hopes were raised into a kind of Assurance; and there was Joy, great Joy seen in the Countenances of all good People, and heard from their Mouths; and, I believe, it was very warm in their Hearts. But alas! we saw what a few Hours could bring forth. That Joy endur'd but for a Day; and that Day was clos'd with a very Dismal Night. The Disease shew'd itself in various Forms, and small Hopes of Life were now left. Then it was that he who perform'd the Holy Offices [Tenison] believ'd himself oblig'd to acquaint the Good Queen with the Apprehensions all had of an unlykelyhood at least of Her Recovery. She receiv'd the Tidings with a Courage agreeable to the Strength of her Faith. Loth she was to terrify those about her, but for Her Self she seem'd neither to fear Death, nor to covet life. There appear'd not the least Sign of Regret for the leaving of those Temporal Greatnesses which make so many of High Estate unwilling to die. It was (you may imagine) high Satisfaction to hear her say a great many most Christian Things, and this amongst them: 'I believe I shall now soon die, and I thank God, I have from my Youth learned a true Doctrine that Repentance is not to be put off to a Deathbed'. That Day she call'd for Prayers a third Time, fearing she had slept a little when they were the second Time read; for she thought a Duty was not perform'd if it was not minded. On Thursday she prepared Her Self for the blessed Communion, to which she had been no Stranger from the fifteenth Year of her Age. She was much concern'd that She found Her Self in so dozing a Condition (so she expressed it). To that she added, 'Others have Need to pray for me, seeing I am so little able to pray for myself'. However, she stirr'd up her Attention, and pray'd to God for his Assistance, and God heard her; for from thenceforth to the End of the Office, she had the perfect Command of her Understanding, and was intent upon the Great Work She was going about; and so intent, that when a Second Portion of a certain Draught was offer'd Her, she refus'd it saying, 'I have but a little Time to live, and I would spend it a better way'. The Holy elements being ready, and several Bishops coming to be Communicants, she repeated piously and distinctly, but with a low Voice (for such her Weakness had then made it) all the parts of the Holy Office which were proper for her and receiv'd with all the Signs of a strong Faith and fervent Devotion, the bless'd Pledges of God's favour, and thank'd him with a joyful heart that she was not depriv'd of the Opportunity. She own'd also that God had been good to her beyond her Expectation, though in Circumstance of smaller Importance; She having without any Indecence or Difficulty taken down that Bread when it had not been so easy for her to swallow any other. That Afternoon she call'd for Prayers somewhat earlier than the appointed time, because she fear'd (that was her Reason) that she should not long be so well compos'd. And so it came to pass: for every Minute after this 'twas plain Death made nearer and nearer Approaches. However, this True Christian kept her Mind as fix'd as possibly she could upon the best things; and

with cynical indifference.[1] A constant thorn in Mary's side had been the attention which William paid to Lady Villiers (later wife of the Earl of Orkney), "with whom it was well known he had been too familiar".[2] Mary had largely suffered in silence, but on her deathbed she gave to Tenison a letter she had written to William "on his conjugal infidelities". The Archbishop, not unnaturally, decided to take the opportunity to urge upon the King a stricter way of life, and (we quote Whiston), "whether . . . desired by the Queen before her Death, or of his own voluntary Motions, he took the freedom, after the loss of so excellent a Wife, to represent the great Injury he had done that excellent Wife by his Adultery with the Lady Villiers". William "took it well and did not deny the same, but faithfully promised the Archbishop he would have no more to do with her".[3]

To encourage him in this good resolve, Tenison preached at Kensington before the King "in his Chamber" on the Sunday after the Queen's death, and took as the subject of his sermon "Holy Resolution". In view of the above circumstances, the following words must have come with a special emphasis:

"It must be confessed, that when those who have been enchanted with sinfull pleasures, begin to think of reforming themselves, there is a great Strife between the Flesh and the Spirit, and they are ready to think they cannot by any means get the Victory, and they cry out with Anxiety and say, ' Men and Brethren, what shall we do?' What shall they do? Doubtless they should encourage themselves in God, who is greater than those who are against them, and will come unto their Aid, if

there were read by her directions several psalms of David, and also a Chapter of a pious Book concerning Trust in God. Toward the latter end of it, her Apprehension began to fail, yet not so much but that she could say a devout Amen to that Prayer in which her Pious Soul was recommended to that God who gave it. During all this Time, there appear'd nothing of Impatience, nothing of Frowardness, nothing of Impertinence, nothing of ill Sound, and scarce a number of disjointed Words. In all these Afflictions the King was greatly Afflicted; how sensibly and yet how becomingly, many saw; but few have skill enough to describe it: I'm satisfi'd I have not. At last, the Helps of Art, and Prayers and Tears not prevailing, a quarter before one on Friday morning, after two or three small strugglings of Nature as in such cases are common, having (like David) serv'd her own Generation by the will of God she fell asleep. Thus piously, thus resignedly, thus calmly departed this Wise and Great and this Good Princess, who could never have learn'd the Art of dying so well, if she had not first well understood, and duly practis'd the Art of living so".

Tenison, "A Sermon Preach'd at the Funeral of her late Majesty, Queen Mary", 1695, pp. 23-30.
[1] D.N.B. lxi. 306 and xxxvi. 354. Even Bishop Watson admits that William was "very much grieved". H.M.C. Hastings MSS. II. 243.
[2] Whiston, Life and Writings, Pt. 2, 1749, p. 113.
[3] Ibid.

they pray to him, and repeat their Holy Vows in sincerity of Heart. It cannot be denied but that the first Step in our Ascent towards Christian Perfection is very laborious. Yet how can we thus contradict ourselves? How shall we do this great Wickedness, and sin against our Conscience, our Baptismal Engagement, our Righteous Purposes, and our Holy Just God, who keepeth his Promise for ever".[1]

How far the King permanently amended his ways we cannot tell, though Burnet asserts that "he turned himself much to the Meditations of Religion, and to secret Prayer", and Whiston states that "the Lady Villiers wondered she could never see the King after the Queen's Death".[2] Certainly he asked the Archbishop to send him a prayer for his private use, and Tenison replied on 6 January 1695, enclosing a very long one, "to be used (especially on ye Lord's Day) before One goes, either Morning or Afternoon, to the Public Worship of God".[3]

William at first wished the Queen to be privately interred, but he later decided that she should be buried in great state in the Abbey. Hence on 5 March 1695, amid much "funereal splendour", Tenison preached a solemn oration on the text: "In the day of prosperity be joyful, but in the day of adversity consider".[4] In this discourse he moralized at length on the severity of the loss they had sustained, and reminded his congregation that "it was the Immorality, the sin of the Nation which had hastened it as a judgment". He described in some detail the Queen's last hours,[5] and concluded with these words:

"May God give us All Grace to live as this Blessed Princess did, that we may die like her: that we may fight the good fight and finish our Course by all the Exercise of our Holy Religion and keep the Faith inviolate to the last minute of our days, that from thenceforth there may be laid up for us a Crown of Life, by our Lord Jesus, the righteous Judge of all Men".[6]

According to the invariable custom of those days, this sermon was published in due course, when it gave rise to several bitter

---

[1] Tenison, "A Sermon Concerning Holy Resolution", 1695, p. 26.
[2] Whiston, *Life and Writings*, Pt. 2, p. 114.
[3] Tenison to King William, 6 January 1695. Lambeth MSS. 930, f. 198.
[4] Eccles. vii. 14.
[5] See note 1, pp. 402-3.
[6] Tenison, "A Sermon Preached at the Funeral of her late Majesty, Queen Mary", 1695. This sermon was even translated into French: "Oraison funèbre de très haute et très puissante Princesse Marie Stuart, Reine d'Angleterre . . . Traduite en Francois par L. D. Amstermdam", 1695. In English the sermon went through several editions.

attacks on the Archbishop "from . . . persons neither well affected to the Government nor entertaining a good Opinion of the Preacher".[1] By such sympathisers with James II, Queen Mary was regarded as "a most unnatural daughter", who although "cherished beyond expression and loved so tenderly" had yet "persevered to her death in such a signal state of disobedience and disloyalty".[2]

The exiled monarch himself gave vent to his feelings somewhat as follows:

"Even that dull man, Dr. Tenison, then Archbishop of Canterbury, who with his languid oration at her funeral rather divert'd than edifi'd the company, rank'd it among her highest praises that by long and laborious contradictions, she got the better of her duty to her parents, in consideration of her religion and her country. Thus she was canonised for a sort of parricide, by usurping her father's throne, and sending him together with his Queen, and the Prince her brother, to be vagabonds in the world, had not the generosity of a neighbouring monarch receiv'd, entertain'd, and succour'd them when their own subjects and even children had lost all bowells of compassion and duty".[3]

Tenison's sermon certainly gave "great offence" to non-jurors generally, and this found expression in "A Letter to Dr. Tenison, upon Occasion of a Sermon at the Funeral of her late Majesty, Queen Mary". This pamphlet, attributed by some contemporaries to Bishop Ken (though not by Tenison, who wrote to Evelyn that this good man had "more wit and less malice"),[4] was probably written by the nonjuror George Hickes (1642–1715).[5]

---

[1] *Memoirs of the Life and Times*, etc., p. 31.
[2] *The Life of Bishop Ken by a Layman*, 1854, p. 685.
[3] *Ibid.*
[4] Tenison to Evelyn, 20 April 1695. Evelyn, *Diary*, iii. 345.
[5] Ken's authorship of this pamphlet has been more or less disposed of in Round's preface to *The prose Works of Bishop Ken*. (a) This pamphlet, he writes, "abounds in severe reflections on the Archbishop for his not having awakened the conscience of the dying Queen to a sense of her guilty conduct towards her father, and for not having called on her to show some tenderness to him in her last moments . . . In style and sentiments the whole letter betrays that it was not the production of Ken". (b) This "Letter" was reprinted in 1752 in the *True Briton* (III, 589), a periodical of a political character, renowned as "a bitter assailant with more malevolence than ability of the House of Hanover and the memory of William III". The correspondent who sent it in stated that it was "indisputably drawn up by the same incomparable hand that so effectually chastened Bp. Burnet at an earlier period". Ken never published anything against Burnet, a fact which suggests Hickes as the author.

The author of this "Letter" attacked the Archbishop principally because he did not direct the Queen to confess the "crimes" which she had committed against her father. "The peculiar Favour of Heaven", he wrote,

"seem'd to have indulg'd you in all that inestimable Day, on purpose that you might carefully employ it, in clearing her Conscience with God and Man, and in perfecting her Preparation for Eternity; . . . I therefore challenge you to answer before God and the World, Did you know of no weighty Matter which ought to have troubled the Princess's Conscience, tho' at the present She seem'd not to have felt it, and for which you ought to have mov'd Her to a special Confession, in order to Absolution. Were you satisfy'd that She was in Charity with All the world? Did you know of no Enmity between Her and Her Father, no Variance between Her and Her Sister? Did you know of no Person who ever offended Her, whom she was to forgive?[1] Did you know of no one Person whom she had offended, and of whom she was to ask forgiveness? Did you know of no one Injury or Wrong she had done to any Man, to whom she was to make Amends to the uttermost of her Power".[2]

There then followed a personal attack on the Archbishop, which we quote as showing how vehement were the passions raised against him at this time.

"Was the whole Revolution manag'd with that Purity of Intention, that perfect Innocence, that exact Justice, that Liberty and that unreproachable Veracity, that there was nothing amiss in it, no remarkable Failings, nothing that deserves one Penitent Reflection. If you lay to Heart how much you have acted against your own Knowledge and Conviction; what ill example you have given to the Clergy, what Scandal to all good Men, what Wounds to our most Holy Religion, and what Occasion to the Enemy to blaspheme, what have you to do but to testify your repentance before God and the World and to mourn in Sackcloth and Ashes, all the Remainder of your Days . . . Believe me, Sir, you have given the World reason to conclude that your Conscience misgave you, being Sensible, that in reproving her, you must have reproved yourself".[3]

Despite the violence of this attack, Tenison maintained a dignified silence, feeling, doubtless, that the death-bed of a queen

---

[1] The reference of course is to William III. See p. 403.
[2] "A Letter to Dr. Tenison", etc., 1695, p. 36.
[3] *Ibid.* pp. 36, 37.

was hardly a fitting matter for controversy. An apologist appeared, however, in the author of "A Defence of the Archbishop's Sermon on the Death of her late Majesty of Blessed Memory". This writer began by sensibly observing that the weakness of the former pamphlet lay in its being based entirely on nonjuring presuppositions, which most people, and particularly the Archbishop, entirely repudiated.

"We have already seen", he wrote, "how little reason there was to insist upon that subject to the Queen who had so deliberately weigh'd and was so fully satisfied as to what she had done. Nor can there be a cause assign'd why any such thing should have been expected of the Archbishop, whose Past declares him not to be of the late Archbishop Sancroft's Principles to disown the present Government; and therefore it was highly unreasonable to expect of him that he should go about to instil Principles in the Queen which he does not maintain himself".

Politically the death of Mary without children brought to the fore the question of the succession to the throne. It was a subject in which Tenison could not fail to be interested, and it is to a discussion of his attitude to this major problem that we now turn.

The short reign of James II convinced Tenison once and for all that no greater misfortune could possibly befall England than a return to Jacobite rule. A Roman Catholic sovereign, imbued with the principles of continental monarchy, was an impossible "ingredient" in a country, Protestant in religion and constitutional in government. It was therefore part of the Archbishop's unshakable political (and religious) faith that the Catholic Stuarts must at all cost be excluded from the succession to the English throne.

Had William and Mary been blessed with children, the succession would have been comparatively secure. As it was, Anne, Mary's sister, and the second daughter of James II by his first wife, Anne Hyde, came next in the succession. This Princess, perhaps one of the most unhappy of women, married Prince George of Denmark in 1683, a union which produced a tragic series of miscarriages.

At the beginning of William's reign, relations between the King and Princess Anne were far from cordial, due in the main to his studied neglect of her husband, although the latter had taken part in the Irish campaign in 1690 at his own expense. This bad feeling resulted in Anne's virtual banishment from

27

Court, and the abandonment of her royal estate. Anne and Mary also found it difficult to agree, but there seemed a prospect of better things when William consented to stand as godfather to the only child of Anne's who seemed likely to survive. In gratitude, the Princess christened the child William, and the King soon after created him Duke of Gloucester. Thus in this little boy, a weakling from his birth, the hopes of the Protestant Succession were placed.

Whatever satisfaction William may have found in being difficult to Anne at times, he could not fail to see the necessity of coming to terms with her. The Court at St. Germains represented a menace to the security of the English throne, which it is difficult for us now fully to appreciate. Anne, certainly, was a staunch Protestant and had little love for her father, but William could never be quite certain that some kind of reconciliation would not take place between them, particularly since she had written to James in 1691 begging that he would be as "indulgent to receive her humble submissions as she was to make them in a free and disinterested acknowledgment of her fault".[1]

Tenison saw the danger, and it was due to him, soon after he became Archbishop, that better relations were established between the King and the Princess. The opportunity presented itself after the death of Mary, when, as we have seen, William was thrown into a "chastened mood". Anne very sensibly, and maybe at the suggestion of the Archbishop, used the occasion

"to write a most kind and respectful letter to the King, wherein she begg'd his Majesty's favourable Acceptance of her sincere and hearty sorrow for his great afflictions in the loss of the Queen : And did assure his Majesty she was sensibly troubled with his Misfortune, as if she had never been so unhappy as to fall under his Displeasure. She did earnestly desire his Majesty to give her leave to wait upon him, that she might have an Opportunity in person not only of repeating this but of assuring his Majesty of her real intention to omit no occasion of giving him constant proof of her sincere Respect and Concern for his personal Interest and Safety".[2]

The Archbishop saw in this tactful letter a means of reconciliation, and he proceeded to use it for this most desirable end. Accordingly, so a contemporary historian writes, "he represented

---

[1] T. E. S. Clarke, *Life of James II*, p. 477.
[2] White Kennett, *A Complete History of England*, iii. 668.

to his Majesty the prudent and loyal conduct of her Royal Highness and the Prince of Denmark during their recess from Court", and pointed out that during this time she did not "obstruct" public affairs, but "had always been in the same publick Measures with him", even instructing her place-men [1] in Parliament to vote as the King wished. Tenison's timely intervention was completely successful, and Luttrell reports (on 1 January) that "His Majestie yesterday was pleased to send the Archbishop of Canterbury to wait on the princesse of Denmark; and 'tis said she will be allowed a guard as heir of the crown".[2] On 6 January Tenison wrote to the King: "I waited on ye Princess last night and she desired to wait on your Majestie on Monday next at four in ye Afternoon, in some room of Your Majesty's lower Apartment by reason of her present condition".[3] Hence it came as no surprise when, a short time later, the Princess was invited to "keep her own Court at Whitehall", and the King made over St. James's Palace to her use.[4] The dignitaries of the Church, under the leadership of Tenison, were not slow in recognizing the changed status of Anne, and on Wednesday, 6 February 1695, "being the princesse of Denmark's birthday, the Archbishop of Canterbury, with 14 other bishops and judges, went to Berkly house to compliment her upon the same, where was a great court of ladies".[5]

The possibility of the Jacobites making political capital out of the strained relations between Anne and William was thus for the time being removed, but the hopes for the Protestant Succession which had been placed in the little Duke of Gloucester were destined to prove in vain.

This young Prince was never strong, and he presented a pathetic figure when, in 1698, he paraded at the head of his little soldiers in Hyde Park. Tenison was, of course, particularly interested in the education of this young man, for whom in 1698 the King selected Gilbert Burnet, Bishop of Salisbury, as instructor, although Anne was not very pleased with this choice, and the Bishop himself was reluctant to take up the post. William, however, was insistent, and he left it to the Archbishop of Canterbury to persuade a weary Burnet to assume this responsibility. The Bishop

---

[1] i.e. members elected through her interest.
[2] Luttrell, *A Brief Historical Relation*, etc., iii. 420.
[3] Tenison to King William, 6 January 1695. Lambeth MSS. 930, f. 198.
[4] White Kennett, *A Complete History of England*, iii. 668.
[5] Luttrell, *A Brief Historical Relation*, etc., iii. 437.

of Salisbury had just lost his wife, and in a letter to him on
28 June 1698 Tenison, after saying that the King had "expressed
himself with great tenderness", went on:

"He still desires you to come as soon as with decency you
can. He looks upon you as a divine who in such cases had
comforted many and thinks it will look best, not to suffer such a
cross to get such power over you as to make you decline so
public a service. He spoke to this effect without my urging
my private opinion which is what it was . . . It is true that
if no steps had been made in this affair, your excuse could
easier have made its way, but seeing things are so far advanced,
it seems not proper to go back. If upon this, that hopeful Prince
should fall into such hands as are unfit, your Lordship would
then repent".[1]

Burnet allowed himself to be thus persuaded, and took up his
position at Windsor, where he proceeded to enforce an educational
curriculum which would horrify a modern teacher. This, and
other things, proved too much for the young Prince (whose portrait
shows him to have been a weakling) and in July 1700 he was taken
suddenly ill. Burnet was in attendance at Windsor, and rumours
as to the serious nature of the illness soon travelled to London.
The Archbishop, at Lambeth, anxiously awaited news, and day by
day Burnet kept him informed of the patient's condition. On
27 July the Bishop of Salisbury sent the following first letter to
Tenison.

"This is by the Princesse's orders to prevent all stories or
misapprehensions. The Duke was a little ill the day after his
Birthday which we imputed to the fatigue of that day: it went
off and he was pretty well till last night that he was feaverish,
his head ached and he had a sore throat. So the Princesse sent
for Dr. Howe who fearing Quinzy has let him blood three
hours agoe 5 or 6 ounzes. Since that time his feaver is abated;
no ill symptoms of no sort appears but the Duke desires assistance in case of accidents; upon this Dr. Gibbons [2] is sent for
only out of precaution that an affair of this consequence
requires. This is the true state of the matter which I am commanded to signify to your Grace that you may communicate
it to any of their Excellencies".[3]

[1] Tenison to Burnet, 28 June 1698. Quoted Clarke and Foxcroft, *A Life of Gilbert
Burnet*, 1907.
[2] William Gibbons (1649–1728) was a well-known physician of the time. See
D.N.B. xxi. 265.
[3] Burnet to Tenison, 27 July 1700. Lambeth MSS. 953, f. 76.

At 10 a.m. on 29 July Burnet reported that all the doctors agreed that the Prince was suffering from a "Malignant Feaver", although Dr. Ratcliffe feared that smallpox might result.[1] At 7 p.m. on the same day, the Bishop of Salisbury sent off another letter to the Archbishop: "Things were not worse but rather better", he wrote, and Dr. Ratcliffe "begins now to give over the apprehensions he had of the smallpox".[2]

Such comfort as Tenison might have taken from these reassuring reports was soon dashed to the ground, for at 2 a.m. on 30 July, a sleepless Burnet dispatched the following letter to Lambeth:

"God has now thought fit to put an end to the Prince's daies, and to all our hopes from him. At 9 last night the doctors applied two new blistering plasters: the blisters of the former were fair and full and everything seemed promising but before even there was a terrible change. The inflamation in his throat grew to that degree that it choaked him. The doctors ordered him to be tapped and some ounces of blood were taken from him but without successe for he panted on till one o'clock this morning and then just as we ended the commendatory prayer he died. I can say nothing and indeed think nothing after the dismal night. God be merciful to a sinfull nation. I need not tell you how much the Prince and Princesse are sunk with this. God of his mercy support them and preserve the King".[3]

Windsor Castle that night was indeed sunk in gloom, and perhaps to relieve his feelings Burnet sent off another note to the Archbishop a few hours later. "I have nothing more to inform you of", he said, "but that we here a sorrowful company, God knows. Our Princes are as it were dead silent and astonished, a great many sick and all of a shock. God grant this may have its due effect on us and on the whole nation".[4]

The death of this little Prince brought the question of the succession to the fore once again. Hopes began to run high at St. Germains, and it was rumoured that Anne herself was favourable to pretensions in this quarter, rather than to place the succession in Princess Sophia, a grand-daughter of James I. Many Protestants were anxious for William to marry again, but the King preferred

---

[1] Burnet to Tenison, 29 July 1700. Lambeth MSS. 953, f. 74. It was this John Radcliffe (1650–1714) who left the funds from which the Radcliffe Infirmary and Observatory at Oxford were built.
[2] Ibid. f. 70.
[3] Burnet to Tenison, 30 July 1700. Ibid. 952, f. 75.
[4] Ibid.

to place the succession in Sophia, in whose favour he had unsuccessfully introduced a Succession Bill into Parliament in 1689. It came as no surprise, therefore, that in opening the Parliament in 1701, the King recommended that provision be made to secure the succession to the throne in the Protestant line, and that as a result an Act of Settlement was passed on 12 June, which placed the succession in the Princess Sophia and her Protestant heirs.

Tenison was wholehearted in his support of this Bill, and in a letter to the Electress Sophia (written some time later) he said in reference to it: "It is true that in conjunctiō with my B^n, my Endeavours towards ye Obtaining ye late Act of Succession, how weak soever, was yet very honest and heartie: And by God's blessing they will continue such, however ye maintaining ye rights of it".[1]

It was idle to pretend, however, that with such a legal provision the succession was secure, for the person of the monarch would be determined as much by political events as by merely legal considerations. The wisest policy for the Electress Sophia, now that she found herself placed in the succession, was simply to wait upon events, and at all costs to avoid becoming embroiled in party politics in England. Such a course of behaviour was quite congenial to her son George, whose interests were centred in the Electorate of Hanover (and fortunately for English constitutional development, continued to be so when he later became King George I of England); but the Electress, a brilliant and vivacious woman, despite her age, found it difficult and irksome to play this waiting game. She was, therefore, constantly seeking an opportunity to promote the interests of her House in some active manner, and it was Tenison's constant endeavour to restrain her zeal, and to prevent her playing into the hands of the extreme Tories. Fortunately the Archbishop was on terms of some intimacy with the Electress, and an interesting series of letters passed between them. No one could doubt the sincerity of his attachment to the Hanoverian succession, and this enabled him to write to Sophia with complete frankness, and to give advice which was often unpalatable. Particularly she had to be prevented from any rash or hastily conceived plan which might give the impression that there were divided counsels between the two Courts of Hanover and England.

---

[1] Tenison to Electress Sophia, 17 December 1702. Lambeth MSS. 930, f. 197.

The bishops, under Tenison's leadership, were amongst the most zealous supporters of the Succession Bill, and after it had passed, the Archbishop dispatched a letter to the Electress in Hanover by the hand of the Count Macquefait, in which he offered their congratulations at this happy event. The Princess replied in a letter dated 16 August, expressing in very warm terms her gratitude to the Archbishop, and "la plus part de Messieurs les Évecques" for the part they had played in championing her cause in Parliament. "Je ne saurois attribuer ce qu'ils ont fait moy", she wrote, "qu'à une zelle de religion".[1]

Sophia now occupied a position of importance as second in succession to the Throne, and Tenison felt that a united gesture of loyalty by the bishops would be of great value. Hence, after securing the king's permission, he drew up a declaration in their name and sent it over to the Electress.[2] In this paper the bishops declared their "Duty and Zeal to her Electoral Highness's Person and royall extraction", together with their respects to "those Two most Serene Houses", from one of which she was descended, and the other in which God had made her "so happy a Mother". This address of loyalty concluded with these words:

"Our Church has bin signally distinguished by the zeal for ye reformed Religion, and by her Fidelitie and Loyaltie to ye Crown. In both which we that are Bishops of this Church do by our Character hold o'selves oblig'd to give example to all other Persons. We do, therefore, crave leave humbly to assure your Electorall Highness that it shall be our endeavour in our Stations and Callings to maintain ye succession to ye Crown as it is now establish'd, and that according to our most especial duty, we will offer up our Prayers to God continually for your Electoral Highness's Person and Family. We are all with ye profoundest Submission, May it please your Electoral Highness, Yr Electoral Highness's most humble, most obedient and most faithful Servants".[3]

There was certainly nothing ambiguous in this address, and Sophia replied with a letter of thanks (10 December), saying that she would be obliged to them for the rest of her life. She well knew the value of such ecclesiastical support (for want of which James II had lost his throne), and writing again some

[1] Sophia to Tenison, 16 August 1701. Lambeth MSS. 930, f. 81.
[2] Ibid., f. 199.
[3] Ibid.

time later, she reminded Tenison that "she counted herself a member of his Church in which she had been born", and informed him that Lord Stamford had given her some books of Common Prayer, though unfortunately "there were not enough English to pray with her".[1]

This last statement leads us to notice that the Archbishop was very anxious that the Court of Hanover should be made familiar with the liturgy and ethos of the Church of England, particularly since it now seemed probable that the Electress (or more likely her son) would one day become its "supreme governor". To further this object, Tenison sent over to Hanover early in 1702 the Rev. James Cressett ("a person much esteemed of her") in order that he might influence the Court and establish a Church in the Electorate where the English liturgy could be performed. Cressett also took over with him a letter from the Archbishop,[2] which, he wrote to Lambeth on 31 January, "was received by her Highness with great civility and very kind expressions".[3] "I shall take no merit", he added in this report to Tenison,

"for only having done justice to yt of yr Grace in relation to the Court, and making both yr Justice and Piety known to it in that manner it ought to be. I know yr Grace will be so just and generous as to assist in my setting up a decent worship in my house here: when Mr. Lambert is ready to come over, I shall first order him to wait upon yr Grace to receive any commands you may have here for me, which I shall at all times receive and perform with great pleasure to the best of my power. I hope a little plate to be lent out of the Jewell Office for the Communion table and such ornaments as are proper for the pulpit to be furnish'd from the Wardrobe will meet with no difficulty in being dispatched; . . . I covet nothing for splendour or goodly show but since these Princes will sometimes honour my Chapell with their presence, it must be fitted up as it ought to be. I doe not forget the four Bibles wch yr Grace was pleas'd to offer for this use. . . . a dozen or two large handsome Common Prayer Books must likewise be provided and sent with the Bibles".[4]

[1] Sophia to Tenison, undated. Lambeth MSS. 930, f. 212.
[2] This letter thanked the Electress for her kind acknowledgment of his efforts on behalf of the Protestant Succession and concluded: "But all this is a just due to yr E. H. ye most excellent Pr. ye Elector, the most hopeful El. Pr. the true Interest of England both in Church and State; and to the Protestant Religion in General". Tenison to Sophia, 17 December 1701. Ibid., f. 197.
[3] Cressett to Tenison, 31 January 1702. Ibid., f. 16.
[4] Ibid.

The Succession Bill came none too early, for on 8 March 1702 William III died. The Archbishop was almost continually with the dying King "from his first Illness of a Fall from his Horse, whereby his Majesty broke his collar bone, to his last moments; after having given and receiv'd with him the Blessed Sacrament of the Lord's Supper, and prevail'd with his Majesty before his Death, to give the last Hand to a Bill in Parliament for the better Security of the Protestant Succession in the Illustrious House of Hanover, and another for attainting the Pretender".[1]

On 23 April, amid scenes of great splendour, Tenison crowned Anne in Westminster Abbey, the Archbishop of York, fittingly enough, preaching the sermon.[2] The Electress Sophia was now next in the succession.

Party politics in England during the reign of Queen Anne had their repercussions abroad, and the struggle between Whig and Tory at home was felt on the Continent. In 1704 the fortunes of the Tories were in the ascendant, and with this inevitably came a rise in the prospects of the High Church party. As part of this reaction there came a scheme to bring over to England either the Electress Sophia, or her grandson and his recently wed Caroline. Behind this move lay the counsels of Laurence Hyde, Earl of Rochester, the great rival of Marlborough, who saw in it a means of identifying the Tories with the Protestant Succession, and so, by being more loyal than the reputed loyalists, preventing the Hanoverians from becoming exclusively "the kings of the Whigs". So seriously did the Duke of Marlborough regard the prospect of this visit, that he waited on the Princess Sophia in Hanover in 1704, and again in 1705, and appears to have exercised his undoubted charms so successfully as to have dissuaded her from such a step, at least for the time being. The Duke's exhortations had the entire support of the Archbishop of Canterbury who, as a consistent Whig, was strongly opposed to this projected visit, although many of the clergy, eager to flaunt their Toryism under the Caroline reaction, were only too willing to greet Sophia in England.

It was to express both his attachment to the succession, and the supreme need for caution, that Tenison wrote to the Electress Sophia on 30 July 1705: "Tho' I have had many Interruptions", he began, "yet after having been guilty of so long a silence, I

---

[1] *Memoirs of the Life and Times*, etc., p. 101.
[2] Luttrell, *A Brief Historical Relation*, etc., v. 166.

think it becomes me rather to begg pardon for it of yr Highness (as I now humbly do) then to send my Apology". Yet this silence, he went on, did not mean that he had been inactive on her behalf. "Never shall anything induce me", he declared, "(as long as God continues his assistance to me) to entertain a contrary view. I say this of myself with much assurance and I believe I may say the like of the people of England who seem very steddy [sic] in yr favour". The excessive enthusiasm of some, however (the Tories and High Churchmen), was not really in her interest. "It is true", he wrote, "some both of the Clergy and Layty, have been less temperate in their zeal than real Churchmen . . . could have wish'd", but these were in a minority, "though they make much the greater noise".[1]

This letter was taken over to the Electress by Dr. Hutton, a physician whom the Archbishop commended to the Princess.[2] Although Tenison was unaware of it, it was rumoured in certain quarters that this man was in fact being sent to Hanover by the Earl of Rochester and his party, in order "to acquaint the Electress that they would invite her Royal Highness into England the next session of Parliament, and to endeavour to gain her Royal Highness to their Interest as their best Friend".

Dr. Hutton himself wrote to Tenison on 14 September 1705, reporting that he had safely delivered his letter, "for which", he said, "her Royal Highness was, and is, extremely pleased with Your Grace, to whom she will make as suitable a Return as she can".[3] The Doctor then continued in a strain which could not have been very welcome to the Archbishop, since it showed only too plainly that the idea of a visit to England had not been abandoned, and that Hutton himself was not averse to such a scheme. "She hopes", he wrote,

"all the bishops in England will follow your directions, and wisheth they may be all off the same spirit and principle of union and concord with your grace, then she believes she and you should soon meet in England, for the Safetie off both Churches Salvo Jure to Her Majestie; in all things relating both to whose person and vertues She Heath [sic] a High Value, and estime for; who, she firmly beleaves together with her great Counsell, Will allways be careful to preserve the succession entire for Her and Her Issue as established by the Law".

---

[1] Tenison to Sophia, 30 July 1705. Lambeth MSS. 930, f. 181.
[2] There is an interesting article on Dr. Hutton (d. 1712), who began life as a herd boy (this is reflected in his spelling), in D.N.B. xxviii. 354.
[3] Hutton to Tenison, 14 September 1705. Lambeth MSS. 930, f. 221.

He then went on, amidst the vagaries of grammar, to assure the Archbishop of the high regard in which he was held by the Electress and her son.

"The Elector was told by his Mother", he wrote, "How good a man your grace is, and what a kind Leter She had received from you: His Electoral Highness askt me some Questions about your Health with great kindness, and wisht you long Liffe, for you can, he sayes, Hope for no Higher place nor no more Trust on earth than what you possess".

Hutton then commented on the marriage of the Electress's grandson (the future George II) on 2 September to Wilhelmina Charlotte Caroline, daughter of John Frederick, Margrave of Brandenburg Ansbach. His comments, once again, were probably not entirely welcome to the Archbishop.

"The marriage of the Prince Electoral is a wonderfull satis-faction to all parties concerned and indeed the young Princess Hath all the good Qualifications necessarie to make up a well accomplished Lady, but above all her Steddiness in Religion, which she was so firmly adhered to, when so many wrought on her to make a change; and was promised to be Queen of Spain.[1] 'Tis certain these young princesses' presence in England would transform the minds of all trimmers, and put men who are for the pretender out of all Hopes ever to put ye nations into any disorder for the future".[2]

The Electress herself wrote to Tenison in more guarded language on 1 October, and seemed a little uneasy at what she regarded as certain false representations made concerning her to the Archbishop; in particular that "she had had a design to cabal [3] against the Queen and against others, as if the safety of England was indifferent to her". Hence she begged the Arch-bishop, whose "character, honour and friendship" she knew she could depend upon, to disabuse people of this notion.[4]

The Archbishop did not entirely depend for his knowledge of events at the Court of Hanover on the letters of Dr. Hutton and the Electress, for he was also kept informed of the progress of

[1] The reference is to the project to marry her, in 1704, to the Archduke Charles, afterwards titular King of Spain and Emperor Charles VI. Her conversion to Catholicism was necessary before the marriage could take place, but despite the strenuous efforts of the Jesuit Ortanus, Caroline (under the guidance of Leibnitz) remained firm in her Protestantism. *D.N.B.* ix. 139.

[2] Hutton to Tenison, 14 September 1705. Lambeth MSS. 930, f. 221.

[3] French "caballer".

[4] Sophia to Tenison, 1 October 1705. Lambeth MSS. 930, f. 224. She signed herself "Votre très affectionée Amie".

affairs by Sir Rowland Gwynne who, though not directly in the pay of English Government, yet kept a watchful eye on events, and was by no means entirely opposed to Sophia's proposed visit.

On 1 August 1705 the Archbishop had sent a letter to Gwynne by Hutton, asking for precise information as to the reactions in the Court of Hanover to the proposed journey to England. Gwynne replied on 6 October, and began by acquainting Tenison with the rumours concerning Dr. Hutton and his doings.

This Doctor "was civilly received by the Electress and the Elector", he wrote, "but yet not so well as to presume, as I believe, to make these propositions [i.e. a visit to England]. He says he will be going in a little time, but I believe he stayes for further instructions from England".

Gwynne then gave his own opinions at large on this projected visit. "It would be a great honour to the Electress", he said,

"to be invited over to England and it would surprise people to see a person of her age of soe good sense and health but yet I am of opinion that the Electress and Elector doe submit this entirely to the Queen's pleasure, and they do not desire their friends to make any step in it without her Majesty's approbation. I suppose that her Majesty will consider this matter before the Parliament does meet and that if she finds it likely to be proposed in Parliament (for the Whiggs will certainly join with the Tories, if it is moved) she will rather propose it herself in her Speech, then let herself be obliged to it by an Address which she cannot refuse to comply with".

Should it be decided to send an invitation to Hanover, then he thought it ought to be confined to the Electress,

"without mentioning the Prince Electoral; he is third in the succession, he is lately marryed, and it would be advisable to let him live here in quiet, till he hath issue; he is bred up here in great virtue and sobriety but if he came into England he might be exposed to many temptations which a young Prince of a gay Temper who hath a great deale of fire, might not, perhaps, resiste, when he would see quite a different world from what he does here . . . He hath good qualities, but I believe it would not be amisse if your Grace would write to the Elector and Electress to seek some Englishman to instruct him perfectly in the English language. I doe all Service I can in it, and he will speak English with me, but not with others, and he hath had a German to teach him whose pronunciation was not good. I am not wanting in informing them of the Constitution of our

Government and I have offered my Service to His Highness to instruct him in the English language. I believe it would not be amiss if your Grace would recommend to the Electress that an able divine or two should be sent over to instruct him in the doctrines of the Church of England, for tho' it should please God to give the Queen Issue to succeed her Majesty yet this knowledge would be noe burthen to him, and if her Majestye should not Have any his Highness is soe much younger, that he may probably survive her Majesty and succeed to the Crown of England. He is most happy in being marryed to a most excellent Princess, who hath showed herself soe steady and firme to the Protestant Religion, in opposition to great temptations, that she ought to be honoured and esteemed by the English nation, and it is a demonstration that the Elector is a wise Prince that he hath made choice of this Princess for his son".

The writer then acquainted the Archbishop with the general gossip of the Court of Hanover, and related at length the movements of a certain Countess Bellamont, whose Catholic activities were suspected of a Jacobite origin. This lady is not without interest. Her father, Henry Bard (1604?–1660) was created Viscount Bellamont by Charles I in 1645, and she herself became a mistress of Prince Rupert and had a son by him. With her at the Court of Hanover were two nieces who had been sent out by their parents "to be bred up in this Court, the Countess promising that they should not be perverted in their religion". The lady's zeal, however, triumphed over her honesty, and "she did endeavour to change them", and apparently with such success that Sir Rowland Gwynne advised the Elector to have them sent home. "I often represent the scandall", he said, "that would be given to the Church of England and to the Protestant succession, that such a thing should be suffered in a Court from which we expected the support of the Protestant Religion and the use that might be made of it by the enemies to the Succession".

Gwynne then went on to relate that James Drummond (1675–1720), second titular Duke of Perth, a life-long Catholic and Jacobite, had been living for the last two years at Hamburg, a fact which "gave too much reason to believe that he continued there only to carry on a correspondence between France and Scotland". Perth had with him an old man named William, generally thought to be a Jesuit, who had secretly visited Lady Bellamont not long previously, which made it more imperative than ever that Tenison should write to the Elector asking for her removal.

The Duke of Perth himself, so Gwynne concluded his long letter, was coming to Lambspring, and this seemed to suggest "some further designe", of which the Archbishop might be entirely ignorant, since "Mr. Wych, the Resident at Hamburgh was a most notorious Jacobite".[1]

This letter shows with what interest Tenison followed events in Hanover, and how he was thought to have some influence over the Electress and her son.

It was now obvious that Sophia's proposed visit to England had passed beyond the tentative stage and that a scheme to promote it by raising the question in Parliament had been decided upon. A contemporary historian writes:

"The secret management of this scheme was from Hanover. Some indigent persons, and others employed by the Tories, had studied to infuse jealousies of the Queen and her ministers into the Electress Sophia. She was then seventy five, but had still so much vivacity that she was the most knowing and entertaining woman of the age, so she seemed willing to change her scene, and to come and shine here in England".[2]

Whatever doubts the Archbishop may have entertained as to the accuracy of these rumours were removed by a letter from the Electress herself on 3 November. This epistle, worded in cautious terms as her letters usually were, yet made her intentions abundantly clear. True, she reiterated, she would not come without the consent of the Queen and Parliament, but it was just the endeavouring to secure this consent which Tenison and the Whigs dreaded; the fear lest the whole affair should become so public, and arouse so many passions, that the Government dare not refuse if it would. To the Archbishop it was obvious that Sophia was submitting to rash and headstrong advisers: for himself he was too much of a statesman ever to precipitate a crisis, and *quieta non movere* was as much his own as Sir Robert Walpole's motto. We quote liberally from the Electress's letter:

"My Lord,

I Receiv'd Your Grace's Letter; You have no reason to make any Excuse that you have not writ to me more often: For I do not judge of People's Friendship for me, by the good Words

---

[1] Gwynne to Tenison, 6 October 1705. Lambeth MSS. 930, f. 222.
[2] Quoted Cobbett, *Parliamentary History*, v. 474.

they give me, but I depend upon your *Integrity* and what you
tell me in General of the Honest Men of England. I desire no
further Assurance of their good Will and Affection to me,
unless they think it necessary for the good of the *Protestant
Religion*, the Publick Liberties of Europe and the People of
England. I thank God I am in good Health, and live in Quiet
and Content here, therefore I have no reason to desire to
change my way of Living on the Account of any Personal
Satisfaction that I can propose to myself. However I am ready
and willing to comply with whatever can be desir'd of me by
my Friends, in case that the Parliament think that it is for the
good of the Kingdom to invite me into England. But I suppose
they will do this in such a Manner, as will make my Coming
agreeable to the Queen, whom I shall ever Honour, and
Endeavour to deserve her Favour, of which she hath given me
many Publick Demonstrations. . . . Mr. How has acquainted
me with her Majesty's good Inclination for my Family which
makes me think that, perhaps, Her Majesty sees this is a proper
Time for her to express Herself in Our Favour, But whether
I am right in this Point or not, my Friends in England can best
judge. It is but reasonable that I should submit myself to their
Opinion and Advice; and I depend most upon what your
Grace shall advise, which will ever have the greatest Weight
with me. Therefore I write more plainly to You, to tell You my
Thoughts, that you may communicate this to All you think fit.
For they will then see I have a great Zeal for the good of
England and a most sincere Respect for the Queen".[1]

This letter was obviously intended to sound the Archbishop
and prepare the ground in England, and it seems probable, from
the fact that it was later included in a pamphlet,[2] that she drew it
up in consultation with her advisers. Gwynne's intimacy with
Sophia was further emphasized in another letter of a more definite
character which he himself sent to the Archbishop on 6 November.
In this he said that the Electress had ordered him to require the
Archbishop to consult Lord Haversham and Sir Richard Onslow
concerning the scheme (both of whom were known to be in its
favour!), and also to find out the general feeling in England on
this question. "Noe man in England", he wrote, "knows anything of this matter but you four [*sic*]; they have letters to the
same purpose, and she does entirely confide in your wisedom,

[1] Sophia to Tenison, 3 November 1705. Lambeth MSS. 930, f. 218.
[2] See later, p. 425. "A Letter from Her Royal Highness the Princess Sophia",
1705.

fidelity and friendship, that you will doe what is fit to be done at present for this family, and for the coṁon Good of England and Europe".

Gwynne concluded with what we may regard as a semi-official appeal for the Archbishop's support, in the following words:

"She desires that your Grace will alsoe communicate the letter to her friends, and If you think fit, that it may be printed and published. Your Grace may perhaps and reasonably wonder at the new conduct of this Court, which was so quiet till now, but they have good reasons for what they doe, of which your Grace shall soon have a further Account. Her Royal Highness is confident that your Grace will give the best advice both in Parliament and here, and if you think fit to write hither, that you doe it by sure hands".[1]

It was now high time for the Archbishop to state his own position, and this he proceeded to do in a letter written to the Electress on 9 November,[2] which expressed his own emphatic disapproval in no uncertain terms. We quote the letter in full:

"I have latelie, within very few daies, the double honour of receiving two letters from yr Electoral Highness. I beg leave to say that the subject matter of both of them is of too much weight for my shoulders. I have not ye vanity to think I am able; but faithfull (by God's Grace) I ever will be to that which I shall judge without byass to be the true interest of her Majesty, yr El. Highness, and these Nations. In pursuance of this Principle, I presume to say with ye humblest submission, that if I have any insight into the present state of Affairs, the Experiment which some may have offered at this time to yr El. H. out of their abundant zele, and which others may have insinuated out of ill designe, carrys with it a great deal of dang'; Neither my L' by Dr. Hutton (of wch I have a copy) nor any discourse with him (full of respect as it was and was felt to be), did lead to it.[3] Nor has it got to Me . . . that her Majesty has, in this juncture, been consulted about it: And each step taken by ye most well meaning of yr servants without knowing her mind, is sett in a wrong way. I verily believe that other Persons whom I can well remember as respectfull to yr El. H. and as hearty Friends to ye Protestant Succession as by Law established,

[1] Gwynne to Tenison, 6 November 1705. Lambeth MSS. 930, f. 223.
[2] Tenison to Sophia, 9 November 1705. *Ibid.*, f. 189. The Archbishop seems to have taken great care in drawing up this letter, and there is an experimental draft of it at Lambeth (930, f. 188).
[3] This seems to suggest that Hutton had represented Tenison as favourable to the scheme.

as are in ye world, [think] in this poynt as I do. The Parliament (God be thank'd) has been happily begun and there are great hopes it will as happily proceed. And if (which God avert) any bone of Contention should be thrown in amongst them . . . the Consequences would be fatal. Yr El. H. will (I doubt not) pardon ye playness of an incurable but well intentioned old Man, whilst he meddles with so little Art in a business so very delicate and of such high concern, And prejudicial [?] (I can't but think) it would prove to be were it once put into practice. I fear this rather because such as were far frō forward in promoting ye Protestant Succession as now by law established seem, in this juncture, favourers of ye Project against which I have taken the confidence to declare my poor opinion".[1]

Such a letter could admit of no ambiguity, but the scheme had now gained such momentum and was so favoured by the Tories, that it was too late to stay its course. Queen Anne was as fearful as Tenison, and writing to the Duke of Marlborough, she expressed her disgust at the "disagreeable proposal of bringing some of the House of Hanover to England", a scheme which she had "been afraid of so long", and had done her best "to discourage".[2]

The Archbishop's hopes for a quiet Parliament were not realized, for in November Lord Haversham seized the opportunity of raising the whole question in the House of Lords. This nondescript politician, who beginning life as an advanced Whig and Dissenter had later for personal considerations assumed an extreme Toryism, was anxious to make party capital out of this affair, by giving the impression that it was the Tories who were really the guardians of the Protestant Succession.

"The last thing, my Lords", so he concluded his speech in the Upper House,

"is that which I take to be the present concernment to us all both Queen and people. I love to speak very plain and shall do so at this point. My Lords, I think there can be nothing more for the safety of the Queen, for the preservation of our constitution, for the security of the Church and for the advantage of us all; then if the presumptive heir to the Crown, according to the Act of Parliament in the protestant line, should be here amongst us. It is very plain that nothing can be more for the security of any throne, than to have a number of

---

[1] Tenison to Sophia, 9 November 1705. Lambeth MSS. 930, i. 189.
[2] Coxe, *Memoirs of the Duke of Marlborough*, 1845, i. 361.

successors round about it, whose interest is always to defend the possessor from any danger, and prevent any attempt against him, and revenge any injury done him. Is there any man, my Lords, who doubts that if the Duke of Gloucester had been now alive, her Majesty had not been more secure than she now is? We cannot think of that misfortune without the greatest grief; but yet we are not to neglect our own plain safety: and though a successor be not a child of the prince, yet he is a child of the Queen and of the people. Besides my Lords, the heat and differences which are amongst us make it very necessary that we should have the presumptive heir residing here; the duty and respect we pay her majesty and the authority of the law can hardly keep us in peace and union amongst ourselves at present: What may we not fear when these bonds shall ever happen to be broken? And would it not be a great advantage for the Church for the presumptive heir to be personally acquainted with the right reverend prelates? Nay, would it not be an advantage, that whenever the successor comes over, he should not bring a flood of foreigners along with him to eat up and devour the good of the land? I will say no more to your Lordships but will conclude with the motion: 'That a humble Address be presented to her Majesty by this House, that her Majesty will be graciously pleased to invite the presumptive heir to the Crown of England according to the Acts of Parliament made for settling the succession of the crown in the protestant line in this kingdom to reside here'".[1]

There then followed a debate of some hours, in which Haversham found himself supported by the Lords of Rochester, Buckingham, Harwich, Abingdon and Winchelsea.[2] The Whigs, amongst whom the bishops and what we may call the Crown Tories formed a solid block, rallied their forces, however, and the motion was defeated, although eleven Tories had the doubtful satisfaction of entering a protest because, as they asserted, "the having a presumptive heir to the crown residing within the Kingdom would be a great strengthening to her Majesty's hands in the administration of the government, security of her royal person and the succession to the crown by law established in the protestant line".[3]

For the moment the Tories were disappointed, but their resentment was seen when on 19 November the Lords carried a

---

[1] Cobbett, *Parliamentary History*, vi. 459.
[2] *Ibid.* p. 468.
[3] *Ibid.*

motion to introduce two Bills, one for "the better security of her Majesty's person and government and of the succession to the Crown in the protestant line", and the other for "the naturalisation of such of the House of Hanover as were Protestants".

This session of Parliament had certainly been an anxious one for such as Tenison, and more was to follow. On 6 December the Earl of Rochester began a long and facetious debate on the specious motion that "the Church was in danger" (a favourite political device), while on 14 December Sir Thomas Hanmer, taking his cue from the Upper House, proposed in the Commons that the heir presumptive to the throne should be brought over to England.

The power of the Whigs, however, was too strong to be thus broken, and these attempts against their position were for the time being unsuccessful. It was now their turn to show resentment, and they did so in the following manner.

When the scheme for bringing Sophia over to England was first mooted, the Earl of Stamford, a violent Whig, had written in very strong terms to Sir Rowland Gwynne condemning the whole project, since it would have the effect of setting up "two Courts that would oppose each other". On 12 January, Sir Rowland replied at great length to this letter, setting out in detail the advantages, which (so he maintained) would result from such a visit, but making it clear that the Electress had no intention of coming over unless requested to do so by both Queen and Parliament. As to her public behaviour, Gwynne wrote, the Electress had merely let it be known that "she refused to subscribe to a declaration that 'she would not approve of the Motion to be invited to come over'".[1]

This letter, together with the private one which the Electress had written to Tenison on 3 November, was now published in the form of a twopenny pamphlet.[2] The Whigs, rather naturally, were furious, first because of the publicity which this occasioned, and secondly because it showed clearly that the Electress was to some extent at least a party to the scheme. Both Houses immediately sent up a joint address to the Queen, declaring "that the said pamphlet was a scandalous, false and malicious libel, tending to create a misunderstanding between your Majesty and the Princess Sophia and highly reflecting upon your Majesty,

[1] "A Letter from Her Royal Highness, the Princess Sophia", p. 4.
[2] "A Letter from Her Royal Highness, the Princess Sophia".

the Princess Sophia, and upon the proceedings of both Houses of Parliament".[1] They therefore prayed the Queen, "since this seditious libel had been of late with great industry dispersed among her subjects, to give instant orders for the discovering of the author, printer and publishers to the end that they might be brought to condign punishment according to the utmost rigour of the law".[2] The Queen, in acknowledging the petition, declared that she was "fully sensible of the very ill design of the paper", and she duly instructed her legal officials to proceed with investigation and prosecution. Gwynne was apparently left unmolested (he was in Hanover, and this might have led to complications), but the printer, one Charles Gilden, was fined £100, and had it not been for the intervention of a friend, would have been humiliated in the pillory.[3]

Thus the refusing in Parliament of Sophia's projected visit, from which Tenison had anticipated "a greater flame", passed off without serious incident, although another less energetic and equally unsuccessful attempt was made in 1707. The danger from these negotiations, however, lay in the strained relations which they left behind between the two Courts of England and Hanover. Such a state of affairs might easily have proved dangerous if left to fester, and it was the preoccupation of Tenison and the Whigs generally to remove this estrangement. To create a more friendly atmosphere, it was decided to elect George Augustus (who had kept himself completely aloof from the above negotiations) a Knight of the Garter, and Lord Halifax was sent over to confer it upon him, and at the same time to discuss the position of Sir Rowland Gwynne. When this Peer set out on his embassage of peace, he took with him, besides the insignia of the Electoral Prince's new dignity (and a letter from the Queen to the Elector),[4] the following epistle from the Archbishop to the Princess Sophia.

"Madam,
 Yr Electoral Highness having condescended to favour me wth a most obliging L^{r}[5] somewhile after ye Answer I had made, out of ye plainess and simplicitie of my heart, to yours of Nov. 3, 1705; I believ'd it to be my duty as well as it was my inclination, to make as I now do such my humble and thankfull

---

[1] Cobbett, *Parliamentary History*, vi. 519.
[2] *Ibid.*
[3] *Ibid.*
[4] Anne to the Elector, 2 April 1706. S.P.Dom. Anne.
[5] This letter is unfortunately not included amongst Tenison's MSS.

acknowledgment of It. It is true, I did think it proper to forbear the troubling of Yr El. H. whilst ye great affair of ye Succession was agitated in Parliament, and in ye meantime to do my duty according to ye best of my power, and to wait for ye event during that Agitation : a good deal fell out as I presum'd to acquaint yr El. H. it was likely to do. At ye beginning the true Friends of ye Succession had cause to fear that a greater flame would have broken out than there did, tho' there was more than enough of it. . . . But (God be thank'd) ye event went according to ye desires and ye wise management of those, who, in both Houses, had from ye first been true to ye Succession of yr most illustrious house. But it would be a great vanitie in me to enlarge further upon ys subject, seeing the Noble Lord who is pleased to undertake the delivery of this to ye E. H. hands has had a great part in that matter from ye beginning, and prevented it with sure judgment and indefatigable application, and is as able as any person to give an Acct. of all the Steps that have hitherto bin taken. I hope that both ye progress and conclusion of ys great Affair may be answerable to ye success wch God has already given to the wisdom of our most excellent Queen and the unanimitie of ys good Parliament".[1]

Tenison was now over seventy, and politics were beginning to move in a direction which he did not approve, but which he lacked the energy or the influence to prevent. Anne was for the most part surrounded by Tory and High Church advisers, and the Archbishop retired more and more into the privacy of Lambeth, where, except among intimates, he kept his own counsel.

With the Electress he appears to have maintained a desultory correspondence, but it was a correspondence of formal friendship, devoid of political significance. This vivacious lady was herself now nearing eighty, and it became evident that the hopes for the succession must be placed in her son. To him, in 1707, there came an accession of dignity when, "after some well warranted hesitation, he accepted the supreme command of the army of the Empire on the upper Rhine".[2] The Archbishop felt it fitting to offer his congratulations, and writing to the Electress at this time, he commented :

"I cannot go on without a most hearty congratulation upon ye Account of ye station [?] which his Electoral Highness has been pleased to accept of. Great things are hoped for from his

---

[1] Tenison to Sophia, 10 April 1706. Lambeth MSS. 930.
[2] D.N.B. xxi. 146.

conduct and authoritie; and both ye Queen and Parliament
have publicly declared their satisfaction in that poynt; And
the body of ye People of Britain do think that if the German
Affairs on ye Rhine are to succeed and prosper (as God grant
they may) the work is, under God, to be brought about by his
hand. I cañot end without a further congratulation upō ye
late happy accession of a Prince of your El. H. illustrious
Family".[1]

Tenison's optimistic hopes from this Prince's military command
were unfortunately not realized. The troops placed under him
were largely undisciplined, and neither Marlborough nor Eugene
initiated him into their counsels, or allowed him to share their
laurels. It is true that he tackled his difficulties with great energy,
but he resigned in disgust in 1710.

Tenison followed the fortunes of the war on the Continent with
much interest, believing that the future of Protestantism was
bound up with its result. His active share in the national effort,
however, was confined to consecrating its success in prayers of
thanksgiving, and in assisting corporate repentance after defeat by
"sanctifying a fast". Thus Marlborough's great victory over
Marshal Villeroy at Ramillies in 1706 brought rejoicing to the
Whigs, and the Archbishop, at the request of the Queen, composed
a special collect, which he distributed to the ministers of the London
churches for use on 19 May, while 26 June was observed throughout the country as a day of general thanksgiving.[2] The next year
brought no such triumphs. There was no great victory on land,
and the autumn was clouded by the wreck of Admiral Sir
Clowdisley Shovell's flagship *Association* with nine hundred men.
Depression was widespread, and the Archbishop secured a
royal proclamation announcing a general fast.[3] The fortunes of
war soon changed, however, and on 11 September 1709, Marlborough gained the decisive victory of Malplaquet, and once
again Tenison arranged for a general thanksgiving.

With Anne, Tenison was never on terms of personal friendship,
and it was probably not only his "manifold infirmities" which
prevented his attendance at Court.

But old ties were being broken. The Electress Sophia died full
of years on 8 June 1714 (having again fallen out of favour with

[1] Tenison to Sophia, B.M. Stowe MSS. 223, f. 107.
[2] Hedges to Tenison, 17 May 1706. Lambeth MSS. 929, f. 57.
[3] *Ibid.* 952, f. 60.

Anne a little before her death),[1] and on 1 August 1714, after a life of tragedy, the Queen herself passed to her rest. "Sleep", said Dr. Arbuthnot, "was never more welcome to a weary traveller than death was to her".[2]

No sooner had the news of Anne's passing been brought to Lambeth, than "the Archbishop midst all the Pressures of his Gout and Old Age, carried his Black Box, wherein the Elector of Hanover's Instrument for declaring the Lords Justices was deposited, and in Conjunction with the Lord Chancellor, and the Hanover Resident, who had each of them one for the same use, caus'd it to be open'd. His Grace as Lord Archbishop of Canterbury was the first in the Commission, and he discharg'd that High Trust with the greatest Application and Fidelity till the arrival of the King when the Regency ceas'd".[3]

The most important thing, after the death of the Queen, was to get the new King, George I, over to England as soon as possible. To this end he embarked at Oranie Polder on 11 September, and it was arranged that he should be received in state at Greenwich, when the bishops in a body were to be present.

The old Archbishop was eager to discharge his last responsibilities to the full, and on 6 September he wrote to Joseph Addison, then Under Secretary of State:

"I propos'd to have this morning waited on the Ld Regents at St. James'. But having water'd over to ye Cockpit on Friday last upō summons, frō ye Committee concerning the Coronation, at my return I was disordered and so continu'd on Saturday tho' with some intermissiō. But yesterday and last night I was seized with frequently sudden and very violent vomitings, so yt, instead of watering over ys day, I thought it necessary to send for my Physician. I hope, by his help, yts course may be stopp'd. For I have a great desire, if possible, to attend his Majesty at Greenwich together with my Br. ye Bps . . . In two things I would desire yr opiniō and directions . . . 1st Whether if I come, It may be proper to Address his Majesty with a short speech wch I have prepared, or only kiss his hand. *Secondly*, whether, if I find myself . . . then so much indispos'd, I may not have leave to return home without attending Him . . . which I feare will be to me an insupportable judgment. My

---

[1] There was a rumour in May 1714, that the Electoral Prince was coming over to England, and Anne expressed her indignation in strong terms both to the Prince and the Electress.

[2] Quoted H. Paul, *Queen Anne*, p. 124.

[3] *Memoirs of the Life and Times*, etc., p. 111.

Heart is with him, I wish my Strength were equall to my Will".[1]

Tenison was indeed anxious, in spite of his age, to greet the new King as soon as his feet touched English soil, and Edmund Gibson wrote of him on 7 September: "I found his Grace very hearty; and he still determines, with God's leave, to attend his Majesty at Greenwich, and to come in the procession as far as Southwark but as yet the wind is full against him".[2]

Whether the Archbishop managed to get to Greenwich we have failed to discover, but he was certainly able, with "a peculiar joy",[3] in spite of "great Pain and Difficulty",[4] to crown George I in Westminster Abbey on 20 October, which he might well do, considering how much he had worked for, and what hopes he set upon, the Hanoverian succession. The strain of the coronation day undoubtedly told on his weakening constitution, for although Gibson wrote later that "My Ld Archbp appears not to have suffered at all by his great fatigue on the Coronation Day", he yet added: "he was thoroughly tired and by Advice lay in bed all next day; and had the honour of a message from the King to know how he did".[5]

His extreme weakness, however, did not prevent him from paying

"his attendance on the King at St. James', where he was in private with his Majesty who was so very much taken with the plainness and open Sincerity of his Conversation, that when a certain Nobleman who had been a great Solicitor for Grants upon all Occasions ask'd him, How his Majesty lik'd the Archbishop, he was pleas'd to give for Answer, to the greatest Degree of Satisfaction, since that Venerable Old Man had been above an Hour and a Half with him, and in all that Time had not ask'd one Favour of him, for himself or his Friends".[6]

There remained but one more public duty for the Archbishop (in conjunction with the rest of his fellow bishops) to discharge, namely, to express his abhorrence at the attempted Jacobite rising which followed the death of Anne. Whatever chances this

---

[1] Tenison to Addison, 6 September 1714. Lambeth MSS. 930, f. 202.
[2] Gibson to Nicolson, 7 September 1714. Bod. Add. MSS. 269, f. 34.
[3] Calamy, *An historical Account of my own Life*, ii. 301.
[4] *Memoirs of the Life and Times*, etc., p. 111.
[5] Gibson to Nicolson, 30 October 1714. Add. MSS. Bod. 269, f. 35.
[6] *Memoirs of the Life and Times*, etc., p. 111. This was the last time the Archbishop left Lambeth till his death.

half-hearted and ill-conceived attempt at revolt ever possessed were shattered when Louis XIV died on 1 September of the following year (1715) and the prospect of effective French help disappeared.

Tenison felt it incumbent on him to condemn publicly this rash revolt, and to exhort his flock to loyalty, although by reason of his age and ill health he no longer took the initiative. A declaration was first drawn up by the Bishop of Gloucester (Richard Willis) and was then approved by the Archbishop and most of the bishops. "Without their privity", however, the document appears to have found its way into the hands of the Government, "who altered something in it and thus retarded it a week". This intervention occasioned some dismay, and a few of "the Bps who had approved, expressed their dislike of handing papers to Lords wch only concerned Bps and flocks".[1] As a result of this interference, the Bishops of Chichester (Manningham) and Rochester (Atterbury) refused to sign. Thus when the document was eventually published, it appeared under the title "A Declaration of the Archbishop of Canterbury and Bishops in or near London, Testifying their Abhorrence of the Present Rebellion". Although not from his own hand, it certainly expressed the sentiments of the Archbishop.

"We are all the more concerned", it said, "that both Clergy and People of Our Communion should upon this Occasion Vindicate the Honour of the Church of England, because the Chief Hopes of our Enemies seem to arise from Discontents artificially raised amongst Us, and because some have valued themselves, and have been too much Valued by others, for a pretended Zeal for the Church, and have joined with Papists in these wicked Attempts". The present was not the time "to stand Neuter when all lies at Stake", nor had "Popery become so Innocent of late that it was indifferent whether a Popish or Protestant Prince be on the Throne".

A hearty loyalty, the address continued, would discourage the rebels, encourage the Government, and

"put an End to our Troubles and Support his Majesty in the just possession of the Crown which was settled upon his Family with every Mature Consideration, and for Just and Weighty Reasons, as being the next Family of the Royal Blood that were Protestants; from whom only we could expect Protection in

[1] Gibson to Nicolson, 13 November 1715. Add. Bod. MSS. 269, f. 45.

our Religion and Civil Liberties which are the birthright of the People of England and which no one has a right to invade".[1]

The rebellion was short lived, and came to an end in the usual miserable toll of executions. The stage was now set for Sir Robert Walpole to stabilize the new dynasty by wedding wealth to loyalty. It was a marriage which Tenison would have approved.

[1] "A Declaration of the Archbishop of Canterbury and Bishops in or near London, Testifying their Abhorrence of the Present Rebellion", 1715.

EPILOGUE

ARCHBISHOP TENISON'S health began to deteriorate about the time that Anne came to the throne, and gout, that eminently respectable complaint of the eighteenth century, made increasing inroads upon his constitution. References to his health become more frequent in his letters, and he often found it necessary to consult the physician Hans Sloane (1660–1753). Writing to him in 1709, and thanking him for the "care of his dear sister", Tenison said of himself: "At present I cannot stirr out, being exceeding tender by having kept in so long, and the gout hanging about me in some degree, and being ready to return with more violence upō catching a little cold".[1] Two years later, we find him complaining to Sloane that he was "again afflicted with very severe Fits of the Gout". "Nor am I yet rid of it", he said, "it being in both my Shoulders, Arms and Hands, tho', I thank God, with some abatement of pain and swelling in my right Arm".[2]

In 1712 the newspapers reported that he was seriously ill, a statement, however, which was subsequently contradicted, the Archbishop having merely "intermitted his public days [3] . . . the Town being thin". "You may depend upon it, he is hearty and well", Gibson wrote to Nicolson, Bishop of Carlisle, "and like enough to live to see bett⟨r⟩ days". [4]

---

[1] Tenison to Sloane, 30 December 1709. B.M. Add. MSS. 4042, f. 80.

[2] Tenison to Sloane. 11 March 1711. *Ibid.* 4043, f. 289.

[3] An interested guest at one of these public days was the German traveller von Uffenbach, who has left the following account of his visit: "When the prayers were over we went with other strangers into a room, through which the Archbishop with his household was led by a marshal into the dining room: we too followed and sat down to table with them. On this occasion there were some sixteen persons dining there, for the most part English divines. On several days in the week he kept open table, of which both the London clergy and those of the country avail themselves. We should, however, have greatly preferred if so many of these people had not been present on this occasion, for they left us small opportunity of conversing with him. This Archbishop Tennison is a fine looking old man; we were much amazed to see how, at his advanced age, he sat bare-headed at table during the meal. He spoke little, and though the victuals were tolerable, the meal did not last over an hour and a half. No health was drunk but the Archbishop's, except any that an individual might himself propose. When the meal was finished we made our bow to the Archbishop. After he had asked what was our native land, and who we were, and inquired after some men of learning in Germany, he dismissed us". (Quarrell and Mare, *London in 1710*, p. 149.) Von Uffenbach during his stay in England also visited the Archbishop's library at St. Martin's (p. 114).

[4] Gibson to Nicolson, 4 October 1712. Bod. Add. MSS. 269, f. 17.

His wife, meanwhile, was also approaching the end of her long life. In January 1713, she was attacked with "a stroke of the palsie" on one side, and as a result lost the use of her speech, and though she later rallied a little, it was obvious that "considering her great age she could never be out of danger in such circumstances".[1] She lingered for another two years, however, till February 1715. Gibson, writing at the time to his friend in the north, commented:

"The publick newspapers will have inform'd Your L[p] of my L[d] ABp's great loss in the death of his Lady, of whom it may truly be said, That she was full of days (being 80 years of Age) and of good works, being for many years past the great support of the poor of this parish.[2] Upon a stroke of the palsie two years agoe, she had removed to a separate apartment; which makes the Change less to his Grace than it would have been, and I hope Your L[p] will find him full as well as you expect".[3]

They had been a devoted couple, and amongst friends she was known for her great strength of character.[4] She always took a special interest in her husband's educational experiments, particularly in the girls' school at Lambeth. A "Picture of his dearest Wife" remained in the Archbishop's bedroom till his death, and he left it by will "to be fix'd up in the School-House . . . there to remain in perpetual Memory of that great Affection which she had for that Society, and that constant and prudent Care which she took of it, from the first Institution of it till the Day of her Death".[5]

It was certain that the old Archbishop would not survive many months, and his two devoted servants, Luke Evans and Thomas Lloyd, were now constantly in attendance. On 11 April 1715 Tenison revised his will, and could still thank God that he was of "sound and perfect Mind and Memory, tho' very aged and infirm in Body".[6]

"My Lord seems to sink apace", reported the faithful Gibson on 13 October 1715, "troubled with his Tenesmus and Shortness of Breath, and if these continue he is not like to continue long. He cañot bear the sight of meat, nor will his Stomach

[1] Gibson to Nicolson, 23 January 1713. Bod. Add. MSS. 269, f. 21.
[2] i.e. Lambeth parish.
[3] Gibson to Nicolson, 1 March 1715. Bod. Add. MSS. 269, f. 39.
[4] See Chap. 16, p. 365.
[5] *Memoirs of the Life and Times*, etc., p. 118. See illustration.
[6] *Ibid*. p. 113.

endure Wine. He has brave Stamina, and he will wear well, but I cañot think (unless there be a speedy change for the better) that he can conquer this Winter".[1]

In November the rapidly failing Archbishop seemed still more "thin and feeble", and he alarmed his household by a severe bout of sickness, "physic as well as the rest". In December, Gibson confessed that his master was "sunk in Strength and Spirits", and added: "My Lord grows weaker; and keeps his Bed, which he began to do when the weather was piercing, but now, I doubt he is not able to rise".[3] Two days later, all Gibson could say of him was that "His Grace is still alive but grows weaker and weaker and takes very little Nourishment of any kind nor does he care to speak".[4] On 13 December, he sent off the following report to Nicolson:

"The fears we were under for his Grace prove to be too well founded and this I doubt is the last time I shall write to you during his life, being now *in extremis* and having been soe ever since 4 this morning. He takes noe notice of anybody, but God be thanked dies quiet and appears not to be in great pain, soe that we hope he will have an easy passage, tho' ye Doctor is afraid there will be a struggle towards the conclusion. God support him and us all in our last hour!"[5]

It could have come as no surprise to Nicolson, when a few days later he received the following letter from Gibson, written on 15 December:

"Yesterday, a quarter past 3 in the afternoon dy'd my good Lord and Master, without any Agony more than a few groans, which were succeeded by new motions of the underlip, and dyed soe quietly, y^t I am apt to believe he was really dead some minutes while we took him to be lying in a kind of dying slumber".[6]

The funeral took place in the following week according to the instructions which the Archbishop had very carefully drawn up in his will.[7] It was his wish that the interment should be as "private as consists with Decency". "I have always had an aversion to Funeral Pomps", he had written, "and would by no means at my

[1] Gibson to Nicolson, 13 October 1715. Bod. Add. MSS. Tanner, 269.
[2] Gibson to Nicolson, 8 December 1715. *Ibid.*
[3] Gibson to Nicolson, 8 December 1715. *Ibid.*
[4] Gibson to Nicolson, 10 December 1715. *Ibid.*
[5] Gibson to Nicolson, 13 December 1715. *Ibid.*
[6] Gibson to Nicolson, 15 December 1715. *Ibid.*
[7] *Memoirs of the Life and Times*, etc., p. 126.

own Interment give Countenance to them". His body was carried out of Lambeth Palace "in a Coffin under a Black Velvet Pall" (which he had bought for "the use of the said parish on solemn Occasions") by twelve bearers. Dr. Edward Tenison preceded the coffin as chief mourner, followed by the mistress and twelve girls of the Charity School which he had founded in Lambeth. The body was carried after "two Turns about the Palace-Yard" directly into Lambeth Church, Dr. Gibson and the two Curates of the parish going "leisurely" before. The former conducted the whole of the service, but the dead Archbishop had "strictly forbidden" either "Funeral Sermon or Oration". His body was buried in the chancel of the Church "in the same Vault and under the same Marble Stone" as that in which his wife had recently been interred.[1] On the stone there was placed the following simple inscription: "Here lieth the Body of Thomas Tenison, late Archbishop of Canterbury, who departed this life in Peace on the XIV Day of December MDCCXV".

Tenison's will is a model of intelligent forethought and typical of his care. We have often had occasion throughout this work to notice his charitable benefactions, and of his posthumous bequests Gibson wrote: "The greatest part of his Estate (wch had been greatly lessened by his benefactions while living) is given . . . to public charities, and the rest distributed in legacies, which for the most part are small, among his relations".[2] Edward Tenison, his heir, commented later: "It was not his Intention to aggrandize and raise a Family. He was so far from aiming at this, that his Legacies to Benet College and the Society for Propagating the Gospel in Foreign Parts, do together amount to a greater sum than he gave to any one of his Relations".[3] To Gibson he left, as a token of his affection, "two silver Candlesticks upon the Chest of Drawers in his Bed Chamber", and the first offer of his option on St. Martin-in-the-Fields.[4]

---

[1] This vault, which the Archbishop had "long designed with both their approbations", was made by a certain Ambrose Warren in February 1713. See H. Farrant, "A Letter to Mr. Archdeacon Tenison", 1717, p. 14.

[2] The benefactions under his will amount to some £7,000.

[3] E. Tenison, "The True Copies", etc., Pt. 2, 1716, p. 5.

[4] Most of his benefactions have been noticed already. Perhaps we may add, however: (a) £50 to the University of Cambridge "for the benefit of the Press and advancing Printing there". (b) A portrait of his "dear father-in-law, Dr. Love sometime Master of the College of the Body of Christ and the Blessed Virgin Mary . . . to be placed either in the Dining Room or Gallery of the Lodge of the Master of the said College". See illustration.

There are many documents at Lambeth which witness to Tenison's constant

It is with regret that the biographer must admit that of Tenison's private life he knows really nothing. The Archbishop was reserved by nature, a despiser of enthusiasm, and his correspondence (though he could be petulant with Sharp) is for the most part formal, official, and hardly ever discursive. He deals with the subject in hand, and takes his leave. It may be that among his friends at Lambeth—Wake, Gibson, Green, and Potter—he at times cast aside his reserve and spoke freely; but if this were so, we have no record of these conversations. His marriage proved childless and this may well have accentuated the loneliness of his later years: there is something almost pathetic in his isolation at Lambeth during the last years of his life.

We are forced therefore to judge his character from his conduct and from the opinions of those who knew him, since he has left behind him no diary, no revealing documents which lay bare the whole man.

Contemporary estimates of Archbishop Tenison reflect, as we might expect, the political and religious passions of the day, though those who were privileged to be on terms of friendship with him bear unanimous testimony to his disinterested goodness, and his concern for the welfare of the Church of England.

Swift, who probably had little personal dealings with the

vigilance in this matter of charity. We select the following as typical: (a) 1037, f. 59. This is headed "Coales for ye poor . . . 1715", and concludes with the injunction that "no drunken who is like to sell ye Coales for Ales to have any". (b) 954, f. 11. This contains a list of the poor parishioners in St. Martin's parish who received relief in 1699, with an account of their condition. (c) 1100. This document is headed: "Received Jan. 31st 1709 by the hand of the most Rev. Father in God, Tho. Ld ABp of Cant. 30 guineas for ye poor distressed Weavers in and about Spittlefields in ye Parish of St. Dunstan's, Stepney, disposed of as follows . . ." This and a similar document (1101) throw an interesting light on contemporary conditions among the poorer classes. There are references to unemployment; "leprosie"; to one family living in a cellar, "and nothing to cover 'em"; to "3 small children, 2 of 'em down with the smallpox almost starv'd, no bed to lie on, all their goods pawned". Henry Richards, an unemployed engraver in Houndsditch, was found to be in a miserable condition. He had "sold all their goods to buy bread", and they "lay on the Boards"; the husband "had not a Shirt to his back for 12 months", and "ye whole family was almost starv'd to death". We read that they were given "12 yards of ordinary linen at 3d yard for a bed, wch they stuft with straw . . . to him, Wife and Children each 1 Shift etc.", the whole amounting to 15s.

We conclude this notice of Tenison's devotion to "charity", with words taken from his sermon preached at the anniversary meeting of the Corporation for the relief of Poor Widows and Children of Clergymen (to which Society he left £500 by will), on 3 December, 1691: "Charities must be done. For seeing the God of Order has not set all Men upon the same Level, because he would not put them in a State of Competition and War; and that the Poor shall always be with us, there is necessity of supplying them; and seeing they have not an Estate which might enable them to do it; and Age and Accidents prevent labour in many of them; therefore charity must keep them from perishing; And for the Publick Supplies, as they are manag'd, they seem not to be sufficient for these things".

Archbishop, though he suffered from his disfavour, charac-
teristically observed that he was "a very dull man who had a
horror of anything like levity in the clergy, especially of whist",
and that "he was hot and heavy like a tailor's goose".[1]

To the extreme Tories, Tenison was the great bar to their
hopes, and he was judged accordingly.

It is not surprising that Thomas Hearne, for example, employed
his usual violence in condemning the Archbishop. In his eyes,
Tenison was "ye heavy Archbp of Canterbury", one of "ye
virulent Enemies of ye Church of England and Universities, such
as are for bringing in a Comprehension and establishing everything that makes for the Whiggs and Presbyterians".[2] How little
confidence we need place in this estimate can be seen from the
fact that Hearne goes on to make the ridiculous and scandalous
assertion that Tenison was a man of "mean spirit", who having
"put the money of a certain School into his own pocket, [yet]
preaches up and often talks of Charity, but has the least share of
it of almost any man in England".[3] Even when he heard the news
of the Archbishop's death, Hearne, though admitting that he
was a man of "some learning", yet felt it incumbent to add that
"he had no principles of Honesty and Conscience".

Such language witnesses to the violence of religious and
political animosities in those days, but it has little other value.

Of similar interest is the testimony of Thomas Bruce, the
Jacobite Earl of Ailesbury (1655?–1741), who could hardly be
expected to constitute an impartial critic. "They advanced
him", he writes, "for what he really was, a very tool. He lived
many years despised by all people of one party or other that had
good sense. He was cruel in his nature, not only in the House of
Peers but in Cabinet Council in examination . . . To conclude
this long and tedious subject; the bishop was greatly neglected,
and for some years before the queen's death he was not summoned
to Council, and stirred not from Lambeth and pretended
infirmity".[4]

Those who were Whigs and his friends, and consequently had
better opportunities of knowing him, are equally unanimous in
their tributes of praise.

With John Evelyn, a discerning critic, the Archbishop was on

---

[1] Swift, *Works*, ed. Doble, x. 231.
[2] Hearne, *Remarks and Collections*, 1886, ii. 115.
[3] *Ibid.* p. 349.
[4] Thomas Bruce, Earl of Ailesbury, *Memoirs*, 1890, i. 301.

terms of close friendship, and their esteem for each other sprang from a common devotion to the welfare of their fellow men. It was the Vicar of St. Martin's who first told the diarist on 10 August 1688, "of the Prince of Orange intending to come over", and it was Evelyn whom Tenison consulted concerning the foundation of a free library and his other educational experiments. They worked together as trustees of the Boyle lectureship,[1] and collaborated in the founding of the maritime hospital at Greenwich, to which Tenison gave £500.[2] Tenison christened Evelyn's granddaughter, and when his "dear and worthy friend" became Archbishop of Canterbury, the diarist rejoiced in his elevation to a position for which his "learning, piety and prudence" made him so suitable. In July 1695 he visited Tenison at Lambeth and records his impressions as follows: "I dined at Lambeth making my first visit to the Archbishop, where there was much company and great cheer. After prayers in the evening, my Lord made me to stay to show me his house, furniture and garden, which were all very fine and far beyond the usual Archbishops".[3]

The two men had much in common. Both were zealously attached to the Revolution and its principles, and sincere in their devotion to the Protestant religion. Evelyn's considered judgment on Tenison, though that of a friend, carries great weight: "I never knew a man", he wrote, "who was of a more universal and generous spirit, with so much industry, prudence and piety".[4]

In the opinion of Edmund Calamy, the Dissenter, Tenison was a "very steady man", who had "all along been firm to the succession of the family of Hanover". "This upright ABp", he said, "was more honoured and respected, even by the Dissenters than by many of the Established Church".[5]

The writer of the *Memoirs of the Life and Times of . . . Thomas Tennison*, thus concludes his study:

> "He was a Prelate, who through the whole Course of his Life, has always practis'd that Integrity and Resolution he first set out with, nor was influenced by the Changes of the Age he lived in, to act contrary to the pure and peaceable spirit of the Gospel, of which he was so bright an ornament. He always

---

[1] See Chap. 2, note 1, p. 34.
[2] Evelyn, *Diary*, 20 April 1695, iii. 345. An interesting correspondence took place between the two on the subject of earthquakes.
[3] *Ibid.*, 6 July 1695, ii. 336.
[4] *Ibid.* 19 July 1691.
[5] Calamy, *An historical Account of my own Life*, ii. 334.

29

stood in the Gap, as often as Popery and Arbitrary Power made its Advances, and was a strenuous Opposer of certain Persecutions fomented by another Set of Men, who, tho' they call themselves Churchmen, and would be thought so by others, profess, and have lately put in Practice, such Principles, as not only scandalize the Character, but tend to destroy the very Being of that Church to which they pretend to belong; and also to subvert the Foundation of that happy Government to which they are obliged by Gratitude and the most solemn Oath, to pay a most cheerful Obedience. That Great and Good Dignitary in the Church deceased, as he was an Exact Pattern of that Exemplary Piety, Charity, Steadfastness, and good Conduct, requisite in a Governor of the Church, so perhaps since the Primitive Age of Christianity, and the Time of the Apostles, there has been no Man whose Learning and Abilities have better qualified him to discharge and defend a Trust of that high Importance".[1]

These contemporary verdicts are in the main the reflection of the passions of the day. The foregoing study, however, makes certain things tolerably clear above and beyond such party strife. Tenison, as a bishop of the Church, was diligent (so long as his health permitted), conscientious, and well meaning. He wished to make the Church more efficient in the discharge of its duties; to secure a higher standard in the personnel of the clergy; to keep pluralism and non-residence within the limits of the law; and to use the Church to improve the declining "morale" of the nation. The good which he did in this respect lived after him, for it formed the inspiration of Archbishop Wake and Bishop Gibson's disinterested zeal.[2]

In his enthusiasm for education, manifested in so many practical ways, and in his respect for the achievements of Bacon, Tenison may be said to represent the renaissance spirit at its best.

Those, however, who still regard the "glorious Revolution" of 1688 as a great step forward towards responsible government and religious freedom (and this is the writer's standpoint) will wish to say more. Tenison was whole-hearted in his championship of the principles of '88, and he wished the Church to give full expression to the spirit of ordered and reasonable liberty. Thus the ever-present fear of Rome made him desire a comprehensive Church

---

[1] *Memoirs of the Life and Times*, etc., p. 112.
[2] We may notice that, before he died, the Archbishop recommended William Wake as his successor.

and he "thought that the narrow notions of all the Churches had been their ruin". If the comprehension for which Tenison laboured so strenuously in 1689 had been established (although a modern writer has described it as a "ludicrous Reunion Scheme prompted by the Government for political purposes", and thrown out as "contrary to Anglican Doctrines"),[1] it may well be that some of the apathy of the later eighteenth-century Church, with the consequent secession of Wesley, would have been avoided.

Tenison's position as the protagonist of "1688" was certainly a difficult one during the years of Anne's reign, when he was never *persona grata* at Court. Atterbury, with his gift for leadership and dynamic personality, was a constant thorn in his side, and it was even rumoured that if Tenison died during Anne's reign, he would be his successor.[2] Personal antipathy, and the privileged position which he held in the counsels of Anne, prevented co-operation with Sharp. Tory counsels, with their burning desire to have revenge on the Dissenters, met with a sympathetic response at Court, and were reflected in the Convocational disputes. Against all these assaults, Tenison, entrenched at Lambeth with his Whig "entourage", remained firm and obdurate. His visits to Parliament were not frequent, but he generally managed to be present (or inspired others) when some Tory scheme was on foot. In his latter years, Tenison felt that the succession would be best secured by quietly waiting upon events, and by avoiding as far as possible theological controversy. The seventeenth century, he felt, had known enough religious upheaval. In his eyes, a return to Jacobite rule, probably in alliance with Louis XIV, whom he had described in 1689 as a "selfish and violent Persecutor",[3] would mean the end of liberty both religious and political for the time being. It was therefore the duty of Churchmen to harvest the fruits already gathered. Those who to-day subscribe to a similar view will rejoice that Atterbury and his followers were not given a free hand to restore "the King over the water", which had it been successful might well have led to a more violent revolution later on, as in France. That such a situation did not arise was in a measure due to the care and devotion to duty of Thomas Tenison.

We leave the reader to reflect upon the facts which we have placed before him, and as a consequence to accept, qualify, or

[1] *Theology*, September 1941, p. 167. The writer is the Rev. Dom. Gregory Dix, O.S.B.
[2] Calamy, *An historical Account*, etc., ii. 333. It is extremely unlikely (see p. 186) that Anne would ever have consented to Atterbury's going to Canterbury.
[3] Tenison, "A Sermon against Self Love", 1689, p. 26.

reject, the judgment of Edmund Gibson, written a few days before the Archbishop's death. "In losing him (whenever that happens) we shall lose the wisest and best Man that I know in the World; many others have more state politicks, but he had the true Christian policy; great Goodness, and Integrity improved by long Experience and a natural sedateness and Steadyness of Temper, and a general knowledge of men and things; had it not pleased God to raise up such an One to steer in the stormy times that we have had (for these last 20 years) the Church in all human probability must have been shipwrecked over and over".[1]

[1] Gibson to Nicolson, 8 December. Bod. Add. MSS. 269.

FINIS

APPENDIX

From an MS. in Lambeth Library (8065) entitled "Croydon School Orders".

"Heads of orders for the Charity Schools for ten poor Boys and ten poor Girls, founded by Thomas Tenison, Lord Archbishop of Canterbury, at Croydon, March 25 1714.

1. This schoole is to consist at present of a schoolmaster and mistress Mr. Henry Zealy and Mary his wife, who shall teach no other children but what belong to this school, namely ten poor boys and ten poor girls.

2. The Master and Mistress shall always be profest members of the Church of England of sober life and conversation; either [both] to be twenty five years of age at the least; they must frequent the holy communion and understand well the principles of the Christian Religion.

3. The Master shall be able to write a good round hand and understand the grounds of arithmetic and teach the children the true spelling of words with the points and stops to true reading.

4. The Master shall twice a week at the least instruct all the children in the Church Catechism and by some expositions approved of.

5. No boy or girl to be under eight years old when admitted nor to stay till after fourteen unless it be to even the quarter then going on.

6. Each boy or girl to be sent in, cloathed, whole and clean.

7. A Common Prayer Book and Bible to be provided for each boy and girl.

8. The boys are to be taught to read, write and arithmetick; the girls the same, also to spin, knit, sew and work.

9. They are to come to school in the summer at seven in the morning and stay till eleven; to come again in the afternoon at one and stay till five. Summer to be reckoned from Lady Day till Michaelmass.

10. In winter to come at eight in the morning and stay till eleven, to come again in the afternoon at one and stay till four.

11. Every Lord's Day and every holiday, and every Wednesday and Friday, they are to go to Church two by two; to sit orderly in their proper seat and make the answers at prayers and sing the Psalms.

12. They are to break up at Christmas, Easter and Whitsuntide, and have the usual liberties as at other schools.

13. On Thursday they are to leave school at 3 of the clock in the afternoon.

14. On Saturday in the afternoon the girls, five at a time in such order as may be most easy, are to help to clean the house.

15. Absence from school or great crimes as lying, swearing, stealing, profanation of the Lord's Day, shall be noted in weekly bills to be laid before the Trustees at their meeting, in order to their correction or expulsion.

16. The Mistress shall weekly chuse one girl to be her particular assistant for the week.

17. If the parent, brother, or sister of anyone in the school shall steal anything from Norwood, the child relating to them shall immediately be expelled and forfeit the school cloathes and books.

18. If anyone of the children of the school shall leave or be taken from the school before they have learnt what the statutes shall direct, the cloathes and books belonging to such shall be left for another.

19. If the parents and friends send not the children clean and decent, washed and combed, or not at the school hours, or anyways hinder them from observing the orders of the school, such children to be dismissed.

20. No child whose parents frequent the meeting house shall be admitted or continue if admitted.

21. The Trustees are to meet on the Tuesday after every quarter day, to look into the state and conditions of the school; and then these orders to be read publickly before them, the Master and Mistress and all the Children.

22. The Trustees shall pay unto the Master and Mistress each —— pounds quarterly out of estate purchased by the founder, Thomas, Lord Archbishop of Canterbury, for the perpetual support of this very charity school.

23. It shall be lawful for me, Thomas, the now Archbishop of Canterbury, founder of the same schoole, to abrogate, add unto, change or alter, these orders; to place or displace any part thereof, and wholly to govern the same according as shall seem to me reasonable, during my natural life without any other person intermeddling therein.

24. The school master and mistress to sit rent free in the new school house, purchased and fitted up by his Grace Thomas, Lord Archbishop of Canterbury, situate in the parish of Croydon.

25. No child to be admitted whose parents are not legally settled as inhabitants of the Parish of Croydon.

26. At their coming in the morning, the Master, or one of the scholars appointed by him, is to begin with the prayers 'Prevent us O Lord in all our doings etc.'; then the Collect for the day, and then the collect for the fifth Sunday after Trinity, 'Grant O Lord we beseech thee that the course of this World may be so peaceablie ordered etc.'

27. At night at their going away they shall say the collect for the day and then the collect for the fourth Sunday after Trinity, 'O God the protector of all that trust in thee etc.' and also 'Lighten our darkness etc.'.

They must be charged when they go to bed to say (as in Psalm, 4th unto verse 9th): 'I will lay me down in peace and take my rest for it is thou Lord that makest me dwell in safety'".

PATERNAL DESCENT OF ARCHBISHOP TENISON

(Based on parish registers, wills, and other contemporary documentary evidence.)

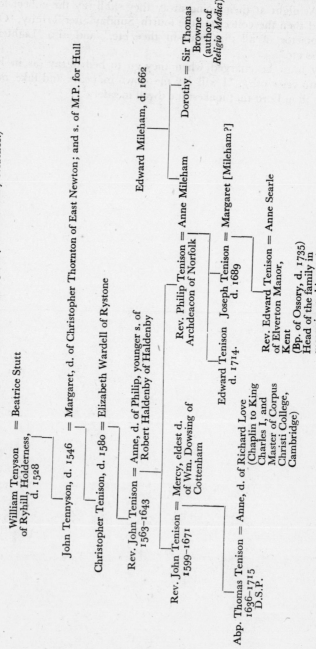

William Tenyson = Beatrice Stutt
of Ryhill, Holderness,
d. 1528

John Tennyson, d. 1546 = Margaret, d. of Christopher Thornton of East Newton; and s. of M.P. for Hull

Christopher Tenison, d. 1580 = Elizabeth Wardell of Rystone

Rev. John Tenison = Anne, d. of Philip, younger s. of
1563–1643　　　　　Robert Haldenby of Haldenby

Rev. John Tenison = Mercy, eldest d.
1599–1671　　　　of Wm. Dowsing of
　　　　　　　　　Cottenham

Abp. Thomas Tenison = Anne, d. of Richard Love
1636–1715　　　　　(Chaplin to King
D.S.P.　　　　　　Charles I, and
　　　　　　　　　Master of Corpus
　　　　　　　　　Christi College,
　　　　　　　　　Cambridge)

Edward Mileham, d. 1662

Rev. Philip Tenison = Anne Mileham
Archdeacon of Norfolk

Dorothy = Sir Thomas
　　　　　Browne
　　　　　(author of
　　　　　Religio Medici)

Edward Tenison　Joseph Tenison = Margaret [Mileham ?]
d. 1714.　　　　d. 1689

Rev. Edward Tenison = Anne Searle
of Elverton Manor,
Kent
(Bp. of Ossory, d. 1735)
Head of the family in
succession to his cousin
the Archbishop

446

BIBLIOGRAPHY

MANUSCRIPT AUTHORITIES

Lambeth Library:
  Tenison and Gibson MSS.
  Act Books of the Archbishops of Canterbury.
  Tenison's register.

British Museum:
  Additional MSS.
  Cole MSS.
  Stowe MSS.

Public Record Office:
  State Papers Domestic. William and Mary, William III, and Anne.

Bodleian Library:
  Ballard MSS.
  Tanner MSS.

Christ Church, Oxford:
  Wake MSS.

Fulham Palace:
  Fulham MSS. relating to the Plantations.

Society for Propagating the Gospel:
  Archives, London.

Lloyd-Baker-Sharp MSS.

Parish registers:
  St. Andrew the Great, Cambridge.
  Cottenham.
  Downham.
  Hollywell and Needingworth.
  St. James', Piccadilly.
  St. Martin-in-the-Fields.
  Mundesley.
  St. Peter Mancroft, Norwich.
  Topcroft.
  Witherley.

Private Papers in possession of E. M. Tenison, including: Notes for the Life of Thomas Tenison, by C. M. Tenison.

Historical Manuscripts Commission:
  Marquis of Bath MSS. 1904.
  Devonshire MSS. 1924.
  Egmont Diary, 1920–24.
  Portland MSS. 1897, etc.
  Hasting MSS. 1930.
  10th Report, Pt. 4.
  10th Report, App. 9.
  13th Report, Pt. 7.

448

BIBLIOGRAPHY

General Printed Authorities Used Throughout

Abbey and Overton: The English Church in the Eighteenth Century. 1878.
Brown, B. C.: The Letters of Queen Anne. 1935.
Carlisle, N.: Topographical Dictionary of England. 1808.
Cobbett, W.: Parliamentary History. 1806, etc.
Cunningham, A.: Lives of Eminent Englishmen. 1836.
Hallam, A.: Constitutional History of England. 1827.
Howell, T. B.: State Trials. 1809–15.
Jesse, J. H.: Memoirs of the Court of England from the Revolution in 1688 to the Death of George the Second. 1843.
Lathbury, T.: A History of the Convocation. 1842.
Lecky, W.: England in the Eighteenth Century. 1892.
Luttrell, N.: A Brief Historical Relation of State Affairs from September 1678 to April 1714. 1857.
Lumby, J. R.: Compendium of English Church History. 1883.
Macaulay, T. B.: History of England. Ed. C. H. Firth. 1913.
Nichols, J.: Literary Anecdotes of the Eighteenth Century. 1812.
Overton and Relton: A History of the Church of England from the Accession of George I to the end of the Eighteenth Century (Hunt and Stephens, Vol. VII).
Phillimore, R.: The Ecclesiastical Law of the Church of England. 2nd edition, 1895.
Sykes, N.: Church and State in England in the XVIIIth Century. 1934.
White Kennett: A Complete History of England. 1719.
A Dictionary of English Church History. Ed. Ollard, S. L. and Crosse, G. 2nd edition, 1919.
Encyclopædia Britannica. 9th edition.
Alumni Oxonienses. Ed. J. Foster. 1892.
Alumni Cantabrigienses. Ed. J. and J. A. Venn. 1926.

Other Authorities Arranged Under Respective Chapters
Chapter I

Mullinger, J. Bass: History of Cambridge University.
Parkin, C.: History of Norfolk. 1775.
The Victoria History of the County of Norfolk. 1906.
White Kennett: A Register and Chronicle, Ecclesiastical and Civil. 1728.

Chapter 2

Burgess, M. A.: A History of Burlington School. 1924.
Cunningham, P.: The Story of Nell Gwyn. 1927.
Evelyn, John: Diary and Correspondence. Ed. W. Bray. 1850.
Gibson, E.: Librorum Manuscriptorum in duabus insignibus Bibliothecis; altera Tenisoniana Londini; altera Dugdaliana Oxonii Catalogus. 1692.
Le Neve, J.: The Lives and Characters of the Protestant Bishops of the Church of England. 1720.
Masters, R.: The History of the College of Corpus Christi. 1753.
Psalmanazar, G.: Memoirs. 1764.
Extract of a Deed of Settlement of the School and Chapel in King Street. 1814.

Chapter 3
Pamphlets concerning the Catholic Controversy

Gother, J.: Good Advice to the Pulpits. 1687.
Gother, J.: Pulpit Sayings. 1688.

Meredith, E.: Some further Remarks on the late Account. 1688.
Pulton, A.: A true and full Account of a Conference held about Religion. 1687.
Pulton, A.: Remarks of A. Pulton, Master of the Savoy. 1687.
Ward, T.: Speculum Ecclesiasticum. 1688.
Ward, T.: The Roman Catholic Souldier's Letter. 1688.
Wharton, H.: The Pamphlet entitled Speculum Ecclesiasticum Considered. 1688.
Williams, J.: Pulpit Popery true Popery. 1688.
An Apology for the Pulpits. 1687.
The Vindication of A. Cressener Schoolmaster. 1687.
A full Discovery of the false Evidence produc'd by the Papists. 1687.
A full Answer to Dr. Tenison's Conference concerning the Eucharist. 1687.
Popery not founded on Scripture. 1687.
The present State of the Controversie between the Church of England and the Church of Rome. 1687.
The Arts of the Missionaries Discovered. 1688.
Reflections on the Author and Licencer. 1688.
The Protestant's Plea for a Socinian. 1686 (taken from Abraham Woodhead's Guide in Controversies. 1673).
An Account of the Persecutions and Oppressions of the Protestants in France. 1686.

Other Authorities

Duruy, J. V.: History of France (Everyman Library, 1917).
Life of Bishop Ken by a Layman. 1854.
Higgons, B.: Remarks on Burnet's History. 1725.

CHAPTER 4

Sacheverell: The Loyal Catechism. 1710.

CHAPTER 5

Pamphlets relating to Convocation of 1689

Bassett, W.: Two Letters and a Vindication. 1689.
Prideaux, H.: A Letter to a Friend relating to the present Convocation. 1689.
A Letter to a Friend concerning some Quaeries about the new Commission. 1689.
Vox Cleri, or the Sense of the Clergy concerning the making Alterations in the established Liturgy. 1689.
To the reverend and merry Answerer of Vox Cleri. 1689.
An Answer to Vox Cleri. 1690.
A Just Censure of Vox Cleri. 1690.
Remarks upon the two Letters. 1690.
Vox Populi. 1690.
Remarks from the Country in two Letters relating to Convocation. 1690.
Vox Regis et Regni. 1690.

Other Authorities

Birch, T.: Life of Tillotson. 1753.
Cardwell, E.: A History of Conferences and other Proceedings connected with the Revision of the Book of Common Prayer. 1840.
Hyde, Henry, Earl of Clarendon: The Correspondence and Diary of Ed. Singer, S. W. 1828.
Nicholls, W.: Defensio Ecclesiae Anglicanae. 1707–08.
Taylor, J.: The Revised Liturgy of 1689. 1855.

Copy of the Alterations in the Book of Common Prayer prepared by the Royal Commission for the Review of the Liturgy. 1689. Parliamentary Papers, Vol. L.

CHAPTER 6

Bruce, Thomas, Earl of Ailesbury: Memoirs. 1890.
Clarke, T. E. S. and Foxcroft, H. C.: A Life of Gilbert Burnet. 1907.
Garth, S.: The Dispensary. 1699.
Newcourt, R.: Repertorium Ecclesiasticum Parochiale Londinense. 1708–10.
Nichols, J.: The History and Antiquities of Leicestershire. 1795–1815.
Stanley, W.: A Sermon preached at the Consecration of . . . Thomas Tenison. 1692.
White Kennett: The Case of Impropriations and of the Augmentation of Vicarages. 1704.
The Victoria History of the County of Lincoln. 1906.

CHAPTER 7

Beresford, J.: The Diary of a Country Parson. 1926.
Churchill Babington: Mr. Macaulay's Character of the Clergy in the latter part of the seventeenth Century Considered. 1849.
The Life of the Reverend Humphrey Prideaux. 1748.
Gentleman's Magazine. 1783. Vol. LIII, Pt. 2.
Brett, T.: An Account of Church Government and Governors. 2nd ed. 1710.

CHAPTER 8

Coxe, W.: Memoirs of the Duke of Marlborough. 1848.
Foxcroft, H. C.: A Supplement to Burnet's History of my own Time. 1902.
Le Neve, J.: The Lives and Characters of the Protestant Bishops of the Church of England. 1720.
Nichols, J.: Letters on Various Subjects to and from William Nicolson. 1809.
Sykes, N.: Queen Anne and the Episcopate. English Historical Review. Vol. L.

CHAPTER 9

Life of Bishop Ken by a layman. 1854.

CHAPTER 10

Pamphlets dealing with the charges brought against Watson, Bishop of St. David's, and Jones, Bishop of St. Asaph

The Case of many Protestant Freeholders and Inhabitants in the County and Town of Cambridge.
Ten Modest Quaeries, etc. 1691.
A Letter to a Person of Quality concerning the Archbishop of Canterbury's Deprivation of the Bishop of St. David's. 1699.
The Extraordinary Case of the Bishop of St. David's further cleared. 1703.
A Summary View of the Articles exhibited against the late Bishop of St. David's. 1701.
A Short Narrative of the Proceedings against the Bp. of St. A. 1702.
Watson, T.: Articles to be enquired of . . . in the triennial visitation of . . . Thomas, Lord Bishop of St. David's. 1691.
A Letter to a Member of the House of Commons. 1701 [?]

Other Authorities

Churchill, I. E.: Canterbury Administration. 1933.
Shippen, W.: Faction Display'd. 1704.
Wood, Anthony: Athenae Oxonienses. 1691–92.

CHAPTER 11

Atterbury, F.: The Epistolary Correspondence of. Ed. J. Nichols. 1783–90.
Cardwell, E.: A History of Conferences and other Proceedings connected with the Revision of the Book of Common Prayer. 1840.
Nicholls, W.: Defensio Ecclesiae Anglicanae. 1708.
Bp. Nicolson's Diary, Transactions of the Cumberland and Westmorland Antiquarian and Archæological Society. Vol. I (1901). N.S.
Sykes, N.: Edmund Gibson. 1926.
Tindal, N.: The Continuation of Mr. Rapin's History of England. 1763.
The Complainer further Reproved. 1704.

CHAPTER 12

Burrows, Montagu: Worthies of All Souls'. 1874.
Remarks and Collections of Thomas Hearne. Ed. C. E. Doble. 1886.

CHAPTER 13

Burn, J. S.: History of Fleet Marriages. 1833.
Howard, G. E.: A History of Matrimonial Institutions. 1904.
Jeaffreson, J. C.: Brides and Bridals. 1872.
Nichols, J.: Letters on Various Subjects to and from William Nicolson. 1809.
Sharp, T.: Life of John Sharp. 1825.
Wilson, J.: Daniel Defoe.
A Letter from Several Members of the Society for the Reformation of Manners. 1710.

CHAPTER 14

Pamphlets concerning lay baptism

Bingham, J.: The Scholastical History of lay Baptism. 1712, 14.
Bingham, J.: Dissertation upon the 8th Canon of the Council of Nicea. 1716.
Sacerdotal Powers, or the Necessity of Confession. 1710.
The Bishop of Oxford's Charge Consider'd. 1712.
Lay Baptism Invalid. Pts. 1 and 2. 1712, 1713.
Dissenters and other unauthoriz'd Baptisms Null and Void. 1713.

Other Authorities

Muss-Arnolt, W.: The Book of Common Prayer among the Nations of the World. 1914.
Sharp, T.: Life of John Sharp. 1825.
Whiston, W.: Sermons and Essays. 1709.
Whiston, W.: Articles objected to Mr. Whiston.

CHAPTER 15

Burrows, Montagu: Worthies of All Souls'. 1874.
Calamy, E.: An historical Account of my own Life. 1829.
Cross, A. L.: The Anglican Episcopate and the American Colonies. 1902.
Godwin, T.: De Praesulibus. 1743 (ed. Richardson).
Sharp, T.: Life of John Sharp. 1825.
Steven, W.: The History of the Scottish Church in Rotterdam. 1883.
Newton, W.: Life of White Kennett. 1730.

CHAPTER 16

Carstares, W.: State Papers and Letters. 1774.
Forster, J.: The Life of Jonathan Swift. 1875.

Killen, T. Y.: The Ecclesiastical History of Ireland.
White Kennett: The Case of Impropriations and of the Augmentation of
    Vicarages, 1704.
Mant, R.: History of the Church of Ireland. 1840.
Patrick, Simon: Autobiography. 1839.
Timberland, E.: The History and Proceedings of the House of Lords. 1742.

CHAPTER 17
Pamphlets

A Letter to Dr. Tenison upon Occasion of a Sermon at the Funeral of her late
    Majesty, Queen Mary. 1695.
A Defence of the Archbishop's Sermon on the Death of her late Majesty
    of Blessed Memory, 1695. (Attributed to John Williams, later Bishop of
    Chichester.)
A Letter from her Royal Highness, the Princess Sophia. 1705.
A Declaration of the Archbishop of Canterbury and the Bishops in or near
    London, Testifying their Abhorrence of the Present Rebellion. 1715.

Other Authorities

Bruce, Thomas, Earl of Ailesbury: Memoirs. 1890.
Calamy, E.: An historical Account of my own Life. 1829.
Clarke, T. E. S.: Life of James II. 1902.
Coxe, W.: Memoirs of the Duke of Marlborough. 1845.
Paul, H.: Queen Anne. 1906.
Whiston, W.: Life and Writings. Pt. 2. 1749.
The Life of Bishop Ken by a Layman. 1854.
True Briton. 1752. Vol. III.

Epilogue and Appendix I
Pamphlets relating to dispute over dilapidations

Farrant, H.: A Letter to Mr. Archdeacon Tenison. 1717.
James, J.: The Survey and Demand for Dilapidations Justified. 1717.
Tenison, E.: The True Copies of some Letters occasion'd by the Demand
    for Dilapidations in the Archiepiscopal See of Canterbury. Pts. 1 and 2. 1716.

Other Authorities

Bruce, Thomas, Earl of Ailesbury: Memoirs. 1890.
Calamy, E.: An historical Account of my own Life. 1829.
Hearne, T.: Remarks and Collections. 1886.
Quarrell and More: London in 1710.

A COMPLETE LIST OF THE BOOKS AND PAMPHLETS WRITTEN, EDITED
OR TRANSLATED BY THOMAS TENISON, WITH THE DATES
OF THEIR EDITIONS

The Creed of Mr. Hobbes Examin'd. 1670, 1671.
A Discourse on Idolatry. 1678.
Baconiana or Certain Genuine Remains of Sir Francis Bacon. 1678.
A Sermon concerning Discretion in giving Alms. 1681, 1688.
An Argument for Union. 1683, 1685, 1694, 1718.
A Discourse concerning a Guide in Matters of Faith. 1683, 1687, 1738, 1748.
Certain Miscellany Tracts, written by Thomas Brown, Kt. and Doctour of
    Physick, late of Norwich. Edited by Thomas Tenison. 1684.
An Account of the Persecutions and Oppressions of the Protestants in France.
    (Translated by T. T.) 1686.
The Difference betwixt the Protestant and Socinian Methods. 1687.

The Present State of the Controversie between the Church of England and the Church of Rome (edited by T. T. and W. Clagett). 1687.

The Tenth Note of the Church Examin'd, viz. Holiness of Life. 1687.

A True Account of a Conference held about Religion. 1687, 1687, 1687, 1687, 1687.

Mr. Pulton Consider'd in his Sincerity. 1687.

An Answer to the Letter of the Roman Catholic Soldier. 1688.

Six Conferences concerning the Eucharist. By J. de la Placette, translated by T. T. 1687.

Of the Incurable Scepticism of the Church of Rome. By J. de la Placette, translated by T. T. 1688.

Of Transubstantiation, or a Reply to a late Paper. 1688.

Popery not founded on Scripture. Edited, and the introduction by T.T. 1688.

A Sermon against Self Love. 1689.

A Discourse concerning the Ecclesiastical Commission. 1689, 1689.

A Sermon concerning doing good to Posterity. 1690.

A Sermon concerning the Folly of Atheism. 1691, 1695.

A Sermon concerning the Wandering of the Mind in God's Service. 1691.

A Sermon preached at the Anniversary Meeting of the Corporation for the Relief of poor Widows. 1691.

A Sermon concerning the coelestial Body of a Christian. 1694.

A Sermon concerning Holy Resolution. 1695.

A Sermon preached at the Funeral of her late Majesty, Queen Mary. 1695, 1695, 1709 (also translated into French, 1695).

A Declaration of the Sense of the Archbishops and Bishops in and about London concerning the irregular and scandalous Proceedings of certain Clergy Men at the Execution of Sir John Friend. 1696.

His Grace the Lord Archbishop of Canterbury's Letter to Dr. Batteley on the Increase of Vice and Profaneness. 1699.

A Collection of Articles, Canons, Injunctions etc. together with several Acts of Parliament concerning Ecclesiastical Matters, edited by T. T. 1699.

A true Copy of the Archbishop of Canterbury's Speech in the Jerusalem Chamber, 1702.

His Grace the Lord Archbishop of Canterbury's Letter to the Archdeacons and the rest of the Clergy of the Diocese of St. David's. 1703.

Articles of Visitation and Enquiry to be answer'd unto at the Visitation of Thomas Lord Archbishop of Canterbury. 1706.

His Grace the Archbishop of Canterbury's Circular Letter to the Bishops of his Province. 1707.

To the Reverend the Minister of ——, a Circular Letter addressed by the Archbishop to the Clergy recommending a Collection on behalf of the distressed German Protestant Refugees. 1709.

Archbishop Tenison's Form for receiving Converts from the Church of Rome. 1714, 1827.

A Declaration of the Archbishop of Canterbury and the Bishops in or near London, Testifying their Abhorrence of the Present Rebellion. 1715, 1715, 1752.

Work reputed to Tenison (Master's History of the College of Corpus Christi) but no longer extant: The Grievances of the Church of England which it is not in the power of its Governors to remedy.

First Biography of Thomas Tenison

Memoirs of the Life and Times of the most Reverend Father in God, Dr. Thomas Tennison, late Archbishop of Canterbury. 1715, 1715, 1716.

INDEX

30   455

30*

Convocation on death of prolocutor, 260; long address, 260–61; tries to make interest with the Earl of Godolphin, 262; attends conference with Viscount Hatton and Abp. of York, 263–4; issues reply to complaints of Lower House, 265; exhorts to peace at prorogation, 266; determines to make no further concessions, 267; sends circular letter to bishops, 268; receives letter from Queen, 269; appraisal of Tenison's leadership, 271; is appealed to by Proast, Chaplain of All Souls', 274; decides in favour of Proast, 275; refuses "physic place" for Grevile, 277; helps to secure dispensation from orders for Blencowe, 278; forced to rescind this, 280–81; holds visitation of All Souls', 282–3; abolishes warden's right of veto on dispensations, 283; sends letter to bishops on increase of vice and profaneness, 286; supports Societies for Reformation of Manners, 287; proposes Bill to control press, 288; concerned about stage, 289; tries to prevent clandestine marriage, and promotes three Acts of Parliament, 290–96; endeavours to keep theological peace of the Church, 297; protests to the Vice-Chancellor of Oxford, 299; relations with William Whiston, 301; advises caution, 302; concurs in condemnation, 304–9; writes to S.P.C.K. concerning Dutch translation of the Book of Common Prayer, 310–14; tries to secure episcopal declaration on lay baptism, 315–20; his distrust of Louis XIV, 323; organized relief for Protestant refugees, 326–34; draws up terms of union with foreign Churches, 335–9; cautious conduct towards introduction of English liturgy into Prussia, 340–44; supports founding of S.P.G., 344; first President, 345; encourages conversion of West Indians, 346–7; amends General Codrington's will, 348–50; works for settling bishops in America, 350–52; interest in American Church, 352–5; receives letter from Rev. Charles Marsham, and from "Theneriffe", 355–7; concern for Greek Church, 358; serves on Ecclesiastical Commission for Ireland, 362; offered archbishopric of Dublin, 364; declines it, 367; receives information concerning Dr. Walkington, 373–5; secures bishopric of Meath for Richard Tenison, 376; disappoints Swift, 376; moderate attitude to Presbyterians, 377; seeks to prosecute John Macbridge, 379; searches precedents for Irish Convocation, 381; receives

long letter from Narcissus Marsh, 383; draws up "Memorial" concerning Episcopal clergy in Scotland, 388–9; writes to Secretary Johnstone on their loyalty, 390; one of commissioners to treat for union, 392; supports Bill in Parliament, 393; draws up paper, "Some methods to propagate English Liturgy in Scotland", 396–9; friend of William and Mary, 401; attends Mary on death-bed, 402; preaches at her funeral, 404; sermon attacked, 405–6; sermon defended, 407; reconciles William and Anne, 407–9; persuades Burnet to act as preceptor to Duke of Gloucester, 410; sends address from bishops to Princess Sophia, 413; sends Rev. James Cressett to Hanover, 414; attends William on death-bed, 415; corresponds with Sophia, 416; receives letter from Sir Rowland Gwynne, 418, and from Princess Sophia, 421; condemns Sophia's proposed visit to England, 422; writes again to Sophia, 426; anxious to meet George I at Greenwich, 429; crowns him, 430; concurs in condemnation of 1715 rebellion, 431; his health, 433; death of wife, 434; his own death, 435; funeral, 435–6; his will and charities, 436; contemporary estimates, Swift, 438, Thomas Hearne, 438, Earl of Ailesbury, 438, John Evelyn, 439; Edmund Calamy, 439; author of *Memoirs of Life and Times*, 440; biographer's estimate, 440–41; Gibson, 441–2.

Tenison's Grammar School, Abp., 27, 28

Test Act, 116, 394

Thorpe, Dr., chaplain to Abp. Sancroft, 16

Thynne, Thomas ("Tom of Ten Thousand"), 18, 20

Tillotson, John, Abp. of Canterbury, 63, 85, 98; draws up list of "concessions", 100; 113 n.5, 115, 120 n.1, 122; death, 131; 134, 150; opinion on dispensations, 152 n.1; reluctant to oust Sancroft, 194 n.1; 195; proceeds against Bishop Watson, 211; 250, 273, 274, 277, 323, 325, 362, 367, 368

Tindal, Mathew, deist, 272

Todd, Hugh, Prebendary of Carlisle, 154, 190

Toft, Mary, 301

Toleration Bill, 70, 77

Toland, John, deist, 254, 301, 383

Townsend, Charles, 2nd Viscount, 188

Transubstantiation, 54, 71

Trelawney, Sir Jonathan, Bp. of Bristol; Exeter: Winchester, 100 n.1, 101, 132, 180, 187

Printed in Great Britain by William Clowes and Sons, Ltd.,
London and Beccles